THE CHURCH AND THE PAPACY

By the same author

This our Sacrifice.   Mowbrays.

The Life and Times of St. Leo the Great.   S.P.C.K.

THE CHURCH
AND THE PAPACY

A HISTORICAL STUDY

BEING EIGHT LECTURES DELIVERED
BEFORE THE UNIVERSITY OF OXFORD,
IN THE YEAR 1942, ON THE FOUNDA-
TION OF THE REV. JOHN BAMPTON,
CANON OF SALISBURY

BY

TREVOR GERVASE JALLAND, D.D.

VICAR OF ST. THOMAS THE MARTYR, OXFORD

LONDON
SOCIETY FOR PROMOTING
CHRISTIAN KNOWLEDGE
NORTHUMBERLAND AVENUE, W.C.2
NEW YORK : MOREHOUSE-GORHAM CO.
1944

Extract
from the Last Will and Testament
of the late
Rev. John Bampton, Canon of Salisbury

'. . . I give and bequeath my Lands and Estates to the Chancellor, Masters, and Scholars of the University of Oxford for ever, to have and to hold all and singular the said Lands or Estates upon trust, and to the intents and purposes hereinafter mentioned; that is to say, I will and appoint that the Vice-Chancellor of the University of Oxford for the time being shall take and receive all the rents, issues, and profits thereof, and (after all taxes, reparations, and necessary deductions made) that he pay all the remainder to the endowment of eight Divinity Lecture Sermons, to be established for ever in the said University, and to be performed in the manner following:

'I direct and appoint that, upon the first Tuesday in Easter Term, a Lecturer be yearly chosen by the Heads of Colleges only, and by no others, in the room adjoining to the Printing-House, between the hours of ten in the morning and two in the afternoon, to preach eight Divinity Lecture Sermons, the year following, at St. Mary's in Oxford, between the commencement of the last month in Lent Term and the end of the third week in Act Term.

'Also I direct and appoint, that the eight Divinity Lecture Sermons shall be preached upon either of the following subjects—to confirm and establish the Christian Faith, and to confute all heretics and schismatics—upon the divine authority of the holy Scriptures—upon the authority of the writings of the primitive Fathers, as to the faith and practice of the primitive Church—upon the Divinity of our Lord and Saviour Jesus Christ—upon the Divinity of the Holy Ghost— upon the Articles of the Christian Faith, as comprehended in the Apostles' and Nicene Creeds.

'Also I direct, that thirty copies of the eight Divinity Lecture Sermons shall be always printed, within two months after they are preached; and one copy shall be given to the Chancellor of the Univer-

v

sity, and one copy to the Head of every College, and one copy to the Mayor of the city of Oxford, and one copy to be put into the Bodleian Library; and the expense of printing them shall be paid out of the revenue of the Land or Estates given for establishing the Divinity Lecture Sermons; and the Preacher shall not be paid, nor be entitled to the revenue, before they are printed.

'Also I direct and appoint, that no person shall be qualified to preach the Divinity Lecture Sermons, unless he hath taken the degree of Master of Arts at least, in one of the two Universities of Oxford or Cambridge; and that the same person shall never preach the Divinity Lecture Sermons twice.'

PREFACE

'History should be studied always as a process; not as a picture.'
These words of a well-known ecclesiastical historian may serve as a
pretext, if not a justification, for the present work now offered for
consideration by those interested in one of the more remarkable and
impressive phenomena in the long record of human achievement.
Its aim has been to comprise within the compass of the eight lectures,
delivered on the foundation of the Reverend John Bampton, Canon
of Salisbury, a survey of the relations of the Papacy and the Christian
Church, paying particular attention to their character within the
first six centuries. It will be generally allowed that such a method is
justifiable, if only because it was within that period that certain main
principles came to be formulated which served as a basis of thought
and action for something like ten centuries. There may perhaps be
some who would suppose that the ground covered in a survey of this
kind has already been so well trodden as almost to exclude the possibility that anything which has not already been examined and re-
examined could conceivably come to light. Yet if it should prove that
these pages contain little or nothing which may fairly be represented
as a new or strictly speaking original discovery, it may yet be found
that a reconsideration of well-known as well as less familiar evidence
may not have been wholly without value in the cause of historical
truth. The fact, which scarcely admits of denial, that 'the Papacy has
often been treated with an admiration too blind or a hatred too fierce'
to make it difficult for any conclusions which might in any sense be
described as impartial to be presented, suggests that there may still
be room for reopening a discussion, the general lines of which have
become unhappily hardened by prejudice and mutual intolerance. It
must, of course, be admitted that such a goal as absolute objectivity,
however important as an ideal, must in the last resort be unattainable;
yet its very elusiveness should only serve to stir the scientific historian to further effort, even though in the end it eludes his grasp.

A further consideration may seem to justify the present undertaking. In the course of the last half-century or so, progress in the
sphere of textual research and criticism has been, relatively speaking,

so rapid and its results often so far-reaching, that studies which pre-date the more recent discoveries will now appear, through no fault of the authors concerned, misleading where they are not actually erroneous. Typical examples of monuments of modern scholarship, especially in the realm of patrology, are to be seen in the *Ecclesiae occidentalis monumenta iuris antiquissimi* of the late Professor Cuthbert Hamilton Turner, and in the edition of the *Acta Conciliorum Oecumenicorum* by Dr. Eduard Schwartz now in the course of completion. And these are only two of many possible illustrations of the development just mentioned.

Finally, it cannot well be gainsaid that one of the most remarkable, and perhaps to ecclesiastical historians of the future one of the most welcome, movements of our time is the one which is leading to a better understanding and a deeper sympathy between Christians holding widely differing traditions and adhering to contradictory systems of Church Order. Speaking generally, however, it remains a fact that those of the Papal Obedience continue to find themselves normally excluded, whether by authority or by conscience or by both, from any participation in worship or consultation with their fellow-Christians, apart from co-operation in movements of a purely sociological character. Even to a more superficial outlook, there cannot fail to be something arresting in this policy of abstention, sufficient at least to provoke a re-examination of the logical basis of such a position.

It is possible after all that the following pages may contain an element of the unexpected. Here and there it may emerge that there is better support for the papal case than has been hitherto acknowledged: elsewhere evidence which has often been regarded as providing unmistakable proof of its acceptance will appear to be more readily capable of a quite different interpretation. But to those to whom the ultimate demands of papal doctrine seem in the end unacceptable there must come inevitably a sense of tragedy that so great gifts as those which the Roman see appears to have enjoyed did not in fact prove capable of better use in the interests of Christendom as a whole. It may be that by a fuller recognition of its status in the history of our Faith there will grow a more generous acknowledgment of its appropriate place in the glorious reunited Christendom of the future.

In the preparation of these lectures and in the laborious task of setting them out in a form suitable for publication, the writer desires to express his very deep gratitude to many friends who have helped him by their advice, sympathy, and encouragement, more particularly to the Rev. Dr. N. P. Williams, Canon of Christ Church, Lady Margaret Professor of Divinity in the University of Oxford, former Lecturer on this foundation, Dr. A. Hamilton Thompson, formerly Professor of History in theUniversity of Leeds, the Rev. Dr. F. L. Cross, the Rev. T. M. Parker, and the Rev. E. Kemp, Librarians of Pusey House, Oxford, Dom Gregory Dix, O.S.B., of Nashdom Abbey, all of whom have given generously of their time in reading the lectures in manuscript and typescript; to the Rev. E. H. W. Crusha, for kindly assisting in the heavy task of proof-reading; and finally to the Rev. R. L. Lewis, who has liberally given of his skill in compiling the Indices; to which he would add his grateful acknowledgment of the painstaking care shown by the printers in handling a highly intricate text, and as always of the generous consideration shown to him by the S.P.C.K. and its indefatigable Secretary.

TREVOR JALLAND

Oxford,
November, 1942.

CONTENTS

I

The Modern Papacy

But the majestic River floated on,
Out of the mist and hum of that low land
Into the frosty starlight, and there mov'd,
Rejoicing, through the hush'd Chorasmian waste,
Under the solitary moon: he flow'd
Right for the Polar Star, past Orgunjè,
Brimming, and bright, and large: then sands begin
To hem his watery march, and dam his streams
And split his currents; that for many a league
The shorn and parcell'd Oxus strains along
Through beds of sand and matted rushy isles—
Oxus, forgetting the bright speed he had
In his mountain cradle in Pamere,
A foil'd circuitous wanderer—till at last
The long'd for dash of waves is heard, and wide
His luminous home of waters opens, bright
And tranquil, from whose floor the new-bath'd stars
Emerge, and shine upon the Aral Sea.

Matthew Arnold, *Sohrab and Rustum*,
l. 875.

Acts xv, 6. 'And the apostles and elders came together for to consider of this matter. And when there had been much disputing, Peter rose up, and said unto them, Men and brethren, ye know how that a good while ago God made choice among us, that the Gentiles by my mouth should hear the word of God, and believe'.

On the morning of Monday, July 18, 1870, as the early glow of dawn was slowly spreading across the sky of north Italy, an express train which had left Rome at half-past seven o'clock on the previous evening was clanking on its way across the plains of Lombardy. For some weeks past the stifling heat of summer in the papal capital had been quite unbearable, and as the train neared the frontier of Piedmont, the fresh air blowing down from the mountains must have reached the weary travellers like a breath of new life. Awakened by the glimmering daylight and the cool of dawn, Monsignor Felix Dupanloup, bishop of Orleans, felt in the pocket of his *douillette* and drew out his breviary. As he turned over its pages to find his places for the current feast of St. Camillus of Lellis, his companion, Monsignor Louis Haynald, archbishop of the metropolitan see of Kalocsa, in Hungary, who was occupying the opposite corner of the compartment, leaned forward in the direction of his fellow-bishop. 'Monseigneur', he said, 'nous avons fait une grande faute'. The bishop of Orleans looked up, paused for a moment, and then, gently raising his hand, showed that he had already begun the recitation of his Office.

Unless we are familiar with the series of remarkable and portentous happenings which had preceded this apparently commonplace and unimportant train journey, we are likely to find the archbishop's remark puzzling, if not merely trivial. That it was in no sense the latter might have been judged from the evident seriousness with which the words were uttered; yet even to those who are well acquainted with its historical setting its precise meaning must necessarily remain something of an enigma.

That others too have found the archbishop's words enigmatic is shown by the divergent interpretations put forward by biographers. Thus Maynard, in his life of the bishop of Orleans,[1] explains that the speaker intended to express his conviction that the attitude adopted by his companion and himself at the recent Vatican council, in common with some of the most prominent and influential members of the Catholic hierarchy, had been altogether mistaken. On the other hand, Lagrange, also in the course of a description of the character and work of Monsignor Dupanloup,[2] suggests an almost contradictory view. In his opinion Monsignor Haynald was deploring, not the fact that the bishop of Orleans and his supporters had resisted the proposals of the majority at the council, but, on the contrary, that they had not been sufficiently resolute in their opposition.

Is it possible to decide which of these rival interpretations is the correct one? To form an opinion it is necessary to recall briefly the later stages of the council, from which the two bishops had now finally withdrawn. From March 6 onwards, when the *schema* on the Primacy and Infallibility of the Roman Pontiff had first reached the assembled bishops, both Dupanloup and Haynald had maintained an unrelenting opposition to its adoption in any form, chiefly, as it will appear, on the ground that such a definition at that particular historical juncture would be in the highest degree 'inopportune'. Some, in fact, of those who supported this attitude had been prepared

---

[1] Maynard, *Vie de Mgr Dupanloup*, vol. iii, p. 282.
[2] Lagrange, *Vie de Mgr Dupanloup*, vol. iii, p. 162, quoted by Mourret, F., *Concile du Vatican*, 1919, p. 308.

to go even further and had actually questioned the historical basis on which the proposed definition was supposed to rest.[1] What is more, the opposition of the 'inopportunists', as they are often called, had been maintained as late as July 13, when at the eighty-fifth congregation held on that day out of six hundred and one votes received, as many as eighty-eight had registered *non placet*, while of the rest no less than sixty-two recorded *placet iuxta modum*.[2] The significance of this minority vote can be better appreciated when it is realized that membership of the congregation in question (from which not less than seventy bishops then in Rome were absent and so refrained from voting) included a large 'official' element, i.e. twenty-three Cardinals *in Curia*, forty-one superiors of religious orders, and no less than forty-three bishops possessing no actual jurisdiction of any kind, while among those who voted *non placet* were many of the most distinguished and outstanding members of the Roman Catholic hierarchy. After the congregation, however, the counsels of the Minority appear to have become divided, and to a joint letter intended to be presented to Pius IX on the morning of the fourth public session which had been announced for Monday, July 18, not more than fifty-five signatures could be obtained. The purpose of the letter was to explain and justify the absence of the signatories from that session, among whom were the two travelling companions Dupanloup and Haynald. It was drawn up on the explicit proposal of Dupanloup himself, but for whom the inopportunists would probably have followed the lead of Haynald in resolving to appear at the session if only to record for the last time a final and inexorable *non placet*. As it was, the gentle persuasiveness of the bishop of Orleans carried with him the majority of those present. 'We could not vote *placet*', he pleaded, 'for nobody would believe us; we could not vote *non placet* for the Catholic world would not understand us, and might be scandalized'.[3] The letter itself, which is patently sincere in expression and unmistakably pathetic in tone, pointed out that the signatories (who included, besides the two already mentioned, the archbishops of Prague and Besançon, the Cardinal primate of Hungary, the archbishops of

---

[1] The opinions of the Minority are discussed by Butler, Dom C., *The Vatican Council*, 1930, vol. i, pp. 106–129, who gives an excellent account of the proceedings of the council based on reliable sources.

[2] Mansi, *Concilia*, vol. lii (iv), 1243 ff.

[3] Butler, *op. cit.*, vol. ii, p. 157 ff.

Paris, Lyons, Munich, Olmütz, and Milan) had arrived at the conviction that no real good could possibly result from their presence
at the session then imminent, since they could not do otherwise than
renew the negative vote already recorded at the eighty-fifth congregation. They were proposing therefore, they said, to return to
their dioceses, with the unhappy feeling that they would find serious
uneasiness of conscience among their flocks on their arrival.[1]

Their action in thus abandoning the council before the session
without formal permission to do so may be thought to have been
justified by the general *venia abeundi* issued by the Pope and published at the eighty-sixth congregation held on July 16,[2] though it is
doubtful whether Pius had really intended that it should have effect
before the public session already fixed.

If, therefore, we take into account the proposal made by Haynald
at the inopportunists' meeting as well as his consistent attitude
throughout the debates on infallibility, it would seem most improbable that Maynard is justified in interpreting the archbishop's words
as implying a conviction that the position taken up by the Minority
had been fundamentally in error. Similarly, although Dupanloup's
eventual answer after finishing his Office has not been recorded, his
known expression of opinion at the private meeting just mentioned
makes it unlikely that he had undergone a complete change of view
in such a comparatively short time. On the contrary, all the evidence
points to the conclusion that Haynald's real meaning was that he and
his fellow inopportunists had been guilty of a grave error in not
carrying through their resistance to the end, concluding with a
spectacular demonstration of their disapproval at the public session,
and thus that of the two interpretations of the remark in the train
the one supplied by Lagrange is the more correct.

In actual fact the almost complete abstention of the inopportunist
party had the effect, as we shall see, of enabling the definition of the
primacy of the Roman Pontiff, contained in the Constitution *Pastor
Aeternus*, to be passed with a vote only a little short of unanimity,[3]
sufficiently harmonious at any rate to satisfy the few remaining
scruples of the more critical among the bishops, as to the legitimately
oecumenical character of the dogma. Thus Lagrange observes,

---

[1] Mansi, *Concilia*, vol. lii (iv), col. 1325 ; *Collectio Lacensis*, 1890, vol. vii, col. 994.
[2] *Coll. Lac.*, vol. vii, col. 760 ff.
[3] Mansi, *Concilia*, vol. lii (iv), col. 1335 ; *Coll. Lac., ibid.*, col. 487.

'From this point of view, if mistake there was, let us call it a fortunate mistake! *Felix culpa!*'[1]

Opinions may differ, however, assuming the correctness of Lagrange's explanation, as to whether in saying that he and the inopportunists had made a great mistake Haynald was actually correct. It might be argued, of course, that it would have been more consistent as well as more honest, though perhaps more dangerous, to have stayed in Rome a few hours longer, and to have recorded a final negative opinion at the fourth session. On the other hand, it is possible to say that the adoption of the Constitution at that session was a foregone conclusion, and that, as the signatories of the minority letter had pleaded, no further protest could conceivably do any good. Some, no doubt, would take a quite different view and be disposed to ask whether the Vatican Constitution in whole or in part was not itself 'une grande faute', while others would find in it a real safeguard of the integrity and permanence of the authentic Christian tradition. Yet others again would roundly describe the whole Roman Catholic position as altogether a sin against reason and historical truth, and would treat the Constitution as no more than a hopeless attempt to save an already doomed ship.

That some such view as the one just mentioned was firmly held by the majority of the thinking population of these islands at the close of the last century is so probable as not to be in need of demonstration. In fact, it is not too much to say that from the sixteenth century onwards the greater part of the Anglo-Saxon race has looked on the Papacy with suspicion if not with active hostility. In more recent years, however, it has been possible to observe some slight but unmistakable modification of this attitude. Hostility has indeed often been replaced by indifference or even contempt. But in other quarters deep-rooted suspicion has gradually softened into more generous and perhaps more intelligent appreciation. No doubt the revolution in thought and ideas which accompanied or followed the war of 1914–18 considerably accelerated this process, and it is perhaps not too much to expect that it will be aided rather than impeded by the experience of the present conflict.

Not only have English politicians come to recognize that the Papacy, in spite of its loss of Temporal Power, as the head and centre of administration of by far the largest organized body of Christians,

---

[1] *Op. cit.*, vol. iii, p. 162, quoted by Mourret, *Concile du Vatican*, p. 308.

is a political force to be taken into account in international affairs, and have therefore thought it worth while that this nation should have its diplomatic representative at the Vatican, but it is becoming apparent to some of the leaders of the Established Church, though perhaps scarcely as yet to a large proportion of its rank and file, that the Roman Communion at least represents an important aspect of Christian life and thought which ought not to be ignored. This latter point of view has also been clearly shown in a number of official pronouncements issued not only by Anglicans, but by conferences in which representatives of various non-Roman Christian bodies, including Anglicans, have recently taken part. On these and like occasions the significance of the Papacy has almost inevitably emerged, particularly when the problems of Christian reunion have been the chief subject of discussion. We may quote as an example the official report of the Lambeth Conference of 1908, where it was formally stated, with reference to the subject of Christian disunity, that 'there can be no fulfilment of the divine purpose in any scheme of Reunion which does not ultimately include the great Latin Church of the West'. As these words are reiterated *verbatim* in the report of the Conference of 1920 as well as that of 1930,[1] they may be regarded rightly as something of an approximation to an official, and certainly up-to-date, expression of opinion on the part of the Anglican hierarchy on this subject. As such, it is clear they are undoubtedly deserving of serious attention at least by members of the Anglican Communion.

Yet if we examine their meaning carefully, we shall find ourselves faced with a somewhat surprising conclusion. The statement affirms that no reunion scheme which leaves the Roman Catholic Communion out of account (for this we take to be the allusion in the not strictly accurate phrase—'the great Latin Church of the West') can

---

[1] The statement first makes its appearance in the Report of the Lambeth Conference held in 1908. See *The Six Lambeth Conferences*, 1929; 1908, p. 422; 1920, p. 144; *The Lambeth Conference*, 1930, p. 131. The statement as given in the report of the Conference of 1908 goes on, 'But they (sc. the Committee appointed to consider and report upon the subject of Reunion) realize that any advance in this direction is at present barred by difficulties which we have not ourselves created, and which we cannot of ourselves remove'. It should be noted, however, that the expression occurs in each case in the Report of the Committee concerned with the Unity of the Church, and that it forms no part of the formal Resolutions, for which alone the Conference, as a whole, is responsible (see 1930, p. 63, and cf. Resolution 32, 1930, p. 48).

conceivably be regarded as in accordance with God's will. It is, of course, unnecessary to point out that the Roman Catholic Communion as it is to-day, and possibly as it has been from the beginning, is bound up with the belief that the Roman see, as the see of St. Peter the Apostle and of his successors, exists *de iure divino*. Do these words mean then that 'ultimately' some belief in the divine origin of the Papacy must be accepted by all, if such a scheme of Reunion is to become practicable as may be held to be in accordance with the will of God? Conceivably not. Yet what is the alternative? Apparently the idea that when the 'great Latin Church of the West' has 'ultimately' rid itself of the incubus of papal authority, it will become a suitable partner in a co-operative society of Christians. Perhaps we can only suppose that the real implications of this remarkable statement have never been fully thought out. Yet never has the need for such consideration been greater than at the present time. Not only is Christianity in many countries faced with active hostility, if not with actual persecution, but surely it is scarcely an exaggeration to say that at the present moment its very principles are at stake. Can we afford therefore to neglect any longer the paramount need for a united Christian front against that alliance of the forces of secularism which unhappily finds its supporters not only on the side of our most determined political enemies, but even among those whom we count our staunchest and most loyal friends? Dare we neglect to explore afresh the differences which exist between Christians, particularly those which divide the 'historic churches' of Christendom?

We have seen that to a considerable degree the importance of the Papacy in the world of politics has already been recognized. It thus appears that much prejudice in that sphere has already been overcome. But what of the religious sphere? Faced by a philosophy of life which has thrown down a challenge to Christian ethics, is it sufficient for us to explore, as is already being done, ways and means by which Christians of all kinds, not excluding 'the great Latin Church of the West', can co-operate for the social welfare of mankind? Are we not bound to go deeper than this and examine afresh the dogmatic basis of those ethics, and in so doing to reconsider the problems of Faith and Order, which have given rise to fundamental differences of belief and discipline among Christians? Is it not possible that after all the Papacy is a Christian institution which can only be discarded or ignored at the cost of some serious loss to Christianity as a whole? And if that is true, as the evidence of history would appear to suggest, ought we not to go further still and ask, with suitable respect, 'Is the Papacy of heaven or of men'? It will be the purpose of these lectures to examine these and cognate questions anew, in the hope that by applying to them what may be described as modern methods of historical criticism we may find ourselves better equipped to give a fair and, as far as may be, strictly objective reply.

We shall begin with a description of what may be called the 'apotheosis' of the Roman see at the Vatican council, and then consider briefly the encyclical letter of Leo XIII, *Satis Cognitum*, as a typical papal utterance on the questions debated at the council. This will lead us to examine afresh the grounds for the belief that it was part of Christ's intention that His disciples should be an organized society. In the second lecture we shall inquire how far the evidence of the New Testament justifies the assignment of a peculiar status in relation to that society of the Apostle St. Peter, and shall go on to describe the origin and primitive organization of the church of Rome. Next we shall discuss the surviving evidence as to the attitude of non-Roman Christians to that church or to its bishop, during the period previous to the council of Nicaea. At the same time we shall analyse some of the earlier signs of what may be called papal self-consciousness in the same period. Then will follow in the fourth lecture the consideration of the last organized persecution, and of the great reaction which followed, particularly in its effects, not only upon the Church at large, but especially upon the Roman see. Here too we shall watch the effort made by the Church to substitute for an inchoate federal order a closely knit oecumenical organization, with a machinery capable of dealing with an embarrassingly well-disposed Empire on its own terms. The period which next calls for treatment is that which is marked by the consolidation of papal authority in the West and by the rapid development of the eastern concept of an *imperator sacerdos*. The last three lectures will show the essential continuity of the papal theory and practice amid a changing historical environment from the beginning of the seventh century to the present day.

We have devoted by far the larger proportion of our space to the first six centuries, not merely because it was during those centuries that the principles which subsequently governed the relations between the Papacy and the Church gradually emerged, but also because nothing less than a right understanding of the evidence as to those relations can possibly qualify us to pronounce aright on the legitimacy or otherwise of the principles themselves. It is here chiefly that we hope to shed some new light on old problems. If the present treatment of the later history may appear somewhat abbreviated it is because it seemed best to direct attention chiefly to those periods in which the leading ideas of later centuries were formed and developed. Yet for the completeness of our project, namely to show that the Papacy is not only an interesting subject for historical study, but a living religious force no less integral to the life of the twentieth century than to that of the first, it was inevitable that we should include in our survey the whole process of its majestic evolution.

I

Let us betake ourselves now to Rome and watch the drama which unfolded there on the very morning when the returning bishops, including those two whose conversation has already formed a subject for discussion, were being speedily conveyed across the Swiss frontier. At nine o'clock, in accordance with normal procedure of the Vatican council, the fourth public session was due to begin. As the hour approached, a crowd of interested spectators, already assembled in the *Piazza di S. Pietro* and in the nave of the great basilica, gazed at an almost interminable procession of Cardinals and Patriarchs, primates and archbishops, bishops and abbots, including the generals of a number of religious orders as they entered and passed up the centre of the church. On arriving under the central dome, each one knelt before the high altar in adoration of the Most Holy Sacrament exposed, and then proceeded to the north (or right-hand) transept, which since the opening of the council had been used as the conciliar *aula*. To-day, as previously on the occasion of public sessions, the folding screen which normally separated the *aula* from the rest of the building had been removed, thus making it possible for at least a proportion of the more inquisitive of the crowd which thronged the nave of the church to feast their eyes on the amazing pageant unfolded before them.

With its back towards the general public and in the middle of the arch leading into the transept stood the conciliar altar, while within each side, eastern and western, ranged four tiers of seating, making a brave display with their red plush cushions. In the highest tier were the seats for Cardinals and Patriarchs, below it those for the archbishops, bishops, and abbots, while lower still were the places for the heads of the religious orders. In the centre, within the transept itself, stood the movable pulpit, provided for the use of those who wished formally to address the council. Beyond, at the far end of the *aula* and most conspicuous of all, was raised the papal throne, its impressiveness enhanced by a broad flight of steps. The throne itself was draped with a shimmering cover of white silk, bespangled with gilt stars, and surmounted by an immense crimson canopy. Below it were the seats of the Cardinal presidents. Two texts in gigantic lettering adorned the walls, the one immediately above the papal throne being an appropriate quotation from Luke XXII, 32, and the other a petition addressed to the Blessed Virgin Mary.

Such was the stage. Now for the actual drama. After the bishops, wearing their red copes and white linen mitres, had taken their places, the proceedings began with a votive Mass of the Holy Ghost, celebrated without chant by the Cardinal priest of St. Agnes, after which, in accordance with ancient custom, the open text of the holy Gospels was set upon the altar. At this point Pope Pius IX himself, accompanied by the Cardinal deacons Gasparri and Mertel, makes his entry. There follows the Litany of the Rogations. The Gospel of the *Tu es Petrus* is sung by one of the Cardinal deacons, and at its conclusion the Pope intones *Veni Creator Spiritus* in his familiar high-pitched voice. The hymn ended, everyone rises and sits down.

The great moment is now at hand. Had we been there we should have seen Mgr Fessler, bishop of Sankt Polten, and Secretary-General of the Council, proceed to the throne and humbly present to the Supreme Pontiff the text of the Constitution *Pastor Aeternus*, who thereupon handed it to Mgr Vallenziani and directed its contents to be read. This was done in clear and more than usually audible tones, compared with the rest of the proceedings. There followed the formal vote-taking. While this was in progress a storm, which had evidently been brewing since the early hours of the morning, broke over the city with a sudden and almost supernatural violence. No doubt to the more imaginative this striking phenomenon seemed to be an expression of the voice of heaven itself, though obviously the interpretation of its significance must have varied according to the standpoint of the individual observer. To the more phlegmatic, however, it was no more than a coincidence that the recurring *placet*, uttered successively as their names were called by five hundred and thirty-three bishops and other members of the council, was punctuated by the most vivid shafts of lightning. As each flash shot through the gloom, the broad expanse of Fontana's dome resounded with re-echoing peals of thunder. Thus to a scene already sufficiently impressive as a work of human agency, nature itself might seem to have added dramatic effect far beyond the capacity of the most ingenious theatrical artist. By this time the *aula* was filled with a lowering darkness, so that when the moment had arrived for the result of the voting to be formally announced to the Pope, and the solemn formula of papal confirmation to be proclaimed, the ceremonial light of the pontifical *bugia* had acquired an unusual, though no doubt, on this occasion at least, most practical convenience.

Out of the surrounding gloom came the Pope's thin, silvery voice: 'The Decrees and Canons, which are contained in the Constitution just read, have with two exceptions pleased all the Fathers; and We, with the approval of the most holy Council, define both the Decrees and Canons, as they have been read, and confirm them with apostolic authority'.[1]

Then with the singing of the familar words of the western Church's solemn act of praise, the *Te Deum*, in which the bishops were joined by the assembled multitude, the fourth public session of the Vatican council was brought to a triumphant close. So at least it must have seemed afterwards to the frail Sovereign Pontiff, whose reign had already all but equalled the traditional years of St. Peter, and who had had the additional satisfaction, so it is said, before he finally left the *aula*, of receiving the submission of the only two bishops who had dared to record their *non placet* and thus to persist to the very end in an attitude of opposition to the Constitution, now finally approved and confirmed.

II

It is well known that this Constitution defined the infallibility of the Roman bishop in the twin spheres of faith and morals. But it is

---

[1] *Coll. Lac.*, vol. vii, col. 487 f.

not always appreciated that the language used is carefully balanced nor that the document was in origin, and therefore presumably remains in fact, only an isolated fragment detached from its original context. It follows from this that if we are to understand aright the precise nature of the jurisdiction and authority here assigned to the Roman bishop, we are obliged to take into account not only the Constitution as a whole, of which the definition of infallibility forms only the concluding chapter, but its general historical context.

In studying this we are bound to begin with the rules of procedure which governed the general conduct of conciliar business. These had been laid down by the brief *Multiplices inter*, published at the pre-synodal congregation held on December 2, 1869.[1] Here it was prescribed that the initiative in proposing questions for the council's consideration was to be considered as belonging solely to the Pope, and although the bishops were permitted to address requests to a special congregation *De Postulatis* appointed to receive them, the decision as to whether the matter contained in them should in fact be introduced was most strictly reserved. No doubt in so large and heterogeneous an assembly some such regulation was indispensable, and we have no right necessarily to regard as an oppressive limitation of the bishops' freedom a measure in the absence of which it is doubtful whether business of any sort could have been conducted. Further, following the precedent of the council of Trent, it was provided that there should be two modes of assembly: the general congregation, the proceedings of which were held *in camera*, and the public session. Here again we have no ground for criticizing the adoption of the same distinction which certainly exists in principle as a part of the most democratic parliamentary procedure and is frequently followed in practice.

As to the introduction of actual matter for debate, it was prescribed that all questions submitted to the council were to be carefully prepared and examined by a commission of theologians and canonists, nominated by the Pope in person, and only after they had been printed and circulated in the form of a *schema* among the bishops

---

[1] Mansi, *Concilia*, vol. l (ii), col. 215* ff.; *Coll. Lac.*, vol. vii, col. 17 ff. It should be realized, however, that in consequence of the decree issued by the presidents of the council, February 20, Mansi, *op. cit.*, vol. li (iii), col. 13 f., this procedure was subsequently modified in order to expedite the work of the council.

could they be formally introduced. Those who desired to address the council had to send in their names beforehand. Others might speak subsequently, if sufficient time permitted. In the event of serious difficulties or amending proposals arising, they were to be referred to one of the four deputations or committees, elected by the council itself, of which by far the most important was the deputation *De Fide*. These bodies reviewed the various proposals and amendments, added their own comments, printed and circulated them to the bishops and eventually brought them forward at a general congregation. Once a *schema* had reached its final form and received the approval of a substantial majority, a public session was held at which the Pope presided in person. At such a session a public recitation of the decrees with the relevant canons in their final form took place, the bishops being entitled to vote *placet* or *non placet* but not otherwise, after which the result of the voting was formally made known to the Pope. In the event of the result being favourable, he would direct their promulgation in the manner already described and accord to them final confirmation.

It is only if we bear these rules of procedure in mind that we shall find it easy to follow the successive stages through which the *Constitutio Dogmatica I de Ecclesia Christi*, usually known as *Pastor Aeternus*, actually passed, before reaching the form with which, as approved and confirmed on that fateful Monday, July 18, 1870, we are here concerned. It was on January 21 of the same year that the original *schema De Ecclesia Christi*, already drawn up by the papal theological and canonical commission, had been circulated in print among the bishops. It consisted in all of fifteen chapters, to the first of which thirteen canons were attached, to chapters eleven and twelve three canons, and to the remaining chapters five more; thus there were originally not less than twenty-one canons in all. The first section, chapters one to ten, treated of the nature of the Church as the Mystical Body of Christ, as a supernatural and yet visible society, of the necessity of its communion for the attainment of eternal salvation, of its indefectibility, its infallibility, and of its jurisdiction. Next, chapters eleven and twelve dealt with the primacy of the Roman see and with its right to exercise temporal power, though surprisingly enough making no mention whatever of the question of the day, namely the infallibility of the Roman bishop. Finally, the last three chapters contained a description of the proper relations of Church and State. That its contents appeared to the council to be of a highly controversial character may be judged from the fact that when on February 22 the bishops were invited to submit their observations on the *schema* to the deputation *De Fide*, no less than three hundred separate statements of opinion were received. Thus it soon became evident that to debate and carry through the Constitution in anything like its original shape and length would be likely to occupy the attention of the council for many months, if not for years.

Meanwhile, however, the congregation *De Postulatis*, which had met on February 9, was recommending the immediate introduction of some definition of papal infallibility. Probably a good deal took place behind the scenes of which no record has been preserved, and this may sufficiently explain the delay which ensued. Not till March 1 did Pius IX give his formal approval to the recommendation just mentioned, and even then allowed five more days to elapse before actually making the fact of his approval publicly known. On the same day that this was done a new formula, prepared by the original papal theological commission, was published. This document treated outright the subject of papal infallibility and an additional period of ten days was allowed, in which the bishops might submit any comments which they saw fit to be made on the eleventh chapter of the *schema* and also on the new additional formula. Yet further delay followed, and it is said that not till April 20 was it generally known that the Pope had taken the momentous decision of 'bringing on the infallibility question after the (third) session, the first thing, and out of its course'.

We may perhaps feel disposed to ask why so much apparent hesitation and procrastination was necessary. The answer is perhaps supplied by various entries which appear in a diary of the proceedings of the deputation *De Fide*, of which the authorship is probably to be assigned to Mgr Ignatius Senestréy, bishop of Ratisbon, one of the more prominent supporters of the definition of infallibility. These show that the council had no sooner opened than the Roman Curia began to realize that, if the procedure outlined by the brief *Multiplices inter*, which we have already described, were to be strictly followed, it was unlikely that the debate on the first *schema De Fide* would conclude before the following autumn (i.e. of 1870), and that consequently the second *schema De Ecclesia* could not be brought forward before the winter 1870–71, with the quite staggering prospect that the chapters dealing with the Roman primacy might well not be reached till the beginning of 1872.

There is every sign that at first as much freedom in debate as possible was permitted by the Cardinal presidents; some might even say more than was reasonable or consistent with efficiency. It is certainly not true that in the earlier stages the machinery of closure was improperly applied. Yet those responsible were bound to face certain unpleasant yet undoubtedly relevant facts. First there was the prevailing uncertainty of the political situation, particularly in central Italy; secondly there were the vast and ever-mounting costs of the council's maintenance ; and in addition the unmistakable impatience on the part of many bishops, and especially, so it is said, of Pius himself, that 'the question' should be settled with so much expedition and finality as might be possible. Hence it is in no way surprising that the demand for some modification of the original programme became quite irresistible.

Day after day fresh petitions and counter-petitions in vast mass were pouring into the office of the Cardinal presidents; many were even addressed to Pius in person. All the same the presidents, no less than Cardinal Bilio, head of the deputation *De Fide*, remained adamant in insisting that the council must adhere to the original programme. The suggestion made to their doyen, Cardinal de Angelis, that he should support the project of taking the chapters on the Roman primacy out of turn was rejected by him with courtesy and firmness. This made it perfectly clear that nothing short of personal intervention on the part of the Sovereign Pontiff could conceivably extricate the council from its impasse. As, however, he had already caused it to become reasonably clear which of the two sides of this particular question he was personally disposed to favour, the promoters of a change of programme must have felt distinctly confident of eventual success. Yet even they had to endure some measure of disappointment. The best answer, and in fact the only answer, which they received from the Pope's private secretary was quite delphic in its ambiguity, namely, that the Holy Father would do what seemed fitting (*quod congruum videretur*). From one who in an emergency had not hesitated to say 'La tradizione son' io', such a reply must have sounded a little commonplace. Meanwhile the impatience of the fathers was only accentuated by the dogged persistence of the deputation *De Fide* in continuing a seemingly interminable discussion of the dogma of the Most Holy Trinity. It is not surprising therefore that yet a further appeal was addressed to the Pope, once again praying that decisive instructions be issued that that part of the *schema De Ecclesia* which concerned the Roman primacy be introduced without further delay. It was immediately followed by a personal letter addressed by Dupanloup to the Pope, imploring him in terms of the strongest possible urgency 'while there is yet time, to spare the Church and the Holy See from evils that may become disasters for Christendom during long ages, and cause the loss of an incalculable number of souls'.[1] All was in vain. Pius had by now finally made up his mind, and the course of events was irrevocably set.

Even so it was not till the month of April had almost run out that on the 27th the attention of the deputation was suddenly diverted to the consideration of 'the question'. Then at the forty-seventh congregation on the 29th it was dramatically announced by the Cardinal presidents that the chapters on the Roman primacy would be considered forthwith.[2]

It has been necessary to describe in detail the long and rather tedious process leading to the debate and gradual formulation of the *schema*, from which Constitution *Pastor Aeternus* was evolved, in order to appreciate the fact to which we have already called attention, that, properly speaking, the Constitution itself is no more than an isolated fragment, torn from its context, and considered and adopted in detachment from its appropriate setting by sheer force of circumstances. But it has been possible by this means to acquire some insight into the methods by which the business, particularly the unofficial business, of the council was conducted.

We must now turn to the Constitution itself.[3] It opens with a short preamble in which it is affirmed that 'the Eternal Shepherd and Bishop of our souls, in order to ensure the permanence of His saving work of Redemption, enjoined that a holy Church should be built, in which as the household of the Living God all faithful

[1] Mourret, *Concile du Vatican*, p. 270.
[2] Mansi, *Concilia*, vol. li (iii), col. 467 ; *Coll. Lac.*, vol. vii, col. 740.
[3] Mansi, *Concilia*, vol. lii (iv), col. 1330 ff. ; *Coll. Lac.*, vol. vii, col. 482 ff. ; Denzinger-Bannwart, *Enchiridion symbolorum*, 14-15th ed., 1922, 1821 ff.

people would be included in a bond of united faith and love'. To this end, it is stated, our Lord had prayed in the words of John XVII, 20, 'that they all may be one'. So besides giving a divine commission to His Apostles, He also willed that there should be apostles and teachers in His Church to the end of time. Moreover, to secure the abiding unity of the episcopate, He set St. Peter at the head of all the rest, and appointed him as a perpetual source and visible foundation of the common faith and life of the Church, on whose stability its sublime structure would rise to heaven. It was added that because the gates of hell did not cease to attack this divinely laid foundation, the Pope had determined with the approval of the council to proclaim a doctrine as to the institution, perpetuation, and content of the apostolic primacy, which, in accordance with the ancient and continuous faith of the universal Church, was to be accepted by all the faithful; and in addition to condemn all errors prevailing to the contrary.

The first chapter of the Constitution, therefore, under the title 'of the establishment of the apostolic primacy in blessed Peter', opens with an affirmation of a primacy of jurisdiction, promised to and actually conferred upon St. Peter by Christ, in support of which the Scriptural texts, Matt. XVI, 16 ff., John I, 42 and XXI, 15 ff. are adduced, and concludes with a formal repudiation of the view which would deny that St. Peter received any primacy of jurisdiction beyond the rest of the apostles either severally or collectively, as well as the one which argues that he received it only through the Church and not immediately from Christ Himself. In the canon which follows, the opinion that St. Peter was not appointed by Christ as *princeps* of all the Apostles, and head of the Church Militant, as well as the view that he received only a 'primacy of honour' and not of 'real and actual jurisdiction', is condemned.

The second chapter which bears the heading 'of the perpetuation of the primacy of blessed Peter in the Roman bishops' begins with the declaration that for the sake of the endurance and stability of the Church it was indispensable that all that our Lord assigned to the office of St. Peter should possess the character of permanence. In support of this are cited three well-known patristic quotations: the first derived from the speech of Philip, Cardinal presbyter of the 'title' St. Peter *ad vincula*, and legate of the Roman see to the first council of Ephesus (431), as it was addressed to the council, with a few unimportant explanatory glosses;[1] the second from the familiar description of the primitive Roman church given by Irenaeus in his *Adversus haereses;*[2] and the third from the petition, probably composed by St. Ambrose, addressed by the council of Aquileia (381) to the Emperor Gratian, in which reference was made to the Roman church as 'the source from which go forth the privileges of sacred communion'.[3] As before, a canon follows, this time denouncing the belief that St. Peter did not possess successors to his primacy over the universal Church *de iure divino*, and that the Roman bishop is not in fact his successor in that primacy.

The third chapter deals with the subject 'Of the scope and nature of the primacy of the Roman bishop'. It opens with an explicit reaffirmation of the decree of the council of Florence, in which it was defined that 'the apostolic see and Roman bishop holds a primacy in relation to the whole world', that 'the said Roman bishop is the successor of blessed Peter, the prince of the Apostles and the true Vicar of Christ, the head of the whole Church, father and teacher of all Christians', and that 'to him has been entrusted by our Lord Jesus Christ a *plena potestas* of ruling and governing the Church universal; even as it is contained in the *acta* and holy canons of the oecumenical councils'.[4] It goes on to declare that the Roman church

---

[1] Schwartz, E., *Acta Conciliorum Oecumenicorum*, Tom. I, vol. i, pt. iii, p. 60 f. (*Acta graeca* 106, 31). The citation omits 'καὶ αὐτῷ δέδοται ἐξουσία τοῦ δεσμεύειν καὶ λύειν τὰς ἁμαρτίας'. It inserts 'et praesidet' although there is nothing corresponding to this in the Greek text. This session does not appear in the *Coll. Casinensis*. Schwartz, *op. cit.*, Tom. I, vol. iii, p. 94 (Act. lat. 35, 20). Cf. *Acta*, Tom. I, vol. i, pt. iii, p. 59.

[2] *Adv. Haer.*, 3, 3, 2. For a full discussion of the significance of this passage, see below, p. 109 ff.

[3] Mansi, *Concilia*, vol. lii (iv), col. 1330. *Coll. Lac.*, vol. vii, col. 483 f. 'ea Sede, e qua venerandae communionis iura in omnes dimanant'. The text in Ambrose, *Ep.* 11, 4, *M.P.L.* 16, 986, reads: 'totius orbis Romani caput Romanam ecclesiam, atque illam sacrosanctam apostolorum fidem ne turbari sineret, obsecranda fuit clementia vestra (sc. imperatoris); inde enim in omnes venerandae communionis iura dimanant'. The context shows that Ambrose is eager to prevent a renewal of the local schism in the Roman church in consequence of the Emperor's indulgence to the anti-pope Ursinus; the phrase 'inde . . . dimanant' would, therefore, seem to involve no more than an acknowledgment of Damasus as the true bishop of Rome, though it implies that the Emperor was believed to possess the right to decide between the rival claimants.

[4] Mansi, *Concilia*, vol. lii (iv), col. 1332; *Coll. Lac.*, vol. vii, col. 484. 'Ipsi (sc. Romano pontifici) . . . pascendi, regendi ac gubernandi universalem ecclesiam a Domino nostro Iesu Christo plenam potestatem traditam esse; quemadmodum etiam in gestis oecumenicorum conciliorum et in sacris canonibus continetur'. Butler, *op. cit.*, vol. ii, p. 117 f., examines the question as to whether 'etiam' in a

possesses a *principatus* of 'ordinary' authority over all other churches, and that this power of the Roman bishop's jurisdiction, being in very deed episcopal in character, is in fact immediate. Consequently all the clergy and faithful everywhere are subject to him in matters of faith and morals, as well as in other questions which pertain to ecclesiastical discipline. At the same time it is pointed out that this power in no way infringes that of the ordinary and immediate jurisdiction exercised by the bishops as successors of the Apostles over their own people, but rather has the effect of strengthening and safeguarding it, as was taught by Gregory I.[1] Nevertheless, for the due exercise of this supreme power the Constitution insists that it is indispensable that the Roman bishop should enjoy freely means of unhindered communication with bishops and churches everywhere, and that as a consequence no State can be permitted to exercise any veto on such communication.

In addition to the foregoing, it is affirmed that the Roman bishop is the supreme judge of all the faithful, and that in all ecclesiastical causes an appeal lies to his judgment, which is to be final and irreversible, and to admit of no appeal to an oecumenical council. The concluding canon rejects the opinion that the judicial power of the Roman bishop is not all-inclusive, but is only one of inspection or direction, and that he enjoys only the larger share of such power, as well as the view that his power is neither ordinary nor immediate.

In the fourth and concluding chapter of the Constitution, entitled 'of the infallible *magisterium* of the Roman bishop', it is defined that his apostolic primacy includes the supreme power of declaring doctrine, a belief always held by the Roman see, confirmed by the continuous practice of the Church and proclaimed by oecumenical councils, especially by those in which the East and the West have been assembled in a bond of faith and charity. In support of this

confirmatory sense is the true reading in the Florentine decree (see Denzinger, *Enchiridion*, No. 649) as against 'et', which would naturally make the scope of the 'potestas' dependent on the correct interpretation of the 'gesta conciliorum' and the 'sacri canones'. In the Greek version of the decree the reading is καί.

But Butler points out that 'etiam' is found in the original text preserved at Florence and hence concludes in its favour. He does not, however, appear to have noticed that the most natural equivalent of the Greek διαλαμβάνεται is not 'continetur' but 'definitur'.

[1] *Ep. ad Eulog. Reg.* VIII, *Ep.* 30. *M.P.L.* 77, 933. 'Meus namque honor est honor universalis Ecclesiae. Meus honor est fratrum meorum solidus vigor. Tum ego vere honoratus sum, cum singulis quibusque honor debitus non negatur'.

assertion quotations are included from the celebrated formula of Hormisdas (actually in the form in which it was received by the so-called eighth oecumenical council), and from the formulae of union adopted at the second council of Lyons and later at the council of Florence.

In fulfilment of their office, it is stated, the Roman bishops have ever concerned themselves with the spread and maintenance of the purity of Christ's teaching, and from all time bishops, whether severally or collectively in councils, have had recourse to the apostolic see for the remedy of injuries to the faith. Consequently the Roman bishops, either after the assembly of oecumenical councils or by ascertaining the mind of the Church at large, whether through local synods or other methods, have defined the doctrines, such as they had learnt by divine aid to be consistent with the holy Scriptures and apostolic traditions, to be held by the Church. At the same time it is denied that the Popes had been promised the Holy Ghost to enable them to promulgate fresh doctrine, but rather to safeguard jealously and to expound faithfully the revelation of the 'deposit of faith' delivered by the Apostles. This doctrine, the Constitution affirms, has always been loyally accepted and followed by orthodox bishops and teachers, since they have realized that, in virtue of our Lord's promise contained in Luke XXII, 32, the see of St. Peter must ever be secure against every kind of error. Thus a *charisma* of truth and of indefectible faith was conferred on St. Peter and on his successors, chiefly for the purpose of preserving the integrity, unity, and permanence of the whole Church.

The Constitution goes on to say that in spite of the evidence of history it has become necessary, in view of the disposition on the part of some to depreciate the authority of this apostolic function, to assert in solemn terms the precise character of the prerogative which it pleased Christ Himself to associate with the highest pastoral office.

Up to this point we have summarized and to a considerable extent abbreviated the terms of the Constitution. But in view of its general importance to our subject, though not perhaps without some risk of exaggeration of its significance at the expense of its context, it may be desirable to render the final paragraph of the fourth and concluding chapter *in extenso* :[1]

---

[1] Mansi, *Concilia*, vol. lii, col. 1334 ; *Coll. Lac.*, vol. vii, col. 487. 'Itaque Nos traditioni a fidei Christianae exordio perceptae fideliter inhaerendo, ad Dei Sal-

'So We in sincere loyalty to the tradition received at the very starting point of the Christian faith, to the glory of God our Saviour, the promotion of [the Catholic religion and the well-being of Christian nations, with the approval of the holy council, teach and define as a dogma divinely revealed that when the Roman bishop speaks *ex cathedra*, that is to say when, in performing his office as pastor and teacher of all Christians in virtue of his supreme apostolic authority, he defines by means of the divine aid promised to him in blessed Peter a doctrine regarding faith or morals to be held by the whole Church, he enjoys that infallibility with which the divine Redeemer willed that his Church should be endowed in defining a doctrine concerning faith or morals; and that for this reason, definitions of the Roman Pontiff of that kind are irreformable of themselves and not as a consequence of the consent of the Church.' The chapter (and so too the Constitution) concludes with a very brief canon prohibiting any contradiction of the foregoing definition.

We have given particular emphasis to this document, in view of its value as a summary of the whole doctrine of the origin, status, and function of the Roman see, as it had come to be generally held by members of the Roman Catholic Communion in the nineteenth century.

It would be a matter of considerable interest to examine at this stage not only the implications of the Constitution, but also the history and significance of the numerous technical terms of Christian theology which it employs. In the interests of due proportion, however, we are bound to refrain from such investigation here. We shall therefore venture to hope that for the moment a series of comments mainly of a general character will suffice.

The most remarkable characteristic of the Constitution *Pastor Aeternus* to the careful student of papal history, apart perhaps from the precise form of the phraseology in which the definition of the infallible *magisterium* is cast, is its striking lack of genuine originality. To

vatoris nostri gloriam, religionis Catholicae exaltationem et Christianorum populorum salutem, sacro approbante Concilio, docemus et divinitus revelatum dogma esse definimus: Romanum Pontificem, cum ex cathedra loquitur, id est, cum omnium Christianorum pastoris et doctoris munere fungens, pro suprema sua Apostolica auctoritate doctrinam de fide vel moribus ab universa Ecclesia tenendam definit, per assistentiam divinam, ipsi in beato Petro promissam, ea infallibilitate pollere, qua divinus Redemptor Ecclesiam suam in definienda doctrina de fide vel moribus instructam esse voluit; ideoque eiusmodi Romani Pontificis definitiones ex sese, non autem ex consensu Ecclesiae irreformabiles esse'.

3

put the point in the opposite way we might say that its most notable feature is its close adherence to that which long before the nineteenth century had become immemorially traditional. Nor is this really surprising in view of the evidence which we are proposing to consider. This will show, we believe, that the Roman see was recognized by other churches as possessing from very early times, if not in fact from the beginning, an undoubted primacy in the sphere of doctrine, at least in the sense of a right to be heard in preference to others. Even those who would favour an ambiguous or even a negative verdict cannot forget the fragmentary nature of the evidence at our disposal, nor the extent to which, in this case as with many other historical problems, particularly of the first and second centuries, we are dependent on inference and reasonable conjecture. Equally, as we venture to believe, it will emerge that the primacy of jurisdiction here claimed so insistently, namely the right of the Papacy to act as supreme judge in matters of discipline, if not traceable so far back as the doctrinal primacy, is at least contemporary in respect of its development with the evolution of episcopal jurisdiction. If therefore the Constitution is in any respect in error, it is so not so much because it is false to the facts as it presents them, but rather because the historical presuppositions on which it rests, though accepted as axiomatic at the time of its composition, have in more recent years come to be regarded as in need of considerable reshaping, if not of complete reconstruction. This need not mean, however, that we must necessarily conclude that a large proportion of organized Christianity took a false road at a comparatively early stage in its career, nor that we shall reach a higher degree of consistency by admitting some measure of divine providence behind the Church of the Apostles, while denying any such grace to the Church of those who succeeded them whether in time or in office. The best than can be hoped is that our presentation of history may more accurately describe the actual course of events, and that we may succeed in some measure in resisting that temptation, which so constantly besets every historian, even the most objective, of depicting earlier periods with the lines and forms of a later age.

The Problem of the Church

Our subject concerns the mutual relations of the Church and the Papacy. We have already studied at close quarters the most authoritative and recent account which the Papacy has given of itself. It will therefore be not irrelevant to examine as its sequel the account which the same authority has given of the Church. It is perhaps surprising that so little attention has been directed to ecclesiological doctrine. Yet the explanation may be simpler than it appears. May not this apparent neglect be due at least in part to the prevailing conviction among Christians that St. Paul in his Epistles had already treated the doctrine so exhaustively that no further definition was felt to be necessary? The fact of the Church was accepted and little thought was given to its place in Christian theology till the nineteenth century, when, after the prevailing spirit of criticism had challenged the very title deeds of the Christian religion, it was felt to be inevitable that this doctrine among others should be re-examined and restated.

As we have already seen, had it been possible for the Vatican council to complete its immense programme (and there seems no inherent reason why at some future date this might not be taken up afresh), we should be in possession of a formal and authoritative definition of the nature and meaning of the Church, which, though compiled essentially from the Roman standpoint, would necessarily be deserving of the most serious attention on the part of Christians, and particularly of those who are unable to envisage any divinely sanctioned scheme of reunion which does not 'ultimately include the great Latin Church of the West'. All the same, we are fortunate in possessing in the encyclical letter *Satis cognitum*[1] issued by Pius IX's immediate successor Leo XIII, June 29, 1896, what may be regarded as a convenient summary of the principal contents of the *schema De Ecclesia* as originally submitted to the Vatican council.

In this letter, after repudiating the view that the Christian Church belongs to that class of things which both in respect of their origin and of their constitution belong to the realm of the purely contingent, the Pope asserts that it was not of a federation of Christian groups but of a single structure (*aedificium*) that our Lord Himself was

---

[1] *Acta Apostolicae Sedis*, Commentarium Officiale, 1909– (in progress), vol. xxviii, p. 708–737. See review of *Satis cognitum*, by Stone, D., in *C.Q.R.*, Jan. 1897, p. 289–317.

speaking when He promised 'I will build My Church'. He goes on to say that since the purpose of the Church is to secure the benefits of salvation to all mankind, it is indispensable that it should have the character of permanence. Moreover, since permanence is only possible on condition of internal coherence, there arises the necessity for a duly authorized and constituted authority, namely the episcopate, the responsibility of which is the propagation of a pure and unimpaired faith as well as the government and administration of the whole Christian society. Of this hierarchy, it is declared, the Papacy is the divinely constituted centre of unity, from which emerges the necessary consequence that to its control all other bishops are both individually and collectively subject.

The principal affirmation of the encyclical may be summed up thus: Christians are organized in a single, visible, coherent, and permanent society, governed and administered by an established hierarchy, of which the principle of unity is to be found in the Papacy, and that it possesses this character and constitution by divine appointment.

A noticeable feature is its elaborate appeal, in spite of the well-known *dictum* attributed to Cardinal Manning, to the authority of history. We may therefore feel some confidence that a similar appeal to historical evidence is at least in harmony with the outlook of its distinguished author, and that one of the greatest figures of modern times would not have been wholly unsympathetic towards our examination of the evidence as to the character and constitution of the Christian society on modern historical principles.

Those who are familiar with the *Satis cognitum* will be aware that the author appears to assume the truth of a number of important presuppositions, which a rigid application of the historical principles just mentioned would no longer permit us to take for granted. Among these is the view that all the sayings attributed to Christ in the New Testament are to be taken as nothing less than His *ipsissima verba*, and are therefore of equal validity as historical evidence. Unhappily from the point of view of a simple treatment of the subject in the face of modern criticism we can no longer adopt such an attitude without some reasoned defence, and if this is to be made, we must inevitably examine the more recent forms which the wide variety of present-day criticism has taken.

In the first place, we have to meet the denial that Christ had any intention of leaving behind Him a 'single, visible, coherent, and permanent society'. Thus it has often been asserted that in view of the considerable place taken by apocalyptic concepts in His teaching, such a plan must have been altogether beyond the range of His thought, if not fundamentally inconsistent with a *Weltanschauung*, which presupposed an immediate or almost immediate 'consummation of the end'.

As an example of such an assertion we may quote the words of Loisy: 'We can only speak of a Church when the Church has come into existence, that is to say, following the rejection of the Apostles' preaching by Judaism, when Christian groups were obliged to organize themselves more and more, and finally outside the religious organization of Israel . . . In the place of the expected "kingdom", the Church came into being, and the conception of the Church took the place of that of the "kingdom" in accordance with the accomplished facts'.[1]

Besides the denials of the 'eschatological' school we must notice an opinion widely prevalent in certain critical circles during the last half-century, to the effect that neither of the two passages, found in the Gospel of St. Matthew alone, in which the word ἐκκλησία actually occurs, can be admitted to have formed part of the strictly authentic oral tradition, on which it is supposed the authors of the original sources, used by our evangelists or else actually embodied in their works, must have relied. Thus Bultmann dismisses Matt. XVI, 18–19, as an utterance, not of Christ Himself, but of a Christian prophet of the first generation, which only subsequently acquired Dominical status. Similarly, he attributes the three preceding verses of the same passage as a 'name-legend' devised by the early Christian community.[2] Martin Dibelius, though less radical in his conclusions, equally rejects as unhistorical the whole passage describing St. Peter's confession, even in the form presented by Mark VIII, 27–29, adding that in Matthew 'it has become a typical legend, name-giving and *vaticinium ex eventu* included'.[3]

Though each of these types of criticism properly requires separate discussion, it is not without relevance to remark at the outset that the principles of the *Formgeschichtliche* school have in some measure at least spared us the trouble of meeting the arguments put forward

---

[1] Loisy, A., *Les évangiles synoptiques*, 1907–8, vol. ii, p. 18 f.
[2] See Redlich, E. B., *Form Criticism*, 1939, p. 136 f.   [3] *Ibid.*, p. 187.

by the more advanced exponents of a purely eschatological interpretation of the Gospels. It is relevant to quote in this connexion the
words of an eminent former lecturer on this foundation : 'It seems,
then' he writes, 'that the form of the earthly no less than of the
heavenly Christ is for the most part hidden from us. For all the
inestimable value of the Gospels, they yield us little more than a
whisper of His voice; we trace in them but the outskirts of His ways'.[1]
If this were really true, we might perhaps feel disposed to abandon
any attempt to recover a strictly reliable and authentic picture of
His real intentions, as a journey without sign-post, map or compass,
on which there would be none to redirect us if we went astray. Unless,
therefore, we are willing to acquiesce in such a relative agnosticism,
we must be prepared to face the eschatological problem on its own
ground.

It may be suggested that writers such as Loisy do not state the
facts with strict accuracy, when they argue that in the present form
of the Gospel tradition the 'kingdom' has been displaced by the
Church.[2] It is, of course, undeniable that *logia* exist such as those contained in Mark IV, 11, and Luke XII, 32, in which the society composed
of the original disciples is clearly distinguished from the 'kingdom'.
Yet there are others in which the 'kingdom' appears to be not so
much the subject of hope or expectation as an entity already realized
under existing conditions.[3] Again, there are those in which, so far
from its coming being associated with a catastrophic *parousia*, the
'kingdom' is clearly described as the fruit of slow and patient development.[4] But even supposing that the chief contention of the eschatolo-
gists holds good, and that the Gospel is in essence an *Interimsethik*, it
may be disputed whether this necessarily excludes the possibility
that our Lord envisaged the existence of a permanent society which
would be characterized by the adoption of such an *Ethik* as a principle of conduct. There is in fact much that is attractive in the point
of view represented by von Hügel : '(The writer) would take his stand
very deliberately with those who indeed find a genuine and full

---

[1] Lightfoot, R. H., *History and Interpretation of the Gospels*, Bampton Lectures
for 1934, p. 225.

[2] *Op. cit.*, vol. ii, p. 9.

[3] E.g. Luke XVII, 20 f., where 'in your midst' as a rendering of ἐντὸς ὑμῶν is
much to be preferred. Cf. Plummer, A., *St. Luke*, 1898, p. 406.

[4] E.g. Mark IV, 30–32 = Luke XIII, 18 f. = Matt. XIII, 31–32; Luke XIII, 20 f. =
Matt. XIII, 33.

eschatological element in our Lord's life and teaching, yet who discover it there as but one of two movements or elements—a gradual, prophetic, immanental, predominantly ethical element; and this sudden, apocalyptic, transcendental, purely religious element. Indeed, the interaction, the tension between these two elements or movements is ultimately found to be an essential constituent, and part of the mainspring, of Christianity, of religion, and (in some form) even of all the deepest spiritual life'.[1] Or, as it has been said by a more recent Anglican author, ' "Crisis" is to be the permanent condition under which the Church works. The eschatological stage will last until the end of the world. Christians can never settle down, and the conduct suitable to an *interim* must last indefinitely'.[2]

We may remark, however, that Form Criticism has undoubtedly performed a valuable task in warning us to be on our guard against a certain complacency in regard to our sources, and in helping to indicate the extent to which even the genuine Dominical *logia* may have been modified, or even expanded and supplemented, under the influence of the various points of view represented in the early Christian community.[3] Thus we should be prepared to allow for the possibility that some part at least of the eschatological element in the Gospels may reveal the impress of a predominantly apocalyptic outlook on a largely ethical and prophetic original, with the possible result that teaching which made deliberate provision for a visible and lasting organization may have been obscured or even misinterpreted by means of an unbalanced eschatological emphasis. What is indeed more likely than that the more enthusiastic and unpractically-minded members of the original group of disciples in a white heat of excited expectation should have succumbed to the temptation to anticipate the future, and by this means antedated the fulfilment of a process, which in our Lord's own mind may well have required, not a few years, but even centuries, for its full accomplishment?

Yet even if we are certain that the eschatological school has misrepresented or misinterpreted the evidence, it does not necessarily follow that the actual community of our Lord's original disciples and their adherents was more than an accidental aggregation of

---

[1] *Eternal Life*, p. ix. 1912.
[2] Lowther Clarke, W. K., *Divine Humanity*, 1936, p. 160 n.
[3] A possible example of such influence may be seen if Mark IX, i = Luke IX, 29 is compared with Matt. XVI, 28.

individuals. Indeed, such a view has frequently been upheld by competent and distinguished advocates. Thus an eminent Liberal Protestant has argued: 'Individual gifts ($\chi\alpha\rho\acute{\iota}\sigma\mu\alpha\tau\alpha$) imparted by the Spirit to different members of the community answered all needs. It was the Spirit acting in each one of the faithful, which determined in this way particular vocations, and assigned to this one or that, according to the individual's capacity or zeal, ministries and offices, which apparently were meant to be provisional in character'.[1] Such a theory, however, seems to be open to at least two main objections. First, if it were true that the experience of direct personal inspiration was an integral element in the primitive Christian consciousness, and was itself bound up with the conviction that within the lifetime of the first generation the existing world order, temporarily infused with a fresh and transient outpouring of the Spirit, was presently to be replaced by another, it becomes difficult if not impossible to explain the considerable success of Christian propaganda among communities predominantly Gentile in race and outlook, to whom such conceptions were almost wholly unfamiliar. Secondly, we may note the lack of any clear signs of an inevitable reaction, such as would naturally have followed had these ideas formed a leading element in the Gospel; nor can we account for the survival of the religion itself, when the imminent cataclysm, which on this view must have appeared to be its principal *raison d'être*, in actual fact altogether failed to occur.

No doubt a variety of explanations has been devised to meet these objections and to account for the fact of survival. These generally take the form of a description of the supposed process by which formless, spirit-moved communities were gradually transformed into a hierarchically ordered Catholic Church. Thus Harnack has suggested that the emergence of a visible organized society was due solely to the irresistible impulse of the common Christian consciousness to realize an ideal unity which would provide a substitute for the racial unity of the people of God.[2] Yet he does not appear to meet the obvious rejoinder that to the Gentiles, who unlike Jewish Christians had no experience of racial unity, the need for finding such a substitute would not have appeared obvious. On the other

---

[1] Sabatier, *Les religions d'autorité et la religion de l'Esprit*, 1904, p. 59 f. A similar view appears in Sohm, R., *Kirchenrecht*, vol. i, 1892, pp. 22–28.

[2] *Dogmengeschichte*, vol. i, 1931, p. 50 f.

hand, a wholly different explanation has been put forward by Sabatier. In his view the concept of a universal Church was solely the product of the creative imagination of St. Paul.[1] We are bound, of course, to admit that as 'children of the same father', united by 'the closest bonds of relationship', the communities which owed their origin to him, such as those to which his extant epistles were addressed, would be readily disposed to recognize themselves as forming part of a larger unity and that even this recognition was due in some measure at least to Pauline inspiration. Yet we have to beware of a temptation to exaggerate a distinction between the Pauline and non-Pauline communities, and to ignore the fact of a perfectly free interchange of ideas and of a community of life and outlook between the two groups, as well as the presence of non-Pauline elements within the Pauline churches themselves. No church provides a more striking illustration of this than the Roman church itself, which no doubt owed much to St. Paul's work, yet had in fact in some sense come into existence before his actual arrival. In such a church it is scarcely conceivable that any theory of Christian organization would have been accepted solely on St. Paul's own individual and personal authority.[2]

There remains the concept of a society which is in essence invisible. After making an occasional, spasmodic appearance both in the primitive and mediaeval periods, it was resurrected, at least in some form, by the reformer Martin Luther. Even in our own time it has not lacked its advocates. Thus Hatch, whose Bampton Lectures marked the beginning of a new epoch in the study of Christian origins, affirmed that although it is 'indisputable that our Lord founded a Church', yet in primitive Christian thought, and so presumably in the mind of our Lord Himself, the Church is in fact 'synonymous with the elect'.[3] Since, however, the precise number and extent of the elect *ex hypothesi* is known only to God, we are evidently face to face once more with the 'invisible' conception. The lead given by Hatch was quickly followed by others, notably by Sohm.[4] Yet the view advanced by this latter author markedly

---

[1] Sabatier, *op. cit.*, pp. 61–63.

[2] The influence of others beside St. Paul, such as that of Apollos at Corinth, must not be forgotten.

[3] *The Organization of the Early Christian Churches*, 1888, pref., p. xii.

[4] *Kirchenrecht*, in two vols, 1892, 1923; further developed in *Wesen und Ursprung des Katholizismus* in *Abh. d. K. Sächs. Gesells. d. Wiss.*, Phil. hist. Kl., 1909, vol. xxvii, pt. 3, pp. 335–390.

diverges from that of his forerunner. Insisting no less strongly than Hatch on the distinction already drawn between the Church as a religious idea and the Church as a concrete organization or institution, he comes to the surprising conclusion that it was the Christians of the first generation who were responsible for confounding the two, or rather were guilty of the crime against religion involved in identifying the idea with the concrete society. It is, of course, perfectly possible that the true character of Christianity remained concealed from the first to the sixteenth century. But it has to be remembered that on Sohm's own showing the process of confusion had already begun in the period to which the greater part, if not the whole, of our existing canonical Christian literature is to be assigned, and hence it would seem that the very sources of evidence are themselves vitiated. This he himself is bound to acknowledge, and for him the only escape from an agnostic impasse lies in a quite arbitrary insistence on the essential purity of the supposed ecclesiological opinions of Martin Luther. Yet it is by no means certain that that great, but possibly wrong-headed reformer, is so convenient a *deus ex machina* as Sohm himself would wish. It is, of course, notorious that Luther's original teaching on the subject of the Church was considerably modified, if not distorted, by those who claimed to be his disciples, and we are left with an uneasy suspicion that Sohm has unconsciously been guilty of a confusion, less perhaps in degree but not less real in fact than the one which he so boldly attributes to the *Urkirche* itself. After all, Luther was nothing if not a child of his age. And it was an age distinguished neither by a clear perception of historical and critical principles nor by a high standard of Christian ethics. Thus we must allow that his theories were inevitably conditioned by his environment. In fact, it is perhaps not too much to say that they were a product of sheer logical necessity. As one who had consciously and deliberately revolted from 'historic Christianity', he was compelled to deny the identity of the hierarchically organized Catholic Church with the true Church of God, and to postulate the existence of a new church '*sola fide perceptibilis*'. Yet this does not mean that he would have easily recognized his own doctrine in the quasi-Platonist concept of an 'ideal' Church, so dear to Lutherans of a later period, and more recently to Sohm himself. Though driven by the logic of his position to avoid using the besmirched phrase *die Kirche Gottes*, and to substitute for it *die Gemeinde der Heiligen*, in his vernacular bible, he did not *ipso facto* transform the *q'hal Yahweh* into a *civitas Platonica*, or substitute for a sensuous object one of merely noumenal perception. On the contrary, he believed himself to be reviving a strictly Hebraic concept, and to be restoring the authentic teaching of St. Paul. What he failed to perceive was that the Scriptures themselves supplied, by means of their ineluctable evidence for the existence of a visible objective *Urchristentum*, a refutation of his own subjective doctrine.[1]

It will further serve to support our argument that so far from misrepresenting our Lord's intention in regard to the future, the canonical authors were strictly faithful to His thought, if we explore for a moment one of the sources of which He made use to give that thought formal expression. Attention has frequently been drawn to the probability that the description of Himself as 'the Son of Man' is derived from Daniel VII, 13. (We do not think it necessary to discuss the hypothesis that our Lord Himself actually used the expression to denote the mythological Messiah, dear to apocalyptic and pseudo-epigraphic writings, but that Gentile influence was responsible for the form of those sayings in which He appears to identify Himself with this eschatological figure.) It is now appreciated that the Danielic 'Son of Man' is a collective symbol rather than an individual person. He is in fact a personification of the 'people of the saints of the Most High'.[2] It is thus entirely reasonable to suppose that in applying this expression to Himself (as we believe Him to have done), our Lord intended to display His conviction, to quote a recent author, that 'God's plan must be to include others with Him. Hence the dominant motive of His life was to form a band of those predestined to be the true Israel, the corporate "Son", in prophetic language, "the remnant". . . . So He chose the Twelve to be the nucleus of His kingdom. For a time He was alone, for they listened to His teaching and wondered at His signs without realizing their

---

[1] Sohm's assertion, *Kirchenrecht*, 1923, vol. ii, p. 135, to the effect that the failure of primitive Christianity to regard the society of the 'people of God' as essentially invisible inevitably gave birth to 'Catholicism' is doubtless true, though the author himself missed its real significance. As to the merit which he assigns to Luther, we may note the comment of Kattenbusch, F., *Die Vorzugstellung des Petrus*, p. 351, where he affirms of St. Paul 'noch jedem, der von der Kirche "gelehrt" hat, auch Luther, weit überlegen geblieben ist'.

[2] Daniel VII, 13, 18 *et al.* Note especially v. 27. On this idea and its place in our Lord's thought, see Lowther Clarke, *Divine Humanity*, 1936, pp. 9–40, esp. pp. 16 ff.

implications. The turning point came when Peter confessed that
He was the Messiah. Then the Church, which had hitherto consisted
of Himself, Who alone realized God's will for His people, came into
existence . . . the spiritual house began to be built'.[1]

We have cited these words at length because they seem adequately
to sum up the conclusions of recent scholarship both in this country
and abroad, conclusions which if accepted (and it appears to us that
no others based on reason or sound judgment are actually possible)
are unmistakably far-reaching in relation to the subject in hand.

No doubt it may be true that *Tu es Petrus* contains no more than
a promise, and it might conceivably be argued, assuming for the
moment the genuineness of the saying, that even if it was our Lord's
intention to create a society, the intention was never actually realized.
Those who attempt to argue on these lines appear to ignore the highly
significant character of the liturgical act performed on the eve of
His Passion. For even if *Tu es Petrus* only foretells the foundation
of the Church, *Hoc est enim Corpus meum* certainly postulates its
achievement. The Church is present in the Upper Room, made
visible in the persons of our Lord and the Twelve. It is symbolized
in the sacrificial act by which Broken Bread and Outpoured Wine are
offered, like the life of the Messiah Himself, to be 'a full perfect
and sufficient sacrifice, oblation and satisfaction for the sins of the
whole world'. His Body and His Blood are Himself, with whom He
solemnly identifies the ἐκκλησία of His institution to be 'a reasonable,
holy and lively sacrifice'. The historical sequence and logical connexion is continuous and unbreakable. The identification of the true
Messiah with the ideal Israel does not exist only in the heavenly
sphere. It becomes incarnate in the Church of the Upper Room.

It seems then that we have every reason to discard any theory of
the original character of the Christian Church which would identify
it with a purely invisible society. Yet a serious problem still remains.
If the new society is visible, what is its character? To answer this
we may begin by asking what is the primary meaning of ἐκκλησία in
the New Testament. Is it the local community or the universal
society? Of the importance of this question there can be no doubt,

---

[1] Lowther Clarke, *op. cit.*, p. 161. Cf. Gloege, G., *Reich Gottes und Kirche im NT.*
=*NTliche Forschungen*, 2, 4, 1929, pp. 218, 228. 'Der Retter ist nur Retter als
Schöpfer eines neuen, erlösten gerechtfertigten Volkes': Linton, O., *Das Problem
der Urkirche*, Uppsala, 1932 (1). Teol. 2, p. 148, 'Der Messias ist keine Privat-
person. Zu ihm gehörte eine Gemeinde. Zu ihm gehört die Herde'.

for with but a single isolated exception [1] it is the only collective noun (as distinct from expressions, significant no doubt, but evidently metaphorical), which is used to describe a group or society of Christians in the canonical books.[2]

We may inquire first of all why this word was chosen in preference to an obvious alternative in συναγωγή. Each could claim the authority of the Septuagint version, though of all Greek renderings of *q'hal Yahweh*, ἐκκλησία is by far the most common.

Yet, with the single exception already mentioned, it is ἐκκλησία which is used exclusively in the New Testament to denote the Christian society, whether local or universal. Perhaps the real explanation lies in the fact that it is a term which even in classical Greek usage was not wholly secular in meaning, and in the later canonical and deutero-canonical books of the Old Testament is used without qualification of a gathering or assembly unmistakably national, and hence, in the case of Judaism, undoubtedly also religious in character Hence it was felt to be specially appropriate to the Christian community. In actual fact, its adoption served to emphasize three important beliefs: first, that the new society was not strictly speaking new at all; it was nothing less than the ancient ἐκκλησία τοῦ κυρίου re-formed and re-established by the true Messiah; second, that it was no mere confederation of local communities more or less loosely associated in the pursuit of common ends and linked together by the possession of common ideals, but a single organic people, the true Israel of God; lastly, that it owed its existence, not to human convenience or mutual arrangement, but to the 'calling out' of the elect from the world by the Word of God; in brief, that its title deeds had been drawn up and signed by the hand of the Lord of Hosts Himself.

There is thus a very strong presumption that it is the universal sense of ἐκκλησία which is primary, and it may be noted that in spite of some disagreement still prevailing among lexicographers, the general trend of opinion lies unmistakably in this direction.

We may now take account of the probability that, as used by the early Greek-speaking Christians, it served as a rendering of some already current Aramaic term. Can we identify the word which it

---

[1] James II, 2.

[2] See Excursus A, 'The significance of ἐκκλησία', where the evidence for conclusions summarized here is set out in greater detail.

represented? To essay this task we are bound to take the evidence
of the New Testament as a whole into account. Out of the hundred
or so occurrences of ἐκκλησία there, about a quarter of the total
are to be found in the Acts of the Apostles. Careful examination of
these shows that nearly half are used to denote the original community of Jerusalem (mostly without any qualification; for whenever
it refers primarily to the Church in some other locality, the place-
name is added, unless the reference is already clear in the context).
Only two examples are found of its use in the plural, these being to
some extent offset by two other passages where it undoubtedly
describes the universal Christian society. From this evidence we
are bound to infer that, at least so far as the author of the Acts was
concerned, the word denoted primarily the whole Church of God,
not merely a local congregation. Historically speaking, it begins as a
small community localized in Jerusalem, and at first the congregation
in Jerusalem is *the* Church. Later, as Christianity spreads, the content
of ἐκκλησία comes to include congregations in other places, yet
without modification of the original concept of a single community.
Evidence of a similarly universalist meaning of the word in St. Paul
is abundant. He speaks, for example, not of 'the Church of Corinth'
but of 'the Church of God which is *in* Corinth'. And if this is true
of his earlier writings, it is certainly more and not less true of those
belonging to the end of his ministry. On the other hand, in the later
canonical books, such as the Apocalypse and the Catholic Epistles,
in perhaps a majority of instances ἐκκλησία appears to denote a local
congregation, though again even there examples of its use in a universalist sense are certainly not lacking.

We turn now to the Gospels. Before considering the only two
actual occurrences of the word, both of them in St. Matthew, we
must call attention to the frequent use, if not of the word itself, at
least of suitable metaphors in order to express its meaning. Just as
the simile of 'shepherd' or 'ruler' is freely applied by our Lord to
Himself as the ideal Head, so 'sheep' or 'flock' is used of the ideal
Israel now realized in the body of His disciples. And it is particularly
striking that it is this metaphor which, either in quotation from Old
Testament prophecy or in passages which appear to be actual
Dominical *logia*, occurs not in one, but in all four of our existing
canonical Gospels. Where the Church is not described as a 'flock',
it is called a 'kingdom', which our Lord does not hesitate to identify

with the Messianic dominion assigned to Him by His heavenly
Father. The evidence is far too extensive to be considered in detail
here, but sufficient has perhaps been said to make it highly probable
that the concept represented by these metaphors is universal before
it is narrowed to the particular.

It is possible now to render this conclusion final and incon-
trovertible in the light of the two isolated Gospel instances of the
word ἐκκλησία itself.

The context of the first of these, including the famous *Tu es Petrus*,
which blazes down in gigantic letters from the inner circumference
of the cupola of St. Peter's, is sufficiently well known to need no
description. But for the sake of clearness we include a rendering of
the two passages :

In Matt. XVI, 17–19, we read : 'And Jesus in His reply said to him
(i.e. St. Peter) : "Blessed art thou, Simon, son of Jonah, since flesh
and blood did not reveal this to thee, but My Father who is in heaven.
I Myself also say to thee, Thou art *Kephā*', and upon this *kephā*' I will
build My ἐκκλησία and the gates of hell shall not overpower it. I
will give thee the keys of the kingdom of heaven : and whatsoever
thou bindest on earth shall be bound in heaven ; and whatsoever
thou loosest on earth shall be loosed in heaven" '.

In Matt. XVIII, 15–18, there is : 'But supposing thy brother does
[thee] a wrong, go, reprove him privately ; if he listens to thee, thou
hast won over thy brother. But if he does not listen, bring with thee
one or two besides, that "at the word of two or three witnesses every
saying may be confirmed". But if he disregards them, report it to the
ἐκκλησία ; and if he disregards the ἐκκλησία as well, treat him as a
pagan or an alien. Of a truth I say unto you, whatsoever ye bind on
earth shall be bound in heaven ; and whatsoever ye loose on earth
shall be loosed in heaven'.

For the moment we must assume that both these texts contain
either as a whole or in part genuine Dominical *logia*, and ignore
the possibility that the compiler of this Gospel in his characteristic
way has put together in a single context sayings actually delivered
on quite distinct occasions. Even so some very evident difficulties
remain. If, as seems clear, ἐκκλησία in the first passage denotes not
only a universal society which exceeds the limitations not only of
space but of time as well, we are confronted with a sense of the word
which goes considerably beyond the meaning already recognized

as its primary one in the rest of the New Testament. On the other hand, in the second passage it is apparently used with primary reference to a local congregation seemingly small in membership, though the possibility cannot be excluded that a saying originally 'universalist' has been 'localized' in the process of transmission. If, however, as seems probable, the local church mentioned is in fact the primitive Judaeo-Christian community in Jerusalem, it is by no means inconceivable that the concept of the ideal Israel identified with the local community is in the background here no less than in the earlier examples of the use of the word by the author of the Acts. Is it possible that conjectural restoration of the actual Aramaic term or terms used by our Lord himself, here rendered in both passages by the single Greek expression ἐκκλησία, may throw further light on our Lord's meaning? Of the possible terms used to render either the Hebrew race collectively or a single Hebrew community the most common one in Rabbinical usage of the first century is kenīshta'. The probability that this was the actual word on our Lord's lips is definitely strengthened by the appearance of the form kenūshtā in those Syriac versions of the passages under discussion which have the closest linguistic affiliation to the Palestinian Aramaic probably spoken by our Lord and His Apostles. Although the word itself primarily denotes a 'gathering', its meaning is certainly not confined to that of a merely local assembly—in fact, there is evidence that in the pre-exilic period individual synagogues were disposed to identify themselves with the true or ideal Israel of God to the exclusion of the rest of the Jewish race. Thus it would seem most probable that the kenīshta' māshīyāh Jêshu'ah represented here by τὴν ἐκκλησίαν μου is no mere individual localized congregation; it is nothing less than the ideal 'Synagogue' of the Messiah Jesus—the true universal Church and Israel of God, soon to become actual in the Christian fellowship.

We may claim then to have shown grounds for belief not only that our Lord Himself intended to create a permanent, universal, while at the same time exclusive, society of His disciples, but also that He conceived of this society, not as a new creation but rather as a refoundation of the original Israel henceforth to endure for all time.

Yet in a human environment desire for permanence demands some provision for organization and control in order to secure under changing conditions preservation of identity. It is reasonable there-

ore to expect that our Lord would have provided also for this. In our
ucceeding lecture the evidence for such provision will be examined
vith particular reference to the place assigned to St. Peter in the new
rder.

Excursus A.—*The Significance of ἐκκλησία in the New Testament*

The normal word[1] used to denote the Christian community in the
New Testament is ἐκκλησία.[2] As there is considerable probability
hat in adopting this term as a description of their society Christians
vere influenced in some measure by the frequency of its use in the
Jeptuagint, it is relevant in the first place to inquire what light that
sage can throw upon the present inquiry.

In LXX it is found in roughly one hundred distinct contexts.[3] In
ll these it serves to render *qāhāl* in the Hebrew original, or else a
rm which is a direct derivative of *qāhāl*.[4] In the earlier writings it
frequently used with some qualification, suggesting that to the mind
f the translators the word by itself was felt to possess a general, non-
eligious significance.[5] In the later books, however, it is often found
sed in an absolute sense without qualification,[6] and by the time we
each the Hellenistic writers, such as Philo, examples occur of the
se of the word in an ideal or supernatural sense.[7]

But in addition to ἐκκλησία as a rendering of *q'hal Yahweh* we
lso find a few instances of συναγωγὴ, which itself is also used to
anslate *'ēdhāh*. Although συναγωγὴ, like ἐκκλησία, originally must
ave been used to express the idea of a gathering or assembly,[8] in

[1] The only other term used to describe a Christian gathering is συναγωγή,
ames II, 2.

[2] Apart from its use to denote the Christain community, it is also found in the New
estament in the classical sense of a meeting of the δῆμος, Acts XIX, 32, 39 f. But it
ust be remembered that such constitutional meetings were endowed with a
ıasi-religious character. Cf Aristophanes, *Equites*, 768 ff.

[3] It is also found occasionally in the other Greek versions of Aquila, Symmachus,
ıd Theodotion.

[4] Found in 1 *Βασ.* XIX, 20 = 1 Sam. XIX, 20; *Ψαλμ.* XXV, 12 = Ps. XXVI, 12; *Ψαλμ.*
xVII, 27 = Ps. LXVIII, 27.

[5] E.g. *q'hāl Yahweh* = ἐκκλησία ὑψίστου, Deut. XXIII, 2 ff.; 1 Chron. XXVIII, 8, etc.
f. *qāhāl lāk* = ἐκκλησίαν σου; Lam. I, 10; Ecclus. XXIV, 2.

[6] E.g. in 1 and 2 Chron., the later Psalms and the Apocryphal writings.

[7] It is a common habit of Philo to assign to it the epithet θεῖα, e.g. in *Conf. Ling.*
4. Such a usage is altogether foreign to the Old Testament and New Testament.
lsewhere he qualifies it as ἱερά, e.g. *Som.* 2, 184, 187. Josephus, on the other hand,
ıly uses the word in a secular sense, e.g. *Ant.* 16, 32; 19, 332.

[8] Num. XX, 4; XXVII, 17; XXXI, 16.

later usage it is normally restricted to mean the building in which
such a gathering would be held.[1]

It may therefore be supposed that these two terms lay ready to
hand as a description of the primitive Christian community, ἐκκλησία
and συναγωγή. Yet of these there must have been a strong bias in
favour of ἐκκλησία, for, as we have seen, συναγωγή, by the beginning
of the Christian era, if not for some time previously, had come to
acquire a localized sense. But there were other reasons which
naturally led to the choice of ἐκκλησία. It served to emphasize the
extension in space of the Christian body and to exclude 'congre-
gationalist' notions, i.e. the view that each local Christian group
constituted in itself the 'people of God'; secondly, it served to stress
the essential continuity between the New and the Old Israel, between
the ἅγιοι of the New Testament and the sh'ērīth of the Old; last,
and perhaps most significant of all, it helped to express the conviction
that the Christian society had not come into being as a matter of
human convenience or by man's disposition, but had in fact been
formed by divine institution and appointment.

Until the latter half of the nineteenth century it was probably taken
for granted generally that in Christian usage the primary meaning of
the word was the 'totality of Christians', its use as a description of a
local or individual community being treated as derived and secondary.
During the latter half of the century, however, a change of view
began to take place, and under the influence of the prevailing outlook
it was widely held that Christian ideas and institutions were deeply
indebted to the organization of the Greek urban communities.
Separate existence, it was held, preceded federation. And even since
that time views of this kind have continued to dominate the attitude
of Protestant scholarship as a whole to this question, as may be
seen from the fact that a number of lexicographers and compilers
of 'word-books' continued to assign to ἐκκλησία as its primary
meaning 'the local community'.[3] More recently, however, a marked

---

[1] Ψαλμ. LXXIII, 8 = Ps. LXXIV, 8, where it is used to render mōēd. In the New Testament, as we have seen, it is used once only of a Christian gathering, James II, 2.
Otherwise it denotes a Jewish place of worship (55 examples).

[2] E.g. Hatch, The Organization of the Early Christian Churches, 1881.

[3] So Preuschen-Bauer, Griechisch-Deutsches Wörterbuch zu den Schriften des
N.T.[3], 1937; Abbott-Smith, Manual Greek Lexicon of N.T., 1922; Köster,
Lexikon f. Theologie und Kirche, 1933, s.v. Kirche (R.C.). For the opposite view see
Gayford, S. G., Art. 'Church', in Hastings' Dictionary of the Bible, and
Robinson, J. A., Art. 'Church', in Encyclopaedia Biblica. Moulton-Milligan,
Vocabulary of the N.T.[2], 1915, appears to support the latter view.

reaction has been noticeable. Thus such modern authors as Zorell, Linton, and Schmidt all agree in giving 'universal society' as the original sense of the word.[1]

It may perhaps seem that this is merely a philological question, possessing no more than a purely academic interest. But it should not be forgotten that 'the practical importance of a right doctrine of the Church is very great. So long as scholars thought that independent communities combined to form the Church in the first instance, reversion to their original independence seemed justifiable'. But if 'the Church was one from the beginning, and by nature cannot be otherwise, disunion is clearly contrary to God's will'.[2]

Let us pass on therefore to consider the light which the evidence provided by the use of the word in the New Testament can throw on the problem. We shall begin with the Acts of the Apostles. By this means we shall be able to follow the chronological order of development,[3] and at the same time avoid having to beg the question of the authenticity of the relevant passages in the Gospels. Out of the one hundred or so instances of the word in the New Testament, no less than twenty-three appear in that book.[4] Of these the word is used absolutely, i.e. without any qualification, in eight passages,[5] in each of which the context makes it clear that the reference is to the primitive community at Jerusalem. In two further instances[6] there is the same reference, but with the addition of ἐν Ἱεροσολύμοις; similarly, in two other cases[7] the use of the phrase ἐν Ἀντιοχείᾳ restricts the meaning to the local community. To these two others[8]

[1] Zorell, F., *Lexicon Graecitatis N.T.*[2], 1931 ; Linton, O., *Das Problem der Urkirche in der neueren Forschung*, 1932; Schmidt, K. L., Art. ἐκκλησία, in Kittel, G., *Theologisches Wörterbuch zum N.T.*, 1936.

[2] Lowther Clarke, W. K., *Divine Humanity*, 1936, p. 155.

[3] In adopting this method we are following the precedent set in the article by K. L. Schmidt, just cited, and also of Dr. Lowther Clarke in his essay on 'The Origins of Episcopacy' in *Episcopacy Ancient and Modern*, edd. Jenkins, C. and Mackenzie, K. D., 1930, pp. 8 ff., who justifies it by arguing that there is 'no reason to doubt the general accuracy of the data given in the Acts. . . . If the Acts is dated about A.D. 80 the development of the ministry must have corresponded with the impression in the minds of his readers'. This line of reasoning seems to provide a case for a similar treatment of the Lucan picture of the primitive ἐκκλησία.

[4] Out of these only nineteen are actually relevant. Acts VII, 38, describes the 'Church' of the O.T. ; Acts XIX, 32, 39, 40, the 'Assembly' in the city of Ephesus.

[5] Acts V, 11 ; VIII, 3 ; XII, 1, 5 ; XIV, 27 ; XV, 4, 22 ; XVIII, 22. If with some authorities we read in 11, 47, τῇ ἐκκλησίᾳ, a further example can be added; but there is better support for the reading ἐπὶ τὸ αὐτό.

[6] Acts VIII, 1 ; XI, 22.   [7] Acts XI, 26 ; XIII, 1.   [8] Acts XV, 3 ; XX, 17.

may be added, in which the word is used without qualification, but where the context makes it clear that the allusion is to the local churches of Antioch and Ephesus respectively. A single example of the expression κατ' ἐκκλησίαν[1] occurs in connexion with the local churches of South Galatia. In two passages, and no more, is the word found in the plural.[2] Finally, there are two contexts[3] in which there can be no reasonable doubt that it is used to denote the universal Christian society.

At first sight it would appear that a stronger case can be made for the view that the primary sense of the word in New Testament usage is the local community. But its strength is only superficial. As we have seen, it was natural that the word should be used in first instance of the original nucleus at Jerusalem,[4] which at least for a short time roughly included the whole of the existing Christian society. But by an equally natural process of extension it came to be used first of Christian communities of Palestine,[5] then of Syria,[6] and finally of the province of Asia.[7] In fact, these communities appear to be regarded in no way as separate entities, but simply as expansions of the original ἐκκλησία of Jerusalem.[8]

Similar evidence is provided by the Epistles of St. Paul. The earliest use of the word here clearly refers to the primitive community at Jerusalem (or perhaps of Judaea).[8] On the other hand, the first Epistle to the Corinthians provides a number of examples of the word used in a universalist sense. Thus at the beginning of the letter the Apostle writes 'the Church of God which is at Corinth,[9] which he then goes on to define as 'them that are sanctified by Messiah Jesus, called as holy ones, with all that call upon the name of our Lord Messiah Jesus in every place'.[10] The same epistle offers a further example of an allusion to the primitive Palestinian community,[11]

---

[1] Acts XIV, 23. [2] Acts XV, 41; XVI, 5.

[3] Acts IX, 31; XX, 28. A variant, though of inferior authority, in IX, 31, is αἰ . . . ἐκκλησίαι.

[4] Acts IX, 31. [5] Acts XV, 4. [6] Acts XX, 28.

[7] Notice that in successive verses, Acts XV, 3, 4, it refers first to the community at Antioch and then to the one at Jerusalem.

[8] Gal. I, 13.

[9] I Cor. I, 2; cf. 2 Cor. I, 1. It should be observed that he does not describe the Christian body at Rome as an ἐκκλησία. See Rom. I, 1–7. Yet contrast Gal. I, 2; I Thess. I, 1; 2 Thess. I, 1.

[10] I Cor. I, 2.

[11] Ibid., XV, 9. Cf. Gal. I, 13, and Phil. III, 6. It is important to observe that St. Paul evinces no special concern for the financial support of the 'saints', except those of Jerusalem. I Cor. XVI, 1–3.

while in saying 'God hath set some in the Church, first apostles, . . .'[1] there remains little room for doubt that the author is referring to the totality of Christians.

A contrast with the usage of the Acts is the frequent appearance in Pauline writings of the qualification 'of God'[2] or 'of Messiah',[3] the former being found once only in the Acts, the latter not at all.[4] Yet if there is one sign above all others that the conception of what constitutes membership of the Christian is the same for St. Luke and St. Paul alike, it is the fact that both equally assign primary importance to the acceptance of the fact of the Dominical Resurrection. If St. Paul pays special attention to the primitive ἐκκλησία at Jerusalem, it must be because he regards it as the divinely called remnant of the ancient qāhāl, from which the new society derives its being.[5]

When we pass on to the later Epistles, a further difference is to be noted. Here attention is directed primarily to the universal society, while the thought of the local community is relegated to the background. Thus out of thirteen examples of the word in the Epistles to the Ephesians and Colossians, not less than eleven are used with a universalist meaning.[6] So too if in Colossians the Church is described as the 'Body of Christ' of which Christ Himself is the 'Head',[7] in Ephesians Christ and the Church are actually placed on the same level.[8] Further, it is in Ephesians that we find a description of the ideal Church as 'holy' and 'blameless', expressions which elsewhere are applied to individual Christians.[9] Some have attempted to draw a sharp contrast between the conception of the Church which appears in St. Paul's earlier writings and that which emerges from this later ones. But such contrast as there is can be explained if the changed conditions are taken into account.

In contrast to the marked emphasis on the importance of the primitive ἐκκλησία at Jerusalem, to which even St. Paul himself appears to have been prone at one time,[10] the Apostle felt bound to

---

[1] 1 Cor. XII, 28.   [2] E.g. 1 Cor. I, 1.   [3] E.g. Rom. XVI, 16.

[4] E.g. 1 Cor. XVI, 1–3. How far any idea of the Church as 'invisible' was from St. Paul's thought may be seen by his use of 1 Cor. XIV, 4 f., 12.

[5] See note above.

[6] Eph. I, 22; III, 10, 21; V, 23–25, 27, 29, 32.

[7] Col. I, 18, 24. Cf. Eph. I, 22; V, 23.

[8] Eph. III, 21, 29b; yet contrast ibid., V, 24, 29a.

[9] Eph. V, 28. Cf. ibid., I, 4; II, 21; V, 27; Col. I, 22.

[10] See above and cf. Acts XV, 1, 24; Gal. II, 12.

insist on the Church's supernatural origin,[1] and even on its identification with the Messiah Jesus Himself. If in the earlier writings he uses the metaphor 'body' to describe the intimate relation of Christians as individuals to one another,[2] it was only to be expected that when the need arose to call attention to the divine institution of the whole Christian society that he should identify the 'Body' with Christ.[3]

A further use of the word calling for mention at this point, the importance of which will be found to be discussed elsewhere, is with reference to places of Christian assembly, or what are sometimes called 'house-churches'.[4]

The evidence provided by the rest of the New Testament apart from the Gospels need not long detain us. All twenty instances of the word in the Revelation clearly refer to local communities.[5] The same appears also to be true of its use in the third Johannine Epistle and in the Epistle of James.[6] On the other hand, in the deutero-Pauline Pastorals the phrase 'God's house, that is the Church of God the Living One, the pillar and foundation of the truth',[7] can only mean the totality of Christians, and the same must hold good also of 'a festal assembly and Church of the first-born, who have been enrolled in heaven', a phrase found in the Epistle to the Hebrews.[8] Though the term itself is lacking in 1 Peter, there can be no doubt that the idea of a universal society underlies the words 'an elect race, a royal priesthood, a holy nation, a people for God's own possession'.[9]

We turn now to the Gospels. In spite of the fact that the word ἐκκλησία is found only in St. Matthew in contexts the authenticity of which as actual Dominical *logia* has been regarded by some as highly suspect, it cannot be denied that even 'if the word is not elsewhere attested. . . . the *thing* is there'.[10] Thus in St. Mark our Lord is represented on the eve of His Passion as deliberately applying the words of Zechariah to Himself and His disciples: 'I will smite

---

[1] Phil. III, 20.   Cf. Gal. IV, 26.   [2] 1 Cor. XIII, 12 ff.; Rom. XII, 4 ff.

[3] See above. Attention may also be drawn to his use of the metaphor of marriage. Eph. V, 28–32. Cf. 2 Cor. XI, 2.

[4] 1 Cor. XVI, 19; Rom. XVI, 4; Phil. IV, 22; Philemon 2; Col. IV, 15 f. Cf. Acts II, 46.

[5] Rev. II-III; XXII, 16.   [6] 3 John 6, 9, 10; James V, 14.

[7] 1 Tim. III, 15; cf. *ibid.*, III, 5. On the other hand, *ibid.*, V, 16, appears to refer to the local community. Cf. also 1 Pet. II, 5; Heb. X, 21.

[8] Heb. XII. 23. *Ibid.*, II, 12, occurs in a quotation from Ψαλμ. XXI, 23 = Ps. XXII, 23.

[9] 1 Peter II, 9; cf. *ibid.*, I, 1; V, 2 f.   [10] Lowther Clarke, *op. cit.*, p. 199.

the shepherd and the sheep shall be scattered abroad'.[1] In connexion with this and with the parallel quotation in St. Matthew,[2] it should be remembered that the term *rōʿēh* (shepherd) is frequently used in the Old Testament as a description of the national ruler,[3] just as *ṣōn* (sheep or flock) denotes the 'people' or nation.[4] It would seem, therefore, that the phrase just quoted was specifically chosen by our Lord because it served to describe His own relation to the new society as well as to stress the corporate unity of the disciples. The same metaphor is also found in an isolated *logion* preserved by St. Luke: 'Fear not, little flock; for it is your Father's good pleasure to give you the kingdom'.[5] It occurs frequently in the Fourth Gospel[6] and occasionally elsewhere in the New Testament.[7] Besides this, we also find the metaphor of the Kingdom applied apparently to the apostolic *collegium*: 'Of a truth, I say unto you, that ye which have followed me, in the new creation, when the Son of Man shall sit upon the throne of His Glory, ye also shall sit upon twelve thrones judging the twelve tribes of Israel'.[8] In the face of evidence such as is afforded by sayings such as these it is impossible to deny that it was part of our Lord's deliberate intention to impress this fact upon the minds of His original disciples, namely, that He and they together constituted the new ἐκκλησία of God, not a fortuitously aggregated assembly, but the true corporate Israel of God.

In the face of what has just been said, it is plainly impossible to reject on purely *a priori* grounds any *logion* in which our Lord is represented as assigning a corporate character to the fellowship of His disciples. At the same time, we must judge each of the Matthaean passages on its merits.

At first sight it would appear that the ἐκκλησια in Matt. XVIII,

---

[1] Mark XIV, 27.

[2] Matt. XXVI, 31. It should be observed that Matthew adds 'τῆς ποίμνης'.

[3] Very common in this sense in Zechariah X–XIV; yet also found earlier, e.g. Jeremiah LI, 23, and possibly in Gen. XLIX, 24. Parallels exist in other Semitic literature; cf. art. 'King' in *E.R.E.*, vol. vii, col. 726. 'Many inscriptions have been found in which a king boasts that his god had appointed him king of his land and shepherd of his people'.

[4] Very frequent in Ezekiel, e.g. XXXIV, 6.

[5] Luke XII, 32. A similar distinction is drawn between the ποίμνιον (=ἐκκλησία) and the βασιλεία in *Didache* 9, 4; 10, 4.

[6] John X, *passim*. Cf. *ibid.*, XXI, 16.   [7] Heb. XIII, 20; 1 Pet. II, 25; V, 4.

[8] Matt. XIX, 28. Although a similar saying is found in Luke XXII, 29 f., the discrepancies are too marked to justify assignment to Q. Cf. Streeter, B. H., *The Four Gospels*, 1924, p. 288.

15–18, is essentially the local community as distinct from the ἐκκλησία in Matt. XVI, 18, which seems to bear a transcendental significance. It is on account of this contrast that some who accept the authenticity of the latter have felt bound to reject the former.[1] Yet it is possible that the contrast is more superficial than real. It is by no means improbable that Matt. XVIII, 15–18, in common with other matter peculiar to the first Gospel, was derived ultimately from members of the original community at Jerusalem, who, as Streeter suggests, had fled to Antioch to escape from the misfortunes of their fellows following the martyrdom of James in 62. The possibility that this *logion* had acquired in their hands a certain change of emphasis favourable to the authority of the primitive Jerusalemite community should certainly be taken into account. Allowance may have to be made for the influence of an interpretation placed upon the ἐκκλησία to which our Lord referred, more restricted in its scope than the original Dominical concept. Moreover, if the hypothesis of an Antiochene origin for the first Gospel in its present form be accepted, it is remarkable that in a community in which presumably by the last decade but one of the first century the Gentile element formed a large proportion, the seemingly harsh expression ἔστω σοι ὥσπερ ὁ ἐθνικὸς καὶ ὁ τελώνης should have been accepted without modification. Yet even if we regard this phrase as a midrash, its almost naïve exclusiveness seems to bear testimony to the genuineness of the remainder. Of the passage as a whole it may be said that, assuming that the *logion* formed part of the tradition derived from Jerusalem, there would be every reason for the 'conservatives', who looked to James as their leader, to treasure a saying which appeared to assign to the ἐκκλησία, identified in their view with the Jerusalemite *Urkirche*, a decisive voice regarding matters in dispute between Christians.[2]

As to Matt. XVI, 16, the genuineness of which as a Dominical *logion* must be assumed here, the context appears to throw no light on our

---

[1] Thus Lowther Clarke, *Divine Humanity*, p. 158, says: 'It is safer to suppose that Christ did not speak these words. On His lips they would refer to the synagogue, which is improbable, or else to the later organized Church, in which case it would mean nothing to the first hearers'. Is it possible that a third possibility, to which in view of the foregoing evidence this latter objection would not apply, has been overlooked, namely that the original allusion was the ideal Israel, a concept by no means unfamiliar to circles accustomed to Messianic expectation?

[2] Thus Foakes Jackson, F. J., and Kirsopp Lake, *Beginnings of Christianity*, London, 1920, vol. i, p. 330, n. 2, point out: 'The advice to lay a quarrel before the community has in itself no sign of date. The same advice might have been given by any Rabbi'.

present inquiry, unless we may also assume the identification of the
ἐκκλησία with the βασιλεία, in which case it seems more probable
that the former word bears a universalist sense.[1]

We could be more confident about this conclusion if it were possible
to reach any certainty as to the Aramaic or Hebrew original, which
is here represented by ἐκκλησία. Assuming the latter to underly the
word in question, we might be reasonably certain that qāhāl was the
original, and thus include this passage along with the rest in which
ἐκκλησία is used to denote the totality of Christians. Still assuming
a Hebrew original, 'ēdhāh is also a possibility, though the meaning
would not be affected to any appreciable extent. Besides these two
terms the Rabbis made frequent use of sibbūr, signifying in the Old
Testament a 'heap' or 'crowd', and used both of the whole Hebrew
nation and of an individual community. Another Rabbinical term is
kenēseth Israel; again the bias would be in favour of a general
rather than a local meaning.

Many, however, prefer to believe that it is Aramaic rather than
Hebrew which underlies the word in question. In this case three
possibilities are suggested by the usage of the Targums, namely,
q'hālā, sibbūra', and most commonly of all kenīshta'. It is remarkable
that in those Syriac versions of the New Testament which have the
closest linguistic affinity with the Palestinian Aramaic most probably
used by our Lord and His disciples, ἐκκλησία and συναγωγή are
represented by kenūshtā; there is thus a high degree of probability
that this or a dialectically related word was actually used by them.

As to its meaning, the fact that kenīshta' or its cognate might be
rendered either by ἐκκλησία or συναγωγή would naturally suggest
that the truly primitive conception of the Christian society was
simply that of a sect within the parent society of Judaism. No doubt
at first official Judaism was content to regard it as such. On the other
hand, it is reasonably probable that the Urkirche, though in fact at
first no more than a συναγωγή, held itself to be the only true Israel,
sharply distinguished from the apostate body now abandoned, thus
making a claim not unlike that of similar communities belonging to an
earlier date. Identification of the sect or local body with the whole
community gives ground for holding in that both the passages con-

---

[1] Bearing in mind what has been said above, this would apply no less to
Matt. XVIII, 15–18, than to Matt. XVI, 16, since for a few years at least the Urkirche
at Jerusalem and the totality of Christians were virtually identical.

sidered above the *kenīshta'* is in fact no other than the ideal *q'hal*
Yahweh, and therefore represents the universal society.

From the foregoing evidence only one conclusion seems possible
namely, that ἐκκλησία signifies in the first instance the totality o
the Christian fellowship, and only secondarily serves to describe a
community domiciled in a particular locality.

St. Peter in the New Testament and the Early Roman Episcopate

Moribus antiquis res stat Romana viresque.
ENNIUS, *Annalia.*

Luke XII, 42. 'And the Lord said, Who then is that faithful and wise steward, whom his lord shall make ruler over his household, to give them their portion of meat in due season?'

'It is not without significance that the title deeds of the greatest of the Christian Churches should rest on a doubtful tradition, an uncertain relic and words which in all probability were not spoken by Christ'.[1] These words occur in an illuminating article on the Papacy contributed to one of our well-known encyclopaedias, and describe supposed characteristics of the Roman church which seem to the author to contain the seeds of decay, of disintegration and of ultimate dissolution. He is, however, by no means the only writer who had permitted himself the luxury of wishful thinking on this subject. Ever since Hobbes sardonically described the Papacy as 'not other than the Ghost of the deceased Roman Empire, sitting crowned upon the grave thereof',[2] its enemies have not been slow to prophesy its imminent decease. Thus in 1875 Renan, who had no doubt good reason to desire such an event, declared his conviction that 'on the death of Pius IX the Conclave, under Jesuit influence, would elect a "fanatical" Pope, who would be expelled from Rome by the Italian Government. Thereupon the moderate section of the Italian Cardinals would put forward a rival claimant to the tiara, who would seek to strengthen his position by coming to terms with the Kingdom of Italy. Mutual anathemas and excommunications would follow, and in the resulting chaos the Papacy and the Catholic Church would founder and disappear'.[3] It seems superfluous to call attention to the falsification of his prophecy.

You will recall, on the other hand, that in a famous *Historical*

---

[1] *E.R.E.*, Art. 'Papacy', vol. ix, col. 628a.
[2] *Leviathan*, pt. iv, c. 47, ed. Smith, W. G. D., 1909, p. 544.
[3] Quoted by Binchy, D. A., *Church and State in Fascist Italy*, 1941, p. 30.

Essay Macaulay, after contrasting the ephemeral transience of the kingdoms of this world and the persistent survival 'full of life and youthful vigour' of the 'august dynasty' of the Papacy, ventured to foretell that the Catholic Church 'shall still exist when some traveller from New Zealand may in the midst of a vast solitude, take his stand on a broken arch of London Bridge to sketch the ruins of St. Paul's'. It is clear from the context Macaulay would have been quite willing to allow the applicability of his words to the Papacy. Since the pessimism of the forecast mentioned above has not been justified by the event, one may reasonably inquire whether its basis is as real as our sceptical author imagines; whether 'the greatest of the Christian Churches' does in fact rest on 'a doubtful tradition, an uncertain relic and words which in all probability were not spoken by Christ'. We may appropriately begin by explaining what we believe to be his meaning

By 'a doubtful tradition' he evidently alludes to the one traceable from at least the last quarter of the second century onwards, if not from a century earlier, which has consistently associated the last years and death of the Apostle St. Peter with the foundation of the church of Rome. By 'an uncertain relic' he means the mortal remains of the Apostle, still believed by perhaps the majority of the Christian population of the world to rest beneath the *confessio* in the great basilica of St. Peter. And finally by 'words which in all probability were not spoken by Christ', he is indicating, though perhaps not exclusively, the *Tu es Petrus*, which is among the *logia* ascribed to our Lord by the author of the first Gospel.

Since we may fairly take the doubts here expressed as representative of a widespread attitude of mind towards the Papacy on the part of a considerable proportion of English people, and not least of those who might claim to belong to the Anglican Communion, and in view of its evident relevance to our subject, it will provide a convenient plan for our discussion to examine each of these criticisms in turn, beginning with the last. At the same time we should wish to point out that in our view it is the 'tradition' alone which appears to be strictly indispensable. For obviously if it could be proved beyond doubt that St. Peter never had any direct connexion with the capital of the Roman Empire, it would follow that the claim of the Roman bishops to be the successors of St. Peter in that see, and consequently

---

[1] Macaulay, T. B., *Historical Essays* contributed to the *Edinburgh Review* 'Essay on Von Ranke,' October, 1840.

ieirs of a supposed privilege, would be difficult, if not impossible, to establish. On the other hand, if it should turn out that the dust enshrined in the *confessio* at St. Peter's were indubitably that of some person other than the Apostle, or even if no more than an agnostic attitude to the question of the relic's authenticity were reasonably possible, it might be held that the papal case had not been seriously affected. So, too, if the arguments against the Dominical genuineness of the *Tu es Petrus* were to prove impregnably strong, it might still be possible to show that the Roman see had enjoyed a peculiar relation to the rest of the Christian Church long before the particular applicability of the Petrine texts to that see had been observed. Yet in view of the significance of those texts, and especially of the *Tu es Petrus*, as possible indications of concepts existing in our Lord's own mind, it is of paramount importance that we should re-examine their claim to authenticity particularly in the light of modern criticism. For it is plain that should the case go against them, the contention that the ascription of a peculiar status to the Roman see, however primitive, must be dismissed as an early corruption inconsistent with the mind of our Lord Himself, would be considerably strengthened. We therefore propose to take this question first, and then subsequently to discuss the evidence for the authenticity of the 'doubtful tradition' and the 'uncertain relic'.

We begin by quoting afresh the version Matt. XVI, 17–19:

'And Jesus in His reply said to him (i.e. to St. Peter): Blessed art thou, Simon, son of Jonah, since flesh and blood did not reveal this to thee, but My Father who is in heaven. I Myself also say to thee, Thou art *Kēphā*', and upon this *kēphā*' I will build My ἐκκλησία *kenīshta*') and the gates of hell shall not overpower it. I will give thee the keys of the kingdom of heaven: and whatsoever thou bindest on earth shall be bound in heaven; and whatsoever thou loosest on earth shall be loosed in heaven'.

So far as our existing manuscript evidence goes, there is absolutely no ground whatever for impugning the authenticity of this passage as part of the original text of the gospel. It is found entire in all known manuscripts and versions, and such differences of reading as exist are trivial and unimportant. It follows from this that attacks on its trustworthiness as evidence of our Lord's purpose must proceed along lines other than those of textual criticism.[1]

[1] See Excursus A, Harnack's theory regarding the *Tu es Petrus*.

Naturally it must seem surprising at first sight not only that this *logion* has been preserved in the first Gospel alone, but that it is lacking in St. Mark's Gospel, which is generally believed to be directly dependent on St. Peter's own evidence as to the facts of our Lord's human life. A common explanation, that St. Peter out of his modesty deliberately suppressed the saying when communicating his material to St. Mark, is by no means convincing. Nor, on the other hand, is it easy to accept the interesting though rather insecure hypothesis that it formed part of the supposed lost ending of that Gospel.[1] Yet even if in the last resort we allow that St. Mark was unaware of its existence, such an admission does not provide a conclusive argument against its genuineness. The very existence of the Synoptic Problem arises from the phenomenon that both Matthew and Luke contain an abundance of matter not found in Mark, and of the genuineness of at least a fair proportion of this matter as representing our Lord's actual words there can be no reasonable doubt. Nor can the fact that this *logion* rests on the sole authority of Matthew be admitted to be negatively decisive; on the contrary, there are reasons, now to be considered, for believing that some at least of Matthew's peculiar matter is derived from a source or sources not less reliable than any other which underlies our existing Gospels.

Whence, then, did the editor of Matthew derive this section of his material? A strong case has been advanced in recent years, by a well-known authority on the Synoptic Problem, for Antioch in Syria as its actual place of origin.[2] He has pointed out that in order to account for its general acceptance, particularly in Rome, where a distinctly critical attitude was adopted to the admission of works of supposedly apostolic provenance to the New Testament Canon, 'Matthew . . . must have been vouched for as Apostolic by some very important Church'. Such a conclusion is attractive, if only for the account which it enables one to give of the evident interest of that Gospel (to quote

[1] Turner, C.H., *Catholic and Apostolic*, Essay on 'St. Peter in the New Testament,' 1931, p. 187, conjectures: 'We cannot indeed say whether the lost ending (sc. of Mark) may not have contained, as it certainly contained an appearance of the Risen Christ to St. Peter, so also a confession by Peter of the Divine Sonship, and a commission by Christ to His chief Apostle; I think, in fact, as we shall see later on, that it did'. On p. 192 ff. he gives the grounds on which his conjecture is based, and suggests further (p. 193) that Matthew, in XVI, 13–20, has 'combined in one episodes that were related indeed, but in actual history quite distinct'.

[2] Streeter, B. H., *The Four Gospels*, 1924, p. 500 ff.

the same author) in the 'doings and primacy of Peter'.[1] It may also
be stated, without discussion, that he gives reasons for postulating
the year 85[2] as the most probable date for the publication of this
Gospel.

If correct, this date would allow ample room for the conjecture
that as a consequence of the political disturbances in Jerusalem
leading to the massacre of James the Lord's brother in 62, the church
of Antioch was enlarged and perhaps embarrassed by a formidable
influx of Judaeo-Christians of the old conservative party, with which
St. Paul had already come into conflict. A direct result of this probable migration may well have been the revival of the earlier tension
between the conservatives, on the one side, who as of old claimed for a
narrow legalistic standpoint the authority of James (now considerably
enhanced by his reputation as a martyr), and on the other the Hel-
lenists, who were rightly confident of the patronage of the great
apostle of the Gentiles. We may take it as highly improbable that
these Judaeo-Christian refugees arrived empty handed. In fact, one
can be reasonably certain that they brought with them something
like a collection of Dominical *logia*, sayings in which the eschatological interest was prominent. For these it may be supposed that the
authority of the Apostle Matthew was claimed, with the counter-
signature of James written in a martyr's blood.

Streeter has suggested that on their arrival at Antioch our refugees
found at least one document already enjoying an established reputation. Nor is it fanciful to identify such a document with our hypothetical Q, in addition to which in all likelihood, during the next
decade or so, the church of Antioch received and immediately
welcomed the Romano-Petrine Gospel of Mark.[3]

With the fall of Jerusalem and the gradual disappearance of mutual
suspicion and prejudice, it would be natural for a demand to arise
for combination of the divergent but by no means mutually exclusive
traditions. Fortunately the church of Antioch was able to claim
close connexion with the one Apostle, namely, St. Peter, who represented in some sense a *via media* between the opposing tendencies.
We may therefore regard it as highly probable that the compiler of a
joint publication would do his utmost to secure any material which
would serve to strengthen the authority of this 'centre of unity', now

---

[1] Streeter, *op. cit.*, p. 504.   [2] Id., *op. cit.*, p. 524.

[3] Id., *op. cit.*, p. 513.

clearly recognized in the person of Simon, son of Jonah, and eagerly
incorporate it in his work.[1]

That much of the peculiar matter in Matthew, as, for example, in
XVIII, 15–18, displays a markedly Judaeo-Christian tone plainly
strengthens the case already put forward. Even if we accept Streeter's
view that the *Tu es Petrus* was derived, not from the material, oral
or written, brought by the refugees from Jerusalem, but 'from the
local traditions of Antioch',[2] which must have jealously preserved
any evidence as to the special status of St. Peter, now claimed
as its own Apostle, it is difficult to see why traditions of this kind
should be necessarily less genuine than those which had emanated
from the mother church at Jerusalem. It is therefore not easy to
admit, except on purely *a priori* grounds, that by the time the conflated Matthaean Gospel came to be set down, 'the written Gospel,
Mark, had been in use long enough . . . to dry up the stream of
genuine independent tradition'.[3] Nor can we altogether exclude the
possibility that a passage such as the *Tu es Petrus*, with its unmistakable Aramaisms and legalistic tone, formed an original part of a
floating tradition, common to the churches of Jerusalem and Antioch
alike.

Arguments against the genuineness of the saying which stress the
singularity of the content here assigned to ἐκκλησία, in view of what
has been said elsewhere, do not appear to demand any further attention. We may therefore pass on to discuss those which take a more
subjective form.

It has been pointed out, for example, that it is inconceivable in
view of the relation of St. Peter to the apostolic Church that there
could have been any general consciousness of a peculiar status such
as seems to be assigned to him by these words. Besides this, it is
argued that the known conduct of the Apostle both before and after
the Resurrection is in no way consistent with the presumed characteristics of a 'Rock', and therefore that this evident inconsistency
must be held to exclude the possibility, assuming the correctness of
the interpretation which identifies it with his person rather than with
his faith,[4] that our Lord could have applied such a term to him.

Taking the latter objection first, we may reply that in spite of the
Apostle's inconsistency of character, his description as a 'Rock' is not

---

[1] Streeter, *op. cit.*, p. 515.   [2] Id., *op. cit.*, p. 259.
[3] Id., *op. cit.*, p. 254.   [4] See Excursus B.

ltogether impossible. Indeed, it may be said in general that it is
ot always the most consistent personality which proves in the end
ɔ be the strongest and most reliable support for others. In fact,
ctual consciousness of past failure such as that of St. Peter often pro-
ides a motive for a fresh and more decisive reorientation of the will.
Ve might even say that St. Peter was chosen because in him most
vidently the new Israel showed itself true to type. St. Peter, like
srael, was selected by the providence of God; like Israel he failed,
ut again like Israel he was converted by the power of God's grace,
nd by the power of the same grace was enabled to strengthen his
rethren.

The historical objection to the authenticity of the *Tu es Petrus*
emands more detailed treatment, and can only be examined
dequately by estimating afresh the significance of the data of the New
'estament and of early Christian tradition as to the status and office
f the Apostle. In connexion with this investigation we should do well
ɔ keep in mind some words of warning uttered by a distinguished
cholar of this University only a few years ago. 'We of the Church of
ɪngland', he wrote, 'and Protestant scholars in general since the
.eformation, have failed to give its due weight to the testimony
ɪpplied by the New Testament, and in particular by the Gospels,
ɔ the unique position there ascribed to St. Peter'.[1]

First of all, then, in regard to the picture of St. Peter presented by
Iark, it is relevant to notice that his record is ostensibly based on
ɪe account of an eye-witness, who was himself one of the Twelve.[2]
'he identity of this witness with St. Peter is sufficiently guaranteed,
ot only by the Apostle's place within the select group chosen to
ccompany their Master on exceptional occasions, but by the
adition, constant from Papias onwards,[3] which associates him in
ɔme way with the actual writing of the Gospel. In addition to those
assages in which St. Peter is mentioned in company with others,
ɪough always first in order, in at least half a dozen others he alone
; specified by name. In this way the author seems to wish his readers
ɔ recognize, either that he acted as leader or spokesman of the rest,[4]

---

[1] Turner, *op. cit.*, p. 181.
[2] Mark i, 21, 29 f.; v, 38; ix, 33; x, 32; xi, 11 (reading of Θ, i, k), 15, 27; xiv, 32,
here the impersonal plural is used. Cf. Turner's essay in *J.T.S.*, vol. xxvi, April,
ɔ25, pp. 228 ff.
[3] Cit. ap. Eus. *H.E.* 3, 39, 15.
[4] Mark i, 36; viii, 29; ix, 5; x, 28.

5

or else for some unexplained reason was to be distinguished from them.[1] It is doubtless true (as we have already pointed out) that if we had this Gospel alone we should indeed know nothing of any explicitly Dominical basis for a peculiar prerogative assigned to him, yet it is perhaps not less remarkable that we should also be ignorant of much that might be said in disparagement of his character.

The impression given by Mark is more than confirmed by the other evangelists. Luke adds new occasions on which his name is the only one of the Twelve selected for mention.[2] To the same writer, in addition to the inclusion of a further question addressed by the Apostle,[3] and of a personal appearance to him of the Risen Lord, we owe the unique Dominical *logion* in XXII, 31, 32, which the evangelist may have derived from the local tradition of the church of Caesarea. This saying reads:

'Simon, Simon, behold Satan has sought to have you all, that he may sift you as wheat; but I have prayed for thee, that thy faith fail not. And do thou, once converted, stablish thy brethren'.

If it is not easy to see here the institution of a permanent office, we can scarcely do less than recognize in it a personal commission of leadership and initiative.[5] Moreover, in view of what has already been said in the previous lecture as to the precise occasion of the constitution of the new ἐκκλησία, it is noteworthy that this saying occurs in close connexion with the narrative of the Last Supper.[6]

Matthew's sketch of the Apostle is distinguished by two opposed characteristics. He omits or blurs certain details which are present or even distinct in the two previous portraits;[7] on the other hand, he

---

[1] Mark, VIII, 32 f.; XIV, 29, 37. Turner, *Catholic and Apostolic*, p. 185, calls particular attention to the use of ἀναμνησθείς in XI, 21, by saying: 'who but Peter would have noted that "Peter *remembered* and said"?'

[2] Thus in two passages VIII, 45=Mark V, 31, and XXII, 8=Mark XIV, 13, the name of St. Peter is introduced by Luke, while in the account of his call, Luke v, 1–11, which appears to be independent of Mark I, 16–20, the words addressed to St. Peter alone (v, 10), 'Μὴ φοβοῦ ἀπὸ τοῦ νῦν ἀνθρώπους ἔσῃ ζωγρῶν', are found.

[3] Luke XII, 41.

[4] Luke XXIV, 34.

[5] The first to interpret this text as implying that St. Peter was set over the Church was Ambrose, *In ps.* 43, *enarr.* 40. *M.P.L.* 14, 1163. *C.S.E.L.* vol. lxiv., ed. Petschenig, M., 1919, p. 292. The earliest Roman writer to make use of it is Leo I, *Serm.* 4, 3. *P.L.* 54, 151; on which see the present writer's *Life and Times of St. Leo the Great*, 1941, p. 67.

[6] The narrative leads up to the solemn consecration of the Twelve (=Matt. XIX, 28) and culminates in the injunction to Peter.

[7] E.g. Matt. XXI, 20=Mark XI, 21; Matt. XXVI, 40=Mark XIV, 37.

ntroduces the name of Peter in connexion with two sayings from
which it is lacking in our other authorities.[1] In addition, he adds two
complete incidents, the walking on the water and the discovery
of the stater in the fish's mouth, in both of which Peter is the central
figure.[2] But none of these rivals in importance the logion *Tu es Petrus*,
asserted by this Gospel as the immediate sequel of the Petrine
confession of our Lord's Messianic office at Caesarea Philippi.[3]

In spite of its great familiarity, the real significance of the words
here ascribed to our Lord has not always been rightly understood
and must therefore be briefly re-examined. First of all, it should be
observed that the saying is introduced by a striking affirmation. Our
Lord declares that the confession just uttered is so tremendous in its
consequences, and so far beyond the wit of man to attain by unaided
intuition or reason, that its origin is to be ascribed, not to human
agency, but to a peculiar revelation imparted to the Apostle by the
eternal Father. Then as the complement of this privilege, the Son
Himself also bestows one of His own giving ('I Myself also say to
thee . . .'). The solemn words which follow proclaim in effect that
the eponym now bestowed upon Simon is no mere nickname like
Boanerges. Πέτρᾳ (*Kēphā*') literally denotes the Apostle himself as
'Rock', and it is on Peter as on rock [4] that the foundations of the new
ἐκκλησία, described in the metaphor of a building, are to be laid.
Against that building so erected, in virtue of the immovable nature
of the substance on which its foundations rest, neither the forces of
evil nor of death can ultimately prevail.[5] Next, to the simile of the

---

[1] Matt. xv, 15=Mark vii, 17; Matt. xviii, 21. Cf. Luke xvii, 4.

[2] Matt. xiv, 28–31; xvii, 24–27.

[3] Matt. xvi, 17–19.

[4] See Excursus C: 'St. Peter as the Rock'.

[5] The meaning of πύλαι ᾅδου has been disputed. Against the more general view
that it is a symbolic expression for 'evil', it has been argued, e.g. by Harnack, A., in
Sitz-Ber. d. köngl. preuss. Akad. d. Wiss, 1918, h. xxxii, pp. 637 ff., and more recently
by Badcock, F. J., *Theology*, July, 1937, vol. xxxv, No. 208, pp. 38 ff., with reference
the Scriptural and apocryphal evidence that it means 'physical death'. Yet in
view of the further evidence presented in *Theology*, Nov., 1937, vol. xxxv, No. 209,
299 f., this conclusion cannot be regarded as decisively established, and some
allowance must be made for passages which 'definitely connect Sheol-Hades both
with sin and with destruction, so that it could be argued that Sheol-Hades represents the powers of evil. Dr. Charles, on Enoch lxiii, 10, has shown how the meaning
of Sheol changed in the period between the Old and New Testament'. In any case,
the fact that πύλαι ᾅδου is used without the article shows that it is a stereotyped
expression. Bernard, J. H., in *Expositor*, June, 1916, pp. 401–9, interpreting the
phrase with reference to Matt. vii, 24–27, makes the interesting suggestion that
πύλαι ᾅδου is a mistranslation of an Aramaic expression, cf. Daniel viii, 2, *'ubhal,*

rock, following the line of thought suggested by the metaphor of the building, is added the metaphorical promise that in the new palace or kingdom (which we here take to be an anticipatory description of the ἐκκλησία conceived of as already constituted) St. Peter is to hold the office of steward or *major domo* (not merely that of porter, as has sometimes been supposed),[1] and in virtue of his possession of the keys, it will be his function to administer the royal substance. But in addition to his administrative authority there is added also legislative power. He is to hold the place of final arbiter or referee, and from his decisions there will lie no appeal.[2]

Against the view that such a prerogative was assigned exclusively to St. Peter, it is natural to find the verse Matt. XVIII, 18, quoted:

'Of a truth I say unto you, whatever things ye bind on earth, they shall be bound in heaven; and whatever things ye loose on earth they shall be loosed in heaven'.

This *logion*, as is well known, is the immediate sequel of the passage, already discussed, referring to the mode of settling disputes between members of the new ἐκκλησία.[3] In view of its editor's familiar practice of assembling his material in paragraphs relating to the same subject, it is insecure in the case of the first Gospel to make use of the immediate context, as a clue to the interpretation of a particular passage. But in this instance there seems no cogent reason against reading the second *logion* as the actual, rather than merely the literary, sequel of the first, and thus explaining its meaning as an assurance that final decisions pronounced by the Church (there is no ground for restricting the scope of the assurance to the Twelve alone) will be ratified by God. Such a promise, however, is not inconsistent with the provision of a final arbiter or referee, whose function is to express ultimately the nature of the Church's decision.

rendered in LXX πρὸς τῇ πύλῃ Αἰλάμ. If what our Lord actually said was 'the floods of Hades' (cf. Gen. VII, 11), it would be easier to account for the use of κατισχύσουσιν.

[1] Thus Leo, *Serm.* 3, 3. *P.L.* 54, 146, calls Peter 'regni caelorum ianitor'. But Goudge, *New Commentary*, 1928, pt. iii, p. 169a, calls attention to the significance of the plural κλεῖς and holds that the place assigned to Peter is not that of porter only but of chief steward. Cf. Luke XII, 42.

[2] As a duly commissioned Rabbi possessed authority to determine questions of casuistry under the Old Covenant, so Peter is given the same power in the new ἐκκλησία. Cf. Acts x, 47. But it should be noticed that it is not primarily a 'power of absolution'. For a late survival of the more strictly correct interpretation, see *Ep. Clementis ad Jacob.* 2, 6. *M.P.G* .2, 26, 41.

[3] Cf. Luke XI, 25.

The fourth Gospel is remarkably well supplied with personal
notes regarding the Apostles. Nor is 'Simon Peter', as he is habitually
called here,[1] any less prominent than in the synoptists. It may perhaps be regarded as significant of the writer's wish to call our attention to his importance in relation to the Gospel narrative as a whole,
that here his naming as *Kēphā'* appears at the very outset of the
Ministry, while a parallel to the Messianic confession at Caesarea is
recorded in connexion with the 'eucharistic' discourse at Caper-
naum.[2] So again at the Last Supper,[3] after the Arrest,[4] on receiving
the report of Mary Magdalene[5] (where St. Peter is apparently the first
to appreciate the meaning of the 'empty tomb'), and finally on the
shore of the sea of Tiberias[6]— in each case it is St. Peter who is the
leader and who is almost unique in showing any capacity for initiative.
The trustworthiness of the whole of this last incident has indeed
been called in question on the ground that it forms part of a chapter
which is demonstrably of the nature of an appendix to the Gospel
as a whole. Without, however, raising either the vexed questions of
the traditional ascription of this Gospel to John the son of Zebedee,
or of its general historical reliability, it is certainly relevant to the
problem of the authenticity of this passage in particular, to point
out the remarkable resemblance which the incident here described
bears to a similar story, assigned by St. Luke to the preliminary stages
of our Lord's ministry.[7] The evident fact that this Lucan episode is
not completely identical with the record of the call of the first four
apostles as set down by Mark-Matthew,[8] may possibly suggest that
Luke has conflated two originally separate traditions, one describing

---

[1] Turner, *Catholic and Apostolic*, p. 197 f. n., points out: 'Our Lord always
addresses the apostle as Simon, save in Luke XXII, 34: Luke is in this respect the
least primitive of the four Gospels. Πέτρος, when used alone, has, as a nickname.
(if one may use the phrase), the article always in Mark (III, 16, obviously does not
come into account) except in VIII, 33—omitted probably because the article has
been used in the preceding verse—and according to W. H., in XIII, 3, where Tis-
chendorf may be right in inserting it with *Aleph* D. 565. Matthew twice, Luke four
times, John three or four times, drop the article; and so later writers like Clement
and Ignatius. On the other hand, Matthew is the only Gospel where Peter, not
Simon, is used in the narrative before the record of the bestowal of the surname'.

[2] John VI, 69, 'σὺ εἶ ὁ ἅγιος τοῦ Θεοῦ'. Cf. I, 41, 49; XI, 27; Mark I, 24; Luke
V, 34. It should be noticed that the Aramaic *Kēphā'* occurs only in the fourth
Gospel, though it is frequent in St. Paul's Epistles: I Cor. I, 12; III, 22; IX, 5;
V, 5; Gal. I, 18; II, 9, 11, 14. Contrast Gal. II, 7, 8.

[3] John XIII, 24.   [6] *Ibid.*, XXI, 2–11.
[4] *Ibid.*, XVIII, 15 f.   [7] Luke V, 1–11.
[5] *Ibid.*, XX, 2 ff.   [8] Mark I, 16–20=Matt. IV, 18–22.

the call and the other the draught of fishes. As a consequence of thi
confusion, Luke may be thought to have substituted for the com
mission to St. Peter, which in the Johannine account follows th
scene by the lake side, a Petrine version of the promise 'I will mak
you fishers of men', elsewhere addressed to Peter and Andrew an
probably intended for James and John as well. Thus in Luke's forr
of the *logion* the words are spoken to St. Peter alone, 'Fear not, fron
henceforth *thou* shalt catch men'.[1] There is also much that is attrac
tive in the view which regards the Johannine appendix as supplyin
the record of that appearance of Christ to Cephas or Simon mentione
by St. Paul and St. Luke. If either of these theories are accepted, th
case for the genuineness of the threefold charge:

> 'Simon, son of John . . . feed My lambs. . . . Simon, son o
> John . . . shepherd My sheep. . . . Simon, son of John . .
> feed My little sheep',[2]

appears reasonably strong. As to its significance, it may be said that
even if these words constitute a formal restitution to the Apostle c
an apostolate forfeited by the thrice repeated denial, it is difficult t
regard such an interpretation as exhaustive, or to exclude the pos
sibility that they also involve the bestowal of at least a personal com
mission, the scope of which is co-extensive with the new ποίμνη (flock)

Does the portrait of St. Peter's status and office as here repre
sented find support in the evidence of the Acts and the Epistles
So far as the testimony of the Acts is concerned, it is evident to th
most casual reader that in almost half the narrative, he is the mos
prominent figure. His is the initiative which leads to the election an
ordination of Matthias to fill the vacant apostleship;[3] his voice firs
bears witness to the nature and reality of the new Pentecostal gift;[4] t
him is accorded by special revelation the divine purpose that th
devout 'God-fearers', no less than those actually 'within the cove

---

[1] See above, p. 54, n. 2, and cf. Bernard, *St. John*, I.C.C., vol. ii, p. 688.

[2] John XXI, 15–17. 'Βόσκε τὰ ἀρνία μου . . . ποίμαινε τὰ πρόβατά μου . . . βόσκ
τὰ προβάτιά μου'. There is a certain progression in the charge. To 'feed
sheep is a greater responsibility than merely to 'tend' them. The earliest-know
example of use of this text in the interests of the Roman see is Leo I, *Serm.* 4, 4
P.L. 54, 152. Yet it should be noted that Cyril Alex., *Comm. in Ev. Ioann.* 12 (o
XXI, 15–17), *M.P.G.* 74, 749, interprets it of a restoration of Peter's apostolate
considered to be forfeit by his threefold denial, cf. Augustine, *Serm.* 295, 4
M.P.L. 38, 1350. Elsewhere Augustine, *Serm.* 296, 3, 5, 11. *M.P.L.* 38, 1353–8
De agon. Christ., 30, 32, *M.P.L.* 40, 308, 'cum ei dicitur, ad omnes dicitur', inter
prets the charge as given to all the Apostles.

[3] Acts I, 15.   [4] *Ibid.*, II, 14.

ant', should be admitted to share the privileges of the Gospel;[1] by him the freedom is secured which one day his fellow-apostle will make known throughout the Roman world. These are but a few yet significant illustrations of the important and outstanding place taken by him in the reconstituted ἐκκλησία of God.

As to the Epistles, we may consider first the evidence of St. Paul in his letter to the Galatians. We shall assume for this purpose the correctness of that reconstruction of New Testament chronology which treats this epistle as the earliest of his extant writings, and would assign it to a period shortly before the apostolic council in 49.[2] In view of its value for the light which it sheds on the person, work, and teaching of the author, it is surprising to discover how much it has to tell us in addition about the relation of St. Peter to the primitive Christian community. For in spite of the author's evident preoccupation with the need of justifying the credentials of his own apostolate in the face of a determined challenge, he does not hesitate to affirm that his chief purpose in visiting Jerusalem three years after the occasion of his conversion was 'to make the acquaintance of Cephas'.[3] He admits that he did indeed encounter James 'the Lord's brother' as well, but makes it clear that this meeting was purely accidental. Why was it so important to introduce himself to St. Peter? Can we exclude the possibility that St. Paul had some problem of a pastoral or administrative nature, regarding which he had reason to think that St. Peter's opinion would be not only valuable but decisive? Following his allusion to this meeting, he goes on to record how on the occasion of a second visit to the mother church fourteen years later, a formal division of work was made between St. Peter and himself, and exclaims, not without a slight hint of sarcasm, but with almost characteristic disregard for grammatical syntax:

'From those who appear to be somewhat (whatever they actually were makes no difference to me—God takes no account of a man's person) I say, those who appear to be somewhat imparted nothing to

---

[1] Acts, x, 2. 'εὐσεβὴς καὶ φοβούμενος τὸν Θεόν', as Turner, op. cit., p. 203, n. remarks: 'Almost a technical phrase for an uncircumcised proselyte' (cf. Acts X, 22 ; XIII, 16, 26). Turner's comment on the episode is, ibid., p. 205: 'Peter has here secured the freedom of the Gospel which Paul is to preach'.

[2] Id., 'Chronology of the N.T.,' in H.D.B., vol. i, col. 424b.

[3] Gal. I, 18. Turner, op. cit., p. 211 f., appears to regard the word ἱστορῆσαι as implying that St. Paul received on this occasion some of the instruction to which he alludes in 1 Cor. XV, 3. Cf. XI, 23.

me in addition. On the contrary, when they saw that I had been
entrusted with the Gospel of the Uncircumcision, as Peter had been
with that of the Circumcision (for He that worked mightily in Peter
to make his apostolate effective worked mightily also in me in relation
to the Gentiles), and when they recognized the grace which had
been given me, James, Cephas, and John, evidently pillars, gave to
me and to Barnabas right hands of fellowship, that our mission should
be to the Gentiles, and theirs to the Circumcision'.[1]

St. Paul then relates how, under pressure of the conservative
influence presumably emanating from the legalist party in the mother
church, St. Peter showed some inconsistency in his attitude towards
the Gentile element of the church in Antioch, in consequence of
which the author had felt moved to make a formal public remonstrance in St. Peter's presence, on the ground that his fellow-apostle's
change of mind belied his earlier, more tolerant conduct.

It is sometimes argued that this description of the authorities of
the mother church, in which St. Peter appears to be no more than
the second of three 'pillars', as well as St. Paul's confessedly critical
attitude towards his fellow-apostle, is utterly inconsistent with any
belief in a peculiar prerogative enjoyed by his colleague in virtue
of a Dominical commission. But can we explain why St. Paul makes
so much of Petrine inconsistency and only notices in passing the
same defect in Barnabas, one who almost from the first had been
his intimate friend and ally? We may admit that St. Peter was
inconsistent, and may even grant that the Pauline protest was
justified, though we should bear in mind that we have no means of
knowing St. Peter's side of the case. Yet St. Paul must have had a
reason for so emphasizing the seriousness of his co-apostle's action.
We can only infer that a decision made by St. Peter, even if hasty and
ill-considered (a view which we must in fairness allow to be unsup-
ported by evidence), was liable to be accepted as the norm, and
that because of this St. Paul realized the urgency of an immediate
protest, before any irremediable harm, as he supposed, might be done.
On his showing, St. Peter seemed likely to bind where he had formerly
loosed, and thus the freedom of the Gospel seemed to be in danger.
Only so does the real implication of the Pauline protest become clear.

[1] Gal. II, 6–9. The word στῦλος is used in I Tim. III, 15, of the Church itself.
Cf. Rev. III, 12. Clement Alex. (cit. ap. Euseb. H.E. 2, 1), has this order of names:
James, John, Peter.

The order of the names 'James, Cephas, and John, evidently pillars', also calls for some further notice. Of the importance of James the Lord's brother (we assume the identity of this James with the person mentioned in I, 19), in relation to the church in Jerusalem, there can be no doubt. In fact, evidence both within and without the New Testament agrees in assigning to him the status of head of the local community,[1] comparable if not identical with that of the single bishop in relation to the local church a century or so later. Moreover, it is clear that after his martyrdom in 62, he was succeeded by his brother Simeon, though perhaps not till after the confusion accompanying the destruction of the city had disappeared and the shattered ruins of the local church had been eventually restored. This early example of an apparently hereditary succession, namely of those who were members of our Lord's own family, has suggested, on the analogy of an oriental Khalifate, that the primitive conception of a Christian 'primacy' was attached not to Rome but to Jerusalem, not to Peter, but to James ; and further that the final disappearance of this idea was a purely accidental consequence of the successive catastrophes which befell the latter city between 69 and 135. Yet it is probable that the tradition of a universal primacy of James does not begin to take shape till the beginning of the third century at the earliest, and then only in the obscure and not very reputable 'pseudo-Clementine' literature.[2] Of evidence that James made decisions of universal application there is none; James gives his vote at the apos-

[1] Cf. Acts XII, 17, ἀπαγγείλατε Ἰακώβῳ καὶ τοῖς ἀδελφοῖς ταῦτα. It is clear from ver. 2 that it is James 'the Lord's brother' who is meant. For a discussion of the relationship of 'His brethren' to our Lord, see e.g. Bernard, St. John, I.C.C., vol. i, p. 84 ff.

[2] The Pseudo-Clementine writings include (1) the *Recognitions* in ten books, the Greek original of which has perished. They are known to us chiefly in a Latin version by Rufinus of Aquileia and in a Syriac compilation, and relate how Clement of Rome came into contact with the Apostle Peter and witnessed his contest with Simon Magus at Caesarea ; (2) the twenty *Homilies* preserved in Greek ; (3) two *Epitomes* also in Greek, derived from the *Homilies* and 'other connected writings' ; (4) a Syriac *Epitome* derived from the *Homilies* and *Recognitions*. Prefixed to the *Homilies* are two apocryphal letters, an *Epistle of Peter to James*, and an *Epistle of Clement to James*, M.P.G. 2, 25–28. This is the only part of the *Homilies* which has survived in Rufinus' version. In the former of these *Epistles* (c.i. M.P.G. 2, 25) the Apostle, in addressing James, seems to imply that he regards him as his superior, calling him :

'Lord and bishop of the holy Church, under the Father of all'.

Similarly, in the latter *Epistle* Clement is represented as describing how he addressed a letter to James, informing him of the death of Peter and of his succession

tolic council and as president of the local church records it last, but
it is the summing up of a chairman, not the verdict of an arbiter.[1]
If anything, the narrative suggests that it was the evidence of
St. Peter which turned the scales of decision in favour of St. Paul.[2]
We cannot therefore regard the order of names as given in the letter
to the Galatians of those who were 'evidently pillars' (a metaphor
which is not the antithesis but the complement of the 'rock' in
Matt. XVI, 18) as dictated by more than a natural inclination to put in
the first place the name of one who was in so unique a relation, not
only to the local church, but also to our Lord himself.

A minor point, though possibly not without significance, is that
(as distinct from our other authorities who use both names, sometimes
separately, sometimes in conjunction) St. Paul, with only two exceptions (each in the Epistle to the Galatians and in successive verses),[3]
consistently refers to St. Peter by his surname in its original
Aramaic form, though graecized as Cephas, thus actually, if unintentionally, calling attention to his character as 'Rock'. In the former
Epistle to the Corinthians, where his usage is wholly consistent, the
position of the name in relation to those of others in the same context is possibly significant. Thus in two passages referring to divisions
in the Corinthian church the order might suggest that St. Paul
regarded him as possessing some priority; a like explanation pro-

---

to the Apostle's see and to his teaching office. Here (*Praef. M.P.G.* 2, 32 f.) he
writes:

'Clement to James, the Lord and bishop of bishops, who rules the holy church of
Jerusalem [of the Hebrews] and the churches everywhere excellently founded by
the providence of God'.

Later (c. 2, *M.P.G.*, 2, 36), in the same letter, Peter is represented as saying:

'I appoint for you this man Clement as bishop, to whom I entrust my chair of
teaching'.

According to Waitz, H., *Die pseudoklementinen Homilien und Rekognitionen*,
Leipzig, 1904, in *Texte u. Unters.*, vol. x, pt. 3, the *Homilies* and *Recognitions* were
put together in their present form c. 300–350 by two different Arian compilers, but
both editors made use of the same source, namely, a lost Clementine romance
entitled Περίοδοι Πέτρου, which probably originated in Rome c. 200–250. This in
its turn was based on the Gnostic-Ebionite treatise Κηρύγματα Πέτρου, to which
the heretical bias of the Clementines is to be traced. (It is to be distinguished from
the Κήρυγμα ἐκκλησιαστικόν, probably known to Hermas and, if so, to be assigned
to the earlier half of the second century.) It was not till the later years of the fourth
century that the 'Clementines' became known in the West through the Latin
version made by Rufinus. Cf. also Chapman, J., 'The Date of the Clementines,' in
Zeitschr. f. N.T. Wiss, vol. ix (1908), pp. 21–34, 147–154.

[1] Acts xv, 19. Contrast κρίνω with ἔδοξε τοῖς ἀποστόλοις (v. 22).
[2] *Ibid.*, xv, 7 ff.   [3] Gal. 1, 7, 8.

bably accounts for the same position of the name in a later passage, while it is noteworthy that of all the Resurrection appearances, both personal and general, cited in the fifteenth chapter, the one to Cephas occurs first in the list.[1] None of these allusions is capable of bearing much weight in isolation, but taken together their combined strength appears to be considerable.

It is probable that neither of the two general epistles traditionally attributed to St. Peter is the actual work of the Apostle, and though a stronger case can be made out for the authenticity of the former than of the latter, its absence from the so-called *Muratorianum*, a Canon of Scripture most probably of Roman origin dating from the period including the end of the second and the beginning of the third century, appears to tell decisively against direct Petrine authorship.[2] In any case, neither of these documents supplies any evidence which might bear upon our present inquiry.

A further passage which might conceivably claim our attention as a possible reference to the apostle is the section in the Apocalypse in which the mission and martyrdom of the 'Two Witnesses' is described. The hypothesis recently put forward that they are to be identified with SS. Peter and Paul has not, however, met with general acceptance, and the passage must therefore be dismissed as irrelevant.[3]

In conclusion, a further argument against the Petrine primacy based on Scriptural evidence calls for some notice. It is sometimes supposed that those passages in the New Testament in which mention is made of our Lord as 'the foundation', or else of the Apostles generally or of the Twelve in particular as 'foundations', tend to disprove the authenticity of the *Tu es Petrus*, and hence the attribution of any peculiar privilege to St. Peter on our Lord's authority. Yet those who argue on these lines appear to have over-

---

[1] I Cor. I, 12; III, 22. Cf. *ibid.*, IX, 5, where in a passage referring to the 'other apostles and the Lord's brethren' generically, Cephas alone is mentioned by name.

[2] It is all but universally agreed that 2 Peter is neither Petrine nor even apostolic, but is to be assigned to the first half of the second century. See *New Commentary*, pt. iii, p. 653 f. As to I Peter, there is some attractiveness in the view advanced by Streeter, *Primitive Church*, p. 128, that the work consists of three parts, a late editorial address and salutations, I, I f; a sermon, I, 3–IV, II, probably given to Christian neophytes; and finally a pastoral letter, perhaps some two or three years later in date. It is far more probable that the place of origin is proconsular Asia than Rome. The actual compilation is conjecturally assigned by Streeter to Aristion the presbyter.

[3] See Turner, *Catholic and Apostolic*, p. 219 f. Charles, R. H., *Revelation*, I.C.C., 1920, vol. i, pp. 280 ff., favours an identification of the 'witnesses' with Moses and Elijah, which appears far more probable.

looked the consideration that the Matthaean metaphor differs from
the rest. There nothing is said regarding a foundation, since the
presence of rock renders it unnecessary. The fact that St. Paul
and the author of the Apocalypse[1] are using a different idea shows
that their words are irrelevant to the question under discussion.

Our survey is now complete. With the evidence before us it is
difficult to imagine that there can be any satisfactory final conclusion but one, namely, that the extensive authority assigned by
anticipation to St. Peter in the *Tu es Petrus* is amply supported, and
that consequently any argument against authenticity on the supposed
ground of its uniqueness must necessarily collapse. Here, then, we
seem to find the true explanation of the frequently recurring phenomenon that whether it be in Jerusalem, Antioch, Iconium or Corinth,
it is St. Peter's point of view and St. Peter's position which has to
be taken into account. No one appears to be concerned with the
views of his brother or Simon Zelotes. It is Simon the Rock alone
whose attitude appears to possess a certain finality, and from whose
decision there would seem to lie no appeal.

II

We now pass on to consider the evidence for a connexion of St.
Peter with the origins of Christianity in Rome. With considerable
ingenuity a previous holder of this Lectureship has sought to defend
the view that the Apostle's earliest contact with the imperial capital
was the immediate or almost immediate sequel of his deliverance
from imprisonment under Herod Agrippa I.[2] We cannot, however,
feel confident that the arguments which he has put forward are
strong enough to support his thesis, and would prefer to adopt a
somewhat agnostic view in regard to that period of the Apostle's life
which intervened between his deliverance and his subsequent
appearance at the apostolic council of 49.[3] Have we any means of
knowing what follows?

At first sight it may appear that the absence of any indubitable
evidence within the limits of the New Testament must tell decisively

---

[1] 1 Cor. III, 11; Eph. II, 20; Rev. XXI, 19.

[2] Edmundson, G., *The Church of Rome in the First Century*, Bampton Lectures for
1913, p. 50.

[3] There is of course a gap in the chronology of St. Peter's career, perhaps of as
much as two years. Cf. Turner, Art. on 'Chronology in the N.T.', *H.D.B.*, vol. i,
col. 424b.

against the trustworthiness of an admittedly post-apostolic tradition. The only possible Scriptural testimony which can be reasonably quoted in favour of St. Peter's residence in Rome is the highly ambiguous salutation addressed by the author of 1 Peter to the recipients of his Epistle on behalf of the 'co-elect lady in Babylon'.[1] But this is surely too fragile a basis on which to stand so tremendous an hypothesis, itself so pregnant of consequences. On the other hand, once we leave behind the canonical literature, we are confronted with a considerable body of evidence strong in quality and widely dispersed both in time and space. Thus in the first Epistle of Clement, which may be assumed to be a work composed in or about 96 and rightly ascribed to a person of that name, whose status in the Roman church was undoubtedly one of some importance, while describing the unhappy consequences of 'jealousy and envy' ($\zeta\hat{\eta}\lambda o\nu$ $\kappa\alpha\grave{\iota}$ $\phi\theta\acute{o}\nu o\nu$) the author alludes to the martyrdom of SS. Peter and Paul.[2] His argument has no doubt a direct relevance as an admonition intended for the 'jealous and envious' in the church of Corinth, in view of the known connexion, direct or indirect, of both apostles with that church,[3] but it would lose much of its needed force if it did not reflect a belief, not less well established in Corinth than in Rome, and one which certainly was to be widely accepted before the end of the second century,[4] that both Apostles had actually lived and died the death of martyrs in Rome itself.[5]

The probable implications of Clement's argument are carried a stage further by a letter of Ignatius[6] written not more than twenty years later and this time addressed to the church of Rome itself, in which he refers to the two Apostles as 'monitors' of Roman Christians. Unless the author had been confident that there were in fact solid grounds for associating both these distinguished names with that

[1] In view of the dubious authorship of this epistle, see above, p. 63, it is difficult to make any use of this expression as evidence in support of the Apostle's residence in Rome. It should be mentioned, however, that parallels to a use of the word as a description of Rome are found in Rev. XVIII, 2, and in *Sibyll.* 5, 143; 2 *Baruch*, 11, 1, ed. Charles, R. H., in *Apocrypha and Pseudepigrapha of O.T.*, 1913, vol. ii, pp. 400, 486.

[2] 1 Clement, 5. See Lowther Clarke, W. K., *First Epistle of Clement*, 1937, pp. 14–18.

[3] So much at least is implied by 1 Cor. 1, 12.   [4] See below.

[5] Clement's argument seems to be that Christians in Rome were well acquainted with the kind of tragedy which might result from $\zeta\hat{\eta}\lambda o\varsigma$ $\kappa\alpha\grave{\iota}$ $\phi\theta\acute{o}\nu o\varsigma$, since they had witnessed the consequence of such in the deaths of 'the heroic apostles'.

[6] *Ad Romanos*, 4.

church, it is difficult to see why he should have chosen them for special mention. On the other hand, if his words are understood as more than a general allusion to apostolic admonition, why, it may be asked, in writing from Asia Minor, should he choose to mention the name of St. Peter, who so far as we can see had no genuine Asiatic connexions?[1]

Yet in the last resort we are bound to admit that evidence of this kind taken alone falls considerably short of positive demonstration. For the earliest known direct affirmation that St. Peter as well as St. Paul lived and died in Italy (the previous sentence in our authority seems to justify our taking this to mean Rome) we have to wait another half-century or so. Such an affirmation is first found in a letter addressed to Pope Soter by Dionysius, bishop of Corinth.[2]

Almost a contemporary of Dionysius, Irenaeus, who was familiar with the traditions of Asia, Gaul, and Rome, describes both Apostles as 'founders and builders' of the church of the imperial capital.[3]

From this point onwards, St. Peter's connexion with Rome is treated as an established and generally acknowledged fact. As examples we may cite from among western authorities the so-called *Muratorianum*, possibly the work of Hippolytus, bishop of Rome, in the first quarter of the third century, but certainly not later than his time, which explicitly mentions the death of St. Peter in a context showing that the author regarded it as a matter of particular interest to Roman Christians;[4] Tertullian, who treats the tradition of the Apostle's life and work in Rome as something beyond dispute;[5] and finally Cyprian, who assumes a connexion between St. Peter and the origin of the see held by his contemporaries Popes Cornelius and Stephen I.[6] Eastern writers of the same period are not less positive,

---

[1] Even the address with which 1 Peter opens, if genuine, is insufficient to prove that St. Peter had actually resided there.

[2] Cit. ap. Euseb. *H.E.* 2, 25, 8. Ed. Schwartz, E., *Eusebii Opera*, vol. ii, *G.C.S.*, 1903, pt. i, p. 178. The other two extracts from this letter cited by Eusebius, *H.E.* 4, 23, 9 ff., ed. cit. *ibid.*, pp. 376, 378, are sufficient to show that Dionysius was familiar with the early history of the church of Rome, though the possibility cannot be excluded that his statement regarding the Apostles is derived from a mistaken interpretation of Clement's epistle, with which he was evidently well acquainted.

[3] *Adv. haer.* 3, 3, 2 f.

[4] *Fragm. Murat.* 37.

[5] *De praescript. haer.* 32, 2; 36, 3; *De baptismo*, 4, 4; *Adv. Marcion.* 4, 5, 2; *Scorpiace*, 15, 4.

[6] *De cath. eccl. unit.* 4. *var. lect.* Ed. Hartel, G., *Cypriani Opera*, *C.S.E.L.* vol. iii, pt. i, p. 212. At the same Cyprian's dominant view is that the 'cathedra Petri'

and though such second- and early third-century evidence as we still possess is confined to Alexandria, as represented by Clement[1] and Origen,[2] there is no reason to believe that the tradition was not in existence elsewhere.

If, then, we may safely repudiate the application of the epithet 'doubtful' to this tradition, so early and so widely attested, can we also reject the allegation of 'an uncertain relic'? Let us hear once again the well-known words of Gaius, Roman presbyter in the last years of the second century:

'But on my side', he writes in reply to the arguments of Proclus, the Asiatic Montanist, 'I can point out the "signs of victory" (τρόπαια) belonging to the Apostles. For if you will please take a walk to the Vatican or along the road to Ostia, you will find the "signs of victory" of those who established this church'.[3]

Gaius, as a presbyter of the Roman church, was presumably a responsible person. And he was evidently running a considerable risk if Proclus had discovered that the 'signs of victory', that is the burial sites, or at least the places of martyrdom, were in fact 'uncertain'.

But possibly it may be felt that this passage falls short of a claim to possess the actual apostolic remains, and that Eusebius in so interpreting it misunderstood his source.[4] If this be so, the earliest positive witness to the existence of the relics will be found in the *Depositio Martyrum*,[5] which, though incorporated in the later *Kalendar* of Filocalus, itself was probably first drawn up in the early years of the fourth century. From this source it is usually inferred that in the later months of the pontificate of Xystus II, as a consequence of a fresh outbreak of persecution under the Emperor Valerian, the remains of the Apostles were hastily removed from their original burial places in the *Vaticanum* and on the *Via Ostia*, and concealed, perhaps originally only as a temporary measure, in the cemetery

is the source of episcopal authority generally, not merely of the Roman see. Cf. also *Ep. Firmiliani, Inter Cypr. Op.* No. 75, 6. 17. Ed. cit. pp. 813 f., 821.

[1] Clement Alex., *Adumbrat. in* 1 *Pet.* 5, 13. *M.P.G.* 9, 732.

[2] Origen, *Comm. in Gen.* 3, cit. ap. Eus. *H.E.* 3, 2. ed. cit. vol. ii, pt. i, p. 188.

[3] Cit. ap. Euseb. *H.E.* 2, 25, 6 f. ed. cit. vol. ii, pt. i, p. 177 f.

[4] For a probable example of such misunderstanding, see below.

[5] *M.G.H., Auct. antiqu.* vol. ix, *Chron. min.* vol. i, 9, p. 71 f. The original text an be restored with some certainty in the light of the derived *Martyrologium Hieronymianum.* Edd. De Rossi, J. B., Duchesne, L. in *A.SS.* (Boll.), November, vol. ii, p. [84]. See Lietzmann, H., *Petrus und Paulus in Rom,*[2] 1927, p. 109 ff.

formerly *Ad Catacumbas*, now called after St. Sebastian, on the *Via Appia*. The date assigned to the commemoration of the Apostles is June 29, 258. Moreover, it should be remembered that the fact of their temporary burial on this site is further guaranteed by a memorial inscription erected by order of Pope Damasus I.[1] With the establishment of religious toleration under Constantine I, and the recovery of its property by the Church, a desire would naturally arise to restore the apostolic remains to places approximately the same as their original traditional burial sites. This desire, no doubt, gave considerable impetus to a plan, which it may in fact have originated, to construct basilicas on these sites to do honour to the twin apostolic founders of the Roman Church. Though the churches themselves have not only been completely rebuilt and undergone considerable modifications at different periods, the Constantinian *confessiones* or reliquaries appear to have remained substantially intact, and for this reason it is held that the apostolic relics themselves still repose in the very places where they were originally deposited in the first half of the fourth century. At the time of the rebuilding of St. Peter's in the sixteenth century careful records were made of the extent and disposition of much ancient material in the vicinity of the *confessio* of the Apostle,[2] while in more recent years, in the light of this and other evidence, a considerable amount of scientific investigation has been undertaken both there, at St. Paul's, and in the catacombs of St. Sebastian.[3] Although the evidence brought to light is scarcely of the quality which would seem to justify a decisive verdict, yet it may be held substantially to have strengthened the case for authenticity.

To sum up the results which our investigation has reached. We may reasonably claim that of the original charges directed against the 'title deeds of the greatest of the Christian Churches', if the one preferred against the authenticity of the relics ought to be returned as

---

[1] Ihm, M. (Teubner edn.), *Damasi epigrammata*, 26, 1895, p. 31. This inscription is in all probability the source of the fantastic story related by Gregory I, *Registrum* IV, 30. Edd. Ewald, P. and Hartmann, L. M., in *M.G.H. Epp.* vol. i, pt. i, 1891, p. 265. Cf. a Eastern form of the legend in Baumstark, A., *Röm. Quartalschr.*, vol. xv (1901), p. 250, referring to the *Chronicon* of Michael Syrus, ed. Chabot, J. B., 1899/1900, pp. 105, 123. For a later mediaeval tradition regarding the temporary burying place of the Apostles, see Rossi, J. B., *Roma sotterr.*, 1864, vol. i, p. 180, *Itinerarium*, col. iii.

[2] The evidence has been collected by Lietzmann, H., *op. cit.*, pp. 189-211.

[3] Cf. Styger, P. *Il monumento apostolico della via Appia*, 1916.

not proven', the evidence submitted justifies dismissal of the other
two; in other words, a decidedly favourable verdict ought to be
given regarding not only the Petrine texts, but also the tradition of
the Apostle's residence and death in Rome.

III

We may now turn to inquire in what sort of environment St. Peter
worked during the short period of his Roman ministry. The answer
must be of the utmost brevity and will as a consequence be inevitably
under the limitation of having to substitute reasonable conclusions in
the place of discussion of a number of points, which would otherwise
deserve fuller examination.

To begin with, we must picture a ghetto in the quarter known as
Trastevere[1] as it existed in the last years of the Roman Republic[2] and
under the early Principate. Mean, squalid houses intersected by
narrow tortuous lanes housed a dense population, a large proportion
of which were descendants of slaves or at best freedmen of the noble
Roman families.[3] Before long the more fortunate and perhaps less
scrupulous members of the Jewish race and cultus succeeded in
improving their social position. In fact, there is good reason to think
that the privileges accorded by the early Emperors to Roman Jews
were due at least in part to a recognition of their financial obligations
to this strange, irrepressible people.[4] As to their numbers, it has been
estimated that by the end of the first quarter of the first century
they could not have fallen far short of fifty thousand out of a total
urban population of something like one and a quarter millions.

Like other oriental cults, Judaism could claim its adherents and
even converts from among the native or at least non-Semitic citizens,
and it may have been due in some degree to its cosmopolitan
character that the cult remained more loosely organized in Rome than

---

[1] A ghetto remained in existence in this quarter of the city as late as 1556, and
to this day the locality retains much of its pristine squalor.

[2] Cf. Cicero, *Pro Flacco* 28; ed. Teubner, p. 224. Sanday and Headlam, *Romans*,[5]
I.C.C. 1914, p. xx, observe that 'Cicero's speech makes it clear that the Jews in
Rome were a formidable body to offend'.

[3] The Roman freedmen were sufficiently important and numerous to possess a
synagogue of their own at Jerusalem; see Acts VI, 10.

[4] Berliner, *Geschichte d. Juden in Rom*, 1893, p. 5 ff. For further details as to the
early history of Judaism in Rome, cf. Schürer, E., *Geschichte des jüdischen Volkes*,[3]
1898, vol. iii, p. 28 (Eng. Trans., 1885, Div. ii, vol. ii, p. 232 ff.). It was Augustus
who first assigned to the Jews the Trastevere region, which had previously served
as an enclave for prisoners of war.

6

elsewhere. Each synagogue, as it seems, enjoyed a considerabl
measure of individual independence, and, unlike those of Alexandri
which were controlled in respect of discipline and finance by a com
mon *presbyterium*, administered its own affairs.[1]

The earliest source to tell of the existence of Christians in th
capital is to be found in the list of greetings appended by St. Pau
to his Epistle to the Romans, which we take to be an integral part o
that letter.[2] The list, while containing a high proportion of common
place names, includes some at least which suggest that even at thi
early date the Roman nobility had not remained wholly untouche
by the new faith. Moreover, it embraces, in addition to a few Jewis
names, ten which are Greek and four Latin, a suggestive proportio
in estimating the composition of the original Christian community.
As to its organization we know nothing. We may, however, infe
from the inclusion of Prisca and Aquila at the head of the list tha
their house was a centre (perhaps at first the only centre) of the ne
society.[4] It may also be assumed that there were leaders to whom th
letter was delivered and who would be responsible for its publication
but they are not specified.

How long Prisca (or Priscilla) and her husband had been Christian
we cannot be certain, but there is some probability in the view tha
the expulsion of Roman Jews, or at least the suppression of thei
social activities, ordered by Claudius in the middle of the century,
must certainly have affected Christians of Jewish origin. In view o
the courteous hospitality shown by this couple to St. Paul, in bot
Corinth[6] and Ephesus,[7] it is natural to assume that they were alread
Christians before the repressive measures of the government rendere
it expedient for them temporarily to vacate their town residence. O

[1] The question as to whether Jewish organization at Rome constituted a unity
or not has been disputed. Cf. Sanday and Headlam, *op. cit.*, p. xxiii; Dix, G.
in *Laudate*, vol. xv, 1937, p. 106 f., who quotes Frey, J. B., in *Recherches de Scienc
Religieuse*, vol. xx, p. 269 and vol. xxi, p. 129, holds that 'the Jewish unit of self
government was the Synagogue-congregation, not the Jewish community as
whole', as against La Piana, C., in *Harvard Theological Review*, vol. xx, 1927
pp. 361 ff.

[2] On the integrity of the Epistle as it has come down to us, see Williams, N. P., i
New Commentary, pt. iii, p. 445 f.

[3] Cf. Sanday and Headlam, *op. cit.* p. xxiv.

[4] Rom. XVI, 5, 'τὴν κατ' οἶκον αὐτῶν ἐκκλησίαν'. Cf. *ibid.*, ver. 15.

[5] Acts xx, 2 f. The comments of Schürer, *op. cit.* vol. iii, pp. 31 ff., on the natur
and extent of this 'expulsion' are important.

[6] Acts XVIII, 1 ff.   [7] *Ibid.*, 18 f.

.eir return, however, which we may suppose coincided with the
ore benevolent rule of Nero in his early years,[1] their house would
turally be once more at the Church's disposal. It would seem,
erefore, that by the time of St. Paul's arrival in the capital, they
d been 'in Christ' for at least eight years.[2] Obviously they must
ve been among the first to welcome the Apostle, and their loyalty
ay well have consoled him in the disappointments and setbacks
hich his ministry in the capital, carried on in spite of the limitations
enforced detention, evidently suffered.

Whether or not, as Eusebius suggests,[3] the Emperor's court to
hich the Apostle had appealed gave a verdict of acquittal, and thus
abled him to enjoy a few years' freedom, must remain undeter-
ined. Our existing evidence is far too fragmentary to enable us to
construct with any certainty the history of the last years of his life
hich followed the conclusion of St. Luke's record in the Acts. In
ct, the silence of our authorities, allowing for the obscurity of the
ronology of the Pastoral Epistles,[4] and for the ambiguity of
ement's allusion to the Apostle's journey to the 'western limit',
ictly permits us to say no more that is positive of him in this
nnexion than of his fellow-Apostle St. Peter. Nevertheless, whatever
ay have been the facts now concealed from us, we can reasonably
ppose that from the beginning of the seventh decade onwards to
e time of their martyrdom both Apostles spent at least some time in
e capital. But to assert more than this involves a dangerous essay in
njecture.

It is appropriate at this stage to make some reference to the
despread, if not early, tradition of St. Peter's alleged episcopate of
enty-five years. And in view of its evident connexion with the
te assigned to the Apostle's death, it will be convenient to discuss
ncurrently these associated problems. We are informed on the
thority of the *Chronicon* of Eusebius, of which only fragments of

---

See Dio Cassius, *Fragm.* 37, 17, on the irrepressibility of the Roman Jews.

For the chronology followed here, see Turner, C. H., Art. 'Chronology of N.T.',
H.D.B., vol. ii, col. 424b. For St. Paul's connexion with the early Roman
urch, see Excursus C: 'St. Paul in Rome'.

H.E. 2, 22, 2 Ed. cit. vol. ii, pt. 1, p. 162. It should be noticed that with his
ual caution, the historian does not readily commit himself to the historicity
this 'period', but safeguards himself by the use of λόγος ἔχει, one of the phrases
ularly employed by him when citing traditions, as to the historical trustworthiness
which he felt some lack of confidence.

See e.g. Harrison, P. N., *The Problem of the Pastoral Epistles*, 1921.

the original have survived (though happily preserved in part in
Latin version by Jerome,[1] in addition to a complete Armenia
version),[2] that St. Peter began his ministry in Rome in the secor
year of Claudius, i.e. 42/43, and was martyred with St. Paul in tl
fourteenth year of Nero, i.e. 68/69. On the other hand, the entry
his name in the fourth century papal list, the *Catalogus Liberianu*
gives 30 and 55 as the terminal dates, while significantly noting t
actual day of the martyrdom as June 29. The discrepancy betwe
these two authorities is obvious enough, yet this should not blind
to the fact of their agreement as to the duration of his ministr
namely, the traditional period of twenty-five years.

We need not pause to discuss how the compiler of the *Catalog*
believed his figures to be reconcilable with the data of the N
Testament. What is important to notice is that both he and Eusebi
alike were evidently trying to do duty to a common and presumal
established tradition. It was formerly believed, notably by that gr
patristic scholar and church historian Lightfoot,[4] that this traditi
could be traced back at least to the *Chronicon* of Hippolytus,[5] that
to say to the first quarter of the third century, but further investig
tion has led to the generally accepted conclusion that, even if t
Chronicon actually included a papal list beginning with the name
St. Peter (and this has been by no means universally conceded),
almost certainly did not contain more than a few scattered histori
entries, and certainly not any figures of regnal years.[6]

---

[1] Eusebius-Hieronymus, *Chronicon*, Olymp. ccxi, Nero xiii in *Eusebii Ope*
G.C.S., vol. vii, p. 185, ed. Helm, R., 1913.

[2] *Eusebii Opera*, *G.C.S.* vol. v, ed. Karst, J., 1911 (German transl.)

[3] *M.G.H.*, *Auct. antiqu.*, vol. ix, *Chron. min.* vol. i, p. 73. It is important to not
that the same date recurs here to which we have already called attention in
Depositio Martyrum, see p. 67, i.e. properly the date of the first translation of
relics.

[4] *St. Clement* in *Apostolic Fathers*, 1890, pt. i, vol. i, p. 260 f. Lipsius,
Bischofslisten des Eusebius in *Neue Studien zur Papstchronologie* (*Jahrb. f. protest. Th
logie*, vol. vi, 1880, p. 233 ff.), assigns a list of Popes to the pontificate of Victo
c. 190.

[5] *Hippolyti Opera*, *G.C.S.* vol. iv, ed. Helm, R., 1929.

[6] Caspar, E., *Die älteste römische Bischofsliste* in *Schr. d. Königsb. Gel.-Gesel*
2. Jahrg. Geisteswiss. Kl., Heft. 4, 1926, p. 170 ff., makes out an elaborate c
in favour of such a list having formed part of Hippolytus' *Chronicon* in its origi
state. For his conjectural restoration of the list, see p. 404. Schmidt, C., in
review of Caspar's work, appended to his *Studien zu den Pseudo-Clementinen*
Texte u. Unters., vol. xlvi, pt. i, Berlin, 1929, p. 357, confesses himself unable
decide between Bauer, A., *Die Chronik des Hippolytos im Matritensis graecus*
in *Texte u. Unters.*, vol. xxix, pt. i, 1906, p. 156 f., who denies that the *Chroni*

It is generally agreed that the victimization of Christians procured by Nero towards the conclusion of his principate, as recorded by the historians Tacitus[1] and Suetonius,[2] took place in 64, and in default of evidence to the contrary it might be supposed that the Apostles were certainly among those put to death at this time. On the other hand, we have no right to assume that the Tacitean 'multitudo ingens' necessarily included the leaders. Our earliest authorities for a downright assertion that the deaths of both Apostles took place in Nero's reign are the apocryphal *Acts of Paul* and *Acts of Peter*,[3] both dating from the last twenty years of the second century. In neither work, however, are their deaths associated with the executions which presumably were an immediate sequel to the Neronian incendiarism. Yet in two respects the *Acts of Peter* shows originality; it places the death of St. Paul a year later than that of his fellow-apostle,[4] and it fixes the arrival of St. Peter in Rome by associating it with the advent of Simon Magus, alleged to have occurred in the second year of Claudius, i.e. 42/43,[5] a date which is scarcely easier to reconcile

contained any papal catalogue whatever, and the view upheld by Caspar, whose more important conclusions will be found summarized in *Die älteste römische Bischofsliste* in *Papsttum und Kaisertum*, ed. Brackman, A., 1926, p. 1 ff. Schwartz, E., *Eusebius Werke, G.C.S.*, vol. ii, pt. 3, c. 7, p. ccxxv, n. 2, 1909, however, asserts roundly, 'Ich stimme hierin den Ausführungen Harnacks *Chronologie*, I, S. 172 ff., gegen Lightfoot um so eher zu, als ich die Existenz einer einzigen alten römischen Liste entscheiden bestreiten muss'.

[1] *Ann.*, xv, 44.
[2] *Vita Neronis*, 16, 2.
[3] *Acta Apostolorum Apocrypha*. Edd. Lipsius, K. A., and Bonnet, M., 1891–1903, pp. 23 ff: 45 ff.
[4] *Ibid.*, *Acta Petri* 1. The *Decretum Gelasianum* 2, 2, ed. Dobschütz, E. von, *Texte u. Unters.*, vol. xxxviii, 1912, p. 7 (the date of this chapter is late 4th cent., see below), ascribes the belief that the Apostles' deaths took place in different years to 'heretics' chatter'. The first known allusion to the opinion that they occurred on the *same day* is found in the *Catalogus Liberianus*, *M.G.H. Auct. ant.* vol. ix, *Chron. min.* vol. i, pt. 9, p. 73. The tradition seems to be adumbrated by Tertullian *De Praescript.* 24, 4. Dionysius Cor. cit. ap. Eus. *H.E.* 2, 25, 8, ed. Schwartz, E., in *Eusebii Opera*, vol. ii, pt. 1, p. 178, is content to say 'κατὰ τὸν καιρόν', an idea which the author may have inferred from 1 *Clement* 5.
[5] *Ibid.*, *Acta Petri* 5. The author holds that Peter spent twelve years in Jerusalem in obedience to a Dominical injunction. Schmidt, C., *Studien zu den Pseudo-Clementinen* in *Texte u. Unters.*, vol. xlvi, pt. 1, p. 360, n. 2, suggests that he derived his idea from the *Kerygma Petri*, cit. ap. Clem. Al. *Strom.* 6, 5, 43. Cf. Apollonius, cit. ap. Eus. *H.E.* 5, 18, 14. ed. cit. vol. ii, pt. 1, p. 478. The Simon Magus *saga* appears in its earliest form in Justin, *Apol.* 1, 26, 56. It is generally believed that Justin's story was derived from a species of false etymology, due to his discovery of an inscription (itself recovered in 1577) to a Sabine deity 'Semoni sanco deo'. Schmidt, *op. cit.*, p. 361, holds that mention of Simon's arrival in Rome in the reign of Claudius was made in Justin's *Syntagma*, now lost.

with New Testament data than those of the *Catalogus* already noticed.

If Eusebius was consciously or unconsciously indebted to this egregious information, whence did he derive his idea of the twenty-five year ministry? We have already excluded Hippolytus.[1] What other source remains? It is known that Eusebius made considerable use of the almost contemporary *Chronicon* of Julius Africanus,[2] a primitive and perhaps somewhat crude, but none the less commendable, attempt to co-ordinate Christian, Jewish, and secular history. This work was based on the Greek chronological unit, the Olympiad, and its author is believed to have arrived at a rough chronology by assigning one or more Olympiads to each of the names which were found in the episcopal lists at his disposal. Thus to each entry in the earliest part of the Roman episcopal list there appears to be assigned three such units, making an episcopate of twelve years. How natural, then, if space permitted, to assign to an Apostle a double allowance! Here then may be some approximation to the real explanation of this enigmatic but evidently unhistorical Petrine pontificate.

IV

If the Christian community at the time of St. Paul's arrival was, as we have seen, still in an embryonic stage of development, particularly in regard to organization,[3] is there evidence to show what kind of organization was in existence immediately after the Apostles'

[1] See above, p. 72. Even supposing his *Chronicon* included a papal list, it was almost certainly a list without regnal years.

[2] Eusebius-Hieron. *Chronicon*, ad ann. Abr. MDLXXI, ed. Helm, R., pt. 1 p. 113. Africanus' work was completed c. 220.

[3] If St. Peter was known to have resided in Rome previous to the sending of the Epistle to the Romans, still more if he was then in residence, it is scarcely conceivable that St. Paul would not have mentioned his name. Some have supposed that he had St. Peter's supposed work there in mind when he explained the cause of his delay in coming: 'making it my aim so to preach the Gospel . . . that might not build upon *another man's* foundation . . . so I have been actually prevented from visiting you' (Rom. xv, 20–22). But this, so far from proving that St. Peter's presence there had been the cause, may rather imply the contrary. For if St. Peter had previously arrived in Rome, his 'foundation' there would have constituted a permanent impediment to St. Paul's plan. In any case, it does not follow that the general principle here enunciated provided the only possible explanation of the hindrance. As to the origin of Roman Christianity, the unknown Italian author, known as Ambrosiaster, has preserved some faint recollection of a pre-apostolic community, which suggests that it was originally dominated by Judaeo-Christian outlook. See his *Comm. in Rom. Prol.* ap. Ambrose, *Opera, P.L.* 17, 47 f.

ifetime? Quite recently the hypothesis has been put forward that, for the first fifty years or so of its post-apostolic existence, the church of Rome 'might not inappropriately be called "presbyterian" '[1] in constitution. This conclusion, if accepted, would have an effect, not only on the history of the Christian ministry in general, but more particularly on any account which might be given of the origins of the Papacy, so far reaching that it necessarily demands a careful re-examination of the evidence.

In view of what has been said about the markedly Jewish antecedents of the Roman Christian community, there are strong *a priori* grounds for supposing that the earliest form of Christian organization in that city was closely modelled on its existing Jewish prototype.[2] But it is obviously impossible to discuss its character in any detail before we have first outlined what we believe to have been the general course of development of the Christian ministry elsewhere.

Till almost the close of the nineteenth century the possibility that that ministry could have taken any other form other than one which was purely local was scarcely envisaged. With the publication of the document known as the *Teaching of the Twelve Apostles*, however, a new phase in the study of the subject may be said to have opened.

As a result, a theory that in its original state the Christian ministry was twofold came to be widely accepted. The highest and most important officers in the Church, it was believed, were those who held the status of 'apostles, prophets, or teachers', and whose qualifications were of an essentially 'charismatic'[3] or prophetic nature. Strictly subordinate to them was the local administration in each individual community, consisting of two orders of bishop-presbyters and deacons.[4] So long as it could be affirmed with some confidence that the so-called *Teaching of the Twelve Apostles* was a document of late first-century origin, views of this kind had a considerable vogue. More recently, however, there have been signs that the tide of enthusiasm which greeted its first appearance as reliable evidence for the immediately post-apostolic period is beginning to ebb. In

---

[1] Streeter, B. H., *The Primitive Church*, p. 221.

[2] See above, p. 69.

[3] E.g. by Harnack, A. von, *Entstehung uud Entwickelung der Kirchenverfassung und des Kirchenrechts*, 1910, p. 19.

[4] A recent exponent of this view is Headlam, A. C., *Doctrine of the Church and Reunion*, Bampton Lectures for 1920, p. 97 and n. 3.

fact, there now appears a marked inclination among modern writers to treat it as an essay in imaginative archaism or else as a handbook of Christian practice pretending to apostolic authority, but actually composed by a Montanist prophet towards the conclusion of the second century.[1] It may well be that the last word on this elusive subject has not yet been spoken, but it is perhaps not temerarious to suggest that as a result of more mature and balanced consideration of the work, much that has been affirmed with some confidence on the whole subject of the ministry during the first quarter of this century may soon be recognized to be in urgent need of drastic revision.

Nor perhaps will revision in this direction alone be necessary. The 'charismatic' hypothesis just mentioned, now somewhat discredited, took over the view popularized by Lightfoot as to the original constitution of the local hierarchy, since at the time of its appearance few were disposed to challenge his interpretation of the early evidence which regarded ἐπίσκοπος (a term which for the moment we may represent by the non-controversial episcopus rather than 'bishop') and πρεσβύτερος (presbyter) as alternative designations of the same office.[2] Nowadays, however, a disposition to treat such a view as open to question can no longer merely be dismissed as 'uncritical'. It has been suggested, for example, that the local ministry in origin consisted solely of presbyters, and that the terms ἐπίσκοπος and διάκονο were used to describe distinctions of function rather than of office. Closely akin to this is a more recent view, which prefers to describe the ministry, at least up to the end of the period covered by the Acts as 'undifferentiated',[4] a theory commendable alike for its simplicity and its inclusiveness. Such a conception of primitive Church order would of course embrace not only the 'seven' of Acts VI, but also the presbyters of Jerusalem, South Galatia, and the 'presbyter episcopi' of the church of Ephesus, as described by Luke.[5]

---

[1] Cf. e.g. Robinson, J. A., in *J.T.S.* vol. xiii, 1911–12, pp. 339 ff., and Donnellan Lectures, 1920, pp. 81 ff.; Muilenburg, J., *The Literary Relations of the Epistle of Barnabas and the Teaching of the Twelve Apostles*, 1929, esp. p. 167 f.; Connolly, R. H., in *J. T. S.* vol. xxxiii, 1932, pp. 237 ff.; *ibid.*, vol. xxxviii, 1937, pp. 364–379 in *Downside Review*, vol. lv, 1937, pp. 339–347; Vokes, F. E., *The Riddle of the Didache*, 1937; Telfer, W., in *J. T. S.* vol. xl, 1939, pp. 133 ff. and 258 ff.

[2] *Philippians*,[4] 1891, pp. 95, 193.

[3] E.g. Parry, R. St. J., *Pastoral Epistles*, p. lix ff., esp. p. lxxii.

[4] Lowther Clarke, W. K., 'Origins of Episcopacy' in *Episcopacy Ancient and Modern*, 1930, pp. 13, 16 f.

cts XI 27; XIII, 1; XV, 32; XXI, 10.

Yet if the ministry was at first 'undifferentiated,' it is clear that by the end of the second decade of the second century, at least in some churches, certainly in those of Asia Minor and Syria, a process of differentiation into three distinct orders of bishops, priests, and deacons had somehow taken place.[1] We need not suppose, and probably have no right to suppose, that this process followed precisely the same course or had been accomplished everywhere by the same date.[2] In fact, the markedly 'parochial' character of early Church history suggests precisely the opposite. It may, however, be regarded as likely that, in general, measures adopted by churches in large centres of population would serve as a model for those of less important cities, and that this applies to the ministry as well as to other elements in the Church's life. Thus it is probable that differentiation began at an earlier date in Rome and Corinth, for example, than in Puteoli.

In the later Pauline period, *episcopi* are distinct from deacons in the Epistle to the Philippians,[3] thus providing evidence for the years 60–64, and by the time the Pastoral Epistles reached their present form, in which we assume them to have appeared shortly after the Apostle's decease,[4] not only is the deacon clearly distinct from the *episcopus*, but the *episcopus* himself, who here always appears in the singular, is apparently also distinct from the presbyters as well. Thus it would appear that in localities near the coasts of the Aegean differentiation of the ministry had already begun at least before the end of the third quarter of the first century.

Hitherto, however, we have found nothing which throws any direct light on the constitution of the ministry in the church of Rome. For this we must wait for the appearance in the last decade of the first century of the famous epistle to the Corinthians, the author of which is undoubtedly Clement, a prominent person, if not an *episcopus*, of the Roman church at that time. The subject of the

---

[1] Ignatius, *Epistles, passim.*

[2] See Streeter, *Primitive Church*, p. 261. In admitting this, we are not committed to acceptance of the author's contention that Episcopacy, Presbyterianism, and Independency may equally claim to have existed side by side as the *de facto* ministry of primitive Christianity.

[3] Philippians, I, 1.

[4] Two recent studies of the Pastoral Epistles agree in the main as to the conclusion that these letters consist chiefly of direction and regulations of a sub-apostolic origin, while incorporating a proportion of genuine apostolic material. See Harrison, P. N., *The Problem of the Pastoral Epistles*, 1921 and Falconer, R., *Pastoral Epistles*, 1937.

epistle, as is well known, is the disorder prevailing in the church of Corinth, information about which had recently been received in Rome. That the Roman church should intervene in the controversy need not be taken, as is sometimes done,[1] as an early indication of the exercise of juridical authority over a neighbouring church, but rather as a very natural reaction to a situation involving the reputation of another Christian community, with which members of the Roman church were probably linked by ties of race and kindred.[2] The fact of this connexion may also be held to justify the assumption that such evidence as the epistle supplies about the organization of the church of Corinth may also be regarded as holding good of the church of Rome, and that the converse may equally be true.[3]

To discuss adequately the various problems raised by the evidence of this epistle would properly demand lengthier treatment than is possible here. Instead, we must be content to summarize a few only of the more probable conclusions. Clement's predominant theme is that of 'common order' in the Church, of which in the latter part of the letter he undertakes to demonstrate the basic principles. The first of these is that such 'common order' is a matter of divine institution; this he shows by calling attention to the existence of a three-fold ministry, together with an order of laity in the organization of the church of the Elder Covenant.[4] On this ground he argues that such 'order' must belong no less to the Christian Church, and in support he calls attention to the practice of the Apostles, who 'appointed their first-fruits, having tested them by the Spirit, to be bishops and deacons'.[5]

He then purports to quote an Isaianic prophecy to show that this appointment equally was a matter of divine pre-ordinance.[6] Nor

---

[1] E.g. by Batiffol, P., *L'église naissante*, 1919, p. 154 f.

[2] Corinth had been refounded in 46 B.C. as a Roman *colonia*, and there is therefore every reason to suppose that many Corinthians were descended from existing Roman families.

[3] If monepiscopacy had existed at Rome at this time and not at Corinth, it is scarcely conceivable that Clement would not have exclaimed at an apparent defect in Corinthian Church Order.

[4] 1 *Clement*, 40 f. Some have supposed that his argument here points to the existence of monepiscopacy at Rome, on the ground that by this time the actual Jewish hierarchy was extinct. If this was his meaning, however, one could wish that he had made it less ambiguous.

[5] *Ibid.*, 42, 4.

[6] *Ibid.*, 42, 5. On the source of this text, Isaiah LX, 17, the significance of which appears to have escaped the notice of Headlam, *Doctrine of the Church*, p. 97, and n. 3, see Lowther Clarke, W. K., *First Epistle of Clement*, pp. 25 and 102; id., *Episcopacy Ancient and Modern*, p. 30.

was this all. After the example of Moses himself, the Apostles deliberately took steps to prevent the possibility of future disorder.

'Our Apostles also knew', he says, 'through our Lord Jesus Christ, that there would be strife over the dignity of the bishop's office. For this reason, since they had perfect foreknowledge, they appointed the aforesaid persons (i.e. bishops and deacons) and subsequently they gave an additional precept, that when they should fall asleep, other approved men should succeed to their ministry. Persons, therefore, who were appointed by the Apostles, or subsequently by other eminent men, and have ministered blamelessly . . . such we consider to be unjustly deposed from their liturgical office. For it will be no small sin on our part if we depose from the episcopate those who have in blameless and holy wise offered the gifts. Blessed are those of an older generation . . . who came to a fruitful and a perfect end. For they have no need to fear lest any one depose them from their assigned place'.[1]

It will be noticed that we have rendered the ambiguous word πρεσβύτεροι as referring not to an order in the ministry but rather, as occasionally in other patristic authors,[2] of an 'older generation', which we also take to be its meaning in c. 47, as earlier in cc. 3 and 21. Such a rendering ought not to be regarded as a drastic cutting of the Gordian knot, since there are undoubted parallels to the use of the word in this sense.[3]

It seems not irrelevant further to ask whom Clement has in mind when he writes in c. 42 of 'the Apostles' and in c. 44 of 'our Apostles'. At the beginning of the epistle he had explicitly named SS. Peter and Paul in a context which seems to associate them closely with the church of Rome.[4] Hence, as he nowhere alludes to the Twelve generally or to any others by name, it may be thought not unreasonable to hold that 'the Apostles' here are the same pair already mentioned. In this case he would appear to say, 'SS. Peter and Paul then (themselves victims of the very sins of which the Corinthian Christians have been guilty), foreseeing the dangers arising from

---

[1] 1 Clement, 44, 1–5 (Lowther Clarke's version in the main). There is doubt as to whether in § 2 we should read ἐπιμονήν (permanence) or ἐπινομήν. The former is Lightfoot's conjecture. See Lowther Clarke, op. cit., p. 103.

[2] E.g. Irenaeus, Adv. haer. 3, 2, 2; 4, 26, 2–5; 4, 32, 1. Cf. Turner, C. H., 'Apostolic Succession' in Early History of the Church and Ministry, ed. Swete, H. B., 1918, p. 124, n. 1.

[3] See below.

[4] 1 Clement, 5.

ambition and disorder, ordained *episcopi* both in Corinth and at Rome; later they made further provision that certain of these should succeed to their apostolic office. Yet although such men have blamelessly performed the liturgical office which is their prerogative, you have improperly removed them from their position'.[1]

Though there are, as we believe, adequate grounds for rejecting the view that Clement formally identifies *episcopi* with presbyters, yet in the face of this evidence it appears equally impossible to deny that he refers to the episcopate in a way that suggests that it was held by more than one person in a single community. It may be pointed out further that we are bound to infer from Clement's description that the function of the episcopate at this time was purely and solely liturgical.[2] Thus it may well be that his frequent use of liturgical language, to which commentators on this document repeatedly call attention, is due to his deep sense of the outrage which has been committed by unjustly depriving ministers of the liturgy of their peculiar office.

If it be asked how this plurality of the episcopate arose, it is impossible to offer more than conjecture in reply. It is probable from the evidence in Acts, 1 Corinthians and Romans that the primitive basis of Christian liturgical organization was the 'house church', such as that of Prisca at Rome.[3] It is equally probable on the same evidence that in large centres of population such as Rome and Corinth, more than one such 'house church' would be acquired at an early date by a rapidly expanding community. Now when an Apostle was present, to him would properly belong the privilege of 'Breaking Bread', as in Acts XIX. But to whom would it be assigned in the Apostle's absence? The natural inference from Clement, who evidently refers to established and recognized custom, is that it would be given to an *episcopus*, and thus a plurality of house churches would at first naturally lead to a plurality of *episcopi*.

If, then, we have succeeded in making a case for what we may call 'polyepiscopacy' as an apostolic institution at Corinth, and may legiti-

---

[1] 1 Clement, 44.

[2] *Ibid.*, 44, 4, where it is explicitly stated that it belonged to the ἐπίσκοποι 'to offer the gifts'. Notice also that they are directly associated with the λειτουργία in 44, 2, 3, 6, and cf. 21, 6; 40, 5, passages which appear to imply a distinction between ἐπίσκοποι and πρεσβύτεροι. For later evidence, see e.g. Ignatius, *Smyrn.* 8; Hippolytus, *Apostolic Tradition*, 3, 4 f., ed. Dix, G., 1937, p. 5.

[3] Acts II, 46; XII, 12; 1 Cor. XVI, 15, 19; Rom. XVI, 5, 14.

mately infer the same form of organization to hold good of the church of Rome at the close of the first century, we may naturally go on to inquire how it came about that in the course of the next century a plurality of *episcopi* disappeared, not only in these churches, but apparently everywhere else, except possibly at Alexandria, and that monepiscopacy, such as has prevailed in the Church ever since, took its place.

In the lifetime of the Apostles, in cities such as Corinth, where we have supposed a number of 'house churches' to have been in existence from an early date, we may infer from St. Paul's own words that periodical gatherings of the whole urban Christian community must have taken place from time to time, possibly on every 'first day of the week'.[1] Since only the largest 'house church' would be sufficient for the purpose, the *episcopus* of that church would naturally preside on such occasions, and in virtue of this prerogative may be supposed to have acquired a certain honorary precedence.[2] But there is yet another factor to take into account. Side by side with the episcopate, we may conjecture that there existed a single corporate *presbyterium*,[3] out of which it may be assumed that under apostolic direction the episcopate and diaconate had originally emerged. To this body still belonged the functions of administering discipline and property, as in the case of its Jewish prototype. But, again, in the absence of the founder-Apostle some chairman would be needed for the proper despatch of business, and one who, as occasion arose, might also represent the local church in its external relations. Can we doubt that the official already mentioned, whom for convenience we may call the *archiepiscopus*,[4] would be the obvious person to occupy such a position? Nor is it difficult to imagine that he would come to be regarded as *the* bishop of the whole community.[5] On the other hand, we have no right to suppose that such a development took place simultaneously in all churches,[6] though we may

[1] In view of Acts II, 45, the possibility that the 'Breaking of Bread' took place on other days of the week as well cannot be excluded.

[2] Cf. Lowther Clarke, *Episcopacy Ancient and Modern*, p. 41.

[3] If, as is possible, the Roman Jews were so organized, the conjecture has considerable probability.

[4] Streeter, *Primitive Church*, p. 260, paradoxically holds that 'archbishops' are more primitive than 'bishops'.

[5] Lowther Clarke, *First Epistle of Clement*, p. 24.

[6] Cf. Dix, G., 'Jurisdiction in the Early Church' II, in *Laudate*, vol. xv, June, 1937, No. 58, p. 112 f.

reasonably hold that in the case of large centres of population, as we have already suggested, such as Rome, Asia Minor and Corinth, where the need was greatest, it would naturally happen there before the rest.

If it be asked what became of the rest of the episcopal college, the obvious inconveniences of plurality in the face of a growing centralization may account for their disappearance in many places. In others, however, it seems that 'polyepiscopacy' lingered on in the office of the *chorepiscopus*, which even in the West managed to survive in some places, in spite of the manifest disapproval of the Roman see, as late as the age of Charlemagne.[1] It is, moreover, remarkable that we have to wait till the middle of the third century before finding a clear-cut assertion of monepiscopacy as a Catholic principle.[2]

In view of the fragmentary character of the evidence at our disposal, not to mention its uncertain chronology, it is difficult to be positive as to a date for the beginning of monepiscopacy at Rome. But if we are justified on the authority of the *Muratorianum* in assigning the *Shepherd* of Hermas to the middle of the second century,[3] it may be inferred from his allusions to the ministry, though by no means free from obscurity, that the change was already complete by this time.[4] Yet, even so, it would seem from his evidence that the position of the bishop as the head of the local church and president of the *presbyterium* was still liable to be challenged, and that the Roman church of his day was not free from dissension arising from rival claims to the 'first seat'.[5]

[1] See Gore, C., *The Church and the Ministry*,[3] 1936, Additional Note D ii, 'Chorepiscopi', p. 330 ff.

[2] *Ep. Cornelii*, ap. *Cypriani Epp.* No. 49, 2, *ad fin. C.S.E.L.* vol. iii, p. 608. Cf. *Ep. Cornelii ad Fabium*, ap. Euseb. *H.E.* 6, 43, 11. ed. Schwartz, E., *Eusebii Opera*, vol. ii, pt. 2, p. 618. It is noteworthy that the earliest examples of such an assertion are found in papal letters.

[3] *Fragm. Murat.*, 73–77. If, as is now widely believed, e.g. by Bardenhewer, *Geschichte d. altk. Lit*, vol. ii, p. 610, this work is to be attributed to Hippolytus of Rome (†235), the author's statement 'Pastorem vero *nuperrime* temporibus nostris in urbe Roma Hermas conscripsit sedente cathedra urbis Romae ecclesiae Pio episcopo fratre eius', seems trustworthy as the assertion of one who was almost Hermas' contemporary. We cannot treat the allusion to Hermas in *Cat. Liber. Vita Pii*, as an independent witness since it is probably derived from the *Muratorianum*. The chief argument against so late a date is based on the allusion to Clement in Hermas, *Vis.* 2, 4, 3. But we have no certainty that this Clement was identical with the author of the epistle to the Corinthians.

[4] *Vis.* 3, 5, 1; *Sim.* 8, 7; *Mand.* 11, 7.

[5] The so-called *Ascension of Isaiah*, ed. Charles, R. H., 1900, p. 22 f. esp. 3, 27, if of Roman origin, may also reflect this struggle.

In view of the testimony already advanced and of inferences which, as we hold, may reasonably be made from it, we should claim that of 'presbyterianism' in the proper sense in the early Roman church there is absolutely no trace. That the *presbyterium* existed at Rome as elsewhere, as indeed it was bound to exist, if the constitution of the Roman church was to be faithful to the primitive Judaeo-Christian model, is scarcely open to doubt. But its administrative authority was, as we should hold, wholly distinct from the liturgical status of the episcopate and diaconate, particularly of the former. And even if episcopacy began as a plurality and later contracted into a single office, it remains not less probable that the primitive *episcopi* were, as we learn on the authority of Clement, appointed by the Apostles. Are we to say that Clement was improperly indulging his imagination, when he leads us to infer that they were so appointed by the authority of our Lord Jesus Christ Himself?

We might at this point appropriately conclude this lecture, if it were not for the existence of an important body of evidence which appears at first sight to shatter at a single blow the case just stated. It is supplied by those intricate and somewhat elusive documents, the early Roman episcopal lists. Few early sources have been subjected to such thorough and minute scrutiny. Yet even to-day it cannot be said that their innermost secrets have been fully probed.

The most important surviving examples are those which appear in the *Adversus haereses* of Irenaeus,[1] in the *History* and the *Chronicon* or *Canon* of Eusebius,[2] in the *Catalogue Liberianus*,[3] in the numerous so-called *Index Catalogues*, nine of which appear in the Introduction to Mgr Duchesne's monumental edition of the *Liber Pontificalis*, and finally in the *Liber Pontificalis* itself.[4] Other lists are those given by

---

[1] *Adv. haer.* 3, 3, 3. ap. Eus. *H.E.* 5, 6, 1. ed. cit. vol. ii, pt. 1, p. 438 ; cf. id., *ibid.*, p. Eus. *ibid.*, 4, 11, 1 f. ed. cit. *ibid.*, pp. 320, 322.

[2] For a summary of Eusebius' lists derived from his *Ecclesiastical History* (completed finally in 325), and his *Chronicon* or *Canon* (311), see Schwartz, E., *Eusebius Werke*, G.C.S., vol. ii, pt. 3, p. 6 ff., where a description of other papal lists will be found. Cf. also Caspar, E., *Die älteste röm. Bischofsliste*, 1926, p. 159 f. ; Helm, R., in *Abh. der preuss. Akad. Phil.-hist. Kl.* for 1923, No. 4, 1924, p. 37.

[3] *M.G.H. Auct. antiqu.*, vol. ix, *Chron. min.*, vol. i, p. 73 ; Mirbt, C., *Quellen zur Geschichte des Papsttums und des röm. Katholizismus*,[5] 1934, No. 125, p. 52 f.

[4] Described by Lightfoot, *St. Clement*, vol. i, p. 311, as 'Leonine'. See Duchesne, ., *Liber pontificalis*, Introd. pp. xiv–xxiv, 14–41, in *Biblioth. d. Écoles Françaises d'Athènes et de Rome*, 1886. Mommsen, Th., *Gesta rom. pont. M.G.H.*, 1898. vol. i, . xxxiii ff.

Pseudo-Tertullian,[1] Optatus,[2] Epiphanius,[3] and Augustine,[4] which though for the most part lacking in dependent value, exhibit a number of points of interest. In addition to all these we may not omit to mention the fragmentary list of Hegesippus,[5] which is thought to represent the surviving portion of an originally complete series now lost, but possibly reproduced by later authorities.

With the exception of the list of Irenaeus, which is unique in making a clear discrimination between SS. Peter and Paul and their episcopal successors, most of the lists agree in supplying what purports to be a continuous series of Roman bishops from the apostolic age down to the time of compilation, including at its starting point the name of St. Peter.[6] As to date of composition, the Irenaean series is plainly the earliest of those which we possess; whether it is in fact the earliest of those of which we seem to have knowledge depends entirely on the view which is taken of the celebrated passage quoted by Eusebius from the *Hypomnemata* of Hegesippus. In the context of the quotation we are told that the author had affirmed the identity of the form of faith as taught by the bishops wherever he went. He then adds, after mentioning the epistle of Clement:

'And the church of the Corinthians persisted stedfastly in the authentic teaching, till the time when Primus was bishop in Corinth. I made acquaintance with them on my voyage to Rome and stayed many days with the Corinthians, during which we shared refreshment in the authentic teaching. And when I came to Rome I made for myself a "succession" (διαδοχήν) until Anicetus, whose deacon was Eleutherus. From Anicetus Soter receives (the teaching) in succession and after him Eleutherus. But in each succession and in each city it (i.e. the teaching) remains exactly as the law and the prophets and the Lord declare . . .'[7]

It should be noticed that in another passage, quoted by Eusebius just below from the same work, the author calls attention to the

---

[1] See Lightfoot, *St. Clement*, vol. i, p. 176.

[2] *De schism. Don.* 2, 2, 3. *C.S.E.L.*, vol. xxvi, p. 36.

[3] *Panar.* 27, 6. ed. Holl, K., *G.C.S.* vol. i, p. 308, 1915.

[4] *Ep.* 53, 2. *C.S.E.L.*, vol. xxiv, p. 153. ed. Goldbacher, A., 1895.

[5] Cit. ap. Eus. *H.E.* 4, 22, 2 f. ed. Schwartz, E., vol. ii, pt. 1, pp. 368-370.

[6] Except *Index Cat. IX.* Corbie ii, ed. Duchesne, *Liber Pontificalis*, vol. i, p. 3, which omits the name of St. Peter.

[7] See note 5 above.

recise juncture to which the beginning of false teaching in the mother
church of Jerusalem was traceable.[1]

What did Hegesippus mean when he wrote that after his arrival in
Rome 'I made for myself a "succession" '?[2] Lightfoot and many
others have believed him to affirm that he drew up for his own
benefit a succession list of the bishops of Rome, inclusive of the
name of Anicetus, i.e. just after the middle of the second century. If
this view could be regarded as certain, it would provide evidence of
the existence of a list some thirty years or so older than the one
preserved by Irenaeus. But Lightfoot was not content with his
exegesis of Hegesippus; he went so far as to claim that the lost list
had been substantially reproduced by Epiphanius,[3] and that the
Epiphanian series was therefore to be regarded as an authority for
the succession of Roman bishops from the Apostles to the middle of
the second century, to which the author himself had added an
appendix bringing it up to date for his own time.

The chief objections which can be raised against the existence of
a list in Hegesippus' *Hypomnemata* are: first, that as it is probable
that Eusebius had the whole of that work at his disposal, it is scarcely
conceivable, in view of his great interest in the subject of episcopal
succession, that he would not have included it intact in his *Ecclesiastical History*. The fact that he fails to do so is most easily explained by
the view that no such list was in existence. Secondly, it has been
argued that διαδοχή, rendered by Lightfoot and others 'succession
list', cannot bear this meaning at so early a date. Those who take this
line urge that even by Eusebius the word is still used in other senses
than this, and that in the pre-Nicene period it normally denoted
either the abstract idea of 'succession' than the concrete one of a

---

[1] *H.E.* 4, 22, 5. ed. cit. *ibid.*, p. 370, namely from the time of Thebouthis, who
appears to have been a disappointed candidate for the episcopate.

[2] 'διαδοχὴν ἐποιησάμην'. Lightfoot, *St. Clement*, vol. i, p. 328, renders the words
drew up a *list of succession*'. *Ibid.*, n. 1, he adds: 'As regards the interpretation
given to διαδοχὴν ποιεῖσθαι it is sufficient to quote [Eusebius] *H.E.* v. 5'. In our
view it is by no means sufficient, since the possibility remains open that διαδοχή
did not bear the meaning in Hegesippus' time which it had come to acquire among
Christian writers by the beginning of the fourth century. The rendering given in
the text is the one proposed by Turner, C. H., 'Apostolic Succession' in *Essays on
the Early History of the Church and the Ministry*, ed. Swete, H. B., p. 118, n. 2,
where his comment is: 'The phrase is odd, but it is not much odder than ἐν ἑκάστῃ
δοχῇ. Obviously the word was already technical to Hegesippus, the symbol of a
whole theory'.

[3] *Panar.* 27, 6. ed. cit., p. 308. It is now coming to be recognized that Lightfoot's
view as to the meaning of this passage cannot stand. See below, p. 87.

7

series of names in succession.[1] But in this case ἐποιησάμην (I mac
for myself) becomes almost unintelligible. Supporters of this objec
tion are therefore disposed to find a textual corruption in this word
Others, however, like Harnack, who also regard Lightfoot's view a
unacceptable, prefer, on the strength of 'permansi ibidem' ('I remaine
in the same place, i.e. in Rome till the time of Anicetus') to emer
διαδοχὴν to διατριβὴν ('I made for myself a succession' to 'I mac
for myself a stay').[3] We cannot, however, place much reliance on th
accuracy of Rufinus' rendering,[4] and his version may well be
courageous attempt to correct a phrase, which in this case may l
supposed already to have become unintelligible by the end of th
fourth century. Finally, there is the objection based on the argumei
of the context, which suggests that succession lists as such are n
Hegesippus' main concern. Rather his object is to show up to wh
point in its history Christians in each local church persisted
undivided loyalty to 'the authentic teaching . . . as the law and th
prophets and the Lord declare'.[5] His information about the Urkirc
of Jerusalem is admittedly somewhat indefinite, though this
doubtless due to loss of continuity, itself a consequence of th
catastrophe which had recently befallen the city.[6] But in the cases
Corinth and Rome he writes from personal experience. He has bee
to both places recently, and has verified the facts for himself. Returne
home he jots down his *Memoirs*, and for the benefit of eastern reade
points out that Anicetus is the last Pope but one. If we wish to pre
the change of tense, we may infer that he had himself been in Ron

[1] Thus Caspar, E., *Die älteste röm. Bischofsliste*, 1926, p. 222 f., who holds th
διαδοχή was at first used in the abstract sense of 'tradition', though by the time
Eusebius it was coming to acquire the more concrete meaning of a succession
bishops as a vehicle of the tradition. Cf. Turner, *op. cit.*, p. 123, n. 1.

[2] So Schwartz, E., *Eusebius Werke*, vol. ii, pt. 1, p. 370, *app. crit.*, where
describes the word as 'alte Schlimmbesserung, um eine Lücke zu fullen'. Cf. i
ibid., vol. ii, pt. 3, p. ccxxv, n. 3, 'Mit dem Excerpt aus Hegesipp., IIII, 22, 3,
nichts anzufangen ; es ist hoffungslos verdorben'.

[3] Adopted by Harnack in *Chronologie*, vol. i, p. 180. Cf. Lightfoot, *op. ci*
vol. i, p. 154 ; Turner, *op. cit.*, p. 118, n. 2, who remarks : 'The egregious propo
. . . comes to grief on the simple fact that Hegesippus did not "make a stay t
Anicetus", but arrived under Anicetus and made a stay till Eleutherus: E
H.E. iv. 11, 7'.

[4] Rufinus is seldom an exact translator.

[5] We know from Irenaeus, *Adv. haer.* 4, 3, cit. ap. Eus. *H.E.* 4, 11, 1. ed. c
vol. ii, pt. 1, p. 320, that Cerdo was excommunicated under Hyginus, who accordi
to that writer was Anicetus' immediate predecessor but one.

[6] I.e. its destruction following the revolt of Bar Cochba in 165.

under Soter, and that Eleutherus was now Pope at the time of writing. On this showing there would seem to be no more reason to 'make for himself a succession' of the Roman bishops than of the Corinthian or the Hierosolymite. Thus we seem to be led back to the second objection, namely that διαδοχή ought not to be rendered by 'succession list'.

If we could be more positive about the meaning of this word, the problem might be regarded as settled in a negative sense. But there is evidence that even in pre-Christian writers it might possibly be used of a series of names.[1] It is impossible therefore absolutely to rule out such a meaning here, however unlikely it may be.

What then are we to say regarding the claim to have discovered Hegesippus' supposed list in Epiphanius?[2] The chief support for this theory lies in Lightfoot's rendering of the passage which describes the beginning of heresy at Rome, in which Epiphanius seems to say:

'A story has come down to our own time how Marcellina was the ruin of a great number of people in the time of Anicetus, bishop of Rome, who succeeded Pius and those before him'.

Lightfoot somewhat arbitrarily discards this rendering and insists that ἦλθεν δὲ εἰς ἡμᾶς must mean 'paid us a visit', and not 'a story has come down to us', in spite of the fact, admitted by him, that the latter rendering is supported by Eusebius. From this he deduces that the papal list which follows is directly dependent on Hegesippus.[3] Most modern authorities, however, such as Holl,[4] have rejected his interpretation and prefer the one given above. We may thus conclude with some confidence that if in fact Hegesippus 'made for himself a succession (? list)', which is by no means certain, it did not lie in

---

[1] Turner, op. cit., p. 197 ff., gives a useful collection of the usage of διαδοχή and its cognates. He shows that it is used in six different senses by Eusebius, with two instances meaning 'list or table of successive bishops' (p. 204: Eus. H.E. 5, 9; 5, 12, 2).

[2] See above, p. 85. The same view is adopted by Turner, op. cit., p. 118, and by Lawlor, H. C., Eusebiana.

[3] Op. cit., vol. i, p. 329.

[4] Holl, K., Epiphanius Werke, G.C.S., vol. i, p. 308: ' "ἦλθεν εἰς ἡμᾶς" ist nicht zu übersetzen "es ist zu uns gekommen"—(das müsste πρὸς ἡμᾶς heissen) sondern bedeutet nach stehenden (übrigens auch sonst verbreiteten) sprach-brauch des Epiphanius (vgl. Index unter ἔρχεσθαι): "es ist auf uns oder an uns gekommen, die kunde ist auf uns gelangt" '. This view is accepted by Schmidt, C., Studien zu den Pseudo-Clementinen in Texte u. Unters., vol. xlvi, 1929, p. 337 f., it is contested by Turner, C. H., in J.T.S., vol. xviii, 1917, p. 119, n. 1.

front of Epiphanius. It would seem, therefore, that even if any such list ever existed, it is now irretrievably lost.

We may look next at our earliest surviving list preserved by Irenaeus, important enough to be set out here in full:

'When therefore the blessed Apostles (i.e. Peter and Paul) had laid the foundations and erected the church (i.e. of Rome), they entrusted the liturgical office of the episcopate to Linus. And Anencletus succeeds him, after whom Clement is ordained to the episcopate in the third place (in the series) from the Apostles. Yet though he actually saw the blessed Apostles and conversed with them, and afterwards had the teaching of the Apostles ringing in his ears and their *paradosis* in sight, he was not the only one; for many were still surviving at that time who had been instructed by the Apostles. . . . And Euarestus succeeds this Clement; and Alexander Euarestus; then in the same manner Xystus is made the sixth after the Apostles, and after him Telesphorus, who also bore noble witness. Afterwards Hyginus, then Pius, after whom was Anicetus. When Soter had succeeded Anicetus, now Eleutherus possesses the order of the episcopate in the twelfth place from the Apostles. By the same order and the same teaching both the *paradosis* in the church and the Gospel of Truth have come down to us from the Apostles'.[1]

Irenaeus' main purpose here is to demonstrate the truth of his assertion in the preceding sections,[2] namely that the doctrine of local churches in his time was identical with the original body of teaching described by him in accordance with the usage of the New Testament as the *paradosis*, the nature of which he illustrates by means of a brief synopsis of the epistle of Clement.[3] His proof consists in showing an unbroken continuity of teachers, whom he identifies with successive holders of the Roman episcopate,[4] a continuity which is also proved to exist in other churches from the logical necessity that their teaching must concur with that of the Roman church on account of its superior origin or authenticity. As this passage will be dis-

---

[1] *Adv. haer.* 3, 3, 3.   [2] *Ibid.*, 3, 3, 1 f.

[3] *Ibid.*, 3, 3, 3, 4.

[4] Whatever Irenaeus' original view as to the relation of one name to the next it is clear that Eusebius took the list to be one of a chronological succession. Lightfoot, *op. cit.*, vol. i, p. 203, accepted Eusebius' view; yet notice that Turner, *Apostolic Succession*, p. 129, n. 3, points out that with Irenaeus it was not so much a question of a succession of 'orthodox' bishops, as of 'good' bishops. The earliest example of the idea of a succession of 'grace' in the later sense appears to be Hippolytus, *Apostolic Tradition*, 3, 5. ed. Dix, G., p. 5.

cussed further in the following lecture,[1] we can postpone more
detailed examination of disputed points for the moment. Here we
are only concerned with the important data supplied by Irenaeus as
to the beginning of the Roman episcopate. But before attempting to
estimate its historical value in connexion with the question of the
origin of monepiscopacy in that church, we must briefly review the
remainder of our surviving lists.

Very careful investigation, such as that undertaken by Caspar,[2]
has shown that all existing lists are ultimately dependent on the one
either compiled or used by Irenaeus. After him they diverge into two
directions, an eastern stream represented by Eusebius in his *History*
and *Chronicon*,[3] and a western one to which belong the anonymous
poet known as Pseudo-Tertullian[4] and the *Catalogus Liberianus*[5] with
its derivatives.[6] Epiphanius' list may be dependent on Eusebius, or
else represents a reversion to an early third-century catalogue such
as Caspar supposes to have been included by Hippolytus in his
Chronicon.[7]

There can be no doubt that the chief, if not the only source of
Eusebius' chronology of the Roman see during the first two and a
quarter centuries was the *Chronicon* of Julius Africanus,[8] which, at
least so far as the Roman see is concerned, provided him with
evidence as to its occupants, and a very rough chronology down to
the fourth year of the Syrian Emperor Elagabalus (221). The purpose
of this work was to show by means of consecutive lists the respec-
ability and historicity of Christian origins in comparison with the
acknowledged history of Judaism and the Roman Empire. But it is
quite clear that in dealing with the problem how he was to include

---

[1] See below, p. 111 ff.

[2] *Die älteste röm. Bischofsliste*, 1926, p. 221.

[3] Eusebius' papal lists are traceable in both these works (see above, p. 88, n. 4).
Of the *Chronicon* only fragments of the original Greek have been preserved by
Syncellus, *Chronographia* (c. 800), e.g. ad ann. 185, in *C.S.H.B.* vol. 41, p. 670
=Eusebius-Hieronymus, *Chronicon*, ad ann. Abr. 2246. See *Die Chronik des
Hieronymus* in *Eusebius Werke*, vol. vii, pt. 1, ed. Helm, R., 1913, p. 215.

[4] See above, p. 84. The date of this work is much disputed. See Bardenhewer,
Gesch. d. altk. Lit., vol. ii, p. 432 ff.

[5] In its original form finished in 336. It was subsequently continued down to
54 in the pontificate of Liberius.

[6] I.e. the *Liber Pontificalis* and perhaps the *Index Catalogues*.

[7] The former view is upheld by Holl, K., *Epiphanius Werke*, vol. i, p. 308; the
latter by Caspar, E., *op. cit.*, p. 414 ff.

[8] On this work, see Gelzer, A., *Sextus Julius Africanus*, 1898.

the list of Roman bishops, the author was beset by the limitation that the catalogues before him were no more than name-lists, and, like Irenaeus' series, gave no indications whatever of chronology. In the case of Irenaeus no doubt chronology in itself was a matter of indifference. To him it was not chronology but continuity which mattered. But to Africanus some kind of chronology, however rough and approximate, was indispensable. As already mentioned,[1] it seems that his solution of the problem was to fit the names at his disposal into a scheme of Olympiads, allowing so many units to each entry according to the number of entries to be accounted for. In this way an important step was taken towards the provision of a thoroughly chronologized list such as we find in the *Catalogus Liberianus*, where at least in its present form, in addition to notes of contemporary consulates and imperial synchronisms, the duration of each pontificate is stated in years, months, and days, for the earlier entries no less than for the later ones. It may be said without more ado that so far as the earlier entries are concerned, all these data are based on pure conjecture, and hence are probably devoid of historical value; in fact, it is not till we reach the resignation of Pope Pontian on September 28, 235,[2] that we find the first trustworthy date in papal history, and only with the decease of Lucius, March 5, 254, that papal obits begin to be reliable.[3]

Hippolytus, rival of Callistus as bishop of Rome, provides in his *Chronicon* a western counterpart to the work of Africanus. Owing to the fact, however, that it has only been preserved complete in three Latin versions, one of which is incorporated in the *Kalendar* of Filocalus,[4] it is difficult to be certain whether or not in its original form it contained a papal list. The version known as the *Liber generationis primus*[5] has a table of contents which mentions such a list, yet no list follows; and a similar table which prefaces the text of the Greek original recently recovered, but unhappily containing only the first part of the work,[6] omits any mention of one.

In spite, therefore, of the elaborate case built up by Caspar[7] in

---

[1] See above, p. 74.   [2] *Cat. Liber.*, Vita Pontiani.

[3] Caspar, E., *Geschichte*, vol. i, p. 44.

[4] *M.G.H.*, *Auct. antiqu.*, vol. ix, *Chron. min.*, vol. i, pp. 89 ff., 138. ed. Mommsen Th., 1892. Cf. also *ibid.*, p. 3, and Duchesne, *Lib. Pont.* vol. i, p. viii ff.

[5] See Caspar, *Die ält. röm. Bischofsliste*, p. 175.

[6] *Hippolytus Werke*, G.C.S. ed. Helm, R. (Bauer, A.) 1929, from the recently discovered *Codex Matritensis*.

[7] Caspar, *op. cit.*, pp. 170–208.

defence of the hypothesis that a catalogue without dates but containing brief historical notes (subsequently incorporated in the *Catalogus Liberianus*), was an integral part of the Greek original, we should prefer to suspend judgment pending the emergence of further and more conclusive data.

Clearly from the beginning of the third century the importance of history was beginning to be appreciated by the Church, though the principles which must govern scientific historical writing were only partially appreciated. Hence it is during this century that divergencies in the lists begin to appear. The list included in his *Adversus Marcionem* by the anonymous author known as Pseudo-Tertullian,[1] plausibly assigned by Caspar[2] to the middle of the third century, inserts before the Irenaean entry 'Anencletus' the name 'Cletus', which we may take to be a shorter form of the same proper noun. The same duplication reappears in the *Catalogus Liberianus*,[3] the date of which in its earlier form is probably not later than 336. But here a further divergence is apparent. The entry 'Clement' occurs immediately after Linus, and before 'Cletus' and 'Anaclitus'. It is clear that the emphasis laid by Irenaeus on the value of Clement's epistle as evidence of the authentically apostolic character of the Roman *paradosis* had created a considerable impression in the West and probably gave rise to the tradition with which Tertullian was acquainted. Whether or not the latter derived it from Rome itself, which he had certainly visited, must remain uncertain, but it is by no means improbable. This tradition affirmed outright that Clement had been ordained directly by St. Peter. That it was due to some knowledge of the Pseudo-Clementine literature is evidently impossible, since the earliest date which can be assigned to these writings in their present form is somewhere in the middle of the fourth century, and we have good reason to believe that they only became widely known in the West through the Latin version provided by Rufinus.

We may therefore conclude that the placing of Clement immediately after Linus by the *Catalogus Liberianus* has nothing to do with the influence of the Pseudo-Clementines. Further peculiarities of the *Catalogus* in its existing form are the complete omission of the entries of Anicetus and Eleutherus, with the result that the years of

---

[1] See above, p. 84, n. 1.   [2] *Op. cit.*, p. 221.
[3] M.G.H., *Auct. antiqu.*, vol. ix, *Chron. min.*, vol. i, p. 73 ff.

Anicetus are assigned to the previous entry, Hyginus, and the years of Eleutherus to his predecessor Soter. Apart from the evident confusion in the list at this point, which appears to have baffled the most ingenious attempts at disentanglement, it is reasonable to suppose that at least the first of the omissions is almost certainly to be explained as a haplographical error, which in some form may also account for the second. There are, in addition, a number of discrepancies in the later dependent lists, of which space forbids mention, but which are probably traceable to these early mistakes.

As to the displacement of Clement, the inversion persists in the lists of Optatus and Augustine (which also show other minor peculiarities), though Optatus, on whom Augustine is probably dependent, retains only Cletus and omits any of the various longer forms of the name.

It was believed by Duchesne that the archetype, from which the lists described by Mommsen as the *Index Catalogues* were derived, could not be earlier than the middle of the fifth century. This view has been somewhat modified by Mommsen, who prefers a fourth-century date, possibly previous to the publication of the *Catalogus Liberianus*. It is at least remarkable that out of the nine complete Latin catalogues, all show Clement in his usual place, while two of them, *Codex Coloniensis* 212 (Saec. VI) and *Codex Albigensis* 2 (Saec. IX from a copy dated 673), enter 'Cletus' as 'Aniclytus' and 'Anelitus' respectively, a phenomenon which points to the composition of the original at a time when the Greek Anencletus was the only form known.[1]

The *Liber Pontificalis*, which in its most primitive form appears as the *Catalogus Felicianus*, belonging to the earlier half of the sixth century, retains the duplication of 'Cletus' and 'Aneclitus,' but introduces Clement between the two, a sign that the more correct Irenaean tradition has made some headway against the 'Liberian' blunder, but has not succeeded in wholly removing it.

The difficulty of reconciling this late fourth-century view of the chronological position of Clement was apparent to Jerome, who mentions it as a variant tradition, but does not consider it worthy of discussion. That valiant *malleus haereticorum*, Epiphanius of Salamis, who visited Pope Damasus I on his own account in 382 must have at once scented in it a potent cause of unorthodoxy

---

[1] *Liber Pontificalis*, ed. Duchesne, vol. i, pp. 24, 26.

nce he thought it desirable to devote a whole paragraph to an
ingenious explanation of its origin. Here most fortunately he took
he opportunity of including a short papal list, which may be copied
om an official catalogue of that time. In view of the use of the later
estern form 'Cletus', it is in any case scarcely probable, as has been
upposed, that it is derived from either Irenaeus or Eusebius. Still
ss are we justified, as has been pointed out above, in supposing that
reproduces the lost list of Hegesippus, even if such a list ever
xisted. His theory that Clement was originally ordained by the
postle, and then withdrew in favour of Linus and 'Cletus', has,
owever, one special point of interest. It appears to suggest that the
host of a memory that the original constitution of the church of
ome had been 'polyepiscopal' still haunted the papal archives.
hat such a ghost occasionally made its presence felt, is shown by a
ngular and otherwise unintelligible entry in the *Index Catalogue*,
odex Coloniensis 212, already mentioned, where after the entries of
Linus' and 'Aniclytus' we read *'isti vivente Dom. Petro sederunt'*,
vhich may be paraphrased 'they were bishops in the lifetime of the
Lord Peter'. Stranger still is the phenomenon also appearing in this
ocument, that while the traditional entry of twenty-five regnal
ears is assigned to Peter, the total number of years allotted to
Linus' and 'Aniclytus' is thirty-three. These figures can only be
aade intelligible on the assumption that the author believed that in
t. Peter's lifetime 'Linus' and 'Aniclytus' for a period at least shared
he episcopate.

A ghost of any sort, even a papal one, may be a frail kind of prop
or an hypothesis. But we should remember that the Irenaean list
insists very strongly on the connexion between Clement and the
Apostles, for which he probably had good authority, otherwise he
ould scarcely have given it so important a place in his argument
vithout running serious risk of attack. In addition, keeping in mind
he total absence of figures from any list previous to those of the
ourth century, we may feel there is some reason for believing that,
hough Irenaeus may have been perfectly correct in his assertion that
ll the names which he cites were names of those who were 'allotted
he episcopate', he was nevertheless mistaken in supposing that the
radition which he found in Rome was simply a list of *successive*
aolders of the episcopal office, and did not include some names
vhich were actually those, not of predecessor and successor, but

rather of contemporaries. If this be so, we seem to have found a
long last a means of ending the conflict between our apparently con
tradictory data. Supporters of traditional episcopalianism may b
disposed to regard our conclusion as a somewhat dubious asset, an
may still believe that the evidence would justify a less revolutionar
explanation. We should be content if it were admitted that som
further ground has been won in the direction of vindicating epis
copacy as an integral and primitive element in the organization of 'th
greatest of the Christian churches', and of its justification as a
apostolic institution.

EXCURSUS A

Harnack's theory regarding the 'Tu es Petrus'.

The most serious attack which has hitherto been made on th
integrity of this passage, Matt. XVI, 18 f., was published by Harnack i
1918.[1] Starting with the contention that πύλαι ᾅδου rightly mean
'death', and not, as is generally held, 'the power of evil', he went o
to argue that the expression 'death shall not prevail' cannot strictl
apply to an abstraction and must properly apply only to a person
Hence it must originally have applied to Peter, and from this he con
cludes that the words καὶ ἐπὶ ταύτῃ τῇ πέτρᾳ οἰκοδομήσω μου τὴ
ἐκκλησίαν are in fact an editorial interpolation.

In support of this conclusion, Harnack quotes in the first plac
the evidence of the works of Ephraem Syrus, in which he comment
on the text of the *Diatessaron* of Tatian. In the Latin version of hi
Hymni et Sermones, on Isaiah LIV, 17,[2] we find 'Vectes inferni no
praevalebunt adversus te'. Similarly, in the Latin version of hi
Evangelii concordantis expositio,[3] he quotes, 'Beatus es Simon . .
et portae inferi te non vincent' and later 'Tu es Petra'. This, i
Harnack's view, shows that the text of the *Diatessaron* knew nothin
of the interpolated clause. As an example of other patristic authors wh
reveal some knowledge of a purer textual tradition of this passage, h
cites Macarius Magnes, *Unigenitus*, 3, 22,[4] in which the author i
probably reproducing an opinion of Porphyry. Yet as we gather fror

[1] *Der Spruch über Petrus als den Fels der Kirche*, Sitz.-Ber. d. k. preuss. Akad.
Wiss., 1918, H. xxxii, pp. 637–654.
[2] Ed. Lamy, T. J., 1882–86, vol. ii, p. 156.
[3] Transl. Aucher Mecharista, ed. Moesinger, G., 1876, p. 153 f.
[4] Ed. Harnack, A., *Texte u. Unters.* xxxvii, 4, 1911, p. 56.

the same work[1] that Porphyry himself was familiar with a text which included ἐπὶ ταύτῃ τῇ πέτρᾳ, we must suppose that he referred αὐτῆς not to ἐκκλησίαν but to πέτρᾳ. It is highly probable that Porphyry derived this interpretation from Origen,[2] in whose works we meet it again and again.[3]

Later authors who retain the memory earlier view areof this Ambrose,[4] and Epiphanius.[5] It last makes its appearance in Jerome,[6] only to be finally rejected. As to our existing text, Harnack points out that our earliest witness in its favour is Tertullian.[7] The evidence of Clement of Alexandria[8] is inconclusive, since in quoting the passage as a whole he omits XVI, 18. Harnack infers from Justin Martyr[9] that nothing was known of the supposed 'interpolation' in his time.

When we come to examine this apparently impressive case, we find that it depends on two main assumptions: first, that πύλαι ᾅδου can only mean 'death', and second, that if the whole text had occurred in Tatian's *Diatessaron*, Ephraem must have quoted it. The fact that he quoted only certain phrases appears to Harnack a sufficient proof that only those phrases were present in the original.

As to the first of these assumptions we must refer to our brief discussion of the point elsewhere. Sufficient has been said to show that the argument in favour of so exclusive an interpretation is not strong enough to bear the weight of Harnack's case. As to the second, we may reasonably ask what evidence there is for the original text of the *Diatessaron*. The *Codex Fuldensis*[10] must of course be discounted, since it is known that the translator made use of the Vulgate in rendering scriptural quotations. But we are fortunately in possession of two ancient versions, one in Arabic[11] and the other in Old Dutch.[12] Whatever the relation of these two versions to the original, it is at least remarkable in this connexion that both versions contain the

---

[1] Quoted by Macarius Magnes, *op. cit.*, 3. 19.

[2] Harnack, *Der Spruch über Petrus*, p. 641, n. 4.

[3] *De princip.* 3, 2, 4. 'Petrus adversus quem portae inferi non praevalebunt'. Cf. *C. Cels.* 2, 77; *Hom.* 1, 10 in Ps. xxxviii; *Hom.* 7, 1 *in Esai.*; *Comm. in Matt.* XVI, 18.

[4] *Expos. in Lucam*, 7, 5.   [5] *Panar.* 30, 24; 80, 11.

[6] *Comm. in Matt.* XVI, 18.

[7] *De Praescr. haer.* 22; *De Monog.* 8; *De Pudicitia*, 21.

[8] *Strom.* 6, 15, 132; 7, 17, 166.

[9] *Dial. c. Tryph.* 100.   [10] Ed. Ranke, E., 1868, p. 85.

[11] French version by Marmardji, A.-S., 1935, p. 225; an English version by Hamlyn Hill, *Earliest Life of Christ*, 1894, p. 136 (cf. also p. 356).

[12] *The Liége Diatessaron*, edd. Plooij, D., and Phillips, C. A., 1929, p. 258 f.

whole of the passage under discussion. Moreover, if we examine Ephraem's commentary, we find in the immediate context of the passage to which Harnack has called attention the following:

'*Dominus quum ecclesiam suam aedificaret, aedificavit turrim, cuius fundamenta omnia, quae erant superaedificanda, portare possent*'.[1]

A natural inference from these words is that the text of the *Diatessaron* which Ephraem had in front of him also included the supposed 'interpolation'.

Yet to make good his case Harnack has to postulate such an interpolation. He has produced abundant evidence from the works of Origen, showing that in the view of the Alexandrine the Dominical promise referred not to the Church but to Peter, a view which appears to have been followed by Porphyry and others. What he has failed to establish is that the words preceding it formed no part of the original text of St. Matthew's gospel.

EXCURSUS B

St. Peter as the 'Rock'

As in the case of ἐκκλησία, it is relevant to a right understanding of this saying to have in mind something of the background of Hebrew thought. The term ṣur is applied to God Himself in Deut. XXXII, 4; 2 Sam. XXIII, 3; Psalm XVIII, 31; Isaiah XVII, 10; *ibid.*, XLIV, 8. Sĕlā is used in the same sense in 2 Sam. XXII, 2, and 'ĕbhĕn in Isaiah XXVIII, 16 (cf. Rom. IX, 33, and 1 Pet. II, 6–8, where the passage is quoted in conflation with Isaiah VIII, 14). The word kēphā' itself is found only in Jer. IV, 29 and in Job XXX, 6 (in the plural), where it is perhaps an Aramaic loan-word.

As to Rabbinical usage, in connexion with Isaiah LI, 1 f., where ṣur is used as a description of Abraham, Goudge, in the *New Commentary*, pt. iii, p. 168a, quotes a midrash (source unverified) which runs: 'God is like unto a king, who wished to build himself a house. He digged and digged, but in each place water sprang up and destroyed the foundation he had dug. At last he chanced to dig, where deep down he came upon a rock (*petra*); then said he: "Here will I build". In like manner God, wishing to create the world, looked upon the generation of Enoch that would be, and that of the flood, and said: "How can I make a world out of such sinners, who will

---

[1] Ed. Moesinger, p. 154.

people it with those who will annoy me"? But when he saw Abraham,
he said: "Ah, here is a rock upon which I can found a world"'.
Goudge points out that here Abraham is represented 'as a rock
prevailing against the flood, and also as bearing the burden of the
whole of creation', and adds with reference to the same passage 'the
rock shuts off the under world and is a stepping stone into the upper
one'.

The patristic authors who comment on *Tu es Petrus* show no sign
of having attempted to interpret it in the light of a hypothetical
Aramaic original. Had some of them been aware of the probability
that the single word *kēphā'* underlies both πέτρος and πέτρα, they
would not have attempted to press a difference of meaning between
the two Greek terms.

In actual fact it is this ignorance which serves to account for a
somewhat remarkable diversity of interpretation traceable not only
as between the writings of one author and another but sometimes
even between those of the same author.

The earliest writer explicitly to comment on the passage is
Tertullian, who in *De praescr. haer.* 22, 4. ed. Rauschen, p. 32 f., and
in *De Pudic.* 21, plainly identifies the 'Rock' with the person of St.
Peter himself. Elsewhere, however, in *Adv. Marcion.* 4, 13, he refers
its meaning to Christ. Origen, on the other hand, interprets it first as
'every disciple of Christ', of whom St. Peter is the type, and then
as indicating the Apostles generally, *Comm. in Matt.* 11. G.C.S.
Origenis Opera, vol. x, p. 86. Cyprian, *De unit.* 4, explains it of St.
Peter. Hilary of Poitiers interprets it of faith in Christ, *De Trin.* 2,
23; 6, 36 f.: the same view reappears in Ambrose, *Expos. in Lucam*,
6, 97 f. *De Incarn.* 33 f. Ambrose, however, also suggests that it
means Christ Himself, *Ep.* 43, 9, but St. Peter in *De Fide*, 4, 56.
'Faith in Christ' reappears in Epiphanius, *Ancor.* 9; in Chrysostom,
Hom. in Matt., 54, 2, *Hom. in Gal.* ad init.; in Ps.-Basil, *Comm. in
Esai.* 2, 66; in Cyril Alex. *In Esai.* 4, 2; *Dial. de Trin.* 4, although the
same author, *In Esai.* 3, had already explained it of Christ Himself. A
quite perplexing diversity of explanation is found in Jerome, who
takes it of the 'Chair of Peter', in *Ep.* 15, 2; of St. Peter, in *Comm.
in Matt.* XVI, 8; of the Apostles generally in *Adv. Jov.* 1, 26; and of
Christ in *Adv. Jov.* 2, 37: in Augustine, 'the apostolate of St. Peter'
in *Psal. c. part. Don.*; 'St. Peter' in *In Psal.* XXX. *Enarr.* 3, 5; *In
Psal.* LXIX. *Enarr.* 4; 'Christ' in *Serm.* 76, 1; *Tract. in Ev. Ioann.*

124, 5; *Retract.* 1, 21 : and again in Leo I, where two views are represented that it is St. Peter and that it is St. Peter's faith, *Serm.* 3, 2; 5, 4 (on which see the present writer's *Life and Times of St. Leo the Great*, pp. 68–74, 476 ff.).

It may be said, however, that the evidence as to patristic views has exegetical interest only, since, to quote a modern Protestant writer, it is 'quite certain, and is now generally admitted, that the words "this rock" refer, not to Christ, nor to Peter's confession or faith, but to Peter himself'.[1]

EXCURSUS C

St. Paul in Rome

The story of St. Paul's direct association with the early Christian community at Rome begins with the welcome given to him at Appii Forum, a town some forty miles distant from the capital, and again at Tres Tabernae ten miles away, as recorded in Acts XXVIII, 15. After his arrival in the city, as a prisoner awaiting trial by the Emperor's court, the Apostle was probably entrusted to the care of the *princeps peregrinorum*, under whose authority he would remain during the two years which appear to have elapsed between the date of his arrival and his trial. In conformity with his status as a Roman citizen, he was kept in *libera custodia*, which permitted him to enjoy free and unhindered intercourse with those who resorted to his rented lodging.

Until comparatively recent times, the traditional story, as recorded for example by Eusebius,[2] as to St. Paul's subsequent career has been generally accepted. Many would still hold that the Apostle's appeal to the Emperor resulted in his acquittal, and that subsequently he found opportunity, not only to revisit the churches of the East, especially the church of Ephesus, but actually travelled as far west as Spain.

It must be realized, however, that there is no direct evidence supporting the historicity of this 'second' period, and that among the chief considerations in its favour is the supposed necessity for finding

---

[1] Stevens, G. B., *Theology of the New Testament*, 1906, p. 139.

[2] *H.E.* 2, 22. Ed. cit., vol. ii, pt. 1, p. 162. It should be noticed that with his usual caution, Eusebius does not actually commit himself to acceptance of the story as genuine. The fact that he uses the expression 'λόγος ἔχει' shows that he felt some doubt regarding its absolute trustworthiness.

a place for the later epistles, including the 'Pastorals', outside the already known period of the Apostle's life. If, on the other hand, we can assign the 'Epistles of the Captivity' if not to the imprisonment at Caesarea,[1] at least to the known internment at Rome, there remain only the 'Pastorals'. As is generally known, serious doubts have been raised in recent years on linguistic grounds against the integrity of these letters in their present form,[2] and there are solid reasons for believing that our letters are post-Pauline in composition, even if, as is highly probable, they incorporate some authentic Pauline fragments.

As to the supposed journey to Spain, it ought to be realized that this rests on somewhat insecure support. For apart from the hope expressed by the Apostle in *Romans*[3] that such a journey might eventually prove to be possible, we have to rely solely on an obscure phrase in the *Epistle of Clement*.[4] Yet it should be appreciated that τὸ τέρμα τῆς δύσεως may be interpreted as 'the goal or objective in the West', i.e. Rome itself,[5] quite as naturally as 'the boundary or limit of the West', a phrase which has been widely understood to mean Spain.[6] For a direct mention of the 'Spanish journey' we have nothing earlier than the late second-century *apocryphon, The Acts of Peter*,[7] whence it is probable that the tradition found its way into the *Fragmentum Muratorianum*[8] and so into the general belief of the Church.[9]

---

[1] Acts XXIV, 27.

[2] E.g. by Harrison, P. N., *The Problem of the Pastoral Epistles*, 1921.

[3] Rom. XIV, 24-8.

[4] 1 *Clement*, 5, 7.

[5] So Harrison, *op. cit.*, p. 107 and n. 1.

[6] Lowther Clarke, *First Epistle of Clement*, p. 89 f., retains this rendering, while admitting that 'such a journey is difficult to reconcile with the data of the N.T.'

[7] Cf. James, M. R., *Apocryphal New Testament*, p. 304, *Vercelli Acts of St. Peter*, 1. The Gnostic author of these 'Acts' had an obvious motive for disposing of St. Paul, in order to the leave the field open for his hero. The document may be as late as 220.

[8] *Fragm. Murat.* 37 ff. 'semota . . . profectione Pauli ab urbe ad Spaniam profiscentis', in a passage in which he appears to distinguish between the credibility of St. Luke's records and of the supposed 'second period'. It is noteworthy that Eusebius omits any reference to the 'Spanish journey' in the passage cited above.

[9] E.g. Athanasius, *Ep. ad. Dracontium*, 4. Cyril of Jerus., *Catech.* 17, 13.

III

The Church and the Roman See before Diocletian

Plures efficimur quoties metimur a vobis, semen est sanguis Christianorum.
TERTULLIAN, *Apologia*, 50.

Rom. 1, 8. 'I thank my God through Jesus Christ for you all, that your faith is spoken of throughout the whole world'.

Almost all students of Church history would to-day be disposed to agree that Eusebius of Caesarea, in spite of his evident shortcomings, his turgidity of style, his inability to digest and arrange attractively or even always intelligibly the vast amount of material which fortune or his own extensive reading had put at his disposal, has received something less than fair treatment at the hands both of our own great historian of the Roman Empire[1] and of a former incumbent of this University church.[2] For when everything possible has been said as to his demerits as a writer, historian and chronologist, few can be so ungenerous as to deny the extent of our indebtedness to his inexhaustible industry, which has placed at the disposal of posterity a very considerable number of citations from earlier writers. But for him works which in his time were still preserved intact in the store cupboards of the libraries at Caesarea, Jerusalem and Alexandria might easily have remained utterly unknown to-day.

Thus it is to Eusebius that we owe almost all that is recorded of the Roman see during the second and third centuries. Even so we could wish that he had been better informed about western literature and the affairs of western Christendom generally, and more particularly as to the main subject of these lectures. For although the information supplied by him concerning the Papacy in the second and earlier half of the third century is scanty, such as he has to tell us on this subject for the thirty years or so immediately previous to his own time is positively meagre and inaccurate in chronology. But in one, who wrote of Tertullian as a Roman,[3] who was ignorant of the location of the see of Hippolytus[4] and who evidently knew

---

[1] Gibbon, *Decline and Fall*. ed. Bury, J. B., 1939, vol. ii, p. 144.
[2] Newman, J. H., *Arians of the Fourth Century*, 1833, p. 282.
[3] Eus. *H.E.* 2, 25, 4. ed. Schwartz, E., *G.C.S.*, vol. ii, pt. 1, p. 176.
[4] Id., *ibid.*, 6, 20, 2. ed. cit., p. 566.

very little about Cyprian,[1] these defects are perhaps not really surprising.

Contrasted with the lively personalities of Ignatius of Antioch, Justin Martyr, Marcion of Pontus, and Irenaeus of Lyons, to mention only a few of the more prominent names in the life of the Church in the second century, the numerous occupants of the Roman see in that period appear to the student of Church history as little more than a series of 'lay figures'. How few, very few, there are of whom a single distinctive fact has been recorded![2] No doubt hagiographers and canonists have done their best to fill the hiatus, but their work is normally of greater interest to students of pious romance and tendentious legislation than to one who aims at the reconstruction of genuine history. Yet for the preservation of such little trustworthy knowledge of the second-century Papacy as we still possess, it is to Eusebius that almost the whole credit must be given.

In appreciating the relative significance, however, of such facts as Eusebius has recorded regarding the history of the Roman see, whether in his own text or in the excerpts which he has included from other writers, it is important to bear in mind his professed object in compiling his famous *Ecclesiastical History:*

'To hand on in writing . . . (a record of) those who led and presided with distinction over this society (sc. the Church) in the most outstanding local churches (παροικίαις)'.[3]

It follows from this that the recording of papal history formed a

---

[1] Eus. *H.E.* 7, 3. ed. cit., p. 638.

[2] Thus Irenaeus, *Adv. haer.* 3, 3, 3, 5, qualifies Telesphorus, 'ὃς καὶ ἐνδόξως ἐμαρτύρησεν', which is often understood to mean that he died as a victim of persecution. It does not follow, however, that 'ἐμαρτύρησεν' is used in any but a quite general sense. The entries in the current Roman *Missale* and *Breviarium* describing Roman bishops from Linus to Marcellus as 'martyrs' rest on no certain historical evidence. The only name to which the title in its later sense can be assigned with any confidence is that of Xystus II, August 6, 258, cf. Cyprian, *Ep.* 80. *C.S.E.L.* vol. iii, p. 839. Even in the case of Cornelius this attribution is doubtful. Cf. Cyprian, *Ep.* 39, 2, ed. cit., p. 582, and Caspar, *Geschichte des Papsttums*, vol. i, pp. 44, 69 f., with note 1. The extent to which legend has supplied the shortcomings of history may be seen by consulting *Vita Cornelii*, in *Liber pontificalis*, ed. Duchesne vol. i, p. 150. As to the other names of second-century Popes, we could say that Pius had an eccentric brother called Hermas (*Cat. Liberianus*), who was the author of the famous document called the 'Shepherd', that Anicetus was of a prudent and generous nature (Irenaeus, ap. Eus. *H.E.* 5, 24, 16), that Soter was distinguished for his charity (Dion. Cor. ap. Eus. *H.E.* 4, 23, 9 f.), and that he showed tolerance to those who differed from the Roman church in matters of discipline (Irenaeus, ap. Eus. *H.E.* 5, 24, 14 f.), but little or nothing more than this.

[3] *H.E.* 1, 1. ed. cit., p. 6.

8

part, perhaps an important one, but in the last resort a part only, ◁
his immense pioneer undertaking. And it is for this reason that w
cannot refuse to pardon his lack of attention to many questions, o
which we might wish to have been more fully informed, nor fail to b
grateful for such details as he has thought fit to supply. But the con
sideration that the annals of the Roman see are in fact only one amon
the many subjects in which he professes himself to be intereste◁
suggests not only that much has perished which might serve to con
firm and deepen an impression already created by what has bee
preserved, but should also remind us that such inferences as a
possible from the material provided fall very far short of providin
a complete and correctly perspectivized picture of the actual relatio
of the Roman church to other churches during this period.

I

It is, however, fortunate that we have also at our disposal a fe
early authorities in addition to those cited by Eusebius. From th
first of these, the epistle of Clement to the Corinthians,[1] there ma
indeed be little to throw light on our subject. Its chief interest for ◁
here lies in the fact of the intervention of the Roman church in th
domestic affairs of the church of Corinth. Yet it must be admitte
that the writer does not claim superior authority for the determinatio
of the crisis. For while he evidently insists on the apostolic (an
perhaps the divine) origin of the episcopate, he does not call attentio
to any supposed privilege attaching to the Roman church. We mus
however, presume that its help had been invoked in some way. If th
aggrieved *episcopi* of Corinth did not themselves report to that churc
what had taken place, the information must have been conveyed
Rome by some means, and it is most natural to suppose that it ha
been transmitted through members of the party which sympathize
with the victims of an act of local injustice.

No doubt the fact that Corinth had been refounded as a Rom
colony in 44 B.C., and presumably now included a high proportion
citizens of Italian stock in its population, made such an appeal ve
natural, nor can we be surprised that the writer should say wi
reference to the legates of the Roman church, who are bearers of t
letter, and who are to 'be witnesses between you and us':

[1] See above, p. 77 ff.

'This we do, that you may know that our concern has been and till is solely that you may soon be at peace'.[1]

Yet it might not be unreasonable to infer from these words that the Roman church was already conscious of some degree of external responsibility, such as does not appear to have been realized by the geographically neighbouring churches of Thessalonica or Philippi, though the latter was also probably linked to Corinth by blood relationship in virtue of a common colonial status. As we shall see, it will not be long before the thought, which seems to underlie this Clementine consciousness of responsibility, acquires a greater measure of precision in papal correspondence, particularly in the light of St. Paul's own words:

'Beside those things that are without, that which cometh upon me daily, the care of all the churches.'[2]

If it is true to say of the Roman intervention that 'the authority is implicit, it being left to subsequent generations to make explicit the reasons which prompted an instinctive action',[3] we are still left with the question as to the source from which the instinct itself was derived. Instincts are usually traceable to habits of past generations. Was the source in this case merely the habituation of the Roman people to the government of others; or was it not rather, as the whole tone of the epistle would suggest, some custom which could claim a sanction Apostolic or even Dominical in origin?

II

The earliest of non-Roman sources for the attitude of other churches to the Roman church is Ignatius, bishop of Antioch, at that time capital of the province of Syria, and according to Josephus, in point of secular distinction, the third city in the Empire. Ignatius, while on his way to suffer death at Rome as a Christian leader, opens his letter to the church of that city with the following words:

'Ignatius, who is also Theophorus, unto the church that hath been favoured with the munificence of the Father Most High, and of Jesus Christ His only Son; to the church that is beloved and enlightened by the will of Him who willed all things that are in faith and love toward Jesus Christ our God; even to her that

---

[1] 1 Clement, 63.   [2] 2 Cor. XI, 28.
[3] Lowther Clarke, First Epistle of Clement, p. 20.

presides in the region of the Romans' country. . . . that presides in love'.[1]

Certain points may be mentioned in regard to this passage. First, it is addressed not to the bishop of Rome, but to the Roman church. Secondly, in estimating the significance of the language used, we must not fail to make allowance for an oriental exuberance of expression. Attempts have been made to read into it a whole-hearted acknowledgment of the Roman primacy. It is true that the word προκαθημένη, here rendered 'presides', might possibly be translated 'has the primacy', provided that 'primacy' were understood according to the primitive sense of *primatus*.[2] But it is not a natural rendering, and would be dismissed by many as tendentious. Further, the meaning of the expression 'in the region of the Romans' country'[3] is certainly not self-evident. If we follow the existing text, we may regard it as a possible description of the West generally, or more particularly of Italy, judged from the standpoint of an Eastern. If, however, we accept the rather attractive emendation which has been proposed, προκαθημένη ἐν τόπῳ χριστοῦ (that presides in the place of Christ),[4] we are still without any indication about the precise content of this 'presidency'. In any case, as we have already pointed out, it is the Roman church which is said so to 'preside', and not the Roman bishop, who is not mentioned. Perhaps the real clue to its interpretation lies in taking this clause in close connexion with one which follows: 'that presides in love'. Efforts to explain ἀγάπης as a synonym for the whole Church have not been very successful.[5] It seems much more natural to suppose that Ignatius awards this title of honour to the Roman church as a just recognition of its abundant merit.

On the other hand, it should be noticed that, in writing to another church, namely of the Ephesians, in spite of bestowing on it abundant praise, he does not describe it as the church which 'presides in the province of Asia'. It is doubtful therefore whether we can simply dismiss this expression as nothing more than a flattering allusion to

---

[1] *Ep. ad Rom. praef.* ed. Lightfoot, J. B., vol. ii, p. 189 ff.

[2] I.e. the status enjoyed by the first-born of a family.

[3] 'ἐν τόπῳ χωρίου 'Ρωμαίων'. The absence of definite articles is at least suspicious

[4] See Phillimore, J. S., in *J.T.S.*, vol. xix, 1918, pp. 272 ff, who compares *Magn.* 6 προκαθημένου τοῦ ἐπισκόπου εἰς τόπον Θεοῦ'. Cf. also *Eph.* 3; *Smyrn.* 8.

[5] E.g. by Funk, F. X., 'Der Primat d. röm. K, nach Ignatius u. Irenaeus' in *Kirchengesch. Abh.* vol. i, pp. 2–12, 1897. Although ἀγάπη is frequently used by Ignatius of a *local* church or churches, e.g. *Trall.* 13, 1; *Rom.* 9, 3; *Philad.* 9, 2, it is never used of the universal Church.

the place of honour held by the Roman church as the church of the imperial capital. And even if we take his language at its lowest possible value, it is difficult not to feel that the author must have had some very serious reason, possibly one additional to the consideration already mentioned, for displaying such evident admiration and respect, which is all the more remarkable as proceeding from one whose own church was itself richly endowed with both secular and spiritual advantages.

No doubt Rome possessed many fascinations for the average provincial, whether his main interest was worldly or religious. As the capital and chief centre of imperial administration of that time, as a focus of art, culture, and education, not to mention its recently acquired architectural grandeur, it must have inevitably drawn many sculptors, painters, men of letters, as well as men of action and practical ability, within the orbit of its attraction. And once they came under its spell, there as a rule they remained.

What was the ordinary Christian's attitude towards Rome itself? Ignatius, as we have seen, writes with great respect for the Roman church, but he nowhere mentions the imperial city for which he had obviously little reason to feel any strong affection. Yet we have constantly been told, and a modern historian has quite recently revived the idea,[1] that such recognition of the Roman primacy as appears in non-Roman writers of this century, and even later, is nothing more than a reflexion in the Christian church of the veneration felt for the city of Rome in the secular Roman world.

What Christians of the period really thought about the *city* of Rome may be judged from the uncomplimentary allusions to it in the Apocalypse,[2] or from Tatian's sardonic reference to 'Roman arrogance'.[3] And in the face of expressions used by those who, like Tertullian, were eager to satirize the methods by which she rose to power,[4] or, following the example of Hippolytus, denounced the whole ordered majesty of Roman rule as a diabolical parody of the Kingdom of God, can we seriously suppose that the respect paid by Christians like Ignatius to the Roman church is explicable solely by the view that it arose from the association of that church in their

---

[1] Kidd, B. J., *Roman Primacy*, 1936, p. 14.
[2] The argument of this section is indebted to Dix, G., 'Jurisdiction . . . in the Early Church' in *Laudate*, 1938, vol. xvi, p. 233 ff.
[3] *Orat. adv. Graecos*, 35. *M.P.G.* 6, 877.
[4] *Ad Nationes*, 1, 7.

minds with the centre of Roman government? Surely it would be
much nearer the truth to say that it was honoured not because of but
in spite of its imperial associations. In view of the evident abhorrence
of secular Rome felt by second-century Christians, it must be
supposed that they had an overwhelmingly strong reason for honour-
ing its church which no mere recognition of worldly prepotence can
be sufficient to explain. It is also remarkable that no other religion,
such as Judaism and Mithraism, which one might have supposed
would inevitably find in Rome a focus of organization, ever came to
attach any special importance to its establishment there. Even the
Imperial cultus itself, in spite of the obvious possibilities of the
capital as a centre of co-ordination and propaganda, remained local
and provincial in character, in such wise that Rome was the one place
where it was not regarded with any great favour.[1]

Yet in spite of the evident distaste of second-century Christians
for the imperial capital, a feeling which its rulers reciprocated by
consistently regarding the new faith as a *religio illicita*,[2] it was
apparently in Rome that Christianity persisted in locating its primatial
centre. During the second century this primacy was accepted as a
matter of practical convenience. As yet no one troubled to ask the
reason. Only when questions began to arise, did it become necessary
to show that the primacy rested not on the secular greatness of Rome
but on the traditional and, as we believe, historical connexion of the
Roman see with St. Peter, the supposed heir of a peculiar Dominical
privilege.

If the emphasis on this connexion and privilege appears earlier in
Africa than elsewhere, and then only in the third century, it may be
explained perhaps either as an accident of survival (for the *lacunae* in
our documentary evidence for the history of the preceding hundred
years are demonstrably large) or else by the serious challenge to
traditional Christian order and discipline which first made itself felt
in the West in that church.

Attention, however, is sometimes directed to the fact that there is no
trace in our existing evidence of any appeal to the 'Petrine texts' in
second-century authors. Yet it must be remembered that the second
century apologists, who laid the foundations of the later definitions of

---

[1] The cult of Rome and Augustus flourished in the provinces, such as Asia
Minor, but was conspicuously absent in Italy.
[2] E.g. Pliny, *Ep.* 97.

Trinitarian doctrine, are equally silent about the familiar texts bearing on that doctrine, and it is noticeable that the period in which Petrine texts begin to be given prominence is the very same as that which is marked by a hitherto unfamiliar appeal to the authority of Scripture in favour of Trinitarianism. To the second century it is the oral apostolic *paradosis* or body of teaching believed to have been delivered to their immediate successors by the Apostles, and not its partial embodiment in the apostolic writings, which is still the primary authority. Hence it is a mere anachronism to treat the Roman primacy in the second century as a thing of purely secular growth, and to justify this view by calling attention to the fact that it is only in the following century that it begins to acquire an *ex post facto* scriptural justification. The scriptural appeal is lacking for the very simple reason that it was not till towards the close of the second century that a collection of Christian writings came to possess a generally acknowledged canonical status. It is often forgotten that it is tradition not Scripture which is, strictly speaking, primary, and that among the criteria, by which the claim of a particular document to canonization was judged, was included that of conformity with a pre-existing body of doctrine.

Let us now see what evidence there is in the period following the martyrdom of Ignatius of what may be called a pragmatic recognition of the Roman primacy. The same evidence may also serve to show how that primacy was conceived.

A very striking feature of the life of the Church in the second century is the immense variety of its speculative activity. Doubtless this is to be attributed mainly to the impact of the Hellenistic genius on the Christian revelation, and to the need of expressing that revelation in an idiom which would satisfy the intellectual outlook of the Graeco-Roman world. To a less extent it is to be explained by a quite deliberate attempt to adjust the principles of the new faith to conform with the categories of oriental theosophy.[1]

At the same time other forces were at work. In spite of the cleavage between Christianity and its parent stock, now complete, the indirect influence of Judaism still persisted. Moreover, in those parts of the Empire remote from large centres of population, in which Graeco-

---

[1] For a description of the real character of Gnosticism, see Kirk. K. E., *Vision of God*, Bampton Lectures for 1928, 1931, pp. 207–219.

Roman culture never obtained a very secure foothold, native enthusiasm was by no means a negligible quantity.

As a result, scarcely half a decade of this century passes without some new development in doctrine or practice. Yet in spite of the immense and often perplexing diversity of these movements, the Christian man of letters, the Christian philosopher or revivalist, each and every one of them appears to betray a common pre-occupation. If it is true that 'in the second century all roads led to Rome',[1] it is also true that those roads were crowded with Christian teachers and writers all intensely eager to purvey their new philosophies. Thus we learn from an eminent ecclesiastical historian that 'from the provinces to Rome in the second century went a constant stream, as Irenaeus tells us, of "the faithful who are from everywhere". . . . To Rome then journeyed Polycarp from Smyrna; Valentinus from Egypt; Cerdo from Syria; Marcion from Sinope; Justin from Samaria; Tatian from Assyria; Hegesippus from Jerusalem; Justin's pupils Euelpestus from Cappadocia and Hierax from Phrygia; Rhodon, Irenaeus, and Florinus from Asia; Proclus and other Montanists from Phrygia; and Praxeas, their adversary, from the same region'.[2] But, as the same writer illustrates further in a later chapter,[3] it was not by any means only the 'faithful' who had recourse to the capital. Those whom Irenaeus regarded as anything but 'faithful' were to be found on the road side by side with those who would by him be accounted orthodox. It can not merely be said that like the well-known Abercius of Hierapolis, they undertook the journey solely in order 'to see the royal palace and to behold the golden robed, golden slippered queen',[4] even if the idea of undertaking it, as he suggests in his own case, may have been due to divine inspiration. For in any case, unlike Abercius, who went home again after his visit, most of them stayed there, and set up their 'warring lecture rooms with which the Roman church was furnished'.[5] As has already been pointed out, we shall not exhaust the possible explanations of this remarkable phenomenon by pointing to the overpowering

---

[1] Prestige, G. L., *Fathers and Heretics*, Bampton Lectures for 1940, p. 55.
[2] Kidd, B. J., *History of the Church*, vol. i, p. 118.
[3] Id., *ibid.*, p. 353 ff.
[4] Abercius Hierapol. in *Enchiridion Fontium H.E. Ant.*[4] ed. Kirch, C., 1923 No. 155. It may be noted that Chavasse, C., *Bride of Christ*, 1940, p. 117, takes Abercius to refer to the local church of Rome.
[5] Prestige, *op. cit.*, p. 65.

magnetism of the imperial capital. For what indeed had Rome to offer to the man of letters, the philosopher or the revivalist, which other cities in the Empire, Alexandria for example, could not provide, and perhaps provide somewhat better? Nor can we readily accept the interpretation of Irenaeus' famous chapter on the Roman see, to be mentioned at a later point, which makes him affirm that 'it was not so much the truth which they found there, as the truth which they brought with them thither that made the Roman church the reservoir of Christian tradition',[1] since exegesis of this kind appears, at least in our view, completely to invert his whole argument. In any case truth which is represented by no more than the highest common factor of widely differing types of experience is not easy to identify with the whole truth revealed by Jesus Christ. For the possibility must always remain that some one among its various and often contradictory exponents has preserved an element in the original presentation of that truth already forgotten or ignored by all the rest. How can we explain then this second century *Drang nach Rom*? May there not have been a conviction, common to Justin, Valentinus, Marcion and the others, that in some way or another, the Roman see had an inherent right to pronounce an opinion on their doctrine, and moreover that the nature of its decision, i.e. whether favourable or adverse, would seriously affect their prospects of success in obtaining for their teaching general acceptance by the Church at large? All the same, if the attitude of the Roman see was unfavourable, as for example towards Valentinus and Marcion, it did not mean that the teacher responsible for the condemned doctrine decamped at once elsewhere. On the contrary, he usually stayed on in Rome, endeavouring to propagate his doctrine in spite of official disapproval, and in extreme cases managed to procure the election of a rival bishop of Rome who could be guaranteed to give it the desired sanction. Thus in a negative no less than in a positive direction there are strong indications that *de facto* if not *de iure* the Roman see was being treated as the universal referee and its doctrine as the norm.

III

If we wish to test the truth of this view we cannot do better than turn to Irenaeus and follow carefully the line of argument used by him to controvert the case of the exponents of the new Gnosis,

[1] Kidd, *op. cit.*, p. 118.

which had then only recently acquired prominence. A common defence put forward by these theosophists of the second century was not to reject the necessity of being in possession of the Apostles' teaching. No one ventured to deny this need. It was accepted by them no less than by their opponents. On the contrary, in reply to those who like Irenaeus might be disposed to point out that there were novel and even original elements in their doctrine, these newfangled teachers did not hesitate to affirm that in the original process of the *paradosis* (or handing over) of the Christian revelation, certain details after being withheld from the whole body of the Apostles had been imparted to a select few only, and that it was from this secret and specially privileged source that their peculiar tenets were derived.[1]

It was chiefly against this affirmation of the existence of a secret element in the original *paradosis* that Irenaeus wrote his famous *Adversus haereses*, in the third part of which he begins his great offensive on the Gnostic position. This part opens with an appeal to the original preaching of the Apostles, which, as the author asserts, was committed to writing in the four canonical gospels. Thus St. Matthew is the originator of the tradition in Jerusalem, which he himself published in writing, St. Peter and St. Paul of the tradition in Rome, handed down in writing by Mark and Luke, St. John of the tradition in Ephesus published by himself.[2] So, says Irenaeus, anyone who chooses to do so can verify for himself in every local church what the actual tradition originally delivered by the Apostles really was. But if he wishes to know how we can prove that it is not defective, it is possible to produce an ascending list of names associating the present-day teaching by an unbroken succession with the Apostles themselves, thus showing that the authentic *paradosis* is wholly comprised in the existing doctrine of the episcopal churches.

For, he argues, even supposing the Gnostic theory of a secret element in the *paradosis* were true, it is inconceivable that the Apostles would not have imparted it to those to whom they committed the charge of their respective foundations.[3]

It has been necessary to paraphrase Irenaeus' words at some length, in order to grasp his method of approach to his subject, of which the crucial section of this chapter in his book forms an essential part.

[1] See below, p. 115.   [2] *Adv. haer.* 3, 1, 1.   [3] *Ibid.,* 3, 3, 1.

Let us see how he proceeds :

'Yet because it would be a very lengthy proceeding in a book such as this to set out the series of successions belonging to all the churches, we are proposing to show that the existing faith of that most noble, ancient, and well-known church, founded and established at Rome by the two most famous Apostles Peter and Paul, the faith, I say, which it still holds, and which comes down to our time by means of a series of successions of bishops, is actually identical with the *paradosis* given by the Apostles, that is "the faith proclaimed to mankind". Thus we refute all those who in different ways, either through private judgment or vainglory, or else in blindness and perversity, make unwarrantable additions. For every church, that is, the faithful in each place, in which the identical *paradosis* given by the Apostles is always preserved by those who preside in each place, is necessarily in agreement with this church because of its superior origin'.[1]

It is obviously impossible to discuss this passage here with the thoroughness which its numerous difficulties naturally demand. We shall therefore devote our attention in the main to the last sentence, wherein the major crux evidently lies. A few preliminary comments are necessary. It will of course be remembered that this section as well as the previous one has been preserved only in a Latin version of the whole work, which a distinguished patristic scholar believes to be almost contemporary with the original.[2] We shall see presently that this question of date is of great importance, in helping us to restore conjecturally the original Greek text. Secondly, we assume that *traditio* represents παράδοσις and have deliberately introduced the Greek word, in order to make it clear that 'tradition' in English does not adequately represent the force of the original *paradosis*, from which, to quote a predecessor in this lectureship, 'the idea of proclamation and the note of authority are seldom or never absent'. As used by Irenaeus it also appears to mean 'the body of teaching originally delivered' by the Apostles.[3]

Further, it is noticeable that *successiones* is here used in the plural, not of several churches, but of one only. This shows that the rendering 'succession' in the singular (assuming that *successiones* represents

---

[1] *Adv. haer.* 3, 3, 2.

[2] Sanday, W.–Turner, C. H., *Novum Testamentum S. Irenaei*, Old Latin Texts, ii, 1923, p. lxiv. But see also p. xcvi.

[3] Prestige, *op. cit.*, p. 22 ff., where evidence as to the early use of παράδοσις is given.

διαδοχαί) does not accurately represent the idea underlying the Latin
or Greek in this context, which being in plural must denote here, not
a mere list of names, but the replacement of one holder of the office
by the next; in fact, 'series of successions', though possibly cumbersome, seems to be needed to convey the real sense of the term.[1]

We now approach the chief problem. What is the significance of
propter potiorem principalitatem, which we take to be the true reading,
and for which we have suggested 'superior origin' as a possible
rendering? A right decision here is of the greatest moment, for on it
must depend the answer given to a number of subsidiary problems.
What is the most probable Greek text underlying these words?
Unhappily this question is rendered vastly more difficult than usual
owing to doubt as to the correct reading. But if we bear the date of
this version in mind, we shall find our first clue by excluding later
meanings of *principalitas* and its cognates, and preferring instead
those for which there is authority not later than the middle of the
third century. This guides us to the senses of 'authenticity' or
'origin'.[2] If we select the latter and reject later meanings, we can
easily account for the *lectio communis* '*potentiorem*' as a later correction of *potiorem* given in the original form of the Clermont MS.,
a correction which must have seemed only natural by the time

---

[1] Cf. Irenaeus, *ibid.*, 4, 33, 8. Used in the singular, it signifies 'one step' in the
series of '*successiones*' from the apostles. This is clear from the use of the expression
'principali successione', which must be the 'original succession' as opposed to later
ones. Cf. for this meaning of *principalis* Tertullian, *De praescr.* 32, 1–3. For the
significance of διαδοχή in the pre-Nicene period, see above, p. 85 f.

[2] It is fortunate that we are able to some extent to check the meaning of *principalitas* as used here by the fact that in the case of three other passages in which i
occurs we still possess the Greek original text. These are *Adversus haer.* 1, 26, 1 bi
and *ibid.*, 1, 31, 1. In the first it is used to render ἐξουσίας in a phrase describing
the 'Demiurge', in the second to translate αὐθεντίας, signifying the 'self-moved
source' (there seems no compelling reason to translate αὐθεντία here as 'absolute
Power'), and in the third, where it again corresponds to αὐθεντία, the meaning of
which is the same as before. The fact, however, that the Greek term is used to
describe Gnostic ideas renders its exact sense somewhat obscure. In 4, 38, 3 i
occurs in the phrase 'principalitatem habet in omnibus Deus' as a translation of
'πρωτεύει ἐν πᾶσιν ὁ Θεός', where its sense appears to be one of 'priority'.

Other instances of the word, where the Greek original is lacking, are *ibid.*, 1, 30, 8
3, 11, 8; 3, 12, 5; 4, 34, 6; 4, 35, 2 *bis*; 4, 36, 1; 5, 14, 1.2. In all of these the mean
ing is akin to 'source' or 'origin'.

The use of the cognate adjective *principalis* and of its adverb *principaliter* serve
to confirm this interpretation. Cf. *ibid.*, 3, 11, 8 *bis*; 4, 26, 2; 4, 35, 2; 5, 14, 2
5, 21, 2; 5, 27, 2. For use of *principalitas* elsewhere in a similar sense, cf. Tertullian
De praescript. 31; *De Anima*, 13; and for *principalis, principaliter*, Cyprian, E
59, 14; Jerome, *Ep.* 124, 14. C.S.E.L. vol. lvi, p. 116.

principalitas had acquired its later authoritarian sense. On this show-ing it would seem that Harvey's suggestion διὰ τὴν διαφορωτέραν ἀρχήν for the Greek original ought to be regarded as highly probable.[1]

It is impossible to pursue here the many other fascinating problems raised by this elusive passage.[2] Instead, in the light of the conclusions

---

[1] Irenaeus, *Adv. haer.* ed. Harvey, W. W., 1857, vol. ii, p. 9, note, where he mentions 'διὰ τὴν ἐξαίρετον πρωτείαν' of Salmasius, 'διὰ τὴν ἱκανωτέραν ἀρχήν' of Grabe and 'διὰ τὴν ἱκανωτέραν ἀρχαιότητα' of Stieren. Cf. *ibid.*, p. 279, n. 5, where Harvey indicates διαφορώτεροι as a probable original of 'differentes', the sense of which appears to be similar to that of 'potiorem' in this passage.

[2] Among these is, first, the question of the true antecedent of 'in qua'. Is it 'Ad hanc . . . ecclesiam', that is, the church of Rome? or is it 'omnem ecclesiam'? The question is of some importance, as the answer appears to affect the precise *nuance* of 'necesse est'. Yet even if it may be argued that a relative clause more naturally qualifies the noun which immediately precedes it, i.e. 'omnem ecclesiam', there is no really insuperable objection to taking it as qualifying 'hanc ecclesiam'. In any case, if it be referred to 'omnem ecclesiam', it would merely serve to supply an additional and not very convincing reason for the 'necessity' of 'having recourse to' or 'agreeing with' (we will not prejudge the sense of 'necesse est convenire [ad]' at this stage), namely that the authentic tradition in the church of Rome has always been preserved, not by the succession of bishops nor even by the local faithful, but 'by those who are from everywhere', by which must be meant presumably either passing visitors or at best those who have settled in Rome comparatively late in life. No doubt it may be said that these visitors or immigrants brought with them the traditions of their own churches, and thus ensured that the local tradition of the church of Rome was kept up to the mark. But it is not difficult to see that such a line of thought makes utter nonsense of the whole argument and is in any case completely at variance with the thought underlying 'potiorem principalitatem'. It would seem therefore that Harvey is less happy in his suggestion that ἐν ᾗ, if it be the correct original of 'in qua', must relate to 'omnem ecclesiam'. His alternative suggestion of ᾗ, 'inasmuch as', is preferable. Secondly, we take 'undique' in its late Latin sense as equivalent to 'ubique'. Cf. Lewis and Short, s.v. *undique*, II, 1. Yet even so it is difficult to believe that Irenaeus' translator could have written: 'Every church, that is, the faithful who are everywhere, in which a tradition im-parted by the Apostles has always been preserved by those who are everywhere'. Bearing in mind the frequency with which Irenaeus stresses his conviction that the successors of the Apostles are the guardians of tradition (e.g. *ibid.*, 3, 3, 1–3), it seems impossible that he could have said simply οἱ πανταχοῦ εἰσίν. Hence we may find some justification for the emendation 'qui praesunt undique' and explain the reading 'qui sunt undique' by assimilation to the preceding line. If adopted, it gives the very suitable rendering 'Those who preside in each place', i.e. the bishops at each local church.

We are now in a better position to consider the next of the chief *cruces* of the passage, namely 'necesse est convenire [ad]'. First of all, is the 'necessity' here mentioned moral or logical? And whichever it be, does 'convenire ad' mean 'have recourse to' or 'resort to', and not rather 'agree with'? Admittedly if 'potentiorem principalitatem' is in fact the correct reading and is to be rendered 'more powerful authority', the 'necessity' would appear to be a *moral* one. But the fact that we have rejected this reading, and preferred 'potiorem principalitatem' in the sense of 'superior origin' renders the possibility that it is logical rather than moral still open. Now we have only to ask how the argument that 'every church . . . in which a tradition imparted by the Apostles has always been preserved by those who preside

already reached, we may summarize what appears to be the author's argument.

Irenaeus states that the task of retailing all the 'successions-series' of all the churches would be impossible.[1] He therefore proposes to give a typical example, the 'successions-series' of the church of Rome, and by this means he believes it possible to prove that the present-day faith of that church represents the whole and not merely a part of the original body of teaching imparted by the two Apostles.

Yet, he adds, to reproduce the 'successions-series' of all the churches would in any case be rather a waste of time, because, with the 'successions-series' of the church of Rome before us we have sufficient proof. For if by the production of this 'series' we can prove

in each place' is *morally* bound to 'have recourse' to or 'agree with' the church of Rome really contributes to Irenaeus' case to see that it is quite irrelevant. For on his showing the authentic tradition already exists in every local church in virtue of the 'series of successions', to which he has referred in the previous chapter (*ibid.*, 3, 3, 1).

We have still to decide how 'convenire ad' ought to be rendered. It should be carefully noted that if the translator wished to express the idea of 'having recourse to' as in *ibid.*, 3, 4, 1, he used 'recurrere [in]'. On the other hand, in his rendering of 2 Cor. VI, 15, we observe that Jerome does not hesitate to write 'quae conventio Christi ad Belial'? We cannot therefore reject this sense, as has sometimes been done, on the ground that it is impossible as Latinity. As a rendering of συμβαίνει πρὸς it would be quite natural. Only some further points of lesser importance need mention. It should be remarked that some commentators and translators appear to have failed to appreciate that 'annuntiatam hominibus fidem' is an allusion to Rom. 1, 8, 'ἡ πίστις ὑμῶν καταγγέλλεται ἐν ὅλῳ τῷ κόσμῳ.' Besides this, the phrase 'praeterquam oportet, colligunt' has occasioned some difficulty. With it we may compare *ibid.*, 4, 26, 2, 'reliquos, qui absistunt a principali successione et quocumque loco colligunt, suspectos habere'. If the meaning in this later passage is 'derive conclusions' it might be thought that such a sense would have demanded 'e quocumque loco'. Yet there is support for this usage without the preposition in Quintilian, *Inst.* 2, 20, 5, *et freq. ibid.* On the other hand, to take 'colligunt' as intransitive, so as to mean 'form themselves into illicit assemblies' (for which Harvey *ad loc.* proposes the Greek παρ' ὃ δεῖ συνάγουσιν), appears harsh here, and in *ibid.*, 3, 3, 2, irrelevant to the argument. Finally, it may be mentioned that the Clermont and Vossian MSS. read 'Paulo et Petro', which in view of the later tendency to prefer St. Peter may represent the original order. Cf. e.g. Eusebius *H.E.* 3, 2. ed. cit. p. 188.

[1] It is perhaps improper though not irrelevant to suggest that Irenaeus had not found it easy to trace any very complete 'successions-series', except in the case of the church of Rome. Eusebius, who deliberately set out at a later date to collect 'succession-lists' as material for his *History*, admits that he was unable to ascertain any reliable dates for those whom he supposed to be the early bishops of Antioch and Jerusalem, while in the case of his own see, Caesarea in Palestine, he could not trace back the succession further than Theophilus, who was himself a contemporary of Irenaeus. Hence our author may have found in his argument regarding the 'potior principalitas' of the church of Rome a convenient way out of the difficulty.

the identity of the *paradosis* of the Apostles with current Roman doctrine (i.e. refute the contention of the Gnostics that what is now taught is not all that was originally imparted), the same proof will show that in other churches the apostolic *paradosis* is identical with that which the bishops (adopting the simple emendation *praesunt* for *sunt*) still preserve. For it is quite unthinkable that the Apostles could have imparted anything to the other churches which was not conveyed to the church of Rome, especially in view of the fact that the latter had SS. Peter and Paul for its original teachers.

Apart from many other respects in which this passage has been misunderstood, it has not usually been noticed that Irenaeus' intention is to prove, not, as we might suppose, that the current teaching of the Church did not exceed the *paradosis* of the Apostles, but the precise converse of this, namely that the scope of the original *paradosis* was exactly coextensive with the doctrine of the Church in his time, and was not 'plus a little something' of which the Gnostics presumptuously claimed a monopoly.

If this interpretation be allowed, we need not delay to consider whether or not *convenire ad* means 'resort to' or 'agree with',[1] nor speculate about the limits of the *principalitas* here assigned to the Roman see. If we are to be faithful to the author's meaning, we shall find here no more than explicit recognition of the Roman see as 'a norm in questions of faith'.[2]

IV

It may, however, be said, 'I admit you have shown some reason to believe that a bishop such as Irenaeus, in whom it may be said with justice that the streams of eastern and western traditional thought to some extent coalesce, unhesitatingly recognized the "normality" of the Roman see in the sphere of doctrine, and that he associated this characteristic with the fact of its origin from the primates of the apostolic band, SS. Peter and Paul, whose eminence was a guarantee of the integrity of its *paradosis*. But can the same be said as to his attitude towards a claim by that see to exercise jurisdiction over other churches? Does not his generally acknowledged rebuke of Pope Victor I give a direct negative to the possibility that any such claim on the part of the Roman see in his time could be justified in virtue

---

[1] The question is examined on p. 114, n.
[2] Cf. Dix, G., in *Laudate*, vol. xvi, 1938, p. 240.

of a supposed legacy from a privilege of arbitration assigned to St. Peter?'

In answering these questions fairly it will be useful in the first place to have before us the traditional account of Pope Victor's action. The sources for it are to be found in the documents quoted by Eusebius and in the interpretation put upon them by him in his record of a controversy on the subject of Paschal observance which took place in the concluding years of the second century.[1] It has been inferred from these that about this time information had been received in Rome that some dissension existed in Asia on this question, whereupon Pope Victor recommended the holding of synods in different places to discuss the matter. As a result, with one exception, it was agreed that Easter should be kept on the Lord's day (i.e. Sunday), and that on this day the Paschal fast should come to an end. The exception was the synod of the proconsular province of Asia, held under the presidency of Polycrates of Ephesus, which duly reported its decision to Pope Victor. It was to the effect that as the churches of that province had always been accustomed to observe the fourteenth day of the Paschal month (it was of course for this reason that they were known later to their opponents as Quartodecimans), they proposed to continue this custom.[2] Yet as soon as Victor knew of this decision, he at once withdrew his communion from the recalcitrants and informed other churches of the action which he had taken.

In some quarters, of which Irenaeus is thought to be typical, the news was received, according to the accepted view, with considerable dismay and even resentment; in fact Irenaeus appears to have believed it to be his duty to utter an open protest.[3] In the end, it is thought, the Pope either withdrew his excommunication in the face of such serious opposition, or else refrained from giving it final effect. In either case it would seem that Quartodecimanism gradually disappeared and was extinct even in Asia at the time of the Nicene council.[4]

Considerable importance has been attached to the affair of Pope Victor I by historians, not less by those who assign a primitive origin

[1] Eusebius, H.E. 5, 23 f. ed. Schwartz, E., vol. ii, pt. 1, p. 488 ff.
[2] Cit. ap. eund. ibid., 5, 24, 1–8.
[3] Cit. ap. eund. ibid., 5, 24, 12–17.
[4] Ps.-Tertullian, Adv. omn. haer. 8. C.S.E.L. vol. xxxvii, p. 225.

the Roman primacy than by those who deny it.[1] That it should be
apable of a diametrically opposed use as a controversial weapon
at least surprising, and might in itself suggest that in some way the
vidence had been misunderstood. Yet in spite of this obvious objec-
on, the traditional view of the affair, which is demonstrably
ependent on the trustworthiness of Eusebius, has gone on being
epeated, till it has become part of the stock-in-trade of ecclesiastical
istorians.

Now we have only to glance at the material supplied by Eusebius
to see that it is not by any means easy to make it form a strictly
oherent story. For while the historian's own words and the extract
uoted by him from the letter of Polycrates refer explicitly to the
cal churches of Asia and to their Quartodeciman convictions,[2]
either of the two citations from Irenaeus appears to have anything
rectly to do with Asia; in fact, the latter one seems to describe
xclusively the attitude of the Roman church towards the practice
residents or visitors of provincial origin,[3] the only reference to
sia occurring in his description of the relations between Polycarp
Smyrna and Pope Anicetus. It is not less remarkable that in the
evious extract Polycrates never once refers explicitly to Pope
ictor or to the Roman see. The more carefully we look then at these
ocuments, the more doubtful we feel that Polycrates and Irenaeus
e really talking about the same thing. In fact, it is only possible to
oduce coherence by making certain assumptions which our existing
xts may permit, but do not necessarily demand. It is usually sup-
sed, for example, that when Irenaeus writes of 'observants' and
on-observants' he refers to the Quartodecimans and their opponents.
ut his actual text does not mention Quartodecimanism. Hence it is
rfectly possible that he is referring either to the observance or non-
servance of the Paschal fast mentioned in the previous extract, or
en to the celebration or non-celebration of the Paschal feast itself,
d is therefore not really discussing Quartodeciman custom at all.

---

[1] E.g. by Batiffol, P., *L'église naissante*, p. 74 ff. and by Scott, S. H., *Eastern
urches and the Papacy*, p. 48. See also authors quoted in Turmel, J., *Histoire du
me de la Papauté*, p. 74 ff.

[2] Eus. *ibid.*, 24, 1, 2–9.

[3] Irenaeus, cit. ap. Eus. *op. cit.*, 5, 24, 14 f. 'τοῖς ἀπὸ τῶν παροικιῶν . . . Πολυκάρπου
δημήσαντος ἐν τῇ 'Ρώμῃ.' Notice also that in c. 25 Eusebius includes a synodical
ter of the province of Caesarea in Palestine, which mentions only that it is the
tom of that province to observe Easter on the Alexandrine date, and hence is
loosely connected with what precedes.

Without, however, examining these and many other problems rais
by this highly perplexing passage at this point, we may briefly sket
the lines along which something like a satisfactory solution can l
reached.

First of all, it must be appreciated that of all the controversi
which had previously disturbed the peace of the Church, Pascha
disputes were among those which would inevitably be of very re
interest to a person in Eusebius' position. The plain reason for th
lies in the fact that it was one of the chief items in the ecclesiastic
policy of his imperial patron and hero, Constantine I,[1] to bring abo
common acceptance of an agreed method of reckoning the Pasch
date.   For this reason we should not be greatly surprised to lea
(though he does not tell us so himself) that Eusebius had ransack
the libraries at Caesarea and Jerusalem in order to trace any sour
which might support the imperial project ultimately carried out l
synodical resolution at Nicaea. This, as we shall see, amounted to
general agreement to abandon the method of keeping Easter accor
ing to the dates fixed by Jewish calculation, and to adopt that whi
was then being followed by the churches of Rome, Africa, Egy
and elsewhere.[2] Eusebius, like his master, was no doubt supreme
anxious to promote uniformity (though probably from tota
different motives), and it was therefore distinctly germane to l
purpose to assemble any evidence which in the remotest possil
way might serve to show that Paschal questions had been previou:
settled by the same method as at Nicaea, namely by a majority vo
and that uniformity had not been imposed by the *fiat* of a sin
bishop, whether it was Victor of Rome or Alexander of Alexandri:

Now any careful reader of his *History* knows well enough th
Eusebius is not particularly discriminating in his use of sources, th
he is just as liable as to include side by side two contradict
authorities without attempting a synthesis, as frankly to misund
stand those whom he quotes.[3] Hence we cannot exclude the possibi
that in this case he may have mistaken what was in fact a pur
domestic dissension within the Roman church for a controversy
almost oecumenical magnitude, and thus succeeded in giving

---

[1] Cf. Eusebius, *Vita Const.* 3, 18. ed. Schwartz, E., vol. i, p. 85.
[2] Id., *ibid.*, 3, 19.
[3] See McGiffert. A. C., 'Church History of Eusebius' in *N.P.-N. Fathers*, vol
p. 50 f., 1890. Bright, *Eusebius*, *H.E.*, Introd. pp. xlvi ff., 1872.

ιite misleading impression about the character of the affair which
ε purports to describe. In other words, it is conceivable that he has
εen guilty in this case of making the very blunder which so con-
antly mars the work of the historian, namely of reading into the
ιst the concepts and practice of his own time.[1]

After studying his authorities afresh, is it possible to derive from
ιem a coherent view of the situation, as they, rather than their
ιonsor, actually present it? Taking first the extract from Polycrates,
ε notice that the writer's principal contention is that, as the
ιuartodeciman custom, still observed and upheld in Asia, forms part
the apostolic *paradosis*, on this ground it can in no circumstances be
ιandoned. On the other hand, the former of the two passages
ιoted on the authority of Irenaeus, as we have already pointed out,
ιes not in itself explicitly mention the Paschal feast (unless 'the
ιy' referred to in the opening sentence be taken as an allusion to it);
ιstead, the author contents himself with saying that, in regard to
versities in individual practice regarding the feast, the church of
ιyons had achieved a *modus vivendi* by simply allowing each of the
ιithful to follow his own private custom, and concludes somewhat
ιradoxically by calling attention to the value of diversity as supply-
ιg evidence of a common faith.[2] Finally, the latter Irenaean passage
almost entirely concerned to demonstrate the fact that up to a
ιrtain recent point in time, a policy of toleration in regard to
ιschal diversity had been consistently pursued by the Roman see.[3]
The whole subject bristles with obscurities, but these need not
ιunt us in attempting some sort of conjectural reconstruction, on
ιe lines suggested by a recent Russian scholar.[4] It may be supposed
the first place that at some date, probably in the earlier half of the
ιcond century, the Roman church had adopted the practice of com-
ιemorating the closing events of our Lord's earthly life on the first
ιy of the week nearest to the day of the Jewish passover,[5] and we

[1] On the difference between the Paschal controversies of the second and the fourth
ιnturies, see Duchesne, L., 'La question de la Pâque' in *Revue des questions
ιtoriques*, vol. xxviii, 1880, p. 5–22.

[2] Cit. ap. Eus. *H.E.* 5, 24, 12 f.

[3] Cit. ap. Eus. *H.E. ibid.*, 14 f.

[4] Zernov, N., 'Eusebius and the Paschal Controversy', in *C.Q.R.*, vol. cxvi,
ιpril, 1933, p. 28 ff.

[5] Duchesne, *op. cit.*, p. 7, holds that the change had already taken place by the
ιne of Xystus I (A.D. 115–125?). But it is not easy to be confident that this is
ιenaeus' real meaning in the passage already mentioned.

may conjecture that it was the adoption of this custom which ga
rise to an association of that day with a yearly commemoration
the Resurrection. On the other hand, those who came from the Ea
particularly, as we may suppose, from *Asia proconsularis*, either
temporary or permanent residents in the capital, quite natural
retained their own custom, to which everything appears to point
being original, of observing the fourteenth day of the Pasch
month.[1] As a result a considerable degree of local diversity arose. F
some time, however, it appears to have passed unnoticed, though v
may perhaps infer from Irenaeus that Pope Soter made son
attempt to impose uniformity. The crisis came after the election
the African[2] Victor I to the papal throne, who being characteristical
Latin in outlook aimed at securing a greater measure of local di
cipline. A tense situation developed in which it is even possible th
a charge of Judaising was preferred against the Asians, and the di
pute finally came to a head at a Roman synod at which a sentence
excommunication was passed against the dissenters.[3] This decisio
as a matter of general interest, was eventually communicated to oth
churches, with the usual request for assent, which seems to have be
freely given, if we follow Eusebius, by all except those of the provin

---

[1] It is clear that later writers treated the Quartodecimans as a species of Judais
See Hippolytus, *Elenchos* (*Philosophumena*), 8, 18, 1. ed. Wendland, P., 191
Ps. Tert. *Adv. omn. haer.* 8. *C.S.E.L.* vol. xxxvii, p. 225. For later evidence as
Quartodeciman survivals, see Epiphanius, *Panar.* 50, *G.C.S.* ed. Holl, K., vol.
p. 244 ff. and Socrates, *H.E.* 6, 11 ; 6, 19 ; 7, 29.

[2] *Liber Pontificalis*, ed. Duchesne, L., vol. i, p. 137.

[3] The only phrase which appears to tell against this interpretation is c. 24, x
'ὡς μὴ ἀποκόπτοι ὅλας ἐκκλησίας', where Eusebius appears to be summarizing t
earlier part of Irenaeus' letter. Our view as to whether the historian fairly rep₨
sented his authority must depend on our general opinion about his trustworthine
On this question, see above, and Lightfoot, Art. *Eusebius of Caesarea* in *D.C.*
vol. ii, p. 326. The view that Victor after all only 'threatened' to excommunica
the Asian Christians appears to be untenable in the face of Eus. *H.E.* 5, 24,
ἀθρόως τῆς ᾿Ασίας πάσης ἅμα τοῖς ὁμόροις ἐκκλησίαις τὰς παροικίας ἀποτέμνειν, ὡς
ἑτεροδοξούσας, τῆς κοινῆς ἑνώσεως πειρᾶται, καὶ στηλιτεύει γε διὰ γραμμάτων, ἀκοινωνήτ₨
πάντας ἄρδην τοὺς ἐκεῖσε ἀνακηρύττων ἀδέλφους. The use of 'στηλιτεύει', an almo
technical term for the action prescribing a condemned person or group of perso₨
shows this clearly enough. The fact that Eusebius uses 'πειρᾶται' means that
his view the sanction was not adopted by the Church as a whole. That
exaggerated the scope of Victor's proscription can be seen from his inclusion in t
ban the whole area (as it appears) of Asia Minor, in spite of the fact that j₨
above he had stated that the only supporters of the Quartodeciman practice we
the churches of the proconsular province (see *ibid.*, 5, 24, 1). The only possi
support for the view just mentioned is in 'τοῖς καταπλησσομένοις' (§ 7), which ne
mean no more than 'amazed'. Cf. Liddell and Scott, *s.v.* esp. on the Middle voi

Asia. These strongly protested in favour of the Quartodeciman
stom. Objection also was made by the church of Lyons, which
ged that the former policy of toleration should be continued.[1]
here is no trace of a protest against Victor's action on grounds of
inciple. No one suggested that he had not the right to act as he had
ne. The sole point at issue is whether in fact the Roman custom
n be upheld as authentically 'apostolic'. And on this question the
nod of Ephesus appears to have been in a minority of one. It would
em therefore that the affair has no bearing whatever on the problem
a papal primacy of jurisdiction. Victor and his synod simply
communicate a group of their own members. The rest of the church
only indirectly affected.

On this interpretation it is evident that the traditional account is
riously misleading. In fact, the more closely it is examined, the more
ident its defects *qua* history become, the most obvious being the
perimposition of the later 'oecumenical' conception of ecclesiastical
scipline on an outlook which at this time remained demonstrably
rochial'. In Eusebius' lifetime the Church, now one of the
igiones licitae of the Empire, was beginning to be oecumenically
nded, but to suppose that it had already begun to be such at the
d of the second century, is to run counter to all our existing
idence and to render the history of the third century quite untel-
ible. We are not then to suppose that Quartodecimanism provides
early example of a challenge to papal authority. If anything is
allenged, it is the right of the Roman church to manage its own

Cit. ap. Eus. *H.E.* 5, 24, 12–17. Irenaeus cites as an example, in addition to
se already mentioned, the charitable behaviour of Pope Anicetus and Polycarp
Smyrna towards one another, in spite of disagreement on Paschal observance.
does not, however, make it clear what was the precise point in dispute. About
s three principal views have been held: (1) it was a question whether or not
Paschal feast should be kept at all, Anicetus being opposed to such celebration
τηρῶν § 17) and Polycarp in its favour (τηρῶν), a view which makes it difficult
account for 'συνήθειαν', a term not naturally used of 'non-observance': (2) it
s a question whether the festival should be preceded by a fast—so Polycarp—
by none—so Anicetus—to which the objection already mentioned equally
lies, though it seems to be supported by the earlier extract from Irenaeus
2 f.): (3) it was a question whether the festival should be kept on the 'fourteenth
' (of the month Nisan)—so Polycarp—or on the Sunday following—so Anicetus
he chief objection to which is the absence of any mention in this extract of the
urteenth day', though we may reasonably infer from Polycrates' letter (§ 4) that
s was Polycarp's practice. On the whole (3) seems the least unsatisfactory, but cf.
a full examination of the problem, Schmidt, C., in *Gespräche Jesu*, Exk. III,
e Passahfeier in der kleinasiatistischen Kirche', in *Texte u. Unters.*, vol. xlii,
577–725, 1919.

affairs. The alarm of Irenaeus, if indeed his letters are right
associated with this affair, seems to be due not so much to his beli
that an act of 'papal aggression' had been committed, as to a fe
lest by precipitate and too rigid discipline over its own members th
Roman church might suppress a part of the apostolic *paradosis*.

In concluding this section it is desirable to pay some attention
the secular background of the events taking place in the life stor
of the Roman see. Hitherto we have made little mention of the co
temporary Roman State or of its system of government. This
largely due to the apparent absence of contact between Church ar
State except in a somewhat incidental fashion during the years alrea
reviewed. The State was certainly aware of the existence of Chri
tianity, as is shown by Pliny's correspondence with the Emper
Trajan,[1] but no occasion had arisen to bring the two into viole
conflict. At least half a century more was to elapse before the late
contradiction between the monotheism of Christianity and tl
official polytheistic theanthropism of the State became impossible
concealment. Henceforth, till the reign of Galerius, the relati
between the two is essentially one of more or less active hostility.

The reign of the Emperor Septimius Severus, whose declinin
melancholy was used by Gibbon to illustrate his dictum that 'tl
possession of a throne could never yet afford a lasting satisfaction
an ambitious mind',[2] has been regarded by secular historians as tl
opening of a new epoch in the annals of the Roman State. There ar
moreover, good reasons for believing that it coincided with the earli
stages of a certain change of ethos within the Roman church, and
is perhaps not without significance that the elevation of a soldier
north-African origin to the principate almost synchronized with t
election of a north-African, Victor I, to the pontificate.[3] Thus in t
last decade of the second century the respective successors
Augustus and St. Peter were alike Latin in culture and African
birth. If the rule of Severus gave impetus to a reaction of the nati
Latin spirit within the western Roman commonwealth against tho
Greek and oriental ideas, which had been so evidently predomina
in the West during the latter half of the second century, the episcopa
of Victor marks unmistakably the beginning of a rapid process
latinization of the western Church, in which hitherto, as the nam

---

[1] *Epp.* 96 and 97.   [2] Ed. cit., vol. i, p. 138 (1929).
[3] *Liber Pontificalis*, ed. Duchesne, L., vol. i, p. 137.

f his predecessors in the episcopal office sufficiently illustrate, ‑reek or at least non-Latin influence had been very considerable.

Victor was almost certainly the first occupant of the Roman see, ho was able to trace the origin of his family from pure Latin stock, nce he was probably a descendant of the legionary-colonists, who, omiciled on the sité of ancient Carthage, had made the *Colonia Julia* centre of Latin thought and culture, more authentically Roman ecause less exposed to the allurements of a decadent Hellenism and ie insidious propaganda of an aggressive Orientalism than the nperial capital itself.

As a promoter of greater cohesion, particularly on the question of turgical observance, but strictly (as we have argued) within the mits of the local Roman church,[1] we have already watched him at ork, and have remarked the stern sanctions with which this clear-ghted provincial, true Latin as he was, inheriting to the full the sciplinary training of his forefathers, attempted to secure a measure local uniformity, even if it meant reversing the tolerant and perhaps esitant policy of his predecessors. We may surmise that he brought ith him to Rome one of the earliest copies of the first Latin version Holy Scripture,[2] and it is scarcely fanciful to conjecture that now r the first time Roman Christians assisted with amazement and erhaps with some feelings of pride at the public celebration in the iom of their forebears of the most solemn mysteries of their ith.[3]

With the pontificate of Victor I the second century comes to an id. We have seen that though Christianity had already reached ome before the actual arrival of SS. Peter and Paul, the tradition hich associates the work and martyrdom of both Apostles, and par-:ularly of St. Peter, with the capital is well-founded. We have aced the development of the Roman episcopate from a primitive age in which it seems to have existed in plurality, to the later one of onepiscopacy. We have considered the significance of the evidence

[1] See above, p. 120 f.
[2] It is possible that previous to Victor's pontificate the only Latin version of ripture current in Rome was the expurgated New Testament produced by arcion. See Harnack, A., in *Texte d. Unters.*, vol. xlv, 1921, pp. 47–54. An early rican version was certainly known to Victor's contemporary Tertullian.
[3] Greek was still in use in the West as a liturgical language in Tertullian's time; e his *De spectaculis*, 25. The persistence of Greek culture in the church of Rome pears to be indicated by the use of Greek characters in the inscriptions on papal nbs so late as the pontificate of Eutychian (†283).

to be found in second-century literature on the question of th
relation of other churches and non-Roman Christians to the Roma
see throughout the period. Briefly summarized, it can be described a
the recognition of that see as in some sense the 'norm' of the whole c
existing Christendom. It may be viewed as a 'primacy of normality
particularly in the sphere of doctrine. Testimony is yet to seek for
Roman self-consciousness of this primacy. It is this evidence whic
the third century begins to supply.

V

Victor's successor, Zephyrinus, may have been unfairly treated b
Hippolytus, yet it is unlikely that he possessed either the initiative o
the inclination to follow in the path already marked out by th
his African predecessor. This was left to the possibly unscrupulous
though certainly successful, Callistus I. Apart from the importanc
of his work as an administrator, the career of this pontifical mounte
bank, even as recounted by his highly unsympathetic biographe
reflects some valuable light on the internal condition of the Roma
church at the beginning of the third century.[1] His story, so full c
undeniably human interest, bears retelling in brief.

Convicted by his master Carpophorus of misappropriation of fund
and by the *praefectus urbi* of disturbing the privileged Jews, Callistu
became the unwilling companion of a group of Christians deporte
some time previously to the Sardinian mines. Here he remained fo
some five years or so until happily rescued under cover of an indul
gence obtained by Marcia, the Christian-minded concubine of th
emperor Commodus. Thus unexpectedly and perhaps undeservingl
awarded not only remission of punishment but freedom from hi
legal owner, the fortunate Callistus presented himself before Victo
who is portrayed as finding himself somewhat embarrassed by thi
surprising turn of events. The election of Zephyrinus,[2] howeve
proved something of a godsend and the miscreant slave, who,
we are to believe Hippolytus, had been fortunate to escape with hi

---

[1] The story is told not without evident relish and probably with some embroide
in Hippolytus, *Elenchos (Philosophumena)*, 9, 12, 1-4. Ed. Wendland, P., *G.C.*
1916, p. 246 ff.

[2] Hippolytus is our sole authority for the character of Zephyrinus, against whor
he prefers charges of venality as well as of incompetence. See *ibid.*, 9, 7, 2 ; 9, 11,
ed. cit., pp. 240, 245.

fe, suddenly appeared in the influential role of archdeacon and
ustodian of 'the cemetery'.[1] Precedent for treating the holder of the
ormer office as preferentially '*papabilis*', already existing in the case
f Eleutherus,[2] and one to be followed with striking frequency down
ne ages of papal history, readily suggested him as the most promising
andidate for the vacancy which presently occurred, and so, in the
cid invective of his opponent, 'he supposed himself to have got
hat he was hunting for'.[3]

It is tempting to pause for a moment to inquire how far Hip-
olytus' character sketch of this remarkable personality is worthy
f credence, especially when we remember that he had every reason
or wishing to give his readers the worst possible impression. Dis-
ppointed and embittered men rarely make good biographers, par-
cularly of their successful rivals, yet even if we make every allowance
or exaggeration and *parti pris*, we must appreciate that it would
ardly have been good policy on the part of the writer to reproduce
othing better than malicious slander. Deliberate misrepresentation
ust have evoked a rejoinder of which some trace, if it had ever
xisted, would surely have been preserved. Can we say none was
ade, because none was possible? Nevertheless, the fact that Hip-
olytus could bring himself to write, as he did, reflects an unfavour-
ble light on the state of his own mind, and contrary to his intention
nly serves to evoke some feeling of sympathy towards the victim of
is unqualified abuse. Perhaps we ought to be ready to allow some
oundness of judgment even in the 'venal' Zephyrinus, who saw in
Callistus a person fit to be entrusted with a position of financial
nd administrative responsibility. Purely selfish avarice is not often
ound in combination with a total disregard for the welfare of
hose concerns in which personal as well as corporate interests are
nvolved.[4]

Before describing the situation prevailing in the Roman church on
ephyrinus' decease, we may notice a few points of historical value
n the Callistus *saga*. In the first place, the small but relatively im-
ortant part played by the lady Marcia not only illustrates a certain
ympathy detectable in high Roman, particularly feminine, society

---

[1] Hippolytus, *Elenchos* (*Philosophumena*), 9, 12, 14. ed. cit., p. 248.

[2] Hegesippus, ap. Eus. *H.E.* 4, 22, 3.

[3] Hippolytus, *ibid.*, 9, 12, 5. It should be noticed that he avoids giving the title
πίσκοπος to Callistus.

[4] For a different view, see Prestige, *Fathers and Heretics*, p. 40 ff.

towards Christianity,[1] such as we have already noticed as existing in
the same circles towards Judaism more than a century earlier,[2] but
is suggestive of the role which before long a 'converted' imperial
court would assume for itself in ecclesiastical affairs, and of the not
altogether healthy influence soon to be felt, particularly among the
clergy, of powerful and richly dowered ladies of fashion.[3] Secondly,
in contrast to the conscientious and stern administration of the Stoic
Emperor Aurelius we may gather that the reign of the athletic
Commodus involved something of a reaction in favour of toleration,
if not indulgence, of Christianity, a policy which it is unlikely that
one so generous and humane as his successor Pertinax did anything
to reverse.[5] If, however, in his later years Septimius Severus in the
supposed interests of social welfare issued an edict prohibiting con-
versions to Judaism and Christianity alike,[6] it is probable that the
effect of its operation scarcely touched the capital itself; in any case
he is said to have shown consideration to Christians among the
official classes.

We may conjecture that it was under cover of a law issued by
Severus confirming the privileges of the *collegia tenuiorum* or funerary
guilds[7] that the possession of property by the church first began to
acquire a semblance of legality, though as Duchesne has pointed out,[8]
the known aversion of the official church for the *collegia* and all their
works[9] makes it highly improbable that any formal step was taken on
the part of the ecclesiastical authorities to obtain recognition of such
a *collegium*,[10] even if it had been possible. In any case, we know that

---

[1] Hippolytus, *Elenchos* (*Philosophumena*), 9, 2, 10. ed. cit., p. 247. 'Μαρκία . .
οὖσα φιλόθεος παλλακὴ Κομόδου'. Hippolytus himself dedicated his 'περὶ ἀναστάσεως'
to the Empress Mamaea. Cf. Hipp. *Op.* ed. cit., vol. i, pp. 251–4.

[2] E.g. Papia Poppoea in the reign of Nero.

[3] Cf. *Coll. Avell.* 1, 9. *C.S.E.L.* vol. xxxv, p. 4; Ammianus Marcellinus, 27,
3, 14.

[4] Eus. *H.E.* 5, 21, 1. ed. cit., 484. The martyrdom of the senator Apollonius in
this reign, related *ibid.*, 2, was no doubt an exception. The fact that it was recorded
is to be attributed to Apollonius' status.

[5] For his character, see Gibbon, *Decline*, ed. Bury, J. B., 1929, p. 108 ff.

[6] Spartianus, *Vita Severi*, in *Scr. Hist. Aug.* ed. Teubner, 1884, vol. i, p. 148.
Cf. Eus. *H.E.* 6, 3, 3, ed. cit., p. 524.

[7] Marcian, *Digest*, 47, 22, 1. See De Rossi, *Roma sott.*, vol. i, pp. 101–8, and
cf. Tertullian, *Apol.* 39.

[8] *Histoire ancienne de l'église*[1], vol. i, p. 384 f.

[9] Cf. the case of Martial, bishop of Merida in Cyprian, *Ep.* 67, 6. ed. Hartel,
G., *C.S.E.L.* vol. iii, p. 740.

[10] The *collegia* seldom exceeded a few dozen in membership, while the church of
Rome at this time may well have numbered close on 30,000 souls.

arly in the third century the church was already in actual possession
f a cemetery,[1] and that under the Emperor Alexander it succeeded
n obtaining an imperial rescript allowing it to retain property (pro-
ably a place of worship) which had been claimed by the guild of
efreshment-room proprietors.[2] That property of this kind was now
wned by the church as a corporate body must be seen as a factor of
onsiderable importance in the life of the Christian community,
ot least because it may well have contributed something to an
ncrease in the Roman bishop's influence and authority. For it is
lain that the fact of having under his care the church's real estate as
ts principal trustee made him increasingly independent of the good
vill of the richer families.[3] Previously it had always been possible for
he legal owners of property to secede to one or other of those
umerous sects, which perhaps to a greater extent in Rome than else-
vhere challenged the claim of the church to be the sole representative
f orthodox Christianity, and by taking their property with them to
eave the church, as yet possessed of nothing which it could call its
wn, in a position of some embarrassment. The fact that it had now
become in some sense a tolerated owner of land, and soon after per-
naps of buildings as well, marks a definite stage in the long process
by which, after attaining State recognition, the Roman see ultimately
icquired the possession of temporal power.

We must now retrace our steps to watch the dramatic turn of
events after the death of Zephyrinus, leading ultimately to a new

[1] The fact that Hippolytus, *ibid.*, 9, 12, 14, says that Zephyrinus 'τοῦτον (sc.
Κάλλιστον) μεταγάγων . . . εἰς τὸ κοιμητήριον κατέστησεν', distinctly suggests that
t was the only cemetery corporately owned by the church at this time. That
here were others in private ownership is shown by the mention of Callistus'
burial, *Liber pont.* ed. Duchesne, L., vol. i, p. 141, as having taken place in the
cemetery of Calepodius on the *Via Aurelia*. The cemetery later known as that of
Callistus came to be regarded as the official burial place, since it was there that all
the bishops of Rome from Antherus (236) to Miltiades (314), with the exceptions of
Marcellinus and Marcellus, were buried, though the graves of Eusebius and Gaius
lay at some distance from the rest. Previous to Zephyrinus, who was buried near the
cemetery of Callistus (cf. de Rossi, J. B., *Roma sott.*, vol. ii, pp. 9-47, and *D.A.C.L.*
vol. ii, col. 1665, n. 1), the earlier bishops had been buried at the Vatican. It has
been suggested that cessation of the practice was due to alterations made in the
neighbourhood of the site. The change may also have been caused by increasing
public hostility to Christianity, and by a desire to avoid any risk of a clash with the
mob such as occurred in connexion with the burial of Callistus.
[2] *Vita Alexandri Severi*, 49. *Hist. Aug.* ed. Teubner, vol. i, p. 290.
[3] The earlier *Coemeterium Domitillae* is an example of a catacomb which, though
used for Christian burial since the end of the first century, had remained in private
ownership.

schism within the Roman church. How this came about may b
briefly explained. In his early days Hippolytus, it seems, had beer
present at the doctrinal lectures which Irenaeus must have giver
during his stay in the capital,[1] and later on had listened with attentior
and sympathy to that great Alexandrine master Origen.[2] As a result
it is not surprising to find him, after his advancement to the pres
byterate,[3] taking a very definite stand in the dogmatic controversie
which distracted the Roman community at the close of the secon
century. Of what nature these controversies were may be appreciatee
when it is remembered that the Church had only recently succeedee
in vindicating the reasonableness of the apostolic tradition as agains
the rationalism of those Hellenistic Orientalists, generally describe
by the term 'Gnostics'. Impelled by a very proper though dangerou
ambition to provide an exposition of the faith 'in terms of moderr
thought', these purveyors of a supposedly true knowledge ($\gamma\nu\hat{\omega}\sigma\iota s$
had devised an essentially dualistic theology and a strangely sub
Christian doctrine of salvation. It was to meet the onslaught of thei
insidious propaganda that writers like Irenaeus had been led to
emphasize, among other points of Christian doctrine, the unity o
God.[4] But in less skilful hands than his such emphasis might easily
distract attention from the Christian limitations of his argument tha
a rational view of the universe demands belief in a single Firs
Principle or *Monarchia*, and by stressing the singularity of God come
to imply that He was also uni-personal.[5] The supreme crux naturally
arose as soon as the question as to the relation of Christ to the God
head had to be answered. It was here that the strict upholders of the
Monarchia, the 'Monarchians' as they were called, found themselves
in a dilemma. It seemed that one had to choose, either to regard
Christ as one who had acquired the status of God, in virtue of the
adoption of the human Jesus by divine election, or else to treat the
being of the Son as no more than a temporary projection of the Godhead, analogous to the self-manifestation of the same Godhead as

[1] Photius, *Bibl.* cod. 121. *M.P.G.* 103, 401 f. who refers to a lost work of Hippolytus, *Syntagma*.

[2] Jerome, *De vir. inl.* 61 in *Texte u. Unters.*, vol. xiv, pt. 1, p. 35 f.

[3] It is not certain whether this took place under Victor or Zephyrinus, though the
former seems more probable.

[4] We are told by Eusebius, *H.E.* 5, 20, 1. ed. Schwartz, E., vol. ii, pt. i, p. 480
that he was the author of a polemical treatise against the Gnostic Florinus entitled
'Περὶ μοναρχίας'.

[5] See Tertullian, *Adv. Praxeam*, 3.

Father and Spirit under other conditions and for other purposes. The three names might thus be regarded as descriptive merely of three successive *modes* of being. Hippolytus sought to evade this dilemma by following the line of thought suggested by the teaching of his master Irenaeus and his contemporary Origen, and interpreted the relation of the Son to the Father in terms of the *Logos* concept, first found among Christian writers in the Fourth Gospel. The chief characteristic of his teaching was that Christ as *Logos* became strictly personal only with a view to creation, but in becoming so assumed the whole character of Godhead. Thus it was only in virtue of the Incarnation that Fatherhood and Sonship could be regarded permanent elements in the unity of God.[1] That such a Christology would not satisfy the demands of Christian consciousness as expressed in the apostolic tradition was evident even to Hippolytus' contemporaries, who, unable to appreciate the more subtle aspects of his theory, roundly accused him of 'ditheism'.

It is possible that Hippolytus was only stating a fact when he alleged that Zephyrinus was 'unfamiliar with the decision of the Church'.[2] Perhaps the Pope found little interest in the interminable wranglings of the Roman *savants* and would have preferred to let well alone, so long as no real danger of schism threatened. But it seemed impossible to avoid making some pronouncement. The 'Adoptionists', following Theodotus the Younger and Artemon on one side, and the 'Modalists,' disciples of Noetus and Sabellius on the other, were equally eager for what they could get of 'official' support. Could Zephyrinus continue to hold aloof? We may perhaps credit the astuteness of Callistus with the discovery of a way out.[3] Let the Pope issue an official statement of doctrine, or make a public profession of faith, which, while embodying the essential elements of apostolic tradition, would satisfy both parties. Zephyrinus complied in the following terms: 'I acknowledge one God Christ Jesus, and beside Him no other as begotten and passible'. He added, perhaps on a different occasion: 'It was not the Father who died but the Son'.[4] Such a statement was undoubtedly meant to preserve the characteristically Roman 'norm' or *via media* in doctrinal controversies. But

---

[1] The sources for Hippolytus' Christology are *Contra Noetum*, 10–15, and *Elenchos*, 10, 33.
[2] *Elenchos*, 9, 11, 1. ed. cit., p. 245.
[3] Id., *ibid.*, 2.
[4] Id., *ibid.*, 3. ed. cit., p. 246.

nothing less than downright approval of their theory could satisfy
Hippolytus and his immediate *entourage*, who from now on adopted
an attitude of uncompromising opposition, not only to the Monarchians, but also to the 'official' party represented by the Pope and his
archdeacon.[1]

At the time of Zephyrinus' death everything pointed to the probability of an open schism. For there was no doubt that Callistus
enjoyed the confidence of the majority including those who saw in
him a skilful diplomatist as well as others who, though probably
indifferent to Christological speculation, recognized a competent
man of business, and thus took proper account of a qualification
which in later times often proved decisive in settling the issue of a
papal election. What is more, some at least of the electors, recalling
the gossip of some ten years or so ago about the escapades of his early
career, may well have thought that it gave some promise of more
lenient treatment in the matter of Christian discipline. Hence the
election of Callistus was almost a foregone conclusion.

How soon Hippolytus decided on definite countermeasures we
have no means of knowing with any certainty, but the fact that the
new Pope made some attempt to conciliate the dissidents by ex-
communicating the Modalist Sabellius[2] suggests that the decision
was not reached till some time after the election had taken place. It
was now Callistus' turn to issue a profession of faith. This he did in
language which, like that of Zephyrinus, dexterously steered a middle
course between strict Monarchianism and the *Logos* Christology of
his intransigent adversary.[3] Yet it is likely that whatever he had said
would have given little satisfaction in that quarter. By some means or
other Hippolytus thereupon procured episcopal consecration,[4] and

---

[1] Hippolytus, *ibid.*   [2] Id., *ibid.*, 9, 12, 15. ed. cit., p. 248.
[3] Id., *ibid.*, 9, 12, 16–19.
[4] This is implied by Hippolytus himself, *ibid.*, *Proem.* 6. ed. cit., p. 3; *ibid.*,
9, 12, 21. ed. cit., p. 249. He is frequently described as a bishop by eastern writers
e.g. by the compiler of the *Canons of Hippolytus* (5th c.) in Riedel, W., *Kirchen-
rechtsquellen des Patriarchats Alexandrien*, 1900, p. 193 ff., and others quoted in
Lightfoot, J., *St. Clement*, vol. ii, pp. 328, 343. The view that he held the see of
Portus, based on the *Chron. Pasch.* (see Lightfoot, *op. cit.*, p. 344), upheld by Otto-
boni in 1771 and once widely accepted, has now been generally abandoned in spite
of Lightfoot's gallant effort, *ibid.*, p. 432 ff., to save it even at the expense of some
concessions. It is equally clear that he denied the title καθολικὴ ἐκκλησία to the
adherents of Callistus, *Elenchos*, 9, 12, 25. ed. cit., p. 250, and insisted on describing
them as a διδασκαλεῖον, *ibid.*, 9, 12, 20 f., 23, 26. ed. cit., p. 249 ff., or even a
Καλλιστίανοι, *ibid.*, 9, 12, 26.

om now on represented himself as the true bishop of Rome and his
ollowers as the true church.[1]

Callistus, however, was not content to restrict his interest to the
eld of dogmatic definition. Various problems of discipline affecting
ae moral conduct of clergy and laity and the relation of Christian
aarriage law to the law of the State insistently demanded attention
nd were solved with marked promptitude. The first of these con-
erned the exercise of the Church's power of absolution. During the
revious century, at Rome and possibly elsewhere, there appears to
ave been a tradition that the Church had power to remit, even if
nly once, the gravest offences.[2] Yet towards the end of that period
wave of rigorism had been steadily spreading, and it now became
ecessary to reassert the Church's competence. This was done by
allistus in the form of a pronouncement that he was prepared after
enance to reconcile to the Church those guilty of grave sexual
ffences.[3] Next there was the question as to the treatment of a bishop

[1] Hippolytus, *ibid.*, 9, 12, 20 f. ed. cit., 2, p. 249.
[2] Such a view must have been held by Pope Hyginus (*c.* 135), who according
o Irenaeus, *Adv. haer.* 3, 4, 3. cit. ap. Eus. *H.E.* 4, 11, 1. ed. Schwartz, E., vol. ii,
t. 1, p. 320, repeatedly absolved Cerdon of the sin of heresy. Tertullian, *De praescr.*
o, 3. ed. Rauschen, G., in *Flor. Patr.* 1906, p. 41, affirms that the same treatment
ras given to Valentinus and Marcion. A similar standpoint, namely that sins
gainst faith or morals may be absolved, was defended by Dionysius of Corinth
orty years later, see Eus. *H.E.* 4, 23, 6. ed. cit., vol. ii, pt. 1, p. 374. No doubt it
aay be thought that Dionysius was exceptionally liberal, though he seems to imply
hat the same sort of generosity was shown to Marcionites at Rome. Further
vidence for the Roman attitude in this matter, at least so far as heresy is concerned,
aay possibly be found in treatment of Montanists apparently recommended to
'ope Eleutherus (178) by Irenaeus, cit. ap. Eus. *H.E.* 5, 3, 4. ed. cit., vol. ii, pt. 1,
. 432, and even if Eusebius is somewhat ambiguous about the precise nature of the
equest addressed to Eleutherus, there is no doubt that the possibility of remission
f the sin of heresy is implied. On the other hand, Tertullian, whom Kirk, K. E.,
'ision of God, 1931, p. 222, takes to be representative of 'the general Catholic
iew on reconciliation in the second century' allows penance but no remission for
aurderers, adulterers, and apostates, and for 'an intermediate class of grave sins
ne reconciliation after penance' (cf. *De poenit.* 7, 9, 12). On the progress of
igorism, see Kirk, *op. cit.*, p. 224 ff. It should be noted, however, that the problem
f reconciliation after apostasy did not become acute until after the persecution of
Decius. Tertullian, however, seems to imply, *De pudic.* 5, that apostasy and murder
vere still regarded as irremissible at Rome in his time. Cf. Origen, *De orat.* 28, 8.
J.C.S. vol. ii, p. 380.
[3] Hippolytus, *op. cit.*, 9, 12, 20. ed. cit., p. 249. The sin of heresy is particularly
nentioned. Galtier, P., *L'Église et la rémission des péchés*, 1932, p. 168 f., argues on
he basis of Hippolytus, *ibid.*, that the real 'edict of Callistus' was concerned only
vith the admission of schismatics and heretics, and that, in so far as it mentioned
he possibility of absolution, it was not concerned with the cases of criminous bishops
nd of clergy who married after ordination, nor with the legalisation of concubina

convicted of a capital sin. Callistus ruled that such a bishop was n‹
to be degraded.[1] In addition he showed himself prepared to treat wi›
tolerance clergy who married twice or even three times, and al‹
those who had contracted such a relationship after ordination›
Besides these problems, some answer had to be given to the questi‹
arising from the refusal of Roman civil law to recognize the uni‹
of a free woman and a slave or freedman as legal marriage. Callist›
decided to accord to these unions ecclesiastical recognition, there›
insisting upon the slave's right to enjoy the common privileges of
Christian.[3]

Each one of the Pope's decisions was used by Hippolytus as t›
ground for a charge of laxity, lack of scruple or worse.[4] Yet there

unions, since in none of these was any question of absolution at stake. But it
difficult, in the face of §§ 20, 24, to deny that Hippolytus seems to have seen
Callistus' ὅρος a licence to sexual indulgence, and that quite apart (καὶ γὰρ κ‹
from his attitude towards 'concubinage'. Nor can we be certain that Tertullia›
De pudic. 1, 6, represents with any degree of fairness what Callistus actually sai›
It has to be remembered that our sole evidence regarding his action comes fro›
embittered opponents, never a reliable source for the conduct of an adversar›
Galtier, op. cit., p. 182, points out that while Tertullian refrains from charging h›
opponent with innovation, Hippolytus does not hesitate to do so, and regards th›
as a proof that they are not referring to the same topic. Yet the possibility remai›
that both were correct. The real enemy was rigorism, and it appears to have be‹
met by safeguarding what was traditional and by solving new problems in a spir›
at once evangelical and just. If applied tradition is innovation, innovation it mu›
have been, but not otherwise.

[1] This question had perhaps not previously arisen. Probably Callistus on›
allowed such treatment to those guilty of heresy or sexual sin. But Callistu›
attitude involved the recognition of an important principle, on which Stephen
acted at a later date (see below p. 172), namely that the effect of ordination ›
imparting 'character' is indelible.

[2] It was generally held that 1 Tim. III, 2, cf. Lev. XXI, 13 f., Ezek. XLIV, 2›
excluded 'digamous' marriages in the case of bishops. Cf. the present writer
Life and Times of Leo the Great, 1941, p. 108, et al.

[3] Callistus' decision merely accorded the same recognition as had already be‹
given, in spite of State law to the contrary, to marriages between freedmen an›
bondwomen. See Hippolytus, Apostolic Tradition, ed. Dix, G., 1937, p. 27 f. For
later Roman view of these marriages, see the present writer's op. cit., p. 146 f. an›
n. 126.

[4] Hippolytus, op. cit., 9, 12, 15, 25. ed. cit., pp. 248, 250, where he calls his riv›
a 'cheat' (γόης), a 'blackguard' (πανοῦργος) and a 'lawbreaker' (ἄνομος). H›
evidently wished to represent that the effect of Callistus' measures was simply ›
licence the three capital sins of murder (§ 25) by condoning the procuring ‹
abortion, adultery (§§ 20, 24, 25) and heresy (§§ 20, 21), and went so far as to hi›
that the practice of allowing a second baptism had been introduced (§ 26) by th‹
Elchasaïtes with Callistus' connivance, ibid., 9, 13, 1, 4 ff. Finally, he charges h›
opponent with simony, Com. in Ruth. ed. cit., p. 120, l. 12, probably the earlie›
example of such a charge against the Papacy.

ood reason to believe that Callistus did no more than reaffirm
aditional Roman practice, and that if there was innovation it was
ither on the side of his opponent.[1] In any case, the latter can scarcely
e acquitted of a very unattractive form of self-righteousness and
iight even be charged with a certain lack of sincerity.

Whether or not the *Elenchos* (or *Philosophumena* as this work of
Iippolytus was till recently more usually known) was published
uring the lifetime of Callistus, it is probable that his inveterate rival
ersisted till the day of the Pope's death in unrelenting opposition.
eader of a group, which even at the first cannot have been very
umerous, and which probably tended to dwindle as the weary
chism dragged on, the anti-pope upheld with undaunted courage and
:nacity the cause of which he believed himself to be the divinely
iosen protector, the purity of the faith and discipline of the Roman
iurch. Nothing more is known of the pontificate of Callistus. Yet
iart from the great cemetery which still bears his name, his memory
 perpetuated in more than one Roman locality, even if allowance
iust be made for the influence on topography of late and untrust-
orthy legends.[2] It is equally significant of the sparseness of our
aterial for the early history of the Roman church that of the thirteen
ears covered by the pontificates of his two successors, Urban I and
ontian, only one certain fact has been recorded, namely the approval
:corded by the Roman synod of the sentence against Origen com-
unicated by Demetrius of Alexandria.[3] There is, however, good
ason to believe that during this period amicable relations existed
etween the church and the Roman government, as represented by
ie religious connoisseur Alexander Severus, and that the measure of
leration which it had enjoyed at the hands of his predecessors was
:rceptibly enlarged.[4] That the influence of Hippolytus at this time
id not sensibly diminished may be judged from the fact that he felt

[1] See above, p. 131, n. 2.
[2] We learn from the *Passio Callisti* that he was a victim of Alexander Severus'
:cret police, which in view of the known tolerance of that Emperor's policy seems
ghly improbable, though it is possible in view of his burial having taken place,
t in the episcopal vault near Zephyrinus but in the cemetery of Calepodius,
at he died in some sort of public disturbance. It has also been suggested that
e ancient place-name *iuxta Callistum* is to be explained by the existence in that
:ality (associated with sailors with whom *Liber pont.* ed. cit., vol. i, p. 141,
mnects Callistus' origin) of the earliest 'titular' church founded under his
spices.
[3] Jerome, *Ep.* 33, 5. *C.S.E.L.*, vol. liv., p. 259.
[4] Eus. *H.E.* 6, 21, 3, 4. ed. cit., p. 568; 6, 28.

himself competent to address to the Empress-mother a treatise on th
Resurrection,[1] though with what result is not known.

A successful conspiracy led by the Thracian peasant-gener
Maximin not only extinguished the reigning dynasty but led to
reconciliation between the opposing parties in the Roman churc
More from political than religious motives the barbarian tyra
directed a vigorous though short-lived attack on its leaders,[2] who m
have been among the more prominent supporters of the previo
regime. Of this attack the reigning Pope Pontian and the anti-po
Hippolytus were the principal victims.[3] Condemned alike to a linge
ing death of hard labour in the Sardinian mines, it is probable th
the two rivals became reconciled, and that the fruits of this reco
ciliation were to be seen in Pontian's voluntary resignation of h
office,[4] in which he was followed by his rival, who is said to ha
urged his adherents to be reconciled with the bishop elected to f
the vacant see.[5] Since scarcely any trace is to be found of his schis
in the years after his death, it is highly probable that some such appe
was actually made, and that it was not unheeded. It must therefore l
reckoned to his credit that his resistance to the 'official' church, u
like that of both earlier and later schismatics,[6] at least caused
permanent cleavage in the Roman community.[7] Further proof of h
final reconciliation with his opponents might be derived from
entry appearing in the *Feriale ecclesiae romanae*,[8] a primitive Rom
liturgical kalendar recording the dates and places of burial

[1] See above, p. 126, n. 1.

[2] Eus. *H.E.* 6, 28. ed. cit., p. 582. It is unlikely that any general edict w
published. So far as we know only Rome and the province of Syria, the la
Emperor's country of origin, were affected. Probably less prominent Christia
were left undisturbed.

[3] *Cat. Lib.* Vita Pontiani: 'Eo tempore, Pontianus episcopus et Yppolitus pre
byter exoles sunt deportati in Sardinia in insula nociva (?) Severo et Quintiano co
[235]'.

[4] *Ibid.*, 'in eadem insula discinctus est IIII Kal. Octobr'. This date is remarkal
as being the earliest in the history of the Roman church, September 28, 235, whi
can be regarded as chronologically dependable. See Caspar, *op. cit.*, vol. i, p. 44.

[5] We owe this sidelight on Hippolytus' character to an inscription set up
Damasus I. *Damasi Epigrammata*, 37. ed. Ihm., p. 42.

[6] E.g. Novatian, on whom see below, pp. 160, 168 ff.

[7] Unless perhaps we can find a hint of the schism's persistence in Eus. *H.*
6, 46, 5. ed. cit., vol. ii, pt. 2, p. 628, where reference is made to the letter address
to the Roman church by Dionysius of Alexandria, which the historian ca
'διακονικὴ διὰ Ἱππολύτου', on which see Dix, G., *op. cit.*, p. xxxiv and note †.

[8] Included in the chronographic compilation of Filocalus, ed. Mommsen, ʾ
M.G.H. Auct. antiqu. vol. ix, *Chron. min.* vol. i, p. 71 f., 1892.

umerous local martyrs covering the whole of the third century,
vhere it is stated that, while the remains of Pontian were buried in
he papal crypt at the cemetery of Callistus, those of Hippolytus were
•laced in the catacomb bearing his name on the *Via Tiburtina*, thus
howing that they had been brought back from his place of exile with
he official approval of the church.

Yet it must always remain one of the strangest paradoxes of history
hat within a hundred years of his death the memory of Hippolytus'
eal place in the life of the Roman church had been almost com-
letely obliterated. Even Eusebius, who quoted from his works with
vident approval and appreciation, and was aware of the fact of his
piscopate, was evidently ignorant of the location of his see.[1] The
radition that in some way he had been connected with a schismatic
1ovement holding rigorist views on discipline was plainly known
orty years later to Pope Damasus I, who was responsible for an
1scription placed to his memory in the Hippolytean cemetery.[2]
3ut by describing him as an adherent of 'Novatus' (*sic*), even the papal
rchaeologist reveals some measure of ignorance about his actual
istory. Similarly Jerome, who like his master Eusebius, supplies
s with the titles of many of Hippolytus' works, some of which he
•robably cites without acknowledging his indebtedness, shows that
1e knew him to be a bishop while confessedly remaining ignorant
f the see in which he presided.[3] The same is generally true of the
nnumerable eastern writers who from the fourth to the fourteenth
entury not only were aware of his existence, but frequently quoted
rom his writings.[4]

All the same the admiration and respect felt for him by at least
hose of his contemporaries who shared his opinions was shown by
he erection to his memory, possibly within his lifetime, of a statue
epresenting him as a Christian bishop teaching from his *cathedra*.
This memorial, which by a happy accident was rediscovered in 1551
•n the *Ager Veranus* near the site of his chief sanctuary, has come
lown to us in a sadly mutilated condition, yet sufficiently well pre-
erved for it to be possible to read the inscriptions on its base, which
et forth a list of some seventeen of his works and, in addition, a

[1] *H.E.* 6, 20, 2. ed. cit., vol. ii, pt. 2, p. 566.
[2] *Damasi Epigrammata*, 37. ed. Ihm, p. 42.
[3] *De vir. inl.* 61, in *Texte u. Unters.*, vol. xiv, pt. 1, p. 35.
'Citations from these authors are conveniently collected in Lightfoot, *op. cit.*,
p. 326–350.

description with a table of dates for the years 222–333 of his well
known Paschal cycle.[1] Yet even so the list is not exhaustive, for
besides those enumerated at least eighteen other writings are known
to have existed, including some which have come down to us in a
more or less perfect state, others of which only later versions have
survived, and yet others of which only the titles are known.[2]

These works by their comprehensive range and diversity of
subject-matter reveal their author at once as the father of methodical
exegesis of Holy Scripture in the West, a pioneer in the intricate
labyrinth of sacred and profane history, a formidable controversialist,
a sober apologist, acquainted with the elusive science of chronometry
and skilled in liturgiology, homiletics, perhaps even the delicate art of
poetry. With such a record before us how can we explain the strangely
unappreciative treatment accorded by the Roman church to one of
her most distinguished sons?

No doubt the fact of his schism and of his bearing towards the
'official' church will account for much. Yet this alone is insufficient
in view of the probability of his rehabilitation at any rate shortly
after his death.[3] It cannot be doubted that the real explanation lies
partly in the traditional indifference of the Roman mind toward
those things which lay outside the immediate realm of the practical
and the concrete, but chiefly in his use of Greek as a medium of
self-expression at the very time when, as we have seen, the Roman
church was becoming conscious of itself as a western, non-Hellenic
institution, and when Latin was becoming its official literary and
liturgical idiom.[4] Possibly, if he had been fortunate like Clement and
Irenaeus in finding convenient though not always lucid interpreters,
it might not have been left to the East to preserve most of his writings
and to modern scholarship to appreciate them afresh at something
like their true value. It is a strange irony that the ignorance and
superstition of later centuries experienced some hesitation between
a legend which depicted his martyrdom in somewhat sadistic language

---

[1] The probability that the statue was erected during Hippolytus' lifetime
at the latest shortly after his death becomes all the stronger if it is remembered that
his Paschal cycle had already been discovered to be unworkable within eight
years of that event and replaced by another.

[2] A detailed description of them will be found in Lightfoot, *op. cit.*, vol. i
pp. 388–403; cf. also *D.T.C.* vol. vi, col. 2493–2505.

[3] Included in the chronographic compilation of Filocalus, ed. Mommsen, in
M.G.H. Auct. antiqu. vol. ix, *Chron. min.* vol. i, p. 71 f., 1892.

[4] The next anti-pope, as we shall see, wrote in Latin.

the images of which had been borrowed from his namesake in classical mythology,[1] and one which made of him a pagan gaoler to St. Lawrence, appropriately converted by the archdeacon's edifying behaviour.[2]

Of his surviving works three alone are perhaps sufficient to illustrate at once his diverse genius and inexhaustible industry. We have already become acquainted with his *Elenchos*,[3] through the use which we have made of the abundant material contained there for a reconstruction of the inner history of the Roman church in the first quarter of the third century. In actual fact, however, this material is of the nature of a lengthy parenthesis within an elaborate and methodical defence of the truth as embodied in the authentic tradition of the Church, following the now familiar model of the author's master, Irenaeus. In this treatise, of which perhaps the most valuable part to the student of dogma is the concluding chapter, Hippolytus surveys the whole field of religious and philosophic speculation, his purpose being to demonstrate that while every heresy has its roots in either pagan philosophy, sensual mysteries, or pseudonymous astrology, none but the teaching of the true Church is identical with the *paradosis* of the Apostles, of which the canonical New Testament is regarded as a satisfactory presentation.

Equally typical of the wide scope of his learning, this time in the sphere of chronography, is his *Chronicon*.[4] Though perhaps somewhat indebted to other works like those of Julius Africanus and Clement of Alexandria, who enjoy the credit of being the first to present

---

[1] Prudentius, *Peristephanon, De Passione S. Hippolyti* (c. 401), quoted by Lightfoot, *op. cit.*, p. 332 ff.

[2] Ado of Vienne (†874), *Martyrologium*, sub. IV. Id. Aug.   *M.P.L.* 123, 322 f.

[3] Until 1842, when a considerable part of this work (possibly the whole of the remainder) was recovered in a fourteenth century MS., only the first book was known to be in existence. At the time of the publication of the additional matter in 1851 it was at first attributed to Origen. Two years later Döllinger contended that Hippolytus was its real author, and this is now generally acknowledged. Cf. Duchesne, *Histoire*[6], vol. i, p. 313.

[4] Its existence was known from the list of Hippolytus' works inscribed on the base of his statue (see above), and was confirmed by an allusion to it in *Elench.* 10, 1. d. cit., p. 265. Until the recovery of a portion of the Greek original in a Spanish MS. (*Codex Matritensis saec. x*) in 1905 nothing was known of the text except through three Latin versions: The *Liber generationis I* and *II*, the latter forming part of the compilation of Filocalus (354), and in the so-called *Chronicon Alexandrium* (Barbarus Scaligeri). For these texts, see *Hippolytus Werke*, *G.C.S.* vol. iv. 1. Bauer, 1929, and *M.G.H. Auct. antiqu.* vol. ix, *Chron. min.*, vol. i, pp. 78 ff. ed. Mommsen, Th., 1892.

Christianity as an essentially historical religion, it is the earliest systematic essay on the part of a western writer, the purpose of which is to harmonize the biblical data with the generally accepted evidence handed down by secular historians. By this means the Incarnation of the Word is shown to be the focal point of all human events, whether sacred or profane.

Finally we must notice his *Apostolic Tradition*,[1] once known to scholarship as the 'Egyptian Church Order', so-called from the fact that until 1900 its contents were known only in Coptic, Arabic, and Ethiopic versions. This work is particularly valuable for the light which it throws on the liturgical and disciplinary practice of the Roman church in the second and third centuries. In addition, the book affords an intimate view of the inner life and devotional habits of the Roman community at this period of an altogether unique character, since we possess nothing resembling it in regard to any other church. Through it we learn how bishops were consecrated and presbyters ordained, what was the Roman church's attitude towards confessors, how baptism was given, and above all how Christians worshipped. The heritage of Christendom has been enriched by such a legacy.

The tale of the gradual recovery of these three works and of their eventual restoration to their true literary parent may be regarded as somewhat symbolical of the return of their author, already noticed, to the stage of sober history. Nor can any serious doubt remain as to the rightfulness of their attribution. The same, however, cannot be said as to the view which ascribes to Hippolytus the so-called *Muratorian fragment*,[2] in regard to which present-day scholarship is by no means as yet unanimous. This document, containing the earliest known catalogue of Christian writings described by its author as 'received in the Catholic Church', is probably a later Latin version

[1] The *Apostolic Tradition* has come down to us 'in a more deplorably battered condition than that of any other important early Christian document' (ed. Dix, G 1937, p. ix).

[2] First published in 1740 from an eighth-cent. MS. by Muratori. As early as 1890 it was pointed out by Lightfoot, *St. Clement*, vol. ii, p. 408, that it was impossible 'to explain the phenomena of this document, if it is preserved to us in its original language. The whole cast and connexion of the sentences are Greek'. Even if the paronomasia (l. 67) 'fel enim cum melle misceri non congruit', is not itself a sufficient proof of originality, seeing that a parallel phrase from the Greek of Irenaeus, *Adv. haer.* 3, 17, 4, was probably familiar to the author, its ascription to Hippolytus has recently been upheld by Bonwetsch in *Nachr. d. Gött. Ges. Wiss.*, 1923, p. 27 ff.

of a lost Greek original. Whether it represents a formal decision upon the limits of the New Testament issued for the specific purpose of excluding heretical writings, or merely a description of the standpoint of the Catholic Church, which at the time of its publication had already become traditional, is still an open question. The fact, however, that it appears to have exercised but little influence on the subsequent attitude of the Roman hierarchy towards this question, as well as the presence of a number of parallels with his acknowledged writings, suggest strongly that we have here yet another work of forgotten Hippolytean authorship, rather than an official document.

Mention of this enigmatic fragment, the date of which undoubtedly falls within the period of Hippolytus' lifetime, makes it necessary to call attention to some developments observable during this period in the life of the Roman church, which as often in the course of history provided precedents for similar developments elsewhere. Out of the struggle with oriental Hellenism it emerged that appeal to an oral *paradosis*, the authenticity of which, as we have seen, was believed to be guaranteed by an uninterrupted succession of authorized teachers leading back to the time of the Apostles, was insufficient in itself as a proof of authenticity. Parallel with the struggle between rival oral *paradoses* there was developing a contest between rival documentary traditions, the issue of which could only be determined by some decision as to which documents were in fact in accord with the authentic *paradosis*.[1] It is probable, however, that the views expressed by the author of the *Muratorianum*, like the description of Church Order given by the *Apostolic Tradition*, represent a standpoint which was already obsolescent at the time of its composition.[2] Nevertheless it has preserved evidence of an important and undoubtedly primitive phase in the evolution of a Christian Canon of Scripture.

The need for fuller documentary statements of tradition to serve as a basis for catechetical instruction must have been apparent at an early stage in the Church's career, but it is important to observe that the earliest sign of its fulfilment is to be found in the records of the

---

[1] It should be appreciated that the admission of any book to a place within the Canon of a local church depended chiefly on its conformity with the local *paradosis*. Not even real or supposed apostolic authorship sufficed as a criterion for this purpose. The point is important to bear in mind in any discussion of the mutual relations of 'Scripture' and 'tradition'. In the fourth century 'Scripture' became paramount as the only authoritative *paradosis* possessing universal validity. In the third century the local *paradosis* still remained primary.

[2] Dix, G., *op. cit.*, p. xi.

church of Rome. Discussion of the origin and development of the creeds can find no place here. It must suffice to say that in view of the evidence of the *Apostolic Tradition*, the origin of the old Roman creed, from which our present Apostles' Creed is directly descended, is to be set back at least as far as the middle of the second century and may well be considerably earlier.[1]

Not less important, however, were the changes taking place in regard to the accepted view of the ministry.[2] Hitherto, after the emergence of monepiscopacy, the early conception of the nature of succession ($\delta\iota\alpha\delta\sigma\chi\dot{\eta}$) had remained substantially unaffected; all that happened was that it became generally acknowledged, as the testimony of Irenaeus sufficiently indicates, that the bishop for the time being of the local church was the embodiment of its unbroken tradition, while it was tacitly assumed, again by Irenaeus, that the links in the 'successions-series' which antedated this monepiscopal development were themselves the names of successive bishops. Here too the need for documentary evidence came to be appreciated, and thus there were drawn up those episcopal catalogues of which once more the Roman lists provide certainly the best and most ancient surviving examples. The purpose of these episcopal lists as distinct from the earlier successions-series was to vindicate, particularly in event of a disputed claim, as for example between Hippolytus and Callistus, the title as a successor of the Apostles possessed by any given claimant.[3] It is, however, in Hippolytus that we seem to see the earliest clear traces of the process by which St. Peter came to be accounted the first bishop of Rome. That he was so reckoned by Irenaeus seems highly improbable.[4] Yet the description of Victor by Hippolytus as 'the thirteenth bishop in Rome from Peter' renders it almost certain that this author treated the Apostle as a bishop,[5] and

[1] For recent discussions of the origin and development of creeds, see Lietzmann, H., 'Die Anfänge des Glaubenbekentnisses' in *Festgabe f. v. Harnack*, 1921; id. 'Symbolstudien', in *Zeitschr. f. N.T. Wiss.* vol. xxi–xxii, 1922–3; Badcock, F. J., *History of Creeds*[2], 1938.

[2] For a brief account of the origins of the Christian ministry, see above, Lecture II.

[3] This consideration suggests the *a priori* probability that Hippolytus' *Chronicon* included a papal list. Yet, as we have seen above, p. 90, the existence of such a list must remain at least doubtful.

[4] See *Adv. haer.* 3, 3, 2 f.

[5] Ap. Eus. *H.E.* 5, 28, 3.

It is well known that there is some uncertainty about the number assigned by Irenaeus to Pope Hyginus in the series. In *Adv. haer.* 3, 3, 3, cit. ap. Eus. *H.E.* 5, 6, 1. ed. Schwartz, E., *G.C.S.* vol. ii, pt. 1, p. 438, it may be inferred that he is

this way a highly pregnant contribution to the past history of the
Roman see and to its future development in relation to the rest of the
Church was made. Yet it was not his own church alone which was to
feel the influence of this remoulding of the 'succession' concept.
We find in the preface to his masterpiece the *Elenchos* a terse and
highly significant description of the office of a bishop. Here, after
speaking of the importance of his work as a means of laying bare the
errors of pagan culture, he proceeds:

'These, however, will be refuted by none other than the Holy
Ghost conveyed in the Church, Which the Apostles were the first to
receive, after which they imparted It to those who had accepted the
faith aright; of these men we are in fact the successors, sharing the
same spiritual endowment ($\chi \acute{\alpha} \rho \iota s$), the same high priesthood, and
the same *magisterium*, being in fact accounted as guardians of the
Church'.[1]

eighth' (no number is given in his case, but Xystus I, his predecessor but one, is
described as ἕκτος ἀπὸ τῶν ἀποστόλων and here the Latin version is in agreement).
On the other hand, *ibid.*, 3, 4, 3, ap. Eus. *H.E.* 4, 11, 1. ed. cit., vol. ii, pt. 1, p. 320,
we read 'ἐπὶ ῾Υγίνου ὃς ἦν ἔνατος ἐπίσκοπος', and again in *ibid.*, 1, 27, 1, ap.
Eus. *H.E. ibid.*, 2, ed. cit. p. 322, 'ἐπὶ ῾Υγίνου ἔνατον κλῆρον τῆς ἐπισκοπικῆς
διαδοχῆς ἀπὸ τῶν ἀποστόλων ἔχοντος'. Yet in each of these passages the Latin
version reads '*octavum*'. Cyprian, *Ep.* 74, 2. ed. Hartel, p. 801, probably following
Irenaeus, *ibid.*, 3, 4, 3, writes 'sub Hygino episcopo qui in urbe nonus fuit,' and
Epiphanius, who appears equally to be following Irenaeus, *Panar.* 41, 1. ed. Holl,
I., *G.C.S.* vol. ii, p. 91 ; *ibid.*, 42, 1, ed. cit., p. 95, writes ἔνατος in both passages.
It is certain that Epiphanius definitely regarded St. Peter, with or without St. Paul,
as a bishop, and it is likely, in view of the statement made by Hippolytus mentioned
below, that this view was accepted by Cyprian, though we cannot altogether exclude
the possibility that his figure arose from the duplication of Anencletus with Cletus
(see above). As to the statements of Irenaeus, it should be remembered that the
Greek text of *Adv. haer.* 1, 27, 1 ; 3, 4, 3, has only come down to us through
Eusebius, and it is noteworthy that Eusebius himself reckons Hyginus as 'eighth'
by implication, for in *H.E.* 4, 5, 5, ed. cit., p. 306, he describes Telesphorus,
Hyginus' immediate predecessor, as 'ἕβδομος', and in *H.E.* 5, *praef.* 1. ed. cit., p. 400,
Eleutherus, his fourth successor as 'δωδέκατος'.
It has been argued from this discrepancy that even in Irenaeus' time the precise
order of the names was still uncertain. So Schwartz, E., *Eusebius Werke*, vol. ii,
pt. 3 (vii), p. ccxxv. Caspar, E., however, *Dic ält. röm. Bischofsliste*, p. 243, holds
that it is probable that Cyprian is responsible for the confusion, since by the middle
of the third century the theory that St. Peter was the first bishop of Rome had
become firmly established. It should be noticed that in his Latin version of Eusebius,
H.E. 4, 11, 1. ed. cit., p. 321, Rufinus writes: 'sub Hygino, qui erat in urbe Roma ab
apostolo nonus episcopus', perhaps reproducing Cyprian, while dotting his 'i's'
and crossing his 't's'. It is therefore not impossible that by this means the Latin
version exercised a reflex influence on the text of Eusebius citing the original Greek
of Irenaeus. Yet in his version of *H.E.* 4, 5, 5, Rufinus writes 'Telesphorus septimus', and of *H.E.* 5, *praef.*, 1. 'duodecimus . . . Eleutherus', ed. cit., pp. 307, 401.

[1] Hippolytus, *Elenchos*, 1. *praef.* 6. ed. cit., p. 6.

The fact that Hippolytus uses the ambiguous term χάρις (he
rendered 'spiritual endowment') makes it difficult for us to be prec
about his meaning. Yet it is not hard to see here an early source of th
later view of episcopacy, in which the emphasis lay on the va
communication and reception of sacramental grace rather than
the sure transmission of an immutable *paradosis*.

Yet so far as the mutual relations and respective spheres
authority of the episcopate, presbyterate and diaconate are co
cerned, Hippolytus, as illustrated by the ordination rites incorporat
in his *Apostolic Tradition*,[1] is strictly traditional. We should noti
carefully how these rites differentiate the functions of the three orde
In the case of the episcopate, spoken of as receiving the 'origir
spirit' which was bestowed on the Apostles, they include 'feeding t
flock', 'serving as high priest', 'ministering' (λειτουργοῦντα
'propitiation' (ἐξιλάσκεσθαι), and 'offering the gifts' (προσφέρειν
δῶρα), to which are added 'authority to forgive sins', 'to assign lo
(διδόναι κλήρους), and 'to loose every bond'.[3] On the other han
while the prayer for the ordination of a presbyter is composed par
of the same formula as that to be used for a bishop, yet at the preci
juncture where episcopal functions begin to be enumerated,
diverges with a petition specifying 'the spirit of grace and couns
that he may share in the presbyterate and govern', and compares
office to that of the Mosaic elders.[4] As to the diaconate, the writ
insists that the deacon 'is not ordained for the priesthood, but f
the service of the bishop', not to be 'the fellow-counsellor of t
clergy but to take charge of property and to report to the bishop
and goes on to insist that he is not appointed to share the 'Spirit
the presbyterate'. Similarly the ordination prayer is content
specify as his functions 'bringing up' (sc. the gifts already mentione
and 'ministering'.[6]

For the moment we must be content to notice two salient points
the evidence of Hippolytus. First the episcopal office, as here describe
is still primarily and essentially liturgical. The same is equally tr
of the diaconate, except that mention of the duty of taking care
the Church's material resources is included. On the other hand, t
presbyterate is shown to be only indirectly concerned with liturg

---

[1] Ed. Dix, G., *op. cit.*, iii, p. 4 f.
[2] Id., *op. cit.*, p. 5.
[3] Id., *op. cit.*, *ibid.*

[4] Id., *op. cit.*, viii, p. 13 f.
[5] Id., *op. cit.*, ix, p. 15 f.
[6] Id., *op. cit.*, p. 17 f.

a presbyter participates in the ordination of a fellow-presbyter, it explicitly specified that he does not ordain but only 'seals', by which the author appears to mean that he expresses outwardly his approval of the admission of a new member to the *presbyterium*, the function of which is evidently judicial. Clearly evidence of this kind as to the differentiation of ministerial functions during the pre-Nicene period is of the utmost importance. Let us see to what extent there exists confirmatory testimony. First during the period before Hippolytus, it is clear that in Ignatius sole authority in liturgical matters is reserved to the bishop,[1] while, if we may trust Epiphanius, the heretic Marcion appealed for the judgment of his case, not to the bishop but to the *presbyterium*;[2] this clearly accords with the view expressed by Hippolytus, that if the bishop enjoys the exclusive privilege of the *sacerdotium*, he does so as a lineal successor, through the Apostles, of Aaron 'the liturgical priest', while judicial functions belong exclusively to the *presbyterium* as the heir of the prerogatives of Moses 'the consecrated judge'.[3] Again, in the third century even so strong an episcopalian as Cyprian believed that the consent of the *presbyterium* was necessary before giving absolution,[4] and felt constrained to apologize for ordaining without their approval,[5] and that in spite of the fact that he can say elsewhere that every function of the Church is to be controlled by the bishops.[6] Similarly not even a former bishop of Rome, according to Pope Cornelius,[7] felt qualified to give the presbyterate to one who had received only clinical baptism without previously obtaining the sanction of the Roman *presbyterium*. Thus paradoxically the presbyter of the second and third centuries was far more a Christian 'magistrate' than a 'priest'. If Cyprian recognizes (and he is not only the first explicitly to do so, but in the third century seemingly unique) that under conditions of persecution a single presbyter, accompanied by a single deacon, may 'offer' in the

---

[1] *Smyrn.* 8, 1. It should be noticed, however, that the phrase used by Ignatius ἂν αὐτὸς ἐπιτρέψῃ', does not *of itself* exclude a layman, still less a deacon, though it is improbable in view of the importance attached by this author to the ministry, that the former is intended. Nevertheless the passage provides no secure basis for the assignment of liturgical functions to members of the *presbyterium* at the beginning of the second century.

[2] *Panar.* 42, 1, 7. ed. cit., p. 95. Cf. Hippolytus, *C. Noetum*, 1, where he mentions the excommunication of Noetus by the *presbyterium* of Smyrna.

[3] Dix, *op. cit.*, p. 4 f., 13 f.   [5] *Ep.* 29. ed. cit., p. 547 f.

[4] *Ep.* 20, 3. ed. Hartel, G., p. 528.   [6] *Ep.* 33, 1. ed. cit., p. 566.

[7] Cit. ap. Eus. *H E.* 6, 43, 17. ed. Schwartz, E., *G.C.S.* vol. ii, pt. 2, pp. 620, 22.

presence of confessors in prison,[1] we are in no way compelled
draw the usual conclusion that the *presbyterium* under perfectly no
mal conditions had already begun to assume the exercise of liturgic
functions. At this time the only proper priest was the bishop, and
far from the presbyter being regarded inevitably as his liturgic
deputy, there is evidence that, for a time at least, in many places
absence of the bishop his liturgical function was supplied not by
presbyter but by a deacon.[2]

The significance of these developments will be discussed mo
fully in the following lecture. It must suffice for the moment to sta
that it helps to explain the absence of evidence for the exercise
jurisdiction by the bishop of Rome up to the period of Constantine

VI

We may now turn to inquire what evidence there is as to ho
other churches regarded the Roman see during this period. Our fir
important witness must be the north-African Tertullian.

As soon as the news of Callistus' 'reforms' spread to North Afric
the dour old presbyter, blazing with the fire of Montanist enthusias
and indignation, sat down to indite in his *De Pudicitia*[3] a scorchin
rejoinder. Serious attempts have recently been made to show th
the bishop here censured by this author is his own ecclesiastic
superior, and not Callistus at all.[4] Yet if this be so, it is difficult to se
why he should have refrained from mentioning the object of h
reproof by name, while, if it was the bishop of Rome whom he ha
in mind, in view of the outbreak of the Hippolytean schism, uncer

---

[1] *Ep.* 5, 2. ed. cit., p. 479: 'presbyteri quoque qui illic apud confessores offerun
singuli cum singulis diaconis per vices alternent'. Cyprian's argument in the co
text is that if several presbyters make a practice of visiting the confessors togethe
the prison authorities may forbid such visits altogether. Yet it is scarcely possib
to believe that he has in mind anything more than a temporary expedient.

[2] That at the beginning of the fourth century deacons were already in the hab
of celebrating the Eucharist in certain local churches seems to be a natural inferen
from the prohibition of the practice issued by the council of Arles (314), canon 1
'de diaconibus quos cognovimus multis locis offerre, placuit minime fieri debere
See Kirch, C., *Enchiridion Fontium*[4], No. 373.

[3] Esp. c. 1, 9–10. He describes Callistus' measures as 'edictum . . . peremp
torium', and assigning to him the title 'Pontifex maximus, quod est episcopu
episcoporum' professes to quote as the Pope's own words, 'Ego et moechiae
fornicationis delicta paenitentia functis dimitto'.

[4] It is difficult to believe that he could have assigned a title so peculiarly Roma
as 'Pontifex maximus' to the bishop of Carthage even in irony. Lawyers are usuall
careful to get their local colour correct.

inty as to the rightful occupant of the Roman see might sufficiently
xplain the omission.[1] It may be remarked, however, that his con-
ntion as a Montanist is not so much that the decisions reprobated
e improperly lax, as that they are altogether *ultra vires*. Only the
ue 'Church of the Spirit' can pardon sins, and even it will not remit
1ose which the incriminated bishop has claimed to absolve.[2]

To this work we shall have to return presently. Attention must
rst be called to certain other passages in which mention is made
ther of St. Peter, of his Dominical commission, or directly of the
oman see. Let us look first at the *De Praescriptione*.[3] In this book,
1e of Tertullian's earliest surviving works (*c.* 200), the main purpose,
ke that of Irenaeus, is to refute the 'exception' of the Gnostics that
their doctrine differs from that of the 'official' Church, it is because
is derived either from scientific investigation or from secret know-
dge not imparted to the Apostles. After rejecting the former as futile,
e demands whether it is conceivable that those to whom 'it was given
know secrets which it was not lawful for the people to understand
uld have been ignorant of anything';[4] then with inexorable logic
e inquires:

'Was anything concealed from Peter, named the rock of the Church
on to be built, who actually obtained the keys of the kingdom of

---

[1] The case in favour of identifying the object of Tertullian's censures with the
shop of Carthage has been urged very strongly by Galtier, P., *L'Église et la
mission des péchés*, pp. 141–183. The possibility that 'benedictus papa', *ibid.*,
5, 7, could refer not to the bishop of Rome but to the bishop of Carthage cannot
e excluded, in view of e.g. *Acta Felicitatis et Perpetuae, Texts and Studies*, vol. i,
. 2, p. 82, ed. Robinson, J. A., Cambridge, 1891; cf. Cyprian, *Epp.* 8, 1. ed. cit.,
485; 23, *tit.* ed. cit., p. 536. On the other hand, 'apostolice', *ibid.*, 21, 5, applied
rectly to a bishop would seem to point to the see of Rome rather than that of
arthage. It has been argued by Adam, K., *Das sogennante Bussedikt des P. Kallistus*,
17, that the 'edict' to which Tertullian referred was simply a decision in the
rticular case of bishops guilty of mortal sin. Yet it should be noted that in *De Pud.*,
4, he appears also to allude to Callistus' attempt to regularize slave marriages.

[2] Tertullian's doctrine of forgiveness of sins is admittedly ambiguous. For his view
hile still belonging to the 'Great Church', see above, p. 131, n. 2. The *De Pudicitia*,
owever, was written after his conversion to Montanism, and in it he repeatedly
serts that only the Montanist prophet under the inspiration of the Spirit can grant
ardon, *ibid.*. 16 and 21. In addition, an increasingly rigorist outlook caused the
uthor to enlarge the catalogue of sins for which no human pardon was possible,
id. 19, and for which not even the intercession of Christ would be available, or, if
vailable, could not avail. For a discussion of Tertullian's theory of Penance, see
irk, K.E. *op. cit.*, p. 514 ff.

[3] Ed. Rauschen, G., in *Florilegium patr.*, fasc. 4, 1906.

[4] *Ibid.*, 22, 1–4. ed. cit., p. 32 f. Note that in the same work, c. 23 (ed. cit., p. 34 f.),
1e author refers to St. Peter's controversy with St. Paul, Gal. II, 11.

heaven, and authority both to loose and to bind in heaven and c earth?'[1]

It is difficult to believe that Tertullian here conceives of th Dominical charge as conveying more than a privilege personal St. Peter himself, yet the passage is noteworthy as supplying th first known allusion to the *Tu es Petrus* in patristic literature. At th same time it is significant of its future use in connexion with th primacy of the Roman See that our author interprets the words meaning that the Apostle was endowed thereby with a prerogativ which was operative beyond the limits of the terrestrial sphere.[2]

The most characteristic argument of this treatise occurs in a lat chapter, where he says: 'whatever is original is Dominical and tru whatever is of subsequent introduction is extraneous and false'.[3] L the Gnostics therefore bring out their spiritual pedigrees, and it w be seen at once that only churches of indubitably apostolic foundatic can 'make a return' showing their apostolic descent by way of uninterrupted 'series of successions'.[4] Giving examples, he cites th traditions of the church of Smyrna about the appointment of Polyca by St. John and of the church of Rome about the ordination Clement by St. Peter.[5] Whatever evidence of the kind the Gnosti may produce he roundly asserts to be plain forgery. The passage also of interest as providing evidence for the currency in Africa of belief in St. Peter's residence in Rome.

We now come to one of the crucial texts, believed by some point to an explicit acknowledgment of the Roman primacy. Let note carefully what it says.

The author is enumerating the more outstanding churches apostolic origin, such as Corinth, Philippi, and Ephesus. He then add

'If, however, you are near Italy, you have Rome, where a tit deed lies handy for us as well. Ah, that church! How fortuna

---

[1] *De Praescriptione*, 22, 3. ed. cit., p. 32 f.

[2] *Ibid.*, 'consecutum et solvendi et alligandi in caelis et in terra potestatem This is of course a somewhat misleading paraphrase of Matt. xvi, 19. Note th Origen, *Comm. in Matt.* 12, 11. *G.C.S.* vol. x, pp. 86 ff., in commenting on th passage repudiates the view that the promise included one of immunity fro physical death. See also above, p. 95.

[3] *Ibid.*, 31, 3. ed. cit., p. 44.

[4] *Ibid.*, 32, 1–3. ed. cit., p. 44 f. It may be remarked that Tertullian uses (v lect.) 'episcoporum . . . succession*es*'. Cf. Irenaeus, *Adv. haer.* 3, 3, 2, 'succe siones episcoporum', on which see above, p. 111 f.

[5] On the origin of this tradition see above, p. 91.

is! to whom the Apostles gave all the fulness of their doctrine
d their life-blood too, where Peter attains the Lord's passion;
here Paul is rewarded with the death of John'.[1]

That Tertullian recognized a primacy in the Roman see can be
arcely open to doubt, though as we shall see, so far as our evidence
kes us, it is not a belief to which he felt it necessary to call much
tention. But to suppose that he has it exclusively in mind in this
assage makes nonsense of his argument. His point here is not
imacy, but 'title deed to possession' (*auctoritas*), based on the
ct of direct or indirect apostolic origin. It is only by ignoring the
chnical meaning of this legal term that any idea of primacy or
risdiction can be read into his words.[2]

We may remark that besides the passage already mentioned there
e at least three others which appear to imply his acceptance of the
adition about St. Peter's residence and death in Rome.[3] A further
assage from his treatise *Scorpiace*, belonging to the later or Mon-
nist period of his life, provides a characteristically 'individualist'
oplication of the *Tu es Petrus*.

He is writing of the free access to heaven granted to every Christian
d demonstrating the falsity of pagan myths which assigned a
ower of exclusion to certain inferior deities. Then he proceeds:

'For even if you suppose that heaven is still closed, be mindful that
ie Lord has left behind here His keys to Peter, and through him to
ie Church, which every single person who has been questioned and
id confessed will take with him'.[4]

Evidently there is nothing to be gleaned here as to belief in any
rerogative peculiar to the Apostle; in fact such a prerogative appears
• be implicitly denied by reason of his assertion that it belongs to the
hurch as a whole and so to every baptized Christian. But it is
teresting to remark how far the author has travelled by means of
is paraphrase from the plain meaning of his text.[5]

---

[1] *De Praescriptione*, 36, 3. ed. cit., p. 50.
[2] Tertullian appears to be thinking of someone going to Rome to fetch the
uctoritas, after the fashion of a lawyer's clerk procuring a deed of transfer. For this
nse of 'auctoritas', see Lewis and Short, s.v. II, H, where the *XII Tabulæ* ap.
icer., *Off.* 1, 12, 37 and other Ciceronian examples are given. There is reason to
elieve that legal terminology is, if anything, more conservative than ecclesiastical.
[3] Tertullian, *De baptismo*, 4, 4; *Scorpiace*, 15, 3 f.; *Adv. Marcionem*, 4, 5, 2.
[4] *Scorpiace*, 10, 12. The *Scorpiace*, i.e. the antidote against the scorpion's sting, is a
ter treatise against Gnosticism.
[5] Cf. *De praescript.*, 22, 3. ed. cit., p. 32 f

Finally we have to consider certain further points arising from l
Montanist treatise the *De Pudicitia* already mentioned.[1] In t
relevant chapters, which, as we have argued, appear to allude direct
to the disciplinary regulations of Callistus I, he has already repudiat
the doctrine that the Church has power to remit after penance tl
sins of adultery and fornication.[2] Later on he reverts to the Pop
claim to have power to forgive such sins and demands wi
indignation:

'As to your present decision, I should like to know on what grou
you assume this privilege of the Church: can it be that, because tl
Lord has said to Peter: "Upon this rock I will build my Church,
thee I have given the keys of the heavenly kingdom"; or becaus
"Whatsoever things thou shalt bind or loose on earth, shall be boun
or loosed in heaven", for this reason you infer that the authority
loosing and binding has descended to yourself as well, that is to sa
to the whole church of Peter's kin? What kind of a person are y
who contradict and misrepresent the evident purpose of the Lor
when He conferred this privilege on Peter simply in his own persol
"Upon thee", says He, "I will build my Church", and "I will gi
the keys to thee", not to the Church, and "whatsoever things th
shalt bind or loose", not what they have bound or loosed. My poil
is confirmed by what follows. On him the Church has been built u
I mean, through his own agency; he himself has inserted the key'.[3]

Following this line of thought, the author goes on to give exampl
of the use of the 'key' by St. Peter, in giving baptism to the Jev
for the forgiveness of past sins, in binding Ananias with the bor
of death or loosing the lame man from his infirmity, and in decidir
under the inspiration of the Spirit to what extent converts we
obliged to observe the Mosaic law.[4]

The studied rhetoric of Tertullian's style raises a number
exegetical problems. What does he mean by 'the Church'? Has tl
word the same connotation all through the same passage? How fa
if at all, does he quote here, as he seems to be doing just above, tl
ipsissima verba of the bishop's 'edict'? What is meant, above all, l
the phrase which we have rendered 'the whole church of Peter's kin

---

[1] *C.S.E.L.* vol. xx, 1890, p. 249 ff.   [2] See above, p. 145 f.

[3] *De pudicitia*, 21, 9–11. ed. cit., p. 269 f. It should be observed that accura
in quotation is not one of this author's strong points. Note 'dedi' in § 9, 'dabo'
§ 10.

[4] *Ibid.*, 21, 13.

As to the first of these, we should notice that earlier in the same chapter he explicitly acknowledges that the Church has the authority to remit sins, but speaking on behalf of the Montanist sect, and presumably citing a Montanist utterance, adds 'I will not do it, lest they commit other sins as well'.[1] There he is vindicating the exclusive right to exercise this power for the Montanists, and it is not less probable that the 'Church' has the same connotation in the section under review,[2] though with an exception shortly to be noticed.

The question whether or not Tertullian is repeating here the actual words of the decision which he criticizes, is obviously of cardinal importance. For evidently, if it were possible to show conclusively that he does so, we should have before us the earliest instance, and that of early third-century date, of use by the Roman see (we assume, it will be remembered, that the 'edict' is Roman and not Carthaginian in origin) of the famous Petrine text. Even so, however, it would scarcely follow that it was being used in support of the Roman primacy, unless we could be certain that the phrase the whole church of the kin of Peter' also formed part of the supposed papal utterance.[3] Yet it seems clear from the form which the argument takes that Tertullian himself was aware that he was not quoting Callistus. Else why in citing the *Tu es Petrus* as a possible justification should he employ such obvious irony? Had Callistus used the text himself, it is hardly conceivable that his critic could have written the words 'On what ground do you assume this privilege of the Church? Can it be because . . .?' If he knew quite well that the

---

[1] *De pudicitia*, 21, 1 f.: 'Sed habet, inquis, potestatem ecclesia delicta donandi. Hoc ego magis et agnosco et dispono, qui ipsum Paracletum in prophetis novis habeo dicentem: "Potest ecclesia donare delictum, sed non faciam, ne et alia delinquant" '. Cf. *ibid.*, 1, 9.

[2] *Ibid.*, 21, 9. 'unde hoc ius ecclesiae usurpes?' Galtier, P., *L'église et la rémission es péchés*, 1932, p. 147 ff., discusses whether the author is alluding to the 'official' r to the Montanist church, and whether 'ecclesiae' is genitive or dative. Shortly before Tertullian has asserted that the Church has the power to forgive sins (*ibid.*, 1, 7), but there he clearly means the Montanist church, so he goes on to inquire ironically 'whence do you usurp this right of the (sc. Montanist) church'? But cf. Koch, H., *Cathedra Petri*, 1930, p. 5, n.; Caspar, E., *Primatus Petri*, in *Zeitschr. d. Sav.-Stift. f. Rechtsgesch.* Kanon. Abt. xvi, 1927, p. 11, note 3. Here we take ecclesiae' to be genitive, which is not excluded by 'dabo tibi claves, non ecclesiae', since in Tertullian's view the authority of the Montanist church is independent of scripture, being derived from direct inspiration.

[3] *Ibid.*, 21, 9. 'idcirco praesumis et ad te derivasse solvendi et alligandi potestatem, id est ad omnem ecclesiam Petri propinquam'.

text had already been cited by his opponent, it would scarcely have been necessary to use such a form of expression.

Furthermore, if the Pope had in fact thus argued in support of his claim to give such decisions, and had actually written (or said) that in virtue of the Petrine promise he had authority to loose and to bind, it is likely that Hippolytus, who must have been at least as well informed as Tertullian, would have mentioned the fact, at any rate in connexion with the legalisation of concubinal unions,[1] though Callistus might have regarded it as a proper use of Petrine authority in its original sense. We may therefore conclude that, with the possible exception of the words quoted earlier in this chapter of the treatise (and even these may be a rhetorical exaggeration), none of the phrases or arguments used is necessarily Callistine.

But what is the meaning of 'every church of Peter's kin'?[2] Does it refer to a view possibly already current in some parts of the West that each church enjoyed its authority to forgive sins in virtue of a direct or indirect derivation from the Roman see? May we not say that the logic of the context demands rather an allusion to a claim that the Roman church itself possesses this authority chiefly because it is more 'related to Peter' as its 'hero' and 'Oecist' than other episcopal churches?

Harnack, however, in arguing[3] against the conclusion to which we have already alluded,[4] that the bishop here censured is not of Rome but of Carthage, has urged that the word which we have rendered 'kin' (*propinquam*) ought to be understood in a strictly geographical sense, but in order to sustain his case he is obliged to treat 'whole' (*omnem*) as a corruption of 'Roman' (*romanam*). It is perhaps not surprising that his view has not been generally accepted.[5] For so far from showing that 'kin' does not give the right sense, he has rather confirmed this rendering by the nature of the expedient necessary in order decisively to exclude it. Nor does he appear to

---

[1] See above, p. 132.   [2] See p. 149, n. 3.

[3] 'Ecclesia Petri propinquam' in *Sitz.-ber. d. preuss. Akad. d. W.* Phil.-hist. kl. 1927, vol. xviii. Cf. also Köhler, W., *Omnis ecclesia Petri propinqua*, 1938, where the hypothesis is put forward that the expression reflects the influence of hero-cults especially prevalent in the East, though not without parallels in the West. We may note esp. (p. 31) 'Aber von einem "Primat" des römischen Bischofs darf man nicht sprechen, diesen Anspruch hat Kallist nicht erhoben'.

[4] See above, p. 144.

[5] It has been solidly refuted by Caspar, E., *Primatus Petri*, 1927, and by Koch, H. *Theol. Quartalschrift*, 1928, p. 169.

ave noticed the extent to which Tertullian's writings are impreg-
ated with the thought of spiritual relationship,[1] and that such a
nse is wholly consistent with the context.

VII

It is now time to see what had been happening at Rome following
e receipt of the news of Pope Pontian's resignation, while a prisoner
a the island of Sardinia, and of the submission of the anti-pope
ippolytus. Probability suggests that Antherus, the common choice
the now reconciled parties, was already of an advanced age at the
me of his election. At all events his death occurred after a pontificate
little more than a month.[2]

The reign of his successor Fabian introduces us to a fresh develop-
ent in local organization. From the *Catalogus Liberianus* we learn
at 'he apportioned regions to the deacons'.[3] As his pontificate out-
sted the rule of Maximin the Thracian by some eleven years or so,
is by no means impossible that during the constant disorders which
flicted the peace of the Roman State for the six years of the colour-
ss reign of Philip[4] following Maximin's assassination, the Roman
urch enjoyed sufficient immunity to enable it to set its house in
der, and to reorganize its resources to meet the possibility of a new
tack. Fabian's successor Cornelius has preserved for us in his letter
Fabius of Antioch[5] a valuable record of the constitution of his
hurch at this time, in which he affirms that besides the bishop,
here were forty-six presbyters, seven deacons, seven subdeacons,
rty-two acolytes, fifty-two exorcists and readers including door-
epers, and more than five thousand widows and persons in a state

---

[1] See Koch, *Cathedra Petri*, p. 22.

[2] *Cat. Lib*. Vita Antheri.

[3] *Ibid*. Vita Fabiani: 'hic regiones divisit diaconibus'. The phrase may mean
ther that he assigned two of the fourteen Augustan *regiones* to each of the
ven deacons, or that he originated the seven diaconal regions, the earliest
liable evidence for which is not earlier than 400. Gregory I, *Reg*. 8, 14, says:
nge retro'.

[4] Eus. *H.E*. 6, 34. ed. cit., vol. ii, pt. 2, p. 588, relates with some caution a story
at when Philip wished to take part in the Easter rites of some church not specified
was not permitted to do so until he had received absolution after penance. Cf.
ron. Pasch. M.P.G. 92, 668. Caspar, *Geschichte d. Papstt*., vol. i, 50, is mistaken
identifying the bishop in question with Fabian.

[5] Cit. ap. Eus *H E*. 6, 43, 11. ed. cit., vol. ii, pt. 2, p. 618. JK 106. The letter
of interest as being (unless 1 *Clement* be so reckoned) the earliest genuine papal
cument which has survived.

of distress'.[1] It is probable that these statistics were derived fro
some official account books, containing lists of persons to who
regular salaries or maintenance allowances were due.[2] If this be s
they reveal not only the extent of the financial and economic respoi
sibility, to which by now the episcopal government of the Roma
church was committed, but also the important fact that the Roma
clergy had already become a salaried body, independent of any ci
occupation for their means of livelihood. Furthermore, the form
the list suggests that stipends were graded according to status, tl
lower offices being grouped together as sharing the same rate of pay
Finally it should be noticed that the seven orders, minor as well
major, bearing the same titles as those familiar to the Western Chur
in after ages, are already in existence; following the three highest, tl
origin of which, as we have seen, lies in the most primitive perio
come those of more recent introduction; the subdeacons first, who
institution is stated by the *Liber Pontificalis* to have been due
Fabian himself,[4] as the coadjutors of the deacons; then the acolyte
whose number suggests that one was assigned to each presbyter as ;
assistant; and finally the fifty-two exorcists, readers and doorkeepei
How these latter were distributed we have no means of knowing, b
if, as we shall see, there were probably some eighteen *tituli*[5] or pi
vately owned buildings in Christian use at this time, it may be co
ectured that one of each order was seconded to a particular churc

It was inevitable, owing to its strictly limited numerical co
stitution of seven, that the diaconate would tend to overshadow tl
presbyterate in influence and importance; in fact, as we have pointi
out, from early times and for many centuries the archdeacon,
head of the diaconal *collegium*, was usually regarded as the obvio
candidate when it became necessary to fill a pontifical vacancy.[6] N

[1] It is possible, especially in view of Dion. Cor. ap. Eus. *H.E.* 4, 23, 9 f. ed. c
vol. ii, pt. 1, p. 376 f., in which he speaks of the charity of the Roman church un(
Soter to provincial Christians, that some of the 'dependents' of that church belong
to other churches. Otherwise, the number seems almost fantastic. Cf. Zernov, 1
in *C.Q.R.* vol. cxvii, Jan., 1934, p. 333.

[2] Caspar, *op. cit.*, vol. i, p. 51.

[3] *Ep. Cornelii*, ap. Eus. *ibid.*: 'ἐξορκιστὰς δὲ καὶ ἀναγνώστας ἅμα πυλωροῖς δύο
πεντήκοντα'.

[4] Ed. Duchesne, L., 1886, vol. i, p. 148, *Vita Fabiani* 'Hic . . . fecit \
subdiaconos'.

[5] The word *titulus* (Lewis and Short, *s.v.*) is originally used of an 'inscriptio
then in a special sense of a 'notice' exhibited on property, thus the 'property' its

[6] See above, p. 125.

there lacking evidence that for some centuries to come this body
ormed the dominant element in the local church, and often exercised
onsiderable influence on papal policy.

On the other hand, the presbyterate continued to fulfil its original
unction as a judicial and disciplinary corporation,[1] of which the
piscopus remained as before the *ex officio* chairman. Yet already signs
f a change to come are apparent, for which no doubt the steady
rocess of numerical expansion of the church was largely responsible.
The diaconal college was becoming increasingly absorbed in financial
dministration in addition to personal attendance on the bishop in his
iturgical capacity. Hence as the need for some measure of decen-
ralization became clear, it was obvious that of the two orders the
nore numerous presbyterate was in a better position to supply the
eed.[2] But the peculiar conditions of the third century supply a
urther explanation. Hitherto persecution, so far as it affected the
hurch of Rome, had not seriously disturbed its normal life, and
vhen a vacancy in the pontificate occurred it was speedily filled. The
Emperor Decius, however, as we shall see, introduced a new policy of
reating confusion and disorder by striking at the heads of the
Christian communities,[3] with the result that following the execution
f Pope Xystus II and the entire diaconal college under his successor
Valerian, a period of no less than eleven months had elapsed before
t became possible to elect a successor. During the interval the con-
luct of the church's worship and affairs must have been solely in
he hands of the *presbyterium*.[4] Privileges once acquired in time of
emergency are not readily abandoned or withdrawn when normality

---

[1] We can infer from *Sacramentarium Serapionis*, 27 (13), ed. Funk, F. X., 1905,
. 188, that this was so in Egypt, where the duty of a presbyter is described as
ϙἰκονομῆσαι'; equally we learn from *Constitutiones ecclesiae Aegyptiacae*, 2 (32),
d. cit., p. 103, which probably reproduces a source emanating from Asia Minor
elonging to the third century, that the presbyterate's chief function was to
dminister discipline. What was true both of Egypt and Asia at this time may be
aken as some indication of prevailing practice at Rome.

[2] In view of the evidence in the *Apostolic Tradition* of Hippolytus, we ought
irmly to resist the temptation to read later theory based on already established
ractice into a more primitive environment. There is really nothing to show, as
ve have already pointed out, that the presbyterate, as distinct from the diaconate,
vas originally regarded as possessing an inherent right to be regarded as the only
ossible order to which the bishop's liturgical functions could be delegated.

[3] See below, p. 156.

[4] *Cat. Lib.* Vita Xysti: '<et presbyteri praefuerunt> a cons. Tusci et Bassi
258] usque in diem xii Kal. Aug. Aemiliano et Basso cons. [259]'. On the authority
or the words bracketed, see *Liber pont.* ed. cit., vol. i, p. 155 f. and note 5.

is restored. Hence we are not surprised to find that it is reported
Xystus' successor Dionysius that 'he gave churches and cemeteries t
the presbyters'.[1] Doubtless this suggests some delegation of liturgic;
functions, though it may really mean much less. The same source
i.e. the *Liber Pontificalis*, describes a measure adopted by Pop
Marcellus early in the fourth century by saying 'this (Pope) establishe
the twenty-five *tituli* in the city of Rome in the manner of spheres c
jurisdiction, in regard to baptism and penance of many who wer
coming over from the heathen, and in regard to the burial places c
martyrs'.[2] As it is highly probable that public administration c
baptism continued to be restricted under normal conditions to th
bishop until late in the fourth century at Rome,[3] the reference t
that sacrament must be taken to mean baptismal preparation. Suc
preparation together with the disciplinary decisions necessary i
regard to penitents must always have formed part of the norm;
pastoral functions of the *presbyterium*. Care of cemeteries, as we hav
seen, belonged to it already, a natural assignment in view of th
necessity for determining the rightfulness of any particular clair
for burial within the Church's property. It seems therefore abundantl
clear that the presbyters in the third century had as yet no regula
responsibilities of a liturgical character. Any idea that at this time the
had become the normal *locum tenentes* of the bishop in celebratin
the Eucharist is altogether excluded. And if further proof wer
needed, we might anticipate by pointing out that even at the beginnin
of the fifth century, while consecration of the elements has been con
ceded to surburban and rural presbyters, the non-liturgical characte
of the office is preserved at least to this extent within the urban limit
that instead of consecrating themselves the city presbyters receiv
the *fermentum* or consecrated loaf from the Pope's Mass by the hand
of acolytes for distribution to their own congregations.[4]

[1] *Liber pont*. ed. cit., vol. i, p. 157: 'Hic presbyteris ecclesias dedit et cymiteria e
parrocias diocesis constituit'. We are to understand the last phrase of the assign
ment of episcopal spheres in the rural area of Rome, not of the establishment c
some sort of parochial divisions within the city. 'Paroechia' at this time still denote
what we now describe as a 'diocese'.

[2] *Ibid*., ed. cit., vol. i, p. 164: 'Hic . . . XXV titulos in urbe Roma constituit
quasi diocesis, propter baptismum et poenitentiam multorum qui convertebantu
ex paganis et propter sepulturas martyrum'.

[3] Caspar, *Geschichte*, vol. i, p. 56, n. 5.

[4] Innocent I, *Ep*. 25, 5. JK 311, 5. The *Lib. pont*. ed. cit., vol. i, p. 168, credit
Pope Miltiades († 314) with the adoption of this expedient. We may admit that i
all probability the custom antedated Innocent I, and may well have been in origi

To return to Pope Fabian. From such evidence as we possess we may well judge him to have been a man of imaginative foresight and practical energy. If he was deficient in any quality it was probably inability to form a correct judgment of character. His successor has a good deal to say in his letter to the church of Antioch about the antecedents of his formidable rival Novatian,[1] and describes how this man, in whom we shall presently recognize the second great antipope, had been ordained presbyter by a former bishop (whom most authorities have identified with Fabian),[2] in spite of his having received baptism clinically and thus, according to the view prevailing at the time, being in some sense a defective member of the Christian *ecclesia*.[3] It would also seem that the bishop had acted in the teeth of an adverse vote supported by all the clergy and a large section of the laity.[4] How injudicious was his neglect of so important an expression of opinion will be seen in the subsequent course of events.

VIII

The Emperor Decius, who is probably to be reckoned among the more conscientious as well as the more disinterested of the Roman princes, found himself, perhaps not without some feeling of distaste, master of the empire in the later months of the year 248. His accession marked the close of a long succession of undistinguished principates, of which the latest has left but one enduring impression on the pages of history, the celebration of the *Ludi saeculares*, as is generally sup-

temporary measure, at first necessitated by the circumstances of the persecution and then continued in time of peace. It should be observed that Duchesne, *op. cit.*, p. 169, n. 4, in citing Innocent appears to overlook the fact that urban clergy are excluded from the scope of the concession granted to the suburban and rural presbyters. In the case of the former, communion of the people by means of the *fermentum* is to continue in force. This seems to imply at least that only the suburban and rural presbyters were permitted to consecrate (conficere) as a normal practice, and may thus be taken to imply that the city presbyters were not at this date permitted to do so.

[1] *Ep. Cornelii*, ap. Eus. *H.E.* 6, 43, 17. ed. cit., vol. ii, pt. 2, pp. 620, 622.

[2] Cornelius, *ibid.*, 13, speaks of Novatian as one who had been afflicted with an evil spirit in his youth, and had received prolonged treatment by exorcism. He was therefore probably already middle-aged at the time of his admission to the presbyterate. This points to Fabian rather than one of his predecessors as the bishop responsible.

[3] The earliest known synodical allusion to clinical baptism as an impediment to ordination is *Conc. Neocaesar.* Canon 12.

[4] For other references to the requirement that a bishop must consult at least the clergy before proceeding to ordination, see above, p. 143.

posed, for the last time. A hard-living provincial, bred in the mou
tains of Pannonia, and eager to effect a political as well as a mor
regeneration of the Roman State, he believed, like Julian a centu
after him, that these ends could best be attained by demanding a
expression of common loyalty by all its citizens to the primitive ar
austere cultus of the Roman people. From indirect, though con
temporary evidence,[1] we may infer that an edict was publishe
requiring everyone to give proof of such loyalty by conformity
the traditional ceremonies associated with pagan sacrifice, ar
threatening in the event of refusal the penalty of exile involvir
confiscation of property and loss of civil rights.[2]

It is by no means certain, as has often been supposed, that th
measure, as such, was directed primarily against the Christian Churc
Yet that every Christian was faced with the necessity of choosir
between conformity and refusal is, of course, obvious. The fa
that the Emperor could say, as it is reported of him, that he woul
endure with more forbearance the advancement of a rival in th
principate than the election of a new bishop to the see of Rome
suggests that he was not blind to the formidable opposition whic
might be engendered by a Church determined on grounds of cor
science to withstand his will. In any case, so far as we know, Christian
furnished the only considerable body of nonconformists; chief amon
them were a number of bishops, including Pope Fabian himself, wh
appears to have succumbed to the consequences of imprisonment
The number of those who were actually put to death was probabl
not large. Far more serious than losses on this score were the defec
tions, real or fictitious, of a multitude of the Church's adherent
and even of some outstanding bishops. In certain churches speci:
problems made their appearance. Those at Carthage arose chiefl
from too liberal and perhaps often injudicious distribution o
superfluous merit by confessors to persons who, less stalwart tha
themselves, were seeking to evade the disciplinary consequence
of their failure. And everywhere, in a greater or less degree, an

[1] Although the actual text of the edict has not been preserved, much may l
inferred about as contents from allusions in Cyprian, De lapsis, 3, 8. C.S.E.L. vol. i
pt. I, pp. 238, 242; Ep. 43, 3. ed. cit., p. 592; Dionysius Alex. ap. Eus. H.E. 6, 4
I, 23.

[2] Cf. Anti-manichaean Edict, Cod. Greg. XIV, iv, 4–7. ed. Haenel, p. 44.

[3] Cyprian, Ep. 55, 9, 1. ed. cit., p. 630.

[4] Cat. Lib. Vita Fabiani. For the character of the persecution in Rome itself, se
Acta Tryphonis, ed. Cavallieri, F. de, in Studi e testi, vol. xx, 1908.

ot least at Rome, there arose the general question of the conditions
hich should govern the readmission of those guilty of actual or
rmal apostasy.

Evidence shows that it was chiefly division of opinion on this
atter which gave rise to a fresh schism within the Roman church.
nce again the tolerant practically-minded diaconate found itself in
pposition to the more vigorous and perhaps more spiritual pres-
yterate, whose leader and spokesman on this occasion was the
resbyter Novatian.

It is an unfortunate though not uncommon accident of history that
e know of his character and conduct chiefly through the evidence
f Cornelius, his successful rival in the papal election, which was
robably held after the receipt of news of Decius' unexpected death
a battle against the Goths.

Cornelius has represented that Novatian was one who had always
herished the secret ambition that he would one day sit on the
rone of St. Peter, though publicly protesting his unwillingness to
ccept the office.[1] Yet from what we can learn from other sources,
is by no means improbable that his protests were sincere and that
e accepted his position as anti-pope with the genuine conviction
at only so could the church be saved from moral and spiritual
isaster. The legacy of his writings[2] handed down to posterity, many
f them pseudonymous and only recently restored to their true
thor, shows him to be a man of painstaking study and ascetic zeal.
is *De Trinitate* was the first and for long remained the only sys-
matic treatment by a western writer of this cardinal doctrine of the
hristian faith.[3] It was a tragedy that such a personality should have
een alienated from the corporate life of the 'great Church'. Yet
ad the policy of rigorism triumphed, with which his name was to be
ssociated, the Church would have lost her power to heal the wounds
f human frailty, to extend hope of new strength to the stumbling
d the fallen, and must in the end have dwindled to an insignificant
andful of self-righteous sinners, no longer intent upon the salvation
f others because oblivious of their own.

---

[1] *Ep. Cornelii*, ap. Eus. *H.E.* 6, 43, 7. ed. cit., pp. 614, 616.
[2] *D.T.C.* vol. xi, col. 817–21.
[3] Ed. Fausset, W. Y., 1909. Jerome, *C. Rufin.* 2, 19. *M.P.L.* 23, 464, shows that
his time this work was still known as Novatian's. In *De vir. inl.* 70, ed. cit., p. 39,
mentions the titles of a number of Novatian's writings which have since perished.
f. Bardenhewer, *Geschichte*, vol. ii², p. 630 ff.

How did it come about that the Church was saved from tl disaster? As we have seen, the first impact of the new imper: religious programme on the Christian communitiës resulted in : alarming proportion of defections from strict loyalty to the exclusi claims of their religion. Everywhere, and particularly in Rome ai Carthage, were to be found those unfortunates who, rather than ri imprisonment or worse, had performed some perfunctory religio: act, sufficient at once to satisfy the official requirement and to exclu them from the Church. Swift was the bitter and ineluctable remor: Yet what hope remained of restoration to Christian communion?

We have already seen that the dominant policy in the Rom: church had hitherto been one of leniency towards those guilty capital sins. Schism, heresy, carnality, each in its turn had four therapeutic rather than excisive treatment at the hands of a soverei; healer. Now it was the turn of apostasy. Could the same mer already freely accorded to the rest be denied? Opinion on this questi was sharply divided both in Rome and Carthage and passions we running high.

At Rome the presbyters, who were responsible, as probably st elsewhere, for the maintenance of discipline, many of them perha of an older generation with little sympathy for the foibles of yout now favoured a policy of extreme caution; in fact some were willi: to concede restoration only on the imminence of death. The da gerous factor was that in maintaining this attitude they were confide of the support of those members of their order who had acquir honorary presbyteral status by suffering imprisonment for th refusal to conform to the imperial requirements. There seemed ther fore every likelihood that this time a policy of rigorism would triumphant. Yet as on a previous occasion[1] it was the practi common sense of the Roman diaconate which saved the situation a: upheld the Church's prerogative of mercy.

At Carthage almost exactly the opposite peril was threatenin Cyprian, recently elected to the episcopate,[2] and faced with the choi of conformity or punishment, had withdrawn from the scene.[3] T Carthaginian presbyterate however, especially those of its numb who had recently acquired similiar status as presbyters in co

---

[1] In the election of Callistus rather than Hippolytus, see above, p. 130.
[2] 248 or early 249.
[3] *Ep. diac. rom.* ap. Cypr. *Ep.* 8, 1. ed. cit., p. 485 ff. Cf. Cypr. *Epp.* 7, 12, 14,

quence of their imprisonment,[1] and may perhaps have been unduly
ated at receiving an unexpected and possibly unmerited dignity,
pears to have set about exercising its disciplinary authority with
ngular lack of prudence and discrimination.[2] As a consequence it
emed that the whole penitential system of the Church was in danger
rapid dissolution. A timely letter from the Roman diaconate,
hich *sede vacante* was in charge of that church's external affairs, not
thout an undertone of reproof at what may have appeared cowardly
nduct on his part, showed Cyprian that he could count on its
oral support in enforcing some measure of discipline.[3] Even so the
uation in Carthage was precarious in the extreme, and its delicacy
is rather aggravated by the presence of a minority of the pres-
terate under the leadership of a certain Novatus, perhaps a defeated
ndidate for the Carthaginian episcopate, who, probably indifferent
the crucial question regarding restoration of the lapsed, saw in the
easures being taken by their bishop a direct challenge to the
iditional judicial privileges of their order, which they now deter-
ined to vindicate at all costs. Believing that much depended on
curing the support of his fellow-presbyters at Rome, Novatus
d a few accomplices made off thither. What he found there must
ve been scarcely to his satisfaction.[4]

As soon as the tension created by the first execution of the terms
the edict had relaxed, a process which may well have been
stened by the news of the Emperor's death in the Gothic campaign,[5]
e Roman clergy and laity met to elect a new bishop. The clear choice
the majority was Cornelius,[6] a man, to judge by Cyprian's estimate,
somewhat limited attainments,[7] yet whose very mediocrity under
e circumstances probably constituted an important qualification.
deed his election seems to supply a signal example of that occasional

[1] On the honorary presbyterate of a confessor who has suffered imprisonment,
Dix, G., *Apostolic Tradition of Hippolytus*, X, p. 18.
[2] *Ep. confess. afric.* ap. Cypr. *Ep.* 23 ; cf. Cypr. *Epp.* 15, 16, 17, 26 *et al.*
[3] *Ep. diac. rom.* ap. Cypr. *Ep.* 8. The evidence that it was written by the Roman
acons is to be found in the omission of that order among the salutations in § 3
488). The problem created by indiscreet leniency on the part of confessor-
esbyters did not exist at Rome, where the presbyterate favoured a rigorous policy.
e Roman diaconate was evidently willing for the reconciliation of the lapsed
er penance, with the exception of catechumens.
[4] Cypr. *Ep.* 52, 2 f. ed. cit., p. 617 ff.
[5] Gibbon, *Decline*, ed. Bury, J. B. (1929), vol. i, p. 269.
[6] Cypr. *Ep.* 55, 8. ed. cit., p. 629.
[7] *Ibid.*, 'quietus alias et modestus'.

intervention, by means of which a watchful Providence appears
have saved the Roman church from imminent disaster.

The attitude of the Roman presbyterate in regard to the burni
question of the hour remained on the side of caution. If it was l
prone to leniency than the diaconate, it was as yet, however, or
moderately rigorist.[1] But the election of Cornelius served as a sigr
for the advocates of rigorism to gather their forces. It was precise
at this stage that Novatus and his fellow-presbyters arrived fro
Carthage. Any disagreement there might have been about the co
ditions under which the lapsed could be reconciled was quick
relegated to the background, and from now on a considerable pr
portion of the Roman and Carthaginian presbyterate were united
common resistance to the episcopate.[2] Strong in the support of l
new allies, Novatus felt that the time had come to take a decisi
step. Novatian permitted his election to the Roman see to take pla
perhaps with some reluctance, and once his consecration had be
procured, the schism was a *fait accompli*.[3] For the second time with
half a century there was an anti-pope in Rome who was assured
the backing of a large section of the presbyterate, both ordained a
honorary.

Naturally letters notifying the fact of Cornelius' election were t
first to reach Carthage,[4] but they were quickly followed by oth
telling of the counter-election of Novatian.[5] The synod of Cartha
naturally hesitated between the rival claimants, until it had be
assured that the appointment of Cornelius had been carried out wi
due regard for democratic precedent and ecclesiastical custom. It th
acknowledged his claim and condemned Novatian as a schismati

[1] *Ep. presb. rom.* ap. Cypr. *Op.* No. 30. ed. cit., p. 549.
[2] It is clear that at first the confessor-presbyters at Rome, especially such o
standing personalities as Moses, Maximus and Nicostratus (cf. *Cat. Lib. V*
Fabiani) were on the side of rigorism and opposed to Cornelius and the diacona
We may note that Novatian and Novatus are frequently confused by Greek writ
who usually identify the former with the latter, e.g. Eus. *H.E.* 6, 43, 1 *et*
Socrates, *H.E.* 4, 28.
[3] Cornelius, *Ep. cit.* ap. Eus. *H.E.* 6, 43, 8, describes Novatian's consecrators
'simpletons' brought to Rome from some obscure places in Italy for the purpo
and adds that at the time of the consecration they were not even sober. To th
acquainted with the devices of religious controversy, the story has a strang
familiar ring.
[4] Cyprian, *Ep.* 45, 2 f. ed. cit., p. 600 f. It is clear that he heard of it only on
eve of the first synod held in April, 251.
[5] *Ibid.*, 2: cf. *Ep.* 68, 2. ed. cit., p. 745.
[6] *Ibid.*, 1.

the same time other letters were addressed by each of the two
oman parties to the heads of the 'greater' churches, Dionysius of
exandria and Fabius of Antioch.[1] Dionysius evidently decided to
cept Cornelius, perhaps chiefly because he disapproved of the
gorism represented by Novatian;[2] Fabius, on the other hand,
cording to Eusebius, preferred to suspend judgment.[3] It was no
ubt on this account that both Cyprian and Cornelius personally
dressed letters to Antioch informing its bishop of the decisions of
e recent Roman, Italian and African synods; and in a later letter
ornelius supplied his correspondent with a lengthy and probably
mewhat tendentious account of the origin of the schism, the greater
rt of which has been fortunately preserved by Eusebius.[4]

It must have been about this time, i.e. after the first synod of
arthage, that Cyprian drew up the first edition of his well-known
eatise *De catholicae ecclesiae unitate*. Undismayed by the rejection
his claims by the churches of Africa, the Roman supporters of
ovatian resolved to set up a schismatic organization at Carthage,[5]
d it is likely that the arrival of their mission headed by Novatus
imulated Cyprian to supply his ally Cornelius with substantial
erary aid. Meanwhile Cornelius and his synod decreed the ex-
mmunication of the anti-pope, his consecrators and supporters.[6]
is against such a background that Cyprian's important and

[1] This is to be inferred from Dionysius Alex. ap. Eus. *H.E.* 6, 45 f. ed. cit.,
. 626, 628.

[2] It is probable that the letter of Dionysius preserved *ibid.* was not the only or
en the first reply sent to Novatian.

[3] *Ibid.*, 6, 46, 3. ed. cit., p. 628. In summoning Dionysius and other important
shops to a synod at Antioch, Fabius was perhaps setting a precedent. He evidently
lieved that the question at issue, whether purely disciplinary or involving in
dition a decision between the rival claimants of the Roman see, was one of major
portance, which no merely local church was competent to adjudicate on its own
thority.

[4] Eus. *H.E.* 6, 43, 3 f. ed. cit., p. 614. Only what appears to be the last of these
ters has survived (§§ 5 ff.). To judge from Eusebius' description (§ 3) it is probable
at Cornelius wrote in Greek.

[5] *Ep. Cornelii*, ap. Cypr. *Epp.* No. 50. ed. cit., p. 613 f. In a previous letter ap.
pr. No. 49, ed. cit., p. 608 ff., Cornelius mentioned that a group of confessor-
esbyters had abandoned Novatian and returned to him. For the Novatianist
ission, see Cyprian, *Ep.* 52, ed. cit., p. 618 ff.

[6] *Ep. Cornelii*, cit. ap. Eus. *H.E.* 6, 43. ed. cit., p. 614 ff. The repentance of one
the consecrators is recorded in § 10. He was deposed, but received into lay com-
union at the request of the Roman laity. Successors to the other two were con-
crated by the Pope and 'provided' for the vacant sees. Cf. *Ep. Cornelii* ap. Cypr.
p. No. 50. ed. cit., p. 613 f., where the substitution of Zetus for Euaristus is
entioned though without specifying the name of the see.

much-debated treatise is to be studied, and here again the purpo
of the writer, an appeal for loyalty to Cornelius, must always
kept in mind.

Much confusion in this regard has been caused by the peculiar
disordered state of the manuscript tradition, resulting in serio
difference of opinion of the actual history of the treatise itse
Difficulties arising from striking discrepancies between manuscrip
had been observed so early as 1563, when the edition of Manuti
was published, but it was not till the appearance of Hartel's editio
in the *Vienna Corpus* in 1868 that the controversy reached its heigl
The real crux arises from the different forms in which Chapter IV ar
the first five lines of Chapter V have come down to us. These diffe
ences can be readily observed by comparing the text of the passa;
in the Benedictine edition (reprinted by Migne)[1] with that edited
Hartel.[2] It is easy to see at a glance that the former text includes
number of phrases emphasizing the need of communion with the s
of Peter, while in the latter stress is laid on the importance of uni
within the episcopate. Archbishop Benson in his *St. Cyprian*[3] argu
that the Petrine or 'Primacy' text had been evolved by an ingenio
editing of the 'episcopalian' text, which alone he believed to
Cyprianic, and by the unscrupulous introduction of a number
spurious and tendentious interpolations.

It has been pointed out recently that a satisfactory solution of tl
problem can only be reached by a thorough examination of the who
body of textual evidence contained in the manuscripts.[4] An ear
contribution to this study was made when Chapman published tl
results of his investigations in 1902–3.[5] Chapman, however, st
believed that the 'episcopalian' or non-interpolated text was tl
primary document, though he concluded that the Primacy text w
a later edition of the same passage written to support the cause
Cornelius at Rome, and that both were equally Cyprianic in autho
ship. Strangely enough, by means of the same evidence, Batiffo
reached a conclusion which was practically the opposite of Chapman
namely that the Primacy text was primary, the 'episcopalian' a lat

---

[1] *M.P.L.* 4.   [2] *C.S.E.L.* vol. iii, pt. 1, pp. 212–4.
[3] Benson, E. W., *Cyprian, his life, his times, his work*, 1897.
[4] See p. 163, n.l.
[5] *Revue bénédictin*, 1902–3. Cf. the same author's *Studies on the Early Papa*
1928, pp. 28–50.
[6] Batiffol, P., *L'église naissante*[7], 1919, pp. 440–7.

odification by Cyprian's own hand. Clearly a final verdict had not
en reached.

Quite recently Fr. Bévenot, S.J., has re-examined the whole
estion.[1] His conclusions which are of far-reaching importance may
briefly summarized. After comparing more than a hundred of
one hundred and fifty manuscripts of Cyprian's works known to
st which contain this treatise, he has pointed out that they
y be divided into seven groups. Starting with those in which there
the whole of the alternative Primacy text, followed by the text as
en by Hartel, and comparing them with the manuscripts giving
s latter text conflated with additional matter, that is the text on
ich Benson founded his hypothesis of 'interpolation',[2] he argues
t the so-called 'interpolated' text is simply a conflation of the
macy text and the Hartel text in that order, and not, as Benson
pposed, a modification of the latter by means of additions from the
mer.[3] Thus at a single blow the whole theory of 'interpolation' is
ttered. Nor is this all. By carefully analysing the order in which
Cyprianic treatises occur in different groups of manuscripts,
venot reaches the conclusion that the single manuscript which
es the Primacy text alone, those which contain the Primacy text
lowed by the Hartel text and distinguished by the transposition of
entence from one to the other (i.e. differing from that group of
SS. which gives both texts, as Bévenot says, 'end on' and intact),
d finally those having the 'conflated' text, all go back to a common
hetype.[4]

Chapman had already shown that on linguistic grounds alone no
e against the Cyprianic authorship of the matter additional to the
rtel text could possibly be upheld.[5] Bévenot carries the argument
stage further, pointing out that whether the Primacy text is the
ginal or not, the author of either text undoubtedly had the other in
nt of him. As on his showing that the Primacy text did not include
last four lines of Chapter IV and the first five lines of Chapter V
given in the Hartel text), it follows that if the Primacy text were
ondary, the author in composing it must have deliberately omitted
s passage. The high degree of improbability that he would have
rificed lines which, though certainly not irrelevant to his argument,

Bévenot, M., 'St. Cyprian's *De Unitate*' in *Anal. Greg.*, vol. xi, Scr. Fac.
eol. Sect. B. No. 5, Rome, 1938.
Benson, *op. cit.*, pp. 200–21.   [4] Id., *op. cit.*, p. 51.
Bévenot, *op. cit.*, c. vi.   [5] Id., *op. cit.*, p. 53.

were more relevant to the argument of the Hartel text, lends considerable support to an already strong case in favour of the originality of the Primacy text.[1] We may note in conclusion that the result of Bévenot's work has been to correct the results arrived at in the course of their investigations by his predecessors, Chapman and Batiffol, and to show that while Batiffol was right as against Chapman in postulating the priority of what Bévenot calls the 'end on' text (i.e. where the Primacy text and the Hartel text appear side by side) to the 'interpolated version', the French scholar had not succeeded in distinguishing the Primacy text as a distinct version from the one supplied by the Hartel text of the same chapter (with the additional lines of the following chapter) in the same treatise.

Now that the two texts have been decisively, and, as we believe finally distinguished, the task of ascertaining what light the *De Unitate* can throw on the nature of Cyprian's real attitude towards the Roman see is considerably lightened. Once it is admitted that the text containing the passage on the Petrine primacy is not only authentic but actually the original, we can see clearly the reasons which led the author to adopt this particular form of argument as a defence of the position of Cornelius as opposed to that of Novatian. The jurisdiction of the presbyterate had hitherto not been seriously challenged in any church. But what was to happen if the bishop and the presbyterate (or at least an influential section of that body) were at variance? How could the superior validity of the bishop's judgment be established in particular against the claim of a rival bishop? Cyprian, using an idea which he probably derived from Tertullian, appeals against the jurisdiction of the presbyterate to a Dominical institution, and shows that Cornelius, as the heir of St. Peter's see, has thereby inherited the promise made to St. Peter,[2] and thus is the living embodiment of the *paradosis* delivered to the Apostle by none other than our Lord himself.[3] Let no one in the Roman church presume, he argues, to dispute

---

[1] Bévenot, *op. cit.*, p. 55 ff.

[2] In view of *Ep.* 55, 8. ed. cit., p. 630, there can be no doubt that Cyprian regarded the bishop of Rome as the actual successor of the Apostle.

[3] Cyprian also uses the commission given to St. Peter as the basis of his argument against the laxist policy of the confessor-presbyters at Carthage, and in favour of a single *cathedra*, regarded more as the source of disciplinary than of dogmatic authority. Cf. *Ep.* 43, 5. ed. cit., p. 594.

It may be remarked that with Cyprian the content of the original *paradosis* has almost wholly lost its former doctrinal character, and instead has become a *paradosis* of unity, i.e. unity of discipline. See esp. *Ep.* 45, 3, ed. cit., p. 602, 'unitatem Domino et per apostolos nobis successoribus traditam'.

ciplinary judgments endorsed by the successor of St. Peter, for
have proof that the judgments of St. Peter are endorsed by no
s than divine authority. They are in fact the judgments of God. In
church of Rome as elsewhere by divine appointment there can
only one episcopal *cathedra*, to which the claims of Novatian are
oved to be false by the fact that it is Cornelius and not he, whom the
t of the episcopate has acknowledged.[1]

It remains to inquire what is the precise meaning of the striking
rase usually rendered 'but the primacy is given to Peter'.[2] Are we
suppose that these words, taken together with other expressions
erring to the Petrine origin of the Roman see and to its heritage
his privileges in the sphere of discipline, imply an acknowledg-
nt of a Roman primacy of jurisdiction? Much of course depends
what our author means when he writes primacy (primatum),
ecially as, so far as we know, he is the first Latin author to employ
as a description of the Petrine commission. Yet in view of its use
ewhere by the same author of the 'preferential rights' of Esau as
first born,[3] it is most unlikely that the writer meant it to imply
periority' or 'pre-eminence', still less 'predominance' in relation to
er sees. Its use seems rather to express the belief that St. Peter
sessed a certain 'right to take the initiative',[4] a belief not incon-
ent with the conclusions already reached about the significance of
evidence supplied by the New Testament. Thus if we render the
rd 'primacy' we must bear this sense in mind. Cornelius, as we

It is in connexion with the process of verification of Cornelius' claim to be the
bishop of Rome that we must read *Ep*. 48, 3. ed. cit., p. 607: 'ut te (sc. Corne-
a) collegae nostri et communicationem tuam id est catholicae ecclesiae unitatem
ter et caritatem probarent firmiter et tenerent'. It may be noted that some MSS.
t 'id est'.

'Sed primatus Petro datur'. This is the reading of Bévenot's Primacy text, *op*.
p. 40.

De bono patientiae, 19. ed. cit., p. 411: 'Esau . . . primatus suos per impatien-
a lentis amisit', *Ep*. 73, 25, ed. cit., p. 798: 'Esau primatus suos inde perdiderit'.
lently Cyprian had Heb. XII, 16, in mind.

That this is the true sense of 'primatum' here receives some support from
71, 3. ed. cit., p. 773, where he writes: 'Nam nec Petrus quem primum Dominus
it et super quem aedificavit ecclesiam suam, cum secum Paulus de circum-
ne postmodum disceptaret, vindicavit sibi instanter aut adroganter adsumpsit,
iceret se primatum tenere et obtemperari a novellis et posteris sibi potius
tere . . .' Cyprian does not reject the view that St. Peter held the 'primatus'.
that he denies is that St. Peter did not appeal to his possession of it to justify a
and for obedience. Yet if 'primatus' at this time really denoted a 'juridical
acy', it is difficult to see how St. Peter could have refrained in Cyprian's view
insisting on his authority.

2

have said, was confronted by a recalcitrant group among the Rom
presbyters, who were claiming, and in view of prevalent custom
without some show of justice, that the presbyterate had the right
determine questions of discipline. Cyprian's purpose therefore v
to prove that in virtue of a power of disciplinary judgment believ
to have been entrusted by our Lord to St. Peter, the bishop,
addition to his recognized liturgical privileges, inherited a like pow
The clue to a right understanding of this part of his argument wo
seem therefore to lie in the gradual acquisition of disciplin
authority by the episcopate at the expense of the presbyterate, and
the parallel development by which the presbyterate in losing
judicial prerogatives was slowly acquiring most of the liturg
privileges hitherto confined to the episcopate.[1]

We may now direct our attention to two other passages in Cypria
writings of this period where reference to the Roman see appears.
a letter addressed to Cornelius he states that:

'We know that we have implored persons journeying (to Ror
alone . . . to acknowledge and hold fast to the womb and root of
Catholic Church'.[2]

At first sight this might seem to presuppose the view that
Roman see is the only source of the Church's being. Yet this is m
than doubtful. The letter was written when the proof of the valic
of Cornelius' election had only just been received and at a time wl
in some quarters certain doubts may have still remained. Cypr
appears therefore only to express his concern lest through ignora
or lack of certainty some Africans should mistake the false for
true episcopate at Rome.

In the second of these passages, which also occurs in a lette
Cornelius, Cyprian writes:

'As if it were not enough for these (schismatics, i.e. the laxist pa

---

[1] On this development, see above, pp. 142 ff., 153 f.

[2] *Ep.* 48, 3. ed. cit., p. 607: 'nos enim singulis navigantibus . . .
scimus hortatos esse ut ecclesiae catholicae matricem et radicem agnosceren
tenerent'.
Other examples of 'matrix' in Cyprian are *Ep.* 71, 2. ed. cit., p. 772, where
allusion is to Catholic baptism; *De Unitate*, 23. ed. cit., p. 231, in a metapho
passage referring to the local Roman church. The following instances of 'ra
may be noted: *Ep.* 45, 1. ed. cit., p. 600, used of the Church generally, with
ticular reference to the relations of a Roman schismatic with the local Roman chu
Ep. 73, 2. ed. cit., p. 779: 'nos autem qui ecclesiae unius caput et radicem tener
in which he appears to be speaking of the rightful bishop of Rome, in a pas
repudiating Novatian's claim.

t Carthage) . . . to have set up for themselves outside, apart from he Church and against the Church, a conventicle of a wretched sect . . on the top of all that has happened up till now, they have the ffrontery, after a bishop has been provided for them by sectarians, to ail off to the very *cathedra* of Peter, and to take with them letters from chismatics and those who are no Christians to the "original" church, hence the one society of bishops has been derived, without reflecting hat the Romans are the people whose faith is praised in the words of he apostle, men to whom an erring faith has no access'.[1]

At first sight this is a very impressive description of the Roman hurch. Yet it is important to bear in mind that Cyprian is chiefly reoccupied with anxiety lest any countenance whatever should be iven to the Carthaginian schismatics. This latter party does not seem) have appealed to the Roman see against the rejection of their stand- oint by the synod of Carthage, but simply to have followed the ormal procedure of sending letters to foreign churches notifying them f the election of Fortunatus[2] in the place of Cyprian, who was egarded as having forfeited his right to be bishop. In speaking of the hurch of Rome as the 'original' church,[3] Cyprian makes no notice- ble advance on the language of Tertullian;[4] he is simply alluding to ne usual theory of the origin of the episcopate in western churches, hich identified its apostolic source with St. Peter.[5] Yet it would be ifficult to deny that Cyprian acknowledges his profound respect for ne Roman see, and by phrases such as these materially contributed, lough perhaps unconsciously, to a fuller recognition of it as the rimatial see of Christendom. Such an expression as the *cathedra etri* could not fail to appeal to the imagination even of the least naginative.

Yet before long even Cyprian was to find himself in serious

---

[1] *Ep.* 59, 14. ed. cit., p. 683 : '. . . navigare audent et ad Petri cathedram adque l ecclesiam principalem, unde unitas sacerdotalis exorta est'. The allusion to the ords of the apostle' is probably to Rom. 1, 8.

[2] *Ibid.*, 9. ed. cit., p. 676. Felicissimus who headed the mission to Cornelius ld acted as deacon to Novatus, before the departure of the latter to Rome; *Ep.* , 2. ed. cit., p. 618. In reporting the election of the anti-bishop Fortunatus, his pporters acted precisely as Cornelius' and Novatian's respective parties had done, e above, p. 160.

[3] *Ibid.*, 14. 'ecclesiam principalem'. Possibly the 'authentic' as opposed to hismatic church. For the significance of 'principalis' and its cognates, see above, 112, n. 2.

[4] See above, p. 146 f.

[5] Cf. Irenaeus, *Adv. haer.* 3, 3, 2 ; Cyprian, *De unitate*, 5.

disagreement with the Roman disciplinary tradition. To explain how this came about we must resume our account of the events which followed the establishment of Cornelius.

The elevation of Gallus to the principate appears to have occasioned a revival of Decius' policy of compulsory conformity with the State religion. Among the victims on this occasion was Cornelius himself. He was banished to Centum-cellae where he died, possibly from the effect of ill-treatment.[1] After a brief interval Lucius was elected his successor, only to be banished in his turn. The successful revolt of Aemilian[2] was probably responsible for a prompt revision of his sentence, though he survived his return only by a few weeks. The date of his death is the first of a series of papal *obits* to be recorded in the *Depositiones episcoporum*.[3]

The new Pope, Stephen I, had been Lucius' archdeacon and like him was of Roman origin.[4] His pontificate is chiefly remarkable for his treatment of an appeal addressed to him by the churches of Leon and Merida, and for his controversy with Cyprian on the validity of schismatic baptism. Normally these two affairs are treated in isolation from one another. We shall, however, attempt to show that there is in fact a close connexion, which has not generally been observed.

It may fairly be conjectured that the schism created by the support given by the distinguished personality of Novatian to a rigorous treatment of the lapsed did not quickly disappear. For a time at least his influence, in spite of all that Cyprian might write against him, continued, and even in some degree may have come to overshadow the less distinguished *auctoritas* of Cornelius. The problem which faced the latter, namely of restoring unity within the Roman church, must

[1] Although Cyprian, *Ep.* 61, 3. ed. cit., p. 696, cf. *Ep.*, 67, 6. ed. cit., p. 747 describes Cornelius as a martyr, we cannot be certain that he is not using the term in its general sense. *Cat. Lib.* Vita Cornelii, reads : 'cum gloria dormitionem accepit' and in his sepulchral inscription 'martyr' is clearly a later addition. His remains were subsequently translated to the cemetery of the *Gens Cornelia* near the papal crypt in the cemetery of Callistus.

[2] Bury, J. B., in his edition of Gibbon, *Decline* (1929), vol. i, p. 272, gives May–June to September, 253, for the reign of Aemilian. His concessions to the Senate probably led to a stricter application of the Decian edict.

[3] *Cat. Lib.* and *Lib. Pont.* assign three years and a few months to his pontificate in error. The correct date of his death, March 5, 254, appears in the *Depositiones* M.G.H. *Auct. antiqu.*, vol. ix, *Chron. min.*, vol. i, p. 70. Cf. Lietzmann, H., *Petrus und Paulus in Rom*[2], p. 9.

[4] *Lib. Pont.* ed. cit. vol. i, p. 153 f. Vitae Lucii et Stephani. For the view expressed here about the character of the controversy between Stephen I and Cyprian, the present writer is indebted to Zernov, N., in *C.Q.R.* Jan. 1934, vol. cxvii, p. 304.

therefore have remained under his successors Lucius and Stephen. This may help to explain an apparent inconsistency in Stephen's policy, namely his seeming indifference to the progress of Novatianism in the Roman *colonia* of Arles.[1] Faced by a formidable minority, he may have believed that the utmost possible tolerance of a different standpoint should be allowed, and that the return of schismatics to the Church should be facilitated by every legitimate means.

Cyprian is our sole informant regarding the Arelatine situation.[2] Both he and Stephen, it appears, had received from Faustinus of Lyons and from other Gaulish bishops letters showing that Marcian of Arles had adopted an extreme form of Novatianism and had abandoned the communion of the Catholic episcopate.[3] He writes therefore to Stephen urging him to represent to the bishops of Gaul that Marcian should be excommunicated forthwith,[4] and also to the church of Arles instructing them that their bishop has been replaced by another, who will supply spiritual needs of the lapsed.[5] If Stephen acts rightly, the writer adds, he will be upholding the glorious reputation of his predecessors; and once action has been taken, he should report the name of the bishop who has been substituted for Marcian so that the church of Carthage may know with whom to communicate.

What was the sequel to Cyprian's action? In view of the absence of reference to the affair in any of his surviving letters, it seems highly probable that Stephen, faced with the problems created by Novatianism in his own church, preferred to leave the Gaulish churches to settle their own difficulties.

[1] It received this status probably under Augustus, see *Dict. Greek and Roman Biog.*, vol. i, p. 196b.

[2] *Ep.* 68. ed. cit., p. 744 ff.

[3] *Ibid.*, 1. That Marcian's Novatianism took an extreme form appears to be implied by 'sine spe pacis et communicationis'. The Roman Novatianists were willing at least to give communion *in articulo mortis*. Marcian had carried the rigorism of his master a stage further.

[4] That he had not yet been excommunicated even by the bishops of Gaul seems to be implied by *ibid.*, 2, 'necdum a nobis abstentus' and *ibid.*, 4.

[5] The phrase 'abstento Marciano', *ibid.*, 3, need not imply that in Cyprian's view the right to excommunicate him rested with Stephen alone—in fact such a view seems to be excluded by *ibid.*, 4. Marcian is to be excommunicated by Stephen *and* the bishops of Gaul, and Stephen is to nominate his successor (presumably because the local church of Arles could not be trusted in the circumstances). Cyprian probably did not appreciate the nature of the precedent which he was thus creating; yet cf. Cornelius' action above, p. 161 n. 6. The fact that there existed between Rome and Arles a close political connexion would give Stephen reasonable opportunity for selecting a suitable candidate for the local church.

But it is also possible that by this time the question of the validi
of schismatic baptism had arisen, and that Stephen's attitude ha
already brought him into conflict with other churches. The usu
view is that he came into collision with Cyprian first and only sul
sequently with the Easterns.[1] Yet is this strictly correct? A passage i
the famous letter of Firmilian of Caesarea in Cappadocia[2] on tl
subject seems to imply that the friction between Stephen and tl
East preceded rather than followed his controversy with Cypriar
moreover the relative shortness of Stephen's pontificate[3] appears i
make it necessary to assign an early date to the beginning of the who
affair. We have already seen that there was some support to be foun
for Novatian in the eastern churches,[4] probably including Firmilian
own church, and it is possible that on the deaths of Cornelius an
Lucius, Novatian renewed his efforts to win their favour. Hence whe
Stephen initiated a policy of seeking to win over his rival's Roma

[1] E.g. Kidd, B. J., *History*, vol. i, p. 469 f.

[2] Ap. Cypr. *Epp.* No. 75. ed. cit. pp. 810–27. (Foɪ ɪne view that this documeɪ
is a north-African version of a Greek original, see Benson, *op. cit.*, pp. 372–7,
Note particularly § 25, p. 826: 'modo cum orientalibus, quod nec vos latere coɪ
fidimus, modo vobiscum qui in meridie estis'. Benson, *op. cit.*, p. 353, n. 6, argu
that the usual view is tenable. (1) Because that order is accepted by Eusebiu
(2) On account of Dionysius' statement in Eus. *H.E.* 7, 5, 4, ed. cit., p. 64
'ὡς οὐδὲ ἐκείνοις κοινωνήσων διὰ τὴν αὐτὴν ταύτην αἰτίαν', which he takes to ref
to an earlier collision with the African church on the same subject. (3) Becau
during the three years of Stephen's pontificate, Dionysius addressed to him on
one letter, while no less than three of his on the same topic belong to the single ye
of Stephen's successor. For an early view identical with that put forward in tl
text, see Dom Maran, *Vita Cypriani*, 29.

The following considerations are to be weighed as against Benson. (1) Even
Eusebius believed, as he appears to do, *H.E.* 7, 2, 3. ed. cit., p. 636–8, that tl
controversy began with a clash between Stephen and Cyprian, we cannot be certa
that he was correct. Not only was he very imperfectly informed as to Stephen
pontificate, of which he has very little to say, cf. *H.E.* 7, 5, 3. ed. cit., p. 640, b
we cannot always trust him to interpret his sources aright (see above on tl
second century Paschal controversy, p. 118 f.). (2) Dionysius, writing to Xystus I
ap. Eus. *H.E.* 7, 5, 4. ed. cit., p. 640, speaks of Stephen's letter to the Eastern
'ἐπεστάλκει μὲν οὖν πρότερον'. (3) The letters quoted by Eusebius from tl
Dionysian *corpus* are not necessarily exhaustive, in fact *H.E.* 7, 5, 3, p. 64
'δευτέραν . . . περὶ βαπτίσματος . . . ἐπιστολὴν' clearly shows that his letter
Xystus was not the first which Dionysius had written on this subject. It seems muɪ
more likely that Dionysius became acquainted with Stephen's controversy wi
Firmilian, at the beginning of Stephen's pontificate, but only *after* he had writtɪ
the letter quoted in *H.E.* 7, 5, 1 f. ed. cit., p. 638.

[3] Stephen died August 2, 257. Cf. Eus. *H.E.* 7, 2. ed. cit., p. 636: 'μησὶν . . . οɪ
ὅλοις ὀκτώ'.

[4] See above p. 161. Possibly there were some who persisted all along in regardiɪ
Novatian as the rightful bishop of Rome.

)porters by reaffirming the traditional Roman attitude towards
\ismatic baptism,[1] thereby acknowledging that of the Novatianists,
: anti-pope's eastern supporters would naturally express some
\lignation. To this Stephen's reply may well have been a threat
)ssibly not more) of excommunication.[2] Realizing that this would
"olve the severance of economic as well as spiritual relations, it is
t inconceivable that Firmilian felt bound to withdraw his protest,
)ugh he refrained for the time being from openly expressing his
lings.[3] Only so can we sufficiently explain the bitterness of his Car-
\ginian letter when at last the opportunity had come for showing his
\approval of the Roman policy in consequence of Cyprian's report.
Meanwhile a grave disciplinary problem had arisen in the West.
hat was to be done if a bishop was found guilty of apostasy; ought
to be deposed? In the course of a recent attempt in Spain to pro-
"e conformity with the State religion it seems that two bishops,
silides and Martial, whose sees were probably Leon-Astorga and
erida respectively, had compromised themselves in pagan prac-
es.[4] Subsequently Basilides had accepted penance and resigned his
\ice, apparently in the hope of being admitted to lay communion.[5]
\en changing his mind, as it seems, he had made his way to Rome
th the intention of procuring restoration.[6] Meanwhile the church of

---

For Callistus' policy and the question of whether or not this represented
traditional practice of the Roman church, see above, p. 131 f. Rufinus, *H.E.*
3 (Eus. *H.E.* ed. cit., p. 639), affirms that the traditional liberal practice was
\lorsed not by Stephen but by Cornelius. If Stephen was responsible for some
\ovation, it is scarcely conceivable that he could have said, as Cyprian alleges,
ihil innovetur nisi quod traditum est'. Had the contrary prevailed hitherto, it is
d to imagine that some evidence of local protest would not have survived.
* *Ep. Dionysii Alex.* ap. Eus. *H.E.* 7, 4. ed. cit., p. 640, in a letter addressed to
stus II, mentions that Stephen had written to him regarding the churches of
ia Minor, 'ὡς οὐδὲ ἐκείνοις κοινωνήσων'.
* It is clear from *Ep .Dion. Alex.* ap. Eus. *H.E.* 7, 5, 1 f., that the eastern churches
eed to recognize Stephen. Dionysius, however, does not say that they repudiated
)vatian's disciplinary standpoint.
* Cyprian, *Ep.* 67. ed. cit., p. 735 ff. In § 1 their crimes are described as 'idolo-
\riae' and 'nefandorum facinorum'; in § 6 he adds that according to the letters of
lix and Sabinus of Leon-Astorga, and another of Felix of Saragossa, 'Basilides
. in Deum blasphemaverit et se blasphemasse confessus sit', while 'Martialis
. praeter gentilium turpia et lutulenta convivia in collegio diu frequentata
filios in eodem collegio exterarum gentium more apud profana sepulchra
)ositos et alienigenis consepultos, actis etiam publice habitis apud procuratorem
cenarium obtemperasse se idololatriae et Christum negasse contestatus est'.
* *Ibid.*, 6.
* *Ibid.*, 5. Cyprian does not say that Stephen had actually acceded to his request,
)ugh the letters already received from Spain make this probable.

Leon-Astorga, or at least a section of it led by the presbyter Fel
had elected a new bishop for that see in the person of a certa
Sabinus. On hearing of the favour shown to Basilides by the Rom
church, the electors of the new bishop wrote to the see of Cartha
(and possibly to other churches) hoping to win its support.

Before describing the significance of Cyprian's reply, one or t
points deserve attention. In the first place, so far as the Spani
bishops are concerned, he represents that Basilides had voluntar
resigned;[1] of Martial's resignation, still less of his deposition, he sa
nothing. Even with Basilides it is not a case of a formal revision by t
Roman see of a verdict pronounced by a local church. In any eve
Martial appears to have succeeded in retaining his episcopate ar
hence had no need to appeal to Rome or to anyone else. Next, wheth
or not Stephen had actually acknowledged Basilides,[2] Cypri
evidently believed that he would do so, and held that, in view of O
Testament precedent,[3] violence would thereby be done, not merely
ecclesiastical but to divine law. It was this, and not any suppos
usurpation of authority on the part of Stephen, which roused h
indignation. Lastly, there is some reason to hold that in refusing
regard a lapsed bishop as *ipso facto* deposed, as Cyprian wishe
Stephen was upholding the traditional attitude of the Roman chur
to this question.[4]

The true significance of Cyprian's letter is that it marks the end
his patience with Stephen's policy, by which in the writer's opinio
the unanimity of bishops had long been seriously endangered. T
Spanish affair had finally convinced him that in spite of his earli
repudiation of Novatian and the loyalty which he owed to Corneliu
successor, he could hold his hand no longer. For in addition to t
question of the lapsed bishops, there was also the earlier proble

[1] *Ep.* 6.

[2] *Ibid.*, 5. Cyprian describes Basilides' journey to Rome thus: 'Romam perge
Stephanum collegam nostrum longe positum et gestae rei ac veritatis ignaru
fefellit, ut exambiret reponi se iniuste in episcopatum de quo fuerat iure depositu
This clear mention of Basilides' deposition contradicts the evidence about his volu
tary resignation in § 6. It seems likely that Cyprian was relying on inaccurate info
mation. As to the result of Basilides' 'appeal' to Stephen, the form of expressio
used by Cyprian does not necessarily imply more than awareness on his part th
such an 'appeal' had been made. His contention is that Basilides' apostasy ha
ipso facto caused him to lose his episcopal status. In any case he is careful
describe Stephen as a victim of ignorance or deception.

[3] Hebrew precedents as to the treatment of an unworthy or illegitimate pries
hood are cited in §§ 1–4.

[4] See above, p. 131 f.

reated by the recognition of the validity of schismatic baptism by the
oman see, of which Cyprian had been aware for some time. He had
efrained from mention of it in the hope that Stephen would go no
irther in the direction of compromise with schism. Now the report
f the Pope's action in the case of Basilides had finally shattered his
ost cherished ideal—the solidarity of the episcopate. Cyprian's dis-
ppointment is one of the tragedies of history, but there is a sense
erhaps in which it was inevitable.

Quite soon after Stephen's election, as it seems, the question
hether Novatianist baptism should be treated as valid or not had
een raised. Cyprian's personal decision[1] against validity, in spite of
ie Novatianist use of Catholic formulas, was based on the principle
at there can be no sacraments outside the one Church.[2] Yet he
akes it plain that in so deciding he is not expressing more than a
ersonal opinion, and implies that every bishop has a right to decide
e question for himself.[3] It was probably as a consequence of some
quiry that he first became acquainted with Stephen's policy in the
atter. Probably the Pope had argued, as no doubt Callistus had
one before him, that those who differed from the Church only on a
uestion of discipline and who otherwise shared the Church's faith
ught to be treated differently from those who were openly opposed to
at faith.[4] As we have seen, he had every reason for wishing to make
e widest possible concessions in facilitating the return of those who
pported his rival Novatian.[5] Cyprian, on the other hand, was faced
two mutually hostile rivals and may have believed that unity would
more speedily restored by a policy of more rigid exclusiveness.
In following it he could show that, at least in some measure, north-
frican tradition was on his side.[6] Yet outside the province of *Africa*

---

[1] *Ep.* 69, ed. cit., p. 749, addressed to a certain layman Magnus, perhaps a Roman
o had felt uneasy about the policy followed by Stephen.
[2] *Ibid.*, 1: 'dicimus omnes omnino haereticos et schismaticos nihil habere potes-
is ac iuris'. The Roman view was that schismatics enjoyed 'potestas' without 'ius'.
[3] *Ibid.*, 17: 'nemini praescribentes quominus statuat quod putat'.
[4] It seems from § 7 that Magnus had cited this argument.
[5] Probably Stephen's position locally was by now a good deal stronger than Cyprian's.
[6] In *Ep.* 71, 4. ed. cit., p. 774; *Ep.* 73, 3. ed. cit., p. 780, he alludes to his earliest
thority against validity, namely a synodical resolution adopted at Carthage
der Agrippinus, *c.* 213, to which Tertullian may also refer in *De baptismo*, 15
S.E.L. vol. xx, p. 213. Cf. *De pudicitia*, 19, ed. cit., p. 262. For further
pport of Cyprian's view see the anonymous author of *Adv. Novat. de lapsis*, 3,
. Cypr. *Op.* ed. cit., p. 55. It was also upheld by some churches in Asia Minor,
cording to Firmilian, ap. Cypr. *Epp.* No. 75, ed. cit., p. 823, and Dionysius Alex.

proconsularis, it seems, a more liberal view prevailed,[1] and awarenes
of divergence inevitably led to inquiries being addressed to the see c
Carthage on the subject. Eighteen Numidian bishops[2] and two fror
Mauretania[3] addressed Cyprian on different occasions, with th
result that a corporate expression of opinion against validity was give
by a synod held under his presidency.[4] Information about this decisio
was sent not only to the bishops of Numidia and Mauretania,[5] but t
Stephen as well.[6] It is likely that Cyprian in his turn was beginnin
to feel the need of Stephen's support in a rather delicate situation.
We are not surprised therefore to find that in writing to Rome h
insists that every individual bishop must be free to act according t
his own judgment.[8]

News of the reception of the Carthaginian mission there gav
occasion later for much criticism of Stephen's conduct on the pa
of Firmilian.[9] Yet in fairness it must be admitted that we have onl
the Cyprianic version of the affair and do not know what there was t
be said on the other side. Even if Stephen may have shown himse
unduly conscious of his position as occupant of the see of St. Peter,[1]
and perhaps insufficiently sympathetic towards the Cyprianic policy

Ep. ap. Eus. *H.E.* 7, 7, 5. ed. cit., p. 644, mentioning synods on the subject a
Iconium and Synada. Dionysius himself, however, states, *ibid.*, 7, 7, 4. ed. cit
that his predecessor Heraclas took the opposite view and evidently favoure
tolerance of diversity (§ 5). It would appear that when Jerome in *De vir. inl.* 6
ed. cit., p. 38, affirmed that Dionysius supported Cyprian, he was not quite exact

[1] This is clear from the large number of abstentions at Cyprian's synods. C
the anonymous author of *De Rebaptismate*, ap. Cypr. *Op.* ed. cit., p. 69 ff.

[2] Their names are mentioned in the address of *Ep.* 70. ed. cit., p. 706.

[3] See *Ep.* 71, ed. cit., p. 771 ff; *Sent .Episc.* ed. cit., p. 435. Cyprian's first rep
to Jubaianus is lost. Our *Ep.* 73. ed. cit., p. 778 ff., is his second letter on the subjec
It is probable from *Ep.* 71, 2, that validity had never been denied in Mauretania.

[4] The names of thirty bishops who took part in it are mentioned in *Ep.* 70, *ibi
p. 766.

[5] *Ibid.*

[6] *Ep.* 72. ed. cit., p. 775 ff. Soden, H., 'Der Streit zw. Rom und Carthago üb
die Ketzertaufe' in *Kgl. Preuss. Hist. Inst. in Rom*, vol. xii, 1909, argues that th
letter belongs to the second synod of eighty-seven bishops in 256. Yet the referen
(§ 1) to the letter to Quintus (*Ep.* 71) as 'nuper expressum', and to the synod a
'nuper' seems to link the first synod, *Ep.* 71 and *Ep.* 72 together.

[7] Just as earlier no doubt Cornelius had felt the need of Cyprian's support.

[8] Cf. *Ep.* 73, 26. ed. cit., p. 26, and *Sent. Episc.* ed. cit., p. 435 f.: 'neminel
iudicantes aut a iure communicationis aliquem si diversum senserit amoventes'.

[9] *Ep. Firmil.* 25. ap. Cypr. *Op.* ed. cit., p. 826.

[10] *Ibid.*, 17: 'qui sic de episcopatus sui loco gloriatur et se successionem Pet
tenere contendit' . . . 'qui per successionem cathedram Petri habere se praedicat
  tmay be that Firmilian is recalling expressions used by Stephen in his reply t
Cyprian's *Ep.* 72. ed. cit., p. 827.

ich he evidently treated as an arbitrary innovation, there is no reason
believe that the behaviour of the Carthaginian legates, judged
m the standpoint of tact and diplomacy, was wholly above censure.
owing only some of the facts, we should hesitate to pronounce
lgment. Moreover it is by no means impossible that the unhappy
acy of the Spanish affair and of Cyprian's rather rash conclusions
s in great measure responsible for a certain stiffness on the side
the Pope.[1] Finally it should be remembered that if Stephen had
nsented to change his attitude, he would have conceded at one
oke the correctness of the Novatianists' position, whose practice
s identical with that of Cyprian in the matter.[2] His choice there-
e may be said to have lain between resigning or retaining his see.
In such a situation it is not surprising that he offered little en-
uragement to Cyprian's legates, and that when they persisted in
manding his support, he gave instructions that they should be
used all hospitality.[3] The mission had only one course open, since
mmunion with Novatian was impossible, namely to return home.
esently an aggrieved but quite uncompromising letter reached
rthage from Stephen, as we may infer from the few sentences
ich have been preserved :

'If therefore any persons shall come over to you from any schism
atsoever, let no innovation be made contrary to the tradition, that
e hand be laid on them with a view to penance, for the schismatics
emselves do not baptize on their own part those who come over to
em from one another, but merely give them communion'.[4]

[1] See above. Cyprian in *Ep.* 72, 2. ed. cit., p. 776 f., had urged that the clergy
o had compromised themselves with schism should only be received back into
communion. Yet, as we have seen, this was also the attitude of Cornelius to
promoters of Novatianism ; see above, p. 161, n. 6.
[2] That some Novatianists were rebaptizing converts from the 'Great Church' is
ar from *Ep.* 73, 2. ed. cit., p. 779. At first sight Stephen, ap. Cypr. *Ep.* 74, 1. ed.
., p. 799, appears to deny this, yet 'alterutrum' should be noticed. Is it possible
t Stephen is alluding to an understanding which had been reached between the
vatianists and survivors of the earlier Hippolytean schism?
[3] The sole witness is Firmilian, ap. Cypr. *Op.* No. 75, 25.
[4] Cit. ap. Cypr. *Ep.* 74, 1, 2, 4. ed. cit., pp. 799, 802. 'si qui ergo a quacumque
eresi venient ad vos, nihil innovetur nisi quod traditum est, ut manus illis in-
natur in paenitentiam, cum ipsi haeretici proprie alterutrum ad se venientes non
ptizent, sed communicent tantum'. For the interpretation of this terse Roman
ctum, see Dölger in *Antike und Christentum* I, 1929, pp. 79, 319, and Weyman,
st. *Jahrb.*, vol. xlix, 1929, p. 323. It is to be noted that Stephen makes no dis-
ction between those who differ from the Church in matters of faith, and those
o differ only on a question of discipline, but says broadly 'a quacumque heresi'.
ephen like most of the Roman bishops had little patience with subtle distinctions.

Stephen's appeal is to the *paradosis*. No more and no less. But
insinuates not without some irony that certain Roman schismati
are in fact more faithful to tradition than Cyprian himself. To t
latter such a reply must have come as a serious shock. But its effe
was not only to destroy at a single blow his ideal unity; it serious
menaced his own status. How in such circumstances could he a
longer conduct himself as true bishop of Carthage and as the u
holder of episcopal government based on the impregnable Petri
origin and foundation of the episcopate?[1]

His failure to win the support of the Roman see now made it
the more urgent that he should find allies elsewhere, and strength
so far as he could his own position in relation to other Afric
churches. Probability suggests that he addressed a number of t
'greater sees', but of their replies, if any, only one has been preserve
the letter of Firmilian, bishop of Caesarea in Cappadocia.[2] Tl
document, to which we have already called attention, in spite of
outspoken criticism of Stephen's disciplinary policy,[3] at tim
bordering on invective, and of its attitude towards those who held
divergent view, bears a certain unwilling testimony to the prestige
the Papacy in his time.[4] If, however, as it has been said, 'he mak
short work' of the papal claims,[5] it is rather because Stephen h:
asserted no more than the fact that he as the legitimate bishop
Rome had a right to define what was the traditional custom of tl
Roman church;[6] of 'papal claims' such as later centuries were
experience, there is no trace. But it must surely be admitted that
arrogance and self-righteousness Firmilian was *facile princeps*.[7]

Encouraged by the Pope's attitude, a number of Cyprian's o
ponents in Africa now took the offensive, and roundly accused h:

[1] *Ep.* 33, 1. ed. cit., p. 566. Here the author frankly interprets Matt. XVI, 18
as the title deed of the episcopate as a whole. Cf. *Ep.* 43, 5. ed. cit., p. 594: 'cathed
una super Petrum Domini voce fundata'.

[2] Cit. ap. Cypr. *Epp.* No. 75, ed. cit., p. 810 ff.

[3] Not disdaining the tones of the bitterest irony, e.g. § 25. The letter as a whc
is in no sense a model of Christian charity.

[4] Notice, *ibid.*, 17: 'Petri . . . super quem fundamenta ecclesiae colloca
sunt . . . Stephanus qui per successionem cathedram Petri habere se praedica
It is noteworthy that Firmilian makes no attempt to refute his opponent or to de:
these statements.

[5] Kidd, B. J., *History*, vol. i, p. 470.

[6] See above, p. 175.

[7] Firmilian, *op. cit.*, § 24. His assertion that Stephen supposed that he cou
excommunicate anyone from the universal Church is a sheer imputation, even if
represents what Stephen may have believed.

behaving as a 'bishop of bishops', tyrannously seeking to impose
will on his fellow-bishops through fear of what might be the
come of resistance.[1] It was probably at this time that Cyprian
ught it wise to re-edit his *De unitate*, and by removing its allusions
the peculiar Petrine heritage of the Roman bishop, and sub-
uting phrases which expressed more fully his favourite doctrine
the co-ordination of the episcopate, to stimulate a greater desire
real unity among the African churches.[2] But it was also necessary
the same time to check the growing movement of opinion adverse
himself. With this object in view another general synod of the
rican provinces was assembled, at which eighty-six bishops under
prian's presidency reaffirmed his policy in regard to schismatic
otism.[3] Full of relief at this tactical success, Cyprian informed
tain of his correspondents among the bishops of its result, so
portant for himself.[4] But in each of these letters there was a
nificant omission. The writer utters not so much as a word against
: treatment of his legates at Rome following the previous synod.
rely there can be only one explanation of this remarkable silence.
prian was unwilling that his strained relations with Stephen should
widely known, since he realized that communion with the apos-
ic see of the West was an essential element in his theory of an
iscopate enjoying together a common Petrine inheritance.[5] It seems
it Stephen and Cyprian have shared each in his own way the same
merited fate—the misunderstanding of posterity. But Cyprian
more than Stephen deserves to rank as one who successfully

Cyprian's words quoted at the beginning of *Sent. episc.* ed. cit., p. 435 f., are
ally thought to refer to Stephen. It is, however, far more probable that he is
oting a charge made against himself. The synod appears to have made no
ntion of Stephen's behaviour, but the bishops present had good reason to fear
t opposition to Cyprian might have had serious consequences for their own
urches. Evidence of their material dependence on the see of Carthage is supplied
Epp. 2, 2; 62; 77; 79. For this reason Cyprian had reason to fear a lack of
nkness in the debate. His frequent insistence that bishops were free to follow
ir own line in disciplinary questions, e.g. in *Epp.* 55, 21; 69, 17; 72, 3; 73, 26,
uld scarcely have been so necessary if he had not given the impression that he
ned at enforcing conformity with his own practice by means of economic pressure.
[2] The re-edited text is the one referred to above, p. 166 ff, as the Hartel Text, ed.
.rtel, p. 209. The changes are in cc. 4 and 5.
[3] *Sent. episc.* ed. cit., p. 435 ff.
[4] *Epp.* 73 and 74. ed. cit., p. 778 ff., 799 ff. Cyprian did not hesitate to criticize
ephen privately, e.g. *Ep.* 74, 1.
[5] *De unitate*, 5. ed. cit., p. 214: 'episcopatus unus est cuius a singulis in solidum
rs tenetur'. Cf. *Epp.* 66, 8. ed. cit., p. 733; 68, 3, p. 746 and note 311.

vindicated his primacy over other bishops and who testified b
significant silence to the importance of the verdict of the see of Rc
in the ordering of the Church.

IX

Yet if Stephen's pontificate had been troubled by continu
schism within his church and controversy without, it remained larg
undisturbed by conflict with the State. His successor Xystus II v
less fortunate. The reigning Emperor Valerian, faced like Decius
the menace of hostile invasion from the East, revived his predecesse
religious policy in his later years.[1] Cyprian and Dionysius of Al
andria suffered banishment (257),[2] and in the following year
Roman church in the person of its higher clergy felt the extre
rigour of the law. In a single day, August 6, 258, there perished P
Xystus and four of his deacons.[3] Three days later came the pass
of the famous archdeacon Laurence, and at about the same time
remaining two members of the diaconal college were put to deat
During the following month Cyprian was crowned with martyrdor
For eleven months the Roman see was left desolate. Stunned by th
blows, not till the ill-fated Emperor had himself become an ig
minious prisoner of the Persians did the church of the capital ne
itself to elect a new chief pastor.

Its choice fell upon the presbyter Dionysius,[6] whose reign has so
ecclesiological interest, already mentioned,[7] but is also remarkable
the light which it throws on the relations of the sees of Rome a
Alexandria. This is supplied chiefly by what is known of the cc
respondence of the two bishops,[8] both named Dionysius, arising c

[1] *Acta proconsularia* ap. *Cypr. Op.*, pt. 3. ed. cit., p. cx. On the eastern mena
see Gibbon, *Decline*, ed. Bury, J. B. (1929), p. 289 ff.

[2] *Ibid.*, and Eus. *H.E.* 7, 11. ed. cit., p. 654 ff.

[3] This was a consequence of a new edict imposing the death penalty, the ter
of which are given in Cyprian, *Ep.* 80, 1. ed. cit., p. 839 f. The *Depositic
Martyrum, M.G.H. Auct. antiqu.*, vol. ix, *Chron. min.*, vol. i, p. 71, assigns
August Xystus, buried in the cemetery of Callistus, together with Agapetus a
Felicissimus, buried in the cemetery of Praetextatus; the *Liber Pontificalis*. ed. c
vol. i, p. 155, supplies the names of two other deacons. As to the effect of th
executions on the Roman church, see above, p. 153 f.

[4] *Lib. pont.*, *ibid.*

[5] *Acta proc.* ap. *Cypr. Op.*, p. cxi ff. Cf. *Vita Cypr.*, *ibid.*, p. cvi ff.

[6] *Lib. pont.* ed. cit., vol. i, p. 157.

[7] See above, p. 154.

[8] Eus. *H.E.* 7, 26, 1; Athan. *De sent. Dion.*, *M.P.G.* 25, 479; id. *De decr
M.P.G.* 25, 459; id., *De synodis, M.P.G.* 26, 770; Basil, *Ep.* 9; id., *De Spiritu S.*

f the success achieved by the teaching of Sabellius, at one time almost
ominant in the church of Rome,[1] but now, it seems, highly popular
ɪ his native country.[2] Uneasy at its progress, Dionysius of Alex-
ɪndria had already sent a word of warning to Pope Xystus,[3] but it was
ɪot till his return from banishment under the more benevolent regime
f Gallienus that he felt able decisively to intervene.[4] The churches
ʰhich were the objects of his criticism appealed against his teaching
ɔ the *paradosis* of 'superior origin' found at Rome,[5] whereupon
ɪe Pope assembled his presbyterate to examine the doctrine con-
ɪained in the documents forwarded to him by Dionysius' opponents.[6]
ʰhe outcome of this was that the bishop of Alexandria received an
ɪvitation from Rome to explain his position more precisely, together
ʲith a concise statement of the official Roman doctrine.[7] The state-
ɪent is highly characteristic of the mind of the Roman church in all
ɔctrinal questions; a direct appeal to an inherited *paradosis*, enforced
ʲy relevant quotation from Holy Scripture, and apparent indifference
ɔ verbal contradiction. It is essentially the formulation, not of a
peculative theologian, but of a 'plain man'.[8]

The election of Pope Dionysius coincided with the beginning of
ome forty years of peaceful relations between the Church and the
ʀoman State, of which the rescript of the Emperor Gallienus to
)ionysius of Alexandria and other Egyptian bishops authorizing them
ɔ resume occupation of all buildings dedicated to the Christian *cultus*,
lienated in the periods of persecution, is a signal example.[9] It is
ɪnnecessary to assign any special motive to the imperial bounty,
•ther than a desire to win a greater measure of public support
gainst his numerous rivals. A less favourable estimate of his character
ʲould ascribe it to a distaste for problems of administration, or to a
ɪerveless indolence.

---

[1] See above, p. 129 f.

[2] The Libyan Pentapolis, i.e. Cyrene, Berenice, Arsinöe, Ptolemais, Sozusa.

[3] Eus. *H.E.* 7, 6. ed. cit., vol. ii, p. 642.

[4] Athan. *De sent. Dion.* 5.   [5] 'Potiorem principalitatem', see above, p. 112 f.

[6] Athan. *De synodis*, 43.

[7] *Ep. Dion. Rom.* ap. Athan. *De decretis*, 26. A fragment only was addressed to the
Church of Alexandria; id., *De sent. Dion.* 13, mentions a personal letter from the
Pope to the bishop. The Alexandrine sent an Ἔλεγχος καὶ ἀπολογία contained in
our books, *ibid.*, 17.

[8] See Harnack, A., *Lehrbuch d. Dogmengesch.*⁴, vol. i, p. 771 ff., where he compares this document to Leo's letter to Flavian, JK 423, and to Agatho's letter to
he Emperor, JE 2109. See below, pp. 307, 365.

[9] The rescript is preserved in Eus. *H.E.* 7, 13, ed. cit., p. 666.

Edicts of real toleration, however, are still in the future. A maof imperial recognition scarcely less significant is the intervention
Aurelian on the side of the opponents of Paul the Samosatene, an
his assignment of the cathedral church of Antioch 'to those with whothe bishops of the "sect", in Italy and the city of Rome, were i
correspondence'.[1] The bishop of Rome in question was Felix I, whos
chief claim to notice is that in the course of the next century and
half he came to be accounted the putative author of a doctrintreatise of Apollinarian origin.[2] Yet even the fathering of pseudony
mous eastern writings on the Papacy may be regarded by some as
direct if undesirable testimony to its prestige.

The two Popes who followed, Eutychian and Gaius, have left n
deep impression on the memory of history, and it is only with th
episcopate of Marcellinus that the Roman church can once mor
usefully claim our attention. His reign is distinguished by its coin
cidence with the most systematic attempt to destroy Christianit
which the Roman State ever essayed, and by his own ignoble conduc
under persecution, of which evidence has been preserved only by
remarkable vicissitude of history. It is to the nature and extent of tha
attempt, as well as to its far-reaching results, that we shall turn ou
attention in the following lecture.

[1] Eus. *H.E.* 7, 30, 19. ed. cit., p. 714.
[2] In spite of the fact that Jaffé-Kaltenbrunner, *Reg. pont. rom.*, vol. i, p. 2
includes this among the genuine papal letters, there can be no doubt at all that it
pseudonymous. By the time of Cyril of Alexandria it was certainly being quote
as an actual letter of Pope Felix I (see his *Apol. c. Orient.*, Anath. 4. *M.P.G.* 7(
343), and was so cited by the Alexandrine presbyter Peter at the first council
Ephesus, Mansi, *Concilia*, vol. iv, 1183 ff. The use of forged documents by th
Apollinarians was first exposed by Leontius Byz. *Adv. fraud. Apoll. M.P.G.* 86,
1947–76. The Felician forgery was not detected till 553, see Mansi, *Concilia*, vo
viii, 821. Cf. Lietzmann, H., *Apollinaris und seine Schule*, 1904, p. 124.

IV

The Papacy and the Constantinian Autocracy

Ahi, Constantin, di quanto mal fu matre,
non la tua conversion, ma quella dote
che da te presse il primo ricco patre!
DANTE, *Inferno*, xix, 15.

ıke VI, 26. 'Woe unto you, when all men shall speak well of you
⸱ so did their fathers to the false prophets.'

At the outset of our study of the relations of the Church and the
pacy during the fourth century, it is most desirable to call atten-
n to two important developments, one affecting the character
the Church as a universal society, the other the organization of the
al community, both interacting on each other, and in various
pects modifying the relation of the Roman church to other
ırches. In the first place we must recall that although there are
eady evident signs in the preceding century of the growth of a
nmon mind between local churches in regard to questions of
ctrine and discipline, and even, as we have seen, about the source
m which decisions on disputed points were rightly to be sought, it
qually clear that like the *civitas* itself in the quasi-federal organiza-
n of the pre-Diocletianic Empire, the local church of the *civitas*
nained to some extent an independent unit, and in consequence
stions were usually settled locally in the *paroechia* affected. As
third century proceeded, this 'parochialism' began to give way to
ider outlook, yet of regular 'inter-parochial' organization there is
le or no sign. Cyprian indeed gathered synods of bishops, but he
so only to meet an immediate need.[1] Everywhere there are the
ns of *ex tempore* improvisation. Yet future developments were
eady being foreshadowed. Thus Pope Cornelius 'provided' suc-
sors somewhere in Italy to the consecrators of his rival Novatian.[2]
apion of Antioch and Dionysius of Alexandria made decisions for
ırches other than their own and appear to have expected them to be
yed.[3] It remains, however, something of a paradox that, so far as
evidence goes, if the interpretation placed here on the action of

---

[1] See above, p. 174 ff. [2] See above, p. 161, n. 6.
[3] See Eus. *H.E.* 6, 12, 4. ed. cit., p. 544; id., *ibid.*, 7, 6. ed. cit., p. 642.

Victor I and Stephen I is correct, the Roman see seems if anyth
to have been somewhat behind the other two great sees in exert
authority of this kind.

From this it would appear that those who are seeking evidence
the exercise of universal jurisdiction on the part of the Papacy in t
pre-Nicene period are after all on the trail of a chimaera. The em
gence of an accepted view about the extent of the Roman se
authority lags slightly behind a parallel development in the Churc
self-consciousness. It is only when the Church has begun graduall
abandon its primitive 'parochial' outlook, and under sheer press
of circumstances to face the consequence of the new relation betw
itself and the Empire, that it begins to create the necessary oecume
cal machinery in order to meet an oecumenical Empire on eq
terms.

An important by-product of this process is seen in the grad
formulation by the Church of its own universal law. Just as it
been found necessary to meet the varied attacks of false teaching,
only with an oral *paradosis*, authentically apostolic, but with the do
mentary evidence of recognized Christian writings, so to equip
Church for its new oecumenical function something more than
written local or even general 'custom' was demanded. The fou
century, however, shows us no more than the beginning of this p
cess. Hence it has to be remembered that at the time of the cou
of Nicaea the idea of a code of ecclesiastical law of universal vali
is still in the future.

In the second place we have to notice an important change tak
place in the organization of the local community. We have alre
seen how towards the middle of the third century the bishop
beginning to lose that monopoly of liturgical functions which he
hitherto possessed.[1] No doubt deacons and even presbyters (at l
in baptism) had co-operated in liturgical acts, but for all that
bishop and the bishop alone remained the *sacerdos*. In conseque
however, of various circumstances, local expansion, persecution
the like, episcopal deputies were increasingly in demand. Thu
came about, perhaps at first as a temporary expedient and only l
as an established custom, that in Rome and elsewhere presbyter
some places (at least for a time) deacons, were being author
under certain exceptional circumstances to consecrate the Eucha

---

[1] See above, pp. 80, 138, 153.

Meanwhile the replacement of the primitive 'parochialism' by a
more oecumenical outlook was leading to recognition of the bishop
as the representative of the local church. His growing contact with
other churches tended naturally to endow his opinions with an enlarged prestige, and thus gradually to give him a prescriptive right to
a deciding voice in questions which earlier might have been regarded
as belonging primarily to the jurisdiction of the *presbyterium*.[1] In this
respect it is scarcely an exaggeration to say that the fourth century
witnessed something very much like an exchange of functions
between the episcopate and presbyterate in the local church.

This consideration has an important bearing on the question of the
expansion of papal authority. For in view of what has been said it is
as unreasonable to expect to find the bishop of Rome exercising jurisdiction, universal or otherwise, as to exclaim at its absence, during a
period in which the bishop's office was essentially doctrinal, litur-
ical and sacramental. Only when we see bishops generally beginning
to act as judges have we the right to expect similar evidence of the
Roman bishop exercising analogous authority. It is certainly not
lacking in the fourth century.

I

The period which now claims our attention includes a series of
events, which taken together constitute an historical crisis of such
magnitude and far-reaching effect that even to-day its consequences
are not yet fully exhausted. Among its causes will be found the unexpected and seemingly accidental acquisition of supreme power by
the Emperor Diocletian, who in spite of his obscure Dalmatian origin
appears to have been endowed with a more than ordinary share of
political foresight and common prudence. On account of his intimate
connexion with the latest and most severe persecution of the Church,
it has not always been easy even for the most impartial of ecclesiastical
historians to include in their portrayal of his character sufficient
recognition of the qualities of integrity and mildness, for which,
judged from a strictly objective standpoint, he would seem to have
been distinguished. Hence if he has been represented as a monster
of cruelty and sadistic vice, it is chiefly because legend has not

[1] It should be remembered that the bishop was in any case chairman of that body,
since monepiscopacy had been established.

scrupled to besmirch the memory of a strong and perhaps con scientious ruler.

To describe at length the nature of the constitutional and admin strative changes inaugurated during his regime does not of cour fall within the scope of our subject, although much might be writte of their influence on the future character and organization of tl Church. Here it is chiefly to his politico-religious policy that v must restrict our attention. How far this was envisaged at first eith by Diocletian, or by his colleagues in the principate, as necessari involving a war of extirpation against the universal Church may w be doubted; yet we can scarcely imagine that passive opposition even active hostility to any plan of imposing conformity to a pag cultus approved by the State, in view of experience already gain from previous attempts of a similar kind in the reigns of Decius ai Valerian, had not been in some measure anticipated by the imperi government from the first.

But while Decius and Valerian may have believed that such policy was demanded in order to extinguish possible *foci* of 'fif column' activities at home in the rear of the army defending tl Empire's life on the Gothic frontier, to Diocletian it must ha appeared at any rate at the outset much more as an essential eleme in the restoration of military discipline seriously weakened by tl indulgent administration of his immediate predecessors. So much least must be judged from the restriction of the scope of the fir Diocletianic edict to those engaged in active service with the army The extension of its application in the following year to the civil se vice showed that the movement for the restoration of discipline w being carried a stage further. This time, however, it became cle that the Christian society was regarded as the chief obstacle to satisfactory fulfilment of the official policy. A law was issued forma declaring all Christian assemblies illegal and ordering their proper and buildings to be confiscated or destroyed, and in addition measur more radical than any of those which had preceded required t surrender (*traditio*) and public destruction by fire of all Christi sacred literature.[2]

[1] The first of these anti-Christian measures appears to have been promulgat by Galerius: Eus. *H.E.* 8, 4, 3. ed. cit., p. 746.
[2] Eus. *H.E.* 8, 2, 4 f. Cf. Lactantius, *De morte pers.* 13, 1. *C.S.E.L.*, vol. xx p. 187.

Such extreme action against a not inconsiderable proportion of the population of the Empire could scarcely be expected not to provoke some active resistance. Spasmodic acts of sabotage[1] took place, and even in some provinces an actual military revolt.[2] These acts, however, only had the effect of driving the government still further in the direction of a policy of complete suppression, and to issue edicts requiring conformity to be extorted by means of imprisonment and even torture from those of the clergy who declined to conform to the pagan cultus. Finally, this time reviving the policy of Decius, proof of loyalty to the State religion was demanded of the whole population.[3] It should be noted that in none of these edicts was the penalty of death formally imposed. On the other hand, the possibility that it might be exacted on a parallel charge still remained open.[4]

If we ask how the Roman church fared under this regime, we find ourselves dependent on scattered and fragmentary information. From mutually independent sources,[5] however, it may be inferred that Pope Marcellinus together with a number of his clergy obtained immunity from further persecution by performing some gesture of outward conformity. Moreover, it would appear that in the eyes of Christians their offence was considerably aggravated by the surrender, doubtless under pressure, of a number of sacred books to the imperial authorities.

Legendary inventiveness used this unfortunate lapse as a source of edification by adding a sequel, in which Marcellinus was represented as repenting of his cowardice and expiating his offence by martyrdom. Thus at least the *Liber pontificalis*.[6] It is, however, unfortunate for his good reputation that there is some convincing, if somewhat obscure, evidence that a quite serious attempt was made to effect in his case a *damnatio memoriae*.

What actually happened may be inferred with some probability

---

[1] Lact. *op. cit.*, 13, 3 ; id., *ibid.*, 14.   [2] Eus. *H.E.* 8, 6, 8. ed. cit., p. 750.

[3] Eus. *Mart. Pal.* 3, 1. ed. cit., vol. ii, pt. 2, p. 910.

[4] Eus. *H.E.* 8, 2, 5, in referring to the edict mentions the penalty of imprisonment, but says nothing about death as a punishment. Probably Diocletian hoped to avoid its use, perhaps more from a motive of prudence than from considerations of humanity.

[5] Augustine, *C. litt. Petil.* 2, 92 (202). *C.S.E.L.* vol. lii, pt. ii, p. 125 ; id., *De unico baptismo*, 16, 27. ed. cit., p. 28 ; *Acta synod. Sinuessae*, Mansi, *Concilia*, vol. i, 1250, on which see Duchesne, *Lib. pont.*, vol. i, p. lxxi ff.

[6] Ed. cit., vol. i, p. 162.

from the significant testimony of the papal lists. The *Catalog.*
Liberianus includes his name with a regnal period from June 30, 29
to October 25, 304.[1] As this latter date coincides with Diocletian
Vicennalia in Rome, a time when the application of the law is like
to have been at its strictest, it is probable that he died a violen
death. Yet if his name actually appears in the *Depositio Episcoporu*
it is evidently a slip, for the date given shows that Marcellus his su
cessor and not Marcellinus is the person meant.[2] Moreover he
passed over in silence by the compiler of the *Martyrologium hierony*
mianum. Similarly in the *Index Catalogues*,[3] which as we have see
depend on an early, perhaps fourth-century, original, mention
made either of Marcellinus or of Marcellus, usually of the latte
but always with the regnal years of the former. It seems therefore n
impossible that those who knew what had happened did their best
exclude the name of Marcellinus from the annals of the Roma
church.[4] But the popular appeal of legendary romance is alwa
stronger than that of sober fact, and it was thus that the apostate wa
forgotten and the repentant martyr took his place.

On the death of Marcellinus the Roman see remained widowed fo
over a year. Meanwhile, as before, there followed in the wake o
persecution an array of disciplinary problems, more especially
this time a new offence against Christian loyalty, the crime o
traditio or handing over sacred books, had been created in con
sequence of the recent legislation. The newly elected Marcellus,
Roman presbyter, to judge from the evidence of a Damasine in
scription, soon showed himself a stern disciplinarian.[5] From a secon
inscription dedicated to his successor Eusebius[6] we also gather th
the measures taken by him were bitterly opposed by a certa
Heraclius, who perhaps for this reason ought to be reckoned
belonging to the pathetic line of anti-popes. In consequence of seriou
disorders resulting from the schism, Marcellus incurred the penal
of banishment.[7] In this way we can account for the singular parad

---

[1] *Cat. Lib.* Vita Marcellini.

[2] *M.G.H. Auct. antiqu.*, vol. ix, *Chron. min.*, vol. i, p. 70.

[3] *Lib. pont.* ed. cit., vol. i, p. 14 ff.

[4] Constantine I procured a similar condemnation of the memory of his form
colleagues, Maximian and Licinius, see below, p. 190, n. 1. The treatment of t
name of John Chrysostom early in the fifth century provides a further example
the adoption of the same procedure by the Church.

[5] *Damasi Epigr.* No. 48. ed. Ihm., p. 51.

[6] *Op. cit.*, No. 18, p. 25.   [7] *Op. cit., ibid.*

at the very fate which he probably intended for his predecessor rrowly missed Marcellus himself. It is clear that the regnal ars of Marcellinus as originally given in the Liberian Catalogue[1] .ve no room for his rigorist successor, and though the name Marcellus also appears, his regnal period has only been conciled with the dates already inserted by means of a makeshift eration.

The widespread confusion which befell Diocletian's 'new order ' er his resignation of the principate and the subsequent usurpation Maxentius, was probably responsible for a less rigorous application the 'conformity' laws. Thus it is far more likely that the banish- nt of Pope Eusebius was a police measure to check civil disturb- ces arising from divided counsels within the Roman church than rt of a deliberately anti-Christian policy on the part of the urper'.[2] How serious this division had become is suggested by e interval of two years which elapsed before a generally recognized ndidate for the vacancy was found in the person of Miltiades. Of brief but undisturbed pontificate of three and a half years it will time enough to speak when we watch the amazing and in some pects unhappy revolution which the Church underwent as a direct nsequence of the policy of general toleration under Constantine, once its benefactor, tyrant and evil genius.

Let us return for a moment to the secular background of events. e ancient capital of York, which holds an honoured place in the litical and ecclesiastical annals of this country, may claim with tice to be among the natural localities where supernatural issues ve been determined, in that it was in this city that the dying nperor Constantius I designated Constantine as his successor.[3] It is a choice of the son born to him by Helena his divorced wife in eference to his younger sons, whose more royal descent might ve recommended, if their youth had not forbidden their selection,

Vita Marcellini : 'ann. viii. m. iii, d. xxv'.

Not only did Maxentius with good reason cultivate friendly relations with the urch, in the face of strong opposit ion to his regime on the part of the pagan bility and senate, but he gave proof o f his friendship in a rescript requiring the toration of Church property. See Augustine, *Brev. collat. cum Donat.* 3, 34. S.E.L. vol liii, p. 84.

Anon. Auctor 2, 4 in *Fragm. Hist. Graec.* ed. Müller, vol. iv, p. 191 ff.; Zosimus, t. nov. 2, 9; Eus. *Vit. Const.* 1, 21. ed. cit., vol. i, p. 18; Lactantius, *De mort.* s. 24. *C.S.E.L.* vol. xxvii, part ii, b., p. 201; Aurel. Vict. *Caes.* 40, all imply that nstantine found his father on his death-bed.

a judgment which suffices to justify his place among the m[
prudent if not the more distinguished holders of the Rom[
principate.

Acclaimed Augustus by the loyal enthusiasm of his fathe[
legions, Constantine I nevertheless began his imperial career in t[
face of very considerable disadvantages. Thus, for example, it v[
highly improbable that either of the dominant partners in the dyarc[
created by Diocletian would readily acquiesce in his irregu[
elevation; Maximin Daza in the East, because he found hims[
once again face to face with an old rival, and Galerius in t[
West, who had intended the succession to Constantius for [
own favourite Severus. At present therefore Constantine had to [
content with receiving legal recognition, not as Augustus, but [
the subordinate rank of Caesar. But it soon became evident [
him, as it had to others, 'that if he wished to live, he m[
determine to reign'.[1]

For the moment, however, he was forestalled by the revolution[
creation as Caesar of Maxentius, son of the ex-Augustus Maximi[
who regardless of his solemn engagements with his former colleag[
Diocletian to remain in retirement took occasion by his so[
elevation himself to reassume the purple. Yet after all, from the po[
of view of Constantine, the pride of the aged but by no means inco[
petent Emperor proved a valuable ally. The revived ambition of t[
father fatally encouraged the innate indolence of the son and [
directly hastened the disappearance of the only serious rival [
Constantine's growing influence in the western provinces, furth[
testimony to which was presently given by Maximinian in his offer[
Constantine of his own daughter Fausta in marriage, together w[
the legal status of Augustus. Following the abortive Italian expediti[
of the Emperor Galerius, his hurried promotion of Licinius to eq[
rank with himself and his reluctant recognition of the claim [
sovereign power of Maximin Daza, in addition to the assumpti[
of Augustan rank by Maxentius, a bewildered empire found its[
the subject no longer of two only, but of six supreme masters. [
these Maximian was defeated and allowed to commit suicide [
Constantine two years later. Even so there still remained four to t[
his way to absolute and unrivalled authority.

It has been necessary to retell in brief the tangled story of imper[

[1] Gibbon, *Decline*, ed. Bury, J. B. (1929), vol. i, p. 430.

olitics during the five years which elapsed after the death of his
ather, Constantius I, in order to call attention to an important
lue for a right understanding of Constantine's religious policy,
specially of the motives which led him to accord toleration to
Christianity. But it must not be forgotten that in spite of the
wealth of praise which has been showered upon Constantine by
Christian historians and panegyrists, the real credit for being the
rst to cancel the Diocletianic programme of compulsory conformity
with the state religion probably should be given not to him, but
o Galerius.

The edict which was published on April 30, 311, was issued
riginally in the names of the four Augusti, Galerius, Maximin,
Constantine and Licinius, and in view of its importance for the
uture of Christianity deserves to be quoted in full:

'Among the various measures which we are constantly adopting
or the advantage and profit of the State, we had in truth formerly
urposed for our part to effect a general reformation according to
he ancient laws and common order of the Romans and specially to
nsure that even the Christians, who had abandoned the religion of
heir forefathers, should revert to a sound belief, since for some cause
uch wilfulness and such folly had attacked and possessed the said
Christians that they no longer followed the customs of the ancients,
which perchance their own ancestors had first established. On the
ontrary, in a spirit of caprice and self-pleasing, they made laws
or themselves to keep, and assembled together people of all kinds
ver a wide area. Finally, when we had issued a precise order that
hey should conform to the customs of the ancients, many were
educed to submission because of their peril, many too were dis-
ossessed. Since, however, the majority of them adhered to their
urpose, it became evident that while refusing the worship and duty
wed to the gods, they were not revering the god of the Christians
ither, in consideration of our most merciful kindliness and having
egard as well to our continual practice of granting pardon to all men,
we have decided that our most generous licence should be granted to
hem too, so that there may be Christians once again, and that they
may assemble their meetings, provided that they do not act contrary
o good order. We shall inform the judges about their procedure in
nother letter. So, according to this our licence, they will be bound
o pray their god for the safety of ourselves, of the State and their

own, that the State may be kept unharmed on all sides, and they ma
be able to live at peace in their homes'.[1]

In view of the 'prescriptions' there can be no doubt that this edi
possessed full legal force in all parts of the Empire. It recalls th
purpose and scope of earlier legislation on religious conformity an
specifies the obduracy of Christians as the only obstacle to i
execution. Of special interest is the opinion here expressed that th
welfare of the State depends on the fulfilment of religious obligatior
by every citizen. Thus the dilemma of Christians, who are said t
have been prevented by their own wilfulness from conforming to th
religious practices of the State, and by the law from following the
own, is to be resolved by permitting them to enjoy corporate existenc
provided that no breach of order is thereby created.[2] It can scarcel
escape notice that this legislation looks back to the early days of th
principate and confers on the Christian society almost precisely th
same privileges of exemption from the religious obligations impose
by the custom of the State and of corporate freedom as had bee
assigned by the earlier Emperors to the Jews, and that the conditio
on which it was granted, namely that no disorder should ensu

[1] The edict is given in full by Lactantius, *op. cit.*, 34. ed. cit., p. 212 ff., b
without the 'prescriptions'. These are to be supplied from the version provid
by Eusebius, *H.E.* 8, 17, 1 ff. ed. cit., pp. 790, 792, 794. Yet in his first edition
the *H.E.* Eusebius had mutilated them by the omission of the name and titles
Maximin Daza (perhaps also of Maxentius), while in the later (common) edition tl
name and titles of Licinius are also omitted. This is to be explained by the *damnat
memoriae* applied to them by the victorious Constantine. Eusebius, moreover, ha
not hesitated to tamper with the sense, apparently to support his own standpoin
For example, he renders 'multi etiam deturbati sunt', which may mean 'deprive
of property' or perhaps 'deterred', '$\pi\lambda\epsilon\hat{\iota}\sigma\tau\omega\iota$ $\delta\grave{\epsilon}$ $\tau\alpha\rho\alpha\chi\theta\acute{\epsilon}\nu\tau\epsilon\varsigma$ $\pi\alpha\nu\tau o\acute{\iota}o\upsilon\varsigma$ $\theta\alpha\nu\acute{\alpha}\tau o$
$\acute{\upsilon}\pi\acute{\epsilon}\phi\epsilon\rho o\nu$', which has the effect of heightening the penal character of the earli
laws, and consequently increasing the credit which he seeks to assign to his he
Constantine. Similarly 'conventicula sua componant' might mean 'build the
meeting places'; yet 'componere' in the sense of 'build' has only poetical authorit
and 'conventiculum' can as easily mean an 'assembly' as the place in which it
held (cf. Lactantius, *ibid.*, 48, 9. ed. cit., p. 232; Turner, C. H., *Eccl. occi
mon. iur. can.*, vol. i, p. 190a, 192a, note). Eusebius, however, boldly translate
'$\tau o\grave{\upsilon}\varsigma$ $o\check{\iota}\kappa o\upsilon\varsigma$ $\grave{\epsilon}\nu$ $o\hat{\iota}\varsigma$ $\sigma\upsilon\nu\acute{\eta}\gamma o\nu\tau o$ $\sigma\upsilon\nu\theta\hat{\omega}\sigma\iota\nu$'. Equally his rendering of 'disciplina' b
'$\acute{\epsilon}\pi\iota\sigma\tau\acute{\eta}\mu\eta$' instead of '$\epsilon\mathring{\upsilon}\tau\alpha\xi\acute{\iota}\alpha$' obscures the real character of the condition o
which the imperial 'indulgentia' was granted. The expression 'denuo si
Christiani' looks back to the quasi-legal status assigned to the Church by vario
third-century Emperors, such as Alexander Severus, Gallienus, and Aurelian ; s
above, pp. 127, 179.

[2] Notice, *ibid.*, ed. cit., p. 213, 'ita ut ne quid contra disciplinam agant'. F
evidence about the growth in this period of the sense of a religious obligation to tl
Divine and of monotheism, see Batiffol, P., *La paix constantinienne*, Excursus
Summus Deus, p. 188 ff.

alls the circumstances which had led to the occasional suspension
their privileges.[1]

The next two years witnessed the disappearance from the scene of
perial politics of both Galerius[2] and Maxentius, the latter as the
feated opponent of Constantine's occupation of the capital.[3] Six
onths later Maximin Daza in his turn was defeated by Licinius.[4]
eanwhile as undisputed master of the West, Constantine proceeded
turn the edict of 311 to good account within his own dominions.
we have seen, it had indeed accorded toleration to Christians, but
had apparently been silent as to their right to recover real estate
t during the period of compulsory conformity. Yet as Maxentius
d already returned confiscated property to the Roman church, so
nstantine now applied the same measure to other churches, at any
e in Africa.[5] Later, in concert with Licinius, who was paying a
ort visit to Milan to espouse his colleague's sister Constantia,[6] it
s further decided that such restoration was to be effected without
mpensation. It is probable, however, that the formal instructions
the subject, which we still possess, sometimes mistakenly described
the 'Edict of Milan', come from the hand not of Constantine but
cinius.[7] To a later age, and even to some of his contemporaries, it

See above, p. 70.

Lactantius, *op. cit.*, 33. ed. cit., p. 210 f.; Eusebius, *op. cit.*, 8, 16. ed. cit.,
. 788, 790.

Lact. *op. cit.*, 44. ed. cit., p. 223 f.; Eus. *op. cit.*, 9, 9. ed. cit., pp. 826, 828, 830.

Zosimus, *op. cit.*, 2, 17; Lact. *op. cit.*, 45–50, ed. cit., p. 225 ff.; Eus. *op. cit.*,
o, ed. cit., p. 838 ff.

This rescript is known only from its preservation by Eus. *H.E.* 10, 5, 15–17.
cit., vol. ii, pt. 2, p. 887. The fact that it follows after Eusebius' version of the
called 'Edict of Milan' is no reason for supposing that it was not published till
er March 313, as Seeck, O., *Regesten der K. u. P.*, 1919, p. 160, suggests. On
contrary, it is far more probable that Constantine issued decisions of this
t immediately after the fall of Maxentius in October, 312. After all, Maxentius
d already set a precedent by restoring church property to the church of Rome,
above, p. 187, n. 2. The allusion to τῇ ἐκκλησίᾳ τῇ καθολικῇ reflects the existence
rival claims to church property in North Africa and may owe something to the
luence of Miltiades.

Lact. *op. cit.*, 45, 1; 48, 2. ed. cit., pp. 225, 228.

Lactantius, *op. cit.*, 48. ed. cit., p. 228 ff., attributes a rescript to Licinius pub-
ed at Nicomedia, in which he refers (§ 4), 'prius scriptis ad officium tuum datis'
d (§ 7), 'certa antehac forma' to some earlier decision. This was in all probability a
cument defining an agreed policy adopted by Constantius and Licinius as to
e vexed question of the restoration of church property, about which, in our
w, the edict of Galerius of 311 had said nothing or at most was ambiguous.
e new rescript had the effect of removing all conditions limiting such restoration
), 'amotis omnibus condicionibus' (which Eusebius, *H.E.* 10, 5, 6. ed. cit.,
884, mistakenly renders, 'ἀφαιρεθεισῶν παντελῶς τῶν αἱρέσεων'), and was in

was almost unthinkable that such a mark of benevolence towards t
Church could have been to the initiative of any but the first Christi
Emperor. By such means was formed the legend of Constantine, t
ideal *Basileus*, a saga which in due time gave birth to a strange a
monstrous brood. Yet the Constantinian μῦθος was already in bei
before Eusebius laid down his pen.

The legacy of the now abandoned policy of the Diocletia
regime, however, was not confined to problems connected w
property. A more serious difficulty, and one which was to test t
diplomatic skill of Constantine to the utmost, was that created
the attitude of the rigorist party in the Church, particularly in Afri
towards those who in time of persecution to a greater or less degi
had conformed to the former imperial injunctions, and especia
towards the *traditores*, i.e. those who had been responsible for handi
over sacred books to the authorities. In the opinion of a major
of the African church such an act constituted a very grave form
apostasy and rendered the culprit liable to the most extreme ecclesi
tical sanctions; and if, as often happened, he was a bishop, it w
held in accordance with the rigorist standpoint generally prevalent
that region that his episcopal status was *ipso facto* void.[1]

News of disorder had evidently reached the Emperor soon after I
defeat of Maxentius, since to this period belongs a rescript of I
addressed to Caecilian, bishop of Carthage,[2] informing him about t
disposal of an imperial bounty to 'servants of the legitimate a
most holy catholic religion',[3] and observing that instructions h

this respect directly opposed to the policy of Maximin, who though loyal to t
edict of 311 in his rescript, as quoted by Eusebius, *H.E.* 9, 9a, 1–9. ed. cit., pp. 8
836, 838, addressed to the praetorian prefect Sabinus (cf. Sabinus' own edict a
Eus. *op. cit.*, 9, 1, 3–6. ed. cit., pp. 802, 804, omitted in Eusebius, *H.E.* 2nd ed
nevertheless actively discouraged the restoration or re-erection of Christ
buildings; see Eusebius, *op. cit.*, 9, 9a, 11. ed. cit., p. 838. Licinius' rescript gi
the appearance of being an official decision interspersed with explanatory not
Cf. Batiffol, *op. cit.*, p. 232–240. The absence of formal 'prescriptions' makes
most unlikely that it is a document possessing the full force of an imperial edi
and may well be traceable to the hand of Licinius alone (so Seeck, O., 'I
sogennante Edikt von Mailand' in *Zeitschr. f. KG.* vol. xii, 1891), for the issue
which Eusebius, by introducing a short preface from the hand of Constanti
op. cit., 10, 5, 1–3. ed. cit., p. 883 ff., attempted to procure the credit for his hero

[1] On the edict requiring 'traditio', see above, p. 184. For the view that for a
grave sin a cleric was reduced to lay communion, see above, p. 161, n. 6.

[2] Cit. ap. Eus. *H.E.* 10, 6, 1 ff. ed. cit., p. 890.

[3] *Ibid.*, 'ὑπηρετῶν τῆς ἐνθέσμου καὶ ἀγιωτάτης καθολικῆς θρησκείας', probabl
denoting the clergy and perhaps the bishops in particular. It is noteworthy tl
Hosius is first mentioned here in the capacity of the Emperor's confidential advi
for ecclesiastical affairs.

en given to the proconsul Anulinus and to the *vicarius* of the
rican provinces to check certain disturbances. Caecilian himself
s enjoined to bring any obdurate offenders to judgment before the
il courts.

Unfortunately for Constantine's project of a universal monarchy
pported by a united loyal Christendom, the recalcitrant Africans,
o declined allegiance to Caecilian as the ordinand of a bishop sus-
cted of the offence of *traditio*,[1] insisted on presenting an appeal to
e Emperor, urging him to appoint an impartial commission of
ulish bishops to judge between them and their catholic op-
ents.[2] The immediate sequel of this was a rescript addressed to
pe Miltiades,[3] instructing him with the bishops of Cologne, Autun,
d Arles as assessors to hear the case presented by either side of the
rican or Donatist controversy (as it later became known after the
me of the rigorist leader Donatus). In addition to the assessors,
iltiades, probably with Constantine's approval, assembled fifteen
shops from north and central Italy to assist him in judging the
se.[4] Thus a Gaulish commission under Miltiades' presidency had
come in effect an Italian synod. Its verdict went in favour of
ecilian, as we learn from Optatus, on the positive ground that
natus had confessedly rebaptized and admitted lapsed bishops to
nance, and on the negative one that real evidence against his
ponent's character was lacking.[5] Nothing daunted by this adverse
cision the importunate Donatus once more solicited the Emperor's
tervention. After a vain attempt to dispose of both claimants,[6] it

[1] See above, p. 184.
[2] The choice of bishops in Gaul to act as judges was perhaps due to the absence
any general persecution in those provinces. Cf. Optatus, *Lib. c. Don.* 1, 22.
S.E.L., vol. xxvi, p. 25 f. It is unfair to argue, as Augustine did, *Ep.* 88, 1.
S.E.L. vol. xxxiii, pt. 1, p. 407, that the Donatists were the first to invoke State
against their opponents. Actually they were only following the precedent
eady set by the appeal of the synod of Antioch to Aurelian.
[3] Cit. ap. Eus. *H.E.* 10, 5, 18 ff. ed. cit. p. 887 ff. Cf. *Ep. ad Chrestum*, ap.
s. *H.E.* 10, 5, 24. ed. cit., p. 889.
[4] *Ibid.*, 'ἡ ὑμετέρα στερρότης'. It appears that considerable latitude was left to
e Pope to determine the precise mode of procedure to be adopted. In such a case
e Emperor realized that he was on unfamiliar ground. Notice that in addressing
iltiades as 'τιμιώτατε' the Emperor assigns to him honorary rank as proconsul.
[5] The effect of Miltiades' action was to create a solid majority in favour of
holding Roman tradition about the questions in dispute. For the tradition on
baptism and the treatment of lapsed bishops, see above, p. 172 ff.
[6] Optatus, *op. cit.*, 1, 23 f. ed. cit., p. 23 f. The synod assembled in the Lateran
lace, which now makes its appearance in ecclesiastical history for the first time.
obably it had already been assigned to the Pope as an official residence. It is to

was decided to investigate the charges preferred against Caecilia
consecrator, Felix of Aptonga. Yet even when these were held to
groundless by the judgment of a presumably impartial civil tribun
the Donatists persisted in complaining that their case had
received full and adequate examination. Finally Constantine su
moned a representative gathering of western bishops to meet
Arles, which once more gave its verdict against them,[2] while maki
the concession that those who could prove that at their baptism th
had testified to their belief in the Trinity were to be admitted
communion by imposition of the hand alone; others who could
satisfy this test to be baptised *de novo*.[3] The members of the syn
conveyed their decisions to Pope Silvester I, who had succeed
Miltiades at the beginning of 314, and requested that if the Emper
approved, they should be made known through the Roman see to t
rest of the Church.[4]

It is unlikely that the idea of summoning such a council came fr
Miltiades himself, who must have regarded the verdict already pr
nounced at Rome against Donatism as sufficient. Indeed the let
addressed to the bishop of Syracuse clearly proves that on th
occasion it was Constantine himself who took the initiative.[5] T
execution of his plan for the restoration of 'good order' showed th

be noted that Miltiades speaks last as the presiding judge in accordance w
senatorial procedure. For an explanation of the lack of evidence against Caecilia
character, see Augustine, *Ep.* 43, 14. ed. cit., p. 96.

[1] The effect of Donatus' appeal was to cause both litigants to be detained,
op. cit., 1, 25 f. ed. cit., p. 27 f. In their absence, perhaps on the advice of t
Emperor, an attempt was made to procure the consecration of a candidate agreea
to both parties, but it was thwarted by Donatist obstinacy.

[2] The minutes of the trial of Felix are given in Optatus, *Opera*, App. II, A
purgationis Felicis, ed. cit., p. 197 ff. The words of Aelianus, *ibid.*, p. 203: 'Caesa
ita pietatem christianis exhibere dignantur, ut disciplinam corrumpi nolint',
most probably an allusion to the condition of tolerance laid down in the edict
311, 'ita ut ne quid contra disciplinam agant', on which see above, p. 189 f. n. 1
The absence of any allusion to the supposed edict of Milan strengthens the ca
against its existence. A second investigation was held in the following year with
similar result. Cf. Seeck, *op. cit.*, p. 163.

[3] Optatus, *Opera*, App. III. ed. cit., p. 206 f. For other texts, see Turner, C. F
Ecclesiae occid. mon. iur. ant. Tom. I, p. 381 ff, 1899. A letter from Constanti
summoning Chrestus, bishop of Syracuse, is preserved by Eusebius, *H.E.* 10, 5, 21
ed. cit., p. 888 f., which is remarkable, if as is probable Chrestus was at this tim
suffragan of the Roman see.

[4] Thus showing that the Roman see was regarded as the normal intermedia
of correspondence among the western churches. Cf. Cyprian's request to Stephe
above, p. 169.

[5] See above, n. 3.

e intended to make the already existing, Empire-wide Christian
ociety into an important instrument for supplying the necessary
ohesion between the various subject races of his dominions. For the
rst time representatives of no less than forty-four local churches[1]
aet together and—highly significant—at the bidding of the Emperor.[2]
Their synodal letter, already mentioned, which now claims our notice,
id not hesitate to express the regret of the writers at the absence of
ae Pope (who was actually represented by two presbyters and two
eacons), and their conviction that his presence would have lent
reater success to their labours, more weight to their verdict, deeper
oy to their gathering. The clause in which they agreed that his
bsence was explained by sufficiently serious reasons[3] is unfor-
anately mutilated of its conclusion, though as it stands it speaks
ignificantly of the honour of Rome as the throne of the Apostles and
ae place of their martyrdom.[4]

At this point follows a short paragraph explaining that the
ssembled bishops had taken the opportunity of their meeting to dis-
uss a number of disciplinary problems, which, though specially
ateresting to themselves, would in their opinion be regarded as
elevant to all.[5] The letter (according to the text given in the Vienna
Corpus) proceeds:

'It has been our good pleasure therefore in the presence of the
Holy Ghost and His angels, that in the existing state of peace (de
uiete praesenti) we should pronounce decisions on those matters
vhich were causing concern to each one of us: it has also pleased us
hat a letter should be written first by you, who hold the greater

---

[1] For their names and sees, including the bishops of York, London and (?)
Lincoln; see Turner, op. cit., p. 398 ff. It is to be noticed that the Roman legates
ppear in the fifth place in the series. It is highly probable that Marinus, bishop of
Arles, whose name appears first in the prescription of the letter, presided at the
ouncil; see Turner, op. cit., p. 381 b.

[2] Turner, ibid.

[3] Turner, op. cit., p. 382b, 'sed quoniam recedere a partibus illis minime
ootuisti . . .'. We can only conjecture that on this earlier occasion some internal
lisorder, such as had occurred under Popes Marcellus and Eusebius (see above,
o. 186), rendered his presence necessary in the capital. Thus accidentally, as it were, a
aluable precedent for absence from important synodical assemblies was established,
vhich in the fifth century was to provide Leo I with sufficient excuse for declining
o attend the council of Chalcedon. For Silvester's election, see M.G.H. Chron.
nin., vol. i, p. 76.

[4] The passage also shows signs of corruption. Turner, op. cit., p. 382b, con-
ectures 'apostolorum corpora usque hodie sedent'.

[5] Optatus, Opera, app. III, ed. cit., p. 206 f.

dioceses (*qui maiores dioceses tenes*), to be conveyed by you especial
to all. But as to the nature of our opinions, we have added somewh
to the letter of our humility'.[1]

The text as it stands, being evidently corrupt in more than o
place, even in the Vienna text defies a satisfactory translation, ar
has thus given rise to a number of ingenious emendations. Leavir
aside minor points, we may proceed directly to the consideration
the phrase 'you who hold the greater dioceses', usually taken to ref
to Silvester. An obvious difficulty here arises from the improbabili
that any bishop, even the bishop of Rome, could be described at th
time as 'holding a "diocese" '. The first clue therefore to a bett
and probably the only correct interpretation of this elusive expressic
lies in taking the word 'diocese' in its contemporary meaning of
civil circumscription. Following this line of thought Turner has pr
posed a very attractive emendation (*annuente qui maiores dioces
tenet*) which gives the simple rendering 'with the approval of hi
who holds the greater dioceses',[2] an intelligible phrase and a
accurate description, yet not of Silvester, but of Constantine himsel

In any case the unemended text provides a highly insecure bas
for the view sometimes held that the fathers of Arles bear witness to
current belief that an extensive sphere of authority was enjoyed b
the Roman see.

On the other hand, it may be remarked that a further emendatio
(*quasi te praesente*), proposed by the same editor for the irrelevar
phrase 'in the existing state of peace' (*de quiete praesenti*), gives th
following highly satisfactory rendering :

'It has been our good pleasure . . . that we should pronounc
decisions as though you yourself were present . . .'[3]

If this be accepted, it is not difficult to see in these words som
further confirmation of our hypothesis that even in the pre-Nicen

---

[1] Optatus, *Opera*, p. 207 : 'placuit ergo praesente spiritu sancto et angelis eius, ut e
his, quae singulos quoque movebant, iudicare proferremus de quiete praesenti; placu
etiam antea scribi ad te, qui maiores dioeceses tenes, per te potissimum omnibu
insinuari'. 'et angelis eius' looks suspicious. The *Codex Novariensis* reads 'prae
sentibus patribus sanctis evangelistae eiusdem'. It is tempting to read for 'angeli:
'evangeliis', explaining the error by haplography.

[2] *Cod. Par. lat.* 12097 reads : 'placuit etiam antequam ante qui maiores dioecesec
tenes . . .' *Cod. Col. biblioth. cap. ccxii* gives a fragment of the letter and read
'antiqui diocisis'. *Cod. Novar. biblioth. cap. xxx* reads 'ante' omitting the res
Turner, *op. cit.*, p. 383b, proposes the emendation mentioned in the text.

[3] Turner, *op. cit.*, *ibid.*: 'Placuit . . . ut . . . iudicia proferremus quasi t
praesente'.

riod, at least in the West, the Roman see was regarded as qualified
some sense to give a decisive opinion on disputed questions of
ctrine and discipline.

'He who held the greater dioceses' was evidently at this stage pre-
red to allow the Church a considerable degree of independence,
least so long as he happened to be in sympathy with its prevailing
tlook.[1] But if it appeared to him at any time that the Church's
cisions were in need of amendment, Constantine was not one to
sitate in taking the necessary steps to that end. Yet in view of his
bsequent treatment of the Donatists,[2] the favour originally shown
Catholics can scarcely be regarded as prompted by any but purely
litical motives.

II

It was not till ten years after the council of Arles, however, that by
 final defeat of Licinius at the battle of Chrysopolis he achieved
 last and greatest ambition.[3]

Hitherto the effects of Constantine's policy had been felt directly
the West alone. But from 324 onwards they were to be experienced
o in the dioceses of Thrace, Pontus, Asia, and the East.[4] There
 the religious policy of the dyarchy had left a legacy of dis-
linary problems for the Church, particularly in Egypt,[5] in addition
which there had arisen a serious doctrinal controversy, the origin
which went back six years or so before Constantine's final victory.
 Alexandrine presbyter, Arius, of independent outlook and out-
ken opinions, had censured what he believed to be Sabellianism in
 teaching of his bishop Alexander, only to find himself con-
mned.[6] His appeal to the bishops of Bithynia was favourably

See Optatus, *Opera*, App. V, ed. cit., p. 208 ff. Yet in spite of p. 209, 'dico
m, ut se veritas habet, sacerdotum iudicium ita debet haberi, ac si ipse dominus
dens iudicet', he did not consider himself lacking in competence personally to
ise an episcopal *iudicium*. See Augustine, *Epp.* 43, 7, 20. ed. cit., p. 101; 88, 4.
cit., p. 410; *c. Cresc.* 3, 70, 81. ed. cit., p. 485.

Augustine, *C. part. Don. post gesta.*, 33, 56. ed. cit., p. 158.

For date 324 (Gibbon, ed. Bury, 1929, vol. i, p. 475, gives 323), see Seeck, O.,
esten d. Kaiser u. Päpste, 1919, p. 174.

Until the middle of the fourth century Egypt formed part of the 'Dioecesis
entis.' See Gibbon, *Decline*, ed. cit., 1929, p. 576 ff.

Consequent upon the exile and subsequent tolerant policy of Peter I of
xandria. The leader of the Egyptian rigorists was Meletius, bishop of Lycopolis.

The earlier stages of the controversy are recorded by Socrates, *H.E.* 1, 5. ed.
ght, W., 1878, p. 4 ff. It should be remarked that Alexander thought it necessary
nform Pope Silvester of the action taken. See *Ep. Liberii*, JK. 212, 4. ap. Hilary,

14

received by that Eusebius who had recently become bishop
Nicomedia,[1] and was in due course transmitted to the Emperor. ,
a result a rescript conveyed by Constantine's ecclesiastical advis
Hosius, bishop of Cordova in Spain, peremptorily ordered bish
and presbyter to compose their differences.[2] But unfortunately f
the success of this imperial method of settling controversy a co
siderable number of bishops assembled at Antioch had meanwh
pronounced a verdict which indirectly supported Alexander.[3] T
situation so created made specially urgent the execution of
imperial project, of which perhaps something had already be
heard, namely of assembling the largest possible council of bishop
the original purpose of which appears to have been to bring to
end the long and wearisome controversies connected with t
calculation of the correct date for the observance of Easter.[4] T
ultimate choice of Nicaea as the actual place of assembly instead
Ancyra[5] may well have been due to the suggestion of the ambitio
Eusebius, who as a consequence of the change probably hoped
influence the course of its deliberations.

Coll. Antiar. Par. Ser A, vii. ed. Feder, A., in C.S.E.L. vol. lxi, pt. 1, p. 89, wh
it is said that Alexander mentioned the excommunication of eleven of the hig
clergy of Alexandria, including deacons as well as presbyters. Alexander, Ep.
Theodoret, H.E. 1, 4, 61. ed. cit., p. 25, mentions five presbyters and six deaco
together with two Libyan bishops. Cf. Sozomen, H.E. 1, 15.

[1] Eusebius had formerly been bishop of Berytus, the second most import
see in the region of Antioch. Cf. Athanasius, Apol. c. Arian. 6. M.P.G. 25, 2
id. Hist. Arian. 7. M.P.G. 25, 701. Possibly he owed both his original appointm
and his translation to Nicomedia, the see of the then imperial capital of the E
to the influence of Constantia, wife of Licinius. It is clear that he was aiming
acquiring for his see a primacy over the whole of the 'Diocese of the East' as it th
existed.

[2] Eus. Vit. Const. 2, 64 ff. ed. cit., vol. i, p. 67 ff.

[3] A synodal letter surviving only a Syriac version, Cod. Par. 62, is our author
for this. Attention was first called to this document by Schwartz, E., in Nachr.
Gött. Ges. d. Wiss., 1905, p. 271 ff. It is addressed to 'the bishops of Italy subjec
the great see of Rome'. Mention is also made of an answer of approval recei
together with twenty-five canons for transmission to the eastern churches. U
happily the scribe did not fulfil his promise of including them, with the result t
nothing is known about their contents. See on the same synod, Seeberg, E.,
N. Studien z. Gesch. d. Theol. u. d. Kirche, vol. xvi, 1913. The fact that it co
demned Eusebius of Caesarea is perhaps sufficient reason for his omission
record anything of it.

[4] In his rescript to the council, the Emperor laid particular stress on this as
main business before the assembled bishops. See Eus. Vit. Const. 3, 17 ff. ed. c
vol. i, p. 84 ff.

[5] On the imperial letter transferring the venue of the council to Nicaea,
Schwartz, art. cit., p. 278.

At this gathering, known to posterity as the council of Nicaea, some
two hundred or more local churches were represented,[1] among them
the see of Rome, the legates of which were two presbyters.[2] Apart
from these, and of course Hosius of Cordova, not more than fourteen
churches belonging to the western dioceses sent representatives.[3] At
the council's deliberations, it may be remarked, though their names
appear in the second place in the series, the Roman legates did not,
so far as we know, occupy the place of presidents, as some would
have wished to find.[4]

Of the results of its work, by far the best known is the Creed.[5] Its
subsequent prominence, however, was due not so much to the
council's action as to the use made of it by Athanasius, bishop of
Alexandria, chiefly as a safeguard of traditional doctrine. For contrary to the usual view it is doubtful whether either in East or West,
except perhaps in Alexandria, it was at first regarded as possessing
any really crucial importance. Council after council attempted to
improve on it, and it probably owed its ultimate survival, though in a
considerably modified form,[6] to the belief that it represented an
authoritative decision on doctrine pronounced by an impressive number of assembled bishops, which had established uniformity in the
East in regard to Paschal observance,[7] and had incidentally provided

---

[1] Turner, *op. cit.*, vol. i, p. 36 ff.

[2] A reason for Silvester's absence is supplied by Theodoret, *H.E.* 1, 7, 3. *G.C.S.*
1. Parmentier, L., p. 30, namely advanced age. More probably he did not think it
worth while to appear.

[3] It must be remembered that at this time the whole of the Empire west of the
province of Thrace belonged to the western sphere of administration. It is, therefore,
not strictly accurate to account as 'westerns' only the representatives of churches in
Italy, Gaul, Spain, and Africa.

[4] The question as to who actually presided is, in the presence of ambiguous
evidence, difficult to answer. No doubt Constantine when he was present did so.
Eus. *Vit. Const.* 3, 13, ed. cit., p. 83, speaks of '$\pi\rho\acute{o}\epsilon\delta\rho\omega\iota$', though it is probable
that the term is used to denote bishops generally. The fact that Hosius' name occurs
first in all lists of subscriptions suggests that he presided as the Emperor's representative, though probably not as Gelasius Cyz. *H.E.* 2, 5, 3. *G.C.S.* ed. Loeschke,
., p. 44, states as a legate of Silvester.

[5] There is no critical edition of the original Creed of Nicaea. For different texts,
see Athanasius, *Ep. ad Iov.* 3. *M.P.G.* 26, 817; Basil, *Ep.* 125, 2; Eus. ap,
Socrates, *H.E.*, 1, 8, 29. See also Badcock, *History of Creeds*, p. 180 ff. A convenient collection of creeds is Lietzmann, H., *Symbole d. alt. Kirche*, 1906.

[6] See below, p. 251.

[7] *Ep. Concilii ad episc. Aeg.* cit. ap. Theodoret, *H.E.* 1, 9, 12. ed. cit., p. 41,
stating that in future all the churches of the East would keep the same day as was
observed at Rome and Alexandria, but ignoring the fact that these two churches
at that time were not in agreement about the basis of its calculation.

the Church with a nucleus round which the Canon Law of the futur
was to be formed.

It is not without significance that the term 'of identical being
(ὁμοούσιον)[1] as a description of the relation of the Son to the Fathe
(which became in later years in some sense the battle cry of thos
who contended for the use of the Nicene definition as the onl
permanently satisfactory basis for a restoration of ecclesiastical unity
appears to have been accepted by the council only with some reluc
tance. In fact, if we are to believe Eusebius, its adoption was definitel
recommended, or in other words imposed, by Constantine himself.
It has been held that its chief recommendation from his standpoin
was its ambiguity, and that as originally used it was patient of inter
pretation not less satisfactory to the rationalists of Antioch than t
the allegorists of Alexandria. Yet if this were so, it is difficult to se
why it was avoided or even implicitly rejected by numerous sub
sequent synodical definitions. Hence it may be that the imperi
preference was due to a quite different consideration. Obviously w
cannot exclude the possibility that its introduction was suggested t
the Emperor by his ecclesiastical confidant Hosius, who in his tur
had in all likelihood been influenced in its favour by the bishop c
Alexandria. If this be admitted, it is not improbable that Hosiu
became its willing advocate, for no reason other than its evider
convenience as the Greek counterpart of the traditional wester
definitions regarding the Trinity, as exemplified by the writings c
the anti-pope Novatian. In a word, ὁμοούσιον was at first recom
mended, and later came to be accepted, as the most convenient Gree
expression of the western *paradosis* on this central mystery.[3]

Of the twenty canons issued by the council only the one usuall

[1] References to the use of the term are to be found in Athan. *De Synodis*, 4
M.P.G. 26, 773 ; Hilary, *De Synodis*, 81, 86. *M.P.L.* 10, 534, 538 ; Basil, *Ep.* 52,
ed. Venet. vol. iii, p. 207 f. in connexion with the synod of Antioch (269) whi
condemned Paul of Samosata, see above, p. 180. Unfortunately our authorities c
not make it certain whether Paul himself used it or objected to its use.

[2] Eusebius, *Ep. ad Caesarienses*, cit. ap. Soc. *H.E.* 1, 8, 29, explicitly says s
Yet he may have exaggerated the Emperor's personal responsibility in order
exculpate himself in the eyes of his own church of having acquiesced, even r
luctantly, in its introduction.

[3] It is possible that by this time it had become a traditional Alexandrine ter
to describe the relation of the Son to the Father. It is used twice with referen
to God or Christ in Clement Alex. *Strom.* 2, 16. *G.C.S.* ed. Stählin, O., vol.
p. 152 ; 4, 13. ed. cit., p. 288, and in the former passage in such a way as to sugg
that he would agree with the Nicene usage. It is likely, if we may judge fro
Rufinus, *Apol. pro. Orig. Pamph.* 5. *M.P.G.* 17, 581. a Latin version of Pamphil

reckoned as the sixth need be quoted here. The text of this canon in its original form runs as follows :—

'Let the ancient customs in Egypt, Libya and the *Pentapolis* prevail in such wise that the bishop of Alexandria has authority over them all, since this is also customary for the bishop in Rome; similarly both in the case of Antioch and in the other provinces, so that the privileges belonging to the churches are safe-guarded; moreover it is generally evident that if anyone becomes bishop apart from the approval of the metropolitan, the great council has determined that such an one ought not to be bishop; yet if two or three by reason of (individual) contentiousness oppose the agreed opinion of all, one which is well justified and according to ecclesiastical custom, let the opinion of the majority prevail'.[1]

To understand this canon aright, as well as the two which immediately preceded it,[2] it is necessary to have in mind the background of recent events. As to the fourth canon, we must recall that at least from the middle of the third century the see of Alexandria had begun

original work, in which Origen, *Comm. in Heb.* is quoted, that Origen himself used the word to denote identity of the Son's being with the Father. We may surmise that it was first suggested to Hosius by Alexander of Alexandria on the occasion of the former's mission, see Sozomen, *H.E.* 1, 15, 6; Socrates, *H.E.* 3, 7, 12, and by him communicated to Constantine. Athan, *Hist. Arian.*, 42. *M.P.G.* 25, 744 (if the usual interpretation of 'οὗτος καὶ τὴν ἐν Νικαίᾳ πίστιν ἐξέθετο' be correct), evidently believed that Hosius' part in the evolution of the Nicene symbol was a decisive factor. Yet that 'ὁμοούσιον' was ambiguous is undeniable. Apart from the phrase 'τοῦτ' ἐστὶν' ἐκ τῆς οὐσίας τοῦ Πατρός' it was consonant with Sabellianism; on the other hand, if the latter component of the word were stressed, it might accommodate a materialist view, with which, as Arius himself pointed out, Manichaeans could easily come to terms. Cf. Ottley, R. L., *Doctrine of the Incarnation*,[6] 1919, p. 315 ff. But it should not be forgotten that it was convenient as a Greek rendering of Tertullian's phrase, 'unius substantiae', *Adv. Praxeam*, 2, or of Novatian's 'communionem substantiae', *De Trinitate*, 26, which in spite of the author's rigorism in discipline, doubtless, as he himself says, authentically represents the *regula veritatis* of the Roman see. It is remarkable, however, that Athanasius himself seems on occasion purposely to avoid its use. Thus in his earlier *Orat. c. Arian.*, 1, 9. *M.P.G.* 26, 29, he uses the term only once, and avoids it even where the context seems to demand it. Cf. *ibid.*, 1, 20, 21, 58. But in his later *De synodis*, 54. *M.P.G.* 26, 789, he emphasizes its indispensability as a bond of union.

[1] Hefele-Leclercq, *Conciles*, vol. i, p. 552; Mirbt, *Quellen*[5], No. 111: τὰ ἀρχαῖα ἔθη κρατείτω, τὰ ἐν Αἰγύπτῳ, καὶ Λιβύῃ καὶ Πενταπόλει, ὥστε τὸν Ἀλεξανδρείας ἐπίσκοπον πάντων τούτων ἔχειν τὴν ἐξουσίαν, ἐπειδὴ καὶ τῷ ἐν τῇ Ῥώμῃ ἐπισκόπῳ τοῦτο σύνηθές ἐστιν. ὁμοίως δὲ καὶ κατὰ Ἀντιόχειαν καὶ ἐν ταῖς ἄλλαις ἐπαρχίαις τὰ πρεσβεῖα σώζεσθαι ταῖς ἐκκλησίαις. καθόλου δὲ πρόδηλον ἐκεῖνο, ὅτι εἴ τις χωρὶς γνώμης τοῦ μητροπολίτου γένοιτο ἐπίσκοπος, τὸν τοιοῦτον ἡ μεγάλη σύνοδος ὥρισε μὴ δεῖν εἶναι ἐπίσκοπον. ἐὰν μέντοι τῇ κοινῇ πάντων ψήφῳ, εὐλόγῳ οὔσῃ καὶ κατὰ κανόνα ἐκκλησιαστικόν, δύο ἢ τρεῖς δι' οἰκείαν φιλονεικίαν ἀντιλέγωσι, κρατείτω ἡ τῶν πλειόνων ψῆφος.

[2] Canons 4 and 5.

to exercise a sort of primacy over the provinces to the west of the
Nile delta.[1] It is unlikely that all the Libyan bishops readily acquiesced
in this development, and hence we may suppose that in the confusion
resulting from the recent persecutions some had probably succeeded
in regaining a measure of independence. Shortly before the council,
Alexander had evidently attempted to reassert his supposed rights,
and on meeting with opposition had not hesitated to excommunicate
the malcontents, who thereupon probably made common cause with
the local opposition to Alexander in his own church.[2] Moreover, the
verdict recently pronounced at Alexandria against the presbyter
Arius and his associates had been openly challenged by the action of
Eusebius of Nicomedia in admitting the defendants to communion.[3]
We may also conjecture that a recent disputed episcopal election to
the see of Antioch[4] had probably given rise to some controversy
among the churches of Syria, and this may have checked the movement, then rapidly on the increase, which favoured the grouping of
local churches according to civil provinces under the presidency of
the bishop whose see was located in the provincial metropolis.[5]

[1] See above, p. 181.

[2] Canon 5: '$\mu\iota\kappa\rho o\psi\upsilon\chi\acute{\iota}\alpha$ $\mathring{\eta}$ $\phi\iota\lambda o\nu\epsilon\iota\kappa\acute{\iota}\alpha$ $\mathring{\eta}$ $\tau\iota\nu\iota$ $\tau o\iota a\acute{\upsilon}\tau\eta$ $\dot{a}\eta\delta\acute{\iota}a$ $\tau o\hat{\upsilon}$ $\dot{\epsilon}\pi\iota\sigma\kappa\acute{o}\pi o\upsilon$' and '$o\mathring{\upsilon}\tau\omega\varsigma$
$o\mathring{\iota}$ $\dot{o}\mu o\lambda o\gamma o\upsilon\mu\acute{\epsilon}\nu\omega\varsigma$ $\pi\rho o\sigma\kappa\epsilon\kappa\rho o\upsilon\kappa\acute{o}\tau\epsilon\varsigma$ $\tau\hat{\wp}$ $\dot{\epsilon}\pi\iota\sigma\kappa\acute{o}\pi\wp$ $\kappa a\tau\grave{a}$ $\lambda\acute{o}\gamma o\nu$ $\dot{a}\kappa o\iota\nu\acute{\omega}\nu\eta\tau o\iota$ $\pi a\rho\grave{a}$ $\pi\hat{a}\sigma\iota$
$\epsilon\mathring{\iota}\nu a\iota$ $\delta\acute{o}\xi\omega\sigma\iota\nu$', clearly reflect the relations between Alexander and Arius. We learn
from Socrates, H.E. 1, 6, that Alexander excommunicated Secundus of Ptolemais
metropolis of the province of Libya Superior (Cyrenaica), and Theonas of an
unknown see in the province of Libya Inferior (Marmarica). Cf. id., ibid., 1, 9
In view of the allegation by Arius that Alexander's doctrine was Sabellian, id., ibid.
1, 5, and the known prevalence of Sabellianism in Libya in the third century (see
above, p. 179), it may fairly be conjectured that the controversy with the Libyan
bishops was more concerned with jurisdiction than with doctrine. It should be noticed
that effect of Conc. Nic. canon 6 was to give Alexander all for which he was contend-
ing, and we should therefore understand '$\tau\grave{a}$ $\dot{a}\rho\chi a\hat{\iota}a$ $\mathring{\epsilon}\theta\eta$ $\kappa\rho a\tau\epsilon\acute{\iota}\tau\omega$' as an allusion to the
customs which were already in force in the third century. It serves to show that as
yet the Church could only appeal to 'custom' in the absence of any generally recognized 'oecumenical' authority. The intention of the canon was plainly that Alexander
should enjoy metropolitical rights over five provinces, '$\dot{\epsilon}\xi o\upsilon\sigma\acute{\iota}a\nu$ $\pi\acute{a}\nu\tau\omega\nu$ $\tau o\acute{\upsilon}\tau\omega\nu$'.

[3] Sozomen, H.E. 1, 15, 10. Eusebius endeavoured to win support from the
provinces of Palestine (perhaps to counteract the growing influence of the see of
Antioch, to which canon 6 in securing the rights of other churches appears to
allude) by pleading Arius' cause with Paulinus of Tyre. See Theodoret, H.E. 1,
G.C.S. ed. cit., p. 27.

[4] See above, p. 194, n. 3, and Schwartz, E., Nachr. d. kön. Ges. d. Wiss. zu Göt-
1905, p. 272 ff. Cf. Eus. Vit. Const. 3, 62. ed. cit., p. 109 f.

[5] Canon 6: '$\chi\omega\rho\grave{\iota}\varsigma$ $\gamma\nu\acute{\omega}\mu\eta\varsigma$ $\tau o\hat{\upsilon}$ $\mu\eta\tau\rho o\pi o\lambda\acute{\iota}\tau o\upsilon$'. This emphasis on the indispensability of the approval of the metropolitan may have merely rendered per-
manent and normal something which had hitherto rested on 'custom', but it was a
definite step in the direction of hierarchical organization on an 'oecumenical' scale

The fifth canon, while safeguarding the authority of the local bishop, seems to have had as its object the strengthening of mutual episcopal loyalty, and in addition the provision of some restraint on an arbitrary use of the now established episcopal jurisdiction, by prescribing the regular assembling of provincial synods.[1]

In view of these enactments it is reasonable to expect a formal ruling in regard to the privileges of the sees of Alexandria and among others Antioch such as was now provided by the sixth canon. In fact it is possible that its compilers were disposed to regard it as in some sense in the nature of a *quid pro quo*. If Alexander, like other bishops, was to be deprived of absolute authority by the fifth canon, he had at any rate the satisfaction of having his claims over the provinces to the west of Egypt explicitly recognized by the sixth. Even so, the compilers perhaps felt the need of justifying their action, and for this purpose, possibly again at the suggestion of Hosius, went on to invoke the privileges of the see of Rome as a precedent.

In view of what has just been said, it is interesting to note the various accounts which have been given of this sixth canon by writers of widely differing standpoints.

Thus it has been asserted by a learned ecclesiastical historian that the First Oecumenical Council knew nothing of the doctrine of papal supremacy'.[2] Elsewhere the same writer observes that the language of the canon 'is not what would be natural on the part of any assembly of Christian bishops who believed that Christ had given to the Roman see a plenitude of jurisdiction, which differed not only in degree but in kind from that of any other see whatsoever'.[3] The usual answer to this line of argument has been to affirm that only the patriarchal rights of Rome were in question, and that its papal authority can therefore be tacitly assumed to be there in the background.[4] Yet it may be pointed out that it is not patriarchal, but metropolitical rights, which are the subject of the canon, and that the former as distinct from the latter do not clearly emerge till the time of Justinian I, over two centuries later.[5] A more reasonable explanation is that by the first quarter of the fourth century the Church, as we have seen, had scarcely as yet accustomed itself to speak in the language of

---

[1] Canon 5.
[2] Bright, W., *Canons of the first Four Oecumenical Councils*[2], 1880, p. 21.
[3] Id., *Roman See*, 1896, p. 80.
[4] Hefele-Leclercq, *Conciles*, vol. i, p. 560 ff.
[5] See e.g. Mansi, *Concilia*, vol. ix, 178 ff.

jurisdiction whether papal or otherwise, and that in consequence th
crucial question which see possessed its plenitude did not aris
Yet it is clear that some abnormal authority (ἐξουσία) was in fa
assigned to the Roman see and it is not impossible that in the ear
fourth century it extended throughout the whole of Italy. Later o
it suffered some diminution through the acquisition on the part
the see of Milan, as a temporary imperial residence, of a local prima
roughly corresponding to the area administered by the *vicari
Italiae* in the northern part of the peninsula.[1] We may conceiv
therefore, that the compilers of the sixth canon 'knew nothing of th
doctrine of papal supremacy'. Yet we ought not to forget that the
had only lately grown accustomed to the idea of metropolitic
jurisdiction ; and the fact that the council endowed the custom
holding casual and occasional synods of bishops, whose sees lay with
the same civil provincial boundaries, and strengthened the authori
enjoyed by metropolitan bishops, hitherto quite vague and on
spasmodically asserted, with the positive force of written laws, shov
that something in the nature of an ecclesiastical revolution had bee
accomplished. Before Nicaea the local church and its bishop ha
been the only essential and recognized unit of ecclesiastical organiz
tion. Whatever else there was remained accidental and contingen
Now for the first time local churches were recognized as grouped
provinces, and their bishops subordinated to the authority of th
metropolitan.[2] It is clear that the Church was moving in the directio
of providing herself with the machinery for corporate action as a
oecumenical society on an equal footing with an oecumenical Stat

Surprising though it may seem to many who have grown accu
tomed to view the council of Nicaea through the eyes of the fift
century and later, there are good grounds for believing that neithe
those who were present there, nor most of their contemporarie
seriously expected either that the Nicene symbol was a final an
sufficient standard of orthodoxy, or that the Nicene canons woul
serve as a permanent and unalterable basis of Canon Law. As late
history shows, they themselves made little of the symbol[3] an

---

[1] Cf. Bury, J. B., *History of the Later Roman Empire*, 1931, vol. i, p. 27, n. 1.
[2] *Conc. Nic.* canons 4–6.
[3] In its synodal letter to the church of Alexandria, Socrates, *H.E.* 1, 9. ed. ci
p. 20 ff., the council has something to say on the subjects of Arius, Meletius an
the agreement reached about the determination of Easter, but alludes to the canoı
and to the symbol in quite general terms : (ed. cit., p. 21) 'εἰ δέ τι ἄλλο ἐκανονίσθη

adily disregarded the canons when it suited their convenience.[1]
 fact it was probably not least because the Roman see came to
gard first the symbol and then the canons as absolutely binding,
at these ultimately acquired that final character attributed to
em in all parts of the Church[2] roughly a century after their
iblication.

The pontificate of Silvester I would not have called for any special
otice if it had not marked the beginning of an era of material
osperity for the church and see of Rome. The romances composed
 fifth-century Roman authors have at least this amount of historical
isis, that by personal gift of the Emperor and of members of his
mily that church acquired for the first time property and buildings
hich were truly worthy of its status as the premier church in
hristendom. It is probable that even before Constantine's first
pearance in Rome in 312 his wife Fausta had assigned her palace
 the Lateran to the Roman bishop as an official residence,[3] though
e erection of the *basilica Constantiniana* doubtless belongs to a later
riod in his reign.[4] To the Emperor's support, and possibly to his
itiative, was due the building of a new church of impressive
mensions on the place of St. Peter's martyrdom,[5] and a smaller
ilding to the honour of St. Paul on the corresponding site. To
ese churches were translated from their temporary resting-place
 the catacomb of Sebastian the relics of the great Apostles.[6] Among

γματίσθη . . . ἀνοίσει (sc. Ἀλέξανδρος) πρὸς ὑμᾶς, ἅτε δὴ καὶ κύριος καὶ κοινωνὸς
ν γεγενημένων τυγχάνων'. One would not judge from this that the council itself
ached very much importance to either. The conciliar theory of the fifth century
s yet to be born.

[1] Thus in spite of canon 15 prohibiting episcopal translations, Eusebius of
comedia succeeded in obtaining the see of the eastern capital within twelve
ars of the council, and Athanasius cites three Scriptural passages against the
actice, *Apol. c. Arian.* 6. *M.P.G.* 25, 260, but altogether omits to quote the canon
nless indeed παρὰ νόμον be taken to allude to it; on the other hand, it would as
sily mean 'contrary to custom' like παρὰ τὸν κάνονα in the text of the canon itself).
 the canon was later quoted against Arianizing careerists, it was not sufficiently
pported by public opinion to prevent translations. Basil, *Ep.* 188, 1. ed. Paris,
39, vol. iii, p. 391 f., so far ignores the authority of canon 8 as to decide the
atment of Novatianists (κάθαροι) in a sense contrary to its ruling. On the other
nd, canon 15 continued to be observed by the local church of Rome down to
 time of Pope Formosus, who was the first Pope to be translated from another
e, and centuries later, 'translation' was still being treated as a technical irregularity.
[2] Athan. *Ep. ad Afros* 1, *P.G.* 26, 1029, and see below, pp. 235, 292.
[3] Grisar, H., *History of Rome and the Popes in the Middle Ages*, 1911–12, vol. iii,
. 291 ff.
[4] *Ibid.*   [5] Id., *op. cit.*, vol. i, pp. 263 ff   [6] See above, p. 67 f.

other important buildings which came into the possession of t
Roman church at this time was the *basilica Sessoriana,* the gift of t
Emperor's mother Helena,[1] later to be enriched with a relic
the true Cross.[2]

We also learn from the *Liber Pontificalis*[3] that the Emperor r
only made extravagant gifts of sacred vessels for these and oth
churches but liberally endowed them with estates not only in Rome its
and its immediate neighbourhood, but in south Italy and Sicily a
even in more remote parts of the Empire. The revenue derived fr
them must have far exceeded the actual amount needed for the ma
tenance of public worship. It is therefore scarcely surprising th
within fifty years of Constantine's death energetic protests began
be made against the increasing luxury and worldliness of t
'established church' in Rome.[4]

It has already been suggested that the most reasonable explanati
of the whole of Constantine's religious policy is that it was initiat
and carried into effect from purely political motives. With that pic
but misdirected ingenuity, with which his Christian admirers fr
Eusebius of Caesarea onwards sought to assign even to
commonplace activities a religious character, it was alleged that t
Emperor undertook the task of refounding Byzantium as his epor
mous capital, because of his supposed disapproval of Rome as
ineradicably pagan city, intending that another altogether unco
taminated by heathen tradition should take its place,[5] or else, a
still later author suggested, because it was his wish that the bish
of Rome should enjoy undisputed possession of the city in which
see was located.[6] There may well be some truth in the allegation t
he found Rome distasteful, but his reason for feeling it so is mt
more likely to have been his impatience with the deeply-roo
democratic traditions and associations of the once proud Repub

[1] Grisar, H., *op. cit.,* vol. ii, p. 136.

[2] The distribution of portions of this relic is first mentioned by Cyril of J
salem (348), *Catecheses,* 4, 10; 10, 19; 13, 4.   M.P.G. 33, 469. 685. 776.

[3] *Liber pont.* ed. cit., vol. i, Vita Silvestri. Caspar, *op. cit.,* vol. i, p. 126, r
holds that this material at least is genuine, and derived from contemporary
ventories.

[4] *Coll. Avell,* 2, 121. *C.S.E.L.,* vol. xxxv, p. 43. Note that in virtue of C
Theod. XVI, ii, 4, the Roman church was legally permitted to receive legacies.

[5] *Chronicon Paschale,* ad ann. 328. *M.P.G.* 92, 708, records the foundation of
city.

[6] *Donatio Const.* (c. 780), 18. See Mirbt, *Quellen*[5], p. 107, No. 228.

wever much ancient Rome might have become reconciled with
lend of monarchical ideas and republican institutions, so charac-
istic of the pre-Diocletianic principate, it was certainly ill-adapted
play the part of a centre of government under the new autocracy.
t only did it represent the old order and a state of imperial
;anization in which local administration still enjoyed some measure
individual freedom, but even its Empire had been little more than
aggregate of loosely federated 'cities' and 'provinces', an association
her than a single homogeneous entity. Under Constantine, however,
: Diocletianic ideal of a closely knit and jealously administered
erium was largely realized. In his 'new order' the city on the
sporus displaced the city on the Tiber. Constantinople was hence-
th in fact, if not in name, the mistress of the world,[1] and even when
: principate was divided and separate spheres in East and West
pectively were recognized, it was not always Rome but some other
y such as Milan, Arles, Trèves, or even Ravenna, which enjoyed the
vilege of imperial residence.

After celebrating his *vicennalia* during one of his brief visits to the
mer capital on July 25, 326,[2] Constantine left the city for the last
ae. His contemporary Silvester died eleven years later,[3] and there
lowed the ten months of the pontificate of Marcus. Within this
ry brief period at least one event of importance took place, which

Cf. *Liber pont.* Vit. Bonif. III, ed. cit., vol. i, p. 316 ; *Conc. in Trullo*, Canon 36,
ich show the logical development of this in the ecclesiastical sphere.

Jerome, *Chronicon*, ad ann. Abr. 2342, ed. cit., p. 231. *M.G.H. Chron. min.*,
. i, p. 232.

M.G.H., ibid., pp. 70, 76. In after years Roman Christians must naturally have
en perplexed by the comparative insignificance of Silvester in relation to his
ster Constantine, and should in consequence have indulged in a good deal of
shful thinking'. It is to this source that we must trace the abundant crop of
vestro-Constantinian legends. Among the more notable and astonishing of these
he one which relates how the Emperor was baptized by the Pope and how as a
rk of his gratitude the former issued an edict which proclaimed that 'throughout
: whole world bishops should respect the Pope as their head, just as all imperial
icials obeyed the king' (Caspar, *Geschichte*, vol. i, p. 128). The famous 'Donation
Constantine', of course, belongs to a much later period (see below), but it is not
ficult to see in the earlier romance its genuine, though perhaps less prolific
cestor. Duchesne, L., *Lib. pont.*, vol. i, p. cix ff., held that these legends were of
ental origin. It has been shown, however, by Levison, 'Konstantinische Schen-
ng und Silvesterlegende' in *Miscellanea L. Ehrle*, ii, 1924, p. 159 ff., that where
: Latin text is the original the place of origin is Rome itself. It may be surmised
at a powerful motive leading to their compilation was a desire to instruct the
rvenu Gothic regime in its proper duty towards the Roman see. For a probable
planation of the source of the baptismal legend, see Duchesne, *op. cit.*, vol. i,
236.

has exercised a lasting influence on the customs and worship
Christians all over the world since that time. It was the appearance
the list of Roman episcopal *obits*, known as the *Depositiones e*
coporum,[1] which records in order according to the yearly kalen
the dates of the decease of the occupants of the Roman see fr
Lucius to Silvester, together with the companion *Depositio*
martyrum or *feriale ecclesiae romanae*,[2] supplying a similar list of
dates and places of annual commemorations of Roman martyrs,
significantly including as its first entry December 25, '*Natus Chri*
in Betleem Judeae'.

The fact that the Emperors themselves from Aurelian onwards
considerable official support to the movement for popularizing
cult of *Sol Invictus*,[3] and the success of this propaganda in Rome
well as a growing enthusiasm for the observance of its chief ann
religious festival, the winter solstice, in the belief that it marked
yearly rebirth of the solar deity, lends considerable probability to
view that the choice of this particular date for the annual co
memoration of the human birth of the 'Sun of righteousness'
dictated largely, if not solely, by a laudable desire to baptize a festi
of pagan origin and endow it decisively with a Christian charact
Not less symptomatic of a more attentive Roman interest in our Lo
human nature was the dedication, probably under Pope Marcus,
a church, later to be known as the *basilica Liberiana*, in honour
His Virgin Mother.[5]

III

By the time Julius I had been elected to the Roman bishop
rendered vacant by the death of Silvester's successor,[6] what is of
described as the 'reaction' to the council of Nicaea had already beg

---

[1] *M.G.H.* Auct. ant. vol. ix, p. 70.   [2] *Ibid.*, p. 71 f.

[3] See Batiffol, P., *La paix constantinienne*,[2] 1914, p. 69 ff.

[4] Lietzmann, H., *op. cit.*, p. 103 ff., shows that January 6 was originally kep
Rome, as at Alexandria and elsewhere, at the annual commemoration of the Nati
a fact to which the Preface of the Epiphany in the existing *Missale Romanum*
bears witness. It is significant, however, of local conservatism that it was not
361 that the Emperor Constantius gave formal recognition to the innovation.

[5] Caspar, *Geschichte*, vol. i, p. 132.

[6] Elected February 6, 337. Since Marcus had died nearly five months previo
the interval seems surprisingly long. Possibly there was some internal dissensio
which we have now no information, sufficient to delay the election. The *L*
pontificalis, ed. cit., vol. i, p. 205, mentions 'exilio fuit mensibus X'. If we could
V for X, we might have a clue to the cause of the delay,

ather force. That Constantine himself was only prepared to enforce
decisions so long as it seemed to him convenient to do so, is
wn by his arbitrary recall of the leaders of the minority at the
ncil without apparently waiting for annulment of their original
tence by synodical action.[1] Soon Arius himself was back in
xandria and local dissension flared up afresh. But on the death of
old bishop, whose claims to primacy in the East had been accorded
he recent council a limited recognition, the pace of the 'reaction'
idly quickened.

The rigorist schism headed by Meletius in Alexandria and dating
m the last of the persecutions probably hoped that its leader,
ose episcopal status had been explicitly recognized by the recent
ncil,[2] would succeed Alexander. It was only to be expected there-
e that, when on Alexander's death his archdeacon Athanasius was
sen and their own bishop ignored, the schismatics would see to it
t Meletius' successful rival would pay dearly for his victory.[3] After
ne four years of wrangling, providing the ambitious Eusebius of
comedia with an admirable opportunity for fishing in troubled
ters, the charges against Athanasius were heard by the Emperor
person.[4] Possibly he suspected that the incriminated bishop was
above using political means for achieving spiritual results,[5] but
atever the truth, nothing as yet could be proved. Athanasius was
refore allowed to return. Little more than three years elapsed and
was once more put on his trial. This time the case was heard by
imperial official, on whose report Constantine decided to repeat the

This is the usual view, e.g. Kidd, *History*, vol. ii, p. 53. Seeck, O., *Geschichte d.
terg. d. ant. Welt*, vol. iii, p. 428, and Stein, E., *Gesch. d. spät-röm. Reichs*,
8, p. 165, note 1. hold that the sentences were annulled in consequence of a
hdrawal of their excommunication at a later session of the Nicene council
lf, late in November 329. Athan. *Apol. c. Arian.* 59. *M.P.G.* 25, 357, mentions
demand of Eusebius of Nicomedia, supported by Constantine himself, that
us should be readmitted to Alexandrine communion. If such a second session of
council ever took place, it was probably attended by a few bishops only, most of
om were in immediate contact with the eastern court.
Conc. Nic. *Ep. ad Alexand.* 6, cit. ap. Socrates, *H.E.* 1, 9, 6.
They began with an appeal to the most influential bishop in the East, Eusebius
Nicomedia, see Athan. *Apol. c. Arian.* 59. *M.P.G.* 25, 356.
Larsow, F., *Die Festbriefe des h. Athanasius . . . aus dem Syrischen übersetzt*,
2, p. 26.
Athan., *ibid.*, 60–62; Socrates, *H.E.* 1, 27, 10; Larsow, *op. cit.*, pp. 27, 77, 80.
some light on a little known side of Athanasius' character, see the Meletian
yrus published in Bell, H. I., *Jews and Christians in Egypt*, 1924, pp. 38–99, esp.
8 ff.

experiment of summoning a representative council.[1] It met at Tyre
the latter half of 335, and after hearing the evidence of a commissi
the members of which according to Athanasius behaved with
scrupulous partiality, voted to deprive him of his see.[2] This ti
as some evidence of political intrigue on the part of the accused
come to light, Constantine deemed it was sufficiently serious
justify sentence of banishment.[3] The place chosen was the city
Trèves, which the Emperor's eldest son, the Caesar Constantine
had made his headquarters.[4]

The following year, on May 22, Constantine I died at Ancyra.[5]
a ruler he certainly merits the eponym 'the Great' bestowed
posterity. Yet we may hesitate to acquiesce in the title of 'Equal
the Apostles' assigned to him by an obsequious oriental clergy, wh
saw nothing incongruous in his self-description as '*episcopus* of
external affairs (of the Church)'.[6]

By his will the Empire was once more divided into distinct sphe
of administration, under his three sons by Fausta. To Constantine
was assigned eventually direct authority in Gaul, Britain, and Spa
with some part of *Africa* or of the 'diocese' of Italy, and a vag
suzerainty over his younger brother Constans in Italy, the rest
Africa, the *ripa Gothica* and Illyricum including the 'diocese'
Thrace, while Constantius II received simply the 'diocese' *Orie*
(including Egypt).[7] Under pressure from his eldest brother, C
stantius agreed, perhaps with reluctance, to rescind the senter

[1] The Emperor's letter to the council of Tyre, Eusebius, *Vit. Const.* 4,
ed. cit., p. 134, shows this clearly.

[2] Larsow, *op. cit.*, p. 28 ; Athan., *op. cit.*, 76. *M.P.G.* 25, 385.

[3] Athanasius, *op. cit.*, 87. The charge was one of attempting to hinder the exp
of Egyptian grain to Constantinople, a measure calculated to endanger the stabi
of the government. The fact that Athanasius mentions it explicitly may show
the charge was false, but it is possible that Constantine knew more than Athana
was disposed to record.

[4] Eus. *Vit. Const.* 4, 61, 2. ed. cit., pp. 142 ff.

[5] Kidd, *History*, vol. ii, p. 68.

[6] Eus. *op. cit.*, 4, 24. ed. cit., p. 126.

[7] Whatever Constantine's real intentions in regard to the succession may h
been, it is certain that mutual jealousies and court intrigues successfully prever
them from being carried into effect. Some uncertainty exists about the extent
composition of the respective spheres assigned to or acquired by the three s
who were all proclaimed Augusti on September 6, 337. For the view stated in
text, see Gibbon, *Decline*, ed. Bury, J. B., 1929, vol. ii, p. 589. As to the religi
policy or convictions of the three Emperors, it is doubtful whether the evide
justifies their being 'pigeon-holed' with the neatness of Kidd, *History*, vol
p. 69.

ainst Athanasius, permitting him to return to Alexandria.[1] Yet as
is was tantamount to setting aside arbitrarily the synodical decision
Tyre,[2] from the very first, in spite of the Emperor's favour, his
osition appeared alarmingly insecure. Two further events, the
signment of the 'diocese' of Thrace to Constantius[3] and the acquisi-
on of the premier see of Constantinople by that unscrupulous
reerist Eusebius of Nicomedia were quickly to make it altogether
atenable.[4] So when new charges of a criminal nature against
m made their appearance, both sides appealed to the Emperors.[5]

As we have already suggested, what may be called the unprepared-
ss of the Church for the new environment, which had come into
ing as a result of the toleration of Galerius, and later of the 'most-
voured-religion' policy of Constantine, is an essential clue to a
ght understanding of the maze of synod and counter-synod, sym-
ols and anti-symbols of this period which confounds the historian
d amuses the sceptic. One point, however, emerges with pellucid
arity—the fourth century gives no support whatever to a doctrine
an intrinsic infallibility in the decisions of oecumenical councils.
or although the council of Nicaea had decisively condemned Arius
d his supporters, ten years later two other councils,[6] inferior per-
ps in numbers but not in gravity, respectively deposed his chief
pponent Athanasius and pronounced in favour of his rehabilitation.
he fact was that the Church had not as yet worked out its own theory
oecumenical authority, and as a consequence was at the mercy of
e only oecumenical power then in existence—the Sovereign Augus-
s—or when there was more than one, either of the dominant partner
the dyarchy, or else of the nearest at hand. The sees of Rome and
lexandria provide almost isolated examples of resistance to the

---

[1] Athan. *Apol. c. Arian.* 87. *M.P.G.* 25, 405.

[2] See above, p. 210.

[3] Gibbon-Bury, *op. cit.*, vol. ii, *ibid.*, assigns this transference to 339. In view
what has been said, p. 210 above, it seems that the 'diocese' and not the province
ly of Thrace is meant.

[4] Athan., *ibid.*, 6. He succeeded Paul, now banished for the second time; cf.
, *Hist. Arian*, 7. *M.P.G.* 25, 701.

[5] Id. *Apol. ad Constantium*, 4. *M.P.G.* 25, 600. The idea of addressing an appeal
the Roman see does not appear to have presented itself at this stage.

[6] I.e. the councils of Tyre and Jerusalem 335. For the former, see above; for the
ter, Eus. *Vit. Const.* 4, 43–7, ed. cit., vol. i, p. 135 ff; Socrates, *H.E.* 1, 3. ed. cit.,
56. An earlier investigation had been ordered by Constantine to take place at
esarea in 334, which Athanasius had declined to attend. For the date, see Bell,
. cit., p. 48.

growing subordination of the Church to the State, though the reaso
for such resistance were perhaps by no means the same in bo
cases. At Rome, where an inherent conservatism impeded an imm
diate appreciation of the change which was taking place, oppositi
was certainly passive and perhaps for a time even unconscious
Alexandria, on the other hand, as represented by Athanasius, reco
nized even before Constantine's death the serious hindrance co
stituted by the new situation, not only to its acquisition of a
undoubted primacy in the East, but even to such exercise of extr
diocesan authority as had been formally endorsed by the sixth can
of Nicaea. If therefore the State adopted the standpoint that ecclesia
tical unity, regarded as an essential element in the maintenance
political order, necessitated the supersession of the doctrinal ar
disciplinary decisions of that council by some compromise to whic
the majority could rally, it was inevitable that sooner or later t
Augustus in the East[2] and Athanasius would come into violent confli

We may reasonably conjecture that the first suggestion of a
dissension in that part of the Empire was conveyed to Pope Juli
through the legates of Eusebius of Nicomedia, now of Constantinop
who came to announce the enthronization of the latter's nominee,
certain Pistus, to the 'vacant' see of Alexandria.[3] Meanwhile, howeve
the nominee withdrew, and to settle the question Gregory of Ca
padocia was solemnly 'provided' by imperial edict.[4] Athanasi
thereupon found it expedient to leave his city and seek allies in t
West. On his arrival in Rome, following that of his own legates,

---

[1] The earliest example of open resistance in any form to the State on the part
the Roman see may be found in the protest of Boniface I against the law of The
dosius II, assigning jurisdiction within Illyricum to the see of Constantinople. Y
in this case the fact that the protest was addressed to and actually supported
Theodosius' own colleague, Honorius, precludes us from regarding it as su
without qualification..On this, see further below, p. 275.

[2] That he did not meet with the same opposition from the western Sovereig
was due partly to their preoccupation in mutual hostilities, and partly to t
drifting apart of the respective policies of the western and eastern spheres
government, which increasing as the years elapsed led to an actual cleavage by t
end of the century, though in name at least the theory of imperial unity persiste
See below, p. 265.

[3] Athan. *Apol. c. Arian.* 24. *M.P.G.* 25, 288. The appointment itself, whatev
may be said against the manner in which it was carried out, was strictly correct. T
council of Tyre had deposed Athanasius, and, properly speaking, the see
Alexandria was vacant. Even if a miscarriage of justice had taken place, Athanasi
put himself in the wrong by affecting to ignore its verdict. Cf. Larsow, *op. cit.*, p. 3

[4] Athan. *Ep. Encyc.* 5. *M.P.G.* 25, 252; Larsow, *op. cit., ibid.*

:ame known that one at least of the Eusebian representatives had
eady taken his departure.[1] Such had been the surprising sequel to
open discussion between the two opposing eastern parties at the
teran. Moreover, besides Athanasius, yet two other plaintiffs,
arcellus of Ancyra,[2] himself perhaps a victim of Eusebius' ambition,
1 Paul of Constantinople[3] appeared in Julius' presence. Letters had
eady been addressed by the Pope to the Eusebians urging the
mission of the whole dispute to a fresh council,[4] a proposal which
elf appears to have originated with the Eusebian legates, and
ually to have included mention of Rome as its appropriate venue.
The evidence of Athanasius himself, however, and the production
the minutes of the recent proceedings showed the Pope clearly
ugh that no ordinary synodical procedure would be sufficient. A
ond letter therefore followed, in which he invited the Eusebians to
sent themselves at Rome and to make out their case against
anasius in person.[5]

t is doubtful whether even Julius himself entirely realized the
mendous significance of his invitation. For, if he had wished, he
ld not very well have asserted in a more unequivocal fashion[6]
rimacy of jurisdiction for his see, which now emerges for the first
e into the daylight of history.

These legates had arrived to announce the election of Pistus; the fact that
gory was to take his place was probably the immediate cause of their return.
s not certain that Athanasius' primary object was to 'appeal' to the Roman see.
bability suggests that the court of Constantine II was his ultimate objective,
ere his earlier favourable reception must have encouraged him in the expectation
nding renewed support. The death of the Emperor, March 30, 340, on the field
Aquileia rendered this project impossible.
A bishop of somewhat reactionary Sabellianizing opinions. If, much to the
dal of the Easterns, he succeeded in satisfying Julius about his orthodoxy,
aay perhaps have been due to a traditionally favourable attitude towards this
esy at Rome, see above, p. 129 f. ; and Epiphan. *Panar.* 72, 2. *G.C.S.* ed. Holl, K.,
iii, p. 256 ff.
Kidd, *History*, vol. ii, p. 75. In view of the later relations between the sees of
ne and Constantinople, the appearance of Paul before Julius has special interest.
Athan. *Ep. Encycl.* 7. *M.P.G.* 25, 237; *Hist. Arian.* 9. *M.P.G.* 25, 704. It does
seem that at this stage Julius proposed that the new council should be held in
ne.
It is one of those decisive incidents in history, the real character of which was
little appreciated at the time of its occurrence. Yet it must be observed that on
us' own showing, the initial proposal to hold a fresh council came not from
self but from the Eusebian legates. See below, p. 214, n. 4, and cf. *Ep. Julii*, ap.
an. *Apol. c. Arian.* 20, 21. *M.P.G.* 25, 279.
It is clear from his letter (*c.* 35), that the Pope considered that after the Roman
ncil had given its verdict, further discussion of the subject would be superfluous.

5

The reply of the Eusebians, unhappily known to us only throug
the Pope's third letter,[1] and in a summary provided by the histori
Sozomen,[2] is highly instructive. Their grounds for refusing t
invitation do not include the obvious one that it was a highly pr
sumptuous act on the part of Julius to have issued anything of t
kind.[3] On the contrary, they contented themselves with saying fi
that the interval was too short, next that the unsettled state of the E
rendered their presence there necessary, and thirdly that the case
Athanasius had already been satisfactorily settled at Tyre. We a
fortunate in possessing the Pope's reply[4] intact, which as the earli
complete papal document of indubitable authenticity, may rightly
regarded as possessing exceptional interest.

Julius' letter is a masterpiece of diplomacy, combining as it does
a remarkably fair measure firmness with the spirit of conciliation. B
perhaps its most remarkable characteristic is its almost complete d
regard of the doctrinal issue and its repeated emphasis on the d
ciplinary aspect of the case. The doctrines of Arius and Marcellus
which it alludes are nowhere examined. All the writer has to say
that the former with his supporters had been condemned by t
'great council' of Nicaea,[5] and that the latter had justified himself
the satisfaction of the Roman see.[6] On the other hand, he devote
considerable amount of space to such questions as the authority
councils,[7] the status of bishops[8] and the importance of 'custom' a

---

[1] See note 4 below.   [2] H.E. 3, 8, 5 ff.

[3] The Eusebians evidently contented themselves with affirming the final vali
of the council of Tyre, see Ep. Julii, 22.

[4] Julius I, Ep. ad Antiochenos, ap. Athan. Apol. c. Arian., 21–35. JK. 186. Fr
the fact that the letter is addressed to members of an Antiochene synod and menti
first in the heading, not Flacillus, who had displaced Eustathius as bishop
Antioch in 330, but Dianius (reading Διανίῳ for Δανίῳ), bishop of Caesarea
Cappadocia, we infer that Dianius and not Flacillus acted as its president. In v
of canon 6 of Nicaea this appears at first sight surprising; on the other hanc
seems to support the view that neither creed nor canons of that council were
yet regarded as finally authoritative.

[5] Evidently Julius knew nothing of its supposed confirmation by the Ror
see. If he calls it 'μεγάλη' (c. 23), he probably alludes not to its 'oecumeni
character, but to its numerical impressiveness, cf. ibid., 29. Note that Athana
uses a similar argument, see below, p. 240, and contrast Ep. Liberii, below, p. 235
later times it was believed that the council had submitted its decisions to Silve
for approval. See the Roman synod of 385, Mansi, Concilia, vol. vii, 1140. For ot
inventions, see below, p. 333, and Duchesne, L., Lib. Pomt., vol. i, p. cxxxv.

[6] Ep. cit., 23, 32.   [7] Ibid., 22 f.

[8] Ibid., 25. It is sometimes supposed that Julius is alluding to an argument of
Eusebians intended to discount the superior value of a judgment of the Roman

nal court of appeal.[1] Yet he nowhere suggests that the decisions of
Nicaea are final. On the contrary, his whole argument presupposes
the possibility that the verdict of one synod may be subsequently
revised or even cancelled by another.[2]

The historian Socrates has asserted that Julius[3] was the first Pope
to enunciate the theory that councils might not make canons contrary to the opinion of the Roman bishop. Even if this were true, it
must be admitted that the historian's mode of expressing the papal
privilege is anachronistic. In the fifth century Canon Law was as yet
immature. In the fourth century the later 'oecumenical' idea of a
canon of universal force and application was quite unknown. The most
that can be said is that Socrates gave expression to a view which by
his time had become widely accepted.[4]

Nevertheless it is more than doubtful whether Julius himself
really says anything of the sort. What he does affirm is that, supposing
the case against the two chief opponents of Arianism, Athanasius and

advance. More probably the Eusebians referred to primatial claims put forward
the see of Alexandria. It is not without significance that apparently the same
Secundus (ibid., 24) who had led the Libyan opposition to bishop Alexander (see
above, p. 201 ff.; cf. Socrates, H.E. 1. 9. ed. cit., p. 20), now takes a prominent
place among the opponents of Athanasius.

[1] Ibid., 21, 'κανόνες ἀποστολικοί'; ibid., 30, 'τοὺς ἀπὸ τῶν ἀποστόλων κανόνας' . . .
παραλελυμένων τῶν κανόνων'; ibid., 32, 34, 'παρὰ κανόνα'; ibid., 35, 'κατὰ τὸν ἐκκλησι-
αστικὸν κανόνα'. It is clear that 'κανών' here denotes either 'unwritten custom' rather
than any specific written canon in the later sense, since at this time universally
acknowledged canons did not exist, or else 'rules' enshrined in writings ascribed to
the Apostles, e.g. 1 Tim. v, 19 f.; Tit. 1, 7.

[2] Ibid., 22. The possibility that a verdict pronounced by Nicaea itself may be
revised is certainly not excluded. Julius appears to argue that Athanasius had not
actually been deposed at the council of Tyre (ibid., 23). This was strictly speaking
true, since the deposition itself did not take place till the council had been transferred to Jerusalem.

[3] H.E. 2, 17, 'τοῦ ἐκκλησιαστικοῦ κανόνος κελεύοντος, μὴ δεῖν παρὰ γνώμην τοῦ
ἐπισκόπου 'Ρώμης κανονίζειν τὰς ἐκκλησίας. Cf. Sozomen, H.E. 3, 10. 'εἶναι γὰρ νόμον,
ἄκυρα ἀποφαίνει τὰ παρὰ γνώμην πραττόμενα τοῦ 'Ρωμαίων ἐπισκόπου', who appears
to be summarizing Julius' own words.

Possibly Socrates had in mind the provision of Sardica (see below, p. 220) and
forgot that this was posterior to Julius' letter. No doubt if, as some have believed, the
historian was a Novatianist, he had good reason to emphasize the superior jurisdiction of the Roman see as a salutary check to aggressive tendencies on the part
the Catholic bishop of Constantinople. The theory finally became a part of Canon
law through its inclusion in a 'false decretal' of Julius JK †195. ed. Hinschius,
456.

[4] Yet as we shall see the council of Ephesus (431) merely reported its findings to
Celestine I without asking for approval; see below, p. 229. The council of Chalcedon
in its synodical letter sought Leo I's confirmation of its canons, but there was good
reason for this action on their part. See below, p. 310.

Marcellus, to have been proved, according to the prevailing custo
of the Church, information should have been sent to 'us all',[1] especial
in view of the apostolic origin of the churches involved, adding th
such action was certainly requisite in a case in which the see
Alexandria was implicated.[2] Yet his insistence on the right of t
Roman see to be consulted is evidently limited by the contex
Julius has a sense of injury, not because a council has given its verdi
without first asking the opinion of the Roman see, but rather becau
the co-operation of the whole Church has not been invited, and th
sense of injury is deepened because one of the bishops just co
demned is in fact bishop of Alexandria. If all bishops ought to
invited to pass judgment on accused members of the episcopa
much more ought the bishop of Rome in a case involving that pa
ticular see.[3] Yet even if this was all that Julius actually said, in sayi
it he enunciated a principle which could easily be applied to oth
cases, for which no exact precedent was in existence.

Historians have usually been so preoccupied with the doctrin
aspect of the mid-fourth century controversy that they have general
overlooked the real cause of Julius' anxiety, which seems to betr
itself in language of brotherly appeal for co-operation, namely t
signs already manifest of an attempt to create an 'eastern Papac
out of the see of the eastern capital. Eusebius was actually overtak
by death before his plans could mature, and his successors for near
a century were men of insignificance in comparison with their co
temporaries in that part of the Empire. But in the long run the se
which he had thus sown began to bear fruit. It was the easte
solution of the new problem created by the changed relation
Church and State, and by the need for a truly oecumenical outloc
Stated in plain language, it involved the replacement of the primiti
conception of the *paradosis* as something received from the Apost
and transmitted by their successors in the teaching office by som
thing entirely new, namely the identification of the *paradosis* with t
δόγμα of Augustus. If the appeal of Julius to the twofold aposto

[1] *Ep. Julii*, 35. 'ἔδει γραφῆναι πᾶσιν ἡμῖν, ἵνα οὕτως παρὰ πάντων ὁρισθῇ τὸ δίκαιο
[2] *Ibid.*, 'ἢ ἀγνοεῖτε ὅτι τοῦτο ἔθος ἦν, πρότερον γράφεσθαι ἡμῖν, καὶ οὕτως ἐ
ὁρίζεσθαι τὰ δίκαια'. There can be little doubt that Julius is alluding to the rep
sent to his predecessor as to the alleged erroneous doctine of Dionysius of Alexand
p. 178 f. On which, see above, p. 179.
[3] *Ibid.*, 'εἰ μὲν οὖν τι τοιοῦτον ἦν ὑποπτευθὲν εἰς τὸν ἐπίσκοπον τὸν ἐκεῖ (sc. Ἀλεξ
δρείας), ἔδει πρὸς τὴν ἐνταῦθα (sc. ἐν τῇ Ῥώμῃ) ἐκκλησίαν γραφῆναι'.

aradosis of the church of Rome[1] shows that he was able to perceive
ne development which was in progress,[2] it is much to his credit. But
has to be remembered that in the interest of his project, Eusebius
f Nicomedia had no alternative.[3] The Roman primacy of doctrine
nd jurisdiction was already in the field. To some it might soon appear
nat it had come into existence, not for the sake of the Roman see
lone, but for the safeguarding of the apostolic *paradosis* throughout
ne whole Church.

The immediate purpose of the papal letter which we have been
onsidering was to announce that at the recent provincial synod of
ne Roman church,[4] held in the 'titular' church of Victor, the same
resbyter who had been Silvester's legate at Nicaea, Athanasius and
Iarcellus had been admitted to communion.[5] The reply of Eusebius
as to use the occasion of the consecration of the new cathedral of
ntioch for holding a fresh council with all the impressiveness pos-
ible, not excepting of course a citation issued by the Emperor Con-
tantius himself.[6] Here for the first time since Nicaea a dogmatic
uestion, namely the temerarious views of Marcellus of Ancyra, the
ashness of which had not been detected by the unspeculative
Vesterns at the recent Roman council, came to the forefront. But
n addition to pronouncing the excommunication of Marcellus the
ouncil formally endorsed the rehabilitation of Arius. We may note
arefully the only argument which the authors of the synodal letter
dduce in favour of the correctness of Arius' beliefs, namely the fact

[1] *Ep. Julii*, 35. 'οὐχ οὕτως αἱ **Παύλου** διατάξεις, οὐχ οὕτως οἱ **πατέρες**
αραδεδώκασιν, ἄλλος τύπος ἐστὶν οὗτος καὶ καινὸν τὸ ἐπιτήδευμα . . . ἃ γὰρ παρειλήφαμεν
αρὰ τοῦ μακαρίον **Πέτρου** τοῦ ἀποστόλου, ταῦτα καὶ ὑμῖν δηλῶ'.

[2] The use of 'καινὸν'='novel' is significant as the precise contradiction of
quod traditum est'.

[3] The see of Constantinople was always at a disadvantage in relation to other
reat sees in being unable to claim direct apostolic foundation. It was only at a later
me that an apostolic 'founder' in the person of St. Andrew, the first of the
postles to be called by Christ, and hence perhaps supposed to be the original
epositary of the *paradosis*, was provided by the inventive genius of eastern his-
orians. See Caspar, *Geschichte*, vol. ii, p. 748.

[4] Athan. *Apol. c. Arian*. 20. *M.P.G.* 25, 281, states that more than fifty bishops
vere present.

[5] We may infer from the same writer, *ibid.*, 33, that other victims of Eusebian
ggression' from the provinces of Thrace, Coele-Syria, Phoenicia and Palestine
vere similarly admitted.

[6] The so-called 'Encaenia' council of 341. Cf. Athan. *De synodis*, 22. *M.P.G.* 26,
20, where a fragment of the synodal letter is preserved. The authors protest that
hey receive no other faith than the original tradition: 'οὔτε ἄλλην τινὰ πίστιν παρὰ
ἣν ἐξ ἀρχῆς παραδοθεῖσαν ἐδεξάμεθα'.

that he had succeeded in satisfying the Emperor Constantius of h
own orthodoxy. That such a contention could be made provid
further illustration of the emergence of this new and altogeth
revolutionary principle, that the right to determine doctrinal que
tions belonged to the Sovereign, or in other words to the State, a vie
which for many centuries was to become dominant in the East, an
but for the almost ceaseless though often passive resistance of th
Roman see would have probably become established throughout th
whole Church.

IV

The diametrical opposition between the supporters and opponen
of Athanasius, as represented by the councils of Rome and Antiocl
showed that an impasse had been reached, from which as things stoo
there seemed no escape. Henceforward the only possible solutio
appeared to lie in making an attempt to summon a truly 'oecumenica
council at which both sides would be fully represented.[1] By arrang
ment of the Emperor Constans, with the acquiescence of his easter
colleague, it was ordered that a council of this character shoul
assemble at Sardica, which, situated as it was on the border betwee
the eastern and western spheres of administration, seemed likely t
provide a kind of 'no man's land' as a meeting-ground for the tw
contending parties. Probably it was the intention of the governmer
that the new council should re-examine the questions at issue *de nov*
The majority of the council, however, insisted on treating the re
habilitation of Athanasius as a *res judicata*.[2] Whether or not thei
attitude was due to the belief that the judgment of the recent Roma
council was final, it had the effect of vitiating the pacific, if mistake
purpose of the Sovereigns from the outset. The minority, compose
mainly though not entirely of Easterns, who evidently did not shar
the belief of their colleagues, can scarcely be blamed therefore fo

[1] Athan. *Apol. ad Const.* 4. *M.P.G.* 25, 601 ; *Hist. Arian.* 15. *M.P.G.* 25, 709.
was significant of the growing subordination of the Church to the State in th
East that the bishops from the *Dioecesis Orientis* were accompanied by two sta
officials belonging to the entourage of the Emperor, a *comes* and the *castrens*
(*s. palatii*; see Bury, *History of the Later Roman Empire*, vol. i, p. 33, n. 2, and *Co*
Theod., VI, xxxii, 1 ; XII, i, 38).

[2] Hilary, *Coll. Antiar. Par.* Ser. A IV, i, 14. ed. Feder, A., *C.S.E.L.* vol. lxv
p. 57 f., in a letter drawn up by the minority council. A strictly impartial view c
the situation is only possible if this and other documents of eastern origin ar
given the same consideration as the evidently biased account provided b
Athanasius.

fusing to have any share in the proceedings, though it may be re-
retted that they saw no other remedy than the holding of a rival
ouncil.[1] Their attitude was ignored by the majority, who quietly went
n with the agenda.

Apart from the confirmation of the verdict in favour of Athanasius
nd Marcellus, already pronounced two years previously at Rome,
nd the reaffirmation of the Nicene definition of faith,[2] which from
ow on begins to play an important part in the controversy, the
najority council of Sardica is chiefly remarkable for its series of
anons'.[3] Like those of Nicaea they are clearly the product of
nmediate circumstances, though in a sense they continue the same

---

[1] Hilary, *ibid.*, 23 ff. ed. cit., p. 63 ff. Cf. Athan. *Hist. Arian.*, 44. *M.P.G.*
5, 745. In the end the dissident minority did not hesitate to declare Julius, Hosius
nd other prominent Westerns deposed. For a convincing demonstration that
oth councils were held side by side in Sardica itself, see Zeiller, J., *Les origines
rét. dans les prov. danub.*, 1918, p. 236, who prefers the testimony of Sozomen,
.E. 3, 11, to that of Socrates, *H.E.* 2, 20. The same author also shows reason to
elieve that the majority council was attended by ninety-eight members, the
ninority by at least eighty.

[2] Not, however, without considering an alternative, see Athan. *Tom. ad Ant.* 5.
I.P.G. 26, 800. The text of the synodal letter has been preserved by Theodoret,
.E. 2, 8. *G.C.S.* p. 101 ff. The comment of Turner in *J.T.S.* vol. iii, 1902, p. 386,
, 2, is important: 'Probably it was only through the stress of the Arian struggle
a the years after the Council of Sardica that first the Creed and then the Canons of
ïicaea came to be placed on a pinnacle of commanding and unique authority.
t. Hilary of Poitiers in 356 was still unacquainted with the Creed; and of the
umerous extant versions of the Canons those that can go back to any part of the
urth century are very few'. See further on the creed of Sardica, Zeiller, *op. cit.*,
. 239 ff.

[3] Turner, C. H., *Eccl. occid. mon. iur. ant.* Tom. I, 1930, p. 452 ff. The genuine-
ess of the canons was vigorously attacked by the Old Catholic historian Friedrich,
., in *Sitz. Ber. d. kön. bay. Akad. d. Wiss.* philos.-philol. u. hist. Kl., 1901,
p. 417–476, *Die Unächtheit der Canones von Sardica*, also *ibid.*, 1902, pp. 383–426,
/ho argued that originally they were drawn up as a forged appendix to the Nicene
anons, and only subsequently, when their falsity had been detected, assigned to
•ardica. To this Turner, 'The Genuineness of the Sardican Canons' in *J.T.S.*
ol. III, 1902, pp. 370–97, produced a wholly satisfactory answer, which reduced
'riedrich's arguments to little more than elaborate special pleading. The only
oint still seriously in debate concerns the question whether of our existing texts
he Greek or the Latin is to be regarded as original. Turner favours the latter; in
upport of the former, see Hankiewicz, G. von., 'Die Canones von Sardica' in
`eitschr. d. Sav. Stiftg. für R.G.* Band XXX, Kan. Abt. ii, p. 44–49, who relies
lmost wholly for the support of his thesis on the originality of our present Greek
ext of canon 6 (as numbered in Turner, *Eccl. occid. mon.*, Tom. I, pp. 498, 500).
t may be remarked that the so-called canons are properly no more than an epitome
f the conciliar minutes. Their peculiar form is perhaps explicable by the lack of
ny competent stenographers among the Westerns, after the secession of the
:asterns along with the 'official' secretariate. But the 'canons' of Arles show similar
haracteristics, see Turner, *op. cit.*, Tom. I, pp. 381 ff.

process of legislation which Nicaea had already begun. The rece
ambitious career of Eusebius of Nicomedia evidently remained
serious preoccupation to the compilers, and gave rise to the impositi
of even more extreme sanctions against episcopal translations th
those which the former council had prescribed.[1] But the inadequa
of the Nicene legislation had become apparent also in other respec
particularly in its failure to provide an appeal from the judgment o
provincial synod. The remedy proposed by Sardica was twofol
first by strictly limiting all personal appeals of bishops to the ci
power[2]; and secondly, in any suit between two bishops, by providi
that neither party should himself appeal to the judgment of t
bishops of another province, but that if one of the parties we
aggrieved, either his own judges or the bishops of a neighbouring pr
vince should address themselves to the Roman bishop; if he decid
that the case ought to be heard afresh, he could appoint judges, othe
wise he was to confirm the verdict already given.[3] It was furth
agreed that in the event of a condemned bishop filing an appeal, I
see was not to be provided with a successor until the case had be
settled by the verdict of the Roman bishop.[4] Finally, in the seco
part of the third canon (as numbered by Turner), it was enjoined th
in the event of a deposed bishop having appealed to the Roman se
the Roman bishop, if he thought fit, might refer the matter to t
bishops of the neighbouring province, who were to decide the matte
But on request of the appellant he might send a personal repr
sentative, and in that event it would be permissible for him
delegate, if he wished, some of those presbyters who had alrea
heard the case at Rome.[5]

[1] *Conc. Nic.* canon 15, contented itself with the requirement that the translat
bishop should return forthwith to his original see, without stipulating any penalt
Conc. Sard. canon 1, ed. cit., p. 452 f., on the other hand, deprived the offend
even of lay communion. Perhaps here we may find a trace of Spanish rigorism.

[2] *Conc. Sard.* canons 5 and 6. ed. cit., p. 462 ff. The provision that those wl
have recourse through their deacons to the Emperor by way of Rome are to deliv
their request to the Roman bishop is to be noted. The Pope, if he finds it justifie
is to expedite the mission to the imperial court. Such a regulation was perha
aimed at defending the correctness of the course of action taken by Athanasius.

[3] Canon 3, ed. cit., p. 455 ff. It is possible that the author had in mind the dispp
which had been going on for some time between bishops of Libya, like Secund
and Theonas, and the bishops of Alexandria, see above, pp. 202, 214, n. 8.

[4] Canon 3, ed. cit., *ibid.*, evidently directed against the intrusion by Eusebi
and his supporters, first of Pistus and then of Gregory into the see of Athanasius

[5] Canon 3 b, ed. cit., p. 460 ff. It should be noticed that this part of the cano
unlike the remainder, opens with the expression, 'Placuit enim'.

One has only to contrast the very limited appellate jurisdiction
hich is here assigned to the Roman see (and assigned, in the view
the bishop responsible for the proposal, as appropriate to the
eculiar office of episcopal jurisdiction regarded as belonging to
t. Peter and thus to the see where his memory was preserved: '*Petri
ostoli memoriam honoremus*') with the more extensive authority
nveyed to that see by the edict *Ordinariorum sententias*[1] some
irty-five years later, or even with the actual procedure already
llowed by Julius himself,[2] to see how eager the council was to do
thing which might be regarded as doing violence to the existing
ghts of the provincial synod. In this connexion we may quote some
ords of the late Professor Turner, 'in a system of judicature which
lowed and yet limited appeals, which left each case to be dealt with
local knowledge, and yet introduced an arbiter superior to local
ejudice, I can see nothing alien to the needs of a generation which
as feeling its way to an increasing closeness of federation, or to the
rcumstances of a moment when the Pope had just earned the special
atitude of all Catholic Christians by giving audience to the protest
Athanasius against his synodical condemnation in the East.'[3]
Both councils of Sardica, that of the minority as well as of the
ajority, issued synodical letters, the former significantly addressed
Gregory of Alexandria and Donatus of Carthage, including a
mber of others such as Amphion of Nicomedia and also perhaps
rprisingly three Campanian bishops;[4] the latter to Pope Julius
ne.[5] This letter of the majority contains a remarkably outspoken
stimony to the belief of the authors in a Roman primacy, which
ads:
'That which has been our constant belief hitherto, remains our
esent conviction; experience serves to prove and confirm, what
ch of us has only heard with our ears.[6] For those words are true,
ich the most blessed apostle Paul, teacher of the Gentiles, spake
ncerning himself: "Ye seek a proof of him, that speaketh in me,
en Christ",[7] though in fact, since the Lord Christ dwelt in him,

[1] See below, p. 246 f.   [2] See above, p. 213 f.
[3] Art. cit. in *J.T.S.* vol. iii, 1902, p. 389.
[4] Hilary, *Coll. Antiar. Par.* Ser. A iv, i. ed. cit., p. 48 ff. The letter devotes
nsiderable space to the doctrinal vagaries of Marcellus.
[5] Id., *ibid.*, Ser. B II, 2. ed. cit., p. 126 ff.
[6] The writers appear to refer to a general belief that the authentic Christian
dition is to be found at Rome.
[7] 2 Cor. XIII, 3. 'ἐπεὶ δοκιμὴν ζητεῖτε τοῦ ἐν ἐμοὶ λαλοῦντος Χριστοῦ'.

there can be no doubt that the Spirit spoke through his mind a
used his body as a means of utterance. So, well-beloved broth
though parted from us in the body, you were present with us ii
harmony of thought and will; the explanation of your absence w
both reasonable and expected,[1] otherwise you might have be
attacked by schismatic wolves, with treacherous wiles, or yelped
by heretical curs raving with madness, or insulted by the devi
poisonous blasphemies, a serpent in very deed.[2] For it will se
best and highly appropriate, if the Lord's bishops, each from l
own province, report to the head, that is to the see of Peter t
Apostle'.[3]

Indirect and perhaps unintentional testimony has been given to t
importance of this letter as evidence for the attitude of a group
bishops towards the Roman see in the middle of the fourth centu
by those who have excluded the last clause as a later editor
addition.[4] Considered in its context, however, the impugned clat
may be seen, not as an irrelevant insertion, but as supplying

---

[1] We have no evidence as to what form Julius' 'excusatio' took. Possibly in v
of the earlier decision in favour of Athanasius at Rome, he held that his prese
at Sardica would be unnecessary. He was represented, however, by the t
presbyters Philoxenus and Archidamus, see Athan. *Apol. c. Arian.* 50. *M.P.G.*
337, and Hilary, *Coll. Antiar. Par.* Ser. B II, 2, 2, where a Roman deacon Le
also mentioned. Transcribers of the Sardican canons, observing that no ment
of Roman representatives appeared in the *Nomina Episcoporum*, remedied
apparent omission by transforming Vincentius of Capua, Januarius of Benevent
and Calipodius of Naples into papal legates, where, as Zeiller, *op. cit.*, p. 244, n
points out, the phrase 'legatus sanctae Romanae ecclesiae' makes its appearance
the first time. See Turner, *Eccl. occid. mon.* Tom. I, p. 546.

[2] Possibly there was some sort of conspiracy on foot to compel Julius, if his per
could be secured, to assent *malgré lui* to the condemnation of Athanasius. If th
was, it is highly probable that it was known to the Illyrian bishops. Julius him
escaped, but his successor was less fortunate. The allusion is of interest as mark
the first of a long series of attempts to compel the submission of the Roman se
the view now rapidly gaining ground in the East that the Emperor was the pro
depositary of the authentic Christian tradition.

[3] Hilary, *Coll. Antiar. Par.* Ser. B II 2, 1. ed. cit., p. 126. It is difficult no
believe that the authors had the *Tu es Petrus* in mind. The reference to St. Pau
well as St. Peter may perhaps look back to the idea underlying Irenaeus, *Adv. h*
3, 3, 2.

[4] The latest exponent of this view is Caspar, *op. cit.*, vol. i, p. 587, who foll
Turmel, J., *Histoire du dogme de la papauté*, p. 251, n. 1. He insists that the
pression 'referre ad sedem Petri' cannot be earlier than the period of the g
decretals of Innocent I; it might be said, however, that the Roman bishops rea
adopted to their own use phrases of this sort which had previously been used
the State. There is plenty of precedent for the use of 'referre' in the sense of 'repo
cf. Lewis and Short, s.v. II B, 2, d.

ditional, though perhaps not very convincing, justification for the pe's absence from Sardica. On the other hand, the real significance the letter can only be appreciated when we take into account the ritorial provenance of those who attended the council. Of the fifty-ie names mentioned in Turner's text, some thirty-nine or so are of bishops whose sees were situated in provinces belonging to the a known as Illyricum, six are from Spain, while only one is from ul, five from northern and four from Southern Italy. In view of s proportion we may rightly regard the opinions here expressed as cially characteristic of those churches which felt the need of some eck on the autocracy of provincial and regional councils, and as rking a definite step forward in the direction of creating that new umenical machinery, the lack of which in the new situation was wly coming to be appreciated. The fact that the Easterns contented mselves with a repetition of the policy of deposing those with om they were in disagreement, without offering any positive tribution to the solution of the Church's common problems, wed that they were far behind their western brethren in realiza-n of the danger of being satisfied with the provisions of the council Nicaea.[1]

or the moment, however, the Sardican canons remained to some ent a dead letter. Yet this is certainly far from being true of the incil's judicial decisions. A general revulsion of feeling in favour Athanasius was their immediate sequel, culminating in the granting Constantius of licence to return to his see, which in any case had n vacant for the past ten months following the death of the in-ded Gregory.[2] It is difficult not to regard this change of attitude on nstantius' part as due to purely political considerations, but what-

---

Turner, *Art. cit.* in *J.T.S.* vol. iii, 1902, p. 386 f., calls attention to the fact : 'At Antioch, in 341, the eastern bishops had indeed contented themselves deciding, in this matter of episcopal trials : (a) that if the bishops of the pro-cial synod—the court of first instance—were divided in opinion, the metro-itan should call in bishops from the next province to help in adjudicating the (can. xiv) ; (b) that if the provincial synod was unanimous, no appeal could lie ll (can. xv)'. Cf., however, as to the date of these canons, Schwartz, E., *Nachr. d. t. Ges. d. Wiss.*, 1911, p. 389 ff. ; Bardy, G., art. 'Antioche' in *Dict. de droit nique*, vol. i, col. 594.

It seems that following his meeting with Athanasius at Aquileia early in 345 han. *Apol. ad Const.* 3, *M.P.G.* 25, 597), Constans exercised his influence his brother on the bishop's behalf. Gregory died June 26 of that year. In gust of the following year Constantius finally confirmed his licence for Athanasius' oration.

ever the cause, Athanasius was left undisturbed for the next six a
a half years.

Meanwhile after securing the eastern frontier against the Persian
Constantius was free to turn his attention to the West, where in
his brother had fallen by the hand of a usurper's emissaries.[2]

V

While Constantius was gradually reasserting the authority of
imperial house, Pope Julius died and was succeeded after an inter
of a month by Liberius.[3] Thus the stage was set for a spectacular t
of strength between two powers, the State in the person of Co
stantius, now sole Augustus and master of the Roman world, and
Church represented by Liberius, bishop of Rome and guardian of
'potior principalitas'; in other words, between two rival concepti
of the source of dogmatic truth, the will of the Sovereign and
apostolic *paradosis*. The struggle has often been misconceived
simply a contest between Nicene and para-Nicene standards
orthodoxy, and insufficient attention has perhaps been paid to
aspect of the struggle just mentioned in which the main offensive w
directed against the person and policy of Athanasius. For it was h
chiefly that the imperial strategy failed of its purpose. To this f
perhaps more than any other Athanasius owes the reputation aware
to him by posterity, as a single-minded, unswerving and impertu
able champion of orthodoxy. Of his single-mindedness the evide
which we have already adduced may suggest some doubt; of
constant and unmovable adherence to the Alexandrine tradition
can be confident. We shall see presently that it was this consta
which in the end secured the victory for Nicene orthodoxy, fina
recognized and imposed by Theodosius the Great.

The main events of this struggle must now be recalled. Co
stantius had scarcely established himself at Milan before news
fresh disorders at Alexandria began to reach the court. Before
middle of 353 an embassy arrived from Athanasius,[4] crossing
passage of an imperial officer already sent to summon him before

---

[1] Following the unsuccessful attempt on the part of the Persians to take Nis
See Gibbon, *Decline*, ed. Bury, J. B., 1929, vol. ii, p. 242 ff.

[2] Early in 350 at Helena in the Pyrenees; Zosimus, *Hist. nov.* 2, 42, 5.

[3] *Cat. Lib.*, reading 'xvi kal. iun. for 'xi kal. iun.'

[4] *Hist. aceph.*, 3. in Turner, C. H., *Eccl. occid. mon. iur. ant.* Tom. ii, p.
Cf. Larsow, F. *Die Festbriefe des h. Athan.*, 1852, p. 34.

nperor.[1] For the time being, however, the summons was merely
regarded. Undeterred Constantius decided to consolidate the
est by calling a representative council to meet to meet at Arles.
ready Pope Liberius appears to have become considerably dis-
ieted by the receipt of letters both for and against Athanasius,[2]
d himself sent Vincentius of Capua[3] to Arles to urge the desirability
a council,[4] while at the same time he despatched a legation to
exandria instructing Athanasius to present himself for re-examina-
n, and even threatened excommunication in the event of refusal.[5]
The new council of Arles coincided with the celebration by Con-
ntius of his *vicennalia* on October 10, 353. Here signatures con-
mnatory of Athanasius were obtained from all the bishops present,
cluding the Roman legates,[6] with the exception of Paulinus of
èves, who immediately received sentence of banishment.
Liberius found himself at this point in a most unenviable dilemma.
hanasius had so far ignored the summons both of Pope and
nperor. The Emperor's reaction had been prompt and decisive.
as Liberius to do no more than utter a feeble echo of the imperial
rdict? Constantius, however, had already supplied the answer,[7] and
e Pope's efforts to avoid so distasteful a course proved wholly
uitless. The only ray of light on an otherwise grey and clouded
rizon was provided by the happy arrival in Rome of Lucifer of

[1] *Ibid.* It is clear that something fresh must have occurred sufficiently serious to
rrant a fresh appeal from the Easterns to Julius, demanding the reversal of the
rdict of 341, and to cause Liberius to summon Athanasius to a second hearing.
e *Epp. Liberii*, JK 212, in Hilary, *Coll. Antiar. Par.* Ser. A VII, 2, ed. cit., p. 90;
.†207, *ibid.*, Ser. B III, 1. ed. cit., p. 155.

[2] See note above and cf. *Ep. Liberii*, JK 212, 2. ed. cit., p. 90, l. 15 ff.

[3] He had been legate of the Roman see at Nicaea, and subsequently as bishop of
apua had been present at Sardica.

[4] *Ep. Liberii*, JK 212, 1. ed. cit., p. 89 f. We may infer from *Ep. Liberii ad Hosium*,
K 209, in Hilary, *Coll. Antiar. Par.* Ser. B VII, 6. ed. cit., p. 167, that Liberius'
wn plan had been for the council to assemble at Aquileia. Notice that besides the
se of Athanasius he refers to 'multa alia' as needing settlement.

[5] *Ep. Liberii*, JK†207. ed. cit., p. 155 : 'litteras etiam ad eundem (sc. Athanasium)
er supradictos presbyteros dedi, quibus continebatur, quod, si non veniret, sciret
alienum esse ab ecclesiae Romanae communione'. In the previous sentence
ention is made of determining a question of 'discipline' in his case. It is clear that
Pharaoh 'which knew not Joseph' now sat in Peter's see. On the genuineness of
is and other letters of Liberius, formerly held by many to be spurious, see below,
229, n. 3.

[6] Besides Vincentius, Liberius had commissioned Marcellus, another Campanian
shop, as his legate. It is clear from the letter of the minority council of Sardica
at there were a number of Campanian bishops who dissented from the policy of
lius, see above, p. 213.   [7] At Arles in 353.

Caliaris, principal see of Sardinia, whose zeal for orthodoxy, which
wholly identified with the cause of Athanasius, was equalled or ev
exceeded by his lack of tact and diplomacy.[1] Possibly Liberius d
played some deficiency in judgment of character in choosing such
person as his legate to the impatient Constantius and in entrusti
him with a personal letter to the Emperor.

In that letter[2] the Pope shows himself only too well aware of t
gravity of the issue.

'I have never acted', he pleads, 'in a spirit of pride nor with des
for honour, but only in accordance with the law (of the Gospel)
reached my present position—my God is my witness—simply again
my will; and my sole ambition, so long as I live, is to continue to ho
it without offence. Moreover I have never executed injunctions of n
own, but those of the Apostles, as they have been for all time laid do
and observed. After the custom and *paradosis* of my predecessors,
have permitted no enlargement, no diminution of the episcopate
the city of Rome. Keeping safe that faith, which has been passed
through a succession of many great bishops, among whom there ha
been numerous martyrs, my constant hope is that it will be preserv
unimpaired'.[3]

Not a strong or original utterance perhaps, but dignified, restrain
and above all characteristically Roman.[4] In fact it may be said th

[1] Also mentioned in JK 211, 213, 215, 216. His lack of diplomacy coupled wi
a complete disregard of canonical principle was shown in his presumptuo
ordination of the presbyter Paulinus to the see of Antioch. Paulinus was the lead
of those who had for various reasons remained loyal to Eustathius, deposed a
exiled by Constantine I in 330. By this rashness Lucifer precipitated a schism whi
lasted nearly half a century. Not content with this, in conjunction with son
Spanish and Italian associates he fomented a minor schism in the West, characteriz
by an attitude of extreme rigorism towards converts from Arianism. See *Coll. Ave*
2, 14. *C.S.E.L.* vol. xxxv, p. 10.

[2] *Ep. Liberii ad Constant. imp.* JK 212 (354). Hilary, *Coll. Antiar. Par.* Ser.
VII, ed. cit., p. 89 ff.

[3] *Ep. Liberii*, JK 212, 3. ed. cit., p. 91: Note the following: 'et nunquam m
statuta sed apostolica, ut essent semper firmata et custodita, perfeci. Secutus more
ordinemque maiorum nihil addi episcopatui urbis Romae, nihil minui passus sun
Et illam fidem servans, quae per successionem tantorum episcoporum cucurri
ex quibus plures martyres extiterunt, inlibatam custodiri semper exopto'.

[4] In these words Liberius refers to his conviction that the apostolic *paradosis* ha
been faithfully transmitted by his predecessors in the Roman see. Later, however,
the same letter, after pointing out the superficiality of the recent proceedings at Arl
(c. 5. ed. cit., p. 92), he urges that a fresh council ought to be called at which th
recent reaffirmation of the Nicene formula at Sardica can be endorsed (c. 6. ed. cit
p. 93). This request is remarkable as being the first explicit reference on the part
a Roman bishop to the Nicene definition as an authoritative statement of belief.

ch strength as it possesses lies wholly in its unoriginality. Con-
iously or not, Liberius laid bare in a few laconic phrases the
emendous issue at stake. If Constantius were to have his way, it
uld not be '*statuta apostolica*', but *edicta* and *sacra rescripta*
hich would determine in future the Church's faith and conduct. In
s path stood only the frail figure of the Roman bishop. It was
idently impossible that such resistance as the Pope could offer
uld in any way avail to avert the inevitable disaster.

Historians have frequently devoted so much of their attention
ther to providing a laboured apology for Liberius' so-called
postasy' or else to placarding his 'fall', that they have had little
isure to mark the real significance of his place in history. Attention
s been quite needlessly and mistakenly directed to his supposedly
aven abandonment of the Nicene symbol in favour of some Arianis-
g formula, or to his treacherous desertion of Athanasius, without
iy serious attempt being made to estimate how far at this date,
en by those bishops who inclined to the support of Athanasius,
e Nicene symbol was as yet regarded as an absolutely final and
ialterable statement of doctrine,[1] or to reflect whether Liberius
ay not have had some fresh justification, about the details of which
e are now ignorant, for regarding Athanasius as an intransigent
sturber of the peace of Church and State alike.

On the Emperor's arrival at Milan, events began to move with
ghtning swiftness. His programme left no room for uncertainty; it
as nothing less than to procure general acceptance of the verdict
cently pronounced at Arles, condemning Athanasius and endorsing
e rehabilitation of Arius. After a determined but altogether fruitless
tempt on the part of Eusebius of Vercelli, acting on behalf of
iberius, to obtain a reaffirmation of the symbol of Nicaea, the
ebate was brought to a decisive issue by its transference from the
iurch to the imperial palace.[2] Even so the pro-Athanasian minority
ept up the struggle and persistently refused to subscribe to the
ishop of Alexandria's condemnation, urging that to do so would be
i uncanonical act.[3] To this we are told Constantius bluntly replied:

---

[1] This is evident from their attitude at Sardica, see above, p. 219, n. 2; and from
e fact that Hilary of Poitiers appears to have been unaware of its existence before
6. See *De Synodis*, 91. *M.P.L.* 10, 543.

[2] Athan., *Hist. Arian*. 31-4. *M.P.G.* 25, 728 ff. Cf. Lucifer, *Moriendum est*, 4.
.P.L. 13, 1015.

[3] *Ep. Liberii*, JK 216 (355) in Hilary, *Coll. Antiar. Par*. Ser. B VII, 2. ed. cit.,
164 ff.

'What I will, let that be accounted a canon; the bishops of Syr
suffer me to speak thus. So either obey, or suffer exile with the rest'

It is doubtful whether either the Emperor himself or those wl
heard him grasped at the time the full implications of his pronounc
ment. But even a specious allusion to the council of Tyre was in
sufficient to cloak the naked shamelessness of his ecclesiastical abso
lutism. His utterance was recognized however for what it was in fac
namely a declaration of war on the apostolic *paradosis*, by three ou
standing western bishops, Dionysius of Milan, Eusebius of Vercel
and Lucifer of Caliaris, who incurred the inevitable penalty for takir
up the challenge.

Weary of councils as perhaps too suggestive of a free and demo
cratic regime, Constantius decided to secure adherence to his pro
gramme on the part of the rest of the episcopate, including the Roma
bishop, by means of signatures to a document drawn up by th
imperial chancery.[2] On Liberius' stubborn refusal he was arreste
and brought under escort to Milan. Threats alternated with entreatie
All was in vain. Liberius remained obdurate,[3] and thus for the fir
time Christians witnessed the unhappy spectacle of a Pope driven int
exile by a Christian Emperor.

In the following year at the Emperor's bidding a further Gaulis
synod, this time at Biterrae, accepted the situation. Of the only tw
dissentients one was Hilary of Poitiers,[4] who probably appreciate
more clearly than most of his western contemporaries the dogmat
issue at stake. He was thereupon exiled to Asia Minor. That valia
old Nicene Hosius equally received a summons to submit, but for th
time being postponed a decision in his case by simply ignoring th
imperial commands.[5]

[1] Athan. *op. cit.*, 33. Even if Athanasius is himself responsible for the opprobrio
epithet 'λεγόμενοι', the utterance loses nothing of its significance in regard to tl
prevailing attitude in the East by its omission.

[2] Caspar, *op. cit.*, vol. i, p. 174.

[3] The genuine record of Liberius' examination before Constantius is in Theodore
H.E. 2, 16. *G.C.S.*, p. 131 ff. The account given by Athanasius, *op. cit.*, 39, is
little historical value.

[4] Hilary, *De Synodis*, 63. *M.P.L.* 10, 522. The other was Rhodanius of Toulous

[5] He had been present at Milan, and in spite of his refusal to agree to tl
council's decisions had been allowed to return home in peace. This fact strengthe
the case for believing that Constantius' motives were far more political tha
religious; obviously a supporter of Athanasius in distant Spain could do far le
harm than in Italy. His letter to the Emperor, cited by Athanasius, *op. cit.*, 4
contains a striking assertion of the proper independence of the spiritual pow

Meanwhile what was happening to Liberius?
After the failure of every possible means to procure his submission
t any rate the Pope showed himself to be entirely proof against
ibery,[1] a practice which now began to make its appearance in
:lesiastical controversy and would soon grow to alarming pro-
:tions) he was despatched to Beroea in Thrace.[2] Worn out by
)re than a year's exile, beset by the advice of friends and the
acks of his enemies, the unhappy bishop at last consented to make
blic his excommunication of Athanasius,[3] already threatened but
t as yet put into effect.[4] In addition he gave his signature to a
tement of belief which had been drawn up at Sirmium five years or
previously.[5] Thus the custodian of the apostolic *paradosis* did
:eisance to the δόγμα of Caesar Augustus.

ssibly the earliest of its kind. When summoned to Sirmium in 357, he consented
communicate with the supporters of Arius, but persisted in his refusal to abandon
hanasius to the day of his death. Cf. Athan. *op. cit., ibid.*; *De fuga*, 5. *M.P.G.*
, 649.
[1] Athan. *op. cit.*, 35, 37.   [2] Soz. *H.E.* 4, 11, 3.
[3] *Ep. Liberii*, JK† 207, Hilary, *Coll. Antiar. Par.* Ser. B III, 1. ed. cit., p. 155.
fé-Kaltenbrunner, *Regesta*, vol. i, p. 32, is evidently mistaken in assigning this
:er to 352–3; it alludes to Liberius' reaction to the letter of the Easterns addressed
Julius I, to his summons to Athanasius on pain of excommunication and finally
the actual pronouncing of sentence. It occurs in the collection of documents
blished by Constant (following Pithou and Le Fèvre, late sixteenth cent.) in
'1 under the title *Fragmenta ex libro S. Hilarii* . . . Constant accepted the
:uineness of this and all other letters included in the collection, but met with
le support. Following their rejection by the Bollandists in *Acta Sanctorum*,
ptember, vol. vi, pp. 754–780, they have generally been regarded as spurious,
. by Batiffol, P., *La paix constantinienne*, p. 516 ff. Already however Duchesne,
bère et Fortunatien' in *Mélanges d'archéol. et d'hist.*, vol. xxviii, 1908, p. 31 ff.,
s disposed to argue for their authenticity, and Feder, A., 'Stud. zu Hilarius von
tiers, 1', in *Sitz.-Ber. d. wien. Akad.*, vol. clxii, 1908–9, No. 4, contending that
Fragmenta were in fact surviving extracts of a larger work by Hilary under the
e *Opus historicum adversus Valentem et Ursacium*, in which the compiler had
quently introduced his own comments, finally and decisively proved their
:uineness. The position of the letter JK†207 at the beginning of the Liberian
lection is to be explained as due, not to its having been written first, but to the
dence supplied in it of an attitude of hostility on the part of the Pope towards
.anasius at the beginning of his pontificate.
[4] *Ibid.*, ll. 14 f.
[5] *Ep. Liberii*, JK † 217. Hilary, *Coll. Antiar. Par.* Ser. B VII, 8. ed. cit., p. 168 ff.
re he mentions his acceptance of 'fidem vestram (sc. orientalium) et catholicam
. quae Syrmio a pluribus fratribus et coepiscopis nostris tractata, exposita et
cepta est'. Much discussion has taken place regarding which of the many state-
nts of belief issued at Sirmium is meant here. The fact that the editor added 'haec
perfidia Arriana' has led some to suppose that it was the 'Anomoean' creed of 357,
which the use of οὐσία with its compounds and derivatives was proscribed. But
date of Liberius' submission makes this most unlikely, and it is far more probable

16

We must now see what had been happening at Rome following t
Pope's secret removal to Milan. On the very day of his arrest t
Roman clergy, deacons and presbyters alike, met in conclave, and
the presence of the laity took an oath that they would never conse
to acknowledge any other bishop so long as Liberius was aliv
Constantius, however, who was probably quite unaware of t
strength of loyalty in the capital to his victim, took steps to provi
an immediate successor. The archdeacon Felix was found after all
be amenable to proposals, and after having been clandestinely co
secrated installed himself in the vacant palace of the Lateran.[2] B
the laity would have none of him and it was seen that when
presided at the liturgy the congregation quietly melted away.[3]

Such then was the unhappy state of affairs when the Emperor pa
the last fleeting visit of his life to the capital.[4] At once he was beset
throngs of women of high social standing, that class of Roman socie
to which successive Roman bishops from Victor I onwards h
managed to endear themselves, urgently entreating him to restore
them their rightful bishop.[5] The imperturbable Constantius turnec

that he was referring to the so-called 'Long' Sirmian creed, see Athan. *De Syn.*
M.P.G. 26, 736 ff., drawn up under the leadership of Basil of Ancyra in 351. T
creed reproduced substantially the 'Dedication' creed of Antioch, 341, Lietzma
H., *Symbole*, p. 27, and was regarded as sufficiently orthodox by Hilary in 356,
Syn. 38. *M.P.L.* 10, 509ff., even if in after years, following the *débâcle* of Arimin
and Seleucia, his editor felt bound to characterize it as 'perfidia', *ibid.*, 9. ed.
p. 170. The gathering of western bishops which was held at Sirmium in 357 a
produced the so-called 'Blasphemy' (Athan. *De Syn.* 28. *M.P.G.*, 26, 740,
Hilary (original Latin text.), *op. cit.*, 11. *M.P.L.* 10, 487), took place on the occas
of Constantius' visit, which occurred after October 17, 357. See Ammia
Marc. *Lib.* 16. 10, 21, and cf. Seeck, O., *Regesten*, p. 204.

[1] This fact is vouched for by the author of the first document, *Quae gesta s
inter Liberium et Felicem episcopos*, contained in the so-called *Collectio Avellana*,
Guenther, O., in *C.S.E.L.* vol xxxv, p. 1. He was doubtless no friend of
'official' church of Rome, but there seems no reason to reject his trustworthiness.

[2] Felix is described as 'archidiaconus' in *Coll. Avell.* 1. ed. cit., *ibid.*, cf. Th
doret, *H.E.* 2, 17, 3. *G.C.S.* p. 137; 'presbyter' in the *Liber pont.* ed. cit., vo
p. 207. Athanasius, *Hist. Arian.*, 75. *M.P.G.* 25, 784, narrates the circumstance
his consecration in contemptuous language. He mentions Epictetus of Cent
-cellae (Civita Vecchia) as the Emperor's principal agent in the matter. Cf. Jero
De vir. inl. 98. ed. cit., p. 47, who includes Acacius of Caesarea in Palestine am
Felix' consecrators. For Epictetus, see *Ep. Liberii*, JK † 218 and cf. Theodo
op. cit. 2, 16. ed. cit., p. 133 ff.

[3] Theodoret, *ibid.*

[4] Amm. Marc. *Lib.* 16, 10, 20; M.G.H. *Chron. min.* vol. i, p. 239.

[5] Theodoret, *ibid.*, records that the women attempted to persuade their husba
to intervene. They, however, ungallantly declined on the specious ground t
interference on their part would incur the Emperor's displeasure, saying, '

af ear to all their prayers and laconically observed that with one
shop already they had no need of two.[1] So when he departed for
e East on May 29, 357, he left Felix II in possession.

The news which greeted him on his arrival in Sirmium some five
onths later[2] must have been at once gratifying and embarrassing.
ie assent of Liberius to the condemnation of Athanasius and his
bscription to a colourless dogmatic formula had removed the
incipal ground for prolonging his exile, already some eighteen
onths in duration. But to permit his return at this juncture might
ly serve to aggravate the disunity already prevailing in the West.
nstantius therefore decided on a last effort to reduce the remaining
itres of western resistance to submission. Once again the aged
osius was summoned to the court, and now at last in common with
ier Westerns approved a formula which excluded the use of the
eek terms οὐσία and ὁμοούσιος from the language of dogmatic
inition.[3] On one point, however—and that probably to Con-
itius the most important—he remained obdurate. Even a year's
ention had no effect; let the Emperor do his worst, he would die
communion with Athanasius. So in the end he was allowed to
urn and to the last persisted in his repudiation of Arius.[4]

Meanwhile Liberius began to grow impatient at his enforced
ence from his see. He successfully approached some prominent
lian bishops to solicit the Emperor on his behalf,[5] and early in the
owing year was brought to Sirmium, where in concert with the
irt bishops[6] and a few Africans he signed a new formula, which
I been drawn up shortly before at a council held at Ancyra under
leadership of Basil, bishop of that see, and incorporated 'of equal

peror will of course forgive you; and you will either get what you want or at
st come away scathless'. It would appear from *Lib. pont.* ed. cit., vol. i, p. 207,
among others the lady Constantia, daughter of Constantine I, had a share in
moting Liberius' recall, and that on his return she provided him with an
um on her estate at St. Agnes on the *Via Nomentana*. The mausoleum built for
by her husband the Caesar Gallus, now described as a 'baptistery', still remains,
is remarkable for its innocence of Christian symbols in its decoration.
Theodoret, *ibid.*
Amm. Marc. *op. cit.*, 16, 10, 21.
This is the famous 'Blasphemy' of Sirmium. See p. 229, n. 5.
Athan. *op. cit.*, 45. *M.P.G.* 25, 749, who asserts that Hosius was already a
enarian.
Epp. Liberii, JK † 218, † 219. On the genuineness of these letters, see p. 229, n. 3.
Germinius of Sirmium, Ursacius and Valens. The latter two were typical
thercock' prelates, who throughout the controversy had veered with every
ige in the imperial policy.

being' (ὁμοίας οὐσίας) as a substitute for the famous Nicene term,[1]
the belief that it expressed the same truth without being liable to t
same objections.[2] At last Constantius decided to allow Liberius
return, and published an edict intimating that the restored exile a
Felix II would for the future share the Roman see.[3] The feelings
satisfaction on the part of the Pope's friends at the prospect of
return therefore were somewhat tempered by their dismay at
flagrant a violation of canonical precedent, and in consequence t
publication of the Emperor's decision was greeted with derisi
mingled with indignation.[4] A conservative Roman *populus* rejected
with scorn and tumultuously gave vent to its disapproval: 'One Go
they shouted ' one Christ, one bishop'.[5]

It is not surprising that the imperial plan proved utterly unworka
from the first, and when at length it came to street riots the Sen
intervened and expressed the popular will by issuing a mild senter
of banishment against Felix. Apart from a single raid on the d
reputable quarter of the Trastevere and the temporary seizure of
Julian basilica, the anti-pope contented himself with the enjoyment
the adequate revenue derived from his estates at Portus, and Liber
was henceforward left in sole occupation.[6]

Even so he must have had little peace of mind. Apart from

---

[1] Epiphan. *Panar.* 73, 3, 1. ed. cit., vol. iii, p. 271.

[2] In view of Hilary's comment on 'ὁμοιούσιος' in *De syn.* 72 ff. *M.P.L.* 10,
the possibility that 'ὁμοι-' was regarded as equivalent to 'par' rather than 'sim
should be taken into account.

[3] *Gesta*, ap. *Coll. Avell.* 1, 3. ed. cit., p. 2: 'habetis Liberium qui qualis a v
profectus est, melior revertetur'. Sozomen, *H.E.* 4, 15, 24, suggests that the
had been proposed at the council of Sirmium held in Constantius' presence,
and had perhaps originated with Basil of Ancyra. It is, however, possible that
imputation is false and that Basil had simply approved of Liberius' return witl
being aware of the problem resulting from the consecration of Felix II.

[4] Theodoret, *ibid.*

[5] *Gesta*, *ibid.*, ed. cit., p. 2. There is a remarkable similarity between this
pression of the convictions of the Roman *populus* and the cry which the confes
presbyters had uttered almost exactly a century before in support of Corne
against Novatian, *Ep. Cornel.*, ap. Cyprian. *Epp.* 49, 2. ed. cit., p. 609: 'nec e
ignoramus unum Deum esse et unum Christum esse . . . unum sanctum spirit
unum episcopum in catholica esse debere'. Cf. *Ep. Cornel.*, ap. Eus. *H.E.* 6, 43,
ed. cit., vol. ii, pt. 2, p. 618. The Roman laity was neither dumb nor ill-instruc

[6] *Liber pont.* ed. cit., vol. i, p. 207. By confusing Felix II with a local Portuen
martyr of the same name, the compiler succeeded in representing him as an
nocent catholic victim of an Arian persecution engineered by Constantius
encouraged by Liberius. The date assigned to his 'martyrdom' (July 29) is prop
the *natale* of his namesake, see *op. cit.*, vol. i, p. 209, n. 13. The correct dat
Felix' death is supplied by *Gesta*, *ibid.*, 4. ed. cit., p. 2, namely November 22,

spicious attitude of several of his former allies,[1] the fact that the
ow important see of Milan was occupied by Auxentius, a bishop of
e court party who had little use for any policy or doctrine which
as in disfavour with the Emperor, meant that the Italian episcopate
as now seriously divided. Moreover the loss of prestige suffered
y the Roman see became only too evident at the new council of
riminum, especially as the advocates of the Nicene formula as the
est solution of the wearisome controversy were not Roman legates,
r none was present,[2] but Restitutus of Carthage and Phoebadius of
gen.[3] Ultimately, however, the will of the majority at Ariminum
as arbitrarily overruled by the Emperor, and the official standard of
thodoxy became the creed of Nice, proclaiming the Son to be
qual to the Father as the divine Scriptures say'.[4] Thus once again
e new *paradosis* replaced the old. The faith of the apostles had been
upplanted by the faith of Caesar.

But for the Persians Constantius might still have reigned long
nough to enjoy for some years the fruits of this highly satisfactory
chievement. As it was, however, the rigours of two winter cam-
aigns undermined his failing strength and his death followed on
ovember 3, 361.[5] His successor Julian regarded Christianity with
staste or even contempt, and in a spirit of fantastic idealism set to
ork to provide an astonished or indifferent Empire with a *réchauffé* of
hristianized paganism as its state religion.[6]

His predecessor's punitive measures against the recalcitrant
lvocates of the Nicene symbol were revoked,[7] and as a consequence
thanasius among others managed to return to his see. He had been
osent for rather more than six years.[8]

Those years had been anything but peaceful at Alexandria. Follow-
g his flight early in 356, steps had been taken by the government to
repare for the installation of its nominee George of Cappadocia,

---

[1] Especially Eusebius of Vercelli and Lucifer of Caliaris.

[2] The absence of Roman legates was perhaps due to the divided state of the local
oman church.

[3] Kidd. ii, 166. For the letter of the majority to Constantius, see Hilary, *Coll.
ntiar. Par.* Ser. A VIII. ed. cit., p. 93 f., and for the definition reaffirming the Nicene
eed, *op. cit.*, ix, 1 ff. ed. cit., p. 95 f.

[4] Athan. *De syn.* 30. *M.P.G.* 26, 748. Socrates, *H.E.* 2, 41. ed. cit., p. 128 f.

[5] *M.G.H. Chron. min.*, vol. i, p. 240; Socrates, *op. cit.*, 2, 47, 4; 3, 1, 1.

[6] Julian, *Ep.* 46, ed. Bidez, J., Paris, 1924, p. 65; *Hist. aceph.* 10. ed. Turner in
:cl. occid. mon.* Tom. I, p. 666.

[7] *Hist. aceph.* 9. ed. cit., *ibid.*

[8] Since Feb. 9, 356. Larsow, *op. cit.*, p. 35; *Hist. aceph.* 5, ed. cit., p. 665.

whom Athanasius describes in the terms of somewhat vulgar abu[s]
customarily applied to his opponents.[1] It is possible that if he had h[a]
a free hand George might have made a good bishop, but the repressi[v]
measures used by the imperial officials against the supporters [o]
Athanasius, who were both numerous and sufficiently active to gi[v]
a considerable amount of trouble, never really gave him a chanc[e]
After some months' absence at the councils of 359 and the followi[ng]
year, he was misguided enough to attempt the reoccupation of h[is]
see shortly after the death of Constantius, only to meet a cru[el]
and perhaps undeserved fate at the hands of the Alexandrine mob[.]

Athanasius marked his return to power by a sparsely attend[ed]
council, at which were present Egyptians and representatives of t[he]
Eustathian party in Antioch and Syria,[3] where Lucifer of Caliaris ha[d]
beguiled the idleness of his exile in creating a new schism, by co[n]
secrating its leader Paulinus as bishop.[4] The new council agreed [to]
treat the less distinguished members of the opposition on the sa[me]
terms as Nicaea had allowed to the Egyptian Meletians,[5] and effecte[d]
a suitable compromise on the use of the term ὑπόστασις (usual[ly]
rendered in the West in dogmatic statements by the term *persona[*]
It also agreed to give to the temerarious opinions of Apollinaris [of]
Laodicaea the benefit of the doubt. Where it failed was in its attem[pt]
to reconcile Paulinus with a section of his opponents at Antioch. T[he]
schism continued, and presently, as is the habit of schisms in need [of]
justifying their existence, or rather the existence of their promoter[s]
took a turn in a rigorist direction.[6] This was shown most clearly [by]
the intolerant behaviour of Lucifer on his return to the West. N[ot]
content with disowning all those who had in any way accepted t[he]
compromise of Liberius, he and his former colleague Hilary t[he]
deacon, legate at the council of Milan,[7] denounced all who were no[t]
prepared to offer reasonable terms to those willing to accept t[he]
Nicene symbol. As a result the task of the Roman see in attemptin[g]

---

[1] *Hist. aceph.* 6. ed. cit. Tom. I, p. 665. Cf. Athan. *Hist. arian.*, 51, 75. *M.P.[G.]*
26; 753, 784. Epiph. *Panar.* 76, 1. ed. cit., vol. iii, p. 340.

[2] *Hist. aceph.* 7 f. ed. cit., p. 665 f.

[3] Athan. *Tom. ad Antioch.*, 1, 10. *M.P.G.* 26, 796, 808; Socrates, *H.E.* 3, 7.

[4] Socrates, *op. cit.*, 3, 9. Cf. Jerome, *Chronicon.* ed. cit., p. 242, and abo[ve]
p. 226, n. 1.

[5] According to Liberius (see p. 235, n. 3, below) the council followed a previo[us]
decision of the Roman see on this point.

[6] Jerome, *Dial. c. Lucif.* 6, 26. *M.P.L.* 23, 168, 189.

[7] Hilary, *Coll. Antiar. Par.* Ser. A VII, 6. ed. cit., p. 93.

rally the supporters of the ὁμοούσιον in the West was rendered
considerably more difficult.

To this period of reconciliation belong a letter addressed by the
Roman see to the bishops of northern Italy[1] and a further letter from
them to the bishops of Illyricum.[2] From the former of these we gather
that the Roman see had formally endorsed the Nicene symbol,[3] in
spite of its supposed defects,[4] as a fitting summary of the 'apostolic
and catholic faith',[5] and was prepared to overlook the fault of those
who had accepted the decisions taken at Ariminum in ignorance of
their true implications, on condition of their repudiation of their error
and the acceptance of the Nicene standard. The letter of the north
Italians, which probably represents the standpoint of those who looked
to Aquileia rather than to Milan as their ecclesiastical centre, was
even more outspoken regarding the adoption of Nicaea as a basis of
orthodoxy, and the need of repudiating the recent council of Ariminum.[6] It also went further than Liberius in specifying Ursacius and
Valens as among the supporters of Arian doctrine who could expect no
pardon.[7]

It seems that the Emperor Julian was highly indignant when he
learned of Athanasius' return and issued an order for his immediate
arrest and deportation.[8] With an almost athletic adroitness, creditable
to a much younger man, but perhaps not surprising in one who not
without some success had managed to defy three Roman Emperors
in succession, the indefatigable old bishop once more eluded capture.[9]
Thanks to Julian's premature death, however, his enforced absence

[1] Hilary, *Coll. Antiar. Par*. Ser. B IV, i. ed. cit., p. 156 f.
[2] Id., *ibid*., Ser. B IV, 2. ed. cit., p. 158 f.
[3] Id., *ibid*., Ser. B IV, 1. ed. cit., p. 156 f.: 'quod iam ex apostolica auctoritate unitum est de pietate.' It seems that the supposed legend of a confirmation by the Roman see of the decisions of Nicaea has some foundation in fact after all; see above, p. 214, n. 5. But it is significant that such confirmation as may be implied here was somewhat belated.
[4] *Ibid*., § 2, 'etiamsi quibusdam leve et remissum videtur'.
[5] *Ibid*., 'fidei apostolicae et catholicae usque ad Nichenae synodi conventum'.
[6] *Ibid*., Ser. B IV, 2. They mention that copies of the Nicene and Ariminian decisions were being enclosed. Had Hilary of Poitiers or Eusebius or Liberius brought back copies of the Nicene creed and canons with them from the East?
[7] *Ibid*., Ser. B IV, 1, 2. 'si aliquis . . . venenum virusque noxium sese vindicare ediderit, et ratione vincetur et auctori perfidiae perdite deputatus ecclesiae catholicae spiritali vigore plectetur'. The claim that a sentence of the Roman see is of universal application could not well be more clearly expressed.
[8] *Hist. aceph*. 10, 11. ed. cit., p. 666 f.
[9] Socrates, *H.E.* 3, 14.

was comparatively brief, and with the new Emperor Jovian h
relations became almost cordial.[1]

The reaction in favour of the Nicene faith now began to gath
strength, and late in 363 a council held at Antioch under the presiden
of bishop Meletius accepted its creed as a statement of belief.[2] Th
process, however, was temporarily checked by the policy of t
Emperor Valens, brother and colleague of Valentinian I, success
of Jovian, under whom the earlier division of the Empire into easte
and western spheres of administration had been revived.[3] Valentini
maintained an attitude of somewhat contemptuous indifference
ecclesiastical controversy, while his younger brother resolved
inferiority complex by supporting the ecclesiastical standpoint of t
bishops of Constantinople. At the synod of Lampsacus held
September, 364, under the presidency of Hypatian, metropolitan
Heraclea,[4] of which the see of Constantinople was still at this tin
properly a suffragan, the ὁμοιούσιον was approved in effect ar
Eudoxius of Constantinople deposed.[5] This rash but probably i
evitable measure was a signal for a fresh outbreak of edicts of banis
ment issued from the imperial chancery. The victims of further ac
of aggression on the part of the Constantinopolitan see resolved

[1] M.G.H. Chrom. min. vol. i, p. 240; Larsow, op. cit., p. 40. For his return, s
Hist. aceph. 13. ed. cit., p. 667. Lucius, the rival bishop of Alexandria, received lit
support. Cf. Athan. (?) Ep. ad Iovianum, Pet. 3. M.P.G. 26, 820 f.

[2] Socrates, op. cit., 3, 25, 14. The suspicion of ὁμοούσιον as a Sabellianizing te
is still evident. Cf. Hilary, De synodis, 71. M.P.L. 10, 527.

[3] This took place at Sirmium. Cf. Ammian. Marc. Lib. 26, 5, 4.

[4] Sozomen, H.E. 6, 7, 8.

[4] Eudoxius, who had played an important part among the opponents
Athanasius and in support of Eusebius, his predecessor in the see of Constantinop
on the deposition of Eustathius of Antioch, had acquired the see of Germanicia in t
province Euphratensis. As such he had attended the council of Antioch in 341 a
of Sardica, where he collaborated with the 'minority' (Hilary, Coll. Antiar. P.
Ser. A IV, 3, ed. cit., p. 75). Neither Socrates H.E. 2, 37, 10, nor Sozomen, H
4, 12, 3 f., appears to have known precisely how he obtained the see of Antioch. (
the deposition of Macedonius in 360 he received the see of Constantino
(Socrates, op. cit., 2, 43, 12), which he held till his death ten years later. He belor
to the group of careerist prelates, characteristic of the history of the eastern Chu
in this period. His opponents included, besides the supporters of his rival Ma
donius, various outstanding bishops of Asia, such as Euethius of Ephesus, Ev
tathius of Sebaste, metropolitan of Armenia prima, and Silvanus of Tars
metropolitan of Cilicia prima, all of whom may well have become apprehensive
the growing power of the see of Constantinople. It was probably with the obj
of acquiring a spurious prestige that its bishop procured on June, 1 356, the rel
of St. Timothy and on March 3 of the following year those of SS. Andrew and Lu
(M.G.H., Chron. min., vol. i, p. 238 f.).

peal against the Emperor to his elder brother in the West.[1] In
cordance with the relevant provisions of Sardica,[2] the eastern
gates presented themselves to Pope Liberius on the way. Addressing
m as 'Lord, brother and fellow-bishop'[3] they professed their
adiness to accept the Nicene symbol[4] and contrasted their own
thodoxy with the heterodox attitude of a recent council of Con-
antinople.[5] It was on condition of this acceptance that Liberius
reed to admit them to communion. But in order to checkmate any
tempt on the part of the see of Constantinople to adjudicate in the
atter, the eastern legates consented to sign an undertaking that, if
y charge should be made against them, they would present them-
lves to judges to be appointed by the Roman see, thus apparently
cepting the applicability of the Sardican canon in their case.[6]

---

[1] Thus following the example of Athanasius, see above, pp. 213, 223. For this
peal to Valentinian I, see Socrates, op. cit., 4, 12. ed. cit., p. 182.

[2] Canon 6, ed. cit. Tom. I, p. 465 ff. It is improbable, as Kidd, History, vol. ii,
230, suggests, apparently relying on Socrates, ibid., that they seriously expected
find the Emperor in Rome, since, as we learn from his edicts, he had resided
ace the beginning of his reign entirely in north Italy or in Gaul. Cf. Seeck, O.,
gesten, pp. 216–228. The legates could not have left the East till after the synods
Smyrna and of other provinces in Asia Minor which followed the council of
mpsacus, and thus probably arrived in Rome not earlier than the beginning of
6. Cf. Batiffol, Le siège apostolique, p. 9.

[3] Ep. Orient. ap. Socr. op. cit., ibid., 'Κυρίῳ ἀδελφῷ καὶ συλλειτουργῷ Λιβερίῳ'.
must not be forgotten that in this period the bishop was still pre-eminently, if
longer exclusively, the 'λειτουργός'.

[4] The Nicene symbol is identified as 'ὑπὸ τριακοσίων δέκα καὶ ὀκτὼ ἐπισκόπων
βαιωθεῖσα', and is here first so described. The mystic number of 'three hundred
d eighteen' (Gen. XIV, 14) is adopted three years or so later by Athanasius,
. ad Afros, 2. M.P.G. 26, 1032, and from then on becomes traditional as part of
e Nicene 'legend'. It is certain that the actual number was nearer two than three
undred. Cf. Turner, Eccl. occid. mon. Tom. I, p. 90. In any case Athanasius' later
ure appears to be inconsistent with his original estimate, Hist. Arian. 66. M.P.G.
, 772. 'τριακόσιοι πλέον ἢ ἔλαττον'. If he was ignorant of the exact number in 356,
w did he come to be better informed three years later?

[5] It had accepted the creed of Nice in Thrace. See above, p. 223.

[6] It is not clear whether or not the final sentence beginning: 'Εἰ δέ τις μετὰ τὴν
τεθεῖσαν παρ' ἡμῶν πίστιν . . .' is in fact part of the original letter, or whether
is an appendix added possibly at Liberius' suggestion. But in either event, it
oves the acceptance and hence knowledge of the Sardican provision, Canon 3b,
. cit. Tom. i, p. 360 f. Batiffol, op. cit., p. 11, appears to be inaccurate when he
cites: 'Cette disposition rappelle celle du concile du Sardique sur les appels à
ome ; elle la depasse même, puisque l'évêque de Rome ici a mission de désigner
s juges de première instance, et non les juges d'appel seulement'. In the case of the
gates and of those whom they represented, the court of first instance which had
onounced against them had been in effect that of Eudoxius. Liberius had examined
eir case and 'ignored the bill'. But, he implies, if their innocence should be called
question, Canon 3b would immediately come into operation.

VI

Before further news of developments in the East arrived, Liberi
was dead. It was September 24, 366. Nine months before this
rival Felix II had preceded him to the grave.[1]

In spite of the generous treatment by Liberius of those clerics w
had deserted him during his period of exile and had opposed
return, a group of them who had supported Felix made up th
minds to secure the succession for one of their own number.[2] But
putting this project into execution they found much to their surpri
that they had been forestalled. Liberius had scarcely breathed h
last when three of his loyal deacons and a handful of presbyte
hurried off to the Trastevere, and after hastily electing one of ther
selves, the deacon Ursinus, in the Julian basilica, had him co
secrated on the spot by the bishop of Tibur, apparently the only o
procurable at the time. The Felicians, however, who seem to ha
included at least a majority of the clergy, were by no means in a mo
to accept a *fait accompli*, and having stormed the basilica rather aft
the fashion of reducing a strongpoint on the battlefield, proceed
further to take violent possession of the Lateran palace. Here on t
following Sunday, October 1, they elected the deacon Damasus, w
was thereupon duly ordained by the traditional consecrator of Rom
bishops, the bishop of Ostia,[3] thus giving to their proceedings
unmistakable impression of regularity, in which the conduct of th
opponents appeared to be lacking. In strategy no less than tacti
they were evidently more than a match for their rivals, for by th
time they had succeeded in winning the support of the civil autho
ties, a most important asset in a disputed papal election. So with he
of the prefect, Damasus managed to procure a sentence of banis
ment from the city against Ursinus and his two deacon-adheren
But when he attempted to get rid by similar means of the sev
opposing presbyters, the Roman laity intervened, and after rescui
its clergy from the police, found asylum for them in the Liberi
basilica. The scene which followed rivalled in horror and trage
that which, as we learn from Thucydides, took place at Corcy

---

[1] So *Gesta* in *Coll. Avell.*, 1, 4. ed. cit., p. 2. It should be remembered that t
Gesta were compiled by the party favourable to Ursinus.

[2] *Ibid.*, 5. For this purpose they held a preliminary election in the basilica of §
Laurence *in Lucina*.

[3] Kidd, *History*, vol. ii, p. 231.

ιen an indignant *demos* took sanguinary vengeance on its defeated
litical opponents.[1]

The tale of this unhappy schism, which in all dragged on for
arly twenty years, is one of a series of appeals to the Emperor by
her side; but almost from the beginning the Damasines had the
per hand, and a final rescript of banishment against Ursinus was
blished early in 368.[2] So it was not till the second anniversary of his
nsecration that Damasus felt sufficiently secure to hold the cus-
mary synod of the Roman church on that day.[3] Its principal work
as concerned with the problem created by the survival of centres of
sistance to Nicene orthodoxy (now, as we have seen, accepted by
e Roman see as the final standard of correct belief), such as still
mained at Milan and in certain parts of Illyricum. It seems that both
Gaul and Venetia (probably at Aquileia) synods had decreed the
position of Auxentius of Milan. In view, however, of the measure
protection which that bishop enjoyed from Valentinian as holding
e see of the imperial capital, Damasus probably held it to be
politic to risk offending the Emperor by openly endorsing their
rdict; instead, in a letter addressed to the bishops of Illyricum,
s synod preferred to emphasize the finality of the Nicene symbol,
hich it justified by calling attention to the presence of Roman
gates at that council, while repudiating afresh the decisions taken
Ariminum, on the express ground that they had not been approved
the Roman see.[4]

Information about the action taken by the Roman synod of 368
as in due course received at Alexandria. In his letter to the Africans,

---

[1] *Historiae*, 4, 48.

[2] It evidently demanded a good deal of effort and perhaps intrigue on the part of
amasus to make good his case with Valentinian. Probably Ursinus could count
a considerable measure of local support, cf. *Gesta*, ap. *Coll. Avell.* 1, 9–11,
. cit., p. 3 f., which shows that the Roman laity who upheld his cause did not
sitate to compare his rival with Antiochus Epiphanes. For the rescript of Ursinus'
nishment, see *Coll. Avell.* 5, ed. cit., p. 48. Even after this Damasus needed the
nperor's help in order to recover possession of the Liberian basilica (Sicinii), *ibid.*,
to get rid of his opponent's supporters, *ibid.*, 7, ed. cit., p. 49 f., and to prohibit
ssident assemblies within a twenty-mile radius of the city, *ibid.*, 8 and 9. ed.
., p. 50 f. *Gesta*, 12. ed. cit., p. 4, mentions liturgical gatherings at St. Agnes,
iich had been Liberius' *pied à terre* on his return from exile (see above, p. 230, n. 5),
nsisting of laity only without ministers of any sort (sine clericis).

[3] *Gesta*, 13. ed. cit., p. 4.

[4] Damasus, *Ep.* 1, JK 232, *Confidimus quidem*. The author of the *Gesta, ibid.*, 13 f.,
marks that the synod firmly declined to give a verdict against Ursinus in his
sence: 'nos ad natale convenimus, non ut inauditum damnemus'.

Athanasius referred to its decisions and expressed some astonishme[nt] that no explicit condemnation of Auxentius of Milan had been pu[b] lished.[1] He intimated that an Egyptian synod had already writt[en] to the Roman see strongly urging this course.[2] The chief interest [of] his letter lies in the view which it expresses about the council [of] Nicaea, asserting that its purpose was to prevent local synods bei[ng] held in the future under pretext of solving a problem regarding t[he] faith, and adding that, if numbers were compared, the Nice[ne] council was as much greater than all the rest, as the whole was grea[ter] than a part.[3]

It is about the same time that a new and somewhat attracti[ve] character comes to the forefront of the eastern stage in the pers[on] of Basil, elected bishop of Caesarea in Cappadocia, September 370.[4] Recent experience had evidently convinced him of the hopeles[s] ness of attempting to restore peace among the eastern church[es] without the co-operation of the West, and in particular of the Rom[an] see. One of his earliest surviving letters,[5] addressed to Athanasi[us] conveyed an explicit proposal that the western bishops should [be] invited to adjudicate between the disputants, and in particular [to] solve the problem created by the Antiochene schism. This meant [in] fact that the Roman see should be persuaded to adopt Basil's ov[n] solution, namely the recognition of Meletius to the exclusion of [his] rival Paulinus.[6] Apparently he was unaware that Athanasius h[ad] already committed himself to communion with Paulinus, and wh[en] all his appeals to Alexandria for help in carrying out this plan m[et] with a cold reception, he evinced quite unreasonable signs of di[s] appointment.

Meanwhile the long drawn out contest between Damasus and [his]

---

[1] *Ep. ad Afros* (i.e. the see of Carthage), 10. *M.P.G.* 26, 1045.

[2] *Ibid.* Athanasius states that it was attended by about ninety Libyan bishops[, as] well as all those of Egypt.

[3] *Ibid.*, 2. He does not mention any confirmation by the Roman see. But [in] addition to a reference to the solution of the Paschal controversy as one of [its] primary objectives, he states that all subsequent synods were aimed solely [at] invalidating the decisions of Nicaea. It is from such material that the Nice[ne] 'legend' has been fashioned.

[4] Gregory Naz., *Orat.* 18, 36. *M.P.G.* 35, 1033.

[5] *Ep.* 66. ed. Paris, 1839, vol. iii, p. 227 ff. But his emphasis on the importa[nce] of the see of Antioch (§ 2), and his description of it as κεφαλὴ in relation to the r[est] of the (? eastern) Church (σῶμα) must have been somewhat distasteful to a bish[op] of Alexandria. See *Ep.* 69. ed. cit., vol. iii, p. 231 ff. and *Ep.* 68, p. 230 f.

[6] See above, p. 234.

ponents at Rome, which had lain dormant for more than two
ars, suddenly sprang to life again, with a development which
rrowly missed eliminating him from the scene. The sanguinary
nflict resulting from the attempt to expel the Ursinians from the
iberian basilica recoiled on the head of the person likely to gain
ost from their eviction, who now found himself arraigned before
e civil court of an unsympathetic *vicarius urbis* on the plain and
ipleasing charge of inciting to murder.[1] For plaintiff Ursinus and
s party had found a useful cat's-paw in Isaac the converted Jew.[2]
etails are scanty, but from the evidence at our disposal it seems
obable that the defendant was found guilty[3] and the case, as
fitting one in which a personage of senatorial rank was involved,
ferred to the Emperor for sentence.

That Damasus owed his eventual acquittal by Valentinian in part
least to the influence of the Antiochene presbyter Evagrius,[4] who
ad thrown in his lot with bishop Paulinus and at the time was
rrying out a special mission to Eusebius of Vercelli, becomes
most certain, if we take into account the Pope's subsequent
titude towards the Antiochene question, to which we must now
turn.

Undismayed by Athanasius' unsympathetic attitude, Basil had
ade a second and even a third attempt to gain his favour. In the
rmer of these[5] he recommended that Damasus should be invited to
nd legates to assist in adjudicating disputed cases; in the latter[6] he
ointed out afresh that the only way to peace lay in a general recog-
ition of Meletius, a step which he urged on the explicit though
ctually false ground that he had already been acknowledged by the

---

[1] The *vicarius urbis* was Maximin, *Coll. Avell.* 12. ed. cit., p. 53 f. The rescript
Ampelius, *praefectus urbi*, in *Coll. Avell.*, 11. ed. cit., p. 52 f., shows that Maximin
ad been given special authority to deal with disturbances arising out of the schism.
n view of *Gesta*, 9, ed. cit., p. 3 f., 'a sede Petri homicidas foras' there can be little
oubt as to the nature of the charge against Damasus, cf. *ibid.*, 12, 'ipsum auctorem
celerum et homicidam Damasum'.

[2] Ambrose, *Ep.* 11, 2. *M.P.L.* 16, 985, holds that Ursinus was the real promoter
f the case. For Isaac, see *Ep. syn. Rom.* 378, *Et hoc gloriae vestrae*, 8. *M.P.L.* 13,
75.

[3] In the course of the examination, with characteristic rigour though with strict
egality, Maximin subjected members of the clergy to torture, *ibid.*, 3, 10.

[4] Jerome, *Ep.* 1, 15. *C.S.E.L.* vol. liv, p. 9, our sole authority for the fact, had
very opportunity of knowing what took place through his friendship with the Pope.

[5] *Ep.* 69, ed. cit., vol. iii, p. 231 ff. On the order of these letters, see Caspar,
p. cit., vol. i, p. 595.

[6] *Ep.* 68, ed. cit., p. 229 f.

Roman see.[1] All was in vain. It took more than a Basil to change t
mind of an Athanasius.

Yet on receiving a copy of the Roman synodical letter of 3
addressed to Illyricum[2], the bishop of Caesarea was emboldened
begin afresh. This time he indicated to Meletius that he should ma
a direct approach to the Roman see.[3] Meanwhile he busied hims
with the composition of a letter to Damasus himself.[4] Meletius w
evidently secure of the support of at least a small section of t
eastern episcopate, since he managed to assemble a synod of son
thirty bishops, who agreed to inform the Roman see that th
assented to the doctrinal position of the recent letter to Illyricum
This letter,[6] together with others addressed to outstanding weste
bishops, such as Valerian of Aquileia,[7] were taken by the Milane
deacon Sabinus on his way home. It was the year (373) of Athana
sius' death. Previous to that event the bishop of Alexandria had take
the very suitable precaution of consecrating his own successo
Peter II, who presently found his position so intolerable that h
quickly made good his escape to Rome.[8] But when at long last
letter arrived from Damasus[9] it was not addressed to Basil, an

[1] Basil appears to have supposed that Liberius' recognition of Eustathius
Sebaste and his supporters (see above, p. 237) included Meletius. Admittedly th
and Meletius were in communion, but Meletius' name does not appear in t
Pope's letter.

[2] See above, p. 239.

[3] *Ep.* 89, ed. cit., p. 258 f.

[4] *Ep.* 70. ed. cit., p. 233 ff. Even if, as is usually held, the letter was never actual
despatched, it is remarkable not only for its allusion to the contact between t
sees of Rome and Caesarea at least since the time of Pope Dionysius (see abov
p. 178 f.), but for its evidently high estimate of the value of the Pope's interventio
(164A): 'τούτων μίαν προσεδοκήσαμεν λύσιν τὴν τῆς ὑμετέρας εὐσπλαγχνίας ἐπίσκεψι
In any case it is difficult to avoid the impression created by this letter and by *E*
69, 1, that, like Eustathius of Sebaste, Basil was not wholly unaware of the pr
visions of Sardica (see above, p. 237).

[5] *Ep.* 1. JK 232.

[6] *Inter Basil. Epp.*, No. 92. ed. cit., p. 262 ff. There appears to be an allusion t
a supposed privilege of the Roman see, i.e. Matt. XVI, 19, in the concludin
sentence: 'τὸ τῇ ὑμετέρᾳ θεοσεβείᾳ χαρισθὲν παρὰ τοῦ Κυρίου, τὸ μὲν κίβδηλον ἀπὸ τo
δοκίμου καὶ καθάρου διακρίνειν, τὴν δὲ τῶν πατέρων πίστιν ἄνευ τινὸς ὑποστολῆς κηρύσσειν

[7] Of these only the letter to Valerian, *Ep.* 91, ed. cit., p. 261 f., has been preserved

[8] *Hist. aceph.* 20. ed. cit. Tom. I, p. 671; Larsow, *op. cit.*, p. 46. For Peter'
escape, see Sozomen, *H.E.* 4, 19; Theodoret, *H.E.* 4. 20. ed. cit., p. 246. Th
scenes at Alexandria which had occurred at fairly regular intervals during Athanasiu
episcopate were renewed on the restoration of the anti-bishop Lucius.

[9] The letter itself has not survived. Its contents can be inferred from Basi
Epp. 156, ed. cit., p. 354 ff.; 138, p. 331 ff.; 140, p. 335 ff. In the last of these h
insists that the Nicene symbol alone is sufficient.

iefly indicated that those Easterns who desired recognition by the
oman see must first sign the doctrinal statement enclosed, and then
nd legates to negotiate terms of reconciliation.

In spite of his disappointment and evident disapproval of Damasus'
ethods, Basil would not even now abandon his object. Western aid
as so urgently needed that this time he contemplated invoking the
lp of Valentinian.[1] Once more it was Damasus who answered.[2] Yet
his attitude had still remained at all ambiguous, the fact that
ortly afterwards a further letter was addressed directly to Paulinus[3]
w left no room for doubt. Basil remained unmoved, and in a
tter to Meletius showed that no dictation from Rome would make
m change his allegiance.[4] As proof of this he refused his support to
further effort to obtain western aid.[5]

By this time, however, a new dogmatic dispute about the com-
eteness of our Lord's human nature was on its way,[6] and it was
neasiness on this score which led Basil to abandon the part of
iomede and this time to approach Peter of Alexandria,[7] who was
ill a fugitive at Rome. Nothing could have been more to Damasus'
king. Thus it came about that in the Roman synod of 378[8] the threads
' the Ursinian and of the eastern 'plots' were united.

In spite of his acquittal by the Emperor, Pope Damasus found that
e memory of the unhappy inauguration of his pontificate persisted
d even led to some measure of insubordination among his suf-
agans.[9] He appears to have decided that his best course of action was

---

[1] *Ep.* 243, ed. cit., p. 539 ff., dated 374 (sc. Schwartz., *Nachr. d. Gölt. Ges. d.
iss.* 1904, p. 368). Basil mentions the possibility of a direct legation to Milan.

[2] A fragment only of this letter, *Ea gratia*, survives. On the date of this and other
agments derived from the *Sylloge* of Theodosius diaconus, see Turner, *Eccl.
id. mon.* Tom. I, p. 625 ff., and Schwartz, *op. cit.*, p. 361 ff.; *Zeitschr. f. N.T.
iss.*, vol. xxv., 1926, p. 42f.

[3] Damasus, *Ep.* 2. JK 235. Jaffé's dates here are misleading.

[4] *Ep.* 214, ed. cit., p. 464 ff.   [5] *Ep.* 129, 3. ed. cit., p. 319.

[6] *Ibid.*, 1, p. 318, concerning the teaching of Apollinaris of Laodicaea. It is proble that the Damasine fragment *Illud sane miramur* belongs to this period.

[7] *Ep.* 266, ed. cit., p. 596 ff. Cf. *Ep.* 263, p. 586, in which he seeks to clear himself
a charge of Apollinarianism, and invites a western opinion on the orthodoxy of
s colleagues and himself.

[8] The dates of the Damasine synods present some difficulties. For the view
opted here, see Schwartz, *op. cit.*, p. 374. It is highly improbable owing to the
cal situation that synods were held in Rome between 368 and 378.

[9] The synodical letter *Et hoc gloriae vestrae*, 5 (see below, p. 245) mentions that
e bishop of Parma and Florentius of Puteoli, the latter in spite of the Emperor's
fusal to hear his appeal, continued to retain their sees in the teeth of a papal
ndemnation.

to obtain a verdict of moral blamelessness from the Roman synod,[1] that when the suffragan bishops[2] and Roman presbyters met ⟨ October 1, 378,[3] they found a full and perhaps unusually interesti⟨ agenda awaiting them.

In reply to the appeal of Basil and the Easterns, the synod endors⟨ a doctrinal statement, sometimes known as the 'Tome of Damasus' which beginning with a Latin version of the Nicene symbol added⟨ series of anathemas against Sabellians,[5] Arius, Eunomius,[6] Mac⟨ donians,[7] Photinus,[8] those who assert belief in two Sons,[9] those w⟨ deny that the Word of God took a rational and intelligent *anima*,[10] a⟨ finally those who argue that the same Word is a temporary extensi⟨ or contraction of the Godhead.[11] To this there appears to have be⟨ added a canon directed against episcopal translations, probab⟨ aimed at Meletius.[12] That the synod pronounced in favour Damasus' innocence is not open to doubt.[13] But it did more than th⟨ It determined to prevent if possible the continuance of episcopal i⟨

[1] *Et hoc gloriae vestrae*, 10.

[2] *Ibid.*, 'severioribus se dedit iudiciis sacerdotum'. This probably means t⟨ suffragan bishops were present, since the use of 'sacerdos' to denote a presby⟨ was still rare at this time.

[3] The fact that the rescript *Ordinariorum sententias*, *Coll. Avell.*, 13, ed. c⟨ p. 54 ff., is written in the names of Gratian and Valentinian, and mentions neith⟨ Valens, whose death occurred on August 9, 378, Seeck, *Regesten*, p. 251, m⟨ Theodosius, elevated January 19, 379, decisively fixes it in the later months of 3⟨ This gives the same year as the most probable date for this synod, to the letter⟨ which the rescript was the imperial reply. Cf. Seeck, *op. cit.*, p. 152, l. 30.

[4] Turner, *Eccl. occid. mon. iur. ant.*, Tom. I, p. 281 ff. See also Caspar, *op. c⟨ vol. i, p. 596.

[5] On the earlier attitude of the Roman see towards Sabellianism, see above, p. 12⟨

[6] Eunomius represented the neo-Arianism of the 'Anomoean' school.

[7] No explicit heresy is here attributed to Macedonius, though he was later ass⟨ ciated with denial of the Godhead of the Holy Ghost.

[8] Photinus (of Sirmium) held a doctrine similar to that of Marcellus of Ancy⟨ but denied any pre-existence to the Son.

[9] The doctrine of which Diodore of Tarsus was held to be a notable representati⟨

[10] Apollinaris the younger of Laodicaea.

[11] Marcellus of Ancyra, see above, p. 213, n. 2.

[12] For decisions of Nicaea and Sardica on episcopal translations, see abov⟨ pp. 205, n. 2, 230, n. 1. This canon, which appears in some Latin texts in a differe⟨ position, or is headed 'Dilectissimo fratri Paulino Damasus', or is omitted (s⟨ Turner, *op. cit.*, p. 387), is evidently distinct from the preceding matter. ⟨ Schwartz, *Zeitschr. f. N.T. Wiss.*, vol. xxv, 1926, p. 65, n. 1. In any case the su⟨ sequent anathemas are a later addition, see Duchesne, *Histoire*, vol. ii, p. 410, n.⟨ It is probable that the Damasine fragment *Non nobis quicquam*, *M.P.L.* 13, 3⟨ should also be assigned to this synod, since it stresses the Godhead of the H⟨ Ghost as well as the completeness of our Lord's two natures, divine and hum⟨ It is perhaps a reply to Basil, *Ep.* 263. See p. 243, n. 7.

[13] Rufinus, *H.E.* 11, 10. ed. cit., p. 1018.

ordination and the recurrence of a situation which must have
peared in the highest degree anomalous, the subjection of the
preme ecclesiastical judge to the jurisdiction of an ordinary civil
urt. Two proposals were addressed to the Sovereigns.[1]

First, in regard to the authority of the Roman see in relation to
her bishops, it was recommended that if a bishop had been con-
nned either by the Pope or by the Roman synod, he should be
nished from his city by the civil power. If, however, he had de-
hed to obey a summons to Rome for trial, the same power, i.e.
prefect of Italy or the *vicarius urbis*, should compel his attendance;
if he belonged to a more remote province he should be tried by
metropolitan. Should the accused however be himself a metro-
itan, he should betake himself to Rome forthwith, or else to judges
pointed by that see. In the former instance, if there were grounds
suspecting the impartiality of the metropolitan, the accused could
her appeal to have his case heard by the Roman see, or by a synod
at least fifteen neighbouring bishops.[2] Secondly, as to the relation

Et hoc gloriae, 9. *M.P.L.* 13, 575. In § 1 the petitioners appealed to a law
lished soon after the elevation of Gratian to the purple (August 24, 367), of
ch only a short quotation has been preserved by Ambrose, *Ep.* 21, 2. *M.P.L.* 16,
5. 'in causa fidei vel ecclesiastici alicuius ordinis eum iudicare debere, qui nec
here impar sit, nec iure dissimilis (haec enim verba rescripti sunt), hoc est,
rdotes de sacerdotibus voluit iudicare. quin etiam si alias quisque argueretur
copus, et morum esset examinanda causa, etiam haec voluit ad episcopale
cium pertinere'. It is probable that this rescript owed its origin to a petition
sented to Constantius by the council of Sardica. See *Oratio syn. Sard.* 1, 1. ap.
ry, *Coll. Antiar. Par. C.S.E.L.* vol. lxv, p. 181: 'iudices . . . a religiosa se
ervantia abstineant neque posthac praesumant . . . se causas cognoscere
icorum'. Thus in virtue of exemption from all civil burdens and obligations,
Theod. XVI, ii, 1, 2, 3, and the privileges already granted by Constantine, *Cod.*
od. XVI, xxvii, 1 (dated by Seeck, O., *op. cit.*, pp. 57, 166, June 23, 318),
icitly designating bishops as judges in cases involving questions of Christian
a and discipline, without right of appeal to a civil court, *Const. Sirmond*, No. 1,
ally provides that in a civil action between Christians, either party might
aand, even if the case were already *sub iudice* before a civil court, to be heard
he bishop's court (although this concession was subsequently withdrawn, *Cod.*
. I, 4, of February 7, 452). Thus the courts of the Church were gradually
airing rights equal to those of the State.
may be observed that here for the first time the title 'pontifex' is applied to
Roman bishop. The title 'pontifex maximus' had been formally laid aside by
tian in 375, Zosimus, *Hist. nov.* 4, 36, ed. Mendelssohn, L., p. 193, where the
y of the indignation expressed by pagans provides an unconscious prophecy of
ater assumption by the Roman bishops.
Ibid., 10: 'quibus etsi aequalis est munere, praerogativa tamen apostolicae sedis
llit'. Here again is the earliest known example of one of the characteristic
gnations of the Papacy. Damasus himself used it later in a letter addressed to
toch, see *Ep.* 7, JK 234, and below, p. 294.

7

of the Roman bishop to the State, it was proposed that he should en
the same exemption from normal secular jurisdiction as was alrea
possessed by other bishops, since, in the view of the petitione
'though he is their equal in office, in virtue of the prerogative of
apostolic see he is their superior'; and in the event of the case be
outside the competence of his own synod, he should be entit
to plead before the Emperor's court. Thus it was hoped that
opportunity for mere calumniation would be excluded.[1]

How far were the Sovereigns prepared to go in the direction
meeting the demands of their petitioners? The synodical letter
received by the young Emperor Gratian[2] and the yet more youth
Valentinian II,[3] the former strongly influenced by the august p
sonality of Ambrose, bishop of Milan since 374,[4] the latter still un
the tutelage of his mother, the Empress Justina, second wife
Valentinian I. Since the defeat and death of Valens at Adrianople
the previous August,[5] Gratian, not yet in his twentieth year, I
been sole effective Emperor. Even so he refrained from granting
that was asked of him. In his rescript *Ordinariorum sententias*[6]
conceded the request touching the trial and appeal of bishops
the jurisdiction of the Roman see;[7] but in regard to proposals for
examination of charges against the Roman bishop he appeared to sh
some hesitation. He does not conceal his contempt for mer
slanderous accusation, but regarding the actual question whether
Pope is to be exempt from the normal process of the law he sli
off into edifying generalities on the natural sense of justice enjo
by Emperors.[8] Possibly he meant it to be understood that he

---

[1] On the privileges of bishops, e.g. in the case of Priscillian, see Sulpicius S
Chron. 2, 49. *C.S.E.L.* vol. i, p. 102. For the rights of senators, *Cod. Theod.* IX, i,
ii, 2; xl, 10, dated 365, 366, 370, cf. Mommsen, Th., *Römisches Strafrecht*, p. 4c
The synodical letter also implored stronger measures against the Roman Dona
(§ 7), and called attention (§ 6) to the failure of Restitutus of Carthage to answ
summons, issued by the Emperors, to justify himself before the Roman synod.
had accepted the final decision of Ariminum, and in the eyes of the Roman
was in need of purgation.

[2] He had been Augustus since 367, and became sole colleague of Valens on
death of his father Valentinian I, November 17, 375. See *M.G.H. Chron. m*
vol. i, p. 242.

[3] He was raised to the principate on November 22 of the same year. *M.G.H. ib*

[4] Elected in the place of Constantius' nominee Auxentius. See Paulinus, *Vita*

[5] *M.G.H. Chron. min.*, vol. i, p. 243.   [6] *Coll. Avell.* 13. ed. cit., p. 5

[7] *Ibid.*, 11. The mention of the 'five' or 'seven' episcopal assessors should
noted. They appear to be the prototypes of the Cardinal bishops.

[8] *Ibid.*, 14. Probably Gratian felt it would be dangerous to detract in any
from the competence of the normal legal authority.

repared to adopt the petitioners' proposal, but if so, he certainly
voided being too precise in his use of language.

It cannot be denied that this earliest formal expression of imperial
upport for the jurisdiction exercised by the Roman see must
ave added something at least to its prestige. Whether it did more
an recognize a situation which ecclesiastically speaking was
ready at any rate *de facto* in Italy, may be disputed. It is, however,
deniable that from this time on the Roman bishops repeatedly
ercise the authority here assigned to them, at first generally in
e West and later occasionally also in the East, as in fact they
d already exercised it, at least in part, before the issue of the
script.[1]

As compared with the powers granted, or perhaps we should
ther say recognized, by the council of Sardica, however, those
entioned in the rescript mark some advance. According to the
solutions of that council, all that was provided was that in the
ent of a suit between two bishops, either the judges or the bishops
a neighbouring province might appeal to the Roman see to examine
e matter and to appoint fresh judges if it thought fit. It was also
owed, in the event of a bishop already deposed filing an appeal,
at the Roman bishop might, if he so judged, either refer the case
a neighbouring province, or else, on the request of the appellant,
nd legates to take part in a fresh hearing.[2] The rescript, on the other
nd, created the Roman see a court of first instance for all metro-
litans, and for all other bishops a final court of appeal, with pro-
ion for overriding metropolitical jurisdiction, if circumstances
peared to warrant such action. Such necessary circumstances, it
y be imagined, would not be difficult to discover when the need
se.

VII

The ecclesiastical scene changed with surprising rapidity as the
hth decade of the century drew to its close. A new colleague in the
ncipate was provided in Theodosius,[3] and the event soon showed

---

See above, p. 213. [2] For reff., see above, p. 219 f.

[3] *M.G.H. Chron. min.*, vol. i, pp. 243, 297 ; vol. ii, p. 60. His elevation took place
January 19, 379. Theodosius was a Spaniard by birth, and this goes far to
ount for the 'western' bias of his first theological edict (see below, p. 249). Later,
r his entry into Constantinople, his edicts undergo a change and have a markedly
tern' tone. Nevertheless his partiality for Nicene theology is perhaps to be
lained, in part at least, by his western origin.

that the Empire had acquired in him a ruler worthy of description $\;$
the last great successor of Augustus. In consequence of an edict
general toleration published by Gratian,[1] Peter of Alexandri
Meletius of Antioch and other fugitive and exiled bishops returne
to their sees. The stage was thus set for a fresh attempt to obta
general consent to an acknowledged standard of faith.

The year 379 was one of considerable importance for the futu
of Church and State. Beset by a war on two fronts, in the Balkans
well as on the Rhine, Gratian decided to entrust his colleague The
dosius with a larger measure of responsibility, and made over t
'dioceses' of Dacia and Macedonia to the eastern sphere of admini
tration, out of which Theodosius thereupon constituted a ne
prefecture of (eastern) Illyricum.[2] He at once made the prospero
city of Thessalonica his headquarters,[3] and by a singular combinati
of diplomacy with strategy secured the Danubian frontier. This ta
accomplished, he began to turn his attention to the more delica
work of pacifying the Church.

The return of Meletius to Antioch[4] marked the beginning
renewed effort to restore unity within the eastern church on
liberal or neo-Nicene basis,[5] and incidentally to heal the loc
schism between his supporters and the strict Nicenes headed
Paulinus. His ability to assemble later in the same year at Antioch
council attended by more than one hundred and fifty bishops ga
some promise of success in the former undertaking, and suggest
that he was already assured of imperial support.[6] As for the latter,
spite of a very reasonable proposal that on the death of either of t
two competing bishops his adherents should be accepted and in the

---

[1] *Cod. Theod.* XVI, v, 5, of August 18 (?) 378, excepting only Eunomia
Photinians and Manichaeans from its scope. Cf. Socrates, *H.E.* 5, 2. It wa
political measure intended to rally the forces of the Empire in a moment of cri
and was subsequently limited, when the immediate danger was past, by a l
generous edict published at Milan on August 3, 379. *Cod. Theod., ibid.,* 'Omi
vetitae.'

[2] Sozomen, *H.E.* 7, 4. For the formation of the new prefecture, aimed at sa
guarding the northern frontier, see Gibbon, *Decline,* ed. Bury, J. B., vol. ii, 19
p. 588.

[3] Hence the later ecclesiastical importance of this see.

[4] Described in glowing language by John Chrysostom, *Hom. in S. Meletium,*
M.P.G. 50, 517.

[5] That objection to the ὁμοούσιον was still strong at this time was shown by
supporters of Macedonius of Constantinople. Cf. Socrates, *H.E.* 5, 4.

[6] Turner, *op. cit.,* Tom. i, p. 625; Schwartz, E., in *Nachr. d. Gött. Ges. d. Wi*
1904, p. 362 ff.; and in *Zeitschr. f. N.T. Wiss.,* vol. xxv, 1926, p. 42 f.

turn acknowledge the survivor, the die-hard rigorism of Paulinus reasserted itself and the plan unhappily came to nothing.[1]

Meanwhile divisions within the church of Constantinople itself were engaging the Emperor's attention. It was probably chiefly in order to remedy these that he issued his famous edict *Cunctos populos*,[2] in which the view now normal in the West on the source of the genuine Christian *paradosis* was formally proclaimed.

'It is our will,' he writes, in the name of his colleagues and himself, 'that all peoples subject to our gracious governance shall conform to the same religious obligations, which are affirmed to have been taught to the Romans by Peter the Apostle of God, and have been handed down by him even to our own time, being followed by the pontiff Damasus and by Peter, bishop of Alexandria . . . namely that according to apostolic instruction and the teaching of the Gospel, we should believe that there is one Godhead of the Father, of the Son and of the Holy Ghost, in equal majesty and undivided Trinity'.[3]

The passage is noteworthy as illustrating the temporary recovery of a more primitive standpoint in the East. But the maxim of Constantius still remained the ruling factor in the situation,[4] and in Theodosius' later edicts the appeal to the apostolic *paradosis* disappears. Its disappearance showed his adoption of the usual eastern standpoint, that the will of Caesar, and it alone, remained decisive.

On November 24, Theodosius made a triumphal and spectacular entry into Constantinople.[5] Without a moment's delay the provisions of the recent edict were put into force, and Demophilus, who had reigned as bishop for the past ten years, being unwilling to accept its terms, found himself an exile and his supporters deprived of church property.[6] This action was further enforced by edict early in the following year,[7] in which it was prescribed that heretical gatherings within cities were to cease and that buildings were to be handed over

---

[1] Theodoret, *H.E.* 5, 3, 14, ed. cit., p. 281, describes some abortive negotiations between Meletius and Paulinus. That something of the kind took place confirmed by Socrates, *H.E.* 5, 5, and by the council of Aquileia (381). Ambrose, p. 12 (cf. Cavallera, F., *Le schisme d'Antioche*, 1905), himself proposed the adoption of a plan of this kind. It is evident that neither side trusted the other.

[2] *Cod. Theod.* XVI, i, 2; ii, 25.

[3] *Ibid.*, 1.   [4] See above, p. 228.

[5] Socrates, *H.E.* 5, 6, 6; *Chron. Pasch.* ad ann. 378. *M.P.G.* 92, 761.

[6] Socrates, *H.E.* 5, 7, 10. Cf. *M.G.H. Chron. min.* vol. ii, p. 61.

[7] *Cod. Theod.* XVI, v, 6, publ. January 10, 381.

to those who accepted the faith of Nicaea, here formally identified
with the Catholic Church.

The see of Constantinople, the importance of which in eastern
ecclesiastical politics now becomes difficult to exaggerate, was
definitely vacant. At once intrigues began in various quarters to
secure the election of an acceptable candidate. Attempts were set on
foot both by Timothy of Alexandria and by Meletius of Antioch to
obtain the success of a man of his own choice, but from one cause or
another in the end neither had his way.[1] The capital was already
thronged with bishops from various parts of the East,[2] each with his
own suit before the new master of the Empire, and it seems to have
occurred to Theodosius that an excellent opportunity was thus provided for settling a number of disputed questions. Possibly he had
already made up his mind that the old struggle on the part of Alexandria, and the more recent though less obvious one on the part of
Antioch, each to obtain a primacy in the East to the exclusion of the
other, must cease now and for ever.

Yet that he seriously intended a council modelled on Constantine's
plan for Nicaea is in the highest degree improbable. If he did so
intend, his purpose hopelessly miscarried, since those bishops who
actually took part in the proceedings were almost without exception
drawn from the prefecture of the East.[3] Even so the 'diocese' of
Egypt was represented only by Timothy of Alexandria and a single
suffragan, and these appear to have arrived merely in time to make
trouble in the matter of the election[4] and then subsequently to have

---

[1] Timothy's candidate was the notorious Maximus, see Greg. Naz. *Carm.* 11
750 ff. *M.P.G.* 37, 1081 ff. He succeeded in imposing on Gregory and later even
on Ambrose, *Ep.* 13, 3, 4. *M.P.L.* 16, 991 f., but not on Acholius of Thessalonic
and his fellow-bishops of Illyricum, who duly reported what was on foot to Pope
Damasus. The latter expressed his emphatic disapproval of the impostor in *Epp.*
5 and 6, JK 237, 238, and in regard to the forthcoming council of Constantinople
of which he had heard, urged Acholius to take steps to see that 'de caetero catholicu
constituatur, cum quo nobis deo propitio possit pax perpetua perdurare'. In *Epp.*
5, 4, he hinted very clearly that he disapproved of the candidate supported b
Meletius, namely Gregory of Nazianzus, on the ground that his election woul
contravene *Conc. Nic.* canon 15; cf. *Conc. Sard.* canon 8, ed. cit., p. 474.

[2] Many citations were issued; none has been preserved.

[3] This is shown by the *Nomina episcoporum*, ap. Turner, *Eccl. occid. mon. iur. ant*
Tom. II, p. 433 ff. Western editors observing the absence of Roman legates adopte
the convenient though unconvincing expedient of borrowing three from the list
of the council of Chalcedon, *ibid.*, p. 434.

[4] Cf. Id., *ibid.* Socrates, *H.E.* 5, 8, states that the election was one of the chi
objects of holding the council. For the part played by Timothy, see Gregory Na
Carm. 11, 1802. *M.P.G.* 37, 1155.

sented themselves.[1] Acholius of Thessalonica was the only bishop
~o could in any sense be accounted a Western, though as he now
longed to the part of the Empire which was being administered at
~nstantinople, and was in all probability personally summoned by
~eodosius as his ecclesiastical adviser, he can scarcely count as such.[2]
~us it would seem that what we may call the 'legend' of Nicaea has
~en equalled if not outstripped by the 'legend' of Constantinople as
essay in imaginative history.

The proceedings of the council[3] fall into two distinct, though con-
~cted stages; a preliminary one, concerned solely with the election
~ a new bishop of Constantinople, including the death of Meletius
~th the election of Flavian to the see of Antioch,[4] and culminating
~ the withdrawal of Gregory and the election of the unbaptized
~ctarius;[5] and a later in which certain doctrinal and disciplinary
~olutions were adopted. These resolutions probably included a
~gmatic statement, or 'Tome',[6] and the endorsement of the Nicene
~nbol, an action which served only to give ecclesiastical sanction to
~ religious policy of Theodosius. The creed ascribed to it by the
~ncil of Chalcedon and appended to its Latin *Acta* was almost
~rtainly a formula of belief produced by Flavian and probably used
~ Nectarius as a profession of faith at the time of his baptism.[7] More
~nificant were the disciplinary decisions.[8] These were evidently

To be inferred from Theodoret, *H.E.* 5, 8, 4. ed. cit., p. 287. The absence of
~mothy would account for the acceptance of canon 2, which appears to correct
~c. *Nic.* canon 6 by the omission of Libya and Pentapolis.

He had baptized Theodosius late in the previous year, see Socrates, *H.E.* 5, 6.
~ advice, which corresponded to the opinion expressed by Damasus, may perhaps
~e been a deciding factor in the exclusion of Gregory.

The exact date of its opening is not certainly known. According to Socrates,
E. 5, 8, it began in May.

Socrates, *op. cit.*, 5, 9. It was later represented, id., *ibid.*, 15, that the supporters
~ Meletius had been guilty of a breach of promise, but perhaps with injustice
~e above, p. 248 f.). For Flavian as an Antiochene presbyter, see Turner, *op. cit.*,
~m. II, p. 441.

Nectarius was praetor and evidently popular, according to Socrates, *op. cit.*,
~. The council which had been summoned to confirm the faith of Nicaea showed
~lf singularly disrespectful to its canons, esp. canon 2. Cf. *Conc. Sard.* canon 8,
cit. Tom. I, p. 472 ff.

Theodoret, *H.E.* 5, 9, ed. cit., p. 289 ff.; *Ep. Conc. $\overline{CP}$.* ap. Mansi, *Concilia,*
~, iii, col. 557. An Arabic version (German transl.) in Riedel, W., *Die Kirchen-*
~htsquellen des Patriarchats Alexandrien, 1900, p. 303 ff. Cf. Turner, *op. cit.*,
~m. I, pp. 284 ff., and Grumel, V., *Regestes des Actes du Patriarchat de $\overline{CP}$.,*
~2, vol. i, p. 2 f.

Grumel, *op. cit.*, p. 1.

Grumel, *op. cit.*, p. 2.

intended mainly to restrict the influence of the see of Alexandria
while safeguarding the privileges of the see of Antioch, and to set t
keystone to the constructive work initiated by Eusebius of Nicomed
over half a century ago. It was resolved that 'according to the cano
the bishop of Alexandria should administer the affairs of Egypt on
and the bishops of the East the East only, saving to the church
Antioch the privileges in the canons of Nicaea'. Similar restrictio
were placed on the 'dioceses' of Asia, Pontus, and Thrace. Bisho
were prohibited from intervening in the business of other (civ
'dioceses' and the 'provincial synod is to order the affairs of ea
province . . .'[2]

'But'—and here is the supreme crux—'the bishop of Constantinop
is to have the privilege of precedence after the bishop of Rom
because it is new Rome'.[3]

This ingenious provision, later known generally as the 'thi
canon', accomplished three remarkable feats. It finally set aside tho
claims to an eastern primacy, which had long been pressed with sor
vigour by the see of Alexandria, and more recently with less vigou
though probably with more scruple, by the see of Antioch; it testifie
even if indirectly, to the traditional primacy of the Roman see; an
it permanently canonized the oriental, and later almost univers
principle, that ecclesiastical dignity ought to correspond to civ
importance.[4]

Theodosius lost no time in complying with the council's reque
for a confirmation of its proceedings.[5] In an edict issued on July 3

---

[1] So Caspar, *op. cit.*, vol. i, p. 233 f.

[2] *Conc. Const.*, canon 2. The re-emphasis of the competence of the provinc
synod was probably directed against the practice of recent origin of settling dispu
by means of synods drawn from more than one province. It represents a reaction
favour of *Conc. Nic.* canons 5 and 6, though tacitly amending its provision as
the extent of Alexandrine jurisdiction.

[3] The expression '$\tau\grave{\alpha}$ $\pi\rho\epsilon\sigma\beta\epsilon\hat{\imath}\alpha$ $\tau\hat{\eta}s$ $\tau\iota\mu\hat{\eta}s$' means a good deal more than 'honora
privileges' and perhaps less than 'primatial privileges'. '$\tau\iota\mu\acute{\eta}$' could denote at tl
time 'office' no less than the 'honour' attaching to 'office'. Strictly speaking t
canon did not contravene *Conc. Nic.* canon 6, which had nothing to say on t
subject of precedence but was concerned solely with the definition of areas
jurisdiction. (See above, p. 201 ff.)

[4] The council was not recognized by the Roman see at the earliest (and so
the West generally) until the time of Pope Hormisdas † 523, as is shown by t
amended form of the *Decretum Gelasianum*, ed. Dobschütz, E. v., *Texte u. Unter*
vol. xxxviii, p. 35, perhaps not till John II, JK 884. Yet even so late as Gregory
ts validity appears to have been open to doubt. See JE 1477, *Reg.* vii, 31.

[5] Mansi, *op. cit.*, vol. iii, col. 557. Grumel, *op. cit.*, No. 4.

[6] *Cod. Theod.* XVI, i, 3.

e enumerated the bishops who were authorized to settle doctrinal
questions throughout the East. At their head stood significantly the
ame of Nectarius of Constantinople.

Unconnected with this council, though in some respects its
estern counterpart, was the council of Aquileia,[1] assembled there
ominally under the presidency of Valerian, though actually under the
ontrol of Ambrose,[2] the purpose of which was to settle a number of
roblems affecting the order of the Church in western Illyricum.
s interest for us lies chiefly in its attitude towards the two bishops,
aulinus and Maximus, who had appealed to its jurisdiction.[3]

After suggesting the same solution of the Antiochene problem as
at which had already been proposed by Meletius, though not
arried into effect,[4] the council listened favourably to the representa-
ons of Maximus against the recent council of Constantinople,[5] and
ter receiving him into communion, possibly in ignorance of Pope
amasus' instructions to Acholius on the subject,[6] it addressed an
mphatic letter of protest to Theodosius[7]—a refreshing sign of
estern independence of imperial control. The outcome of this pro-
est was joint action between the two Sovereigns, in consequence of
hich complementary councils were held in the following year in
ome and Constantinople.

The bishops of the East having already dismissed the case of
Maximus[8] in the previous council made no further direct reference
o it on this occasion (382). But they took the opportunity of passing

[1] It had been formally summoned by Gratian, *Gesta Aquileiae*, 3, ap. *Ambrosii Op.*
P.L. 16, 955 f. Damasus excused his absence. See also Kauffmann, F., *Aus der*
chule des Wulfila. in *Texte u. Unters. z. altgerman. Religionsgesch.*, 1899, vol. i,
p. 31–63. For its date in May previous to the council of CP. 381, see Homes
udden, F., *St. Ambrose*, 1935, vol. i, p. 201 n. 2.

[2] It appears that since the time of Auxentius the see of Milan had exercised
etropolitan jurisdiction in northern Italy. It is possible that on the deposition of
ionysius, peculiar authority had been assigned to it by Constantius as an offset to
e Roman primacy. See Caspar, E., *op. cit.*, vol. i, p. 237, n. 2.

[3] The latter in person, Ambrose, *Ep.* 13, 3, 4. *M.P.L.* 16, 991 f.; the former
rough the presbyter Evagrius, *Gesta Aquil.*, *M.P.L.* 16, 979.

[4] Ambrose, *Ep.* 12, 4–6. *M.P.L.* 16, 988 f.; cf. *Ep.* 13, 2. See also above, p. 248 f.

[5] Id., *Ep.* 13, 4. If the council was still in session in June this would be quite
ossible.

[6] See above, p. 250, n. 1.

[7] Id., *Ep.* 13, 3, 4. Theodosius appears to have been somewhat indignant to
ceive such a letter from bishops. Cf. *Ep.* 14. *M.P.L.* 16, 994 f.

[8] *Conc. Const.*, canon 4, which not only declared Maximus deposed but in-
alidated his episcopal acts.

two further canons,[1] in the first of which they referred to the 'Tome
Damasus',[2] and in the second limited a right of appeal from th
provincial synod to a council composed of bishops summoned fro
the same civil 'diocese,' thus giving a measure of practical effect
the famous Constantinopolitan canon of the previous year. By th
same canon appeals addressed to the Sovereigns or to an oecumenic
council were expressly excluded.

Finally they addressed a courteous but distinctly firm communica
tion to Pope Damasus and the western bishops, emphasizing the
allegiance to the Nicene symbol, for the interpretation of which the
referred the Westerns to the 'Tome of Antioch' as well as to the
own definition issued at the previous council,[3] and represented wit
doubtful ingenuousness that the ordinations of Nectarius, Flavian
Antioch and Cyril of Jerusalem[4] had been in strict conformity wit
the canon of Nicaea.[5]

The council of Rome was held somewhat later, since legates fror
the recent council at Constantinople were present, as well as Paulinu
of Antioch and Epiphanius of Salamis,[6] not to mention the presbyte
Jerome, who evidently stood high in the confidence of Pope Damasus.
Besides these, imperial officials had arrived bringing an official noti
fication of Nectarius' election. The council made no difficulty abou
recognition in his case, but so far as Flavian's claim to the see c
Antioch was concerned, the fact that Paulinus was admitted t

---

[1] Grumel, op. cit., No. 5.

[2] See above, p. 244.

[3] The council of 382 refers to its predecessor as 'τῆς οἰκουμενικῆς . . . συνόδου
see Theodoret, H.E. 5, 9, 15. ed. cit., p. 293. It should be realized that ἡ οἰκουμενικ
was used to denote the Empire, hence the civilized as opposed to the barbaria
world. Its application to the council of 381 was thus a veiled slight on the Western
at which, as we have seen, they were unrepresented.

[4] The fact that both he and his metropolitan, Gelasius of Caesarea (see Theodore
H.E. 5, 8, but cf. Turner, op. cit., Tom. II, p. 436), seem to have been present i
Constantinople suggests that they were there to refer some dispute about jurisdictio
to the Emperor's decision. Socrates, H.E. 5, 8, implies that Cyril had only recentl
accepted the ὁμοούσιον.

[5] Conc. Nic., canon 2, in spite of its prohibition of the election of neophytes.

[6] Epiphanius of Salamis had come as a supporter of Paulinus, but perhap
also in the hope of throwing off the jurisdiction of the see of Antioch, an
of making the church of Cyprus autocephalous. Cf. Jerome, Ep. 108, 6. ed. cit
p. 310 f.

[7] Jerome, Ep. 127, 7. M.P.L. 22, 1091. Damasus addressed to him some persona
letters on Scriptural questions, two of which, Epp. 8 and 9, JK 239, 253, Inte
Epp. Hieronymi, Nos. 19 and 21, C.S.E.L. vol. liv., pp. 103 f., 265 f., have bee
preserved.

ke part in the deliberations showed clearly enough that it was
sallowed.[1]

To this council, as is coming to be believed, a document of singular
terest belongs which here claims our attention. It has actually come
wn to us in a collection, preserved in two editions, the later
blished during or just after the time of Pope Hormisdas, the
rlier in the pontificate of Gelasius I. Hence its usual title *Decretum*
elasianum.[2] Yet the contents and general character of the whole
llection show that it is not in its present form an official compila-
n, such as might have been made at the instigation of Gelasius
mself, but one of purely private and unofficial origin.[3] On the other
nd, we are not bound to exclude the possibility that the compiler has
ade use of some official material. Moreover, it is usually accepted that
e first three chapters of this collection are in fact quite distinct in
igin from those which follow.[4] That they cannot be later than the
iddle of the fourth century is proved by the quotation from the
ird chapter which appears in the preface to the so-called 'Isidorian'
rsion of the Nicene canons.[5] On the other hand, there is internal evi-
nce which points to their composition in the time of Pope Damasus.[6]
hus not only is the influence of Jerome, who, as we have seen, was
mself present at the Roman council, apparently traceable in the
cond chapter,[7] but in the third an argument is used which appears

[1] Sozomen, *H.E.* 7, 11, 3.
[2] Critically edited by Dobschütz, E. von., in *Texte u. Unters.*, vol. xxxviii,
12, who argues that in its primitive form the *Decretum* included cc. 1–5, and
nce could not be Damasine.
[3] See Chapman, J., in *Revue bénéd.*, vol. xxx, 1913, pp. 187 ff., 315 ff., who
ls attention to an inconsistency between cc. 3 and 4, and thus supports Dobschütz,
. cit., p. 343 ff. in his *argumentum e silentio* against its attribution to Gelasius.
. Caspar, *Geschichte*, vol. ii, p. 773.
[4] See Caspar, *Geschichte*, vol. i, p. 598.
[5] Turner, *op. cit.*, Tom. I, p. 274, expresses the view that the codices which con-
n the 'Isidorian' version of the Nicene canons, first used by Maassen, and de-
ted M by Turner, go back to an archetype of Roman origin dated 420–440. The
eface to the canons already appears in this collection and comparison of it with
e *Decretum*, c. 3, shows that it is dependent on the *Decretum*. See the two docu-
ents printed side by side in Turner, *op. cit.*, Tom. I, p. 155 ff.
[6] The only argument against the unity of cc. 1–3 is based on the idea of the
uble procession' of the Holy Ghost, c. 1, 3, which Dobschütz, *op. cit.*, p. 23,
gards as an interpolation from Augustine, *Tract. in Joh.*, 9, 7.
[7] *Decr. Gel.*, 2, 4. ed. cit., p. 28, where the second and third Johannine epistles
e described as 'alterius Johannis presbyteri'. Similarly the phrase used with
erence to the Lamentations, *ibid.*, 2, 2. ed. cit., p. 25, 'cum *Cinoth* id lamentationi-
s suis' seems to be Hieronymian, since it is found word for word in *Prologus*
leatus. Cf. Turner, in *J.T.S.*, vol. i, 1900, p. 554.

to be an indirect rejoinder to the letter brought to that council by t
Constantinopolitan legates.[1]

We seem therefore to be in the presence of an authority of fir
class historical value, the date of which cannot well be other than 3&
Here we are concerned only with the third chapter, the argument
which may be summarized as follows:

The Roman church possesses a primacy over all other churches
virtue, not of conciliar decisions, but of the Dominical promise
St. Peter, i.e. the *Tu es Petrus*, and for its foundation both he and !
Paul were together responsible.[2] It proceeds:[3]

'The first see of Peter the Apostle belongs to the Roman churcl
"having no spot nor wrinkle nor any such thing".[5] And t
second see was consecrated at Alexandria in the name of bless
Peter by Mark his disciple and evangelist, and he after bei
sent forth by Peter the Apostle to Egypt, preached the word
truth and accomplished a glorious martyrdom.[6] Moreover t
third see of the most blessed Apostle Peter at Antioch is held
honour because he dwelt there before he came to Rome, and the

---

[1] *Decr. Gel.*, 3, 3. ed. cit., p. 33. Cf. *Ep. concilii* $\overline{CP}$. (382) ap. Theodoret, *H.E.* 5,
ed. cit., p. 289. In this letter the order of the 'greater churches' is Constantinop
Antioch, Jerusalem, the last of which is described as 'μητρὸς ἀπασῶν τῶν ἐκκλησία
see p. 294.

[2] *Ibid.*, 3, 1. ed. cit., p. 29. It should be noticed that the words 'non diverso (
tempore), sicut heresei garriunt', *ibid.*, p. 31, are lacking in the 'Isidorian' prefa
ed. cit. Tom. I, p. 157, and so are probably an addition by the compiler, cf. a
Turner, *op. cit.*, Tom. I, p. 244 ff. The *v.l.* 'nonnullis' for 'nullis', *ibid.* 3, 1. ed. c
p. 30, may have arisen from the belief that the councils of Nicaea and Sardica h
in fact 'preferred' the Roman church to other churches. Turner, *op. cit.*, Tom.
p. 156, and Dobschütz, *op. cit.*, *ibid.*, both accept 'nullis' as the correct readi
If they are right, the expression is further proof that cc. 1–3 of the docume
cannot be later than the first quarter of the fifth century. Cf. Boniface I, *Ep.* 14,
JK 364.

[3] *Ibid.*, 3, 3. ed. cit., p. 32 f.; Turner, *op. cit.*, Tom. I, p. 157 f.

[4] Turner, *ibid.*, reads 'Romanae ecclesiae', which in spite of Dobschütz' arg
ment, *op. cit.*, p. 258, n. 2, is the reading of the 'Isidorian' preface, Turner, *op. c
p. 158.

[5] Eph. v, 27. This quotation 'non habens . . .' does not really support Dobschü
reading, 'Romana ecclesia', since, as it is not specially attributed to the Rom
church as distinct from the Church generally till Hormisdas, see *Ep.* 26, 4.
Thiel, A., p. 795 and cf. *Lib. Carolini*, 1, 6. *M.P.L.* 98, 1021, it would seem to b
gloss introduced by the editor. It is lacking in the 'Isidorian' preface. See Turn
op. cit., Tom. I, p. 158.

[6] The earliest witnesses to this tradition are Eus. *H.E.* 2, 16, 1, ed. cit., p. 1.
and Jerome, *De vir. inl.* 8, ed. cit., p. 12. Cf. Epiphanius, *Panar.*, 51, 6, 10. ed. c
vol. ii, p. 256 and Dobschütz, E. v., *op. cit.*, p. 259.

st of all the name of the new-born race of Christians had its
igin'.[1]

The significance of this pronouncement is fairly evident. It is
thing less than the Roman answer to the post-Constantinian theory
ecclesiastical authority in doctrine and discipline, at this time
dely, though perhaps never universally, accepted by Easterns, yet
rtainly by those who looked on the sacred person of Caesar as the
edium and interpreter of Christian tradition, and who had adopted
purely secular principle as a basis for the mutual relation between
urches. In the place of this novel conception, the council re-
serts the 'potior principalitas' of the Roman see arising from the
ct of its twin apostolic source, and justifies the status of the sees of
exandria and Antioch as second and third in rank on the express
ound of their supposedly Petrine origin. At the same time it
pudiates by implication the claim made by the third canon of
1 for the see of Constantinople, as one which depends, not on
ostolic foundation, still less on Dominical institution, but on a
nciliar resolution. It therefore represents a gallant, though seem-
gly forlorn attempt to safeguard the primitive conception of an
ostolic *paradosis* against the alien theory that for its faith and
actice Christianity must depend solely on Caesar's will.

In spite, however, of all that Caesar could do, doctrinal con-
oversy in the East persisted, as is shown by further edicts against
retics, following an abortive council at Constantinople in 383.[2]

Evidently there still remained some in the East, as we have sug-
sted, who were not satisfied with faith based on an imperial *Diktat*.
mong these appear to have been the presbyters of the church of

---

[1] The compiler here appears to accept the tradition of the Pseudo-Clementine
erature (and not that of Gal. II, 12 ff., which seems to describe no more than a
ssing visit), although elsewhere the *Decretum*, c. 5, 2, ed. cit., p. 49, excludes such
erature as apocryphal. Was it because he was aware of the untrustworthiness of
s authority that he went on to invoke Acts XI, 26, as a more substantial support'?
f. Eus. *H.E.* 2, 3, 3. ed. cit., vol. ii, pt. i, p. 113 f.; Ammonius, *In Acta App.* xi, 26
Cramer's *Catena*, 1838, vol. iii, p. 199; Innocent I, *Epp.* 23, JK 309; 24, 1.
310; Celestine I, *Ep.* 22, 7. JK 432; Leo I, *Serm.* 82. *M.P.L.* 54, 425. For the
umber of the principal sees, see Walafrid Strabo, *De reb. eccl.* 31. *M.P.L.* 114,
3 f; Nilus Doxopatris, *Notit. patr. M.P.G.* 132, 1093, who recognize only three.
or their order, see *Ep. Aurelii Carthag.* inter *Epp. Bonifacii I*, No. 2. *M.P.L.*
, 751; Boniface I, *Ep.* 15, 5, JK 365. The order in the 'Donation of Constantine'
Antioch, Alexandria, Constantinople, Jerusalem. Cf. Mirbt, *Quellen*[5], No. 228, 11.
[2] Grumel, *op. cit.*, No. 7. Cf. Soc. *H.E.* 5, 10. For the relevant edicts, see *Cod.
heod.* XVI, v, 11; XVI, 5, 12; and in the following year *ibid.*, XVI, 5, 13. For
heodosius' intervention in questions of jurisdiction, see *Const. Sirmond.* 3.

Berytus, who were no doubt extremely gratified that their bish
Timothy,[1] a prominent supporter of Apollinaris, had been depos
by imperial mandate, yet felt the need of a more canonical form
discipline, and in consequence applied to Damasus with a view
obtaining their bishop's formal excommunication. His reply calls on
for brief notice. In the first place it should be realized that to se
a reply of any kind in this case constituted an open challenge to t
validity of the 'second canon' of Constantinople. Appeals to t
Roman see from the East were already becoming more exception
Hence Damasus wasted no time before pointing out the significance
his appellant's action.[2]

'In paying affectionately that respect which is due to the aposto
see' he begins, 'you offer it specially to us, most honoured sons. Y
if it belongs to us to guide the helm entrusted to us more particular
in that holy church, where the holy Apostle had his see and taugh
we nevertheless acknowledge ourselves to be insufficient for such
office'.[3]

Damasus is under no allusion about the dignity of his position
successor of St. Peter. Nor does he scruple, even in addressi
members of a church which was a suffragan of the 'apostolic see'
Antioch, to describe his own as 'the apostolic see' without any qua
fication.[4] We may note too that after insisting on the sufficiency
the Nicene symbol as a statement of the apostolic faith, he goes on
refer to the purpose of the formula recently set forth by the Roma
see as being to serve as a safeguard of the apostolic *paradosis*.[5]

[1] He had been present at the council of C̄P. 381 (see Turner, *op. cit.*, Tom I
p. 439) and according to Leontius Byz., *Adv. fraud. Apoll. M.P.G.* 86, ii, 197
had been on friendly terms with Athanasius. Subsequently, according to Damasu
Ep. 7, JK 234, cf. Leont. Byz., *ibid.*, he was condemned at Rome in the presence
Athanasius' successor Peter. Some of his works have survived, see Lietzmann, H
Apollinaris u.s. Schule, 1904, vol. i, p. 277 ff.

[2] *Ep.* 7, JK 234. It has survived only in a Greek version preserved by Theodore
H.E. 5, 10. ed. cit., p. 295, who evidently misunderstood it when he described i
'τοῦτο τοῖς τὴν Ἐῷαν ἰθυνοῦσιν ἐπισκόποις διὰ γραμμάτων δεδήλωκεν'. That it w
actually addressed to bishops is rendered highly improbable by the twice repeate
phrase, υἱοὶ ἀγαπητοί. So Batiffol, P., *Siège apostolique*, 1924, p. 106. In oth
respects the Greek version betrays errors and obscurities.

[3] *Ibid.* It may be observed that Damasus once more emphasizes the claim of th
Roman see to have preserved intact the apostolic *paradosis*.

[4] Cf. the letter of the Roman council of 378, *Et hoc gloriae vestrae*, on which se
above, p. 245 f. Also Batiffol, P., *Papa, sedes apostolica, apostolatus*, 1925.

[5] *Ep.* 7. JK 234. 'ἐκεῖνο . . . ὅπερ παρὰ τῶν ἀποστόλων παρεδόθη'. The allusio
to the *twin* source of Roman apostolic tradition is noteworthy and may be compare
with *Decretum Gel.* 3, 3, see above, p. 255 ff.

It is necessary, however, to call attention to the absence of perfect
greement even in the West at this time as to the actual character of
the Roman primacy. The anonymous author, described since the
days of Erasmus as Ambrosiaster, thought it desirable to remind
his readers that the New Testament was acquainted with a primacy of
St. Paul as well as of St. Peter.[1] What may have been the real purpose
of the writer can only be conjectured and no definite answer can
easily be given so long as his identity and place of origin remain
undecided. Possibly Damasus' exercise of authority had been so far
in keeping with what is known of the inaugural days of his pontificate
as to call forth some protest against a seemingly excessive use of
autocratic power. Equally the deposed Arian Palladius[2] was constrained to revive the later Cyprianic theory of the common possession of the *cathedra Petri* by the whole episcopate,[3] and not by the
bishop of Rome only to the exclusion of the rest. In particular he
protested strongly against Damasus' behaviour as *princeps episcopatus* in excusing the absence both of himself and others from the
council of Aquileia,[4] and thus, as Palladius argued, showing his unwillingness to take counsel as an equal with his fellow-bishops.

In actual fact, however, his criticisms possess indirectly a considerable measure of positive value. It is clear from Ambrose's report
that the condemnation of their author and of his ally Secundianus at
Aquileia had been simply a foregone conclusion.[5] All that remained
for the council to do was to apply to them a sentence already pronounced by Damasus' predecessor against the supporters of Ariminum.[6] Naturally Palladius himself makes this one of the grounds of
his case against Ambrose, but he bears unwilling witness to the fact

---

[1] *M.P.L.* 17, 45 ff.

[2] *Dissertatio Maximini c. Ambros.*, ed. Kauffmann, F. in *Aus der Schule des
Vulfila*, 1899, pp. 67–90. The passage occurs in the third part, ed. cit. p. 86 f.
which Zeiller, *op. cit.*, p. 487, shows to be the work of Palladius of Ratiaria, who
had been deposed as an Arian at the council of Aquileia, and is entitled by him,
b. cit., p. 489, '*Palladii c. Ambrosium oratio*'. See also Batiffol, P., *Siège apostolique*,
. 27 ff.

[3] All that Palladius succeeded in doing was to show that if the Cyprianic theory
f Church Order was cumbersome under the pre-Constantinian 'parochial' system,
nder the new 'oecumenical' conditions it was quite unworkable.

[4] The 'others' were the bishops subject to the metropolitical jurisdiction of the
oman see. See Kauffmann, *op. cit.*, p. 87.

[5] *Gesta Concil. Aquil. M.P.L.* 16, 955 ff. The proceedings are described briefly
y Homes Dudden, F., *Life and Times of St. Ambrose*, 1935, vol. i, p. 200 ff.

[6] See above, p. 235.

that even in a situation where the influence of Ambrose was pre
dominant, the judgment of the Roman see on a question of doctrin
was regarded as decisive. Moreover his allusion to the 'prerogativ
of the see of Peter', as well as his neo-Cyprianic theory, poin
clearly to a marked revival of interest in the *Tu es Petrus*, of whic
the *Decretum Gelasianum* already mentioned supplies confirmator
evidence.[1] It is reasonably probable that this revival was a dire
consequence of an effort on the part of the Church to find a solid bas
for a new machinery of oecumenical action, such as the menacin
situation created by the adoption of Christianity by Constantin
had shown to be urgently needed, to replace the old, haphazard
'parochial' methods of pre-Nicene days. Yet if Palladius was actuall
trying to bolster up a theory which was already out of date, he was a
the same time sufficient of a realist to recognize that some alternativ
to the practical consequences of the Roman primacy had to be foun
It was therefore in fact nothing less than sheer force of logic whic
extorted from him the amazing proposal that the controversy betwee
the Nicenes and the supporters of Ariminum would be best settle
by its submission to the Roman Senate.[2] On his own admission suc
a proposal would lead to the preposterous situation of pagans an
Jews acting as judges of the Christian faith; yet even so he decline
to accept the only logical alternative apparent.

In contrast to the critical attitude represented by the two author
just mentioned we turn to the more positive views of Ambrose. Her
again we find evidence that attention was being given afresh to th
meaning and value of the *Tu es Petrus*. Commenting on this text, th
great bishop of Milan does not hesitate to identify the 'rock' with S
Peter, as for example when in answer to critics he replies: 'Could no
Christ, who by His own authority confided the kingdom to Pete
have strengthened the faith of one whom He called the rock thereb
declaring him to be the foundation of the Church?'[3] Or agai
elsewhere:

'This is that Peter to whom Christ said, Thou art Peter and upo
this rock I will build my Church. Wherefore, where Peter is, ther
is the Church, where the Church, there is no death, but life eternal'.

---

[1] *Decr. Gel.* 3, 3. See above, p. 255 ff.
[2] *Diss. Max.* ed. cit., p. 90. Cf. Zeiller, *op. cit.*, p. 490.
[3] Ambrose, *De Fide*, 4, 56. M.P.L. 16, 653. Cf. Id., *De Spiritu*, 2, 156. *M.P.L*
16, 808.
[4] Id., *In ps.* 40 *enarr.* 30. *M.P.L.* 14, 1134. Cf. Cyprian, *Ep.* 66, 8. ed. cit., p. 73

To meet the argument that it was against St. Peter's own person, at it was promised the gates of hell should not prevail, Ambrose pointed out that the allusion was to his confession of faith, 'which is shut out more than one heresy'.[1]

There is a similar emphasis, in spite of some confusion of metaphors, on the importance of that faith in a passage where he says:

'To His disciple also He denied not the grace of this name (i.e. the rock), that he also should be Peter, because from the Rock (i.e. Christ Himself) he has the solidity of stedfastness, the firmness of faith. Do thou too strive to be a rock. Seek thou the rock, not without thee but within thee. Thy rock is faith; the foundation of the Church is faith. If thou art a rock, thou wilt be in the Church, for the Church is on the rock; if thou art in the Church, the gates of hell shall not prevail against thee'.[2]

Of a primacy bestowed on St. Peter personally Ambrose had no doubt. Moreover he associated its bestowal with the occasions described in John XXI, 15 ff. and in Luke XXII, 31 f.,[3] being thus the first to call attention to the significance of these texts. Yet though he speaks of St. Peter as 'being preferred to all' and 'governing the perfect',[4] he appears to qualify this by saying elsewhere, 'Peter . . . took on himself a primacy of confession not of office, a primacy of faith not of rank', thereby reviving the earlier sense of *primatus*.[5] And mindful of the dignity of his see, he reverts to the view put forward by Cyprian in his later edition of the *De Unitate*, that judicial authority, being conferred on all the Apostles as well as on St. Peter, belongs immediately to all Catholic bishops.[6] In speaking of the Roman church he emphasizes his belief that it has preserved unimpaired the faith of the Apostles[7] and that to be in communion with that church is a guarantee of correct faith.[8] Similarly he urges that matters in dispute regarding faith or discipline should be referred to for arbitration.[9] Still more striking are the phrases which he uses

[1] Ambrose, *De Incarn.* 33 f. *M.P.L.* 16, 862.
[2] Id., *Exp. ev. Luc.* 6, 97 f. *M.P.L.* 15, 1781. Cf. *Ep.* 43, 9. *M.P.L.* 16, 1180, where Christ is identified with the 'rock' (1 Cor. x, 4).
[3] Id. *In ps.* 43 enarr. 40. *M.P.L.* 14, 1163.
[4] Id., *op. cit.*, 10, 175 f. *M.P.L.* 15, 1942.
[5] Id., *De Incarn.* 32. *M.P.L.* 16, 861. For the meaning of 'primatus' see above, 165.
[6] Id., *In ps.* 38 enarr. 37. *M.P.L.* 14, 1107.
[7] Id., *Ep.* 42, 5. *M.P.L.* 16, 1174.
[8] Id., *De excessu Sat.* 1, 47. *M.P.L.* 16, 1362.
[9] Id., *Ep.* 56, 7. *M.P.L.* 16, 1222. Cf. *Ep.* 13, 7. *M.P.L.* 16, 993.

18

to describe the relation of the Roman see to other churches as, for example, when he writes on behalf of the council of Aquileia to the Emperor, saying:

'Your Grace must be besought not to permit any disturbance of the Roman church, the head of the whole Roman world, and of that most holy faith of the Apostles, for from thence flow out to all mankind the privileges of sacred communion'.[1]

The association of ideas in this passage—the Roman church—head of the world—apostolic faith—sacred communion is very striking and certainly significant. It must mean much more than a mere primacy of honour, even more than a primacy of faith. To some it may appear to imply not less than that primacy of arbitration, of which we have already seen evidence in an earlier period.

In one respect at least the Roman see was left permanently in Ambrose's debt. None was more ready than he to assert the spiritual independence of the Church in its relation to the State.[2] But it was his literary genius which expressed this principle in the words:

'How can greater honour be paid to the Emperor than that he should be called a son of the Church? . . . Since the Emperor is in the Church, not over the Church, a good Emperor seeks the aid of the Church and refuses it not'.[3]

The weapons of the papal cause in its struggle with the later Empire were thus already forged. In the hands of a Gelasius, Nicholas and a Gregory they were soon to be tempered, sharpened and wielded in the vindication of sacerdotal authority against the secular power.[4]

That egregious contemporary of Ambrose, Jerome the Roman presbyter, represents the more middle-class outlook as contrasted with the former's aristocratic standpoint. But for that reason, though often crude in utterance and seldom profound in thought, he was specially qualified to express the opinions of the western 'man in the street' towards the end of the fourth century. Two characteristic observations of his may serve to illustrate his ideas. On the Antiochen

[1] Ambrose, *Ep.* 11, 4. *M.P.L.* 16, 986. See however for a further explanation p. 18, n. 3.

[2] See Batiffol, *op. cit.*, pp. 51, 82, and Carlyle, R. W. and A. J., *History of mediaeval political theory in the West*, 1903, pp. 180–190.

[3] Ambrose, *Serm. c. Auxent.* 36.

[4] It should be realized that before they reached Gelasius they had been hammered on the anvil by the administrative genius of Leo I.

chism his frequently repeated remark was: 'If he's joined to Peter's
ee, he's my man'.[1] Or in writing to his friend Pope Damasus:

'I am speaking to the successor of the fisherman and the disciple
f the Cross . . . by communion I am allied with your beatitude,
nat is to the see of Peter. I know the Church was built on that rock.
Whoever eats a lamb outside this house is a Gentile. Anyone who
not in Noah's ark when the flood comes will drown . . . the man
ho gathers not with thee scatters, I mean, he who is not Christ's is
ntichrist's'.[2]

It is at least to Damasus' credit, in spite of his evident defects,
nat finding in Jerome a scholar of some ability and inexhaustible
ndustry he chose him for the monumental task of preparing a new
atin version of Holy Scripture. He certainly lived long enough to see
ne first edition of Jerome's version of the Gospels, though he may
so have glanced through the rest of his friend's New Testament
nd his hasty text-revision of the Psalter. The old Pope's eighty years,
early twenty of which had been spent in assiduous though by no
neans undisturbed rule of the Roman church, closed on December
r, 384. Of his archaeological and literary achievements we have no
eed to speak, but they are of sufficient importance in themselves to
ave left historians and epigraphists permanently in his debt.

The century which we have reviewed is one of crucial importance
. the history of every aspect of the Church's life. It witnessed a
nange, the like of which has not been seen till almost within our
wn time, when reversing the 'most favoured religion' policy of
onstantine I, the State in some parts of the world has resumed
ne task of suppressing or at any rate discouraging Christianity in
.e supposed interests of social welfare.

It cannot be too often emphasized that the Constantinian revolution
ound the Church largely unprepared. Hence it is not altogether
urprising to discover that when the first wave of reaction to the
nange, so significantly expressed by the fulsome adulation of
usebius, had passed, for the time being at least it was at the mercy
any ambitious adventurer who choose to win the Emperor's
vour. Slowly it began to be appreciated, in consequence of the

[1] Jerome, Ep. 16, 2. ed. cit., p. 69. It is important to consider the significance of
s words in the light of the local situation at Antioch. No one can be surprised
at a visiting presbyter of the Roman church would naturally prefer as bishop of
ntioch one who was in visible communion with his own bishop..
[2] Id., Ep., 15, 1. ed. cit., p. 63 f.

ceaseless controversies resulting from State intervention in th
sphere of religion, that some universal umpire or referee was indis
pensable, and the principle that such a referee was to be found i
the Roman see, already established in the West, began to mak
headway in the East. The check to this development presented by th
policy of the Emperor, who by the end of the century was claimin
to determine questions of doctrine as well as discipline, led to
western re-examination of the basis on which the arbiter's authorit
rested, the results of which were to remain almost unchallenged i
the West for over a thousand years.

V

The Papacy and the Later Roman Empire

The childhood shows the man,
As morning shows the day. Be famous then
By wisdom; as thy empire must extend,
So let extend thy mind o'er all the world.
MILTON, *Paradise Regained*, l. 220.

Ezekiel III, 17. 'Son of man, I have made thee a watchman unto the house of Israel; therefore hear the word at my mouth, and give them warning from me'.

It was perhaps a matter of some significance for the future of Church and State alike, within the framework of the *Imperium Romanum*, that in the course of a principate of some sixteen years' duration Theodosius the Great spent at least eleven in the city of Constantinople. Not even Constantine himself had kept so long a residence in the capital of his own choice, and of his immediate successors none had remained there for more than a few months at a time. It is therefore not unreasonable to hold that it was to Theodosius I more than to any other Emperor of the fourth century that the eastern sphere of imperial administration, and its centre in particular, owed the earliest impress of at least some of those peculiarly Byzantine' characteristics by which it came to be distinguished from the Empire in the West. During those eleven years there took place a rapid process of transformation, so rapid in fact that by the time his degenerate sons Arcadius and Honorius found themselves, perhaps to their dismay, joint masters of the Roman world, the rift between East and West, which had been imperceptibly widening in the course of the century, had already become an almost impassable gulf. The effete orientalized despotism of Arcadius and Theodosius II, both in its resemblance and in its contrast to the irresponsible rule of Honorius and Valentinian III, only serves to confirm the general impression created by the closing years of the fourth century, that almost all that had survived of Augustan imperialism was to be found in Rome on the Tiber, and that the new Rome on the Bosporus had been largely absorbed by a semi-Asiatic Byzantium.

Nor is the contrast less marked between the eastern and western churches. That *obiter dictum* of Constantius II, to which we have

265

already alluded,[1] uttered in the heat of passion some thirty years before, has by now become a normative principle. Henceforward in the East, with but an occasional exception, the nature of which we shall do well to note, it is Caesar's will which is the chief determining factor in questions of doctrine and discipline alike. No doubt a similar outlook had frequently conditioned the attitude of Constantius' father to ecclesiastical problems, but under Theodosius I it became a well-established principle. Henceforth the history of the eastern churches is the record of the gradual elimination of primitive ecclesiastical autonomy, and its replacement by a 'Caesaro-papism', in which the *imperator-sacerdos* becomes the sole fount of disciplinary and dogmatic authority alike. At the same time it is the record of a series of pathetic attempts at resistance in one quarter or another against the intrusion of this sub-Christian concept, with its tragic consequences in the disruption of the Church's visible unity.

So far as the East was concerned the process began after Constantine's defeat of Licinius, but except for a brief period towards the end of the reign of his son Constantius, it had failed until now to make any serious headway in the West. This was due in part at least to limitations of a purely geographical nature. Yet not entirely. so. Racial temperament had made western Christians largely indifferent to theological problems of a speculative character, such as have always fascinated the eastern world. Instead they devoted their attention to questions in which the chief interest was ethical and practical. Thus it was but seldom in the period which preceded the great Christological controversies of the mid-fifth century that the Papacy came into direct contact with problems involved in the formulation of doctrine; its chief concern lay far more in the direction of determining disputed points of a disciplinary or administrative nature. So real in fact was the cleavage between East and West that when at length the great dogmatic controversies came within the papal orbit, we cannot always feel sure that the real issue was clearly apprehended in the West. Yet this at least can be said with confidence, that in each case, as it arose, the Roman see tended as a rule to adopt a mediating standpoint, which, while contributing but little to a satisfactory solution of the problem in hand, nevertheless helped to secure so far as was possible that both sides had a fair hearing, and, most important of all, sometimes proved successful by this means in safeguarding the

[1] See above, p. 228.

nity of the Church. Again and again the unprejudiced and disinterested in either party to a controversy displayed evident satis-
action when they became aware of the attitude adopted by the
Roman see. Thus the history of the period is something more than the
ismal story of a rearguard action on the part of the Church against
Caesaro-papism. It is also in some measure the record of an unremit-
ing struggle on the part of the Papacy to preserve the coherence of
he Church. Here as so often in the annals of that great institution we
an trace unmistakable marks of a reversion to type. As at Jerusalem
nd Antioch of old, it remains largely true even now that 'all could
ally round the name of Peter'.[1]

I

It seems that at the time of his death, December 11, 384, Pope
Damasus I, whose pontificate had been inaugurated, as we have seen,
vith scenes of violence and even tragedy, was able to bequeath to his
uccessor a comparatively peaceful and united church. Even so, there
re signs of some renewal of inner conflict, and it was probably not
ill he had received news of Theodosius' confirmation of his election,[2]
he first of its kind, that the new Pope Siricius felt reasonably secure.
At any rate the Emperor's letter must have ministered the *coup de
grâce* to any hopes still cherished by the presbyter Jerome of succeed-
ng his old friend. But it may well be imagined that his successful
ival breathed a fresh sigh of relief on hearing that the accomplished
scetic, well known as a merciless opponent, had now decisively
haken off the worldly dust of Rome from his feet, and betaken him-
elf to the more exotic and perhaps more spiritual environment of
Ferusalem.

The pontificate of Siricius is chiefly remarkable for the emergence
•f a new phase in papal policy. For the Roman see to adjudicate the
orthodoxy of teachers, to hear appeals and to give rulings on questions
vhich vitally affected the life of the Church as a whole, was, to judge
rom what we have already seen, in no sense fresh. There is unmis-
akable evidence that it had at any rate done some of these things at
east as early as the second century. Moreover, it had addressed letters
•f a pastoral or admonitory character to other churches, with evident

---

[1] Streeter, B. H., *The Four Gospels*, p. 515; cf. above, p. 51 f.
[2] *Coll. Avell.* 4. *C.S.E.L.* vol. xxxv, p. 47 f.

consciousness of a certain responsibility for the welfare of the Churc as a whole.

Siricius continued this tradition. But actually he did more. Wi him we can observe the beginning of a tendency to take the initiativ showing that the Roman see was now disposed to interpret i responsibility, not only as concerned with the redress of existi evils and grievances, but also with their prevention. Those few of h letters which have survived are better preserved than the fragmenta and confused remains of his predecessors' correspondence, and ov their preservation largely to incorporation in some of the earlie western collections of Canon Law.[1] It is significant that a form pronouncement of the Roman see first acquires the technical descri tion of *Decretal* in this pontificate.

We may reasonably regard this new instrument of papal ac ministration as an immediate product of the situation created l the Sardican legislation and by the rescript *Ordinariorum sententi* of 378.[2] The decretal is simply the particular form which the conte of the papal office as that of a universal referee assumes in respon to the demand created by a Christianized *Imperium* for oecumenic machinery at the disposal of the Church.[3] As such it incorporat elements old and new side by side. Like the letters of his pr decessors, the decretals of Siricius make frequent use of Scriptur quotations and allusions, as for example when he writes, speakir of clerical irregularities in his letter to Himerius of Tarraco:

'How deeply we are smitten with grief when we are forced t bewail the misdeeds of those who share our own status, above all those on whom there rests without intermission, according to th words of blessed Paul, daily anxiety and the care of all the churches'

---

[1] See Silva Tarouca, K. *Beiträge zur Überlieferungsgeschichte der Päpstbrie des 4. 5. u. 6. Jahrhunderts* in *Zeitschr. f. kath. Theol.* vol. xliii, 1919, pp. 467–48 657–692. (The promised continuation has not yet appeared.) Cf. Turner, in *J.T.* vol. xxx, 1929, p. 225 ff. on the *Corbie MS. Paris lat.* 12097.

[2] See above, p. 246 f.

[3] It may be remarked that the decretal is in effect a papal adaptation of th imperial rescript, that is to say, an authoritative answer to an inquiry which becomes legal precedent and so a general law. Yet Siricius himself appears to be unconscio of any change, and appeals to the 'general decrees' of his predecessor Liberius.

[4] *Ep.* 1, 6 (7). JK 255. Cf. 2 Cor. XI, 28. The phrase 'praecipue' . . . is ambiguou Only if 'praecipue' be taken to qualify 'deplorare' against the natural order of th words is it possible to relate 'quibus' to 'nos'. If on the other hand, as seems mo consistent with the structure of the sentence, 'praecipue' qualifies the relati clause, the latter seems to refer not to the Roman see but to the episcopate as co trasted with those whose responsibility is less onerous.

His language is not less traditional when he recalls in phrases
scriptive of an almost mystical identity the perpetuation of the
trine primacy in the Roman episcopal succession:

'We bear the burdens of all who are heavy laden; nay more, the
essed Apostle Peter bears them in us, he who, as we hope, protects
d guards us as the sole heirs of his office'.[1]

The composite diverse character of the decretals is shown by their
corporation of the legal phraseology of civil law, side by side
th a style characteristic of recent synodical decisions, and in the
gnment of 'the canons' with prohibitions of Roman origin,[2] or
the juxtaposition of the 'decisions of the apostolic see and the
crosanct canonical definitions'.[3]

Here is something unmistakably new. Yet even so the transition
m old to new is barely perceptible. For if his letter to his suf-
gans[4] and his reply to the inquiries addressed to him by the
shops of Gaul[5] appear to be 'rescripts' issued on his own authority,
hird letter to the Africans[6] communicating the decisions of a recent
man synod is confessedly written on behalf of his synod. It is
ar that no real difference is felt to exist between the personal
thority of the Pope and that of the Roman Curia.

Perhaps the most striking contrast between the decretals and
e earlier papal documents is to be found in the replacement of the
l language of 'appeal' by a new phraseology of 'menace'. Thus we
ad in the letter to Gaul:

'Therefore let the offenders put the matter right in synod, and
move those on whom the (clerical) status has unfittingly been
nferred; else let us be informed of their names, that we may know
m whom we must withhold communion'.[7]

---

[1] *Ep.*, 1 (1). This idea, which approximates to belief in a kind of reincarnation
the Apostle in every successive holder of his office, appears to originate with
icius, but recurs perpetually in later papal documents. See the present writer's
e and Times of St. Leo, p. 71 f. Such a belief goes far to explain the 'impersonality'
the Papacy.
[2] *Ibid.*, 15 (19).
[3] *Ibid.*, 15 (20). Cf. Caspar, *Geschichte*, vol. i, p. 262.
[4] *Ep.* 6, JK 263. That the letter was actually addressed to bishops of the Roman
ovince is Batiffol's view in *Siège apostolique*, p. 159.
[5] It has come down to us anonymously as 'Canones Romani concilii ad Gallos
scopos'. *M.P.L.* 13,1155.
[6] *Ep.* 5, JK 258. It is probable that, like *Ep.* 6., this letter was originally addressed
the Roman province. See Duchesne, L., *Histoire*, vol. iii, p. 185.
[7] *M.P.L.* 13, 1155.

In addition we shall do well to notice carefully the frequent use
technical and legal terminology which from now on becomes
characteristic feature of documents emanating from the pa
chancery. A typical example is the use of the verb 'report' (referr
an expression borrowed from the technical language of civil admir
stration, to describe a communication addressed by a diocesan bish
to the Roman see. Thus once again from the letter to Himerius:

'We have furnished sufficient answers, I think, to each of t
questions, which . . . you have referred to us, as to the head
your order'.[1]

If this letter can be compared to an imperial rescript, the o
addressed to the suffragans of the Roman see already mention
resembles an imperial edict. This earliest known *motu proprio* ope
with the clarion note of a modern encyclical.

'As we meditate in fear on the Judgment of God, beloved brethr
and on the doom which everyman shall receive after this life accor
ing to his works, we dare not keep silence when a scandal arises;
fact, necessity itself compels us to speak. For the prophet sa
"Lift up thy voice like a trumpet". Were I to demur, to whom belor
the care of all the churches, I should hear the Lord saying, "Ye rej
the commandment of God, that ye may establish your own tra
tions" '.[2]

The implicit claim of the Roman see to make decisions
universal application in the sphere of doctrine and discipline ali
of which we have already noticed some early examples, now becom
explicit. Siricius openly proclaims its doctrine and practice
normative for all other churches.[3]

We should considerably underestimate the significance of th
documents were we to regard them as no more than the individu
utterances of a vigorous and dominant personality. When Siric
described himself as the 'heir of St. Peter's office', he gave expressi
to an idea of far-reaching importance; the impersonality of
Papacy. Attention has been called to this characteristic by a rec
historian when he writes: 'Uber den einzelnen Päpsten steht

[1] JK 255, 15 (20). It seems more likely that 'corpus' here refers to the episcop
than to the whole Church.
[2] JK 263. The quotation from Isaiah LVIII, 1, becomes from now on a freque
cited Scriptural phrase in papal letters. For the second quotation, see Mark VII,
and cf. *Ep.* 1, 8 (12) JK 255.
[3] See *Ep.* 10, 3 (5), 3 (8), 3 (9).

stitution, das *Papsttum*, als der historische Organismus, welcher
r eigentliche Inhalt und Gegenstand der Papstgeschichte ist'.[1]

It is in this strange semi-mystical identification of the living Pope
th the survival of Peter that we touch one of the secrets of papal
luence, and find at least one explanation of its enduring *auctoritas*.

If, however, we regard Siricius in detachment from his office as
ir of St. Peter' and compare him with his great contemporary
nbrose, we cannot fail to be impressed by the superiority of the
hop of Milan. Yet it was Rome and not Milan which became the
ief centre of oecumenical Christendom. For a time even after the
se of the fourth century the see of Ambrose enjoyed a prestige
nost greater than that of Rome itself.[2] But its day was short, and
fore the fifth century had run a quarter of its course no one was
iously concerned to court its favour or be assured of its support.
oreover, even at the zenith of its influence its *auctoritas* was con-
ed within the limits of western administration.

The following appears to illustrate the difference in the attitude of
sterns towards Milan and Rome respectively. A synod held at
esarea in Palestine about this time to determine the wearisome
hism in the church of Antioch, wrote to Theodosius and mentioned
o letters addressed to the East in the compilation of which Ambrose
ust have had an important part. But it was evidently to a further
ter from Siricius that the eastern bishops attached major
portance.

'With joy therefore', they write,[3] 'we have received the accurate
ıching of bishop Siricius concerning the church canons, and,
llowing this letter, we have decreed that these things be ratified :
    that we have given legal and just votes, to the effect that
    know one bishop of Antioch only, the religious lord bishop
avian'.[4]

It may, of course, be said that a touch of irony lies behind this
iental courtesy, but it is at least noteworthy that when the Roman

[1] Caspar, *op. cit.*, p. 266.   [2] See above, p. 253.
[3] This letter is known to us from its inclusion in the works of Severus of Antioch.
e *The sixth book of the select letters of Severus*, ed. Brooks, 1903, p. 224.
[4] The allusion is to *Conc. Nic.* canon 4, forbidding consecration of bishops by a
ıgle consecrator, and so excluding Evagrius, a recent claimant to the see of
ıtioch. The same canon is in view in canon 2 of the Roman synod of 386, see
ricius, *Ep.* 5, JK 258. The difference in the attitude of the East towards the see
Rome and towards the see of Milan seems to show at least in some measure that
litical status alone will not sufficiently account for the prestige of the former.

see drew attention to a principle of Canon Law, it was believed to
deserving of serious notice.

II

For further evidence about the relations of the Papacy with the E
at this time we must observe in particular Siricius' connexion with
churches of eastern Illyricum. These serve to throw some light
the attitude of the Roman see to the problems which had acqui
fresh importance as a result of Theodosius' policy of making Co
stantinople the effective capital of the *Imperium Romanum*. Damasu
had already established close relations with the see of Thessalonica
the time of the council of Constantinople (381), which under Siric
became a close bond of alliance. It was essentially defensive
character, and although the potential aggressor was never, so far
we know, explicitly mentioned in papal correspondence, both part
knew well enough the quarter from which aggression was threaten
Unhappily only two Roman letters[1] have survived from Siricius' ti
to show of what character these negotiations were and what was th
result. As to the latter there is at least no doubt.

It is probable that at the end of the fourth century provinc
organization of local churches, such as had existed, for example,
Asia for at least the past fifty years, remained as yet undeveloped in
more backward provinces of the Balkan peninsula. Once more it v
the policy of Theodosius which not only made its creation urgen
necessary, but also in this case supplied the means. Thessalonica h
been used by him as an earlier focus of administration in the sh
period which intervened between his elevation to the rank
Augustus and his formal entry into Constantinople. The distincti
thus acquired, as well as its importance as a commercial cent
marked it out as the obvious see for a bishop of metropolitan stat
But above all, it had a good claim to possess a church of aposto
origin.[2] It was thus well qualified to act as a salutary check on t
growing ambitions of the upstart see of Constantinople.[3] It v
no doubt partly with such an intention, but chiefly perhaps to p
an end to flagrant disregard of the requirements for a canoni
episcopal election, that Siricius took it upon himself to nominate
bishop Anysius as metropolitan, assigning to him the whole of t

---

[1] *Ep.* 4, JK 259; *Ep.* 9, JK 261.
[2] Strangely enough, little if any notice appears to have been taken of this fact
the correspondence now under review.   [3] See above, p. 250 ff.

w prefecture of Illyricum as his sphere of jurisdiction, with the
cial duty of securing the election of fit candidates to the Illyrian
scopate.[1] From later correspondence we learn that these powers
re in some sense confirmed by Anastasius I, Siricius' immediate
cessor, but it is not till we turn to the letters of Innocent I that we
form any precise notion regarding their scope.

It will be convenient at this stage to survey the whole course of papal
ations with the churches of this debatable territory between the
tern and western spheres of the Empire. In this way it will be
ssible to form a coherent picture of the seriousness of the new
nace' to the visible unity of the Church and of the nature of the
pal reaction towards it.

The growing importance of Illyrian affairs in the eyes of the
man see at the opening of the fifth century appears to be
strated by the fact that the earliest surviving letter of Pope
nocent I is addressed to the see of Thessalonica, by which the
hority already assigned to its occupant Anysius by his pre-
cessors is explicitly confirmed.[2]

The next letter known to us is some ten years later in date.[3] In the
erval Anysius had been replaced by Rufus, and something like
rmal provincial organization of the Illyrian churches had come into
ng. Citing Mosaic and apostolic precedents, Innocent enjoins the
w bishop to exercise authority on his behalf (*nostra vice*) as 'the
st among primates' (i.e. metropolitans)[4] throughout the prefecture
Illyricum. He is to act as a means of communication between them
d the Roman see, and in relation to the Illyrian episcopate as a
al arbiter, it being left to his judgment whether or not to refer any
rticular question to Rome for final decision. We may surmise that
fus had been disposed to keep matters too much in his own hands,
d had given occasion for complaint against decisions made in
fiance or in ignorance of Canon Law. Yet in calling his 'vicar' to
count Innocent does not lose his sense of reality. His decision is

See JK 259, 261.

Ep. 1, JK 285. No letters addressed to Illyricum by Anastasius I have been
served.

Ep. 13, JK 300.

It should be understood that 'primas' is a synonym for 'metropolitanus' in
s period. Cf. Siricius, JK 286, 1; JK 258, 2, can. 1; *Conc.* Taur. canon 1, 1;
nc. Carth. (397) 2.7. ed. Bruns, H. T., *Canones apost. et concil. vet. sel.*, 1839];
v. Hippon. 5. *op. cit.*, p. 136; [*Cod. eccl. afr.* 17, 86, *ed. cit.*, pp. 162, 178]. The
erences in brackets are to 'prima sedes'.

that technical irregularities in recent episcopal elections may
overlooked, but must not occur in the future.[1]

We may not pass on to the consideration of his successors' attit
to this sphere of jurisdiction without mentioning, for the sake of
light which it sheds on Innocent's conception of the responsibi
entrusted to the see of Thessalonica, an important contribution ma
by him to the whole practice of papal administration. Its nature
most clearly illustrated in a decretal addressed to Victricius,[2] bish
of Rouen (Rotomagus), one of the principal sees in northern Ga
There it is required that if at a local synod a *maior causa*, a prec
definition of which is not supplied, should arise, the verdict is to
referred to the Roman see for confirmation or amendment.[3] It
probable that the justification for this precept is to be found in
principles underlying the enactments of the council of Sardica,
confirmed or enlarged by the imperial rescript *Ordinarior*
sententias, to which we have already referred.[4] The council of Nic;
had found it necessary to provide some safeguard against 'prelac
and by the middle of the fourth century a similar check on 'p
vincialism' was urgently in demand, so now once again the princi
of the Roman see as the 'universal referee' was invoked. Those w
interpret Innocent's ruling as a sign of papal aggressiveness m
either ignore the realities of the situation or else disregard the earl
evidence in support of the principle which underlies it.

To resume our account of the relations of the Roman see w
eastern Illyricum, the next batch of evidence to claim our attenti
concerns an appeal to that see by the metropolitan church of Corir
against a decision of Rufus, bishop of Thessalonica. Boniface
who was now Pope, saw fit to support the case of the petitioners, a
to overrule the action of his 'vicar', in spite of the fact that the lat
could claim that a Nicene canon was on his side. Nevertheless wh
confirming the election of Perigenes to the see of Corinth, he
plicitly renewed the special authority of the see of Thessalonica.[5]

---

[1] *Ep.* 17, 3, JK 304. Cf. *Ep.* 16, JK 303.
[2] *Ep.* 2, JK 286.   [3] *Ibid.*, 3 (5 and 6).
[4] It should be observed, however, that the *prima facie* justification provided
Innocent I himself is derived from Exodus XVIII, 22. See p. 246 f.
[5] *Epp.* 4 and 5, JK 350, 351. It should be noticed that the concluding sectio
of these two letters have been interchanged in error. Cf. Caspar, *op. cit.*, vol
p. 373 f, n. 3. The fact that Boniface could support his petitioners against Can
Law seems to point to some lack of consistency in papal policy, when it came
dealing with this 'debatable' territory.

f we ask how such direct papal intervention in the affairs of
ricum was regarded in Constantinople, we can find the answer in
script issued at this time by the young Emperor Theodosius II,[1]
o had succeeded his father Arcadius some thirteen years previously.
is provided that disputed questions arising among the churches of
Illyrian prefecture were to be referred to the episcopal synod of
eastern capital, on the explicit ground that the city 'enjoys the
vileges of ancient Rome'.[2] It is important to observe the progress
de by the claims of this see since the days of the famous 'third
on'.[3] In 381 ecclesiastical inferiority to the see of Rome was
nowledged: now we find a clear assumption of nothing less than
ıality. In spite of the attempt made by Boniface through the
ıperor Honorius to obtain the withdrawal of this provision[4] and
ıeodosius' professed willingness to make amends, the law itself
s left undisturbed, and ultimately found a place in the *Codex
eodosianus*.[5] There can be no doubt that it provided one of the
ıst fertile seeds of future schism.

No doubt it was knowledge of the existence of such a law which
couraged renewed resistance to the papal decision in regard to a
puted election to the metropolitan see of Corinth. Boniface's
ıction was responsible for one of the outstanding papal documents
this period.[6] It is a clear and uncompromising restatement of the
ounds on which the peculiar authority of the Roman see was
lieved to rest, namely the Dominical commission of Matt. XVI, 18.
the same time it includes a thinly veiled protest, not unmixed with
reats, against presumptuous interference on the part of the see of
nstantinople. Its most characteristic passage is the following:
'Since the occasion demands it, if you will please examine Canon
w, you will find what is the second see after the Roman church
d what is the third. This group (of sees) has been canonically set
art, so that the bishops of other churches, though sharing one and
e same episcopal status, may realize that there are those to whom
ey ought to be obedient in a bond of love for the sake of ecclesias-

---

[1] *Cod. Theod.* XVI, ii, 45.
[2] *Ibid.*, 'quae (sc. urbs CP.) Romae veteris praerogativa laetatur'.
[3] See above, p. 252.
[4] *Ep.* 7, JK 353, and *Ep. Honorii imp.* inter *Bon. Epp.* No. 10. *M.P.L.* 20, 769.
Ep. Theod. imp., ibid., No. 11.
[5] The original law was issued in 421, the *Codex* published in 438.
[6] *Ep.* 15, JK 365.

tical discipline . . . None has ever been so rash as to oppose t
apostolic primacy, the judgment of which may not be revised; no
rebels against it, unless he would be judged in his turn'.[1]

In his letter to Rufus Boniface is even more outspoken, and do
not hesitate to refer 'to the activities of those who are inspired by
desire for innovation and a lust for importance which is not th
due'.[2] Even the most casual reader of his words could have
possible doubt as to the identity of the object of this censure. In y
a further admonition, this time addressed to the bishops of Thessa
he lays stress once again on the consequences of the Petrine prima
Thus, to quote only the opening words, he writes:

'The universal ordering of the Church at its birth took its orig
from the office of blessed Peter, in which is found both its directi
power and its supreme authority. From him as from a source, at t
time when our religion was in the stage of growth, all church
received their common order. This much is shown by the injunctio
of the council of Nicaea, since it did not venture to make a decree
his regard, recognizing that nothing could be added to his dignit
in fact it knew that all had been assigned to him by the word of t
Lord. So it is clear that this church is to all churches throughout t
world as the head is to the members, and that whoever separat
himself from it becomes an exile from the Christian religion, sin
he ceases to belong to its fellowship'.[3]

Later, with further allusion to the aspirations of the see of Co
stantinople, the same letter reads:

'Let there cease all newfangled presumption. Let none cheri
unlawful hopes. Let no man strive to violate the decisions of t
ancients, decisions of long-standing observance. Let everyone w
holds himself to be a bishop conform to our directions. Let no
presume to ordain bishops anywhere in Illyricum without the conse
of our fellow-bishop Rufus'.[4]

A further letter bearing on the situation in Illyricum, usua
ascribed to Celestine I, Boniface's successor, but recently shown
Schwartz to belong to Boniface himself, has a special point of interes
Speaking generally of ecclesiastical discipline the Pope writes:

---

[1] Ep., 5. There is evidently allusion to Conc. Nic., canon 6, here.
[2] Ep. 13, 1, JK 363.   [3] Ep. 14, 1, JK 364.   [4] Ibid., 4.
[5] Celestine, Ep. 3, JK 366, on which see Schwartz, E., Festschr. f. Reitzenste
1931, p. 146.

'We in particular are under obligation to be responsible for all, whom Christ assigned the duty of universal stewardship in the ly Apostle Peter, when He gave to him the keys of opening and)sing, and discriminated among His Apostles, not so that one ould be inferior to another, but that he should be the first. Law ould govern us, not we the law; if we are to uphold canonical inciples, let us be obedient to the canons ourselves'.

As to the authority of the see of Thessalonica, it is explicitly stated t only that its confirmation is to be obtained for all episcopal ctions, but that even metropolitans are not to assume jurisdiction thout its knowledge and approval. It is also to act as a channel for communications addressed to the Roman see.

Under Xystus III a further change in the political situation took ice, in consequence of which, by arrangement between Theodosius and Valentinian III, the eastern portion of western Illyricum was igned to the political jurisdiction of Constantinople[1], with the tural result that scope for Constantinopolitan 'aggression' was finitely increased. In consequence of renewed difficulties between rigenes of Corinth and Anastasius, the new bishop of Thessalonica, stus endorsed once more the privileges of the latter see, and pointed t that obedience was due to it no less from the bishop of Corinth n from other metropolitans.[2]

It is significant that Xystus actually found it necessary to warn bishops of Thessaly against availing themselves of a right of peal to Constantinople, recently upheld by a synod of that see. insisted that all suits between bishops were to be settled by astasius, now bishop of Thessalonica, or else referred to himself.[3] Under the master hand of Leo I, that indefatigable champion of lesiastical unity and canonical discipline, the privileges of Anas-ius were explicitly renewed with special reference to episcopal secrations. We may note too a significant indication of the growing sion in the relations between the sees of Rome and Constantinople his injunction to Anastasius 'to man the out-post'.[4] Numerous er points of interest must be passed over here, but it may be narked that it is to the longest of Leo's surviving letters in the dex Thessalonicensis that we owe that phrase which so frequently ppears in the later history of the Papacy.

See the present writer's *Life and Times of St. Leo*, p. 201, n. 111.   [2] *Ep.* 7, JK 393.
Ep. 8, JK 394. Cf. Grumel, *op. cit.*, No. 84.   [4] Cf. *Ep.* 5, JK 403.

'We have entrusted you, beloved, with our "vicariate", in su
wise that you have been called to share in our responsibility, not
possess the fulness of power (*ut in partem sis vocatus sollicitudin
non in plenitudinem potestatis*)'.[1]

It is also noteworthy that he interprets the famous sixth canon
Nicaea[2] to imply that even the measure of authority assigned by it
the sees of Alexandria and Antioch does not make them any the le
subject to the one see of Peter. Under Leo the concept of prima
noticed in our last lecture has already undergone some modificatio
By remaining silent about the supposedly Petrine origin of the oth
two sees, he points to its exclusive attribution to the see of Rome.

Yet in spite of the vigilance of successive Popes, Byzanti
imperialism gradually established its control over the Church, fir
in the East and later also in the West. No bulwark which the Papa
might contrive to raise was proof for long against its open or secr
progress. But before describing its advance and its unhappy effect
the unity of Christendom, we must turn back to review the eviden
as to the attitude towards the Roman see of those churches whi
as yet remained immune from its disintegrating influence.

III

The history of the churches of north Africa in this period
deserving of particularly close attention in this respect, because
has frequently been believed that their relation to the Papacy w
marked by an attitude of supposedly primitive independence su
as other western churches had never shown or else had long sin
abandoned. In the course of the fourth century African chur
organization had lost its primitive extempore character and h
become assimilated to the provincial system generally adopt
throughout the Empire. Local differences persisted, however, t
most notable of which was the peculiar status assigned by custo
to the bishop of Carthage, which in certain respects appeared
entitle him to treat with the bishop of Rome as his peer, scarcely
his inferior, and in virtue of which he was accorded the presiden
over the annual plenary African synod.

The closing years of the fourth century witnessed yet furth
attempts to settle the fratricidal Donatist schism, that unhappy lega
of fourth-century rigorism, more recently aggravated and embitter

[1] *Ep.* 14, 1, JK 411.   [2] See above, p. 201 ff., and below, p. 308 ff.

y the blatantly political expedients adopted by Constantine I and
is successors.[1] Diffident about the propriety of certain proposed
measures of tolerance towards repentant schismatics, the African
synod of 401 sought the advice of 'Anastasius, bishop of the apostolic
see, and Venerius, bishop of Milan'.[2] What opinion Venerius expressed we are not told. All we know is that Anastasius I appears
to have been unfavourable to the African proposals. The synod, however, contented itself with a polite acknowledgment of the Pope's
reply, and decided to allow an independence of action to individual
bishops such as Cyprian in his time had stressed with such elaborate
emphasis. Yet in spite of every effort to reach a *modus vivendi* on the
part of the Catholics, the Donatists remained unmoved, and, contemptuous of any form of compromise, persisted in schism. One may
perhaps be pardoned for supposing that at least on this occasion
Anastasius had formed a correct judgment.

Typical of that attitude of cordial respect towards the Roman see,
which is found in Cyprian's earlier edition of the *De Unitate*, the
work of Optatus of Milevis merits careful notice. His book 'on the
Donatist Schism', published in its later form under Pope Siricius,
contains the following testimony to the belief of Africans of this time,
apparently held by Donatists and Catholics alike :

'So you cannot deny,' he writes, 'that you are aware that an episcopal see in the city of Rome was conferred on Peter first of all, in
which Peter sat as head of all the Apostles, whence too he was called
Cephas, and that in that one see unity was preserved by all, lest the
rest of the Apostles should each claim a see for himself—on the contrary, he who would establish another in opposition to the one see
would be evidently a schismatic and a sinner. So a single see, which
is the first of the (Church's) endowments, was occupied by Peter, to
whom there succeeded . . . Siricius, who is to-day our ally; with
whom in our case the whole world is in harmony by interchange of
letters in a single social fellowship. Therefore produce the origin of
your see, who wish to claim the holy Church for yourselves'.[3]

Though Optatus' words have an Irenaean ring, it is difficult to

[1] See above, p. 179.
[2] See Bruns, H. T., *Canones apost. et concil. vet. sel.*, 1839, vol. i, p. 168 f. For an
earlier request for advice addressed to Rome and Milan, see *Brev. Hippon.* c. 37,
cit., p. 133.
[3] *De schism. Don.* 2, 2, 3. *C.S.E.L.*, vol. xxvi, p. 36. The passage includes a
papal list from Peter to Siricius, on which see above, pp. 84, 92.

believe that Irenaeus would have fully endorsed his exclusive
Petrine doctrine. Nevertheless they show that in the face of the
acute difficulties, created by the persistence of a rigorist schism
those who valued the apostolic tradition had perforce to appeal to
centre of unity outside their own immediate organization, from which
at least since Tertullian's time it had been believed that that tradition
had been derived.[1]

During the first decade of the fifth century we know little of any
contact between the African churches and the Roman see. The
resumption seems at least in part to have been due to the political
catastrophes which marked the beginning of that century. Before ten
years had passed Italy lay at the feet of Alaric the Goth, and even
Rome itself had experienced not only the hardships of an intermittent
siege but the ignominy of actual capture and sack at the hands of the
barbarian foe. It was in order to escape the dangers and privation
arising from the presence of a hostile force of uncertain temper
which the Roman imperial government, relying perhaps on the
comparative security of its retreat behind the marshes of Ravenna
seemed impotent or perhaps unwilling to challenge, that a considerable
able proportion of the urban population sought peaceful asylum in
the transmarine provinces of north Africa.

Among these emigrés was Pelagius, a monk, as it appears, of British
origin, and Celestius, a Roman layman. The former, since his arrival
in Rome in the time of Pope Anastasius I, had already acquired
considerable reputation no less for piety than for learning. An even
greater popularity now rewarded their activities in Carthage, with
the result that they rapidly found themselves the acknowledged
leaders of a group of like-minded Christians in that city, in whom
their stoic appeal to human self-confidence evidently awakened a
response. Pelagius' stay was but brief, and it was left for Celestius to
continue the spread of his teaching, and so before long to become the
object of a determined attack by Paulinus, deacon of Milan and disciple of the great Ambrose. His condemnation by the local church
and his appeal to the Roman see[2] had no immediate sequel, since
like Pelagius he chose to seek in the East a less critical milieu for
the propagation of his ideas.

---

[1] See above, p. 147. There is reason to believe that at this time Catholics in
Africa were far fewer in number than the Donatists.
[2] Facundus, *Def. III Cap. Lib.* 7, 3. *M.P.L.* (*Inter Opp. Aug.*, vol. x), 45, 1723

Perhaps nothing more would have been heard of the two in Africa, it had not been for the insatiable curiosity of a certain Orosius, who ad undertaken a journey to the mother Church of Christendom and ad accidentally encountered Pelagius. After consultation with the ld Roman presbyter Jerome, who for the past twenty-five years ad made his home in Jerusalem and seldom rested from con-roversial activity, the too inquisitive Spaniard believed himself to be n the trail of a dangerous heresy, and therefore felt it his duty to hallenge the influence already gained by Pelagius over John the local ishop.

Presently, at a synod of the church of Jerusalem, Orosius delivered vigorous attack against which even John himself seemed powerless o defend his protegé. In the end it was agreed, to judge from Orosius' wn words, 'that brethren and letters should be sent to blessed nnocent, Pope of Rome, and that all should follow what he should ecide'.[1] The charge against Pelagius was subsequently renewed by wo exiled Gaulish bishops at the synod of the province held at)iospolis. This time it seems that the tables were turned and that he accused succeeded in obtaining formal absolution from heresy. ut if Innocent ever received the original letter no record of his eply has been preserved.

Orosius returned to Africa in 416, and in the summer of the same ear, roughly five years after the original condemnation of Celestius, was decided by the provincial synods of *Africa proconsularis* and f Numidia to condemn his teaching afresh, together with that of his lly Pelagius. Both synods moreover were evidently aware of two erious objections to their action: first, that they were condemning the ccused in their absence, and secondly that the sentence of the eastern rovincial synod just mentioned might easily be taken to represent he verdict of the most ancient of all Churches. It therefore seemed ighly desirable to have recourse to the Roman church on account f its *potior principalitas*. For if Pelagius' teaching had been declared) be in line with the *paradosis* of Jerusalem, how could mere African erdicts avail against such an authority? Probably no one in Africa ras more alive to the dangers of the situation than Augustine him-elf, as may be judged from the personal letter sent by him and four ther African bishops to Pope Innocent, to provide a covering note[2]

---

[1] *Liber apologeticus*, 6, 5. *C.S.E.L.*, vol. v, p. 611.
[2] *Inter Innocent. Epp.* No. 28. *M.P.L.* 20, 571.

to the two synodical letters,[1] inviting the opinion of the Roman see o
the matter in hand.

'We have heard it said', writes Augustine, 'that there are people i
Rome, where that man (sc. Pelagius) has spent much of his lifetime
who are favourably disposed towards him on various grounds, whil
in the East, where he is living now, resolutions of the Church hav
been drawn up, in virtue of which he is regarded as vindicated'.[2]

Later on he says:

'If they (sc. Pelagius' supporters) were to understand that the book
which they think or know to be his, has been anathematized an
condemned by himself on the authority of Catholic bishops, an
especially that of your holiness, which we do not doubt will be c
considerable weight with him, we think they will not dare furthe
. . . to perplex faithful and simple Christian hearts'.[3]

It has been said that the African churches of this period uphel
'the old Conciliar Constitution of the Church'.[4] We must how
ever at the same time take account of certain signs of a convictior
in some measure shared by the Africans with the rest of th
Church, that if a local decision (in this case on a point of doctrine
was to possess universal validity, it must in some way be supporte
by a verdict of the Roman see.

It is difficult, therefore, to admit the fairness of those who hav
alleged that in his reply Innocent deliberately distorted these lette
by interpreting them as appeals to the doctrinal *magisterium* of h
see.[5]

'In searching out the things of God', he writes to Carthage, 'whic
the bishops must judge with every care, particularly by means of
really impartial general council, you are following the precedents c
ancient tradition and are mindful of the custom of the Church b
restoring in very deed the vitality of your faith, not only in makin
your recent declaration, but in your present consultation. You decide
that your verdict should be referred to our judgment, with the know
ledge of your duty to the apostolic see, since all of us who are place
in this position desire to follow none other than the Apostle, who
the source both of our episcopate and of the prestige of our name'

When he says later on that the Africans requested that 'a decisio

---

[1] *Inter Innocent. Epp.* Nos. 26 and 27. *M.P.L.* 20, 564 ff.
[2] *Ibid.*, No. 28, 2. *M.P.L.* 20, 572.   [4] Kidd, *History*, vol. iii, 171.
[3] *Ibid.*, No. 28, 14. *M.P.L.* 20, 579.   [5] E.g. Caspar, *op. cit.*, vol. i, p. 333.
[6] *Ep.* 29, JK 321.

may be given which will profit all at the same time throughout the churches of the whole world',[1] he expressed precisely their need. Against a purely African decree there might always lie an appeal to some other council.[2] Innocent, it seems, was invoked precisely in order that the matter might be settled once and for all (omnibus una). If space permitted, it might be possible further to illustrate the point with other relevant quotations from this correspondence.[3] Instead we must turn to inquire how far the views expressed by Augustine himself on the place of papal authority within the Church coincide with those which appear to be implied by the African handling of the Pelagian controversy.

Much has often been made, or perhaps it might be said made out, of a phrase which occurs in a sermon of his delivered shortly after Pope Innocent's reply had been received. Let us look at it in its actual context:

'What was said of the Jews, is wholly appropriate to them (sc. the Pelagians). They have a zeal for God. "I bear them record, that they have a zeal for God but not according to knowledge". What does it mean, "not according to knowledge"? "For they being ignorant of God's righteousness, and going about to establish their own, have not submitted themselves to the righteousness of God". My brethren, be my partners. When you find such people, do not conceal the fact, have no misplaced pity: I repeat, when you find them, do not conceal the fact. Convince those who contradict you or else bring along to us those who remain obdurate. For by now two synodical letters have been sent on this dispute to the apostolic see; from that see in turn replies have come. The dispute is at an end: would that the error too might end at last. So we urge them to take note, we warn them to be instructed, we implore them to change their minds'.[4]

It is, of course, from this passage that the famous but apocryphal paradigm, 'Roma locuta est, causa finita est', has been coined, of which no more than the last three words are authentically Augusinian. To help us to interpret the thought underlying his genuine words, let us inquire what view he takes of the Petrine office. We may

---

[1] Ep., 2.
[2] Cf. Augustine's view on the authority of councils, De baptismo, 2, 1–3 (2–4); 9 (14). C.S.E.L. vol. li, pp. 174–8, 190.
[3] Epp. 30, 31, JK 322, 323; (inter Aug. Epp. Nos. 182, 183. Coll. Avell. No. 41). C.S.E.L. vol. xxxv, p. 92.
[4] Serm. 131, 9 (10). M.P.L. 38, 734.

note first that in writing to the layman Generosus, contemplating conversion to Donatism, he insists that the promise given to St. Peter presupposed his primacy among the disciples. Its actual content in Augustine's view was none other than his endowment as the representative of the Church, with the 'power of the keys'.[1] Yet although at one time he identifies St. Peter himself with the 'rock',[2] later he interprets it rather of Christ, arguing that 'Peter, receiving his name from this "Rock", represents the Church now to be built upon it. For it was not said to him, "Thou art the rock", but "Thou art Peter". The Rock in fact was Christ'.[3] Elsewhere, it may be noted, he expressly rejects the view that 'the power of the keys' was entrusted to Peter alone, and argues that his primacy was simply a personal privilege, not one of office.[4] 'It was not a single individual', he writes, 'but the one body of the Church which received these keys. It is for this reason that the pre-eminence of Peter is declared, because when it was said to him, "to thee I deliver" that which was delivered to all, he provided in himself a symbol of the actual fellowship and unity of the Church'.[5] In another passage Augustine calls particular attention to this representative role of St. Peter, who showed in his conduct failure as well as success, weakness as well as strength, and was thus a type of the Church, which, unlike the Donatist sect included in its membership strong and weak alike.[6] We may now ask how far he regarded the teaching and discipline of the Roman see as normative for the rest of the Church. So far as discipline is concerned admittedly at least one passage of his may be found in which, in a case where no serious principle was involved, namely the practice of fasting on Saturday, he explicitly repudiates any obligation to conform to Roman custom.[7] On the other hand, his theory of authority in such matters emerges quite clearly in his arguments against the rejection of schismatic baptism, where after repudiating the validity of an appeal to Cyprian, he insists that the verdict of Holy Scripture alone can be regarded as final and beyond discussion. At the same time it should be noticed that he qualifies this by asserting that Pope Stephen's ruling represented a custom 'derived from the apostolic

---

[1] *Ep.* 53, 2. *C.S.E.L.* vol. xxxiv, p. 153. The passage is of particular interest in that it contains Augustine's papal list. See above, pp. 84, 92.

[2] In *Ps.* xxx. *Enarr,* 3, 5; In *Ps.* lxix. *Enarr,* 4.

[3] *Retract,* 1, 21, 1.   [5] *Serm.* 295, 2. *M.P.L.* 38, 1349.

[4] *Tract in ev. Joh,* 124, 5.   [6] *Serm.* 76, 3. *M.P.L.* 38, 480.

[7] *Ep.* 36, 2 (4).

dition, since many customs, which do not appear in the apostolic
ters nor in the synods of those who came after them, because they
e observed throughout the whole church, are nevertheless held to
ve been handed down and commended by the Apostles'.[1] Where
en did he believe the norm in matters of doctrine was to be found?
tention has sometimes been called to a supposed difference between
e answer of his earlier writings and that of his later ones to this
estion, since in the former it is the finality of conciliar decisions,
ile in the latter that of Roman verdicts which appears to be
phasized. This difference has led some to speak of a development
der pressure of logic, and others of an anomalous inconsistency.
rhaps the truest explanation is that more importance has been
tached to his views on authority than he would have assigned to them
mself. Rather than as a carefully thought out theory it is possible to
gard them as little more than a series of *obiter dicta* based on per-
nal experience of ecclesiastical practice in north Africa. Had he
tended to formulate a clear-cut theory, it is inconceivable that his
eculative genius would not have compelled him to inquire whence
plenary council derives its authority,[1] who is to determine whether
 not its resolutions are in accord with the supposedly absolute
ctrinal standard of the scriptural tradition, and finally how they
e to be enforced. The eastern churches, as we shall see presently,
d already found an answer to most if not all of these questions,
t it is likely that to one so convinced of the need for the Church's
iritual independence it would have savoured too much of total
bordination to the State to give any permanent satisfaction. It
ay be added that if only the promoters of the fifteenth century
nciliar movement had set themselves to answer these and like
estions, before launching their well-meant but mishandled attempt
 restore the unity and purity of the Church, more immediate and
ore lasting benefit might have followed.

For a more complete picture of the attitude of Augustine and of the
rican churches towards the doctrinal primacy of the Roman see,
is necessary to trace very briefly the subsequent fate of Pelagianism
der Innocent I's successor.

Innocent was succeeded on his death, March 12, 417, by Zosimus.
 spite of all that may be said against him it may be doubted whether
is unfortunate Pope has received sufficiently fair treatment at the

[1] Cf. above, p. 283 n. 2.

hands of historians. Thus even Duchesne has written 'Zosime, l
représente une véritable anomalie. De son court pontificat l'impre
sion qui résulte est celle d'une série d'entreprises peu sages
d'efforts manqués'.[1] That may well be true, but there is perha
another side. There is no need to speak here of his choice of t
intruder Patroclus of Arles as a suitable recipient of exceptio
authority in the provinces of southern Gaul, an obvious enough er
of judgment which had an unfortunate aftermath in the unhap
relations between Hilary and Leo I.[2] Less well founded, as we sh
see, is the charge that he was guilty of hasty and ill-considered acti
in the Pelagian controversy so as to give occasion, as it has be
supposed, for the African churches to assert their independence
the doctrinal authority of his see.

Let us carefully examine the facts. Zosimus had no sooner be
elected than the irrepressible Celestius made his reappearance
Rome. Without any hesitation he revived the question of his appe
made seven years previously, but which he had apparently thoug
better to withdraw.[3] It is unfortunate that we are solely depende
on Zosimus' own account[4] for evidence as to the proceedings of t
Roman synod at which Celestius was heard, and that both t
appellant's *libellus* and his confession of faith have perished. Yet i
a mistake to suppose that he received a clear verdict of acquittal. .
that was done was to allow two months' grace to his accusers to prese
their case. And in view of his profession of willingness to corr
'whatever that (sc. the Roman) see should condemn', he was giv
the benefit of the doubt for the moment. At the same time it shou
be noticed that the existing sentence of excommunication against h
was not removed.[5] Therefore it is not true to say that Zosimus ga
formal approval of Pelagian doctrine on this occasion. As Chapm
has pointed out, his most serious mistake lay in putting too gr
reliance on Celestius' sincerity.[6]

But shortly after this the Pope received two relevant documen
a letter from Praylius,[7] the new bishop of Jerusalem, and a *libell*

---

[1] *Histoire*, vol. iii, p. 228.
[2] See the present writer's *Life and Times of St. Leo*, pp. 113–128, 159–164.
[3] See above, p. 280.
[4] *Ep.* 2. JK 329. *Coll. Avell.* No. 45, ed. cit., p. 99 ff.
[5] Augustine, *De pecc. orig.* 7. *C.S.E.L.* vol. xlii, p. 170 f.
[6] *Studies on the Early Papacy*, 1928, p. 161 ff.
[7] See Zosimus, *Ep.* 3, JK 330. *Coll. Avell.* No. 46, ed. cit., p. 103 ff.

m the hand of Pelagius,[1] in which the latter, like Celestius,
nowledged his readiness to be corrected by him 'who holds both
faith and the see of Peter'. Professions of this kind might well
ceive the good-natured Zosimus. Not so the watchful Africans, who
obably received the Pope's two letters together with a copy of
agius' *libellus* by the hand of the same messenger. An immediate
ly from Aurelius of Carthage was sent, requesting a prolongation
the prescribed interval of two months.[2] Shortly afterwards, about
turn of the year 417/18, a large, but not plenary, African council
s assembled, which reaffirmed the sentence of Pope Innocent,
d urged that the *bona fides* of Celestius and Pelagius ought not
be trusted.[3] To the same date belongs the *libellus* of Paulinus
Milanese deacon, which is of interest as bearing independent
d important testimony to the doctrinal primacy of the Roman
.[4]

But unfortunately for the Pelagians, the African letter just men-
ned contained an embarrassing document—now unhappily lost—
other than the *Acta* of the original synod of 411 at which Celestius
d been condemned.[5]   The disclosure had for its immediate and
amatic sequel the sudden disappearance of Celestius from Rome.
is final proof of guilt evidently convinced Zosimus that his patience
d been unrewarded, and an encyclical letter was thereupon issued
which the condemnation of Celestius and Pelagius was formally
ewed.[6] The matter need be pursued no further. Sufficient has
en said to show, first, that in spite of Zosimus' over-generous
atment of Celestius and Pelagius he had not in fact, as is often
presented, delivered a hasty judgment and subsequently been
liged to withdraw; secondly, that the African churches, in spite
their impatience with the Pope's method, in no way repudiated
eir former deference to the Roman see.

At this stage we can imagine that it might be said: 'Granted that

App. operum Augustini. M.P.L. 45, 1716.
See Zosimus, *Ep.* 12, JK 342. *Coll. Avell.* No. 50, ed. cit., p. 115 ff.
Augustine, *C. duas Epp. Pel.* 2, 3 (5). *C.S.E.L.* vol. LX, p. 463; *De pecc. orig.*
). *C.S.E.L.* vol. xlii, p. 171 f.; Prosper, *C. Coll.* 5, 53. *M.P.L.* 51, 226 ft.
Coll. Avell. 47, ed. cit., p. 108 ff. 'Quod iam diutius latere non potuit, sed
nifestius publicatum spiritali per tuam beatitudinem gladio resecatur, ne
plius ferinis dentibus grex domini secetur in partes, quem pastor bonus sollicita
ervigili cautela custodis'.
See above, p. 280.
M.P.L. 56, 490. Cf. Seeck, *Regesten*, p. 338.

a case may be made for a concession by the African churches to
see of Rome of some sort of doctrinal primacy, at least it must
admitted that there is nothing to show that they allowed to it
primacy of jurisdiction'. Once more let us try to form, so far a
possible, a strictly objective view of the evidence. It begins with
record of an appeal addressed to the Roman see in the last month
so of Zosimus' pontificate by a bishop of the province of *Byzac.*
against the verdict of his provincial synod, which appears in
course of its proceedings to have called in the aid of secular offic
as assessors. We have no information about the details of this af
beyond that which can be inferred from Zosimus' own hig
indignant letter to the synod.[1] In this particular case it may be t
the African bishops had good reason, not known to Zosimus,
summon secular advice in a situation in which financial inter
appear to have been involved. On the other hand there is no evide
that the Pope's intervention evoked any immediate protest, such
might have been expected, if his action had been held to
illegitimate.

The *cause célèbre* of Apiarius, which next claims our attention, ta
us back to the beginning of Zosimus' last year (418). In attempt
to evaluate the evidence, let us constantly bear in mind the fact t
our documents are scarcely adequate as a basis for a compl
reconstruction of the affair. On the Roman side there is actu
nothing beyond the fragments of a *commonitorium* delivered
Zosimus to his legates and a short letter of Boniface I to the sar
while on the side of the Africans, besides some local canons
uncertain date, we have to make what we can of the corrupt
incomplete acts of the plenary African council of May 25, 419,
synodical letter to Pope Boniface, letters to Carthage from Cyri
Alexandria and Atticus of Constantinople, and finally a synod
letter to Celestine I of uncertain date.[2] Such is not the material ou
which it is easy to construct a wholly satisfactory account. Let us
down briefly the assured facts. First, it is clear that in accepting
appeal of Apiarius and in demanding amends on the part of
bishop, Zosimus represented that his action had been justified
canons which he alleged to be Nicene. That the canons cited w

[1] *Ep.* 16, JK 346.
[2] Turner, *Eccl. occid. mon. iur. ant.* Tom. I, p. 561 ff. Note carefully what is s
op. cit., Tom. I., p. 624 *ad fin.* See also his article in *J.T.S.* vol. xxx, 1929, p. 3

t among those actually adopted at Nicaea was subsequently
ved by the Africans in the light of the copies of the original Nicene
ions sent at their request from Alexandria and Constantinople.

Nevertheless there can be little doubt that Zosimus was quite
aware of his mistake. Admittedly he showed lack of needful
esse, but it is difficult to imagine that anyone in his position
uld conceivably have been so foolish as to suppose that he could
pose upon the Africans by a simple fraud. In actual fact the case
unst him rests chiefly on a quite groundless assumption; namely
t by the year 418 no one had any right to be ignorant as to which
ions were Nicene and which were not. Let us look into this question
a moment.

The ninth century Chieti MS. (Vatic. Regin. 1997), also known as
Codex Ingilrami, our earliest existing source for Roman Canon
w, contains besides other canonical matter the Nicene canons
mbered I–XXVIII, and then without a break and with consecutive
mbering the Sardican canons XXVIIII–XLVI, followed by the
cene subscriptions.[1] Yet the fact that the existing titles are no part
the original version, but are borrowed from the later one in the
esnel Collection,[2] makes it quite possible that at least as late
the sixth century (the date of the exemplar from which our Codex
ives) the text was still in a very primitive state, and even at that
ie lacked any precise division into separate canons. A further
estion arises about the date and provenance of the archetype. We
ve already seen that it was not apparently till after the council of
rdica that any serious importance began to be attached to matter
Nicene origin, whether symbol or canons. It may be regarded
highly probable that a copy of these canons found its way to
me by the hands of the Roman legates to Sardica. Nor does it
m unlikely that to the document which they brought with them
re appended the minutes of Sardica. Has any trace of this primitive
cument survived? Careful investigation has shown that the
nity of the Nicene-Sardican section of the Codex Ingilrami can-
t well be later than the fourth century,[3] and we are thus presented
h a very strong probability that it represents the most rudimentary
ge in the development of Roman Canon Law, and that this collection,

Turner, op. cit., Tom I, pp. 105, 113–141; pp. 452–486; Id. in J.T.S., vol.
XI, 1930, p. 15.
Id., Eccl. occid. mon., Tom. I, p. 274.   [3] Op. cit., Tom. I, p. 103.

or something very similar, was accepted as authoritative at Rome
at least the first twenty years of the fourth century and perhaps late

But the question naturally arises, in view of the known presence
Gratus of Carthage at Sardica,[1] how it came about that the Afric
council of 419 appeared to be unaware of its provisions. No one wou
presumably wish to accuse the African bishops of a deliber.
suppressio veri, nor can we ignore the fact that at least one Afric
canon,[2] certainly in existence before 419, bears so striking a resen
blance to a Sardican canon (numbered VI in Turner's collection
that it can scarcely be dismissed as accidental. On the other hand, i
known that Augustine, believing our Sardican council to have be
an Arian assembly, discounted its validity.[4] We may suppose that
opinion of this kind was widely shared among his contemporaries, t
prevalence of which may explain the general ignorance or neglect
the Sardican canons.

Let us now look more closely at the local African canon law.
view of wide differences of opinion on this subject, it is impossi
here to do more than call attention to some questions which have be
raised. Contrasted with the more generous appellate legislation
Nicaea, the earlier African canons are surprisingly severe. Is it po
sible, as Chapman has suggested,[5] that the provision for appe
was made as a direct result of Apiarius' case ? It is usually believ
that the African canons against clerical 'transmarine' journeys we
intended to prevent bishops and others having recourse to the Rom
see. Yet can we altogether exclude the possibility that the origin
purpose of these canons was not to prevent reference to the Rom
see so much as to discourage the practice, already habitual with t
Donatists, of making appeals 'to the court' (*ad comitatum*)?[6] At a

---

[1] *Conc. Carthag.* (348), can. 5. Mansi, *Concilia*, vol. iii, 143. The council
notable for the fact that by canon 1 it reversed Cyprian's policy of rejecti
schismatic baptism.

[2] *Cod. can. eccl. ap.* canon, 106. *M.P.L.* 67, 216.

[3] *Eccl. occid. mon.* Tom. I, p. 465 ff.

[4] Augustine, *C. Cresc.* 3, 34 (38). *C.S.E.L.* vol. lii, p. 445 f.; cf. *Ep.* 44, 3 (
M.P.L. 33, 176. *C.S.E.L.* vol. xxxiv, p. 113 f.

[5] *Op. cit.*, p. 186.

[6] The relevant canons are *Conc. Carthag.* (397), canon 28, ed. Bruns, *op. c*
p. 127; *Brev. Hipp.* canon 27. Id., *op. cit.*, p. 138; *Cod. Eccl. Afric.* canons 23,
106. Id. *op. cit.*, pp. 163, 183, 187. The reference in canon 94 'Recitatae sunt liter
papae Innocentii: ut episcopi ad transmarina pergere facile non debeant' seems
confirm the view that the 'transmarine' appeals which it was sought to exclude
means of these canons were those addressed to the imperial court.

e it is clear that even if canons were actually passed after the
ɔiarian affair, intended to prevent bishops from appealing to the
ɔman see against the decisions of the African plenary or provincial
uncils, they must have been ill-supported by public opinion, since
late as 423 we find cases of appeals, with which Augustine at any
:e appears to have found no fault in principle.[1] Even the famous
ter *Optaremus*[2] is content to express the desire, reasonable enough
itself, that Celestine will not admit to communion those bishops
ɪom the Africans have excommunicated, and that he will not send
 clergy as exactors of dues or penalties (*exsecutores*) such as the
-mannered Faustinus. It is clear that this letter was meant as a
m though courteous remonstrance, but it is too much to say that
explicitly, and in so many words, repudiated the appellate juris-
:tion of the Roman see. It seems, however, that it had a salutary
ect, so that when a quarter of a century later an appeal was
dressed to Leo I, he had the wisdom to remit the case for re-
amination by the provincial council.[3] But if we are to be convinced
ɪt the African churches refused absolutely at least the status of
 occasional referee to the Roman bishop, we seem to be in need of
ɔre decisive evidence than has hitherto been produced.

IV

We have already considered evidence of the indirect relations of the
ɔman see during this period with the see of Constantinople, in
ɪnnexion with its delegation of peculiar powers to the see of
ɪessalonica. It is now time to see what light is cast by the history
 this period on relations of a more direct nature. That Nectarius,
ɪeodosius I's nominee to the see of Constantinople in 381, was
ɪnewhat overshadowed by the forceful personality of Theophilus
 Alexandria is shown by the issue of the Constantinopolitan synod
 394,[4] at which the part played by the bishop of the imperial
ɔital was evidently quite secondary. At the same time it is relevant
 remark that the intervention of the see of Alexandria was due largely
 the commission given to him by Pope Siricius, to whom in the
 ginal instance the question at issue had actually been referred.[5]
 Four years later the election of John as bishop of Constantinople,

---

Ep. 209, 8. *C.S.E.L.* vol. lvii, p. 351.   [3] *Ep.* 12, 12, JK 410 (c. 446).
Turner, *op. cit.*, Tom. I, p. 614.   [4] Grumel, *op. cit.*, No. 10.
    [5] Duchesne, *Histoire*, vol. ii, p. 623 f.

and his assumption of his great name-sake's role in virtue of
denunciation of the morals of the eastern Court, gave Theophilus
further opportunity to assert the primacy of his see. Meanwhile
had already been given further proof of the solidarity of relatio
existing between himself and the Papacy in the letters of Anastasius
supporting the Alexandrine condemnation of certain aspects
Origen's teaching. It may well be true that the Roman synod w
content to accept without serious discussion the view of Origenis
presented to it by Theophilus, but it is equally clear that even t
all-powerful bishop of Alexandria felt more assured of the success
his policy when he was able to show that his verdict had be
endorsed by the Roman see.[1]

Summoned to Constantinople as a defendant, Theophilus so
found opportunity to assume the position of judge, and in allian
with the court succeeded in procuring John's banishment. T
earliest information on the subject to be received by Pope Innoce
came from Theophilus; it was quickly followed by other letters, tl
time from John himself and his supporters. Similar letters were a
addressed to the sees of Milan and Aquileia.[2] It should be realize
however, that the basis of John's appeal was not the provisions
Sardica but the second canon of 381.[3] The Pope's reply to Theophil
calls for some comment. John's final deposition, it appears, had be
justified on the ground that in resuming possession of his see,
spite of the verdict of Theophilus' synod of 'the Oak', he had violat
the fourth canon of Antioch.[4] To this Innocent answers:

'If you are confident in your verdict, appeal to a council he
according to the mind of Christ, and there plead your case with t
canons of Nicaea as witnesses, for the church of the Romans ackno
ledges no other; thus you will render your position proof agai
attack'.[5]

The Pope's advice is highly significant. It shows that the Rom
see at this time (404) knew no Canon Law other than the canons

---

[1] *Ep.* 2, JK 276; JK 281 (see Jaffé, *Regesta*, vol. ii, p. 691, and Gheyn. v.d.
Revue d'hist. et de litt. réligieuses, vol. iv, 1899, p. 5); JK 282 in *Acta concilior
occumenicorum*, ed. Schwartz, E., 1924–6. Tom. I, vol. v, pt. i, p. 3. *Coll. Pal
No. 1*, the first two addressed to the see of Milan, the last to John of Jerusalem
[2] Palladius, *Vita Chrys.* 1–3. *M.P.G.* 47, 5 ff.
[3] Mirbt, *Quellen*[5], No. 137.
[4] Mansi, *Concilia*, vol. ii, col. 1309. Cf. canon 12, *ibid.*, 1313. On these cano
see Hefele-Leclercq, *Conciles*, I, ii, 706 and above p. 217.
[5] *Ep.* 5, JK 288.

caea, i.e. presumably the collection of fourth century origin from
ich our *Codex Ingilrami* was ultimately derived.[1] Innocent
terated his insistence on the unique validity of these canons in a
ter addressed to the supporters of John in the following year,[2] and
l more explicitly condemned those of heretical provenance.
itions and appeals continued to pour in from the 'Johannites', in
isequence of which, at the suggestion of the Pope and a synod of
lian bishops, a request was sent by the Emperor Honorius to his
ther at Constantinople by the hands of a papal legation, that a
incil of the Easterns be assembled at Thessalonica with a view to
restoration of peace. The Emperor Arcadius, however, or perhaps
should say his powerful minister the eunuch Eutropius, had
ady been satisfied. John had been deposed and Atticus reigned
his stead. So in pursuance of a technique soon to become normal
the eastern government's treatment of those who resisted its
lesiastical policy, the papal legation had its post bag confiscated on
arrival, and was immediately put aboard the next ship sailing for
ly. Innocent apparently swallowed the insult suffered in the per-
s of his representatives and contented himself with declaring his
imunion with the exiled John.[3] Yet even if he had chosen a more
nonstrative mode of protest, it is unlikely that Arcadius and his
isters would have given it any serious attention. The debt of the
of Constantinople to Theodosius I was steadily being repaid with
ipound interest.

ohn died in the following year, a martyr to the prestige of his
and to the moral primacy of the Christian Church.[4] His memory
l already been proscribed by the exclusion of his name from the
tycha of Alexandria, Antioch, and Constantinople. A schism
ween Rome and the three greater eastern churches was therefore
v in being.

I.e. a collection which included the canons of Sardica as well as those of
iea proper, the whole being commonly believed in Rome at this time to be
ene'. On the *Codex Ingilrami*, see above and below, pp. 289 f., 309.
Ep. 7, JK 294. *M.P.L.* 20, 501.
Ep. 12. JK. 298, preserved in a Greek version.
Nothing has been said here about John's 'Petrine' doctrine. Of his readiness to
e use of the see of Rome as a court of appeal there is no room for doubt. On the
r hand, it may reasonably be held that his interest in the prerogatives of St.
r arises not so much from his enthusiasm for papal jurisdiction as his concern
he primacy of his native see of Antioch, of which the Apostle was believed to
been the founder. For a different view, see Scott, S. H., *Eastern Churches and
Papacy*, 1928, pp. 125–135.
o

The means by which this schism was . gradually resolved
deserving of brief mention as they are not without significance. F
years had already elapsed by the time the first move was made by
see of Antioch, through the restoration of John's name to the *dipty*
by the newly elected bishop Alexander. The Pope on being acquain
with this decisive step towards reunion did not hesitate to express
heartfelt satisfaction.[1]

In a subsequent letter, also to Alexander,[2] Innocent set forth
view about the appropriate relations between the Roman see and
greater churches of the East, more particularly the see of Antic
which he allowed to be second only to the see of Rome because it
the temporary as distinct from the final meeting-place of the Apost
Referring to the sixth canon of Nicaea, he interpreted it to mean t
to the see of Antioch was assigned authority over the whole 'dioc
of the East', not because of its civil importance but chiefly beca
it was 'the first see of the first Apostle'. As to its bishop's jurisdicti
the Pope directed that all episcopal elections within the 'dioc
were to be subject to Alexander's confirmation, and, while the c
secration of bishops would normally belong to the appropriate met
politan, in the case of sees in the neighbourhood of Anti
Alexander might perform the rite himself.[3]

That Innocent was quite adamant about the necessity for a
rehabilitation of the martyr John is shown by his reply to the sugg
tion of a Macedonian bishop that he should resume communion w
Atticus of Constantinople.[4] Yet in spite of the rupture between t
see and Rome, Boniface, papal apocrisiary, who so far as we know
the first to hold such an office, continued to reside in the east
capital. It was not, however, till after Innocent's death, and perb
as a consequence of Atticus' signature of Zosimus' anti-Pelag
encyclical,[5] that normal relations were resumed. Twenty years l;
still, under the auspices of the civil government, the relics of Jo
surnamed 'Chrysostom', were translated in state to the capital
was a belated act of reparation and must have reminded the dev
no less than the cynical of the saying about 'the tombs of the proph

[1] See *Epp.* 19; 20; 21. JK 305–307. [2] *Ep.* 24. JK 310.
[3] It is important to notice the implication of these instructions. Inno
evidently assumed that he had the same right to order ecclesiastical affairs in
'diocese of the East' as Siricius had claimed over the prefecture of Illyricum.
[4] *Ep.* 22, JK 308.
[5] *Acta conc. oecum.*, ed. cit., Tom. I, vol. v, pt. 1, p. 68. *Coll. Palat.* No. 36.

o sum up, the chief interest of the whole affair from our point of
ew lies mainly in the fact that it shows the readiness of the Papacy
the person of Innocent to treat one of the primary sees of the East
a subordinate agent for the execution of papal policy.

V

We are now approaching the question regarding the attitude of the
stern churches towards the Roman see during the great Christo-
gical controversies of the fifth century. The religious situation in
e East had not changed to any marked extent since the days of
icaea. Then, as now, the see of Alexandria was on the point of
quiring a dominant position in ecclesiastical affairs; then, as now,
e last word lay with the *imperator-sacerdos*. Such differences as
ere were can be found chiefly in the fact that imperial autocracy had
come in the meantime if anything more bureaucratic and the
ethods of the Alexandrine episcopate distinctly less scrupulous.

If one of the commonest *motifs* of tragedy is the punishment of
ρις by a vengeful deity, the use of the word as a keynote of the career
Nestorius, elected to the see of Constantinople in 428, is highly
posite. From the beginning of his episcopate he showed himself
premely conscious of his position as bishop of the eastern capital,
d made his special task the eradication of heresy. It was in con-
xion with this undertaking that shortly after his election he
tempted to learn the opinion of Pope Celestine I regarding the
imerous agents of Pelagianism who had sought asylum in the East,
entioning in passing a growing eagerness to predicate $\Theta\epsilon o\tau\acute{o}\kappa os$
(od-bearer) of the Blessed Virgin. At least two letters on the subject
ere despatched;[1] if any replies were sent, none has been preserved.
sually the Roman see showed some readiness to answer its corre-
ondents. Is it possible that Celestine had momentarily forgotten his
ity, or was carelessly neglecting his role as 'universal referee'? Or
as it because the occasional *faux pas* of Zosimus, the memory of
hich must have been still fresh, had made the Papacy more than
ually wary? Yet if Celestine's silence was due to the innate con-
rvatism of the Roman see, he was evidently not unwilling to use the
vantage of up-to-date methods, as is shown by the presence
a secret agent in the eastern capital in the person of Marius

[1] Schwartz, *op. cit.*, Tom. I, vol. ii, pp. 12–14. *Coll. Veron.* No. 3; id., *ibid.*, p. 14 f.
ll. Veron. No. 4. Latin versions only have survived.

Mercator, a convinced opponent of Pelagianism, who ensured that t
Pope was kept well informed regarding Nestorius' personal attitu
on the matter about which he desired Roman advice. A later letter
sympathy to Celestius seems to suggest that what Nestorius rea
wanted was not advice but support, in this case against the a
powerful influence of the court.[1] Subsequent events, moreover, we
to show that Celestine's caution was amply justified.

Meanwhile the stage was being set for a spectacular trial of streng
between the sees of Constantinople and Alexandria. Cyril, who no
presided over the Egyptian churches, if lacking some of the mer
of his predecessor and uncle Theophilus, was not a whit behind hi
in whole-hearted devotion to the cause of his see. Throughout
seems to have been kept not less well informed than Celestine abo
the trend of events, and particularly of any movements of pub
opinion in Constantinople. Fishing in troubled waters had long beer
favourite amusement of Alexandrine bishops, and Cyril was not o
to let an opportunity for so acceptable a diversion pass him by.
was about the same time that Nestorius, who must have been by
means unaware of intrigue behind the scenes, in writing to Cyril
criticism of his Christology, thanked him for his lively interest
Constantinopolitan affairs.[2] Doubtless we can assume that mu
depended in the last resort in regard to the issue of the impendi
struggle on the success of one or the other of the two prospecti
combatants in gaining the favour of the court. Yet it is equally cle
that both sides recognized the importance of another factor, t
significance of which had certainly not diminished with the passa
of time. What would Celestine have to say? We know that he had l
him some sermons of Nestorius, probably supplied by the obligi
Marius, to help him to make up his mind,[3] and to these was now add
a very suitable letter from Cyril.[4] Let Celestine give the word ar
communion with Constantinople would be suspended forthwit
Otherwise let him beware; Nestorius was on the point of claiming
doctrinal primacy. It is perhaps significant that Cyril for his pa
preferred to remain silent about a possible candidate for a primacy
jurisdiction.

[1] Schwartz, op. cit., Tom. I, vol. v, p. 65. Coll. Palat. No. 35. Also a La
version.
[2] Id., op. cit., Tom. I, vol. i, pt. 1, pp. 29–32. Coll. Vatic. No. 5.
[3] Ep. 13, JK 374. Id., op. cit., Tom. I, vol. ii, p. 9. Coll. Veron. No. 2.
[4] Inter Celestini Epp. No. 8. M.P.L. 50, 448.

A Roman synod pronounced decisively in favour of the orthodox $\Theta\epsilon o\tau\acute{o}\kappa o\varsigma$ (God-bearer) as applied to the Blessed Virgin, at which elestine himself delivered a simple exposition of the western radosis, and in his letter to Cyril readily accepted the more elaborate lexandrine theory of the relation between the divine and human in hrist.[1] But with characteristic pastoral zeal the Pope urged the clamation of the misbeliever. These documents in due course ached Alexandria. It is difficult to believe that Cyril was at all sposed to lend any support to such a laudable programme; at e same time he must have felt considerable satisfaction to read at the Pope had appointed him to act on behalf of the Roman e in the matter. Several other letters were despatched at the same ne from the papal chancery, among them one to Nestorius himself, d in addition, one to the clergy and people of Constantinople self.[2]

By this time the controversial temperature in the East had risen nsiderably, and the unhappy Theodosius II, whom nature appears have better qualified to play the part of *sacerdos* than of *imperator*, deavoured to assume the dual role by summoning an imperial uncil to meet on Whitsunday in the following year (431) at Ephesus. he 'sacred' missives summoning the bishops spoke vaguely of disnsions, but gave little or no hint of the tremendous issues at stake. is likely that the Emperor himself conceived of nothing more nbitious than a representative assembly to restore peace to the local urch of Constantinople.

That Cyril himself welcomed the plan is highly improbable. But e duty already entrusted to him by Celestine provided his hand ith a trump card which if played early enough in the game might ell ensure the discomfiture of his less skilled opponents. On the her hand, Nestorius evidently regarded it as giving real hope of a tisfactory result, and to this end made a further effort to win elestine's support, inviting official Roman approval of his own term $\theta\rho\omega\pi o\tau\acute{o}\kappa o\varsigma$ (Man-bearer) to the final exclusion of its rival $\Theta\epsilon o\tau\acute{o}\kappa o\varsigma$.[3] is manoeuvre received indirect help from the letters addressed, rhaps at his instigation, by John of Antioch and his coterie to the

[1] *Ep.* 11, JK 372. Schwartz, *op. cit.*, Tom. I, vol. ii, p. 5. *Coll. Veron.* No. 1.
[2] *Ep.* 12, JK 373. Id., *op. cit.*, Tom. I, vol. ii, p. 21. *Coll. Veron. No.* 6; *Ep.* 13, 374. Id., *op. cit.*, Tom. I, vol. ii, p. 7. *Coll. Veron.* No. 2; *Ep.* 14, JK 375, , *op. cit.*, Tom. I, vol. ii, p. 15. *Coll. Veron.* No. 5.
[3] *Inter Celestini Epp.* No. 15. *M.P.L.* 50, 499.

principal western churches.[1] The attitude of the Roman see toward this and also towards the counter-move represented by Cyril twelve anti-Nestorian anathemas shows clearly that it was once mo following the traditional *via media* so characteristic of its standpoi in doctrinal controversies.

When the earlier arrivals at Ephesus had assembled, they we confronted with at least two surprises: Cyril, whom everyor except his own supporters expected to be treated as the defendan was found to have taken the double part of prosecutor and judge on the other hand, there was as yet no sign of the representatives of Celestine, bishops Projectus and Arcadius with the presbyter Phili who were said to be still on their way. Thus in spite of a successf issue from Cyril's standpoint of the hurried proceedings of the fir session, it became necessary to start practically *de novo* on the arriv of the Roman legation nearly a month later. It was on this occasic that the recital of Celestine's letter[2] was greeted by the assembly wit great acclamation: 'A just verdict', they shouted, 'Hail Celestine, tl modern Paul! Hail Cyril, the modern Paul! Hail Celestine, defend of the faith, Celestine, who is at one with the council'.[3] The encouraging and doubtless sincere marks of approval gave Philip, tl most astute member of the Roman legation, two incomparable oppo tunities for proclaiming the Roman primacy.[4]

On the latter of these occasions he addressed the council as follow:

'No one has any doubt, on the contrary it has been recognized all ages, that the holy and most blessed Peter, chief and head of tl Apostles, pillar of the faith, foundation of the Catholic Churc received from our Lord Jesus Christ, the Saviour and Redeemer the human race, the keys of the kingdom, and that to him has bec given power for the binding and loosing of sins: it is he who un this day and without intermission both lives and judges in h successors'.[5]

---

[1] Schwartz, *op. cit.*, Tom. I, vol. i, pt. 3, p. 41. *Acta graeca* No. 97.

[2] *Ep.* 18. JK 379. Schwartz, *op. cit.*, Tom. I, vol. ii, p. 22. *Coll. Veron.* No. 7.

[3] Id., *op. cit.*, Tom. I, vol. i, pt. 3, p. 57. *Acta graeca*, No. 106, 19. Bardenhew *Gesch. d. altkirchl. Lit.* vol. iv, p. 615, n. 1., holds that these words referred *Ep.* 13 (see p. 296, n. 3 above), announcing the condemnation of Nestorius, but Caspar, E., *Geschichte d. Papstt.* vol. i, p. 409, n. 4, points out, the counci attitude was to ignore previous action and to treat the whole question afresh. It significant that among the letters of Celestine cited by Firmus of Caesarea (Schwar *op. cit.*, *Acta graeca*, No. 106, 21), no mention was made of *Ep.* 13.

[4] Schwartz, *op. cit. Acta graeca*, Nos. 106, 23 and 31.

[5] Id., *ibid.*, *Acta graeca*, No. 106, 31.

Here is the famous passage cited in the Vatican Constitution, *astor aeternus* of 1870.[1] It is interesting to see that its emphasis is on primacy of jurisdiction rather than of doctrine, and that the *ı es Petrus* is interpreted decisively as a power of absolution, rather an of arbitration.

We may notice further the succeeding context of Philip's words, ıce it illustrates once again the pre-occupation of the Roman see th the safeguarding of the apostolic *paradosis*.

'His (i.e. St. Peter's) successor and rightful representative, our ost blessed Pope, bishop Celestine, has sent us to this council, the sembly of which has been ordered by the most Christian Emperors, substitutes for his appearance in person, in that he is ever mindful the Catholic faith, and in preserving it safeguards the doctrines of e Apostles, as they have come down from your fathers and forbears'.[2]

Thus the sentence against Nestorius was confirmed by the verdict the legates. Meanwhile what was the attitude of the eastern overnment? Consistent with its original conception of the purpose the council, it decided to act with a proper impartiality, and to ıforce not only the recent decision against Nestorius, but in addition e one pronounced by the supporters of Nestorius against Cyril, us bringing the conciliar proceedings to a paradoxical and somehat undignified conclusion. The Cyrilline bishops, however, duly ported their action in an official letter to Celestine,[3] and even the mperor showed suitable deference to him by agreeing, though ossibly with reluctance, at the request of Philip to the withdrawal of s edict against Cyril. The Roman legation, after taking part in the ection of Maximian to fill the place of the deposed Nestorius, set f for Rome in company with two representatives of his electors. nce they had returned, Celestine was not slow to fulfil his assumed sponsibility for the peace of the eastern churches, and by various

[1] It should be noticed that the compilers of the Constitution find it necessary insert 'praesidet' (*Coll. Lac.*, vol. vii, col. 483). It has already been remarked at accuracy in quotation from patristic authors is not a strong point of this ocument, see above, p. 18, n. 3.

[2] Id., *ibid.* Scott, S. H., *Eastern Churches and the Papacy*, 1928, p. 153, argues om the absence of any mention of protest on the part of the bishops against these terances that the doctrine which they contained was accepted *in toto* by the council. is difficult to feel that such an *argumentum e silentio* ought to be accepted in the ce of the record of the conciliar procedure which presupposes independence of tion throughout. It should be noticed, however, that Philip does not find it ojectionable that the council has been summoned by the Emperors.

[3] Schwartz, *op. cit.*, Tom. I, vol. i, pt. 3, p. 5. *Acta graeca*. No. 82.

letters sought to secure acceptance of the recent decisions and
effect the reconciliation of the see of Antioch.[1]

Yet by the time peace was actually restored, Celestine was dea
and his place filled by the Roman presbyter Xystus, the third of th
name. Following the reunion of Cyril and John of Antioch by mea
of the 'Formula of 433,'[2] in the composition of which it is probab
that Proclus, soon to be elected to the see of Constantinople, had
considerable share, John wrote appreciatively of the new Pope in
letter addressed to the Roman see:

'It is for the well-being of the whole world, as we believe, that y
have attained to the apostolic see. The churches of Christ througho
the whole earth now will have a beaconlight, one which lightens n
only the West but the farthest ends of the world'.[3]

A similar testimony to the central position of the Papacy in relati
to eastern controversies came from the metropolitan bishops
Cappadocia secunda and *Cilicia prima*,[4] who in a letter to Pope Xystu
after comparing him to Moses as victor over the Egyptian hereti
and deliverer of the orthodox Israelites, presented this earne
appeal:

'We beg you therefore to arise without delay, and with burnin
zeal to raise a great trophy of victory against the forces of o
opponents, having before your eyes both the care and concern of th
Good Shepherd for a single wandering sheep. Do not suppose th
neglectful treatment of so many shepherds and sheep is witho
danger; seeing that while the sheep are wandering, the shepher
suffer the violence of a tyrant'.[5]

We do not know whether Xystus answered this letter directly, c
whether he considered his communication to John of Antioch[6]
sufficient reply. In the latter the author laid marked emphasis c
the character of the apostolic *paradosis*.

'We wish', he writes, 'that your holiness would proclaim what yo
have written. You have learnt by the outcome of this affair what
means to be like-minded with us. The blessed Apostle Peter ha

---

[1] *Epp.* JK 385–8. Schwartz, *op. cit.* 1, 2, pp. 98, 88, 90, 91. *Coll. Veron.* Nos. 2
23, 24, 25.
[2] Schwartz, *op. cit.*, Tom. I, vol. i, pt. 4, p. 33. *Acta graeca.* No. 130.
[3] Id., *op. cit.*, *ibid.*, pt. 7, p. 158 f. *Coll. Athen.* No. 121.
[4] Eutherius of Tyana and Helladius of Tarsus.
[5] Schwartz, *op. cit.*, Tom. I, vol. iv, p. 148. *Coll. Casin.* pt. 2. No. 205, 8.
[6] *Ep.* 6. JK 392. Schwartz, *op. cit.*, Tom. I, vol. ii, p. 108 f. *Coll. Veron.* No. 3

nded down in his successors that which he received. Who would
sh to be parted from the doctrine of that Apostle, whom the Master
mself instructed first before the rest? It was not hearsay nor speech
mmitted to writing which taught him; he was trained with the others
the lips of the Teacher. He had not to search among writings and
iters; he received the original and direct faith which can admit of
dispute. On that faith we must meditate and in it abide always,
we would be worthy to be reckoned among the disciples of the
ostles, by following them with a pure understanding.'[1]
Yet side by side with this encomium of the apostolic faith a new
ment in papal letters makes its appearance. It is no other than
static praise of the orthodoxy of the Sovereigns.[2] To what extent
rds of this kind were justified history shows reason to doubt. It is
ficult to deny that by using such language Xystus was taking
e first steps along a road which could only lead in the end to
dication by the Papacy of its doctrinal primacy and its surrender to
esar. Thus it seems that the fascination of a semi-divinised
nperor, which had already hypnotized the eastern churches, was
the way to lure even the Roman see within reach of its seductive
arm. The event would show that in time only the more vigorous
rsonalities among the successors of St. Peter would prove strong
ough to resist its overpowering magic.
For the present, however, the relations of that see, both with the
tern Emperor and the Constantinopolitan bishop, remained
dial. Even an appeal against a decision given by Proclus, the new
upant of the see of Constantinople, in favour of Iddua of Smyrna,
ase involving jurisdiction within the province of Asia, was dis-
owed, and that in spite of the complete lack of any canonical
tification for Proclus' intervention. Here again Xystus was treading
lippery path. Had he been less conciliatory the pain caused by his
ccessor's rejection of the famous twenty-eighth canon of Chalcedon[3]
ght perhaps have been avoided.

VI

In Xystus' successor, Leo I, the Roman see found at once a stal-
rt upholder of its traditions and a master builder of its future
wer. Leo was not so much a creator as a mason. The material lay

---

[1] Schwartz., *op. cit.*, Tom. I, vol. ii, p. 109.
[2] Id., *op. cit.*, *ibid.*   [3] See below, p. 310.

ready to his hand, but it was due to his genius that the Papacy emerg
from the trials of his pontificate stronger and, if it be possible to s
so, more impregnable than ever before. The careful student of t
abundant Leonine literature, no less than ninety-six sermons ar
more than one hundred and sixty letters, which the grateful homa;
of later generations has preserved, will find evidence that in him, l
activities, and particularly in his conception of his office, all t
separate strands of papal tradition coalesce to form a single cor
which not even the periodical disasters, material and moral, to bef
the world in succeeding centuries, were able to break. The credit f
this achievement belongs largely, though no doubt not exclusively,
his august personality.

Was it part of our Lord's intention to form a permanent ἐκκλησ
of His disciples? Leo answers, 'The birth of Christ is the beginni
of the Christian people, and the birthday of the Head is the birthd:
of the Body'.[1] What was the place of St. Peter in it? 'He was appoint
before the others for this reason, that we might understand by t
mystical sense of his titles . . . when he is established as porter
the kingdom of heaven, and is set up as judge of things to be bou:
and loosed, of what sort is his association with Christ'.[2] Or agai
'He (sc. the Lord) originally assigned it (sc. the responsibility of t
episcopate) to the most blessed Peter, the head of all the Apostle
and intends that from him, as from the head, His gifts shall be co
veyed to the whole body, so that whoever dares to secede from t
foundation of Peter may know that he is excluded from communi
with God (*mysterii . . . divini*)'.[3] Did St. Peter come to Rome
teach and die there? Leo replies, 'When the regions of the earth we
apportioned among them (sc. the twelve Apostles) the most bless
Peter, chief of the apostolic band, was sent to the citadel of the Rom
Empire; that thus the light of Truth, which was being made know
for the salvation of all nations, might shine forth with grea
efficacy throughout the whole world from the very capital itself
Did other churches consult the Roman see as a universal referee? I
answers: 'Men resort to the see of the blessed Apostle Peter from t
whole world, and require at our hands that general care for the Chur
which was entrusted to that see by the Lord'.[5] Has the Roman se

[1] *Serm.* 26, 2. *M.P.L.* 54, 213.   [3] *Ep.* 10, 1. JK 408.
[2] *Serm.* 3, 2. *M.P.L.* 54, 146.   [4] *Serm.* 82, 3. *M.P.L.* 54, 424.
[4] *Serm.* 5, 2. *M.P.L.* 54, 153.

macy of doctrine? 'That which the Catholic Church everywhere
lieves and teaches on the mystery of the Lord's Incarnation, is
ntained in the letter (sc. The Tome), which I am sending to my
ther and fellow-bishop, Flavian'.[1] Has it also a primacy of
isdiction? Leo reminds the bishop of Thessalonica, 'We have
trusted you . . . with our legatine office, in such wise that you
ve been called to share our responsibility, not to possess the fulness
power'.[2] On what scriptural basis does the claim to such authority
t? Leo's fourth 'anniversary' sermon[3] supplies the answer. Not only
es the familiar *Tu es Petrus* text reappear there (this sermon is the
urce from which the Vatican Constitution *Pastor Aeternus* derives
me of its more impressive phrases), but side by side with it are
ged the Lucan and Johannine texts, in virtue of which he believes
at a peculiar privilege was conferred on St. Peter by our Lord
mself.

In view of the important part played by Leo in the co-ordination
d epitomization of the ideas and contributions made by successive
pes before his time, he has been regarded in some sense as the
rsonification of the Papacy. This view, however, needs some quali-
ation. In spite of his greatness as a ruler, administrator and not
st as a diplomatist, his world was essentially the *Imperium
manum* as it had existed since the days of Augustus. Far-seeing as
s policy may have been in many respects, it remains doubtful to
at extent he visualized the needs and conditions of a society in
ich the landmarks of the old Graeco-Roman world would be
most submerged in a welter of Germanic princedoms, the monarchs
which resembled barbaric counterfeits of the Roman *Princeps*.[4]
t it can scarcely be doubted that when he laid down the office
ich he had adorned, he left it immeasurably stronger in relation
t only to the Church but to society in general, so much so that
r almost half a millenium, as the amazing extent of his literary
mains serve to show, when men recalled the old order which had
rished, it was not the Roman Emperors but the name of Leo which
ey remembered; when they contemplated the former majesty of
ome, it was his commanding presence which stood before them;
hen they were moved with gratitude for the legacy of law and
lture bequeathed to them from a vanished Empire, it was to Leo

[1] *Ep.* 29. JK 424.   [2] *Ep.* 14, 1. JK 411.   [3] *Serm.* 4. *M.P.L.* 54, 148 ff.
[4] Theodoric the Great is perhaps the most typical.

more than to any other of the heirs of St. Peter that they believ
the real credit for this achievement was due.

If such has been the verdict of posterity on this remarkable figu
to whom almost alone among the successors of the Apostles t
epithet 'great' has been bestowed, what was the estimate of his co
temporaries? Even if we ignore the glowing appreciations hand
down to us by his intimate friend, Prosper Tiro,[1] we are still l
with ample material in the actual history of his pontificate. It m
be evident, however, that in so comprehensive a survey of t
relation of the Church to the Papacy as the present, no more th
the barest outlines of this important epoch can be sketched.

Something may be said here of Leo's relations with the Rom
State. There can be little doubt that the grandeur of his genius enabl
him to treat with the government of that degenerate scion of t
Theodosian house, Valentinian III, on more than equal term
Testimony of his ascendancy even over those who were his immedia
Sovereigns is supplied by letters of theirs which have been preserv
among the Leonine *corpus*. Opinion may indeed differ widely as
whether the use which he made of such power as the enfeebl
secular arm could lend to his aid, was in fact in the best interests
the Church. But that his spiritual authority was willingly conced
by a decadent monarchy can scarcely be doubted if Valentinia
own words with reference to the Pope's suppression of suppos
irregularities committed by Hilary of Arles are remembered:

'That (sc. papal) verdict itself would have been valid througho
Gaul even without imperial enforcement. For what limits can the
be to the authority of a bishop so great as he?'[2]

Only one representative example, and that from a letter address
to him by bishops of the province of Arles itself, can be given he
to illustrate the attitude of the western churches to the see of Ror
in this period:

'Through the most blessed Peter, chief of the Apostles, the ho
Roman Church holds the principate over all the churches of t
whole world'.[3]

---

[1] *Chronicon* in *M.G.H. Chron. min.* vol. i.
[2] *Inter Leon. Epp.* No. 8. *M.P.L.* 54, 622 ff.
[3] *Inter Leon. Epp.* No. 65. *M.P.L.* 54, 879. *M.G.H. Epp.* vol. iii, p. 17.

VII

We may now resume our study of the attitude of the eastern
urches, where alone as yet the sub-Christian theory of the *imperator
cerdos* had succeeded in gaining the mastery.

It is scarcely likely that so vigorous a defender of the primacy of
s see as Cyril of Alexandria could view with satisfaction the extent
which his rival in the see of Constantinople had managed during
e intervening years to repair the damage suffered by its prestige in
nsequence of the disaster at the recent council of Ephesus. It was
rtunate that for the propagation of Alexandrine doctrine in the
pital of the Empire, which by reason of its traditional connexion
th the see of Antioch was naturally more disposed to favour a rival
eology, he could count on the support of a vigorous and not wholly
rupulous monastic element. It was left, however, to his successor
ioscorus to reap the benefit or the misfortune of plans which
d already been set in train.

The story of the events by which the see of Alexandria and its
eology of 'one incarnate nature of the Word' gained a temporary
permanent ascendancy need not be retold.[1] It is only necessary to
ll attention to the fact that once more the Roman see was called in as
biter, this time by Eutyches, the Constantinopolitan advocate of the
ore extreme elements in Cyril's teaching, and that it was to Leo
at the archimandrite presented his *libellus*, humbly professing his
llingness to amend should his ideas be found amiss.[2]

The sequence of the synod of Constantinople (448), at which
der the presidency of Flavian, lately elected to the see of Con-
antinople, the 'monophysite' doctrine of Eutyches was condemned,
d the second council of Ephesus, surnamed by Leo himself, per-
ps not without justice, the 'robber-band' (*latrocinium*),[3] which saw
e triumph of Eutyches and his powerful ally Dioscorus, bears a
riking and highly sinister resemblance to the events which had
volved the abdication of Gregory of Nazianzus and the martyrdom
Chrysostom.[3] Two facts, however, stand out with remarkable

---

[1] E.g. in *Ep.* 1 *ad Succensum. M.P.G.* 77, 232. 'μίαν φύσιν τοῦ Λόγου σεσαρκωμένην'.
tley, *Doctrine of Incarnation*[6], 1919, p. 416, says: 'Cyril thought it enough
state the paradox (e.g. the Son of God ἀπαθῶς ἔπαθεν), and to lay stress on its
:omprehensibleness, without contributing in any appreciable degree to the
ution of the problem . . . the work of Chalcedon was not less essential than
at of Ephesus to the preservation of the Christian Faith'.

[2] *Ep.* 95, 2. JK 475.   [3] See above, p. 293.

clearness. First, that the supporters of Eutyches at the seco
council of Ephesus displayed an amazing and certainly significa
anxiety, lest the Roman legates, one of whom was the deacon Hila
Leo's successor in the papal throne, should encompass the recitati
of the Pope's letter to the council';[1] and secondly, that to the victi
of Dioscorus' aggressive policy, supported by a pliant and this ti
wholly prejudiced government, Flavian, Eusebius of Dorylaeu
and Theodoret of Cyrrhus, *doyen* of the Antiochene, that is to s
'dyophysite,' theological school, the one means by which the authen
tradition of the Church could be rescued, and indeed their own p
sonal safety secured, seemed to lie in an appeal to the judgment of t
West, and in particular to the impartial verdict of him, 'to whom',
Theodoret wrote, 'for every reason the primacy belongs', and
whose decision the same writer no less than his opponent Eutych
freely acknowledged himself ready to submit.[2]

The execution of the papal decision and the deliverance of t
eastern churches from the tyranny of the see of Alexandria w
unhappily achieved only at the price of their submitting even mc
completely than before to the principle that the last word on
ecclesiastical questions belonged to the Emperor, and that it was
him to restore a superficial appearance of unity by imperial edi
As a result little scope was left for the programme which Leo hims
had so earnestly desired to put into effect, namely of procuring t
conversion rather than the suppression of the dissidents.

The council of Chalcedon itself sheds some valuable light on t
attitude of the East towards the Papacy in this period. On t
accession of Pulcheria and Marcian to the eastern throne, followi
the death of Theodosius II, July 28 450, Leo did his utmost to ur
that for the appeasement of the disorder created by the interventi
of Dioscorus of Alexandria in the affairs of the see of Constantinop
nothing more was necessary than to re-establish unity on the basis
acceptance of his Tome. Such a policy was unacceptable, however,

[1] *Ep.* 33, JK 427. That it was this letter and not the 'Tome'. *Ep.* 28, JK 4
is shown in the present writer's *Life and Times of St. Leo*, p. 238 ff. The *Acta
this council are incorporated in the *Acta* of Chalcedon, see Schwartz, *op. cit.*, To
II, vol. i, pt. 1, p. 67 ff.

[2] *Libell. Appell. Flaviani*, in Schwartz, E. *Acta conc. oec.* Tom. II, vol. ii, pt.
p. 77 ff. *Coll. Novar. No.* 11; *Libell. Appell. . . . Eusebii, ibid.*, p. 79 ff. C
Novar. No. 12; *Libell. Appell. Theodoreti, Inter Leon. Epp. No.* 52, *M.P.L.*
846, see esp. c. 6.

e new Sovereigns, who insisted that nothing short of a dogmatic
cision approved by a genuinely representative council could achieve
e desired end. It was significant, however, of the extent to which
ey felt themselves to be dependent on the support of the Roman see
at they found it necessary in making known their project to ascribe
mewhat disingenuously the initiative to Leo himself, whom they
scribed 'as having the oversight and leadership in the divine faith'.[1]

The proceedings of the council at Chalcedon show clearly the un-
illingness of the episcopal 'chorus', as distinct from the protagonists
the drama, to commit themselves to any new statement of dogma,
d its evident relief at the publication of Leo's Tome,[2] which with its
refully balanced dyophysitism seemed to fulfil the need of 'a plain
an's guide to the doctrine of the Incarnation'.[3] Their well-known
clamation was a sufficient demonstration of their feelings:
'That is the faith of the fathers, the faith of the Apostles. We all
lieve thus, the orthodox believe so! . . . Peter has thus spoken
rough Leo! The Apostles taught so! . . . Leo and Cyril taught
e same doctrine! . . . Why was that letter not read at Ephesus?
is the letter which Dioscorus concealed'![4]

The question 'Why was that letter not read at Ephesus?' could
ve only been rhetorical, for all those who had been present on
at occasion must have known the real answer.[5] Now, however, the
ssibility of peace seemed already in sight. That it failed of attain-
ent was probably due to two causes which may well be regarded as
fferent aspects of a single factor, namely the desire of the eastern
vernment to obtain for the see of Constantinople a primacy of
octrine and of jurisdiction in the East, equal if not superior to the
e already claimed by the Roman see in relation to the whole
hurch. Marcian's insistence on the council's duty to evolve a dog-
atic definition was probably due far less to a desire for the vindica-
on of the truth than to the fear lest the adoption of Leo's Tome
ithout qualification should seem to ascribe too great an importance

---

[1] *Inter Leon Epp.* No. 73. *M.P.L.* 54, 890. ' . . . ἐπισκοπεύουσαν καὶ ἄρχουσαν τῆς
as πίστεως'.

[2] Schwartz, *op. cit.*, Tom. II, vol. i, pt. 2, p. 93. See for the Tome, id., *op. cit.*,
om. II, vol. ii, pt. 1, p. 24 ff. *Coll. Novar.* No. 5.

[3] For a discussion of some modern criticism of Leo's Christology, see the present
iter's *op. cit.*, p. 492 ff.

[4] Schwartz, *op. cit.*, Tom. II, vol. i, pt. 2, p. 81 [277]. *Acta graeca* No. 23.

[5] It is doubtful, however, whether the question of reading the Tome at
hesus (449) ever actually arose. See above, p. 306, n. 1.

to the verdict of Old Rome, and thus overshadow the upsta
prestige of the see of his own capital. Not less important in this co
nexion was the introduction during the sixteenth session of t
council of a canon, usually reckoned as the twenty-eighth, accepte
be it remembered, by not more than one hundred and eighty-fo
bishops out of a total membership of certainly not less than fi
hundred,[1] which assigned to the see of Constantinople the ordinatic
of metropolitans throughout the 'dioceses' of Pontus, Asia, ar
Thrace. Professing to be no more than a reinterpretation of tl
famous 'third canon' of Constantinople (381), it explained itself
conferring on the Constantinopolitan see the same ecclesiastic
privileges as those enjoyed by the Roman see itself. Whether or n
this legislation was brought forward at the instigation of the Emper
(it was in any case passed in the absence of the imperial commissic
which had presided over the previous sessions of the council ar
may therefore have been taken by surprise), there was evidently
feeling that in spite of protests he was bound to support a measu
promoted by the local bishop. In the case of the Roman legates, c
the other hand, surprise was quickly followed by deep indignatic
at so direct a challenge to the unique prerogatives of the apostol
see. Their protest took the form of an appeal to the sixth canc
of Nicaea, which according to the view current in Rome, probab
since the time of Pope Damasus I, was meant to prescribe the ord
of precedence among the 'greater churches'. The canon as recite
by Paschasinus of Lilybaeum, principal member of the Roma
legation, reads thus:

'The sixth canon of the three hundred and eighteen holy father
"The Roman church has always had a primacy. Let Egypt al:
retain one, such that the bishop of Alexandria may have authori
over all, since this is a custom also in the case of the Roman bisho|
In like manner also he who is established (as bishop) in Antiocl
and in the rest of the provinces let churches of other cities ha\
primacies. . ." '[2]

The quotation raises a number of acute problems. In the first plac
supposing that these words accurately represent what Paschasin\

---

[1] Schwartz, *op. cit.*, Tom. II, vol. i, pt. 3, p. 94 [453]. *Acta graeca*, Actio XVI
No. 9. Scott, *op. cit.*, p. 193, says '84'. The 'canon' is probably a ψῆφος.

[2] Id., *op. cit.*, Tom. II, vol. i, pt. 3, p. 95 [454]. *Acta graeca*, Actio XVII, No. I
See for version of Rusticus, id., *op. cit.*, Tom. II, vol. iii, pt. 3, p. 109 [548]; Turne
Eccl. occid. mon. iur. ant., Tom. I, p. 148. See also above, p. 201 ff.

:ually said, whence did he obtain this text? Comparison with earlier
tin collections of Canon Law of Roman or Italian origin suggests
it he derived that part of the canon which we have quoted from the
irth century version contained in the collection represented by
r *Codex Ingilrami* (or of Chieti).[1] At the same time it should be
ticed that what follows forsakes that text and follows fairly closely
stead the so-called 'Isidorian' version, which in its original form
held to have been in use c. 425.[2] We may perhaps infer from this
it the official book of Roman Canon Law current in Leo's time
s a conflation of the two earlier versions, 'Ingilram' and 'Isidore'.
t how can we account for the origin of the opening phrase? In spite
a generally accepted view it is most unlikely that it had been
vised by some Roman scribe to justify a universal primacy. For
er all *primatus*, in its fourth-century sense, denoted no more
in the office of a metropolitan bishop. A possible motive for its
roduction may have been supplied, however, by the loss of
stige suffered by the Roman see under Liberius and during the
it ten years or so of the pontificate of Damasus. Bearing in mind the
reasing importance of the see of Milan at this time, and the absence
any metropolitical organization in Italy, it is by no means improbable
it there were some who felt the need of reasserting the customary
t quite undefined metropolitical authority of the Roman see within
: Italian peninsula and entered a marginal note to that effect. The
blication of the earliest Latin version of the Nicene-Sardican
ions, which probably remained the official Canon Law of the
man church till at least 418, provided an obvious opportunity for
eassertion of this claim.[3] Thus it is reasonable to suggest that the
rase may in origin have been no more than an explanatory gloss
the phrase regarding 'the custom in the case of the Roman
hop' (*Romano episcopo . . . consuetudo*).

The reply of the officials of the church of Constantinople to this
narche on the part of the Roman legates was to cite the third
ion of Constantinople 381 (that they actually quoted first the Greek
t of the sixth canon of Nicaea is open to considerable doubt).[4]

See above. Cf. Turner, *op. cit.*, p. 151, para. 2.
Turner in *J.T.S.*, vol. xxx, 1929. p. 339; *Eccl. occid. mon.* Tom. I, p. 274.
Turner, *ibid.*; *op. cit.*, Tom. I, p. 329.
The sixth canon of Nicaea in its original form was a witness rather against than
the primacy of Constantinople and hence was quite irrelevant. Though it is given
he Greek *Acta*, it is in Caspar's view, *Geschichte*, vol. i, p. 523, a later insertion.

21

It was now the turn of the legates to protest. Such a canon, they sa
formed no part of the genuine Canon Law. This was, of course, pe
fectly true so far as the Roman church was concerned, the offic
corpus of which did not include the canons of the Constantinopoli
council. The presidents overruled the objection, however, and t
new canon was endorsed by acclamation. The legates, being th
successfully checkmated, insisted that their protest should
entered in the official *Acta* so that it might be clear that their resi
ance had been due not to jealousy but to anxiety for the maintenar
of canonical principles.[1]

Even before the return of the legates news of this decision of t
council reached the ears of Leo. His earliest letters on the subject,
spite of his satisfaction at the acceptance of his verdict on Eutycl
and at the incorporation of his dogmatic teaching in the concil
definition, showed quite clearly his determination to resist the adc
tion of the objectionable canon. Thus in writing to the Empr
Pulcheria he says:

'Resolutions of bishops which are repugnant to the rules of t
holy canons defined at Nicaea . . . we rescind and utterly annul
the authority of the blessed Apostle Peter, since in all ecclesiasti
questions we defer to those laws which the Holy Ghost laid do
through the three hundred and eighteen prelates, with a view
their peaceable observance by all bishops'.[2]

This was in 452. Two years later, under pressure as it seems fr
the Emperor, Anatolius, bishop of Constantinople, presented
apology to Leo.[3] The latter graciously accepted the gesture, on
supposition that it implied willingness to withdraw the twen
eighth canon. Yet whether or not Anatolius' intentions were since
the canon remained in force.

There can be little doubt that Leo was by no means alone in
attitude of protest. Suspicion and mistrust of decisions reached
Chalcedon were widespread, and persisted in spite of all the devi
of imperial policy alternating between suppression and cajolery
the opposition. Resistance was shown in various parts of the East, k
nowhere with greater determination than in Egypt. Alexandria or
again witnessed scenes of violent disorder, which on the death

---

[1] Schwartz, *op. cit.* Tom. I, vol. i, pt. 3, p. 99. *Acta graeca*, Actio XVII, No.
[2] *Ep.* 105. JK 482.
[3] *Inter Leon. Epp.* No. 132. *M.P.L.* 54, 1082.

[M]arcian culminated in the assassination of the bishop Proterius, [so]lely on the ground of his Chalcedonian sympathies. It is clear that [th]e growing nationalism of the Copts had discovered a convenient [fo]cus in Cyril's more extreme theological utterances,[1] and from this [ti]me on Egyptian 'Monophysitism' began to be clearly distinguishable [fr]om the official theology of the Empire. It may well be true that in this [ca]se dogma was the chief cause of difference. But some responsibility [fo]r the embittered relations between Alexandria and Constantinople [m]ust surely be assigned to the twenty-eighth canon, and to its generally [un]happy effect on the corporate unity of the eastern churches.

Marcian's successor, the Emperor Leo I, faced with unrest at [ho]me in addition to a constant threat to his frontiers, did his utmost [to] secure the restoration of peace. A project of holding a new council [to] revise the decisions of Chalcedon was mooted and preparations for [it] were already in hand. The chief opposition to this procedure came [fr]om Pope Leo, who showed obvious signs of disapproval and urged [th]at, while all possible measures should be taken to reconcile the [di]ssidents, no step was justifiable which might endanger the dogmatic [se]ttlement already reached. No doubt the see of Constantinople had [it]s own reasons for fearing what such a new council might bring [fo]rth, and may have had good cause to be apprehensive of the growing [in]fluence of Timothy, surnamed Aelurus, recently elected by the [m]onophysite majority in Egypt to the see of Alexandria. Ultimately [th]e expedient of a kind of plebiscite by provinces was adopted.[2] Each [pr]ovincial synod was required by the Emperor to answer two [qu]estions: 'Ought the council of Chalcedon to be upheld?' and [o]ught Timothy to continue as bishop of Alexandria?' Of the [six]ty-six or so possible answers not more than twenty-two are known, [an]d we may hesitate between suspicion of governmental integrity [an]d admiration of its skill, when we learn that with one exception all [we]re favourable, so far as can be known, to the first, and quite [un]animous about the second. Whatever the truth, the effect of these [m]anoeuvres was that at the time of Pope Leo's death Egypt was all [bu]t lost to the unity of the Church, while signs were not lacking that [ot]her provinces too were on the point of breaking away.

Before closing our review of this important pontificate something

[1] Particularly Cyril's *XII Anathemas*.
[2] See *Encyclia* ap. Evagrium, *H.E.* 2, 9, 10. ed. Bidez, J., and Parmentier, L. [18]98, p. 59 ff. Cf. Cassiodorus, *Divin. et Saec. inst. litt.* 11. *M.P.L.* 70, 1123.

must be said about an outstanding feature of his administratio
Again and again we encounter in his letters the theme of 'unity a
order by obedience to Canon Law'. As to what Leo meant by Can
Law, we can see from his frequent allusions to the subject that l
believed it to embrace the authentic Nicene canons with the additi
of those of Sardica, which at this time were still treated by the Rom;
see as Nicene in origin. It has been argued that those who held su
a view in the middle of the fifth century cannot well be absolved
consciously accepting a fraud. Yet no one who has carefully follow
the spasmodic, even erratic development of Canon Law in the We
could possibly allow such a charge to go unchallenged. Supposi
that the standard Roman Canon Law of the time was the earli
form of the 'Isidorian' Collection, conflated (at least so far as tl
sixth canon of Nicaea was concerned) with the text represented l
our *Codex Ingilrami*,[1] in which the Nicene and Sardican canons for
a single group, no one in the Rome of Leo's time could be said to ha
been guilty of dishonesty if he represented that the canons governi
appeals were actually Nicene. Even the later 'Isidorian' Collectio:
though grouping the canons of Nicaea and Sardica (in epitom
separately, continues to describe the latter with the title:

'Here begins the Nicene council of twenty bishops: the thin;
which are not contained in the Greek but are found in the Latin ;
follows . . .'[2]

And if it be asked why the Roman church failed to correct th
historical error, after the unhappy results of Zosimus' misquotatio:
it may be replied that it is by no means certain that Pope Bonifac
ever obtained the original canons of Nicaea as he was requested
do by the Africans, or that the discovery that the disputed cano
were absent from the Greek text necessarily satisfied the Roma
church about their non-Nicene origin. On the contrary the headin
in the later 'Isidorian' Collection (M) seems to show the opposit
Western Canon Law, it must be remembered, only emerged out
its primitive stage under the skilful hand of Dionysius Exiguus.

Before calling attention to the significance of his attitude or
further point in Leo's conception of what was included in Canon La
must be remarked. He is the first Pope explicitly to insist on the nee
of obedience to the decretals of his predecessors, which thus begi
to take their place as part of the Canon Law of the western churcl

---

[1] Turner, *Eccl. occ. mon. iur. ant.* Tom. I, p. 151.   [2] Id. *op. cit.*, Tom. I, p. 54

ven before the beginning of his pontificate a collection of these
documents from Siricius to Celestine had already come into existence,
tended primarily for local use.[1] Collections of his own letters were
on to form an important addition to this papal *corpus*, and thus
und their way into the archetypes of the fifth and later centuries.

Though Leo himself never uses the phrase, it may reasonably be
id that his whole administration was moulded according to his
edecessor's dictum: 'Law should govern us; not we the law. Let
who uphold canonical principles be obedient to the canons our-
lves'.[2] Thus the fifth-century Papacy was still content to remain
e custodian of the Church's legislation; the time had not yet come
hen it would claim to be its arbiter.

The arts of sculpture and painting have each left us a memorial of
is great Pope. The colossal bronze figure of the Apostle in St.
ter's has been widely believed, though no doubt mistakenly, to
ve been modelled at Leo's order from the molten material of the
lossal statute of Jupiter Capitolinus. Though the tradition may
self be false, as an image of his pontificate, embodying, as we have
en, every aspect of the great papal heritage, nothing could be
ore appropriate. Equally expressive of its significance, not only as a
ndmark in the life of the Church, but as a turning point in world
story, is the Raphaelite wall-painting in the *Stanze della Segnatura*
the Vatican, in which the serene majesty of the Pope and his
tendant Cardinals confronts the barbarous might of Attila. Thrice
his lifetime Leo had seen the Eternal City prostrate before the
rbarian; twice he had himself interceded in person for its pre-
rvation with Hun and with Vandal. Authors of legend may have
aggerated Leo's part in Attila's discomfiture, and the hand of a
aster painter minimized it by introduction of the miraculous. But
ch through his own medium has expressed the truth that much
at was best in the old tradition was saved from the wreck consequent
pon Germanic invasions chiefly through the immovable stead-
stness of the Roman see.

[1] Turner, in *C.Med.H.* vol. i, p. 182.
[2] See above, p. 268, n. 1. Leo's preoccupation with the due observance of Canon
w may be illustrated by the following references: *Ep.* 1, 1. JK 398, 'auctoritatem
nonum decretorumque nostrorum'; *ibid.*, 1, 6.; *Ep.* 4, 2. JK 402; *ibid.* 3 (? *Conc. Nic.*
non 17); *ibid.* 5, 'omnia decretalia constituta, tam beatae recordationis Innocentii,
am omnium decessorum nostrorum'; *Ep.* 10, 4. JK 407; *Ep.* 12, 5, 9, 10. JK 410;
. 19, 1. JK 417; *Ep.* 104, 3. JK 481; *Ep.* 162, 3. JK 539.

VIII

Most of what is known of the seven-year pontificate of his success
Hilary is derived from a few surviving letters concerning that Pop
relations with southern Gaul.[1] It is remarkable that in spite of t
fact that an independent Gothic kingdom had been established
the former province *Narbonensis*, the Roman see did not cease
regulate the affairs of the Catholic Church in that area. More i
portant were Hilary's relations with Spain, now also in German
occupation. It was with reference to the appeals of Ascanius, metr
politan of Tarragona,[2] that the Roman synod of 465 was held, t
special interest of which is that it is the first of which exact minut
of the proceedings have been preserved, including a comple
record of the Pope's allocution. It is significant for the history
Canon Law that we find him once again stressing the need
obedience to the precepts of the divine law and the constitutions
the Nicene canons, and adding 'that only at the peril of his stat
can anyone violate either the divine constitutions or the decrees
the apostolic see'.[3] That Hilary probably followed his predecessc
in recognizing the dogmatic decrees of other councils in addition
that of Nicaea is suggested by an entry in the *Liber pontificalis*, whi
reads:

'This Pope composed a decretal and published it throughout
the East, together with letters concerning the Catholic Faith, co
firming the three councils of Nicaea, Ephesus and Chalcedon, wi
the Tome of the holy bishop Leo'.[4]

Even if the details of this entry are untrustworthy, it is of intere
to note that no mention is made of the council of Constantinople
381.

Under Simplicius, elected on February 25, 468, difficulties wi
the East began afresh. The accession of Acacius to the see of Co
stantinople in 472, and the violent assumption by Zeno of sc
imperial authority there two years later gave some impetus to
increasingly general reaction against the council of Chalcedo
Egypt, as we have seen, was already in revolt, and with the help
the usurper Basiliscus, Peter Fullo, a firm ally of the veteran mon

---

[1] The best edition of papal letters from Hilary I to Pelagius II is that of Thiel,
Epistolae Romanorum Pontificum, 1868 (one volume only published).
[2] Thiel, p. 155, No. 13.   [3] Id., p. 159, No. 15.   [4] *Lib. pont.* ed. cit., p. 2

ysite Timothy Aelurus, regained possession of the see of Antioch.
hus two at least of the 'greater eastern churches' were in the hands
determined opponents of the council. During the two years or so
Basiliscus' usurpation of the eastern throne, Acacius had to suffer
any indignities caused by the presence of Timothy in the capital,
ho obtained from the 'tyrant' an imperial encyclical, formally
ndemning Leo's Tome and the decrees of Chalcedon, and giving
perial recognition to Nicaea and the first council of Ephesus with
e significant addition of the so-called *latrocinium*.[1] It was indicative
the untrustworthiness of the eastern episcopate that when con-
onted with this declaration of the imperial *paradosis* most of the
e hundred who now assented to the edict had only a few years
eviously expressed precisely the opposite opinion.[2]

Acacius, who had already unsuccessfully endeavoured to obtain
pe Simplicius' confirmation of the twenty-eighth canon of Chal-
don, believed that the eastern primacy of Constantinople was in
nger, and not content with obtaining what he wanted from the
urper, first procured his deposition ; then shortly after he extracted
nfirmation of the canon from the restored Emperor Zeno. Among
e evident signs of the growing importance of his see in relation
other eastern churches is the charge later preferred against him by
pe Felix III :

'I know not after what fashion you claim that you are the *princeps*
the whole church'.[3]

It has been conjectured with considerable probability that Felix
as alluding to Acacius' employment of the title 'oecumenical
triarch'.[4] If this is correct, he was the first of the Constantinopolitan
shops to use it, and thus anticipated Gregory I's famous protest
more than a century.[5] In this connexion, however, it should be
alized that the term 'oecumenical' properly speaking did not mean
orld wide', as the protesting Latins appear to have understood it,
it simply 'imperial', and that an identical title had already been
signed to the Popes, and in that sense, by Alexandrine deacons.[6]
s use, therefore, in any period has no direct relevance to questions
garding the Roman primacy.

---

[1] Evagrius, *H. E.* 3, 4. ed. cit., p. 101 ff.
[2] Caspar, *Geschichte*, vol. ii, p. 15.   [4] Caspar, *op. cit.*, vol. ii, p. 747 f.
[3] JK 592, 8. Thiel, p. 232.   [5] See below, p. 355.
[6] Schwartz, *op cit.*, Tom. II, vol. i, pt. 3, pp. 15 [211], 17 [213]. *Acta graeca*
tio II, Nos. 47, 51.

Before the first year of Zeno's restored principate had elapsed, event took place in the West, the historical significance of which ł perhaps been exaggerated, but which at least deserves mention.[1] August 23, 476, the Ostrogoth commander Odoacer assumed t title of 'king' and after occupying Ravenna, as the anonymo chronicler records :

'He deposed Augustulus from the kingdom. Having pity on ł tender years and because the youth was fair, he granted him his ł and awarded him an income of six thousand *solidi* and sent him dwell in freedom with his family in Campania'.[2]

We need not linger further over the pathetic demise of the weste principate, except to remark that its disappearance in no sen affected the theory of the *Imperium Romanum*, which remained, it always had been, a single unity. So little indeed did it change t practice of the surviving *imperator*, who reigned as before in Co stantinople, that the event might have been passed over in silen were it not for the effect on the life of the Church of the final tran ference of the seat of Empire from Rome to the capital of the Eas to which the craven petition addressed to Zeno by the Roma Senate bore perhaps unwilling witness. That prince affected ignore the *de facto* rule of Odoacer and to uphold the legitimist clain of his deposed western colleague. But he must have found it difficu to believe that there still remained any hope of effectively restorir Roman rule in Italy.

It is likely that uncertainty about the political situation goes son way to account for the absence of any positive element in Simpliciu eastern policy. The surety of touch with which Leo I had handled tł kaleidoscopic variations in eastern affairs seemed momentari to have been lost. A keener sense of opportunity might have mac better use of the appeals of Acacius to support the failing cause Chalcedon, and a better appreciation of the delicate poise of easter politics prevented the blunder of giving qualified support to Joh Talaia, a candidate for the see of Alexandria who was in no sense

---

[1] As Bury, J. B., *History of the Later Roman Empire*, vol. i, p. 408, points ou it is 'inaccurate and unfortunate' to describe this event as marking the 'Fall of tł Western Empire'. Romulus Augustulus' title to the principate in any case w doubtfully legitimate, and Julius Nepos, who had reigned for just over a year, ar had perhaps the better claim, survived till May 480.

[2] Seeck, *Regesten d. K. u. Päpste*, p. 422.

rsona grata at the court of Zeno.[1] Instead the initiative was allowed
imperceptibly to pass into the hands of Acacius. Disappointed at the
comparative impotence of the Roman see, he had probably come to
believe that the only means of restoring ecclesiastical unity in the
east lay in asserting the primacy of Constantinople in the sphere of
doctrine. To this end he had recourse to the familiar expedient of an
imperial dogmatic statement, which was believed to be sufficiently
monophysite to satisfy Peter Mongus, the new bishop of Alexandria,
but not so evidently outspoken against the council of Chalcedon as to
cause undue alarm to its adherents. This was the famous *Henoticon*,[2]
which Schwartz has described as 'ein rein politisches, auf dog-
matische Prinzipientreue verzichtendes Dokument'.[3] Like every
other attempt at effecting Christian reunion by means of a deliberate
accidental disregard of principle it proved a failure. Its sole
achievement was the creation of a new schism at Alexandria.

Felix III, who succeeded Simplicius in the year (483) following
the publication of this document, had the satisfaction at an early date
his pontificate of receiving as a suppliant that John whom we
have already noticed as the unsuccessful Chalcedonian candidate for
the see of Alexandria. It may be remarked that his was the first
papal election in which direct intervention on the part of the secular
power is known. The secular power in this case was, of course,
Odoacer, who at the request of Simplicius had instructed the
praetorian prefect Basil to see that the normal procedure was carried
out without any disturbance of public order. That Felix traced
is origin to the old Roman aristocracy, whose descendants, while
recognizing the Gothic regime as a *fait accompli*, continued to treat
the eastern *imperator* as their only lawful sovereign, may help to
explain his extreme deference to the Constantinopolitan government, in spite of his continued intransigence towards Acacius.

It was probably to John of Alexandria that the Roman see owed
earliest direct acquaintance with the contents of Zeno's *Henoticon*.
We may gather something of the effect produced from the fact that
the announcement of his election to the Emperor, Felix included
intimation of the despatch of a Roman legation to Constantinople.
Speaking in the character of Peter, 'prince of the Apostles', the Pope

---

[1] *Coll. Avell.* 68, ed. cit., p. 151 ff.
[2] Evagrius, *H.E.* 3, 14, ed. cit., p. 111 ff.
[3] Quoted by Caspar, *op. cit.*, vol. ii, p. 22.

besought him not to permit the seamless robe of Christ to be to
asunder.[1] With studied caution he passed over the *Henoticon*
silence, while he praised the council of Chalcedon as '*via, ut script*
est, regia mediaque'.[2] A further letter in the form of an appeal, b
with a menacing undertone, was addressed to Acacius.[3] The lega
had scarcely left Italy when, in the course of an investigation
John's appeal, Felix realized the extent to which Acacius had co
ceded the abandonment of Chalcedon. A third letter followed the
fore, citing the patriarch to give evidence in the case of John.[4] J
just as the Pope seemed to model his action on Julius I's treatment
Athanasius, so the reception of the Roman legates at the hands of t
eastern government recalled that of their predecessors in the ti
of John Chrysostom. On this occasion, however, the government us
far greater circumspection and succeeded in persuading the legates
acknowledge the orthodoxy of Acacius and Peter Mongus, an
which was tantamount to the acceptance of the *Henoticon*.

It is with no surprise that we learn how on their return the lega
were at once summoned before a Roman synod, to which th
presented an evasive apology from the Emperor and a defiant rejoind
from the patriarch. At once a sentence of deposition against Acaci
was pronounced and duly notified both to Zeno and to the offendi
bishop.[5]

It is noteworthy that, while among the grounds for Acacius' co
demnation mention was made of his traffic with acknowledg
heretics, the chief emphasis was laid on his contravention of Can
Law by usurping the privileges of others.[6] This significant thrust m
be supposed to have been provoked by the knowledge that, doubtl
as part of the price for the share which he had taken in procuri
Zeno's restoration, the Emperor had agreed to confirm the twent
eighth canon of Chalcedon. The formal sentence, in accordance wi
the verdict of the synod and pronounced by Felix in person with
the majesty of his office, then followed:

'Since Acacius, after being warned by us a second time, has n
ceased to show contempt for beneficial canons (*statutorum sa*
brium), and supposed that I in the person of my (legates) ought
be imprisoned, by a judgment pronounced from heaven God h

---

[1] JK 591. Thiel, p. 222.
[2] With allusion to Num. XXI, 22.
[3] JK 592. Thiel, p. 232.
[4] JK 593. Thiel, p. 239.
[5] JK 601, JK 599. Thiel, pp. 247, 2
[6] JK 599. Thiel, p. 243.

nished him from the episcopate. Wherefore if any bishop, clerk,
onk or layman shall have communion with him after this sentence,
 him be anathema, as the Holy Ghost declares. . . . Know that
ou art thrust forth from the episcopate, as well as from Catholic
mmunion and the number of the faithful, condemned by the judg-
ent of the Holy Ghost and by our apostolic authority, and never
 any time to be loosed from the bonds of the anathema'.[1]
Felix evidently had made the most of his opportunity. His action
eant, of course, nothing less than a declaration of open war between
ose who believed in the Church as an independent spiritual society
d those who were prepared to acquiesce in its identification with
e State. The custodians of the apostolic *paradosis* and the subjects
 upholders of Caesaropapism were now face to face in open con-
t.
Not less significant is the Pope's letter addressed to the Emperor,[2]
e style of which seems to betray the authorship of Gelasius, pre-
ntly to succeed Felix in the papal throne. Signs of the state of
lligerency now prevailing are to be seen in the almost studied
oidance of the usual terms of courtesy characteristic of such
rrespondence. With brutal directness of expression the Pope
lled the Emperor's attention to the essential issue; a choice between
mmunion with Peter the Apostle and Peter Mongus.
'Of a certainty', he writes, 'it redounds to the prosperity of your
airs if, when the matter in hand concerns the things of God, you
ert yourself according to His commandment to submit your
perial will to the bishops of Christ and not to assume leadership,
 learn sacred matters from those who are set over them, not to
ich them, to follow the prescription (*forma*) of the Church and not
 prescribe to it laws to be followed after the fashion of men, nor to
rannize over its ordinances, since it is in very deed God's will
at you should bow yourself in humble obedience'.[3]
It might have been supposed that Gregory VII or Innocent III
as speaking. Instead it is the Papacy of the late fifth century. Yet
ese words do not belong to an isolated episode, such as the conflict
tween Ambrose and Valentinian II. On the contrary they mark
e opening of centuries of struggle between the Papacy and the
npire, between clericalism and laicism, between Church and
ate.

---

[1] JK 600.   [2] JK 601. Thiel, p. 247.   [3] *Ibid.*

If it be asked whether it was necessary for the Papacy to force t
issue in this way, we may reply that properly speaking it had
alternative. Hitherto Emperors had been content to enforce th
ecclesiastical policies by means of councils. This time Zeno h
presumed to use an imperial *motu proprio* to undermine the author
of Chalcedon. Thus Caesaropapism openly declared itself. 'Da
is the comment of a modern historian of the Papacy, 'ist der entsch
dende Punkt, an welchem das kaiserliche Reichskirchenregiment
"Cäsaropapismus" überging.'[1] As to the reaction to the sentence
excommunication, it is noteworthy that, in spite of the appare
indifference of the Constantinopolitan authorities to the thunder
the papal anathema, remarkable ingenuity seems to have been shov
to prevent echoes of it from reaching the Church at large.

Two further incidents of Felix' pontificate bearing on our subje
deserve mention. At the Roman synod of the following year (48
apart from the condemnation of the legates who had communicat
with Acacius during their visit, a resolution was published declari
its 'acknowledgment of the venerable councils of Nicaea and t
first of Ephesus together with that of Chalcedon, against Nestori
and the most impious Eutyches'.[2] It is worth remarking that t
same synod reaffirmed the primacy of the Roman see as the repr
sentative of the whole Italian episcopate, citing the *Tu es Petrus*,
the strength of which it was asserted that the Nicene fathers h
conferred on the Roman church the right to confirm and appro
decisions. It may be supposed that the allusion here was to t
Sardican legislation, and we may perhaps infer from this that t
belief that the Sardican canons belonged to Nicaea remained ev
at this date the official view in Rome.[3]

The same pontificate also sheds a brief ray of light on the attitude
Africa. Those churches, which some seventy years previously h
not hesitated to challenge a papal opinion on Canon Law, for near
half a century had lain at the mercy of the Arian Vandals. T
attempt of Eugenius of Carthage at this time to insist that no
African churches, 'especially the Roman church, which is the he
of all churches',[4] should be invited to take part in a joint conferen

---

[1] Caspar, *op. cit.*, vol. ii, p. 35.

[2] *Coll. Avell.*, 70, 8. ed. cit., p. 158; cf. *Decr. Gel.*, 9. Note the omission
Constantinople (381).

[3] For earlier references to this belief, see above, pp. 288 f., 312.

[4] Victor Vitensis, 2, 43. In *C.S.E.L.* vol. vii, p. 41.

Arian and Catholic bishops only provoked further reprisals against
Catholics. In vain the rhetorical appeal of Victor Vitensis: 'Blessed
Peter, why dost thou keep silence in the affairs of those sheep and
lambs which in His wide protective providence have been entrusted
to thee by our common Lord?' The renaissance of Catholicism in
Africa was not yet. All that Felix could do to bring aid to his appellants
was to invite the Emperor's cautious intervention.[1]

IX

To return now to the relations of the Papacy with the East.
The breach between the Roman see and the supporters of the
Henoticon, Acacius, Peter Mongus of Alexandria and Peter Fullo of
Antioch, was complete. The Roman synod had declared them
deposed, and Acacius in his turn had struck the name of Felix out of
the *diptycha* of the church of Constantinople. The polemical writing
of Gelasius occasioned by the schism continued during the last years
of Felix, and is chiefly represented by his two earlier *Tractates*. The
former of these is a brief compendium of the history of heresy from
Nestorius to his own time (489), and shows such marked differences
of style from his acknowledged writings as to call in question its
ascription to his authorship. An attempt, however, to make it
dependent on Liberatus' *Breviarium* and certain papal letters has
only served to prove the contrary.[2] The second of these *Tractates*,
belonging to the same year, though composed after the death of
Acacius, is a collection of *testimonia* from the time of Pope Simplicius
and directed chiefly against Peter Mongus.[3] Acacius' successor
Fravita, in his letter of enthronization, addressed Felix as 'the successor of Peter, prince of the Apostles, the rock of faith and steward
of the heavenly mysteries by the authority of the keys'. It was all in
vain. For Fravitas, as formerly for Acacius, the choice still lay, as
Gelasius pointed out afresh, between communion with an Apostle and
with a 'stammerer'. A fresh approach on the part of his successor
Euphemius met with a similar answer.[4] It is clear, however, that a
reaction was already on foot at Constantinople which might have
brought the schism to an end, if it had not received a severe check by

Caspar, *op. cit.*, vol. ii, p. 40.
Coll. Avell., 99. ed. cit., p. 440 ff. Cf. Bardenhewer, *op. cit.*, vol. iv, p. 627;
Caspar, *op. cit.*, vol. ii, p. 751.
JK 669. Thiel, p. 524. Cf. Bardenhewer, *op. cit.*, vol. iv, p. 628.
JK 613. Thiel, p. 266.

the elevation of the 'sacristan' Emperor Anastasius I. Moreover,
election of the uncompromising Gelasius to the Roman see on Ma
1, 492, rendered any hope of a *rapprochement* from that quarter
of the question. Reunion was not yet even in sight.

The brief but important pontificate of Gelasius I constitute
definite landmark in the history of the Roman see. Like Victor I
African[1] by birth, he appears to have lacked neither Victor's zeal
discipline nor his tenacity of purpose. No Pope before or after h
more consistently upheld the Roman principle ' *Nil innovetur,*
quod traditum est', even though in his case traditionalism me
chiefly the irretractability of the decrees of Nicaea and Chalced
Thus his guiding principle may be summed up in the words:

'Let us maintain inviolate the rules which the Church has receiv
from the Fathers and there will be peace'.[2]

Not less typical of his outlook is his attitude towards the Acac
schism, which we find clearly expressed in his second *Tractate*:

'The matter is clear: the sole cause in fact of the cleavage in un
and the disturbance of harmony, is that so long as the names
the transgressors are not excluded from the Church, they prev
the restoration of the bond of peace. For if it is permissible to re
in church the names of the successors and partners of Eutyches (si
Peter was his successor and Acacius his partner), why should not
same be allowed in the case of the successors and partners of Ar
or of other heretics? Or is it supposed that Eutyches was less god
and misbelieving than Arius? No one of sound intelligence wo
dare to claim that. If then their godlessness is equal, so must they
equally avoided; otherwise, if once such freedom is granted, for
future anything will be allowed to any one, and, God forbid, su
confusion and disorder will result that, as the prophet says, "Th
is no longer difference between the clean and the unclean". It is
the business of our humility to pass sentence on the schism affect
the whole world; but it is our duty to take care for our own salvati
since each of us will have to give account before the judgment s
of the Everlasting King'.[3]

It has been suggested that desire for a *rapprochement*, which p
sently began to show itself afresh in the East, sprang solely from

---

[1] See *Lib. Pont.*, ed. cit., vol. i, p. 256 f. and n. 1.
[2] JK 611, 19. Thiel, p. 287 f.
[3] *Tract.* 2, 5 f. Thiel, p. 526 f. cit. Ezek. xxii, 26.

sire of the imperial government to reach an understanding with
e sorely threatened western provinces. But some allowance ought
be made as well for an underlying conviction, by no means extinct
the East, that communion with the Roman see was indispensable to
al unity,[1] and equally for no less a sincere longing on the part of the
esterns for a restoration of order and harmony within the Catholic
hurch.

Of the considerable extent of Gelasius' literary remains (at least
4 letters or parts of letters of his have been preserved) by no means
e whole directly concerns us here. We may therefore confine our
tention to those documents which throw light on his conception of
pal jurisdiction, and of the relations of the Christian Church to the
hristian State.

As to papal jurisdiction, his doctrine is to be found most clearly
t forth in his letter to the bishops of Dardania,[2] reflecting the
fficult situation which had arisen in Illyricum, in consequence of
e continuing schism. We may infer from the Pope's letter that a
termined attempt was being made by the see of Constantinople to
in over the Illyrians to the *Henoticon*, and that already Andrew of
hessalonica had given way. In spite, however, of an assurance on
e part of the Dardanian episcopate of loyalty to the Roman see
d their request for a Roman legation, Gelasius found it necessary
put forward an elaborate apology for the Roman attitude.[3]

It may be inferred from Gelasius' argument that the eastern
ffensive' took the following form. It was contended that Acacius had
en improperly condemned, in that, despite his peculiar status as
shop of the imperial city, he had not been deposed by an extra-
dinary synod; moreover, it was said that the sentence of deposition
tered by Pope Felix had not been signified to the eastern episcopate
writing.[4] These and several other objections the Pope met in a
irit of impatience or contempt. Only on occasion did he condescend
attack his critics on their own ground. As an example of such
gument we may cite his thrust at the canonical status of Acacius' see:

---

[1] Some allowance also must be made for the belief that the suppression of
onophysitism would serve to check 'fifth column' activities such as later were to
en the doors of Syria and Egypt to the Saracen invaders.

[2] JK 664. Thiel, pp. 392, 414. *Coll. Avell.*, 95. ed. cit., p. 369 ff. Cf. ed. cit., No
6, p. 617.

[3] *Op. cit.*, 101. ed. cit., p. 464 ff.

[4] *Ibid.*, 1 and 8. Thiel., pp. 392 ff., 403 f.

'Yet we do not hesitate to mention that which is known to the universal Church, namely that, as the see of blessed Peter the Apostle has the right to loose what has been bound by the judgment of any bishops whatsoever, and since it has jurisdiction over every church, so that no one may pass judgment on its verdict, the canons providing that an appeal should lie to it from any part of the world no one is permitted to appeal against its judgment. Therefore it clear that Acacius had no episcopal authority to cancel a judgment of the apostolic see without its knowledge. Let them answer these questions: in what synod did he assume this right, which in any case would have been unlawful apart from the apostolic see? Of what see is he the bishop? Of what metropolitan city is he the prelate? Does he not himself belong to the province of the church of Heraclea? in fact it was lawful for him without a synod to rescind a judgment of the apostolic see without inviting its opinion, was it not equally lawful for the first see, appropriately executing the decisions of the Chalcedonian council, to thrust out a miscreant such as him by its own authority?'[1]

Acacius himself, it was urged, had acknowledged the Roman primacy of jurisdiction by acting as its agent in pronouncing the original sentence against the Monophysites. And if the Eastern objected that notice of his deposition had not been sent to them Gelasius replied that it had not been reported to the Roman see when the Emperor had deposed and restored bishops without a synod. Nor could it be argued that any further synod was necessary, for to hold one such as the Easterns demanded would have contradicted the principle that an irreformable decision against a heresy (i.e. Chalcedon) was sufficient by itself.

Gelasius pointed out further that the Roman see above all others was bound to carry the decrees of all councils which had been approved by the universal Church, 'since it ratifies each council by its authority, and safeguards it by its ceaseless oversight, in virtue its leadership (*principatu*), which the blessed Apostle Peter received by the word of the Lord, and which by common agreement of the Church he has always possessed and still retains'.[2]

Here he plainly acknowledged that the Roman see, as the ratifier

---

[1] K 664, 5. Thiel, p. 399 f. *Coll. Avell.*, 95, § 27, ed. cit., p. 378; cf. § 21, ed. cit. p. 376.

[2] *Ibid.*, 3. *Coll. Avell.*, 95, 10. ed. cit., *p.* 372.

ardian and protector of conciliar decisions on matters of faith, was
elf bound to their observance. Does this involve an admission that
e Roman primacy of jurisdiction was also subject to conciliar
thority? Gelasius supplies the answer:

'The apostolic see has frequently had occasion, as it has been said,
 ancient custom, even without any previous council, both of
solving those whom a council had unfairly condemned and of
ndemning without the presence of a council those whom it ought
condemn'.[1]

No doubt by a 'council' Gelasius meant a 'general' or, as we should
y, 'oecumenical' council. But could he rightly claim that the
storation of bishops condemned by the *latrocinium* was accom-
shed by the Roman see, and not by the council of Chalcedon?[2]
e objection presented no difficulty, for in his view not only did the
man see *alone* annul the decisions of the former council, but
ne was responsible for the summoning of the latter.[3] No doubt
k of an exact knowledge of the actual history of those councils
evented him from being conscious that his version seriously mis-
presented the facts. Yet it is clear that from such an argument in
our of the papal primacy of jurisdiction there followed logically
gative as well as positive consequences. Negatively it implied that
e Roman see could not be cited before any court, whether civil
ecclesiastical. In fact Gelasius himself affirmed as much in his
ter to Faustus when he said:

'The canons . . . ordered it (sc. the Roman see) to give judg-
nts relative to the whole Church, but itself to have recourse to the
dgment of none'.[4]

Yet the disturbing fact that the sees of Antioch and Alexandria had
th been rendered vacant as a result of the recent conviction of their
alcedonian occupants on supposedly criminal rather than ecclesias-
al charges inevitably led to some reconsideration by Gelasius of
e relations between Church and State.

The three chief sources for his doctrine on this subject, the refuta-
n of the eastern case in favour of Acacius,[5] the letter of 494 to

[1] JK 664, 5. *Coll. Avell.*, 95, 28. ed. cit., p. 379.
[2] See the present writer's *Life and Times of St. Leo*, p. 290 f.
[3] This is an excellent example of what Caspar, *op. cit.*, vol. i, p. 302, calls
eisterung der Geschichte durch die Doktrin'.
[4] JK 622, 5. *M.P.L.* 56, 630. Thiel, p. 344.
[5] JK 611. Thiel, p. 287.

22

Anastasius I[1] and the so-called fourth *Tractate*, generally known
the 'Tome of Gelasius',[2] represent roughly three successive stages
the development of his thought. We have already called attention
the warning addressed by him to the Emperor Zeno in the name
Felix III, that it befitted an Emperor 'to learn sacred matters . .
not to teach them'. Writing later as Pope, he took a definite st
forward by calling attention to the implications of the Empero
position as *filius ecclesiae*. In the same letter he proceeds:

'It is his (sc. the Emperor's) business to learn what is the conte
of religion, not to teach it. He has received the privileges of
power in civil affairs from God, and so he should be thankful f
benefits received, and not claim anything contrary to God's order.
is God's purpose that bishops should be responsible for the admir
stration of the Church, not the secular powers; the latter, if they a
Christian, according to His will ought to be subject to the Chur
and to the bishops'.[3]

This was written in 489. Five years later, from delimiting the
respective jurisdictions he turned to comparing and contrasting t
spiritual and secular powers themselves. In the course of his famo
letter to Anastasius I he evolved a description of their distincti
features and mutual relations, which, afterwards known as t
'doctrine of the Two Powers', provided one of the primary sourc
used by canonists and other writers in their treatment of the proble
of Church and State in Europe for almost a thousand years.

'There are in fact two', he wrote, 'Emperor Augustus, by who
this world is originally (*principaliter*) governed: the consecrat
authority of bishops (*auctoritas sacrata pontificum*) and the ro
power (*regalis potestas*). Of these, the responsibility of the bishops
the more weighty, since even for the rulers of men they will have
give account at the judgment seat of God. For you know, mo
gracious son, that, though in your office you preside over the hum
race, yet you bow your head in devout humility before those w
govern the things of God and await from them the means of yo
salvation; you realize that in the use and fitting administration of t
heavenly sacraments you ought to submit to Christian order, not
be its master, and that in these matters you ought to be subject
their judgment, and not to desire that they should be subordinat

---

[1] JK 632. Thiel, p. 349.   [2] JK 701. Thiel, p. 557.
[3] JK 611, 10. Thiel, p. 293.

your will. For if within the limits of the order of civil government
πristian bishops appreciate that sovereignty has been conferred
you by the disposition of heaven, and themselves obey your laws,
as to prevent their seeming to resist a judgment supreme in human
airs, how greatly it befits you in your turn eagerly to give obedience
those to whom have been assigned the privileges of the sacred
ʳsteries. Moreover, as a serious risk has been incurred by bishops
having remained silent through respect for the Sacred Majesty,
was fitting, so a grave danger, which God forbid, threatens those
ιo, when they should obey, behave with contempt. If it is right
ιt the minds of the faithful should be subject to all bishops every-
ιere, who dispose the things of God aright, how much more ought
ɔport to be given to the prelate of that see, whom the supreme
vine Majesty has willed to be preferred above all bishops, and
ɔm the Church has obediently honoured with universal and
failing loyalty'.[1]

We can scarcely do justice to the importance of this passage in
εneral survey of this kind. It is possible, however, to call attention
ɔne or two salient points. In the first place it should be realized that
description as the 'doctrine of the Two Powers' is not strictly
urate. Gelasius does not equate the two authorities; on the
ιtrary he discriminates clearly between what is 'imperial' and
at is 'episcopal.' To the former he assigns *potestas*; to the latter
toritas. Here lies a distinction, familiar to students of Roman
stitutional law. *Auctoritas* belonged to the ideal and moral
ere, and just because its force was derived from tradition or from
ɔlic opinion, it was strictly an ethical concept, as in the case of the
nan Senate, and so differed from the physical *potestas* endowed
h executive *imperium*, which in the republican period belonged to
populus and was entrusted to the magistrates only for the period
heir office. There was therefore a clear though undefined sense
ʰich *auctoritas* if compared with *potestas* could be regarded as the
ɪer of the two, just as moral influence is superior to physical
·e.

ʰat Gelasius should have been willing to draw this distinction is
he more remarkable in view of the fact that Christian bishops,
·ng whom he himself was no exception, had claimed at least
·e the days of Cyprian *potestas* as well as *auctoritas*, not only for

[1] JK 632, on which see Caspar, *op. cit.*, vol. ii, p. 64 ff.

the Church but also for themselves. If, however, we ask what
actually meant by *auctoritas sacrata pontificum*, there can be li
doubt that he was alluding to the *potestas* of binding and loosing,
in other words, to episcopal jurisdiction as understood in the fi
century. Yet it must not be supposed that Gelasius here propou
any final solution of the problem of the relation between Church a
State. His purpose was not so much to solve the problem as to prov
a rational ground for the belief that in the spiritual sphere
authority of the Church could have no superior.

Enough has probably been said to account for the dominant pl
taken in mediaeval thought by Gelasian ideas. But there is perh
yet a further and more subtle reason to be mentioned. It is to
found in his apparently deliberate use of paradox and ambiguity.
an example of the former we may cite his use of the predicate *sacre*
By current imperial usage the word *sacer* was normally employec
qualify that which belonged to or emanated from the Sovereign.
here its cognate participle is applied not to the *regalis potestas* bu
the *auctoritas pontificum*. Did Gelasius then, by his prophetic antici
tion of later papal usage, intend to imply a correction of curr
imperial practice? Again, in insisting that the Emperor himself
subject to the judgment of bishops (*ex illorum te pendere iudic*
he was using a current judicial phrase in a metaphorical sense
describe the Emperor's subordination to the episcopate in
purely spiritual sphere, but in such a way as to leave open
interpretation that in the administration of civil justice the court
the Church were superior to those of the State. Perhaps it is not
much to say that it was the use of phraseology of this sort which
responsible for a new phase in the evolution of the Papacy;
in which the canonist and the lawyer were to play a far more p
minent part than the theologian and the historian.

What further light on his views of this question can be deri
from the third of his works already mentioned, the fourth *Tract*
the Gelasian authorship of which is no longer seriously dispute
Perhaps its most significant feature is to be found in his character
tion of Christ as the only true Priest-King, who, as he writes:

'Mindful of human frailty, by an august disposition appoi
what was fitting for the salvation of His own. In this way He
tinguished the respective duties of each power by its appropi

[1] JK 701. Thiel, p. 557.

ctions and distinctive office, intending that His own should be
ed by the healing of humility, instead of being cut off once more
human pride. Thus it was provided that Christian Emperors would
in need of bishops for the sake of eternal life, and bishops for the
e of the good order of this temporal world would observe imperial
dinances'.[1]

It is unquestionable that Gelasius here, as in other places, shows
nsiderable indebtedness to Augustine. Originality lies chiefly in his
rivation of *regnum* and *sacerdotium* from Christ's immediate
stitution and the comparison and contrast between the functions of
e 'Two Powers'. Not less pregnant was his already familiar dis-
ction between *discere* and *docere* as further expanded in his letter to
ustus:

'As to the religious aspect of the question', he says, 'the final stage
the whole procedure belongs, according to Canon Law, only to the
ostolic see. As to its secular aspect, he (the Emperor) ought to
certain from bishops, and especially from the Vicar of blessed Peter,
at which belongs to God, and not judge the aforesaid matters
mself'.[2]

Gelasius is one of those prodigies of history whose ideas were so
r in advance of their time that not years but centuries were needed
r their full appreciation. No doubt in his case there were, at the
ne, serious hindrances which considerably impeded the process.
it the mere fact of their survival and persistence in the face of the
ost formidable opposition is surely proof of their essential value
the eyes of the more reflective of his contemporaries.

Through Nicholas I, the first Pope seriously to face the challenge
the Byzantine principate, and once again to deny his competence in
e sphere of religion, through Gregory VII and Innocent III, we
n trace the working out of the principles which their great pre-
cessor had already supplied. Thus it may be said that the
erarchical claim of the later Papacy to have not one but 'two
ords' at its disposal was the inevitable and logical outcome of
elasius' thought within the framework of mediaeval society. If
ly deserves the title of forerunner of the mediaeval Papacy it is
rely he.

[1] JK 701, 11. Thiel, p. 567.   [2] JK 622, 9. Thiel, p. 341.

X

Before considering the later course and ultimate settlement of t
Acacian schism we may glance for a moment at the situation of t
Roman see in the West. In 489 the comparatively benevolent ru
of Odoacer had been violently overthrown by Theodoric, who
savage temperament was adorned but not transmuted by a genui
respect for Roman culture. With him and his Arian faith ev
Gelasius could not do other than make terms, and it is sometim
forgotten that since the days of the Gothic 'emperor-maker' Ricime
Rome possessed at least one church assigned by the master race
the Arian *cultus*. Thus it is remarkable and perhaps not witho
significance that the pontificate of one of the most uncompromisir
exponents of papal authority should have fallen within a period durir
which Roman Catholicism was in some sense at least a 'disestablishe
religion.

His successor Anastasius II enjoys a singular title to fame in th
he is thought by many to be the Pope intended by Dante, when th
poet describes the huge tomb in the sixth circle of the *Inferno*:

> *Anastasio papa guardo,*
> *lo qual trasse Fotin della via dritta.*[1]

Whether or not we believe that he was in fact deserving of this ur
happy reputation must depend on the view taken of his eirenic polic
towards the Acacian schism. No doubt his aristocratic origin di
posed him to regard even a monophysite Emperor like his namesal
at Constantinople with greater respect than the Arian king at Ravenn
On the other hand, it is to be remembered that at least one of h
more important surviving letters is unequivocally 'Chalcedonian' i
phraseology,[2] even if he showed himself willing to discuss ambiguiti
in a Greek version of the Tome of Leo I. Yet it is a fact that h
legates entered into relations with the monophysite Egyptians a
Constantinople by receiving at their hands a dogmatic statemer
(*commonitorium*). Among them was the Thessalonian deaco
Photinus, commemorated by the Florentine poet, who with h
colleagues went so far as to endorse the monophysite documen
perhaps because it acknowledged the papal primacy, but otherwi
differed little from the *Henoticon*. By the time they had returne

---

[1] *Inferno*, xi, 9.
[2] JK 746. Thiel, p. 624. See Caspar, *op. cit.*, vol. ii, p. 84.

ıastasius was dead, and the Roman church in the throes of a
sputed election. It is hard to attach any real responsibility to the
parted Pontiff for their action, unless it might be said that he
ould have briefed his emissaries more carefully before their depar-
re. It may be remarked that it was not the first time nor the last
at papal legates were hoodwinked at Constantinople, mainly as a
ısequence of inadequate preparation.

The philo-Byzantine policy of Pope Anastasius, which evidently
d aroused serious misgivings among the rank and file of the Roman
urch, could at least count on the support of the Roman aristocracy
d particularly of the Senate, which at this time, no doubt as a con-
quence of the disappearance of the western principate and the
sumption of authority by the Gothic kings, provided a rallying point
r an interesting renaissance of Graeco-Roman cultural consciousness.
Sharply opposed to this tendency was the outlook of the lower
rata in Roman society, the loyalty of which turned to Ravenna rather
an to Constantinople. The importance of this divergence for the
story of the Church and Papacy can scarcely be exaggerated, since
marks the earliest phase in the emergence of an Italian nationalism
rn not of Graeco-Roman culture, but of a fusion of Latin and
ermanic racial characteristics, and at the same time the widening
the gulf already in evidence between the eastern and western
nceptions of Christian faith and order.

The tension between these rival loyalties led to open conflict on
e death of Anastasius II, and was manifested in sharp divisions of
inion among the Roman clergy and the city populace. The choice
the majority of the former was the deacon Symmachus, Sardinian
birth, baptized in Rome late in life; of the latter the Roman born
ch-presbyter Laurence. The outlook was by no means promising.
harges of bribery were being freely made by either side and street
ts were beginning. Happily more moderate counsels prevailed
d both sides had recourse to the decision of Ravenna. Theodoric,
ho had forcibly displaced Odoacer, was naturally inclined to favour
e 'Italian' party, but succeeded in giving the impression of being
ictly impartial by deciding that the candidate of the majority
ould prevail. Symmachus was therefore accorded general recog-
tion by the clergy, and at his first synod, of March 499, at which
venty-two bishops, seventy-four presbyters, and seven deacons
re present, a resolution against 'lobbying' before elections was

adopted. A further decision prescribed that in any case where t
Pope had not designated his successor (presumably referring to t
almost unbroken tradition in favour of the election of the arc
deacon in office), and in the event of a divided vote, the choice of 1
majority should be final.

It soon became clear, however, that the supporters of Laurer
had by no means accepted defeat. In defiance of the Alexandri
date of April 22 for Easter in the year 501, Symmachus had p
scribed according to the pre-Victorian Paschal cycle, March :
and the resultant controversy became so acute that they were succe
ful in procuring his summons to Ravenna. To a charge of creati
disorder they were careful to add others more seriously damaging
his reputation.

In the end a general synod of the Italian episcopate was assembl
at Rome in the church of S. Maria in Trastevere, at which Laurer
of Milan presided. Symmachus appeared in person, and thou
protesting against the intrusion of his opponents into the Rom
churches committed the tactical mistake of giving the proceedir
his approval. It soon became clear that even the bishops could 1
make up their minds how to handle such a highly unprecedent
situation. Two sessions were held without any decisive resu
Meanwhile the Pope sought asylum at St. Peter's as the o1
ecclesiastical property which had not been seized by his opponen
and thus, we may note, provided a precedent for the transfer of 1
papal *familia* from its original home at the Lateran to the co1
parative security of the Vatican. In desperation the synod attempt
to shift on to the shoulders of Theodoric the invidious responsibil
of condemning a Roman bishop. That he was an Arian by faith o1
serves to enhance the extent of their embarrassment. Finally,
Symmachus declined to appear and Theodoric to intervene, t
synod at its fourth session decided to extricate itself from the impas
by passing a vote of acquittal.

Yet before long it was made evident, as was only to be expect
that the verdict was far from giving general satisfaction. For o
thing, there had been numerous and significant abstentions in 1
voting. Inevitably tongues began to wag, and some even went
far as to draw the cynical inference that the privileges of the aposto
see must include a general licence to commit sin.[1]

---

[1] *Fragm. Laur.* ap. *Lib. Pont.* ed. cit., vol. I, p. 44 ff ; Caspar, *op. cit.*, vol. ii, p. 1c

Yet in spite of the Pope's pathetic situation, enthusiastic champions
the Roman see made a timely appearance in the persons of
￼nodius of Milan and Avitus of Vienne. The latter may well have
pressed the view of the Italian episcopate as well as that of Gaul
￼en he wrote: 'If the position of the chief (*princeps*) is shaken by
cusation, we feel the position of everyone of us to be weakened'.[1]
￼he work of Ennodius on the other hand, as a reply to the Pope's
emies, though characterized by clever evasions, violent abuse and a
￼arked dependence on irrelevant quotations of Holy Scripture, has
￼pecial interest as the product of a church which at one time seemed
￼ely to overshadow even Rome itself as the primatial see of Italy.[2]
￼ him we find the earliest explicit assertion that a distinction is to
￼ drawn between the Pope as an individual and the Pope as the
￼lder of the Papacy. As an individual he will receive just judgment
￼ the Last Day; as Pope he cannot be guilty of anything demanding
dicial punishment. It is not difficult to imagine that such a view
￼uld have been highly acceptable to one such as Gregory VII,
￼der whose inspiration the Ennodian principle was embodied
the *Dictatus Papae*.

Not less remarkable was the abundance of pseudonymous and
￼ocryphal literature which may rightly be regarded as a by-product
this anomalous situation. The chief object of these writings was to
ake good some of the very obvious defects in the papal structure
hich recent events had laid bare. They included, besides other
￼ppositious conciliar *Acta* such as the *Gesta Liberii*, the *Gesta
ysti* and *Gesta Polychronii*, the proceedings of an apocryphal 'synod
Sinuessa' at which the unhappy Marcellinus was supposed to have
￼en arraigned.[3] Encouraged to judge himself, the Pope was repre-
nted as having declared himself guilty, whereupon Miltiades,
￼parently elected and consecrated on the spot, is said to have
marked, "Rightly has he been condemned out of his own mouth,
r no one has ever judged the Pope, since the first see can be judged
y no man." A similar principle emerges in the contemporary sup-
ement to the Silvestrian saga depicting another imaginary Roman
nod, which besides condemning the author of the Paschal cycle,
jected by Symmachus, some hundred years or so before his birth,

---

[1] *Ep.* 34 in *M.G.H. Auct. ant.*, vol. vi, pt. 2, p. 64.
[2] *Ep.* 49 in *M.G.H. Auct. ant.* vol. vii, p. 49. Cf. Thiel, p. 735, No. 6.
[3] See above, p. 214, n. 5.

passed a series of canons of which the last significantly read : 'No m
shall judge the first see'.[1]

It is evident from these strange essays in imaginative history tl
the ideas of Gelasius were already showing themselves prolific, l
it would be unjust to Symmachus to attribute to him direct respc
sibility for the offspring. History as a science is comparativ
modern, and even to-day signs are not lacking that in some parts
Christendom the connexion between history and religion is not
regarded as vital. A tendency to exaggerate the place of the 'mystic;
or to adopt a facile pragmatism, and correspondingly to depreci;
the 'historical,' was almost certainly not less characteristic of a gene;
tion which had grown up in Rome amid the new Italo-Germa;
environment. It was from sources such as the Symmachian forger
that the mediaeval Papacy furnished a considerable part of its co
troversial armoury. Unfortunately, by the time the poor quality
the material so employed was discovered, the weapons had alrea
been forged and could only have been refashioned at considerai
risk, even if the will to undertake so hazardous a labour had be
present.

To return now to the situation of Pope Symmachus. Some twel
months after his ambiguous acquittal he felt sufficiently confide
of his position to reassemble the Italian synod; yet that he shou
have been able to do so at all provides some testimony of his 1
habilitation in public opinion. A resolution on the subject of chur
property was submitted at the suggestion of the Senate to Theodor
who in turn referred it back to be passed in accordance with ancie
constitutional practice by a *Senatus consultum*. This interesti;
example of the survival of senatorial procedure not only reflec
Theodoric's almost scrupulous regard for constitutional correctne;
but serves to illustrate the extent to which by now even the Sena
was turning away from the Greek centre of the Empire at Byzantiu
and towards the nationalist Italo-German monarchy at Ravenr
By this means the process of Symmachus' rehabilitation was hastene
even if it was not till 506 that it could be considered complete.

[1] For the Symmachian forgeries, see *M.P.L.* 6, 1–19, and 8, 822–840. (
Liber pont. ed. cit. Intro. pp. cxxii, cxxvi, cxxxiii ff.

XI

As to Symmachus' relations with the East, we may take as typical
 letter to Anastasius I[1] replying to various complaints by the
iperor, who was no doubt much disturbed by the recent anti-
zantine developments in the West. It combined singular lack of
od taste with a feeble plagiarism of the work of his great pre-
cessor, particularly his doctrine of the 'Two Powers'. No doubt
was true that so long as the Emperor persisted in upholding the
ne of Acacius, he could not expect the Roman see to remain
lifferent, and Symmachus' mistake lay not so much in what he said
in the way he said it. However, a stroke of military good fortune
bled the Emperor to leave the West to its own devices, and to
lress himself with renewed ardour to the fulfilment of his ambition,
nely, the establishment of Monophysitism as the religion of the
ipire.

It was about this time that the patriarch Macedonius, elected
5) in the place of Euphemius to the see of Constantinople, was
sented with a peremptory demand from the Emperor that he
uld issue an official repudiation of the council of Chalcedon. In
te of the certainty that on refusal he would incur immediate
position, he did not lack the courage to declare that apart from
eneral council under the presidency of the Roman bishop no
h repudiation was possible.[2] His sentence followed within the
ar (511).

By the following year the three 'greater churches' of the East were
the hands of Monophysitism, which being now in the ascendant
an to show the usual fissiparous tendency of a successful schis-
tic movement. It is therefore with some sense of relief that we
e up a letter addressed to the apostolic see, illustrating the attitude
the victims of Caesaropapistic tyranny while it bewails the tragic
ie of the Acacian affair. Reminding the Pope that he enjoys the
ver to loose as well as to bind, his petitioners plead:

Of a truth you are possessed of the Spirit of Christ, who are
ly instructed by your holy teacher Peter how to tend the flock
Christ, which has been entrusted to you over all the earth and
eys you not by constraint but willingly; who call to us your sub-
ts with the Apostle Paul and say, "We have not dominion over

----

[1] JK 761.   [2] Caspar, *op. cit.*, vol. ii, p. 121

you regarding the faith, but are helpers of your joy." . . . All of u
both those in communion with them (sc. Monophysites) and tho
who decline it, await next to God the light of your visitation a
admission to favour. Wherefore hasten to help the East, whence t
Redeemer Himself sent forth two great luminaries Peter and Paul
give light to the whole world'.[1]

What answer, if any, Symmachus returned to this pathetic appe
is unknown. All that remains of his eastern correspondence is
letter to the Illyrian episcopate urging them to take warning fro
the fate of the eastern churches :

'For those, who believed they could disregard the admonition
the apostolic see, have deservedly suffered what is bound to bef
those who forsake their duty'.[2]

His pontificate is remarkable for a revival of close relations betwe
the sees of Rome and Arles in the person of its bishop Caesarius, w
has the distinction of being the first recorded recipient of authority
use the *pallium*.[3] Symmachus' choice of Caesarius rather than I
rival Avitus of Vienne as papal vicar of Gaul is deserving of so
credit as an act of diplomacy, since, while Vienne formed part of t
dominions of the Catholic Burgundians, it was the Arian Theodo:
who at this time controlled Arles and its immediate environs. T
Church generally would have cause to thank him in days to con
for his timely intervention in the affairs of southern Gaul, even
at the time his choice seemed to betray an excessive eagerness
conciliate an Arian and therefore potentially hostile government.

The election of Symmachus' archdeacon Hormisdas to succe
him on July 20, 514, was evidently a foregone conclusion. He h
been called one of the great peacemakers of his line, a title which l
generous treatment of the surviving adherents of the anti-po
Laurence alone might justify, but which is confirmed by his pa
in the settlement of the eastern schism. There is, however, room i
some doubt, whether the means by which it was achieved w
altogether to the advantage of the Roman see or in fact to the ultim:
peace and unity of the Church as a whole.

We may not always be justified in tracing ecclesiastical events
political causes, but in this case it can scarcely be denied that t

[1] Thiel, p. 710 f., No. 12, 2.
[2] JK 763. Thiel, p. 722. *Coll. Avell.*, 104, 16. ed. cit., p. 492 f.
[3] Caspar, *op. cit.*, vol. ii, p. 125, *n.* 10

outbreak of revolution in Byzantium disposed the Emperor to look far more favourably than before on the possibility of a rapprochement with Rome. His new *Magister militum* Vitalian, the leader of a successful revolt, had the satisfaction of inviting the new Pope together with his suffragans to attend a projected council at Heraclea. It is not without significance that the imperial letter spoke of the 'archbishop and patriarch' of Rome as the appropriate mediator in a doctrinal controversy.[1]

With deliberate circumspection, and not without the express approval of Ravenna, Hormisdas made his preparations. Profiting by the experience or rather neglect of his predecessors, he took care to provide his legates with most thorough and precise instructions about conditions of reunion. These were: first, recognition of the council of Chalcedon and of the Tome of Leo by means of an imperial encyclical to all bishops; next, formal assent of all bishops in the presence of their churches to the said council, to Leo's letters and to the condemnation of the monophysite leaders by name, besides which the bishops were to sign in presence of witnesses a *libellus* drawn up by the papal notaries; then the reference of the cases of all exiled bishops to the apostolic see with a view to a fresh examination; and finally, reservation to papal judgment of all cases of bishops charged with the persecution of Catholics.[2]

In the *libellus* just mentioned we encounter for the first time the celebrated 'Formula of Hormisdas'. Not less than six variant editions of this document have come down to us from antiquity, to which the latest text included in the Vatican Constitution *Pastor Aeternus*, professedly though not accurately citing it in the form accepted by the fourth general council of Constantinople (869-70), has added yet another.[3]

Though sometimes described as a *regula fidei*, it is far more a definition of the logical consequences of accepting the Roman primacy of doctrine and jurisdiction than an actual statement of faith. Moreover, owing to the comparatively uncertain state of the text, it is by no means easy to be sure of its original argument. Its most authentic form is probably the one which was appended to a

---

[1] *Coll. Avell.*, 107. ed. cit., p. 499 f.; Thiel, p. 742, No. 2.
[2] *Coll. Avell.*, 116 b. ed. cit., p. 520 ff.
[3] The following phrases are omitted: 'et a constitutis patrum nullatenus deviare' . . . 'et patrum sequentes in omnibus constituta'. Caspar, *op. cit.*, vol. ii, p. 134, n. 3, calls attention to the significance of these omissions.

letter addressed by the Pope to the Spanish bishops,[1] since it professes to have been derived directly from the Vatican archives, though in certain cases the readings of the *Codex Berolinensis* are probably to be preferred.[2] We give here only those passages which bear directly on the primacy. Its opening sentence reads as follows:

'The first requisite for salvation is to give heed to the formula of the correct faith and to err in no way from the decrees of the fathers, because[3] we cannot ignore the declaration of our Lord Jesus Christ, when He said: "Thou art Peter and upon this rock I will build my Church". Moreover, the truth of His words is shown by actual fulfilment, since in the apostolic see the Catholic religion has always been preserved "without spot". So, as it is our aim to be parted in no way from that faith and hope, we anathematize all heresies . . .' (here follows a list beginning with Nestorius and including Acacius and the monophysite leaders by name, together with an explicit declaration of acceptance of the council of Chalcedon, on the express ground 'that in conformity with the Nicene council it proclaimed the apostolic faith'. In addition mention is made of the 'catholic letters of Pope Leo I.) It concludes thus:

'Wherefore I hope that I may deserve to be with you in one communion, such as is defined by the apostolic see, where the permanence of the Christian religion is intact and genuine'.

Thus once more the plan was being tried of solving the difficulties of the eastern churches by offering for their acceptance, after the example of Leo I, a formula of Roman origin. But in this case Hormisdas expressed his willingness to do what Leo had refused: namely to appear at the projected council in person.[4] For some reason, however, it seems that at the last moment he changed his mind, so that the legates left Rome without him, only to return a few months later with a polite letter from the Emperor having effected precisely nothing. During the next three years letters and legations passed backwards and forwards. The deadlock remained.

At last the death of Anastasius I in July 518 gave promise of an improvement, and this was quickly made good by the action of the new Emperor Justin I, who at once brought pressure to bear on the

---

[1] JK 788. Thiel p. 793. See Caspar's additional note, *op. cit.*, vol. ii, p. 764 ff.
[2] *Coll. Avell.* in *C.S.E.L.*, vol. xxxv, pt. 2, p. 800 ff.
[3] Omitting 'et' with *Cod. Berol.*
[4] *Coll. Avell.*, 115, 4. ed. cit., p. 511. The change is highly significant of the subservience of the Roman see to the Byzantine court.

triarch John II to declare publicly his acceptance of the council
Chalcedon. In addition the restoration of the names of the deposed
triarchs, Euphemius and Macedonius, together with that of Pope
o, to the *diptycha* of the Constantinopolitan church gave striking
timony of good will. Among the many other unmistakable
nptoms of a changed outlook in the eastern government was the
ter addressed by John to Hormisdas,[1] which, besides a formal
quest for restoration to communion with the Roman see, included a
ofession of faith in the teaching of the councils. It should be
ticed, however, that besides Chalcedon the letter included the
ancil of 381. Mention was made of the insertion of the names of
o and Hormisdas in the *diptycha* of Constantinople, and the writer
acluded with a request that the Pope would send legates 'to give
d receive our satisfaction'.

To a Constantinopolitan legate lately arrived from Justin to
aeodoric the Pope gave letters on his return for the Emperor and
an II. Apparently Hormisdas had not thought it necessary to
swer immediately a communication from the Emperor's nephew
stinian,[2] nor did he pause to comment on the mention of 'four
ancils'. In spite of previous disappointments preparations for a
w papal legation were set on foot. Its members, as before, were
efully briefed with secret instructions, including a provision that
y might, if necessity arose, express themselves as satisfied with
e omission of the names of Acacius' successors from the *diptycha*,
iving the Pope's requirement of explicit condemnation. It is
portant, however, to notice that the *sine qua non* was to be the
blic acceptance in some fashion of the Roman *libellus*.

After some hesitation John subscribed. At first he appears to have
t forward a statement of belief composed by himself, but in the end
d to be satisfied with the 'face-saving' effect of a Constantino-
litan preface to the Roman formula, besides some significant altera-
ns.[3] It must have surprised more acute observers in Rome to find
at an addition treated the council of 381[4] as possessing the same
idity as Nicaea, and to notice that John appeared to regard the
s of Rome and Constantinople as twin manifestations of a single

---

Coll. Avell., 146. ed. cit., p. 591 f. Grumel, *op. cit.*, No. 210.
Though he answered it later with JK 804.
Coll. Avell., 159. ed. cit., p. 607 ff. Grumel, *op. cit.*, No. 212.
This council was not officially recognized by the Roman see till the pontificate
ohn II, in JK 885, *M.P.L.* 66, 23 (534).

episcopate. They must also have remarked a striking omission fr
the *libellus* in that the words 'condemned by the apostolic s
following the name of Acacius were discreetly excluded.

On paper the capitulation of the see of Constantinople seemed
notable achievement. Once again it appeared that the bishop of t
eastern capital had acknowledged the Roman primacy of doctri
But was this all? Everyone in the East knew that in the backgrou
of these negotiations there stood the grim old cavalry colonel Just
now successor of Augustus, and, what was more, the astute p
sonality of his theologically-minded nephew Justinian. Meanwhil
new controversy had arisen on the subject of a doctrinal form
originally sponsored by Peter Fullo and introduced by him into t
liturgy of the Antiochene church, the burden of which was: 'O
of the Trinity . . . was crucified'. By a strange paradox this form
was now being eagerly taken up by a group of monks of Scyth
origin, who appeared to be quite unaware of its heterodox p
venance. After evading the vigilance of Justinian's secret police,
Hormisdas' considerable embarrassment these monastic theologi
had arrived in Rome with the intention of submitting their 'the
paschite' formula to his arbitration. But worse was to come. Ecclesi
tical and political events in Illyricum showed only too clearly t
the initiative lay with the Emperor, and that for evident reasons
was not prepared to accept a Roman primacy of jurisdiction in th
regions. Thus, as we see from the general tone of Hormisdas' la
correspondence, the Pope was inevitably obliged to adopt a r
which was largely passive. Nevertheless the evident eagerness w
which Justinian pressed for a decision in the matter of the The
paschites showed that, like Marcian before him, not even the effecti
master of the East felt able wholly to dispense with the opinion of t
Roman see in a controversy involving doctrine. When the Pop
decision was given, it was found to contain neither approval nor co
demnation of the new formula; its only positive statement was t
the definitions of Chalcedon and of Leo I were decisive and fu
sufficient as a safeguard against heresy.[1] But by this time the east
government had decided itself to sponsor the phrase, in the su
position that it would clear those who supported its policy of accor
ing recognition to Chalcedon and the Leonine letters of any s
picion of Nestorianism. Thus we seem to see how gradually but qu

[1] JK 857, 2. Thiel, p. 960. *Coll. Avell.*, 236, 6. ed. cit., p. 718.

rely even the primacy of doctrine was being wrested from the
pal grasp.

Hormisdas has been charged with weakness of character and an
sence of resolute determination in the execution of his designs.
it the question must remain whether given the existing political
uation he could well have acted otherwise. No one could have
en more insistent than he on the attitude of the Roman see regard-
g the essential point at issue, namely, the repudiation of Acacius.
s offer to travel to the East in order to preside in person over the
ork of reconciliation has been ascribed to Roman vanity. Yet the
ssibility of a simpler explanation such as eagerness to do anything
restore the unity of the Church cannot be excluded. We shall see
at Byzantium was willing enough to welcome the Pope as a sup-
ant, or even as an agent of imperial policy. But for a Pope as the
preme judge in relation to the immediate subjects of the *imperator*
erdos it could find no room. If Hormisdas failed for the time being,
was chiefly because the eastern churches had been misled into a
nfusion of the things of Caesar with the things of God. Yet time
uld show that his eirenic labours had not been in vain.

XII

The project of a papal visit to Constantinople was actually
alized under his successor, John I, though he came rather as the
mble emissary of Ravenna to protest against the closing of Arian
urches in the eastern capital than as an arbiter of questions
uching Christian faith and order. In fact the chief significance of
s pontificate is that it appears to mark a new widening of the rift
tween Italo-Germanic nationalism and Byzantine imperialism, and
e beginning of that period which has been called the 'Byzantine
ptivity', in which the Papacy was often to find itself the pawn of
e or other of the two opposed tendencies.

After summoning Pope John to Ravenna, Theodoric required him to
tain from the Emperor, not only restoration of the Arian churches,
t also the reversion of Arians recently converted to Catholicism.
o the performance of the former task he consented; the latter, in
ite of his evident helplessness, he courageously declined. Thus a
thetic tragedy was enacted, in the course of which the magnificence
John's reception at Constantinople only served to enhance the

23

irony of his position, and the most optimistic supporters of the Rom
see could not deny that even the recoronation of an eastern Emper
was scarcely a sufficient compensation for the serious damage incurr
by papal prestige. As to the outcome of his mission, the unfavoura
reaction of Theodoric on his return appears to suggest that nothi
was achieved. Responsibility for his sudden end, which quicl
followed, was reasonably and not unnaturally ascribed by gossip
the king.[1] John was not the only Pope to die a martyr for pa
independence of action.

The pontificates of his immediate successors call for no spec
notice except to remark that it is to Boniface II's intervention
Illyricum that we owe the survival of that valuable collection
early papal and other documents known as the *Codex Thessalonicens*
and that to John II must be assigned the first explicit recognition
the Papacy of the council of Constantinople (381)[3] as of oecumenic
rank. The brief reign of Agapetus I marks one of the few bright
intervals in the gathering gloom of the Byzantine tyranny over t
Church. As an advocate of Gothic claims Agapetus, like John
travelled to Constantinople in person. The situation there must ha
seemed anything but reassuring. A fresh agitation against Chalced
relying on the support of the Empress Theodora was evidently
foot, and already the new patriarch Anthimus had declared himself
communion with the monophysite leaders, Theodosius of Alexand
and Severus of Antioch. Agapetus on arrival declined communi
with him, and on his resignation had the satisfaction of ordaini
Menas as his successor.[4] More than this, the Pope received at t
hands of Justinian I, Emperor since 527, and also of Menas separa
acts of subscription to the formula of Hormisdas, which includ
an explicit recognition of the 'four councils' and a detailed expositi
of the dyophysite or Chalcedonian doctrine.[5] This served in so
respects to counterbalance the acceptance of the formula 'one of t
Trinity became man and was crucified', which Justinian had

[1] Caspar, *op. cit.*, vol. ii, p. 189.
[2] See Hefele-Leclercq, *Conciles*, 1908, Tome ii, p. 1119. The most recent editi
is by Silva Tarouca, K., in *Textus et Documenta Ser. Theol.* 23, 1937. Besides t
Acta of the Roman synod of 531, it contains twenty-seven letters, preserved
whole or in part. Two letters, Leo, *Epp.* 100 and 132, are included in Schwartz,
Acta conc. Tom. II, vol. iv, p. 167 ff.
[3] See above, p. 251 f.
[4] JK 897. *M.P.L.* 66, 48.
[5] *Coll. Avell.*, 89 and 90. ed. cit., pp. 338 ff., 340 ff.

ıg last managed to extract from John II, and seemed to suggest
at after all Caesaropapism was on the point of acknowledging a
gher authority. Preparations were in hand for an imperial council to
amine various outstanding questions when by an unfortunate
ıncidence Agapetus died (April 22, 536).

In spite of this serious loss the projected council met and con-
.cted the business which had been proposed for it.[1] A remarkable
oportion of its membership was western, and thus, though this
int has not always been noticed, it has a good claim to be treated
some real sense as oecumenical. With impressive unanimity the
nod endorsed the sentence already pronounced against Anthimus
Pope Agapetus, and received among its *Acta* the letters addressed
the Roman see to the Syrian bishops[2] and to Epiphanius of
ınstantinople.[3] It also formally condemned the principal mono-
ysite bishops, including Severus of Antioch and Peter of
ıamea.

In this way it seemed that the philo-monophysite policy of the
npress Theodora had been successfully circumvented by means of
e valuable support of the Roman see. Unhappily the premature
ath of Agapetus during his residence in the eastern capital unex-
ctedly deprived the Emperor of a valuable ally. The Empress had
eady procured the venal support of the Roman deacon Vigilius,
d, it seems, was taking steps to ensure his prompt election to the
most limit of her purse. Yet all the speed that her candidate could
ıke on his return journey to Rome did not succeed in anticipating
e election of Silverius on the nomination of the Gothic king
ıeodahad. It was not to be the last time that the unfortunate and
t too scrupulous Vigilius would find himself overtaken by the
oid march of events.

On this occasion, however, fortune or the undiplomatic behaviour
his rival played into his hands. The Byzantine invasion of Italy
der the command of Belisarius appears to have taken the Goths
surprise and not least Silverius, who after compromising himself in
aat appeared to be a treasonable conspiracy against the imperial
storation, was arrested, deposed and eventually handed over to the
ıder mercy of the disappointed Vigilius.

That Theodora's favourite would quickly make himself master

---

[1] Mansi, *Concilia*, vol. viii, 895 (*Actio* 1).
[2] JK 800. Thiel, p. 820.   [3] JK 861. Thiel, p. 970.

of the situation and procure his own election was of course only to
expected. Yet throughout the unhappy years of his pontificate t
ghost of the unfortunate Silverius seems always to have been at
side, and his subsequent tergiversations may perhaps be par
explicable by an uneasy consciousness of its accusing presence.

Of Vigilius' relations with the West little need be said except
call attention to two points which clearly reflect his compl
dependence on the current imperial policy. In writing to Auxan
of Arles he pointed out that the renewal of the papal vicariate assign
by his predecessors to that see, as well as the grant of the covet
pallium, must be regarded as dependent on the Emperor's approva
A later letter, addressed by Vigilius from Constantinople to Auxani
successor Aurelian,[2] requesting him to solicit the Frankish ki
Childebert to safeguard the interests of the Roman church agai
the Gothic 'usurper' Totila, showed only too clearly the disadva
tages suffered by the Papacy through having hitched the waggon
its fortunes to the star of imperial restoration.

That Justinian now proposed to exploit his favourable position
relation to the Roman see to the full was made clear by his insiste
demand that Vigilius should endorse explicitly the decrees of t
recent Constantinopolitan synod, together with the relevant imper
edict. In complying with this command Vigilius meekly excus
his omission with the plea that he had supposed no further repetiti
of a sentence already pronounced to be necessary and mention
significantly his satisfaction that 'the Lord in His mercy has be
pleased to grant you *episcopal* as well as *imperial* wisdom'.[3]

Sentiments of this kind only serve to betray the extent to which t
Papacy had come to acquiesce in the principle of government of t
Church by an *imperator sacerdos*. Nor was this all. Vigilius went
far as to promise that if Menas of Constantinople, or any other, p
nounced a condemnation, he would readily confirm the senten
This was of course tantamount to giving a blank cheque to his fello
patriarch and very much like an acknowledgment of the equal stat
of the Roman and Constantinopolitan sees.[4]

[1] JK 912. *M.G.H. Epp.* vol. iii, p. 58, No. 39. For the need of obtaining impe
sanction as a condition of granting this privilege, see also JE 1491, Gregory I, *Reg.* 8,
[2] JK 918. *M.G.H. Epp.* vol. iii, p. 64, No. 44.
[3] JK 910. *Coll. Avell.*, 92, 2. ed. cit., p. 348 f.
[4] We should be guilty of ingratitude if we did not recall that it is to this act
submission on the part of the unfortunate Vigilius that we owe indirectly one of

Meanwhile the Emperor was setting in motion a new process ended to satisfy the scruples of the Monophysites regarding the alcedonian settlement. The primary question arose concerning writings of Theodore of Mopsuestia, whose responsibility for Christological doctrine, now known as Nestorianism, had already en suspected at the time of the theopaschite controversy. A nilar suspicion also attached to the anti-Cyrilline writings of eodoret of Cyrrhus. It seemed therefore to the official party that hese causes of offence could be removed, the way to reconciliation th monophysitism might lie open. The chief difficulty remaining s how to overcome the uncomfortable fact that not only had eodore never formally been condemned, but that Theodoret and Antiochene partner Ibas of Edessa (whose letter to the Persian aris against Cyril made up an anti-monophysite trilogy) had been some sense recognized as orthodox at Chalcedon.

Justinian evidently believed at first that the simple and expeditious thod of an imperial dogmatic edict on the lines of the *Henoticon* uld solve the problem. The same means had already been success- in effecting a posthumous condemnation of Origen. How natural at a similar *ukase* against the great Antiochenes should be provided adjust the balance. Yet even if the Roman see had never shown any rked eagerness to defend the famous Alexandrine theologian's mory, from its point of view to attack Theodoret and Ibas was rely to insult Chalcedon and even Pope Leo himself. Little wonder n that the publication of the edict produced dismay, followed alarm and even indignation in Roman quarters. With characteristic ll Vigilius, it seems, decided upon a policy of masterly inaction.

Once more the resourceful Empress intervened, and by a remark- le exercise of *force majeure* managed to procure the Pope's removal m Rome. After many delays and much procrastination, including least six months spent at Catania in Sicily, the sorely tried Vigilius ached Constantinople. Here he found himself between two fires. one side were Justinian and his Empress; on the other the fluential Roman deacon Pelagius. The last-named had already certained prevailing opinion in the West on the question of the day, d could see clearly that if the matter were pressed in accordance

---

liest and most complete collections of the Leonine letters, the *Codex Monacensis*, merly at Ratisbon, the archetype of which was probably derived from the papal hives. See the present writer's *Life and Times of St. Leo*, p. 507.

with the Emperor's programme a serious situation might rapic
develop there. In particular he was assured of the support of t
learned Ferrandus, deacon of Carthage. That distinguished wri
belonged to the brief renaissance of the African church in this peri
before its final submergence beneath the *maelstrom* of Islam, a
is characterized by an insistence on the doctrinal primacy of t
decisions of those oecumenical councils which had been approv
by the Roman church, as second only to the authority of H
Scripture itself.[1] Vigilius, however, preferred to ignore these evide
tokens of future resistance, and after saving his face by means
an *ad hoc* synod published his *Judicatum*, in which the 'Th
Chapters', as the incriminated authors came to be known, we
formally condemned, while the council of Chalcedon was explici
upheld.[2] This took place on Holy Saturday (April 11), 548. But
was to be expected, it only succeeded in creating disappointme
or distress. The Monophysites, such as Theodore Askidas, bish
of Caesarea in Cappadocia, were indignant to find that it presum
to defend the infamous council, while on the other hand the Wester
were shocked that any word should be spoken against those wh
Chalcedon had rehabilitated. Facundus, bishop of Hermiane
north Africa, who was present in the capital at the time, did r
hesitate to show the courage of his convictions by declining Vigili
communion. Soon signs of revolt began to appear within the pa
entourage itself, and before long protests were being echoed
Illyricum and particularly in north Africa, where a plenary coun
went so far as to declare the Pope excommunicate, until the offendi
document should be withdrawn.[3] Simultaneously Facundus pu
lished his lengthy *Pro defensione trium capitulorum*, which though qu
uncompromising on the point at issue, contrived to shift the m
responsibility for recent action on to the shoulders of the Empero

Probably no one was more surprised at the stir which his
timed expression of opinion had caused than Vigilius himself.
the other hand, it is clear from the evidence that he had seriou
hoped to be able to play off one party against the other. At the sa
time he probably guessed that, in spite of the Emperor's autocra
handling of the situation, any final settlement which affected

---

[1] Fulgentius Ferrandus, *Ep.* 6, 7. *M.P.L.* 67, 921.
[2] JK 922. Cf. Facundus, *Pro defensione trium cap.* praef. *M.P.L.* 67, 527.
[3] Victor Tunnun. *Chron. ad ann.* 549. *M.G.H. Auct. ant.*, vol. xi, p. 202.
[4] *Op. cit.*, 12. *M.P.L.* 67, 841 f.

sregard the papal attitude was recognized even in Constantinople be out of the question. He therefore proposed that the whole iestion should be shelved, until a council representative of the npire as a whole could be assembled.[1]

Preparations for such a council were already on foot when heodore Askidas broke the truce. It is difficult to believe that he d so without the Emperor's knowledge and approval, but in any se the only effect of his action was firmly to re-unite the Pope with e rest of the western bishops. Yet their sentence of deposition pro-unced against Theodore, in which they included excommunica-ns of Menas and his suffragans, finally served to convince Justinian at·in a case where the usual means of imperial diplomacy had idently failed, a more crude alternative must be employed.[2]

A tragi-comic scene took place in the church of St. Peter *in ormisda*, whither the western bishops had fled for sanctuary. The ·lice were sent with orders to effect the Pope's removal. Yet in the :e of a hostile mob, who unlike the Emperor had some feelings of spect for the person of St. Peter's successor, they had to make an dignified retreat.[3] Naturally such action had the effect of trans-ring a considerable weight of moral support to the side of Vigilius. more subtle policy of attrition followed, in the course of which no ·vice of detraction, petty annoyance and open violence known to a distic and somewhat unscrupulous oriental autocracy was left tried.

Although Vigilius had by now returned under an imperial guarantee the palace of Placidia, in which he had originally been housed, he ust have already made up his mind to escape from the city at the rliest opportunity. He had by now spent nearly five years in Con-ntinople, and the affair seemed no nearer final settlement than len he arrived. But whither was he to go? No asylum could be und in the East, free from the unwelcome attentions of the perial police; to return to Rome, with the city once more in the nds of the Gothic 'rebel', was out of the question. But an oppor-nity provided by the coincidence of a moonless night and the offer a friendly boatman was not to be lightly declined. So when the nperor awoke next day, he must have been somewhat disturbed to

[1] Mentioned in JK 930. [2] *Ibid.*
[3] These events are described in a letter of the Italian clergy, Mansi, *Concilia*, . ix, col. 440.

learn that the elusive Pope had tactfully installed himself in t
Chalcedonian sanctuary of St. Euphemia, the authorities of which
their timely intervention showed that they were quite undeservi
of the aspersion cast by the oracle upon the perspicacity of th
ancestors. Here Vigilius was presently joined by the rest of t
Westerns. Further use of force on the part of the Emperor seem
henceforth impracticable.

It was now Vigilius' turn to take the offensive. After publishi
sentences of deposition and excommunication against his opponen
he issued an encyclical on the lines of the formula of Hormisd
the purpose of which must have been to reassure western opinio
The effect of this action on the capital was electric. The excommu
cated bishops united in producing a declaration of complete assent
the 'four councils' and a profession of readiness 'to respect a
accept as orthodox therein all that had been said to be such
common consent with the legates and representatives of the aposto
see'.[2]

Vigilius presently returned to Constantinople, and on the dea
of Menas had the satisfaction of receiving a solemn profession of fa
from his successor, Eutychius, in which the new bishop ackno
ledged the 'four councils', the letters of Leo and other Popes, a
supported the project of a new council under Vigilius' presidenc
For obvious reasons the Pope endeavoured to postpone its assembl
and proposed that it be held in the West. But Justinian natura
would have none of this, nor would he entertain any longer the alt
native of a round-table conference, still less the proposal of Pelagi
that the decision on the question of the 'Three Chapters' should
left to the Roman see.

The council, consisting of no more than one hundred and forty-fi
bishops, assembled on May 5, 553.[4] At the first session the n
imperial conception of the Church's constitution came to the fo
It was the theory of 'the five Patriarchates' which henceforward
mained dominant in eastern ecclesiastical circles for many centuri
but which could only claim the support of antiquity by a high
tendentious reading of its history.[5] Nor can it very well be forgott

---

[1] JK 935. *Coll. Avell.*, 83, 3–9. ed. cit., p. 231 f.
　[2] *Ibid.*, 6.　　[3] Grumel, *op. cit.*, No. 244.　　[4] Mansi, *Concilia*, vol. ix, col. 1
　[5] The theory is elaborated in Justinian's letter to the council, Mansi, *op. c
ibid.* Its effect was to reduce the western church to a minority of one in relat
to the four eastern patriarchates.

this connexion that by the middle of the sixth century 'Egypt was ᴀolly monophysite, and the Catholic Patriarch of Alexandria had ᴀrcely a flock. Antioch was sacked by the Persians, and rebuilt by stinian; it was in danger of the enemy, and riddled by heresy'.[1] ᴀ the other hand the tacit recognition by the Roman see of the third ᴀon of Constantinople (381) was not merely a belated concession Caesaropapism. It was just plain and straightforward realism, and such in sharp contrast to the artificial archaism of Justinian's ᴇory of the Church's constitution, which though formally embodied eastern Canon Law and in the *Codex Justinianus*, remained largely ᴛt of correspondence with the *de facto* situation.

The business of the first session of the council was largely taken ᴀ with the reading of the Emperor's letter and a discussion of means be adopted for obtaining the Pope's support. Ultimately it was ᴇcided to allow him twenty days in which to produce a considered ᴅinion. The *Constitutum* of Vigilius[2] was actually conveyed to the ᴀthorities two days in advance, and in it he professed his readiness condemn certain propositions of Theodore of Mopsuestia, but ᴀssed over the other two 'chapters' in silence. It was signed by ᴀteen western bishops.

Justinian now attempted to show that Vigilius had contradicted ᴀnself and had also broken an undertaking to condemn the 'Three ᴀhapters,' which he was alleged to have made shortly after his arrival the capital.[3] He ordered the exclusion of the Pope's name from ᴇ *diptycha* of Constantinople, but insisted at the same time that ᴇ intended to preserve unity with the apostolic see.[4] To this strange ᴀt significant proposition the council assented. In its eighth and ᴀt session it solemnly endorsed the condemnation of the 'Three ᴀhapters,' in accordance with the edict published in 552.[5]

A sentence of exile, already pronounced against numerous ᴀesterns, including the stalwart deacons Rusticus and Liberatus, ᴀw hung over Vigilius himself. Some compromise seemed inevitable. ᴀ a letter to Eutychius the Pope pointed out that though he did not ᴀndemn their persons, he was now willing to add to his previous

[1] Chapman, *op. cit.*, p. 24.
[2] JK 935. *Coll. Avell.*, No. 83. ed. cit., p. 230 f.
[3] It has been suggested that the declaration was a forged one. See Chapman, ᴀ. *cit.*, p. 234, but contrast Caspar, *op. cit.*, vol. ii, pp. 253, 262, and 278.
[4] Mansi, *Concilia*, vol. ix, col. 366.
[5] *Ibid.*, 375 ff.

rejection of the works of Theodore the anti-Cyrilline writings
Theodoret and the letter of Ibas.[1]

The Emperor, however, would be satisfied with nothing short
complete conformity. This was finally given in a subsequent *Co
stitutum* which, while explicitly upholding the authority of Chalced
and of Leo's Tome, and assenting in full to the conciliar decisio
disingenuously explained away the Roman legates' acceptance
Ibas' letter at Chalcedon by arguing that the incriminated docume
was a forgery.[2] The competent Roman deacon Pelagius, who h
openly disowned this abject capitulation to Caesaropapism, was
this time already interned. During his 'protective' custody
employed his leisure in composing *In defensionem trium capitulorun*
a work which shows considerable dependence on Facundus and d
plays little or no concern to gloss over the defects in Vigili
character.

The Pope, by a singular display of ingenuity, had apparently su
ceeded in satisfying Justinian without actually confirming the counc
He took home with him a 'Pragmatic Sanction' containing prescri
tions for the administration of the Italian province.[4] But Rome nev
saw its absentee Pope again alive. He died on the way at Syracu
on June 7, 555, and received burial not in St. Peter's, but in
Silvestro on the *Via Salaria*.

Vigilius is undoubtedly one of those occupants of the pap
throne, who provide a comparatively easy target for censure. Tha
compared with some of the great figures who have held the sar
office, he was weak, impulsive perhaps, possibly even venal and, wh
was more serious, lacking in respect for an undertaking, seer
difficult, if not impossible of denial. But there are other aspects of h
character which ought not to be overlooked. Faced with the choi
between imperial adulation in ease and luxury, no doubt a conside
able temptation to one like himself, a man of advanced age a
wracked by the chronic assaults of a painful infirmity, and, on t
other hand, the interests and reputation of his see, not to menti

---

[1] JK 936, only preserved in a Greek version.

[2] JK 937. Schwartz, *op. cit.* Tom. IV, vol. ii, p. 138 ff. It is clear from Pelagi
In defensione trium cap. 5. ed. Devreesse, in *Studi e testi*, vol. lvii, 1932, p. 55, that
one of Vigilius' deacons at the time of the council, regarded the idea as false a
absurd.

[3] See note above.

[4] *Corp. iur. civ., Nov.* ed. Kroll, G., 1880, vol. iii, app. vii, pp. 799 ff.

e welfare of the Church as a whole and the inviolability of the
:crees of Chalcedon, at the cost of untold suffering, physical and
ental alike, he deliberately put the latter in the first place. Soon
ter the premature and impulsive expression of opinion contained
his early *Judicatum*, he must have appreciated that if Justinian were
lowed to pursue his programme without the salutary check pro-
ded by well-informed criticism, the only result must be not the
conciliation of heresy, as the Emperor appeared to suppose, but a
:w schism. His expectation, as we shall see, was more than justified
₇ the event. If in the end he gave his allegiance to the imperial
plicy, it must have been because he believed that further resistance
ould only harm his friends. Had he considered only himself, he
uld have easily obtained his release at a much earlier stage in the
ntroversy.

Justinian I has rightly earned the gratitude of posterity for his
gacy in the sphere of jurisprudence and for his share in providing
r the wonder and inspiration of future generations one of the
andest monuments of the Byzantine age. His purely political aims
d achievements fall outside the scope of our discussion, though we
ust not fail to give due credit to his ideal of restoration of real unity
the Empire, even by force of arms, and to the remarkable military
ccess of his western campaigns, which his less gifted successors
ere unwilling or else unable to exploit. In his ecclesiastical policy
seems possible to trace two phases. There is an earlier one belong-
g to the reign of his uncle and to the opening years of his own
rincipate marked by a more generous and tolerant outlook, which
aped its reward in the happy relations between East and West
nder Popes Hormisdas, John II and particularly Agapetus, and
ilminated in the harmonious issue of the synod of 536. After this
pint we begin to trace signs of a progressive deterioration, and it
noteworthy that they coincide with indications of an ever-increasing
iterference in ecclesiastical affairs of the ex-ballet dancer, the
mpress Theodora. It is perhaps on her more than any other that
ie real responsibility for the perpetuation of the eastern schisms
iust lie. Unhappily her evil influence on her husband outlived her
ears, and at the last Justinian the 'apthartodocetic' Monophysite
:emed little more than a monstrous reincarnation of her cruel and
nperious spirit.

Few Popes have ever ascended the throne of St. Peter in less

enviable circumstances than Pelagius I, who had found hims(
constrained to procure his preferment at the price of an acknowled
ment of the recent council. It is easy, probably too easy, to accu
him of an ambitious venality, or even of a wholly unprincipled chan
of mind. Yet it is hard not to feel some suspicion regarding the puri
of his motives in making so startling a change of front. His pontifica
is marked by the beginning of a tradition, in virtue of which eve
Pope as a condition of the confirmation of his election by t
Emperor or his representative at Ravenna, was compelled to subn
to the humiliation of presenting a formal profession of faith.[1] A
it is not without significance that this odious reminder of form
subservience to imperial control was first contemptuously cast asi
by that stalwart custodian of the Church's spiritual primacy Grego
VII, though the eastern Emperor's claim to a right of confirmati
had been disowned some three centuries before.[2]

In his declaration of faith Pelagius took up afresh the attitude
Vigilius in his earlier *Constitutum*, and affirmed the essential orth
doxy of Theodoret and Ibas. But this by no means sufficed to disp
very deep anxiety and resentment, signs of which were everywhe
apparent in the West, not only in Africa, but in north Italy and ev
within the area of his own metropolitan jurisdiction. In Ravenna h
name was being omitted from the *diptycha*, and Paulinus of Aquile
felt strong enough in his resistance to assume on his own authori
the title of patriarch. The weakness of the Pope's position, even
relation to the Frankish kingdom, was betrayed further by h
compliance with the request of Childebert I to submit a professi
of faith.[3]

The reigns of John III (561–574) and of Benedict I (575–579) a
among those of which history has almost the least to tell us in t
whole course of the papal succession. The latter is only remarkal
for its coincidence with the beginning of the Lombardic invasion, o
of those periodical incursions of Germanic hordes into the Itali
peninsula, which continuing at varying intervals down to our ov
time, have left such a deep impression on European history and n
least on the character of the Papacy itself.

---

[1] JK 938. *M.G.H. Epp.* vol. iii, p. 81, No. 56.
[2] See below, p. 372.
[3] JK 942. *M.G.H. Epp.* vol. iii, p. 70, No. 48.

XIII

Before summarizing the pontificates of Pelagius II and Gregory I, ~~~ich will conclude this part of our subject by bringing us to the ~ry threshold of the mediaeval Papacy, it will help us better to ~preciate the position of the Roman see in its relation to the Church ~nerally, more particularly to the eastern churches, if we turn back ~ notice the almost indescribable humiliations of which the former ~pital of the Empire had recently been the victim.

If Justinian had been content like his predecessor to treat the ~othic kingdom with watchful though on the whole benevolent con~~eration, it might have been possible for the gradual fusion of ~ermanic and Latin culture in Italy, which under Theodoric had ~ready made considerable headway, to pursue its peaceful course, and ~rhaps in the end to have adapted itself to the new conditions arising ~om the centralization of imperial government at Byzantium. Un~ppily the decline of the Gothic monarchy provided the eastern ~ spot with a most seductive opportunity for putting into execution ~s grandiose plans for imperial restoration. Apart from the tragic ~tcome of this policy in relation to the affairs of the Church, the ~ture of which we have already foreshadowed, its effect in the sphere ~ social economy was more disastrous than can be imagined.

For no less than eighteen years central Italy had been a prey to ~e merciless havoc of war. Four times at least during that period ~ome itself was taken and retaken by besieging armies, Byzantine and ~othic in turn. The aqueducts which provided both the water supply ~d the power of the large number of corn mills in the city, master~eces of the structural skill of the imperial age, lay in ruins. The ~arves of Portus were empty and deserted, on all sides devastation, ~stilence and famine. After the terrible siege of 546, when Totila and ~s Goths had taken captive an almost defenceless city, it was once ~ore the Church, this time in the person of the deacon Pelagius, which ~tervened. Bearing in his hands the sacred volume of the Gospels ~ went to meet the Gothic king on the steps of St. Peter's, and ~torted from him a promise of security for the hapless citizens. ~t the conqueror was not thereby deterred from undertaking an ~most complete evacuation of the desolated city. The historian ~ocopius records that Totila 'took with him the Roman senators, ~d despatched the remaining citizens with their wives and children

to the villages of Campania; not a person was to remain behind
Rome, so that he left it altogether without inhabitant'.[1]

Even if we allow for a measure of rhetorical exaggeration on t
part of the writer, it is evident that in this period the once pro
capital was brought down to the very depths of humiliation. It
easy to understand the urge which many must have felt at suck
time to escape from the miseries of their temporal condition, and
give themselves up to a life such as the rule of the great Bened
seemed to promise, where the worldly anxieties of this life would
transcended by the spiritual consolations of the monastic ide
Moreover the prevalence of these conditions helps to provi
explanation of that strain of self-mortification and repression whi
so evidently forms part of the attitude towards life of Gregory
in some respects a unique figure among the holders of the pa
office, but who is nothing if not a man of his own time.

It is important that we should bear in mind the complete loss
civil importance by the Eternal City in connexion with the theory tl
the Papacy owed its ecclesiastical pre-eminence largely, if not whol
to Rome's secular greatness. Can it be wholly without significan
that even when that greatness had diminished to vanishing point, i
the West only but the East as well, in spite of the tyranny of Caesa
papism, continued to regard 'the Roman Pope' not merely as t
'first of all bishops',[2] but as in some sense indispensable to the mai
tenance of the Church's stability in doctrine and discipline?

Gregory I, the scion of a noble Roman family, began to play
prominent part on the stage of history in the important admin
strative office of *praefectus urbi*. With his extensive patrimony
not only founded six monastic houses on his paternal estates
Sicily, but actually made one out of the palace in Rome which he h
inherited. Ordained deacon and given charge of one of the ci
regions under Benedict I, or possibly under his successor Pelagius
he was quickly promoted to the responsible position of pap
apocrisiary in Constantinople.[3]

With the invasion of the Lombards social and economic conditio
in Italy reached their lowest ebb. So general was the famine in Ror
that even Benedict I succumbed to its effects. Pelagius II, co

---

[1] *De bello Goth.*, 3, 22. ed. Teubner, p. 397 f.
[2] Justinian, *Nov.* 131, 2. *Corp. iur. civ.* ed. Kroll, 9, vol. iii, p. 655.
[3] JE 1368.

:rated without waiting for the customary imperial confirmation,
once besought Childebert II of Austrasia and the Emperor
berius II to deliver Italy from the invader.[1] Neither Franks nor
zantines were able to win a decisive victory, and in the end the
arch of Ravenna, Smaragdus, was constrained to agree to an
nistice, thus leaving the country, in an unhappy state of political
tability.

That relations between Gregory as papal apocrisiary and the new
triarch of Constantinople John IV, surnamed the 'Faster', were
;hly cordial is shown by their close association in literary work.
e bonds of friendship were even strong enough not to be broken
the controversy which broke out between them soon after
egory's return to Rome, regarding the ascription to the bishop of
nstantinople of the title 'oecumenical patriarch'. This had been
ed by Gregory, orthodox patriarch of Antioch, at a synod before
ich he had been summoned to answer certain charges apparently
mped up by monophysite influence. On Gregory's acquittal the
ta of the synod were forwarded to Rome, presumably to obtain
firmation. Pelagius' indignant reply[2] annulling its proceedings,
the sole ground that a proud and pernicious title had been used,
st have caused considerable surprise, followed by not unjustifiable
entment. Unhappily Pelagius' actual letter has not been preserved,
t we may suppose that his objection was based on the supposition
it πατριάρχα οἰκουμενικὸς was to be rendered *patriarcha univer-
is*. Actually, as we have already seen, the proper rendering of
ουμενικὸς was not *universalis* but *imperialis*, and that the title
d not only been used in all probability by Acacius, but since the
ddle of the fifth century had been applied from time to time also
the Pope.[3]

More serious, however, from the papal standpoint was the con-
uance of the western schism over the 'Three Chapters' controversy.
a letter to Elias of Aquileia, Pelagius, in citing Luke XXII, 31 f.,
fended the Roman primacy of doctrine, and while acknowledging
 'four councils' passed over the fifth in silence.[4] A carefully

To be inferred from a letter addressed to Aunachar, bishop of Auxerre. JE
8. *M.G.H. Epp.* vol. iii, p. 448, No. 9.
Mentioned in a letter of Gregory I, JE 1683.
See above, p. 315.
JK 1054. Schwartz, *op. cit.*, Tom. IV, vol. ii, p. 105 ff. *M.G.H. Epp.* vol. ii,
. iii, p. 442 f.

documented reply from the 'schismatics' evoked a more outspok
declaration insisting that the 'fathers' had only confirmed t
dogmatic sessions of Chalcedon, i.e. up to the sixth inclusive, a
that their confirmation had not applied to the later sessions in whi
the cases of Theodore, Theodoret and Ibas had been discussed.
conclusion he quoted the 'Primacy' text of Cyprian's *De Unitate*, 1
which his letter provides our earliest authority.[1] His third letter d
plays a significant change of tone. It strikes a note of gentle p
suasiveness and of friendly discussion, one not always prominent
episcopal argument with opponents. 'Holy Church attaches m
value to the goodness of faithful hearts than to the strict use of word
'It is the content rather than the words which matters'. There can
little doubt that here is the hand of Gregory.[2]

Pelagius died of the plague in February, 590, and it seems that t
delay in Gregory's consecration till the following September was d
solely to his refusal to accept office without first obtaining imper
approval. It is more than an understatement to say that his pontific
is unique in papal history—to affirm that he is almost the only Po
in the first six centuries whom we feel that we know as a m
as a distinct and very human personality, rather than merely as t
heir of a tradition or the possessor of a privilege, is scarcely
exaggeration. We may hold him narrow in outlook, superfici
credulous, even superstitious, but we can never call him intolera
impatient, overbearing or self-seeking. He can be generous as well
firm, sympathetic while remaining discreet. His style is turg
laboured and often full of affectation, but there is an underlyi
moral sincerity which seems to compensate for the lack of t
terseness and simplicity, that austere economy of language alrea
remarked in more than one of his predecessors.

A few only of his more characteristic acts as Supreme Pontiff c
be noticed. After the failure of Pelagius II to convince the no
Italian bishops and to persuade them to accept the Roman asse
to the fifth council,[3] the Greek exarch entered the lists. Forci
methods against the patriarch Severus and three bishops by comp
ling them to accept communion with John III of Ravenna only m
matters worse.[4] Ultimately their case was referred by the Empe

---

[1] JK 1055. Id., *op. cit., ibid.,* p. 108 ff. See above, p. 161 ff.
[2] JK 1056. Id., *op. cit., ibid.,* p. 112 ff.   [3] See above, p. 355.
[4] The Istrian bishops appealed against the exarch to the Emperor. *M.G*
† .vol. i .p. 17, *Reg.* I, 16 a; Paulus diaconus, *Hist. Lang.* 3, 26. *M.P.L.* 95, 5

aurice to Gregory, and though they declined to acknowledge his
risdiction as being a party to the case, their resistance sensibly
minished.[1] The eventual disappearance of the schism was probably
celerated by their judge's magnanimous patience.

Yet if the Istrian 'schismatics' appeared to prefer imperial to papal
risdiction, the same preference was not invariably shown by the
yrian bishops. In eastern Illyricum the change which had taken
ace in the relations of Church and State was the more evident, since
en as late as the Acacian schism the Illyrian episcopate was by no
ans prepared as a whole to accept the authority of Constantinople,
ether of Emperor or patriarch. By now, however, the vicariate of
essalonica had practically ceased to exist, and it was left to the
man see to deal with the Illyrian churches as best it could. That it
s still possible for the Pope to intervene effectively in Illyrian
airs is proved by his successful protest against an attempt on the
rt of the Emperor Maurice to depose the primate of Prima
stiniana solely on the ground of advanced age. In spite of the
perial intention, the primate remained in the possession of his see
d even outlived his Sovereign.[2] Much the same is true of the case
Adrian of Thebes, whose act in deposing two of his deacons was
first referred by the Emperor to John, metropolitan bishop of
rissa. Adrian himself appealed to Constantinople in his turn and
a hearing of his case, at which the papal apocrisiary was present
an assessor, obtained a reversal of the metropolitan's judgment.
ter, however, an imperial mandate was given to John, primate of
stiniana, to investigate the matter afresh. Finally Adrian appealed
the Roman see. Gregory seems to have examined the matter with
upulous care, and, on the ground that the church of Thebes
s neither a suffragan see of Larissa nor subject to the jurisdiction
Justiniana, rehabilitated Adrian with the provision that any further
resentations against him should be made to the papal apocrisiary.[3]
That the word of the Roman see still counted for much in the East,
spite of the predominant position of the Emperor, is shown by his
cessful advocacy of the claim of the deposed Anastasius to the
of Antioch.[4] To assert a primacy of jurisdiction over the see of

---

See foregoing note. Schwartz, *op. cit.*, Tom. IV, pt. 2, p. 132.
To be inferred from JE 1860–1. *Reg.* XII, 10, 11.
JE 1210–1. *Reg.* III, 6, 7.
M.G.H. Epp. vol. i, p. 335; JE 1355. *Reg.* V, 42. Cf. also JE 1489, *Reg.* VIII, 2.
G.H. Epp. vol. ii, p. 2 ff.

4

Constantinople itself was beset with difficulty. Yet even John
yielded in the matter of an appeal by two of his presbyters to
judgment of the Pope, which Gregory justified on suppose
canonical grounds. It is worth mentioning that the case of one of
presbyters, John of Chalcedon, showed only too clearly the need
an impartial court of appeal, such as ideally the Roman see co
provide, since it turned out that the nature of the heresy of wh
John was accused was imperfectly understood even by his accuser

A more serious clash arose between Gregory and John IV, a
result of the reappearance of the title to which Gregory's predeces
had taken such strong exception, namely, the designation of
Constantinopolitan bishop as 'oecumenical patriarch'.[2] The Po
renewed Pelagius II's protest and insisted that 'all bishops of
Church are as the stars in the firmament, the rain clouds in the
to the Church; whoever exalts himself above them loses the gr
of parity with them and true blessedness'.[3] His letter shows a rema
able blend of winning gentleness and outspoken reproof. Yet und
lying it there was a fixity of purpose which even the Emperor's su
port of his patriarch failed to move. Gregory persisted in saying tha
continued use of the title would disturb the peace of the Chur
and urged that even St. Peter himself was not called the 'univer
Apostle.[4] Even if Chalcedon had applied it to the Roman see,
further use had been made of it in that quarter. With disarm
humility Gregory declared 'Cunctorum sacerdotum servus sum'.[5]

No doubt it may be said that Gregory was incorrect about his fac
more particularly in his assertion that the use of the title was a rec
innovation on the part of its present holder; in any case the patriar
of Constantinople had not applied it to himself, but had mer
been so designated in certain synodical Acta.

The controversy did not cease with John's death. Gregory repea
his protest to the new patriarch Cyriacus, who reacted less favoural
than his predecessor to Gregory's rebukes, with the result that
Pope felt obliged to instruct his apocrisiary to refuse the patriarc
communion.[6] Yet not only did the see of Constantinople retain
title, but even Gregory suffered the outrage of having it applied
himself by Eulogius of Alexandria.[7] Hence it could have been lit

---

[1] JE 1394, 5.
[2] See above, p. 355.
[3] JE 1357. Reg. V, 44.
[4] JE 1360, Reg. V, 37.
[5] Ibid.
[6] JE 1476, Reg. VII, 30.
[7] JE 1518, Reg. VIII, 29.

isfaction to the Pope to read in an edict of the Emperor Phocas,
it the see of the Apostle Peter was the ' head of all the Churches',
ile the Constantinopolitan Church described itself as the ' first
all the churches'.[1] Such an outcome of the 'battle of the title'
ild at best be described as 'pyrrhic'. Yet by a strange paradox
)ther Gregory would one day reverse the attitude of his humbler
edecessor by claiming its exclusive application to the Roman see.
His memory is not undeserving of the special honour which has
en paid to it in our country. In his mission to the Anglo-Saxons
see the true pastor at work, unhindered by the limitations imposed
on him by the Byzantine yoke, or by the constraints arising from
hostility of the Lombardic invaders and the self-possession of the
inkish kingdom. Gregory himself records that he gave instructions
Angle boys of sixteen to eighteen to be bought in Gaul with the
inkish money received from papal estates there, and for them to be
ined in monasteries for the worship of God.[2] The Anglo-Saxon
ssion he made his personal care. Yet if conversion of the heathen
glish was his primary object, he certainly did not neglect the duty
rousing the zeal of the neighbouring bishops. Moreover, an
lirect result of the Gregorian plan was to create an important
:post of papal influence on the very flank of the Germanic world
1 thus in some degree to counterbalance the eccentric tendencies
Irish-Scottish Christianity.

To say as Gibbon has done that 'the conquest of Britain reflects
s glory on the name of Caesar than on that of Gregory the First'[3]
y well be true. No doubt like Caesar's, Gregory's 'conquest' was
y limited in extent. Nevertheless it is to him that at least the
dit for taking the initiative must be given. That he deserves to be
led the 'Apostle of the English' may be fittingly acknowledged by
Church of England, which affirms her primate to be the successor
St. Augustine; that he merits his place among the canonized Saints
the Catholic Church will not be denied by those who recognize in
life the genuine tokens of a *Servus Servorum Dei*, reflecting,
haps, more clearly than any other of the Popes, the traits of Him
o said : *Quicumque voluerit in vobis primus esse, erit omnium servus.*

[1] *Liber Pont.* ed. cit., vol. i, p. 316.
[2] JE 1386.
[3] Ed. cit. (1929), vol. v, p. 38.

VI

The Papacy and Mediaeval Christendom

Tu regere imperio populos, Romane, memento
(Hae tibi erunt artes), pacisque imponere morem,
Parcere subjectis et debellare superbos. *Aeneid*, vi, 851.

Luke XXII, 36, 38. 'Then said Jesus unto them, But now, he t[
hath a purse let him take it, and likewise his scrip: and he that ha
no sword, let him sell his garment and buy one . . . And they sa
Lord, behold here are two swords. And he said unto them, It
enough'.

When we speak of a thing as 'changing', we mean that it is in
process of acquiring new or additional qualities or characteristi
and perhaps also of losing some at least of those which it forme
possessed. No doubt there is a sense in which this definition n
apply to the whole history of the Papacy, considered as the l
history of an 'organism'. At one period there is gain, at another lc
Yet in the period which we have examined hitherto 'change' l
been almost entirely in the direction of gain. It may appear to son
as we have suggested, that the source of this gain is to be found i
growing realization on the part of the Church as a whole of the r
implications of what appears to have been part of its original traditi
crystallized in the Dominical *logia* addressed to St. Peter, and i
simply in some factor, in itself external to Christianity, such as
civil grandeur of the city of Rome in relation to the ancient wo1
Yet whether this be true or not, it remains a fact that in spite of
diminution of the city's purely secular importance and the transferen
of the capital of imperial administration to the East, the Roman
continues to a greater or less extent to be the centre of reference, ev
when the influence of Caesaropapism, whether in its eastern or
western form, was at its height.

Yet it can scarcely be denied that gain in spiritual authority a
in prestige was accompanied by some degree of loss, for as we lc
back to the pontificate of Vigilius and compare it with that
Innocent I or Leo the Great, it is difficult not to feel that a cert
diminution in moral stature has taken place. On the other ha1
comparisons of this sort are so evidently subject to the limitatic

posed by the nature and source of the historical evidence at our
posal, at best fragmentary and usually far from impartial, that to
ne it might seem best to refrain from anything of the nature of a
cisive judgment in the matter.

So to revert to our definition, 'change', if it is not to be 'trans-
itation', must not affect essential identity. *Plus ça change, plus c'est
même chose*. Of no historical 'phenomenon' is this more true than
the Papacy. That there has been 'change' even in the course of the
riod which has already been under review is of course undeniable.
some sense it may be said to have been inevitable, since 'change' is
every living organism, such as the Church and the Papacy itself,
ecessary and ineluctable condition of remaining alive. Yet what
rely secular institution can show more unmistakable proofs of an
ntity, not only essential but even in a considerable measure
cidental' as well, at least within the limits of the first six centuries?
In fact it might almost be said that it is only when we reach the
ntificate of Gregory I that the outlook of the Roman see begins
show clear signs of having been affected by the changes in its
litical environment which had been taking place during the two
vious centuries.

In no respect is the change more evident than in the relations of
Papacy with the Empire. In consequence of the concentration of
perial authority and administration at Byzantium, and the ever
sent menace of Lombardic invasion and aggression, it was in-
table that to a steadily increasing extent the Popes would look to
'Roman Emperor' for moral and even material support, and
uld constantly find themselves obliged to make concessions to
esaropapism, such as, given a greater measure of independence,
y would almost certainly have refused. What is much more
narkable is that the princes and patriarchs of the East should have
itinued to feel it to be in any way worth while to consult, still less
occasion to defer to the opinions and judgments of the bishop
what had by now become a third-rate plague-infested provincial
vn.

Thus the importance attached by so autocratic a sovereign as
tinian I to success in obtaining a decision in support of his doc-
al policy from the humiliated Vigilius seems quite unintelligible,
t does not mean that even sixth-century Caesaropapism itself felt
ble to act in the teeth of the moral opposition of the Papacy. It

will be seen that what appears to be true of the sixth century contint
to hold good of its two immediate successors, and that in the mor
thelete and iconoclastic controversies which now claim our attentic
a situation in many respects closely analogous to the one alrea
described does not cease to prevail.

I

The efforts made by Justinian I and his predecessors to rest
ecclesiastical unity in the East by making the greatest possible cc
cessions to monophysite susceptibilities were continued under
successors with varying degrees of enthusiasm, but with little if a
greater success. It might even be said that Chalcedonian orthodc
was in worse case than ever, for by the time Heraclius ascended 1
Byzantine throne, none of the great sees, possession of which h
been hitherto contested by the orthodox against the Monophysit
had even an orthodox claimant. Yet the westward and southw:
progress of the Persians, together with the constant menace of 1
Slavs and Avars to the northern and western frontiers of the shrunk
Byzantine Empire, supplied an overwhelmingly strong argument
favour of arriving at the earliest possible solution of those theologi
differences which had already weakened imperial unity for m
than a century and a half.

The first attempt[1] to reach unanimity with the less recalcitrant d
sidents was made by means of a definition to the effect that the Gc
head and Manhood in Christ shared a single 'mode of activi
($\dot{\epsilon}\nu\acute{\epsilon}\rho\gamma\epsilon\iota\alpha$). It failed mainly owing to the opposition of Sophronius
Jerusalem, who insisted that only the acknowledgment of two 'moc
of activity' acting in co-operation could possibly be consistent w
loyalty to Chalcedon. By this time, however, its author Sergius
Constantinople had reached the conclusion that the dangers involv
in either expression, the former seeming to do violence to the doctri
of the Two Natures, the latter to involve belief in two faculties
volition, rendered it necessary to avoid both alike and to insist or
on the unity of the Agent. Heraclius fell in with the suggestion b
warned by the unfortunate experience of Zeno in the promulgati
of the *Henoticon*, evidently hesitated to act decisively in the mat
without previous consultation of the Roman see.

[1] Grumel, *op. cit.*, No. 285.

The reply of Pope Honorius I[1] came to achieve an unenviable notoriety in later history, in virtue of the support which it was believed by Easterns and others to lend to the doctrine of a 'single will' in the Incarnate Christ. It is probable, however, that the writer of the letter, in which the Pope's opinion was expressed, who later succeeded Honorius as John IV, was quite unaware of the true nature of the problem which faced the Emperor and his patriarch, and was concerned only to emphasize the absolute sinlessness of our Lord's human life.[2] Hence, while he readily agreed that all definitions about 'modes of activity' were vain and lacked support of scriptural or synodical authority, he was equally insistent that the predication of Christ Incarnate with more than one purpose was out of the question, or the simple reason that His human nature was wholly immune from sin.

A little reflection might have shown the Easterns that Honorius (or rather his secretary) had touched upon a far more subtle aspect of the problem than those which they themselves appear to have considered. All that mattered to them was that a doctrine of 'one power of volition' in Christ could now be published to the Empire as possessing the *imprimatur* of the Roman see. Even if they observed that the Pope was actually discussing a psychological problem, while they themselves were concerned with metaphysics, they preferred to ignore the difference.

If Honorius was to blame, it was not so much for his supposed 'monotheletism', which stated no more than was held by all who believed in the reality of our Lord's human experience, but rather for his too ready acquiescence in the dogmatic prompting of Sergius and for his failure to examine the matter with sufficient thoroughness. In fact, it was on the latter ground that he was censured by his successor Leo II, when the new Pope justified Honorius' condemnation together with that of other Easterns by saying, 'So far from quenching the flames of heretical doctrine, as befitted apostolic authority, he actually fed them by sheer negligence'.[3]

The interval between the death of Honorius and the final proscription of his memory by the sixth oecumenical council was

---

[1] JE 2018.
[2] Cf. Maximus Conf. *Disput. c. Pyrrho. M.P.G.* 91, 327 ff.
[3] JE 2119. Note, however, that in JE 2120 he wrote 'qui immaculatam apostolicae traditionis regulam, quam a praedecessoribus suis accepit, maculari consit'.

marked by an unmistakable reaction on the part of the Roman se
against an attitude of too ready compliance with the outlook c
Constantinople. In the conduct of Pope Martin I, however, doctrin;
opposition was combined with political revolt. His consecratio
without awaiting the customary imperial confirmation[1] and th
immediate summoning of a council to meet at the Lateran o
October 5, 649, unite to give the impression that the Roman se
was resolved to declare open war on eastern attempts at dogmati
compromise. Meanwhile, at Constantinople, the new definition sup
ported by the *Ecthesis* of Heraclius and the *Type* of Constans II wa
being actively promoted by a succession of monothelete patriarch;
who, while professing adherence to the doctrine of Honorius, re
mained indifferent to the changed attitude of his successors. Th
Type was in fact an edict strictly on the Theodosian model, whic
aimed at procuring conformity by prescribing severe penalties fc
dissent. It is a significant indication of a new attitude of independenc
on the part of the Roman see that the Lateran council just mentione
is the first of which the minutes have been recorded in full both i
Latin and Greek, and of which the *Acta* include a collection c
relevant authorities, thus following the normal model of the record
of an oecumenical council.[2] It is reasonably certain that the literar
ability and familiarity with the methods of synodical procedure o
the part of those Greek monks who, including Maximus the Confesso
happened to be in Rome at the time, was chiefly responsible for thi
interesting departure. Yet we should miss the real significance c
this document, were we not to recognize in it the rising of the day
star heralding the complete deliverance of the Papacy from it
almost self-imposed thraldom to the ecclesiastical suzerainty c
Constantinople.

Pope Martin's triumph, if spectacular, was at best short livec
Convicted, not perhaps without some show of justice, of treasonabl
relations with a western usurper named Olympius, and subjected t
untold humiliations and sufferings in Constantinopolitan dungeons
he died almost forgotten in exile. We need not seriously dispute hi
title to a martyr's crown, though it is doubtful whether even Con
stans II would have felt justified in inflicting on his unhappy victir

---

[1] Caspar, *op. cit.*, vol. ii, p. 554. It was perhaps due in part to the coincidenc
that no exarch was in residence at Ravenna at the time.

[2] Mansi, *Concilia*, vol. x, col. 863 ff.

:h a refinement of vengeance if he had not been convinced, even
slender evidence, of the Pope's implication in a conspiracy against
throne. Maximus the Confessor was equally subjected to rigorous
mination, but was convicted of nothing more serious than refusal
assent to the dogmatic position of the *Type*, and thus of unwilling-
s to lend his hand to a doctrinal compromise.

It is not till we reach the pontificate of Agatho that we find once
re a personality on the throne of St. Peter possibly worthy to rank
ong the majestic figures of the fifth century. The new Emperor
nstantine IV was evidently convinced that as the conquests of
am had now made the recovery of Egypt and the East an impos-
ility, no obstacle to a full understanding with the Roman see should
permitted to remain. He therefore invited the Pope to send legates
Constantinople with a view to bringing about a complete recon-
ation. Agatho, however, who had evidently profited by the unfor-
ate experience of Vigilius, took steps to assure himself of the
gest possible measure of western support before undertaking
gotiations with the Easterns.[1] No doubt there was more than one
d reason for the Roman see of this time to re-echo the sentiment:

> *timeo Danaos et dona ferentes.*

it was not till the later part of 680 that the Roman legates finally
off. We may regard it as significant of the chastened mood pre-
ling in Constantinople that though the Emperor presided in
rson at the council, which by then had been called into being, the
ates occupied the first place after him. They had brought with them
ters to the eastern Sovereigns of special interest. In them we appear
trace for the first time the setting forth of a new principle of unity
der the changed conditions of a new world, where in the West
lependent Germanic kingdoms had replaced the centralized
ganization of the *Imperium Romanum*, while in the East the
perium itself had shrunk to pathetically insignificant proportions.
re it was declared:

'The Roman church has by God's grace never erred from the
thway of the apostolic *paradosis*, nor has it lapsed into heretical
velties, but from the very beginning of the Christian faith has
eserved unimpaired that which it received from its founders the
inces of the Apostles'.[2]

At a Roman council, March 25, 680. Mansi, *op. cit.*, vol. xi, col. 285 ff. JE 2110.
JE 2109, cf. JE 2110.

The same letter sets forth the orthodox belief in 'two wills', a contrasts in almost Irenaean fashion the variety and inconsistenc heretical teaching. Then cautiously abandoning the independ policy of the 'rebellious' Roman synod of 649, and acting as it wo seem on Sardican principles, it leaves the decision on the treatm to be given to the memory of those Constantinopolitan patriar who had rashly supported Monotheletism to the present impe council.

It is impossible not to notice the striking 'traditionalism' of th documents, which illustrates that strange, almost mystical continu persisting throughout papal history. Even if, when contrasted w the self-confident independence of the Tome of Leo I, they betr alike their indebtedness to Greek theological acuteness, as rep sented by Maximus the Confessor, and their scarcely concea deference to imperial susceptibilities, they deserve attention marking in a sense the dawn of full self-consciousness on the p of the Papacy, as the long night of the 'Byzantine captivity' v giving place to a new daybreak with which it would illumine education of the adolescent nations of Europe.

We need not discuss further the reasons which led to the inclus of the name of Pope Honorius among the list of supporters Monotheletism condemned by the council, though in view of wl has already been said we may feel that there is reason to doubt justice. It must, however, be mentioned that in its final session, o which the Emperor presided in person, the council formally su mitted Agatho's letter to the signature of all present, to which Emperor solemnly appended his own. Then in an effusive panegy the council declared:

'On our side fought the majestic prince of the Apostles, for his ty and successor in his see anointed us and revealed to us the myst of God's providence. Rome, the ancient city, presented to th O Emperor, a confession of faith written by the hand of God, a so brought to us from the West the bright daylight of true doctri Here were but ink and paper, yet the voice of Agatho was the voice Peter'.[1]

At first sight such an acclamation might appear to denote a sig triumph for the Roman primacy of doctrine. But there is another si to the picture. First, we must not forget that, such as it was, t

[1] Mansi, *op. cit.*, vol. xi, col. 657 ff.

iumph had been bought at an alarmingly high price, that is to say, ^thing less than assent by future popes to the condemnation of a ^oman bishop on the express ground of unorthodoxy. It is probable ^at hesitation on the part of the clergy of the Roman church to ^cept such a bargain goes far to account for the unconscionable ^lay of eighteen months which ensued after the death of Agatho, ^fore it was found possible to procure a suitably compliant candidate ^r the vacant see. That Leo II had spent his earlier ministry in the ^rvice of the Sicilian church, and appears to have had no previous ^nnexion with Rome, makes it easier to explain how he came to ^nd his approval to an act which in the eyes of a native Roman must ^ve seemed a sad but inevitable humiliation.[1]

But such was the generally supine attitude of the Roman church in ^e latter half of the seventh century towards the Empire that, unlike ^s predecessor, the sixth oecumenical council evoked no audible ^rotest. Thus in the original formulae of the *Liber Diurnus*, compiled, ^ it seems, for the instruction of junior clerks in the papal chancery, ^e new council takes its place side by side with Nicaea, Constanti-^ople and the rest. What is more, in the very formulae in which the ^opes-elect were required to profess their orthodoxy, both before ^d after consecration, a custom which none of them before Gregory ^II had the wit or perhaps the courage to abolish, the name of ^onorius finds a dishonourable place side by side with the notorious ^eresiarchs of the East.[2]

Among the measures taken by the Emperor Justinian II for the ^feguarding of the Church, of whose faith he declared himself to be ^e divinely appointed protector, an important place is to be assigned ^ the collection of one hundred and two canons issued by the ^uini-sext council of 692. The purpose of the collection was to lend ^ecumenical sanction to the local discipline of the Constantinopolitan ^hurch and to render it the norm for the rest of the Empire. Not only ^as express recognition given to those canons of earlier councils, ^cluding the famous twenty-eighth canon of Chalcedon, which, as ^e have seen, had assigned peculiar privileges to the Constanti-^opolitan see and in theory had always been repudiated at Rome, ^ut in one case, namely the cohabitation of deacons and presbyters

---

[1] Caspar, *op. cit.*, vol. ii, p. 610.
[2] *Liber Diurnus*. ed. Sickel, Th. v., 1889, *Form.* 84, p. 100. See Caspar, *op. cit.*, ^l. ii, pp. 619 and 782 ff.

with their wives, the new legislation explicitly sanctioned wh western Canon Law had forbidden.[1]

While Pope Sergius I openly declared the new Canon La invalid,[2] his successor John VII adopted a less hostile attitud Whether Constantine I, the last of the Popes to make that journey the eastern capital which had already proved so tragic for thr of his predecessors, actually persuaded the Emperor not to insist c its recognition in the West remains obscure. All we know certain is that he had the satisfaction of receiving the submission of Constantinopolitan patriarch, who as a matter of expediency ha temporarily compromised himself with a monothelete reaction.

II

From now on, however, we begin to notice marks of increasin papal independence. The growth of an embryonic Italian nationalism which we have already observed under Theodoric the Great, thoug temporarily checked by a revival of imperialism under Justinian and by the presence of the Lombardic menace, became at th stage more pronounced, and was directly or indirectly responsible f preventing Pope Sergius I and his successor from meeting at th hands of the Byzantine Emperor a fate similar to that which ha overtaken Martin I. The period of violence and revolution Constantinople which followed the assassination of Justinian further weakened the loyalty of Italy towards the Byzantine gover ment, and with the almost contemporary elevation of Leo III the principate and of Gregory II to the Papacy, it may be said that new era in the history of both institutions had begun.

For the first time, as we learn from the *Liber Pontificalis*,[3] a Pop had been found who was courageous enough firmly to oppose th payment of taxes by that area of the imperial domains in centr Italy now known as the Roman duchy, and it is clear that resistanc of this kind was only possible because Lombards and Romans wer learning to make common cause against the imperial administratior Yet to suppose that Gregory II deliberately fostered an Italia

---

[1] *Conc. Quinisext.* Canon 13. Cf. *Conc. Agath.* (506), Canon 9. Kirch, *Enc Fontium*, Nos. 963 ff., 1093.
[2] *Liber Pont.* ed. cit., vol. i, p. 372.
[3] Ed. cit., p. 403.

evolution is to disregard the clear evidence that he was still prepared
to do all that lay in his power to maintain the imperial connexion.

The inherent traditionalism of the Papacy always had been and
was to remain a serious obstacle to the acquisition of a realistic
political outlook. We have already observed that so astute a diplomatist as Leo I showed little awareness of the signs of imminent
dissolution of the *Imperium Romanum* as it had existed for the past
four and a half centuries. It is therefore scarcely surprising that
Gregory II, in spite of the manifest indications of change and
evolution on all sides, not least in Italy itself, gives the impression
that to him the maintenance of the fiction of imperial unity was of
paramount importance, while the possibility of the Papacy adapting
its policy to the evident march of events does not seem to have entered
into his calculations.

Yet side by side with an apparent lack of realism, Gregory, and
to a still greater extent his immediate successors, showed themselves
by no means incapable of making the best use of their opportunities
in the interests of freeing the Roman church from its galling subjection to Constantinople. The process of deliverance was, however,
somewhat hastened on the imperial side by the religious and social
policy of the Emperor Leo III. Known generally as the iconoclastic
controversy, the real character of the struggle, to which the new
policy gave rise, has been very variously interpreted. To call it a
movement of oppression of the artisan and unlettered classes by the
aristocratic and educated sections of opinion in the Empire, is to
ignore its religious character, which, if not essential, was at least
accidental. On the other hand, though the imperial prohibitions of
image worship cut at the very roots of popular religious practice, the
extent to which they were actually directed against those who stood
to gain most from the perpetuation of the existing state of affairs,
namely the monastic element, must not be left out of account. That
the deliberate purpose of the iconoclastic measures was to meet the
susceptibilities of Judaism and Islam finds few modern supporters;
instead, preference is more usually shown for a view which regards
them as a reaction of the Asiatic spirit against Hellenic dominance in
Eastern religion, life and culture. Finally, and perhaps chief in
importance, account must be taken of the possibility that Iconoclasm
was traceable to monophysite influence. Those to whom the reality
of our Lord's manhood was meaningless, would naturally be ex-

pected to disapprove of what to them seemed to aim at expressing t
incomprehensible Godhead in the finite terms of a material imag
Whichever of these theories best meets the evidence, it is necessai
to distinguish two distinct phases in the conflict: an earlier stage,
which the government was content to order the concealment
removal of images and seems to have deliberately avoided viole:
measures against its opponents; and a later one, in which the destru
tion and profanation of objects of religious and artistic value,
addition to the active persecution of monks and other advocates
image worship, undeniably played a considerable part. There is i
occasion here to describe either of these phases in detail. In fact, tl
whole controversy was to so great an extent a domestic affair of tl
church of Constantinople and its immediate dependencies, that apa
from the importance of its influence on the relation of the Papac
not only with the eastern church but with the State in East and We
alike, it would scarcely have demanded notice.

The first imperial edict against the images issued in 726 arrive
in Italy the following year. Its publication was followed by a remar
able uprising of Italian sentiment. On all sides there were revol
followed by the murder or expulsion of imperial officials. It is pr
bable that but for the pacific intervention of Gregory II, wh
acquired possession of the city of Sutri as a gift to the Roman s
by the king of the Lombards, either in reward for his pains, or mo:
likely as a bribe for his support, an open breach with the Empi
would have followed on the spot.[1] It may be remarked with referenc
to the seemingly insignificant gift just mentioned that, contraste
with the spectacular inauguration described by the imaginative ski
of pseudo-historians, the historical beginning of the Temporal Powe
looks singularly unromantic and commonplace.[2]

The day of Byzantine rule in central and north-eastern Italy wa
now drawing to a close, and under Gregory's successor, the third (
that name, a Roman council explicitly condemned the imperi:
iconoclastic policy.[3] The attitude of the new Gregory was, in fac

[1] It may be remarked that Caspar, E., in 'Gregor II und der Bilderstreit' i
Zeitschr. f. KG. vol. lii, 1933, p. 66 ff., is a recent advocate of the genuineness
Gregory's letters JE 2180, 2181, in their original uninterpolated form.

[2] The next stage was the acquisition by the Roman see of the Roman 'ducatus
See Caspar, op. cit., vol. ii, p. 727 f.

[3] Lib. pont. ed. cit., vol. i, p. 416. Note the mention of 'nobilibus etiam cor
sulibus et reliquis Christianis plebibus' as present.

ything but conciliatory, so much so that he marked his growing dependence of imperial authority, which in its turn went so far to assign southern Italy, Sicily and Illyria to the Constantinopolitan patriatchate, by being the first Pope to assert sovereign ghts by the issue of a papal coinage.[1]

It seemed for the moment, however, that with the renaissance of e Lombardic kingdom under its great ruler Luitprand, that the pacy had after all only exchanged king Log for king Stork. By ngular astuteness the last Greek Pope Zacharias succeeded in taining confirmation of Roman authority over a large area in ntral Italy and the restoration of the Church's patrimony in the rth. It was a sign, however, that traces of the subordination of the pacy to the imperial government at Constantinople still remained, at Pope Stephen II[2] felt obliged to undertake the task of ambassdor on behalf of the Byzantine Emperor Constantine V to the ankish court. Yet actually it was a happy misfortune. The king who ceived him was Pepin I, to be distinguished from his grandfather, pin of Heristal, and his great-grandfather, Pepin of Landen, neither whom was actually king of the Franks. Not many years previously had received a favourable reply from Zacharias on the rightfulness a revolutionary proposal, namely, to depose his legitimate sovereign ilderic III and reign in his stead. Pepin had profited by the cision. Now he assured Stephen that all the Pope's wishes would performed, and in return received the crown of France at the pe's hands. Then at the diet of Quierzy by the historic (and storical) donation of Pepin the foundation of the Temporal Power s decisively laid,[3] and after the defeat of Aistulf the Lombard by e arms of the Franks, Stephen II reigned as a sovereign prince. he political connexion between Rome and Byzantium was now oken for ever, and it was no doubt only as a result of the Emperor's timate acquiescence in a *fait accompli* that political severance did t lead to a lasting ecclesiastical schism at the same time.

[1] Martin, E. J., *History of the Iconoclastic Controversy*, p. 78, n. 2, who points out at the coinage in question consisted of square bronze *tesserae*, and adds that if se were more properly tokens, the earliest papal coins are the silver *denarii* of rian I.

[2] 'Confusion in the numbering of the Stephens is explained by the fact that a phen who was elected to succeed Zacharias died before his consecration'. artin, *op. cit.*, p. 79, n. 1. Cf. Jaffé, *Regesta*, vol. i, p. 270.

[3] See *C.M.H.* vol. ii, p. 588, where the possibility that the document is a forgery examined and rejected.

Zacharias had been the last Pope to send off the customary let
announcing his election to the Byzantine Emperor (Constantine
and to the Constantinopolitan patriarch.[1] Hence there could be
more significant indication of the changed conditions than that t
election of Stephen III's successor Paul I was announced not
Constantine but to Pepin. Meanwhile the attack on the images a
their advocates at Constantinople had been proceeding with spa
modic enthusiasm, roughly in proportion to the extent of imper
support. In the end, to set the seal of ecclesiastical approval on
victory over the opponents of Iconoclasm, the Emperor summon
an ecclesiastical assembly intended to be an 'oecumenical' counci
But so far as our evidence goes, no invitations were sent either to t
Pope or to any of the four other patriarchs (the see of Constantinop
was in any case vacant).[4] Nevertheless a moderate Iconoclasm w
endorsed as the official policy. Following the council, Constanti
now realized that if his plans were to succeed, the monasteries, whi
had from the first been the chief centre of resistance, must be fina
rooted out. Among the victims of this phase of the struggle was t
patriarch Constantine, though it is likely that his unhappy fate w
due less to his enthusiasm for images than to his open detestation
the Emperor's inhumane conduct.[5]

It was, however, not till 769, in the year following the election
Stephen III and the death of Pepin, that the image controver
was once more brought formally to the notice of the Roman churc
At a Roman synod held in that year,[6] remarkable for the fact that
included representatives of the Frankish church, a conservati
decision in favour of the veneration of images was reached, whi
did little more than endorse the standpoint adopted by the previo
synod on this question thirty-eight years before.[7]

Following the rather dingy record of the mid-eighth centu
pontificates, the rule of Adrian I, elected soon after Charles (usua
known as Charlemagne) had become sovereign of the whole of h

[1] *Lib. pont.* vol. i, p. 432. Cf. JE 2448.
[2] JE 2336. It is noteworthy that mention of 'cardinals' first appears in the *Lib
pontificalis* of this time.
[3] Martin, *op. cit.*, p. 45 ff. It lasted from February 10 to August 8, 753.
[4] It is sometimes believed that the Pope was summoned, but declined to atten
[5] Martin, *op. cit.*, p. 65. Some allowance for exaggeration of imperial inhumani
by political and ecclesiastical opponents ought perhaps to be made.
[6] Id., *op. cit.*, p. 82.
[7] See above, p. 370.

ther's Frankish dominions, shines with a lustre now somewhat
familiar. If it is dim compared with the brilliance of the Inno-
ntian and Leonine reigns, it is at least sufficient to mark him out
a figure of serenity and dignity in a period of Italian history dis-
guished by neither of those qualities. Following the collapse of
e Lombardic kingdom,[1] most cordial relations were established
tween Adrian and Charles, issuing in a renewal by the king of the
onation of Pepin, that is to say, a recognition of papal sovereignty
thin the duchy of Rome and the exarchate of Ravenna. Although
e *Liber Pontificalis* suggests that a large area in northern Italy was
cluded, other contemporary evidence makes this highly impro-
ble.[2] The most likely explanation of its datum is that the author
s confused recognition of sovereignty with restoration of title to
ntifical estates or patrimony. The statement is, however, certainly
t without interest, since it testifies to the existence at this date
a current of ideas favourable to the creation of a document such
was provided in the forged 'Donation of Constantine'. The date
the 'Donation' has been much disputed. Yet to judge from internal
idence it seems unlikely that it was devised after 800 or earlier
an the historical Donation of Pepin. The situation into which it
s most naturally is one in which papal territorial claims are in need
documentary support. That such a need arose in the period
o–790 is beyond doubt, and in consequence that decade or a few
ars earlier or later gives a date to which its composition may be
signed with considerable probability. That its place of origin was
me scarcely admits of serious dispute.[3]

Nevertheless, in spite of Adrian's favourable position in relation
Charles as shown by the confirmation of Pepin's Donation, there
s never any doubt which of the two was actually the master.
owhere is this to be seen more clearly than in the difference between
e respective attitudes of Pope and king towards the second council
Nicaea, at which was decreed the restoration of the images to the
urches and their veneration by the faithful.[4] After the strictly

---

[1] By the abdication of Desiderius in 774. *C.M.H.* vol. ii, p. 702.
[2] *C.M.H. ibid.*, p. 599 f.; Jaffé, *Regesta*, vol. i, p. 291 f.; *D.T.C.* vol. i, col. 448.
[3] For the text, see Mirbt, *Quellen*[5], No. 228. The document is described and its
e discussed in *C.M.H.* vol. ii, p. 586 f., where it is pointed out (p. 590, *note*),
h reference to JE 2325, that 'it is by no means improbable that it was penned by
same hand as the Donation of Constantine'.
[4] Martin, *op. cit.*, p. 89 ff. For the conciliar definition, see p. 103 f.

25

limited success of the iconoclastic policy of Leo III and his s
already mentioned, the inevitable reaction had followed under Ire
and Constantine VI, who in taking measures to undo the work
their predecessors showed marked deference towards the Rom
see. Not only was the Pope invited to send legates to the new coun
which assembled September 24, 787, but on their arrival they we
treated with signs of the utmost respect and seem actually to ha
presided at the council.[1] A possible cause of disharmony betwe
the Papacy and the East, namely the mention of the standing pa
grievance about the use by the bishop of Constantinople of the ti
'oecumenical patriarch', was cleverly evaded by the simple expedi
of omitting the offending passage from Pope Adrian's letter[2] in t
course of its public recital. The council's decisions, according to
tradition now generally normative in the East, amounted to little mo
than a formal endorsement of the current imperial policy, which
this occasion happened to coincide with the papal attitude. Howev
signs were not lacking of a growing impatience on the part of cert
sections of the eastern church, particularly among the monks,
represented by Plato of Sakkudium and Theodore of Studium,
wards the oppressive dominance of the State. We must theref
take note of the revival of a more independent outlook and o
movement which, turning to the Papacy for support, was to exerc
considerable influence in the next generation.[3]

The Latin translation of the conciliar resolutions, brought b
by the Roman legates and presently forwarded to Charles, was unf
tunate in its choice of words. No care, for example, appears to h
been taken to avoid the undesirable implications of *adoratio* a
rendering of προσκύνησις (reverential salutation), nor to make
clear that this was distinct from the λατρεία (worship) paid so
to God and to Him alone. As a result, in spite of the papal appro
given to the document, Charles and his Franks, pardonably unp
pared for such subtle distinctions, drew up a formal rejoinder to
eastern council in the *Libri Carolini*, and seven years later at Fra
fort solemnly repudiated its decisions.[4]

[1] Mansi, *op. cit.*, vol. xii, 999. Some three hundred and fifty were presen
which a fair proportion were abbots. Martin, *op. cit.*, p. 93, observes 'it was
who supplied the bishops with brains'.
[2] JE 2448, 2449.
[3] *C.M.H.* vol. iv, p. 21. Cf. *Theodore of Studium*, Gardner, A., 1905, p. 125
[4] On the *Libri Carolini*, see Martin, *op. cit.*, p. 228 ff.

Happily, however, for the peace of the Church, Adrian was states-
[ma]n enough not to press these differences and contented himself
[wi]th allowing time to do its work. If it be said that in so doing he
[wa]s preferring the temporal advantages of his see to loyalty to con-
[sci]ence, it must in fairness be admitted that a policy of tolerance in
[su]ch a question may well have seemed to a western mind the only
[rea]sonable course.

[W]hen Adrian died in the following year (795), his successor Leo
[II]I was elected and consecrated with such precipitation that we can
[on]ly infer that he owed his elevation to some sort of party intrigue.
[Th]e fact that he was not like his predecessor a scion of the Roman
[no]bility suggests that he was the candidate of the pro-Italian, as
[op]posed to the pro-Frankish element in the church. In any case, to
[se]cure his position in relation to Charles he found it necessary to
[ma]ke almost abject profession of loyalty,[1] of which the king evidently
[to]ok advantage to increase the measure of undefined control over the
[Ro]man see which he already enjoyed in virtue of his status as
[p]atrician'.

[T]he outrage on Leo's person which followed a few years later, and
[fo]r which his disappointed rivals were almost certainly responsible,
[on]ly served to make him still more beholden to the Frankish Sovereign
[th]an before, by whose support alone, after a lapse of nearly twelve
[m]onths, he was reinstated in his see.

[T]he dramatic coronation of Charles as Augustus by the Pope on
[Ch]ristmas day, 800, has been the subject of much controversy among
[hi]storians. On the one hand, it has been treated by mediaeval sup-
[po]rters of the temporal authority of the Papacy as a signal proof that
[a] ruler who might be called one of the greatest monarchs of history,
[an]d who was in any case one of the creators of mediaeval Europe,
[th]ereby acknowledged that he owed his temporal authority to the
[Ro]man see, that the spiritual power was supreme even within the
[te]mporal sphere, and, most significant of all, that what the Papacy
[ha]d conferred the Papacy could take away. On the other, non-papal
[hi]storians generally have been disposed to lay stress on the reasons
[wh]ich, as the king himself admitted, had brought him to Rome,
[na]mely to investigate charges against the Pope, details of which had
[no] doubt reached him from Leo's enemies during the months which
[ha]d elapsed since the Pope's restoration. At the synod summoned by

---

[1] JE 2492. *D.T.C.* vol. ix, col. 305.

Charles reference was made to the famous principle, *Apostol* *sedes a nemine iudicatur*, and it was decided on the Symmachi precedent to allow the Pope to purge himself by taking an oath innocence, which, in the event of the survival of the accused, w held in a credulous age to be equivalent to acquittal by the verd of God.[1] Hence it has appeared to some that the true significan of the king's act in receiving the crown at the hands of an inc minated Pope was that it was meant to set aside all doubts regardi the royal belief in his innocence.

Against this view, however, it has been pointed out that Leo h in any case resumed his functions twelve months previously, a that actually there is evidence that to Charles the coronation came a somewhat distasteful surprise. We can perhaps dismiss the lat as a form of biographical tendentiousness, and may suggest that ev if it is true that Leo had performed pontifical acts since his retu it does not follow from this that his position was really secur On the whole the best explanation of the event may be the c which holds it to be the result of a suggestion on the part of L himself, in which Charles' pride may well have acquiesced r unreadily, little realizing that one day it would provide a formida weapon in the papal armoury against his successors. At the same tir it should not be forgotten that papal recognition of Charles Augustus gave him a real justification for repudiating the author of Byzantium, now subject to the female government of the Empr Irene, which from the Frankish standpoint was illicit. After all, wl the Papacy needed most was the defence of a powerful protector, r only as a safeguard against Lombardic and Greek elements in Ita but to repress insubordination and disorder in the city of Rome its That Charles' successors failed in this respect was certainly not t fault of the Papacy, though indirectly their weakness materially aid the growth of its power.

We must now give some account of a much misunderstood co pilation which about this time first makes its appearance on t stage of history, the collection of papal letters and a few otl related documents usually known as the *False Decretals*.[3] This l

---

[1] *Liber pont.* vol. ii, p. 7. Cf. above, and Caspar, *Geschichte des Papsttu* vol. ii, p. 110.

[2] See documents quoted in Mirbt, *op. cit.*, No. 240 ff.

[3] The standard edition is Hinschius, P., *Decretales pseudo-Isidorianae et Capi Angilramni*, 1863.

en the cause of a considerable amount of anti-papal prejudice, so
uch so that many have supposed that it constitutes the chief
pport of what have been described as the papal claims. Hence in
: interests of historical accuracy it is well that we should under-
nd its real character. This may well lead to a very different
imate of its part in the development of papal authority.

The collection has come down to us as the supposed work of
dore of Seville, to whom the chief responsibility for the 'Isidorian'
lection of Canon Law (also called *Hispana*) compiled at the end
the seventh century, was commonly assigned. It is in fact an
plification and interpolation, by means of spurious decretals,
a canonical collection in use by the church of Spain in the eighth
tury, all the documents of which are indubitably authentic.
eudo-Isidore' is divided into three parts. The first, entirely
irious, consisting of papal letters up to but not including Silvester I.
cept for two pseudonymous letters of Clement, they appear to be
: work of the compiler. The second part is a collection of conciliar
iterial derived directly from the *Hispana*, to which a few spurious
ces have been added, including the 'Donation of Constantine'.
ially, the third part contains a large number of genuine letters
m Siricius onwards to Gregory I (with some letters of Gregory II).
iese are preceded, however, by forgeries assigned mainly to the
ervening pontificates between Silvester and Damasus I, but with
: addition of others attributed to those Popes whose genuine letters
: included. The author's sources, in addition to the *Liber
ntificalis* which enjoyed a wide circulation at this time, are ecclesias-
al writers generally and also later ecclesiastical discipline which it
his practice to antedate so far as is possible.[1]

As to the date of its compilation, a citation in the statutes pro-
ilgated by Hincmar of Rheims in 852 supplies us with a *terminus
quem*. A *terminus a quo* is less easy to fix. But it is generally agreed
it the work is indebted to the pseudo-capitularies of Benedictus
vita not earlier than 847. Thus the year 850 may be taken as
proximately correct.[2]

Those who have supposed that its primary purpose was to extend
fraudulent means the authority of the Roman see have seriously
isunderstood its *raison d'être*. Careful study of the forgeries which
includes shows that they are almost entirely concerned to emphasize

[1] See *D.T.C.* vol. iv, col. 212.   [2] *C.M.H.* vol. iii, p. 448.

such points as the limitations which ought to govern the preferme
of a charge against an ecclesiastical superior, the necessity for co
fining charges against the clergy to an ecclesiastical court, t
conditions under which a bishop may be tried, and the right of
bishop to appeal to the papal court. A further general characteris
is its marked eagerness to check the authority of the metropolit
bishop. Thus there are grounds for saying that it is episcopal
more than papal prerogatives which the author designs to uphold.

As to its place of origin, France rather than Rome or Spain, as w
formerly supposed, is now the most widely accepted, and the situati
known to have been prevailing at this time in the province
Tours perhaps most nearly corresponds to the features just mentione
The collection was quoted by numerous non-Roman authors in t
ninth and tenth centuries. Though possible allusions to it occur
the letters of Nicholas I,[1] his successor Adrian II was the first Po
actually to make use of it. Throughout the tenth century, howev
the papal chancery observed a remarkable hesitation in its rega
and it is not till the pontificate of Leo IX in the following centu
that it played any considerable part in papal documents. Even th
some restraint continued which was not finally abandoned till t
time of Gregory VII. In fact, as we shall see presently, the r
creator of the Papacy, as it was to be known for the next six centuri
was not, as has sometimes been thought, the elusive 'Pseudo-Isidor
but the genuine historical Nicholas I.

III

Before recording the chief characteristics of that great pontific
it is necessary to resume the history of the controversy on imag
since in its later stages it reflects some light on the attitude of cert
Easterns towards the see of Rome, once they had shaken off t
fetters of Caesaropapism.

Following the rather indecisive policy of the successors of Ire
the deposition of Michael I (813) led to the elevation of Leo
surnamed the Armenian. His success against the Bulgars enab
him to range himself openly on the side of the still numero
iconoclastic party. But the struggle of the previous century h
taught the image-worshippers some important lessons, the m

---

[1] JE 2785. Mirbt, *Quellen*[5], No. 252.

nportant of which were that their case needed a good deal of
rengthening if it was to win the day, and that they must cease
count on the fickle support of the imperial government, but rely
ther on its own merits. At the first clash with their monastic pro-
gonist, Theodore of Studium, the Emperor was bluntly told that
'hurch matters are the province of priests and doctors : the admini-
ration of secular things belongs to the Emperor'.[1] This was tanta-
ount to an enunciation of the thesis of Gelasius I, but this time the
okesman was not a Pope but an eastern abbot. For the time being
eo appears to have been deterred from creating an open breach
ith the Studites. Later, however, he summoned a council, which
stored the situation as it had existed after 753.

For the first time, so far as we can see, since the days of Con-
antine I the more vigorous elements in the Byzantine church now
solved to win complete freedom from the State, and in order to
cure their independence appealed immediately to the authority of
e Roman see against the Emperor. Meanwhile strong measures
ere being taken by the imperial government, particularly as before,
ainst the monks.

Theodore, who had by this time been driven into exile, addressed
gent and pathetic appeals to Pope Paschal I, of which the following
ords are typical :

'Listen to us', he writes, 'O Apostolic Head, charged by God with
e guidance of Christ's sheep, porter of the heavenly kingdom, rock
the faith on which is built the Catholic Church, for you are Peter,
u are the successor of Peter, whose throne you honourably fill'.[2]

Paschal's intervention, however well intentioned, had little effect.
elief to the orthodox came not from the Papacy, to whose voice
eo and his supporters remained deaf, but from a palace revolt in
hich Leo was struck down and Michael II raised to supreme power.
nder his more tolerant rule, the result rather of indifference than
favour to the orthodox, the exiles, including Theodore, were
called. Banishment had done nothing to break down the old abbot's
delity to his principles.

'There is no question here', he said, addressing Michael, 'of
ıman and temporal things, which kings have the power to judge,
ıt of divine and heavenly dogmas, which have been entrusted to

[1] *C.M.H.*, vol. iv, p. 30.
[2] *Op. cit.*, vol. iv, p. 32.

those only to whom God has said: "Whatsoever thou shalt bind
earth shall be bound also in heaven, and whatsoever thou sha
loose on earth shall be loosed also in heaven". Who are they who ha
received this power? The Apostles and their successors. As
Emperors and sovereigns, their part is to lend their support an
approbation to what has been decreed. No power has been grant
them by God over the divine dogmas, and if they exercise such,
will not be lasting'.[1]

Later Michael appears to have arrived at the conviction th
image-worship would disappear if the Pope's support were wit
drawn. He therefore wrote to the Emperor of the West, Louis t
Pious, urging him to exercise pressure on the Papacy to procu
its abolition. Little satisfied with such methods, his success
Theophilus resolved on sterner action. Yet although the records
this reign are full of stories of the barbarities inflicted by him
the recalcitrants, by the end of 842 it was becoming evident th
repression had failed of its object and that the Empire was growi
weary of an interminable and seemingly fruitless struggle.

Under the regency of his widow Theodora during the minority
her son Michael III, after some preliminary hesitation it was decid
by substituting the monk Methodius for John VII in the office
patriarch to reverse the late Emperor's policy and restore imag
worship. The action of the Empress-regent was confirmed by t
council of 843 and the restoration of images was solemnly celebrat
on the first Sunday of Lent, a day still observed in the Byzanti
church as the festival of Orthodoxy. Yet although liberty to worsh
images had been vindicated, we must not overlook the price at whi
it was bought. The opponents of Iconoclasm had with one voic
from Gregory II and John Damascene to the council of 787 a
Theodore of Studium, contested the Emperor's right 'περὶ πίστε
λόγον ποιεῖσθαι' (to have his say concerning faith), yet in the triump
of 843 it was not so much the Church as the Sovereign who w
victorious. Moreover, the evil legacy of Constantine I's success
quickly showed itself in a sanguinary persecution let loose agair
the Paulician sect in Asia Minor, in which it is said one hundre
thousand persons lost their lives.

[1] Note that he does not confine the authority transmitted in virtue of Matt. x
18, to the Papacy, but like Ambrose and Augustine (see above pp. 261, 28
regards it as conferred upon the whole episcopate (ibid., p. 33). See Epp. Lib. i,
and 34. M.P.G. 99, cols. 141, 1017, 1018. See C.M.H., vol. iv, p. 33.

Yet in estimating the true character of Michael's government we
ust make some allowance for a deliberate attempt on the part of
e Macedonian dynasty to discredit its predecessor, and in any case
must be allowed that his uncle the Caesar Bardas, who was the
ective ruler, by a genuine devotion to duty succeeded to a remark-
le degree in restoring the prestige of the Empire.

But conscientious administration was by no means Bardas' only
im to distinction. To his practical ability there was added an un-
mmon interest in education and scientific research, and it was a
sire to promote these objects which led him to procure the removal
the ascetic Ignatius from the patriarchal throne, and to install in
s place the more worldly and certainly more liberally minded
otius, whose scholarship and brilliance in intellectual attainment
arks him out as one of the brightest stars in the Byzantine
clesiastical firmament.[1]

It soon became evident that the abrupt transference of the chief
shopric in the eastern church from the lineal successors of the
nservative image-worshippers to the less rigid and more tolerant
erals would not be accepted without opposition. The discon-
nted element called attention to the fact that Photius was only a
yman at the time of his nomination, and represented that the sole
use of Ignatius' removal had been his too outspoken criticism of
e all powerful Caesar's morals. In spite of evidence that his resigna-
n was voluntary, it was being alleged that he remained the only
gitimate holder of the patriarchate. These and other means of
eating prejudice against Photius were freely used later in the course
the controversy now on the point of breaking out.

It must be remembered that the breach in unity created by the
age-controversy had never been completely healed, and thus the
signation of Ignatius was used by the monastic party of Studium
a means of creating alarm that orthodoxy was once more in danger.
ence it was not long before adverse reports on Photius began to
rive in Rome, on the strength of which Pope Nicholas I felt bound
investigate the new patriarch's claim to the see of Constantinople

[1] Of his industry as a writer there is no possible room for doubt. For what
lows, see the recent studies of Dvornik, F., such as 'Le premier schisme de
otios' in *Bull. de l'inst. archeol. bulgare*, vol. ix, 1935, pp. 301–325; 'Le second
nisme de Photios. Une mystification historique' in *Byzantion*, vol. viii, 1933,
. 425–474; 'L'oecumenicité du huitième concile (869–870),' in *Bull. de la classe
s lettres* (Acad. roy. de Belgique), vol. xxiv, 1938, No. 10.

before formally accepting his *synodicon* or letter of enthronizatio̅
However, at a synod held in the eastern capital (861), at whi̅
Nicholas' legates were present, it was decided to declare Ignat̅
deposed.[2]

Nicholas, on the other hand, remained unconvinced. He theref̅
declined to accept the decision of his legates and persisted in t̅
view that Ignatius remained the true patriarch. Meanwhile a furtl̅
source of disagreement between the sees of Rome and Constantino̅
had arisen on the question of the provision of a hierarchy for t̅
kingdom of Bulgaria. King Boris had at first applied to Photius, l̅
on finding that the new patriarch was intending to treat his kingd̅
purely as a subject province of the Constantinopolitan patriarcha̅
he had changed his mind and was now inviting Nicholas to sup̅
his demands. The Pope who had already claimed the right to regul̅
the ecclesiastical affairs of Bulgaria in virtue of his ancient author̅
over the Illyrian vicariate,[3] eagerly grasped the opportunity̅
asserting a prescriptive right of the Roman see. It was in this c̅
nexion that he drew up his famous *Ad consulta Bulgarorum*,[4] of whi̅
the principal characteristic was a marked insistence on the div̅
gences between western and eastern usages and on the rightfuln̅
of the former to the exclusion of the latter. In particular, it w̅
insisted that the patriarchal sees in order of precedence were ̅
clusively Rome, Alexandria and Antioch; if Constantinople a̅
Jerusalem were accounted patriarchal, there was no precedent ̅
their being so reckoned.

It was not to be expected that Photius would readily accept t̅
position. Letters were therefore addressed to the western Empe̅
Louis II and to certain bishops of his dominions who had good reas̅
to be dissatisfied with Nicholas, urging the Pope's deposition.[5]
addition to this on learning of the arrival of Roman legates ̅
Bulgaria, Photius issued a formal condemnation of western custon̅
in which he specially censured the uncanonical introduction into t̅
creed of the 'double procession' of the Holy Ghost.[6]

---

[1] JE 2682. See also Grumel, *op. cit.*, No. 464.
[2] Grumel, *op. cit.*, No. 464. The synod took the view that Ignatius had uncano̅
cally acquired the patriarchate.
[3] JE 2682.
[4] JE 2812. *M.G.H. Script.* vol. i, p. 568 ff. Mirbt, *Quellen*[5], No. 253.
[5] *C.M.H.* vol. iv, p. 249.
[6] Grumel, *op. cit.*, No. 480 f.

Everything now pointed to a decisive rupture. The final breach
me when following the murder of Bardas and the elevation of
sil the Macedonian in 867, Photius formally excommunicated
icholas at a Constantinopolitan synod held in the autumn of that
ar, and again urged Louis II to procure his removal.[1]
The patriarch was probably well informed about the situation in
e West and particularly of the indignation aroused by the attitude
the Papacy to the Frankish kings. Thus Nicholas' predecessor
regory IV, acting with the support of the Frankish bishops, had
t hesitated to refer to Lothar I as his subordinate:[2]
'Why speak to me', he wrote, 'of the orders of the Emperor? Are
t the orders of the Pope of equal weight? And is not the authority
er souls which belongs to the Pope above the imperial rule which
of this world?'[3]
Nicholas I had found himself confronted with a formidable
tuation arising from the support given to Lothar II by the arch-
shops of Cologne and Trèves in decreeing the annulment of his
arriage. Yet without hesitation he had declared the archbishops
eposed and remained adamant, undeterred even by the arrival in
ome of the Emperor Louis II in defence of his brother at the head
an armed force. Thus the advantage remained with Nicholas, and
e Papacy came out of the struggle with undiminished prestige.[4]
So now in his attitude towards Michael III, Nicholas showed that
regarded all kings and emperors as accountable to him for their
tions and thus subject to his spiritual jurisdiction. In this sense at
ast he may be said to have contributed materially to the formulation
a papal *potestas directa* in temporal matters *ratione peccati*, though
never actually made use of the phrase himself. Some would even
old that, in one of his letters referring to the case of Lothar II,[5]
adumbrates the doctrine of the 'two swords', to which we shall
fer presently, assigning to the Papacy absolute control over spiritual
d temporal affairs alike. At least it must be allowed that, if he did
t actually quote the text, he certainly upheld the idea which it was
bsequently used to justify. The importance of his pontificate is
at it marks the foundation of a number of those principles which
rgely conditioned the relation of the Papacy to the Church during

[1] *C.M.H.* vol. iv, p. 250; Grumel, *op. cit.*, Nos. 482–5.
[2] *C.M.H.* vol. iii, p. 448 ff.   [3] JE 2578. *M.P.L.* 104, 297.
[4] *C.M.H.* vol. iii, p. 450; Jaffé, *op. cit.*, vol. i, p. 351.
[5] JE 2787.

the later centuries of the Middle Ages. Thus he argues that eve
grade in the ecclesiastical hierarchy is essentially subordinate
the see of Rome; archbishops enjoy the exercise of their metr
politan jurisdiction only in virtue of the possession of the *palliu*
received at the Pope's hand; bishops can only be judged by him
under his authority; councils and synods derive their validity on
from papal approbation.[1]

The belief that Nicholas made use of the *False Decretals* to justi
his claims, once widely held, has now been generally abandoned
and it is usually admitted that, as in the case of many of his pr
decessors, material for the formulation of his theory was already
existence before his time. Perhaps his greatest claim to historic
significance is that he made a notable contribution to the extensio
of a conception of Christendom which recognized in the see
Peter its inevitable centre of unity or rallying point, and an authorti
holding sway over every department of human life.

Returning now to the relations of the Papacy with Photius, t
revolutionary elevation of Basil I and the downfall of Michael I
proved a serious menace to the patriarch's position. On his rival
refusal to communicate with the new sovereign Ignatius was hasti
reinstated. By this time Nicholas I was dead. His successor Adrian I
in consequence of a Roman synod which condemned Photius afres
requested the Emperor to summon a council at Constantinople
order to endorse the Roman decisions.[3]

When this council opened on October 9, 869, shortly after t
arrival of the four Roman legates, it began by styling itself 'oecu
menical,'[4] in spite of the fact that it was in no sense representati
of the universal Church, since the highest number of bisho
present at any one session (9th) was sixty-five, while at the earli
sessions scarcely more than half that figure was reached. However,
soon became clear that there was a wide gulf between the point
view of the Emperor and that of the legates. Basil desired the counc
to restore peace; the legates, as in the days of Celestine I and Leo
at the councils of Ephesus and Chalcedon,[5] simply required t
acceptance of Pope Adrian's judgment. Yet in spite of unwillingne

---

[1] *C.M.H.* vol. iii, p. 453.   [2] See above, p. 378.   [3] *C.M.H.* vol. iv, p. 2
[4] There was nothing abnormal in the use of this style, which simply mea
'imperial'. Councils had been in the habit of using it since the days of the coun
of Constantinople 382. See above, p. 254, n. 3.
[5] See above, pp. 298, 307.

the part of the Emperor and the council to condemn Photius un-
ard, they eventually agreed to accept the legates' view that the
nciliar act of deposition was no more than the publication of a
dgment already pronounced. At the same time taking advantage of
eir presence, an attempt was made to persuade them to recognize
onstantinopolitan jurisdiction over Bulgaria. When this failed
natius decided to act in spite of the Roman see, and consecrated
Greek hierarchy for the Bulgarian kingdom. In this way it was
ade clear that in a question involving the extent of Byzantine
risdiction, it mattered little who happened to be patriarch.

Meanwhile by one of those swift changes of opinion, so common
the history of the eastern church, Photius was once more restored
favour, and later on the death of Ignatius was reinstalled in the
triarchate. By this time the Roman legates, after a perilous journey
the course of which their copy of the *Acta* of 869/70 was stolen,
d returned to Rome. The missing information, however, was
nveniently supplied in an abbreviated version of the recent pro-
edings (as appears from comparison with the Greek *Acta*) compiled
r Anastasius Bibliothecarius, who had been present at the council
the representative of the Emperor Louis II.

As was to be expected, Adrian II's successor John VIII, nominated
872, showed great indignation at Ignatius' conduct in the matter of
ulgaria. After pointing out in a letter to king Boris[1] that Ignatius
d presumed to do what even Photius had shunned, the Pope
bsequently wrote to the patriarch himself to the effect that unless
: withdrew the Greek bishops from Bulgaria within thirty days he
ould be deposed.[2] Shortly afterwards he despatched two legates to
onstantinople,[3] to see that his orders were carried out.

Yet, in view of the political situation in the West and the menace
the Saracen invasions, and in spite of the questionable advantages
ined by the successive coronations of Charles the Bald[4] and Charles
e Fat,[5] the Papacy was once more showing signs of being ready to
rn to Constantinople for support, and appeared to be willing to do
e utmost possible to reach an understanding with Photius. We are
erefore not surprised to find that while the Roman legates con-
nted themselves with a somewhat non-committal attitude towards

---

[1] JE 2962. Cf. JE 2996. [2] JE 3130. [3] JE 3135.
[4] Jaffé, *op. cit.*, vol. i, p. 386. December 25, 875.
[5] Id., *op. cit.*, vol. i, p. 417. February 9, 881.

the new situation, in Rome the imperial legates were successful
obtaining his almost unconditional recognition. Thus in a letter
Photius himself John formally stated: 'We have annulled . . . t
council held there (sc. in Constantinople) against you . . . becau
our predecessor Adrian did not subscribe to it'.[1]

We now come to the final act in this strange drama, the Photi
synod of 879/880. Any doubt concerning the authenticity of the *Ac*
of this assembly has been finally removed by the recent research
of a well-known Byzantine scholar; even the sixth and seven
sessions, which were still regarded as spurious even by those w
had accepted his conclusions regarding the others, have now be
proved genuine.[2] The same author is convinced that the pecul
features of these last two sessions, notably the fact that they we
held in the imperial palace, are sufficiently explained by the c
cumstance that the Emperor Basil was at the time in mourning f
the death of his heir. In one respect at least this synod presents
remarkable contrast to its predecessor of ten years before. It w
attended by not less than three hundred and fifty bishops.[3] As to
decisions, all that need be said here is that it completely rehabilitat
Photius and annulled the Ignatian council of 869/870.

The legates returned to Rome in August, 880, and John VIII du
confirmed the *Acta* of the recent council, with the exception
that which the legates had done contrary to the apostolic injunctio
That John himself at no time withdrew from this attitude is prov
from various later allusions to him made by Photius. The questi
remains, however, whether, as has been generally supposed, t
patriarch was subsequently excommunicated by the Roman s
That Marinus I sent him no letter of enthronization two ye
later is to be explained by his personal hostility to Basil I. On t
other hand, not only is it certain that Adrian III sent such a lette
but it is equally clear that although Photius was finally deposed
Basil's successor Leo VI, it was on purely personal grounds, a
there can be no doubt that Pope Stephen V recognized him
legitimate patriarch at the time of his deposition.[6] The interesti

---

[1] *M.P.L.* 126, 874. Cf. *D.T.C.* vol. viii, col. 605.

[2] Dvornik's latest study of this subject has not yet appeared. The view stated
the text rests on his verbal assurance on this point.

[3] A striking and no doubt significant contrast to the numbers present at
Ignatian council of 869/70.

[4] JE 3222 f. *M.G.H. Scriptores*, vol. vii, pp. 227–8. Cf. *D.T.C. ibid.*, col. 608

[5] JL 3399.   [6] JL 3452.

nclusion to be derived from this evidence is that Photius appears
have died in communion with the Roman see.

There can be no doubt that he was a vigorous defender of the
ivileges of the Constantinopolitan see and of the legitimacy of
stern customs against the attempt of Nicholas I to impose Roman
actice on the Bulgarian church. That he rejected the Roman
imacy of doctrine and jurisdiction is proved to be untrue by his
n attitude in submitting to papal judgments.[1] As to his protest
ainst Nicholas it is clear that it was directed not against the Papacy
t against what he regarded as a misuse of papal authority—in a
ord against what is now known as Papalism.

His story, however, has a strange epilogue. In view of the facts
st mentioned, it is surprising to find that the Photian synod of
9/80 was subsequently forgotten in the West, while the Ignatian
sembly of 869/70 was accorded the rank of the eighth oecumenical
uncil. How is this singular inversion to be explained?[2]

First of all it is to be remarked that the belief that the council of
9/70 should be reckoned as oecumenical is referred to first by
incmar of Rheims. That Hincmar himself did not so reckon it is
oved by the fact that with the majority of the Frankish episcopate
accepted only six such councils, and excluded the second council
Nicaea. After him very few western authors up to the middle
the eleventh century paid much attention to their number, but
ne described this council as oecumenical. Equally in Rome itself,
en as late as the profession of faith sent by Leo IX to Peter of
ntioch, an official papal declaration, seven councils and seven
ly are mentioned. Similarly Cardinal Humbert in pronounc-
g sentence against Michael Caerularius, an occasion on which
had every reason to give prominence to earlier condemnations
a patriarch of Constantinople by the Roman see, mentions seven
uncils and no more. Five years later Peter Damian evidently holds
e same view. If further proof of the official attitude of the Roman
urch at this time is wanted, it is contained in the *Liber Diurnus*,
hich, as we learn from Cardinal Deusdedit, was modified during
e eleventh century and appeared in a new edition in 1059.[3] Here too
e papal profession of faith still contents itself with the mention of

[1] Dvornik, *L'affaire de Photius*, p. 86.
[2] For the view stated here, see Dvornik, *L'oecuménicité du huitième concile*,
447 ff.
[3] Id., *op. cit.*, p. 459.

seven councils alone. The same is true of the episcopal profession
faith which it contains, and which certainly belongs to this revisio
In any case it is certain that the seventh council was not add
officially to the oecumenical list at Rome till after 880.[1] Who th
was responsible for the inclusion of the eighth? The way was pr
pared by Anselm of Lucca who, in his collection of Canon La
introduced the eighteenth, twenty-first, and twenty-second cano
of the Ignatian council under the heading *universa octava synod*
borrowing from the *Acta* themselves the epithet *universa* (οἰκουμενικ
Deusdedit in his turn makes use of its canons but shows a certa
hesitation about its oecumenicity. Yet inevitably the eleventh centu
reformers, in their anxiety to check lay investiture, were attract
by the canons of this council, which provided them with the desir
authority. The first canonist explicitly to range it with the sev
councils is in fact Ivo of Chartres, whose source was possibly t
collection named *Britannica*, containing a corrected extract from t
collection of Deusdedit in which the *professio fidei* enumerates r
seven only but eight. Thus the process of the inclusion of t
Ignatian council was begun. Yet even so late as the fifteenth centu
it was possible so far to ignore its status as in a Latin version of t
Acta of the council of Florence to describe the latter, and not t
council of 869/70, as the eighth oecumenical council.

IV

In the latter half of the ninth century there opens a period
spiritual and political decline in the history of the Roman see. Contr
over kings passed out of papal hands, and so far from increasi
their power the Popes found themselves driven to adopt a poli
of almost desperate self-defence. Besides this, the Papacy became f
the time being little more than a secular prize, falling by turns to t
stronger of the contestants, the imperial house of Spoleto and t
local Roman aristocracy. In the end the despairing appeal of t
unhappy Formosus to Arnulf, king of Germany, bore fruit, and
the person of Otto I, following the deposition of the profligate you
Pope John XII, the German Emperors began to exercise a pr
ponderating influence in the direction of papal policy which was
last for over a century. Side by side with the degradation of t

---

[1] Dvornik, *op. cit.*, p. 467.

pacy there is to be remarked in addition a growing loss of authority
the part of the local episcopate, with an ever increasing dependence
the will of kings and particularly of feudal lords, only counter-
anced by the fact that many of the bishops, especially in Germany,
ame lords themselves, in whom temporal interests tended more
more to extinguish any real sense of spiritual responsibility.

t is no doubt highly probable that Otto the Great conceived that
a result of his coronation by John XII in 962 he was actually
iving the Empire of Charlemagne. But whereas Charlemagne
l been the effective sovereign of the lands which formed his
ninions, Otto remained in fact no more than a German prince,
ose possession of the imperial crown endowed him with a certain
lefined prestige in western Christendom as its defender against
ign invaders and as the guardian of justice and peace. His
hority in spiritual matters suffered from a similar lack of precision,
while Charlemagne had exercised unlimited sovereignty over the
urch, Otto was regarded as no more than its benevolent protector.[1]
n if the Papacy was obliged to recognize his temporal overlordship,
emained a fact that it was the Pope and not the Emperor who was
l without question to be the spiritual head of Christendom.
o's control over Italy, though more effective than that of his
cessors, was at best the rule of a foreigner, which inevitably
used deep resentment among the less submissive Romans. That
h a suzerainty would cease to be anything more than nominal
e the Papacy had succeeded in recovering its strength, was there-
only to be expected. Yet it must not be forgotten that the Roman
remained indebted to Otto for having checked its degradation
critical point in its history

he progress of its recovery can already be traced in its earlier
es in the pontificate of Silvester II, the first Pope of French
od, who in 999 succeeded Gregory V, said to have been the first
man successor of St. Peter.[2] Otto III, grandson of the render of the Empire, who was Silvester's contemporary, as a
er showed some strange characteristics, but there can be little
bt that in the nicely balanced relations between Papacy and
pire during his reign, the ideal described at a later date by St.
nard or by Dante came nearest to fulfilment. If relations between

[1] *C.M.H.* vol. iii, p. 164.
[2] John XIV was a Lombard and the first to take a papal name (983).

5

the two powers were not less cordial under the Emperors Henry
and Henry III, it cannot be said that the same equilibrium remain

The pontificate of Silvester II was also remarkable for the f
that he was one of the earliest popes to show any real sympa
with that great movement for reform, which, indebted perhaps
some measure to the foundation of Cluny at the beginning of
tenth century, had been steadily gaining ground since that time
first in Lorraine and then later in Germany.[1] Starting as a rev
against the prevalence of secularism in various forms, it gradu
developed into an attempt to release the western Church as a wh
from the stranglehold of feudalism. If under Gregory VII
clamour for the removal of lay patronage and lay control and
centralization of the Church under papal leadership can already
recognized as inevitable consequences of the whole program
we are reminded by a modern historian that 'the early stages of
process are all dictated by the desire to effect the reform of
Church, which still remains the first object even with Pope Greg
VII'.[2] Doubtless one of the more important of the clues to a ri
understanding of the period is to be found in the recognition of
fact that 'the pontificate of Gregory VII marked the final reject
by the official Church of the old attitude of mistrust towards
world',[3] which itself was not incompatible with the idea of its c
version 'by the action of a divinely instituted kingship' work
through a strictly subordinate clergy. But the conversion of the wo
through a clerical hierarchy centralized under the Pope was a po
which was bound to involve a direct and ineluctable challenge to
concept of a monarchy responsible only to God.

However attractive some may have found that explanation
Gregory's activities which regards them as aimed primarily
ultimately at the establishment of an absolute papal dominion o
Church and State, it is becoming clear that such a simplification
history is only possible if a number of relevant factors is igno
In the first place it has to be realized that the evils which ev
reformer deplored and sought to remedy, chiefly those of sim
and incontinence in the clergy, were not merely the consequence

---

[1] It should be appreciated that modern historians such as Tellenbach, G
Bennett, R. F.), Church, State and Christian Society, are disposed to regard
extent of this influence as far less than was formerly supposed.

[2] Brooke, Z. N., English Church and the Papacy, 1931, p. 28.

[3] Tellenbach, op. cit., p. xi f.

nerally debased moral standard. They were also to a great extent
e direct result of the proprietary church system, the so-called
genkirchenrecht, which had grown up in the West and particularly
Germany as part of the process of the conversion of the Teutonic
tions to Christianity.[1] Such a system was the product of an attempt
christianize society from within, in which the laity acquired
mething more than a merely passive role in the Church's life. Thus
e founder of an Eigenkirche himself appointed its priests, prescribed
eir rule if they were monks, and generally exercised control over
eir manner of life. As a result, episcopal authority became subject
severe limitations by reason of the fact that large areas of their
oceses were withdrawn from their direct supervision. Yet it must
t be supposed that the Eigenkirchenrecht existed in spite of the
erarchy. Bishops and Popes alike availed themselves of the privileges
iich it conferred, and though at times a serious obstacle it might
so on occasion be a powerful asset in the promotion of reform.

V

This proprietary church system gave rise indirectly to a develop-
ent destined to have far-reaching effects on the administration of
e Church and in particular on the progress of its centralization
der the Papacy. This took the form of a revived interest in Canon
aw and especially in its application to the practical administration
a diocese. The need of some convenient collection of the laws of
e Church, arranged not in groups of chronologically related matter,
ch as conciliar law, decretal law and so on, but under subject
adings, had been fulfilled in some measure by the anonymous com-
er of the Collectio Anselmo dicata and by Regino of Prum. But
the beginning of the eleventh century their work was in need of
ing brought up to date, and there was a special demand for its
plication to the peculiar conditions of the Church in the Rhineland.
his fresh need was now supplied (1012–1023) by Burchard of
orms, in his Decretum or Collectarium. The character of his work is
ghly significant of the dominant ecclesiastical ideas of his time in
is borderland between France and Germany. For if he evidently
cepts 'the divine institution of the Papacy and its headship of the
urch', 'employs Papal decretals as his chief authority' and regards

[1] Cf. Caspar, op. cit., vol. ii, p. 4 ff.

them as the sole source of jurisdiction as well as the final court
appeal in all major cases and for all bishops, yet to him the Papacy
not so much sovereign as 'the hinge on which all Christendom turns
On the other hand, much stress is laid on 'the importance of th
bishop and of episcopal authority'.   As yet it is the bishop rathe
than the Pope who is to be agent of the much needed reform; th
Pope is only 'the final arbiter to whom the most difficult cases are
be referred'.[1] The defects of such a collection from the point of vie
of those who saw in the Papacy and the Roman church a sovereig
power, of which bishops were only the subordinates, are so obvior
as to need no emphasis, and it was inevitable that before long a ne
code would be in demand.

The importance of Canon Law from the eleventh to the sixteent
centuries for our purpose lies not only in the fact that it serves
illustrate the extent to which the western church acknowledged th
principle that the Pope is universal arbiter and supreme judge; th
principle had already been long established and was accepted withor
question. It also shows that the Pope was coming to be regarded lil
the *princeps* in the Constantinian autocracy as the sole legislato
whose decretals, apart from the canonical decisions of occasional si
called oecumenical councils, wholly under papal control, were no
the chief source of new law.[2] More than this, the new developmer
of Canon Law serves to illustrate the process by which the Papac
from being regarded as universal referee in the Church comes to
regarded as absolute sovereign over the Church. In view of this
will give coherence and unity to this aspect of our subject if th
whole march of the evolution of ecclesiastical legislation is surveye
together at this point, leaving on one side for the moment a fin
estimate of the significance of the great reform movement of whic
it may be accounted one of the more enduring results.

The earliest collection to put the authority of the Papacy and th
reform programme in the very centre of the picture appeared und
Leo IX about a quarter of a century after Burchard. Known as tl
Collection in 74 Titles, it used almost exclusively the *False Decreta*
and the works of Gregory I as its sources. It is important, howeve

---

[1] Brooke, *op. cit.*, pp. 33, 85 ff.

[2] It should be remembered that Canon and Civil Law were studied side by si
at Bologna, where, as in other centres of North Italy, the tradition of Roman ci
law had survived from classical times. This fact goes a long way to explain the ea
with which the papal monarchy was assimilated to the former imperial autocrac

not for its completeness, for judged from this standpoint it was seriously lacking, but for its basic principles which are traceable in all later collections.

Of the collections dating from the pontificate of Gregory VII, namely those of Otto, Anselm of Lucca and Deusdedit, neither the first nor the last was of much use to the average bishop and his lawyers who had to apply the law, being arranged either as a whole or in part on a chronological plan. Anselm's work, however, was of greater practical convenience, for although like the others it assigned an important place to matter bearing on papal authority and the reform, it also admitted as much non-Roman matter as was judged to be conformable to Roman tradition. Moreover, it was strictly systematic. It is therefore the first of those canonical collections which lead up to Gratian.

After Anselm, under the influence of Bologna, the study of Canon Law became more objective, and under the same influence at the end of the eleventh century the first comprehensive collection under subject headings compiled by Ivo of Chartres made its appearance. His *Decretum*, and more especially his *Pannormia*, exercised a considerable influence far outside Italy and was only gradually superseded by the work of Gratian. The famous *Decretum*, or to give it its full title *Concordantia discordantium canonum*, marks the beginning of the *ius novum*. It followed the plan, not of stating the law, thus differing markedly from its predecessors, but of laying down legal theses and then proving them by quotations. Among its proofs it includes documents, conciliar canons, papal decretals, and even civil laws. One of its chief aims was to remove discrepancies. In arrangement, comprehensiveness and convenience the work marked a greater advance on its predecessors, and as such it soon came to enjoy recognition as the universal text-book of Canon Law in the West. Yet it must be remembered that it was in fact a manual rather than a strictly official code or *Corpus*.

Gratian's material reached down to 1139. During the following century, in the course of which papal authority in relation to civil government attained its zenith, much additional matter became current, and under the hand of Raymund of Pennafort was eventually published by Gregory IX in 1234 as his *Decretales*, which possessed the character of an official code, while Gratian's *Decretum*, as we have seen, remained merely a legal hand-book. Apart from the canons issued at the third and fourth Lateran councils, the work included only papal material, and from the fact that it was no more than a supplement to Gratian's *Decretum* was often quoted as 'extra' or more briefly as 'X'. Although the matter was arranged in chronological order, the decretals were not given in full, and as this meant that it was often necessary for a proper understanding of Raymund's text to refer to the original documents, in later editions the full text of the decretals was supplied.

To the five books of Gregory IX, Boniface VIII added a *Liber Sextus* which embraced, besides papal documents of the thirteenth century, the canons of the first and second councils of Lyons.

Finally, Pope Clement V, after his withdrawal to Avignon, formed the project of publishing his own Constitutions with the decrees of the council of Vienne, intending to call it *Liber Septimus*, but died before the work was complete. It was afterwards issued under his successor John XXII, but as it contained only Clementine material it became known as the *Constitutiones Clementinae*.

These four collections, constituting the so-called *Corpus iuris canonici clausum*, to which later two appendices called *Extravagantes* were added, reached their final form in 1503, though they were not officially added to the *Corpus* till a century later. By such means the imposing structure of mediaeval Canon Law came to be built, the importance of which in schooling the mind of western Christendom to the fact of papal sovereignty is perhaps difficult to exaggerate.

VI

To return now to the reform movement of the tenth century. With the accession of Henry III to the imperial throne, the Papacy was confronted by an Emperor who was wholly devoted to the programme of reform, so that following the installation of Clement II in the place of Gregory VI, deposed by Henry at Sutri, the reformers could claim that at last the movement had secured at least a footing in the capital of Christendom itself. But it was not till Leo IX received the tiara that it was clear the see of St. Peter had been occupied by one of its advocates. The credit for the appointment of this great man is to be given solely to Henry, yet in making the choice, as it has been said, 'he raised up the power that was to cast down his son and destroy the Empire'.[1]

---

[1] *C.M.H.* vol. iii, p. 308.

With Leo the movement tended to take on more definitely the
aracter of a revolt against lay control, a factor which often appeared
be among the chief obstacles to its progress. Yet in spite of all
it he could do by his journeys and active encouragement of
iodical action to make the world outside the Roman patrimony
niliar with his august person and with papal authority in general,
e Roman see continued to be subject to the undefined suzerainty of
e Empire, so long as Henry III remained alive. Hence it was not
after the Emperor's death that it began to be possible to shake off
perial tutelage. Yet an early sign of future independence is to be
en in the Election Decree of 1059, issued by the Lateran council
ld under Nicholas II, by which a preponderating voice in a papal
ction was given to the Cardinal bishops, in co-operation with the
rgy and laity of the Roman church, while leaving to the Emperor
hts which in practice were little more than honorary.[1]

In this intermediate stage of the reform we can still see the two
luences, described by Tellenbach as the 'mystical' and the
ganizational', at work; the former represented by the archdeacon
ter Damian, the latter by Cardinal Humbert. Peter, who later
came Cardinal bishop of Ostia, favoured a policy of co-operation
tween the spiritual and secular powers. It is true that he asserted
at Christ had conferred upon St. Peter *terreni simul et caelestis
perii iura*,[2] but this phrase, originally intended solely as a com-
entary on the universality of the spiritual authority conferred on
e Apostle in Matt. xvi, 17–19, was subsequently misinterpreted as
leclaration of the plenitude of spiritual and secular power claimed
the later Papacy. If he anticipated the later doctrine of the 'two
ords', it is not less clear that he restricted the Papacy to the use
the 'sword of the spirit'.[3] On the other hand, Humbert's analogy
the relation of the soul to the body,[4] as illustrating the primacy of
e spiritual power, provided a basis for a completely theocratic
tlook which would not be content with the perfectly balanced
rmony of relationship between the two powers, but would aim at
e concentration in the hands of the Papacy of all manifestations of
thority, spiritual and secular alike.

[1] Mirbt, *Quellen*[5], No. 270. A right of confirming the election was given per-
nally to Henry III, in consideration of his services to the Roman see, though not
a matter of course to his successors. See *C.M.H.* vol. v, p. 37 f.
[2] See Rivière, J., *Le problème de l'Eglise et de l'État*, 1926, pp. 387–393.
[3] Mirbt, *Quellen*[5], No. 277.   [4] *M.G.H. Lib. de lite*, i, p. 225.

With the election of the archdeacon Hildebrand as Gregory VII,
the Papacy as it was to be known down to the beginning of the fourteenth century comes into existence. Since the death of Humbert
he had been the leading figure in the Roman Curia. As such he had
inherited not only Humbert's position but his ideas as well. 'Grégoire
VII', writes one of the best-known authorities on this period, 'sera le
disciple de Humbert, tout en dépassant de beaucoup son maître'.[2]
The details of his struggle with Henry IV are well known and call
for no detailed description. It will be sufficient for our purpose to
call attention to the extent to which the idea of the Papacy underwent
modification in consequence of his policy and teaching.

What were the sources of his principles. The literary material on
which he made use in his conflict with the Emperor included of course
Holy Scripture, yet it has been said that 'though quotations from the
New Testament are more numerous, it is the spirit of the Old
Testament that prevails'.[3] In addition, he shows an intimate knowledge
of the collections of decretals current in his time, and if he made
extensive use of the *False Decretals* it is fair to assume that he used
them in good faith. He was dependent to a marked extent on
Gregory I, on whom he relied for his knowledge of Augustine and
especially of the *Civitas Dei*. Finally, he was particularly indebted
to the work of his immediate predecessors, who, by their reorganization of the papal chancery on the lines of the bureaucracy which
served the Emperors, provided the necessary machinery for elaborat-
ing the theories on which his claims were built.

It is noteworthy that the same consciousness of the papal office
as a mystical reincarnation of St. Peter, of which examples have
recurred from the end of the fourth century onwards, now springs to
life afresh in the guise of an absolute imperialism. Thus it was in
virtue of his possession of St. Peter's office that Gregory believed in
an unlimited power of excommunication and of absolution which
knows of no human superior. Yet just because he held himself to be
responsible to God alone, he recognized that his authority must be
exercised in accordance with strict justice. For him as for many of
his predecessors, duty was mainly concerned with securing the
proper observance of Canon Law, and it was a natural consequence

---

[1] By popular acclamation in despite of the recent Election Decree.
[2] Fliche, A., *La réforme grégorienne*, vol. i, p. 305.
[3] *C.M.H.* vol. v, p. 54.

this standpoint that his decrees were rather interpretations of
isting law than new legal definitions.

During the earlier years of his pontificate it is clear that he remained
ntent with the Gelasian view on the dual supremacy of the two
wers each within its own sphere. Thus he compared the *sacer-
tium* and the *imperium* to the eyes of the Church's body, the end of
th being alike spiritual. Yet after his clash with the Emperor he
as forced to recognize that this dualism was no longer tenable, and
at the demands of *Justitia* required the absolute primacy of the
iritual power. Thus he reached the conviction that the dominical
pointment of St. Peter and his successors had committed the final
dgment of human conduct, including the conduct of kings, to the
pacy and to it alone. As in the *Dictatus Papae*,[1] which at least owes
uch to his inspiration, the absolute supremacy of the Roman see
ithin the spiritual sphere is affirmed, so Gregory's letter *Quod ad
rferendos* declares its absolute sovereignty within the secular. Driven
 the force of his own logic he came to affirm the diabolical origin of
mporal authority, and to declare that " if kings are to be judged by
shops for their sins, with how much greater show of justice ought
ey to be judged by the Roman Pontiff.'[2] At the same time we must
te at least one argument in this letter which is new, and to be
garded as a typical product of the reforming influence, namely his
rong emphasis on the moral superiority of the Papacy as compared
ith the Empire. It is therefore a direct consequence of his argument
at he insisted more than once on the moral holiness of the Pope for
e time being, as indeed he was bound to do, if papal authority, no
ss in the moral than in the legal sphere, was the one power *sans
reil*.

To summarize what has been said. Within the twelve years of his
ntificate (1073–1085) Gregory came to believe that for the attain-
ent of his goal—the establishment of righteousness upon earth—
e mediaeval theory of two equal and independent, yet not self-
fficient powers was impracticable. He had tried to realize his ideal
ith the aid of a temporal ruler in strict subordination to the
pacy; and on the failure of this experiment he had turned to another
-the attempt to achieve his end against the Emperor's will. In this
o he seemed to fail. Yet his failure was in fact a moral triumph on
e basis of which it would one day be possible for a successor to

---

[1] Mirbt, *Quellen*[5], No. 278.   [2] Id., *op. cit.*, No. 297, p. 157, l. 5 f.

assume the diadem of a *sacerdos imperator*. Thus his defeat inaugurat
the apotheosis of the mediaeval Papacy. Yet at the same time t
subsequent victory contained paradoxically the seeds of futu
disaster, in that it was only achieved by the destruction of the ve
means which had rendered its achievement possible.

No attempt has been made within the limits of our space
examine afresh the varied aspects of Gregory's struggle for mor
righteousness alike in Church and State. Nor have we consider
how far his part was strictly disinterested, though perhaps sufficie
has been said to show that, even if he believed from the first th
only by the triumph of the Papacy and the establishment of i
universal sovereignty could an ideal human society be attaine
it was the victory of the Roman see rather than of Hildebrand whi
was his chief ambition. Nor, again, is there opportunity to estima
the extent to which there was an element of genuinely conscientio
resistance on the part of his opponents whether spiritual or secula
Both sides, it must be remembered, could make out a good case
their own premises. But of the two, Gregory's was by far the mo
impregnable, since even if it could be argued that temporal pow
was a divine ordinance, it was not less true that the primacy of t
spiritual was an essential Christian principle. It only remained
be seen how far, once the supreme power in both spheres had becom
for a brief space united in a single office, the primacy of the spiritu
could be upheld without becoming in its turn subordinated to pure
secular ends.[1]

VII

In one respect at least Gregory, the Papacy and the Church
a whole had undoubtedly been robbed of the full fruit of h
achievement. In his lifetime, though before he had become emine
in the counsels of the Roman see, a fresh estrangement between t
Papacy and the Byzantine Church had come into being. Since t
days of Nicholas I the perennial grievance against the West about t
unilateral addition of the *Filioque* to the doctrine of the Holy Ghos
as contained in the Constantinopolitan-western creed, had flared u
intermittently; on the western side there was the perpetual sore
Byzantine ecclesiastical jurisdiction in southern Italy established

[1] The fact of Gregory's own dependence on Norman military power cannot
ignored, and illustrates the danger mentioned here as already appearing. To ga
its support he had to acquiesce in Robert Guiscard's attack on the eastern Empir

e pontificate of Gregory II; on the eastern side again the offence
eated by the claim of the kings of Germany to be the true heirs of
ugustus in disregard of those put forward by the 'Emperors of the
reeks'.[1] Moreover, if the reputation of the Papacy in the West
uld be restored by the happy alliance of German Emperors and
erman Popes, there was no equally ready instrument for its
habilitation in the East. By the beginning of the eleventh century
e breach had already widened sufficiently for the name of the
igning Pope to be erased from the Byzantine *diptycha*, at the very
ne when the area of the oecumenical patriarch's jurisdiction had
quired a phenomenal expansion by the acceptance of a Greek
erarchy in Russia. Some twenty years later the patriarch Eustathius
deavoured to obtain from John XXI a declaration 'that the church
Constantinople is universal in its sphere, just as the church of
me is in the universe'.[2] It was one of those concessions to Greek
btlety of distinction which, as John himself appears to have
ought, the Papacy might readily have granted without any sacrifice
essential principle; at least it could be said that it left the Roman
imacy unimpaired. Unhappily, so soon as the reform party had
ard of it, they protested at Rome with such vigour that John was
iven to refuse the concession. Even so he was able to show his
nerosity and eagerness to promote an understanding by acknow-
lging the jurisdiction of the Greek metropolitan of Bari with his
elve suffragans. It would seem, therefore, that papal 'absolutism'
s not solely responsible for the enlargement of the breach between
st and West.

Everything goes to show that there was no desire on the part of
eastern church as a whole, or such of it as remained in com-
union with the see of Constantinople, for a breach with the Papacy.
t lack of charity between the respective advocates of eastern and
western usages had done its disruptive work, and it was an unfor-
ate historical accident that the pontificate of a strong willed
ormer in the person of Leo IX happened to coincide with the
triarchate of the ambitious, ungenerous and inflexible Michael
erularius.

The immediate cause of a reopening of the conflict between the
stern and western Churches arose from papal intervention in

---

[1] *C.M.H.* vol. iv, p. 261.
[2] Grumel, *op. cit.*, No. 828; *C.M.H. ibid.*, p. 262.

southern Italy, now in the power of the Normans. Yet from
first the patriarch Michael adopted a keenly hostile attitude towa
any proposals for an alliance with the West; insults directed agai
the Roman see and indignities inflicted on Christians of the La
rite in Byzantium were multiplied with Michael's active encoura
ment, if at any time he made overtures of conciliation, there is ev
probability that he did so only under political pressure.

To arrange the desired alliance Leo IX despatched three legat
among whom by what was perhaps an unfortunate choice he incluc
the ardent papalist and reformer Cardinal Humbert. If Michael is
be blamed for arrogance, the legates certainly displayed a sig
absence of tact, perhaps of ordinary courtesy. Then to an alrea
strained situation further tension was added by the evident ho
expressed by the Pope in his letter to Constantine IX that
Emperor would bring his fractious patriarch to obedience. Afte
good deal of mutual recrimination, during which Constantine
his utmost to preserve peace and safeguard recognition of the Rom
primacy, news was received in the early summer of 1054 of the de
of Leo IX.[1] From this point onwards it became clear that Mich
was determined to engineer a schism by any means possible. T
legates waited for some months at Constantinople, but as no furth
instructions were received from Rome (Leo's successor Victor
was not elected till a year had elapsed) they decided to act on th
own initiative. In the course of the liturgy in the great Church
St. Sophia they entered and laid on the altar a bull of excommuni
tion against Michael.

The only immediate effect of this act was to bring over put
opinion in the capital wholly to the side of the patriarch, so much
that the Emperor himself was obliged to give way and permi
solemn anathema to be published against the Roman see.[2] His
proved in the end far more disastrous to Byzantium than to
Papacy. It lost southern Italy for the Byzantine obedience; it fina
disunited East and West politically and ecclesiastically; and
creating a permanent breach in culture, policy and religion prepai
the way for the final disappearance of the eastern Empire. Strang
enough, however, on the Roman side, the excommunication

[1] Symonds, H. E., *The Church Universal and the See of Rome*, 1939, p. 259.
[2] *C.M.H.* vol. iv, p. 272. It should be observed that the patriarch of Anti
showed no great eagerness to follow the lead of the see of Constantinople in breal
with the West. Cf. Fortescue, A., *Orthodox Eastern Church*, pp. 188 ff.

owever, it must be admitted that a divergence persisted in spite of
anon Law. By a concession of Paschal II, in spite of the decrees of
rban II, it was permitted to an archbishop to consecrate to the
piscopate those who had previously done homage to the king for
heir temporalities.[1] Though Paschal's ruling was intended perhaps
nly as an experiment, Henry I had insisted on homage preceding
onsecration, and then by the confirmation of the custom in
Henry II's Constitutions it became part of normal English practice.
et its comparative insignificance only serves to emphasize the
ompleteness of the sway of Roman Canon Law over the English
hurch in other respects up to the end of the twelfth century and
eyond.[2]

A renewal of the struggle of the Empire with the Papacy was
harked by the excommunication of Henry V by Gelasius II.[3] After
our years of indecisive skirmishing a treaty of peace was drawn up
y the two powers in the Concordat of Worms. Although the Emperor
etained full control of elections in Germany, the Concordat was to
he advantage of the Papacy, for it marked the completion of the
rst stage in the process by which the practical immunity of the
talian episcopate from imperial intervention was secured.[4]

By now it had become clear that the reform movement had
aunched the Popes on a course of temporal aggrandisement, from
hich, even if they had wished, it would have been difficult to draw
ack. Yet there were already some who recognized that the policy of
Gregory VII was leading to the enlarged spiritual and temporal
ower of the Papacy being used for purely secular ends. Typical
f those who watched this development with considerable misgiving
vas Bernard of Clairvaux. His *De Consideratione* addressed to the
Cistercian Pope Eugenius III, while yielding to none in its insistence
f the fulness of papal authority in the spiritual sphere, looked upon
ve possibility of the Pope becoming a secular ruler with undisguised
prror. Though admitting that both swords belong to the Church,
ernard insisted that the Pope should refuse himself to employ the
emporal 'sword', and that in spite of his affirmation elsewhere that

---

[1] JL 6290. *M.P.L.* 163, 284. [2] Brooke, *op. cit.*, p. 154.
[3] *C.M.H.*, vol. v, p. 161.
[4] It has been held that the Concordat took the shadow for the substance, and that
although it put an end to 'investiture', it allowed interference with elections to the
German episcopate to continue unabated. See Brooke, Z. N., *Investiture Controversy.
Proc. of Brit. Acad.* vol. xxv, 1939, p. 26.

the Papacy exists 'to preside over princes, to command bishops an
to order kingdoms and Empires'.[1]

The spiritual sovereignty of the Papacy had been developed apar
by the organizing ability of the eleventh century Popes. The syste
of promulgating decrees at Roman synods, later published an
applied by local synods, established ever more and more firmly th
principle that the Pope was to be regarded as the universal legislato
His legates, permanent and temporary, travelled everywhere, ove
riding local jurisdiction and enforcing conformity to Roman standar
of discipline. The demand that bishops and even archbishops shoul
obey frequent summonses to Rome, as well as the provision that n
metropolitan could exercise his authority as such without fir
obtaining the coveted *pallium* from the hand of the Pope himsel
tended to increase the subordination of the local episcopate, whi
in addition by the creation of the office of primate, somewhat afte
the fashion of the earlier papal vicariates, there was placed over th
metropolitans a regional prelate more directly subject to pap
control.[2]

All this and more is to be regarded as a direct consequence of th
adoption of the reform movement by the Roman see. The onl
question which still awaited solution concerned temporal supremacy
The Concordat of Worms, while solving the minor question c
investiture, had left the major one undetermined. After the reopenin
of the conflict under Adrian IV, it soon became clear that the con
test between Alexander III and Frederick I could only result in
final triumph for the Papacy. The Empire had already suffered
serious breach in its defences by the blows delivered against feuda
ideas by Alexander's predecessors. The fact that Alexander coul
enlist on his side formidable support, Lombardy and Sicily, Franc
and Byzantium, enabled him to wear down Frederick's militar
strength. By the Peace of Venice the ultimate temporal supremac
of the Papacy was assured. Yet it had been bought at a price. Th
nascent power of nationalism, which the Papacy had called into bein
as its ally, was one day to challenge not only its temporal authorit
but its spiritual sovereignty as well.

The pontificate of Alexander III includes two specific points o

[1] Nevertheless the passage from the *De Consideratione* was later used by Giles c
Rome in defence of the temporal supremacy of the Popes, and so passed into th
Unam Sanctam of Boniface VIII.
[2] *C.M.H.* vol. v, p. 109.

erest. It shows the Pope in alliance with the city states and local
nmunes, and thus marks one of the earlier stages in the estab-
iment of a papal suzerainty in Italy. On the other hand, it witnessed
renewed repudiation of the claim that a council solemnly sum-
ned by an Emperor was competent to judge a Pope; and thus once
re the principle *Prima sedes a nemine iudicatur* was vindicated.[1]
yet, however, ideas of representative and constitutional govern-
nt were but dimly conceived by either Church or State. It remained
be seen whether, after they had made their influence felt upon the
urch, such a principle could be safely upheld.

The period which followed the death of Alexander in 1181 included
uccession of short pontificates held by Popes already of advanced
: at the time of their election. It may perhaps be regarded, like
years following the death of Gregory VII, as an interlude mainly
voted to consolidation.

IX

With the election of Innocent III the Augustan age of the Papacy
gins. Long before the latter half of the twelfth century was com-
te, the influence of the great collections of Canon Law, but
haps more particularly of Gratian's *Decretum*, had made itself felt,
1 individual commentators were beginning to assert not only the
olute supremacy of the Papacy over the Empire, but even went
far as to suggest that the only real Emperor was in fact the Pope.
was Innocent who, with a very considerable measure of success,
nslated these semi-official ideas into practice, by welding them into
oherent unity with the canonical doctrine regarding the character
the papal office. For a text illustrative of his pontificate we may
ll take one of his most characteristic utterances, which occurs in a
mon preached on an anniversary of his consecration:

Others were called to a share in responsibility, yet Peter alone was
nitted to the fulness of power. For a token of spiritual authority he
bestowed on me the mitre, for a token of temporal authority he
given me a crown; a mitre representing priesthood and a crown
bolizing the kingdom, making me the Vicar of Him, who has on
vesture and on His thigh a name written, "King of Kings and
rd of Lords: a Priest for ever, after the order of Melchizedek".'[2]
n justification of this ideal, Innocent made full use of the ideas,

[1] *C.M.H.* vol. v, p. 433.
[2] *Sermo* 3, *In consecr. pont. M.P.L.* 217, 665.

metaphors and analogies which for the last century or more ha
formed part of the literary heritage of the Church. It was certain
not without significance that on the occasion of his consecration
chose as his text the familiar words of Jeremiah :

'See, I have this day set thee above the nations and over t
kingdoms, to pluck up and to break down, to destroy and to ove
throw, to build and to plant'.[1]

This text, though he was not the first to apply it to the use
papal authority, is typical of his hierarchical interpretation of t
Old Testament. He insists on the twofold character of the office
Melchizedek as a type of the Papacy, and repeats the analogy of t
sun and the moon already used by his predecessors to explain
relation to the Empire. Naturally the metaphor of the 'two swor(
recurs in his writings. What is perhaps most surprising is the la
of novelty, for, as we have so often observed in previous pon
ficates, Innocent adds nothing strictly original to the basis on whi
his claims to supreme power are made.

Although Innocent argued that he was the superior of all eartl
monarchs and therefore their judge, no less had been maintain
at least in principle by Nicholas I. His most characteristic declarati
about the dependence of the Empire *principaliter et finaliter* (
origin and ultimate purpose) itself only expressed the view implici
held by his predecessors about the significance of imperial coronati
at the Pope's hands. Yet it should be observed that in spite of 1
repeated assertions that the Pope's spiritual power knows no boun(
Innocent allowed some limitation to the use of his temporal authori
It was only normal and continuous within the limits of the pa|
patrimony. Outside this area its exercise was occasional. Thus
writes :

'For we do not propose to pass judgment on a fief, the jurisdicti
over which belongs to him (*i.e.* Philip Augustus), unless some spec
privilege or contrary custom limits the common law (of the relatic
ship between the feudal superior and his vassal), but to decide or
question of sin, the censure of which is undoubtedly within c
province—a right which we are both competent and in duty bound
exercise'.[2]

---

[1] Jeremiah, i, 10.
[2] *Reg.* VII, *Epp.* 42, ann. 1204. The correct reading here is 'contrariam',
Friedberg, *op. cit.*, 243. 'Iuri communi' would seem to refer, not as usually

There is therefore ground for belief that with Innocent the
mporal authority of the Papacy, in spite of the considerable reper-
ssions likely from its use in the political sphere, remained essentially
ligious in respect both of its supposed origin and of the conditions
its exercise.

As a result of Innocent's influence the papal chancery underwent
nsiderable reorganization. Rules for the conduct of business were
early defined, stereotyped formulae for different kinds of letters
ere provided, and minute care taken to ensure the detection of
rgeries. Appeals to the papal court either might be referred to
dges delegate in the country of origin, in which case the Pope
served the right to pronounce sentence, or they might be settled in
ome itself. When this happened the case was usually heard by a
oman commission of *auditores*, though from time to time Innocent
eferred to hear it in person. The case of Giraldus Cambrensis
ows clearly the normal course of procedure in appeals to Rome
this period.[1]

It is beyond doubt that at this time the influence of the Roman
uria, consisting as it did for the most part of men of culture and
ucation, was on the side of maintaining at a high level the finer
tivities of the human spirit. But the mainspring of the whole
mplex machinery was the master mind of Innocent himself, the
ture of which is nowhere seen more clearly than in the decretals
nich he issued, to be incorporated later in the *Decretum* of Gregory
. Among the additions to the general Canon Law of the Church
ere the seventy canons issued by the fourth Lateran council.
itherto Lateran councils, even those held since the beginning of
e twelfth century which later came to be reckoned as oecu-
enical, were in fact only a somewhat enlarged form of the original
cal synod of the Roman church, of which we have already noticed
number of examples in the primitive period. On this occasion,
owever, doubtless on the initiative of Innocent himself, a serious
tempt was made to assemble a body of bishops representative of
e whole of the western church. As a result some four hundred or
ore bishops were gathered, thus constituting an assembly which
cceeded in numbers and perhaps also in decorum many of the earlier

cretals to the 'common law of the Church', but to feudal practices common to
: French *regnum* as a whole. The present writer owes this interpretation to the
urtesy of Professor Powicke.
[1] *C.M.H.* vol. vi, p. 34.

and more famous oecumenical councils. Its title to the epithet w
perhaps scarcely inferior to theirs. For if it was exclusively weste
the great Seven were without exception predominantly eastern
composition. As to its results, it left an impress on the sacramen
life and discipline of the Church which remained for the most p
unchallenged till the authority underlying its enactments was its
repudiated by the forces of reform.

In an outline sketch such as the present it is not easy to do just
to an impressive personality like that of Innocent III, still less to t
grandeur of his ideal of a Christian Europe united in comm
allegiance to the throne of St. Peter. Yet enough has been s
perhaps to suggest that in him the Papacy reaches what may
called without exaggeration the zenith of its influence. Under
successors we become increasingly conscious that though t
semblance of power remains, it is after all only a façade behind wh
there is taking place the slow but seemingly inevitable process
disintegration and decay.

This strange phenomenon, not altogether unfamiliar in t
history of purely secular institutions, has been well described by
modern writer:

'During the first part of the thirteenth century the hold whi
the Papacy had on Christendom was still increasing; whereas ha
way through the century the loss of that hold had become a forego
conclusion, and the only question left was, How long would it ta
for the crash to come?'[1]

In the year of Innocent III's election (1198) the future Empe
Frederic II, then a child of little more than three years, was crown
as Sovereign of the mediaeval kingdom of Sicily. But in order
possess his kingdom he had to face a determined effort on the part
the newly crowned Emperor Otto IV to unite Sicily to the Empire,
in the days of Frederic's father Henry VI. From this very unpromisi
situation Frederic owed his rescue to the timely intervention of t
Pope. The German princes responded to Innocent's invitation
depose Otto and elect Frederic. Nevertheless, as it remained t
Pope's consistent policy to keep the Empire and Sicily disunit
Innocent took good care to extract a declaration from Frederic
this effect. Nowhere more clearly is that strange impersonality of t
Papacy seen than in the relentless perseverance of Innocent's su

[1] Smith, A. L., *Church and State*, 1913, p. 6.

sor, one who differed from him in almost every quality, in the
ne attitude of hostility towards any furtherance of Frederic's
ns for unification. Yet what Honorius III resisted almost uncon-
ously, and perhaps contrary to his own inclination, Gregory IX,
man as he was, opposed with indomitable determination. It was
long before Frederic was excommunicate, and peace was only
tored at the price of important concessions, as a result of which
hold on Sicily if not broken was certainly weakened.

After a fresh breach Frederic was so far successful that he seemed
the moment to have all Italy at his feet. In the midst of the
sis Gregory died, and his successor Celestine IV followed him
the grave after a pontificate of only seventeen days. That the papal
se was ruined must have been the mistaken though not unreason-
e view of Frederic's more optimistic supporters. It was mistaken
y because it left out of account the remarkable capacity of the
pacy, never better shown than in this dark hour, for being able to
e phoenix-like from its ashes.

The election of Innocent IV, conducted by a handful of Cardinals
der most adverse conditions, proved disastrous for Frederic. The
w pontificate was marked, through a strange turn of fortune, by
evival of the eighth-century policy of Gregory III of inviting help
the papal cause from France, which was to prove disastrous to
pacy and Empire alike.[1] All the fixity of purpose of Gregory
, more than the diplomacy of Alexander III, and some, though
haps not enough, of Innocent III's dignity, were reincarnate in
s Genoese successor of St. Peter, even if he was totally lacking in
: moral goodness of the third Honorius. It was he more than any
er who introduced into papal policy and administration a new
d sinister element, an almost unscrupulous subordination of the
ritual to the secular, and displayed an adeptness in this direction,
en imitated but seldom exceeded by his successors. By ruining the
se of the Hohenstaufen he wrecked the Empire; but the spirit
led to his aid and the material instruments which he employed
uld themselves combine to ruin that very power which he himself
d sought to render proof against destruction. Thus it is scarcely
exaggeration to say that in effect Innocent IV was the first Pope to
rifice spiritual primacy for temporal power, and it has been said

Urban II had similarly called in France against the Empire. The policy had
ome almost a tradition of the Roman see.

that Dante's verdict on Celestine V might well stand as a judgment
on the whole Papacy of the thirteenth century, when it bartered the
legacy of St. Peter for the fatal dowry of Constantine.

That Innocent carried the theories of his predecessors a stage
further in the direction of temporal as well as spiritual absolutism is
clearly shown in his declaration *Eger, cui levia*, where he affirms :
'The Lord Jesus Christ . . . being a true king and true priest
after the order of Melchizedek . . . established in the apostolic
see not only a pontifical monarchy but a kingly one as well'.[1]

Thus Innocent assigns a twofold sovereignty to the Papacy, for
which he finds an additional justification in the promise not merely
of a key, but of *keys*. Appealing to the 'Donation of Constantine' he
argued that the Emperor performed his temporal functions only as
the delegate of the Papacy, asserting that both the temporal and the
spiritual sword belong *de iure* to St. Peter, for, even if the exercise
of the former was assigned explicitly to the Emperor, implicitly it
belonged to the Church; a power which was now actual in the Pope's
hands had always been potentially within the Church's control.
In complete consistency with this view he asserted that the Church
in pronouncing judgment on a temporal question acts *indirectly*,
even if it is through the direct action of the secular power that her
judgment becomes effective. Moreover a judgment pronounced by
the Pope in person, as in the case of Frederic, was held to be equivalent to the utterance of a verdict by God Himself.[2]

It is instructive to compare the doctrine of the Papacy as enunciated
by this Genoese Pope with the form in which it appears in the
writings of Thomas Aquinas. In contrast to the juridical formulæ
of the canonists, scholasticism remained content with more
traditional theories, such as we have already found in Gelasius
and Peter Damian. Thus he reproduces the saying of St. Bernard
'It holds the spiritual (sword) alone with a view to its exercise,
yet it holds also the temporal one in being able to command its
use'.[3]

On the other hand, he did not argue that temporal power exercised
by the State is only legitimate when it is conceded or delegated by
the Papacy. On the contrary, he asserted that spiritual and secular
sovereignty are alike both of divine origin (as against Innocent III

[1] Mirbt, No. 358, p. 197.   [2] Mirbt, No. 357.
[3] *In iv Sentent.*, *Dist. xxxvii.*, Q. 2. Art. 2 ; cf. Bernard, *De Consid.* 4, 3, 7.

no treated all temporal sovereignty not delegated by the Papacy as
. abuse). In fact, the secular power is only subject to the spiritual
any case where the salvation of souls is at stake. Thus while he
mitted that Sovereigns who are excommunicated for heresy or for
her causes may be deposed, he insisted that since the spiritual
elfare of their subjects is involved, the infliction of such a punish-
ent has not a political but a religious character. Elsewhere in his
ork, *Opusculum contra errores Graecorum*, he summarizes the
aditional doctrine as to the papal primacy, as for example, when he
·clares that :
'The Vicar of Christ holds a universal prelacy over the whole
hurch . . . he possesses in the Church the plenitude of power'.[1]
It may be remarked that these and other similar affirmations are
pported by quotations from forged *Acta* of Chalcedon and
urious works of Cyril of Alexandria.
It is easy to see that there is a fundamental difference between the
nception of the papal office held by Innocent IV and the one
fended by St. Thomas. In the latter the only concession made to
e canonists is the assertion that the Pope may exercise his deposing
ower for causes other than heresy. Such a concession, of course, pro-
ded a dangerous loophole for action springing from a motive far
ore easily recognizable as political than as religious. But when all
said, it remains true that the Thomist view has little in common
ith the policy of Innocent, in which 'everything spiritual, everything
ligious, became a means to one political end'.[2] If the doctrine of
e great Dominican had prevailed, it seems possible to say that the
apacy might yet have been saved the humiliations of the next two
nturies, and the Church preserved from the disasters of schism.
nhappily the forces released or created by the calculating Genoese
nonist proved far too powerful to be kept in check. After the
attering of the grand imperial ideal a self-confident secular
itionalism rose to take its place. By that time the spiritual credit of
e Papacy had been so far mortgaged in favour of its secular power,
id its policy subordinated to such an extent to temporal gain, that
hen its authority, first in the secular and then in the religious
here, came to be challenged, it was found to be spiritually bankrupt.
) when the need for creating fresh spiritual resources was realized,

---

[1] Mirbt, No. 361.
[2] Smith, A. L., *op. cit.*, p. 228.

irreparable disasters had befallen the Church, which even the heali
power of time has as yet only partly repaired.[1]

X

When Innocent IV died, the problem of finding a suitable candid:
for the Sicilian crown remained unsolved. Charles of Anjou h
declined the original offer, and Manfred who had accepted it prov
far from amenable to the papal will. It was Urban IV, son of a Fren
shoemaker, who revived the plan of finding a solution by means
French support. But his invitation to Charles, this time accepte
marked the beginning of an orientation of papal policy which wou
end in the subordination of the Roman see to the French crown.
soon became clear that in Charles the Papacy had found a serva
who was resolved to become its master. The final shattering of t
last hope of the Hohenstaufen in the pathetic death of the you
Conradin, martyr to the dying ideal of the Empire and victim of t
relentless Innocentian vendetta, left Charles a predominant figure
Italian politics.[2] Gregory X, with a singular gift for make-believe, w
not unsuccessful in erecting at least a façade of political and ecclesia
tical unity at the council of Lyons. But it quickly crumbled in t
face of the *Realpolitik* of Anjou and Castile, and even if the mo
enterprising and practical methods of Nicholas III managed
restore a greater measure of papal independence, the gain secur
was soon lost by Martin IV, whose reign was distinguished by t
renewal of the Byzantine schism, which the recent council h:
unsuccessfully attempted to heal.

With the accession of Philip the Fair to the throne of France fo
years later, a new and remarkable chapter opened in the history
both that nation and of the Papacy. With the fading of the mediaev
ideal of a European unity of peoples loosely federated under tl
common suzerainty of the Empire, nationalist self-consciousness w
growing more and more apparent. Not only France, but Engla:

---

[1] The unhappy effect of the constantly increasing papal taxation necessitated
the 'crusades' against Frederic II and others, and known to be such, must
remembered. The attitude of one like Matthew Paris in England shows how
harmed the prestige of the Papacy and caused its spiritual position to be und
mined. Cf. Smith, *op. cit.*, p. 167 ff.

[2] The war of the 'Sicilian Vespers' seriously injured the reputation of the Pap:
in Italy, where the overbearing conduct of its French allies was found intolerabl

d Aragon as well, were becoming more aware of themselves as
dependent sovereign states, the rulers of which reigning by divine
ght were held to be responsible only to God.

After the drab and undistinguished rule of Nicholas IV the garish
lours of Boniface VIII's pontificate present a sudden and almost
rrifying contrast.[1] It acquired great prominence in the later middle
es, mainly owing to the contest with Philip the Fair, and to the
rect challenge to papal authority which it involved. The remote cause
 this struggle with the new nationalism has already been indicated.
 arose, as we have seen, from the growth of nationalist consciousness
 France and an attitude of growing impatience towards the claims
 the Papacy, which, not content with an absolute spiritual primacy,
d come to assert a temporal sovereignty not less universal and
solute in its turn. The actual form of the conflict was dictated
gely by circumstances of an economic nature. The breakdown of
e feudal military system had been brought about, at least in part,
· the widespread recognition of the possibility that obligations of
rvice could be discharged by means of monetary payment.[2] Hence
ere had resulted an ever-increasing system of taxation, levied by
e section of the community on another for the benefit of its
mediate superiors. Nominally at least all spiritualities enjoyed
emption,[3] but in practice the distinction between spiritual and
mporal property of the Church was not easy to define; for example,
y revenue derived from land, even when it provided for a religious
use, was never able to escape taxation altogether. Yet this does not
ean that the clergy were not taxed in respect of *spiritualia*. Taxes
d dues of various kinds were levied by ecclesiastical superiors, and
· none more generally or more effectively than the Papacy itself.
heir variety and oppressiveness were already considerable; in the
urse of the next century or so they would become intolerable. So
o by the time Innocent IV was Pope, elaborate machinery involving
e employment of a whole host of collectors and officials had come
to existence. Yet if it was asked what became of the money so

---

[1] Yet another and scarcely less remarkable contrast was provided by the brief
ntificate of Celestine V, which itself is sufficient to illustrate the extent to which
e Papacy had become secularized. A saint could not remain Pope for more than
: months.

[2] But also by the eventual recognition of its utter inefficiency when face to face,
at Crécy, with mercenaries skilled in the art of warfare.

[3] Spiritualities meant little beyond fees for spiritual services. The bulk of
clesiastical property was temporality.

collected, it was found that a formidable proportion of it was used
finance the political allies of the reigning Pope. Thus it came abc
that on occasion, as under Gregory X, sums collected from
French clergy were placed at the disposal of the French kingdc
then acting in the papal interest,[1] while under Celestine V the l
disguise of providing for strictly ecclesiastical needs was abandon
The system was gradually extended in France, until by a general le
on all property and the proposed reimposition of the 'tenth', intend
to defray the cost of the war against England, the clergy were be
subjected by the State to a double tax, on *spiritualia* and *tempora*
alike.

When Boniface VIII intervened with his bull *Clericis laicos* it m
not be supposed that he was disinterestedly attempting to protect
French clergy from injustice. There were at the end of the thirteer
century considerable arrears in taxation owed by France to
Papacy, and obviously if Philip had his way there would be neith
the inclination nor the means to defray them. The effect of the b
was to prohibit any taxation of the clergy apart from papal approv
and though it suffered some diminution in value as a bulwark agair
royal exactions, in consequence of *Etsi de statu*, by which such taxati
was allowed to be levied without first obtaining approval if the ki
should judge it expedient, it remained the basis of papal poli
The measure of later papal submission to the French monarc
is to be judged by its repeal by Clement V.

The action of Boniface was in no sense an arbitrary improvisatio
but was a logical application of the principle of papal intervention
temporal concerns, which had been acknowledged generally for
last two centuries.[2]

The case of the bishop of Pamiers, the secret alliance between
French court and the house of Colonna, together with news of fre

---

[1] On the nominal excuse that it was to be used for crusading.

[2] It should be realized that the Pope was actuated by a laudable desire to s
the war then threatening between Edward I of England and Philip by cutting
supplies on both sides. We have here the earliest example in history of the appli
tion of economic sanctions, as usual a total failure. A further remarkable feature
his bull is the assumption implied by its opening words, that clergy and laity
two separate and hostile bodies. The extent to which the idea of the Church as
corpus Christi had broken down is significantly illustrated by the contempor
English use of 'gens de seinte Eglise' as the usual legal designation of a clergym
The claim to immunity from taxation for clerics is to a great extent a logical devel
ment from the *privilegium fori*, which had been the chief matter of contenti
between Thomas Becket and Henry II.

actions from the clergy, combined to convince Boniface that no
derstanding or compromise was possible. His bull *Ausculta fili*,
dressed to Philip in person, was an ultimatum, and following the
feat of France at Courtrai the Pope felt strong enough to summon
e French bishops to a council at Rome. It is remarkable that in
ite of Philip's prohibition, thirty-six out of a total of seventy-eight
mmoned were present.[1] The council was followed by the publica-
n (possibly on November 18, 1302) of the famous bull *Unam
nctam*, a document which has been described as 'the most
solute proclamation of theocratic doctrine ever formulated in the
iddle Ages'.[2]

The bull is in effect a theological statement of the nature of the
urch and its mission. This forms the framework of doctrine into
ich a definition of the functions of its head, the Sovereign Pontiff, is
serted. It contains the following propositions. First, that there is
ne Church, outside which there can be neither salvation nor the
rgiveness of sins. Next, that as the Church is but a single body it
n only have One Head, with which Christ, Christ's Vicar Peter,
d the successor of Peter are identified. Thirdly, that the Church
ssesses and has authority over 'two swords', the spiritual and the
mporal. Yet while the former belongs to the bishop, the latter is to
used by the hand of kings and soldiers, according to the will and
permission of the bishop. For in any event the temporal power is
bordinate to the spiritual. From this it must follow that the
mporal power, since it is established by the spiritual, may be judged
it. So too a lesser spiritual power is to be judged by its superior,
it the highest can be judged by God alone, not by man. The
thority of this supreme power, the bull declares, is in fact divine,
nce to resist the spiritual power is to resist the ordinance of God.
'Wherefore', it concludes, 'we declare, affirm, define and pronounce
at for every human creature it is an indispensable condition of
lvation that he should be subject to the Roman Pontiff'.[3]

There is here, as we have so frequently remarked before in papal
cuments, strikingly little that is actually original.[4] The first pro-
sition can be found already in third-century writers. The mystical

---

[1] Boase, T. S. R., *Boniface VIII*, 1933, p. 316.
[2] *C.M.H.* vol. vii, p. 313. Mirbt, *op. cit.*, No. 372.
[3] Mirbt, *ibid.*, p. 211.
[4] In any case the immediate source of its argument is to be found in the *De
clesiastica potestate* of Giles of Rome, then recently published.

identification of Peter with Christ and the reigning Pontiff with Pet
is in Leo I. The theory of the 'two swords' may be as early
Nicholas I, but is certainly in St. Bernard, though the form in whi
it is quoted here differs in that it leaves no initiative whatever
the temporal power. Yet nothing is said about the authority of tl
spiritual power in strictly temporal matters. Instead, the bull
content to insist on the right of the former to judge the latter, ai
on the very principle *Prima sedes a nemine iudicatur*, which, as v
have seen, goes back to the beginning of the sixth century. I
significance lies chiefly in the fact that its logical issue is to redu
the State to no more than a function of the Church, and the Chur
to little more than an instrument of the Papacy. If opposition to i
temporal claims was immediate and violent, it is not less remarkab
that scarcely twenty years passed before its spiritual claim w
challenged as well; remarkable, yet not surprising, if we recall tl
extent to which during the last half century the political outloc
of the Papacy had tended to subordinate spiritual values to en
directly temporal.

But the pontificate of Boniface served also to show that this sul
ordination was not confined to the political sphere. If we may regai
the decision which assigned a higher rank in the hierarchy of festiva
to the feasts of the four Latin doctors, Ambrose, Jerome, Augustin
and Gregory, and imposed the change on the Latin church at larg
as possessing a purely religious character, the same is by no mea;
true of the institution of the Jubilee in the year 1300. Doubtless
itself it was not strictly an innovation, since it was simply a develoj
ment of the primitive custom of making pilgrimage to Rom
especially to the burial places of the Apostles, for the sake of tl
spiritual benefits to be obtained. On the strength of this traditic
Boniface now assured to 'all who, being truly penitent, visit the
basilicas in this present year, and in each succeeding hundred
year, not only a full and copious, but the most full pardon of a
their sins'.[1] Although nothing was said officially about a connexic
between merit and money, the inclination to reckon spiritual no le
than temporal obligations in terms of a monetary equivalent was tc
strong not to predominate, and even if it had not been foresee.
the Jubilee soon came to be regarded as a highly profitable methc
of financing papal enterprises. Yet the popular view of indulgence

[1] Boase, *op. cit.*, p. 233.

at is to say, official acts by which the remission of temporal penalty
ie to sin was proclaimed by the hierarchy, such as the Indulgence
the Jubilee, tended to divorce moral sincerity from external
actice, and thus open the way to a quantitative assessment of
iritual values in terms of a monetary tariff.[1] Whatever the tem-
rary advantages secured by such methods, there remained all the
ingerous possibilities of an inevitable reaction, not less harmful to
clesiastical authority because a century and a quarter was to elapse
fore it actually took place.[2]

After Boniface's death it seemed at first by no means impossible
at by astute diplomacy, in spite of the intensity of feeling aroused
the one side by the recent blunt assertion of papal privilege, and
the other by the brutality inflicted on the person of St. Peter's
ccessor at Anagni by the emissaries of French nationalism,
nedict XI might be successful in satisfying at one and the same time
e rival claims of Italian sentiments and of French patriotism, the
ter determined to lose nothing of the fruits of its recent victory.[3]
it he was powerless to appease the strife between the Florentine
ctions, and his premature death was believed to have been hastened
those who preferred disorder to peace, and who saw in him a
tent influence on the side of reconciliation.

XII

The prompt election as Clement V of Bertrand de Got, arch-
shop of Bordeaux,[4] marks the beginning of the Avigonese Papacy.
is a mistake to suppose that in abandoning for seventy years their
aditional seat the Popes were carrying out a deliberate policy. The
oice of Avignon, an enclave within the Arelatine dominion of the
cilian kingdom, was originally dictated solely by the consideration
at it enabled the Popes to be near at hand in order to effect that

[1] The idea goes back to the practice of commuting penances for other works
g. by going on crusades) in the earlier Middle Ages. The feudal analogy of com-
itation of personal service had no doubt some influence on its growth.
[2] It is probable that Boniface himself hoped to stave off the growing hostility
the temporal power by impressing pilgrims with his prestige seen at close range.
iere is a story that he displayed himself to them wearing the imperial insignia
d proclaiming 'Ego sum Caesar; ego sum imperator'.
[3] *C.M.H.* vol. vii, p. 17.
[4] As such he was a subject not of Philip but of Edward I of England. France at
e time was not sufficiently united for it to be possible to speak of all its inhabitants
Frenchmen. It is important to bear this fact in mind in thinking of the Popes of
ignon, most of whom were Gascons, Provençals, Limousins and so on.

programme of appeasement between the French and English kir
doms to which they had recently directed so much of their attenti(
Nor was it ever contemplated that the 'Babylonish captivity' wou
be more than a brief interlude.[1] Yet there was a natural inclinati
among Popes and Cardinals of non-Italian origin to be indifferent
Rome as a place of residence, and thus to prolong the anomaly o
bishop of Rome directing the affairs of the Church from a cen
far removed from his own see.[2]

There can be little doubt that in the interests of anti-papal pi
paganda in the fourteenth century, the evils of the Avignonese peri
were considerably exaggerated, not least by Italians, like Petrar(
who realized that Italy stood to lose much by the change.[3] It m
well be true that the standard of morality in the city of Avignon its
left much to be desired, but if it was not higher, there is no evider
to show that it was appreciably lower than that obtaining in m(
mediaeval cities of the time. As to the allegation against the pa]
court of unrestrained luxury and extravagance, it must not be f(
gotten that at least two of the Avignonese Popes, Benedict XII a
Innocent VI, made quite serious attempts to effect reform in gener
and especially to reduce expenditure.[4] And it was, at least to so)
extent, the unpopularity of such measures within the Curia tl
prevented their having any far-reaching or permanent effect.

The renewed struggle belonging to this period between Papacy a
Empire enacted by John XXII and Lewis of Bavaria was far m(
like a stage parody of the classical conflicts of an earlier age thar
real contest. The collapse of feudal principles and the rise
nationalism, together with the loss suffered by the Empire after t
fall of the Hohenstaufen of an effective role in European politi
lent to the whole affair a strange air of unreality.[5] Avignon mi

---

[1] Mollat, G., *Les Papes d'Avignon*, 1920, p. 400 f.

[2] It should be realized that Italy itself was at the time in a highly disturbed c(
dition, and that the Popes were in any case naturally attached to the land of th
birth. This was even more true of the Cardinals, and the prevalent laxity as
residence on the part of all bishops and dignitaries in this period prevented th
absence from Rome from being regarded as a scandal *per se*, except by such peo]
as Catherine of Siena, who were perhaps popularly regarded as 'cranks'. In any c
Avignon became a papal possession under John XXII; hence the Pope's resider
there was analogous to that of the archbishop of Canterbury living at Lamb
or at some other of the archiepiscopal manors outside his diocese.

[3] Mollat, *op. cit.*, p. 302; *C.M.H.* vol. vii, p. 288.

[4] Mollat, *op. cit.*, pp. 67, 98.

[5] Flick, *Decline of the Mediaeval Church*, 930, vol. i, p. 220.

ake with the thunder of papal anathemas, and Rome enjoy the
ʋersion of a papal election by plebiscite, but the attitude of Europe
nained one of indifference not unmingled with contempt.

But if the struggle itself, prolonged under Benedict XII and his
ɔ successors, seemed almost unsubstantial, there was nothing unreal
its literary products. The revolt of the mystical and other-worldly
tlook against the growth of secularism, already foreshadowed at the
d of the twelfth century in the writings of Joachim of Flora, found
rallying point in the attempt of the spiritual Franciscans to recap-
re the spirit of their founder. This force now combined with the
ɛrary ability of the supporters of the Emperor Lewis to present
ɔrmidable challenge, no longer only to the temporal claims of the
pacy, but even to the validity of its spiritual authority. Yet if
ne like the Franciscan General, Michael of Cesena, were prepared
call in question the very foundation of papal supremacy, its
ɩmacy of doctrine, others scarcely less radical in principle concen-
ɩted their attack on the immunity claimed by the Popes from human
lgment, and insisted strongly on the absolute supremacy of a
neral council. Some advocates of this latter view, such as that
ɩtinguished member of Oxford University, William of Occam,
mitted that the Papacy was of the *bene esse* of the Church, while
ʒuing that the Gospel of Christ can alone be regarded as the final
ɩrce of faith. Others, again, like Marsilius of Padua, repudiated the
pal claim to depose sovereigns, attacked the supremacy of Canon
ɩw, and defended the creation of national churches.[1] On all sides
e declaration contained in Gratian's *Decretum*, that a Pope may be
posed for heresy, was being quoted and quoted again.[2] In some
ɩarters mention was made of the view of the canonist Rufinus that
hism and perhaps idolatry would provide sufficient cause,[3] and
ɛre were doubtless a few who were prepared to cite the *Summa* of
ɩguccio in defence of the position that the heresy incriminated
ɛd not be notorious. The axe seemed therefore already to be laid
the root of the tree.

[1] In addition he repudiated the Petrine privileges and even doubted the residence
St. Peter at Rome. His is the first real attack upon the Papacy on downright radical
ɛs.

[2] *Decretum*, VI, *Dist.* xl. ed. Friedberg, vol. i, p. 146. *M.P.L.* 187, 215. Cf.
ʋière, *op. cit.*, p. 111. This was of practical importance in view of the heresy
ʒarding the Beatific Vision preached by John XXII and his condemnation of
ɛ doctrine of apostolic poverty.

[3] *C.M.H.* vol. v, p. 742.

Yet the contest with the shadowy Empire died down, and after t]
half-hearted attempt of Urban V, the Papacy finally returned
reoccupy its ancient seat in the person of Gregory XI. Unfortunatel
however, for the future of Christendom and the unity of the Churc
a great deal of water had passed under the Pont d'Avignon during t]
last seventy years, in consequence of which it proved impossib
for the Papacy to resume precisely the same position which it ha
abandoned at the time of the election of Bertrand de Got.

Two factors, one affecting its relation to the Church, the other :
position in Italy, had meanwhile radically affected its status. In t]
first place the unfortunate policy of territorial acquisition, develope
to such a formidable extent under Innocent IV, had left a lega
which for seven centuries hung like a millstone round the pap
neck, till it was finally shattered by the entry of Cadorna into Ron
One of the chief considerations which had detained the Pope a
Curia so long in Avignon was the instability of papal control ov
its *patrimonium* and Italian possessions, a fact which is clear
shown by the decision to return to Rome once the military exploi
of the soldierly Cardinals Albornoz and Robert of Geneva ha
succeeded in winning for their master almost undisputed control
the Papal States.[1] Out of this factor arose the other, namely, financi
embarrassment. The diminution of papal revenue from Italy,
addition to the steadily rising cost of military campaigns ar
bureaucratic centralization, made it urgently necessary for ne
sources of revenue to be tapped. So to the varied expedients
papal taxation, against which vigorous protests had already bee
made both in England and in France, was added a new method
exploiting the almost boundless wealth of the mediaeval Churc
The claim of certain extreme advocates of papal authority, that
virtue of its supposed sovereign rights over all civil governments a
temporalities were at its disposal, had already been expressed l
Clement IV in the spiritual sphere, by means of a claim that a
benefices and ecclesiastical property throughout Christendom we
papal donatives.[2] The possibilities of this as a source of gain, eve

[1] Mollat, *op. cit.*, pp. 159, 163.

[2] No Pope, however, ventured to put fully into effect the claim of Giles of Rom
that all property, ecclesiastical and civil alike, belonged to the Pope. Nor was t
claim generally admitted. Bishop Pecock in England made himself very unpopu
with the clergy for asserting it of ecclesiastical property, and his misfortunes a
imprisonment were largely due to his advocacy of the papal case.

it might be argued in all seriousness that the Pope as their rightful
owner could not be guilty of simony, are not difficult to imagine,
t the extensive use which was made of the supposed right by means
reservations and expectancies, in addition to straightforward
esentations, utterly beggars the imagination. There can be no doubt
at financially the security of the Avignonese Papacy left much to
desired, yet possible insolvency could scarcely justify the ruthless
ploitation of the Church's substance, not only then but for many
ars to come.[1]

Thus the return of Gregory XI to Rome found the Papacy deeply
volved in two main preoccupations, either of which alone would
ve been sufficiently serious to impair its primitive reputation for a
interested concern in the maintenance of a pure tradition and an
dered discipline in other churches. Combined, they led to a radical
ticism of the whole theory of papal authority. The first of these,
ich amounted to an attempt to solve the problem of providing
the insistent demands of the papal exchequer by making generous
fts on the Church's spiritual and material credit, inevitably pro-
ked the demand that the Church should itself undertake the task
reform in 'head and members', which the Papacy seemed powerless
put into effect. The second, namely the absorption of attention in
maintenance of the integrity of the papal dominions in Italy,
ded to deprive the heirs of the great traditions of Leo and Innocent
heir moral and spiritual ascendancy in Europe, and to reduce them
the eyes of their contemporaries to rank of petty Italian despots,
tenure of whose temporal state depended on the maintenance of
ever-increasingly precarious balance of power.

XIII

Of the great schism in the West, and the vain attempt to remedy
prevalent evils in the Church, by means of the ill-starred and
organized conciliar movement, only so much needs to be said as
rs on the question of the position of the Papacy under the growing
uence of Humanism and the impact of the New Learning on
stern Christendom.

he strange absence of realism in the outlook of the Roman see

Yet it should be borne in mind that papal provisions sometimes served as an
t to the favouritism and nepotism of local ecclesiastical and secular patrons,
hich point see Barraclough, G., *Papal Provisions*, 1935, c. iv.

8

and its Curia following the collapse of the Empire may be regard
as responsible in some measure, though by no means alone, for t
disastrous interlude in its history, during which anathemas a
counter-anathemas re-echoed across Europe, as the Popes of Avigr
and Rome mutually consigned one another to perdition. It was fr
this uneasy nightmare of a two-headed monster that the Church
the theologians, canonists and men of practical common sense w
to new life in the high promise of the council of Pisa.

A new body of pamphleteers descended into the arena, and by
pen of those like Henry of Langenstein, the radical ideas of Occ
and Marsilius found fresh if less revolutionary expression.[1] Nev
theless, in spite of Henry's light-hearted dismissal of canon
impediments, it must have been difficult even for the promoters
the conciliar method of ending the schism really to answer w
complete satisfaction either to themselves or to others, embarrass
questions involving the right to summon a council, the office
conciliar president and the legitimacy of its proceedings.[2] It was
spectre of uncertainty which dogged the deliberations of the succ
sive councils, and in the end led to the almost unconditional surren
of the movement to Eugenius IV at Florence.[3]

As illustrations of the relation of the Church to the Papacy dur
this period two documents seem to deserve special mention.
first of these is the declaration contained in five articles subscribe
the fifth session of the council of Constance. The first of these
an affirmation that the existing council was legitimately assemb
oecumenical in character, and that all persons of whatever rank, e
Popes, were bound to obey it in matters concerning the faith,
extirpation of schism and the reformation of the Church in 'head
members'. Next came the declaration that should the Pope (J
XXIII) decline to obey its decisions he should be subjected to

---

[1] It is important to notice how far less radical Henry of Langenstein was
his predecessors.

[2] *C.M.H.* vol. vii, p. 295.

[3] The conciliar movement served to lay bare the real weakness of papal a
lutism as created by the canonists of the post-Hildebrandine period. With
Popes it had worked well on the whole ; but given a corrupt holder of the off
became an insurmountable obstacle to reform. The chief difficulty in the w
the movement's success is to be found in the fact that its leaders had been br
up in the papal system and, when it came to be called in question, were incapa
proposing a workable alternative. Historical knowledge sufficient to make an a
to the primitive church order was lacking, nor was there any sign of an abil
rediscover fully the organic conception of the Church as the *corpus Christi*.

n legal penalty, and that neither he nor the Curia might leave
nstance without the council's permission. Lastly, it was asserted
t the Pope and all who had been invited to the council had enjoyed
l liberty.

The chief opposition to these articles had come from the Italian
mbers of the council, who had urged the Emperor Sigismund to
event them from being accepted *conciliariter*. In spite of this
otest, however, the council gave them its full approval. When,
refore, after John's deposition and the election of Martin V, the
ure relation of the Pope to the council was discussed, inevitably
further problem about the legitimacy of the decrees adopted by
fifth session was raised, and particularly the question whether
not they were confirmed by the Pope. It has often been argued
t his confirmation of the conciliar *Acta* by means of the bull
er cunctas and also given at the forty-fifth session, was conditioned
the phrase *in favorem fidei et ad salutem animarum*. To argue that
h decrees did not involve questions of faith or salvation would
m at first sight impossible. Hence it is usual nowadays to call
ention to the Pope's own words in the forty-fifth session: 'I
rove therefore and ratify all that has been done in conciliar
aion (*conciliariter*) as to a matter of faith, but not (what was done)
erwise or in any other way'. Yet what is the real meaning of
ciliariter? If it is 'acting as a council', as opposed to *nationaliter*,
ing by nations', then the fourth and fifth sessions are included
the scope of Martin's confirmation, for if at other sessions the
ncil voted by nations, it certainly voted *conciliariter* on that
asion. The question therefore resolves itself simply into one of
umstantial evidence. Did the fifth session behave *conciliariter*?
viously this is not easy to decide, but an impartial consideration
ts procedure might justify the view that its behaviour was not
conciliaris than that of many similar assemblies. We shall see
. in actual fact the influence of the decrees of the fifth session
not disappear with their repudiation by Eugenius IV after the
ncil of Basle. Thus the whole controversy illustrates very clearly
uncertainty obtaining at the time on the qualifications which
e needed for a council to be recognized as truly oecumenical.
happily, Papalists and Conciliarists alike were at the mercy of a
ception of church order and a standpoint regarding church
ory which was very largely devoid of a real historical foundation.

The conciliar theory widely acknowledged in the fifteenth centu
was that for a council to be legitimately regarded as oecumenical
must be summoned by the Pope, and that he or his legates shou
preside; that it should be morally representative of the whole Chur
after a summons had been addressed to all the bishops, of whom
sufficient number must be in attendance; and, finally, that it should
formally approved by the Pope. Papalists and Conciliarists agre
that of these conditions the first two were certainly fulfilled both
Constance and at Basle; only in regard to the fulfilment of the
at Constance was there a difference of opinion, for if Eugenius
did in fact confirm the sixteen first sessions of Basle, the effect
his subsequent acts was to reverse the decision.

Neither side was apparently aware of the real difficulty, name
that the early history of councils had been transformed into a lege
Moreover, judged by these three standards, none of the first ei
oecumenical councils was deserving of the name, still less th
which had been held following the schism between the sees of Ro
and Byzantium; in fact, it seems possible to argue that the o
council completely to satisfy them all was the council of Floren
It is hardly necessary to recall that all the first eight councils w
actually summoned not by a Pope but by a Roman Emperor; t
the gathering of bishops at these could scarcely be called e
'morally' representative of the whole Church, since they were
overwhelmingly eastern in composition, while the eighth, if ind
it has any right to be reckoned even by Roman Catholics as oe
menical, was frequented by a pathetic handful of the Cath
episcopate; and finally, that even if Leo I independently confirm
the dogmatic definition of Chalcedon, the later papal confirmati
seem for the most part to have been accorded under pressure
Caesaropapism, though it may be allowed that failure to annu
conciliar decision was tantamount to its actual confirmation.
formal papal endorsement of the symbol and canons of Nicaea
distinct from their belated adoption by the Roman see, there is
trace except in the realm of legend, nor of any of Constantinopl
Only once, therefore, in the pre-Reformation period does the pa
conciliar theory seem to have been carried out in practice, and t
it was prevented by circumstances, mainly of a political natu
from achieving any lasting results.

Nevertheless the council of Florence managed to bequeath

posterity a historical monument of considerable importance in its
Decretum pro Graecis embodied in Eugenius IV's bull *Laetentur caeli*.
Its significance lies in the fact that it expresses a view of the Papacy
which was actually accepted by representatives of the eastern as well
as of the western churches on the eve of the Reformation.

'We also define', it declares, 'that the holy apostolic see and the
Roman Pontiff holds a primacy over the whole world, and that the
Roman Pontiff himself is the successor of blessed Peter the prince
of the Apostles, and the true Vicar of Christ, and remains the head
of the Church and the father and teacher of all Christians; and that
to him in the person of blessed Peter has been delivered by our Lord
Jesus Christ the full power of ruling and governing the universal
Church; even as it is comprised also in the *Acta* of oecumenical
councils and in the holy canons'.[1]

The effort to prove the complete subordination of councils to the
Papacy as an historical experiment can scarcely be pronounced an
unmitigated success. On the other hand, the theory of conciliar
authority itself is even less proof against close investigation. History
has shown that it is far more the moral consensus subsequently given
to conciliar decisions (and nowhere is this more evident than in the
case of Nicaea I itself), than either the extent to which they were
truly representative or the fact of being due to papal initiative or
of enjoying papal approval, which endows them with such a degree
of *auctoritas* as they may be held to possess.

XIV

The years which intervened between the council of Florence and
the death of Leo X were marked by a rapid deterioration in the
spiritual and moral prestige of the Papacy. The Church was already
beginning to experience the full impact of the Humanistic movement,
for which in the fifteenth century it seems to have been no better
prepared than it had been in the fourth for the embarrassing patronage
of Roman imperialism. Yet in the earlier crisis it had revealed a
power of adaptation which now appeared to be conspicuously absent,
as a result of which there ensued a strange, almost terrifying paralysis
of its nerve centres, which left it ill-fitted to grapple with the forces

---

[1] Denzinger, *Enchiridion*,[14] 1922, No. 694. Mirbt. *op. cit.*, No. 400.

of disintegration soon to be released in all their fury on Christia
society.

The dying glory of the Middle Ages irradiating the otherwise di
mal years of the later fifteenth century shone out for a brief space
the romantic enthusiasm of Pius II. Even if we may be disposed
dismiss as a quixotic enterprise his courageous attempt to assun
once more the role of spiritual and temporal leader of Christendo
in a desperate attempt to rally Christian consciences to the rescue
the prostrate torso of the Byzantine Empire, we must at least acknov
ledge that even in the shadows of the approaching cataclysm tl
Papacy was still capable of rising above the petty claims of nationalis
and of upholding with almost desperate loyalty that ideal of supr
national unity which the Middle Ages had long dreamed of b
never effectively attained.

It was indicative of the coming determination of the Roman s
to make itself once more the indispensable centre of Christendo
that Pius II took the opportunity by means of his bull *Exsecrabilis*
dealing a mortal blow to the theory of conciliar supremacy, and at tl
same time to proclaim the finality and irreversibility of a pap
decision.[1] Strangely enough in doing so he asserted no more tha
the Popes of the fifth century.

With the romanticism of his predecessor, the practical sagacity
Paul II present a striking, though by no means unfamilar contra:
His was the ambition which made of the papal Curia the mc
splendid court in Europe; his the pride of position as 'first citizen'
Rome, which sternly repressed disorder and gave attention to tl
provision of social services to an extent exceptional in a mediaev
prince. To him was due also the restoration of unity and authori
within the Petrine patrimony, so that by the year 1468, by a cor
bination of force and diplomacy, he had succeeded in bringing abo
a general pacification of Italy.

The most spectacular if by no means the most important event
his pontificate was the visit to Rome of the Emperor Frederic I
when the utter humiliation of the once proud *imperium* of the Saxo
and Franconian dynasts was dramatically and symbolically displaye
Once again the fatal plan of attempting to secure the interests of t
Church by fostering disunion between Christian princes and weake
ing a power which might have safeguarded eastern Europe agair

[1] Mirbt, *op. cit.*, No. 406.

e Turkish invader ensnared the Papacy in an embarrassing political
iance. Yet Paul II has not always received sufficient credit for his
alities as a ruler. In a later age, more appreciative of social welfare,
would have been accounted a great benefactor. If his care was
ore for the things of the body than of the spirit, it was because the
pacy as an institution had itself almost learnt to believe that its
inence was due more to its secular associations than to its spiritual
igin.

With Sixtus IV the Papacy became, but for the brief interlude of
Irian VI, finally and decisively Italianized. It was an age in which
ovements in favour of democratic and representative institutions
d almost universally given way to absolutist monarchies. Thus,
id the warring competition of Italian princes, the Papacy, if it was
t to be driven out of Rome or become subject to some petty tyrant,
is compelled to fight a grim struggle for existence. Sixtus realized
at it was no longer possible to rely on a balance of power, still less
spiritual prestige, for his independence. The former had always
en precarious, and in the present disordered state of Italy was
tirely unstable; the latter, thanks to the unhappy results of the
hism, had been well-nigh destroyed. He was the first to adopt an
ashamed policy of nepotism, and to use it for the creation of a
ong unified political power in central Italy sufficient to stand alone
ainst all rivals, singly or in combination. The chief obstacle to his
bition to a secular Italian primacy was to be found in the despotic
vernment of the Medici in Florence, and it is difficult to discharge
m of some measure of complicity in the device for its violent over-
row. Its partial success had ultimately led to a state of open war
tween that city and the Roman see, bringing the Papacy into a
sition of serious embarrassment, from which it was only extricated
a strangely acrobatic and almost wholly unmoral diplomacy. So
Sixtus left behind him a capital remodelled and in part at least
built, and deserved well of posterity by his recreation of the Sistine
apel and the Vatican library, it remains to his eternal discredit
at it was he more than any other who made of an institution, the
tentialities of which for good were unlimited, a secular power which
ly differed from its contemporaries in virtue of its historical
igin, spiritual now in little more than name. The real tragedy
y in the coincidence of the resulting moral degradation of the
ghest ecclesiastical power in Christendom with an age in which

perhaps never more was the Christian faith in need of the support which a higher moral tone in the lives of those meant to be its chief advocates alone could have supplied.

It will be unprofitable for our purpose to pursue further the history of the Renaissance Papacy. The pontificates of Innocent VIII, Alexander VI and Julius II add much to the record of sordid degeneration, but little to our knowledge about the place occupied by the Papacy within the life and history of the Church. And if with the election of Leo X the Roman see passed out of the slough of vulgar prostitution of spiritual grandeur into the more decorous state of self-admiring complacency, its spiritual potency seemed to have utterly vanished.

Politically, in its relation to the secular powers, Leo's pontificate was marked by a return to the diplomacy of an earlier period, namely in the extension of the system of concordats. These originated in their modern form with the attempt on the part of Martin V to stave off organic reform of the whole Church by buying off each nation separately with a minimum of solid privileges. Such questions a the conditions of episcopal election, rights of patronage and appeals to the Roman see were redefined and regulated. The countries involved in these early concordats were first Germany, Poland Hungary and Scandinavia, next the Latin nations France, Italy and Spain, and finally England. Unfortunately the political instability of the Papacy, in consequence of its unhappy position as only one among a number of contending Italian princedoms, deprived them of anything more than ephemeral value, a limitation which not even the fresh agreement of 1448 between Nicholas V and Frederic II was able to overcome. Under Leo X the conflict between the spirit of French nationalism and papal authority, though concealed by the Concordat of 1516, was made evident by the Pope's exercise of his supreme power to cancel the Pragmatic Sanction of the previous century (1438)[1] on the one side, and on the other by Francis I' promulgation of Leo's bull, thus implying the claim to be able to adopt or to repudiate papal judgments. The 'dualism' of mediaeval theory remained unresolved, yet the trend of events pointed to the coming of a time when the relations to the Papacy of churches already increasingly national in character would be subject to the *nutus* of their national sovereigns.

[1] Mirbt, *op. cit.* No. 398.

It remained for the Roman see of the sixteenth century to show how
· it was capable of such spiritual and moral rejuvenation as would
able it to preserve the real values of the Petrine heritage, while
scarding all that was irrelevant or even inimical to the fulfilment
its genuine mission. The question which will call for consideration
not whether the work of the Counter Reformation was well done,
t rather whether it was done well enough. That it was possible at
seems only to be attributable to a strange and to some perhaps
accountable intervention of Providence.

We have surveyed a vast period of history and a great variety of
anging conditions. But if there is any lesson to be learnt from the
arch of events it is that in its struggle to attain some measure of an
al unity of thought and life humanity cannot dispense altogether
th the power of the Spirit. The Papacy which gave promise in the
rlier Middle Ages of possessing the moral force necessary to create
d maintain that unity failed because it essayed to achieve spiritual
ds by temporal means. Thus its true supernatural mission was
scured, and men turned elsewhere to nationalism, secularism, and
en to an unashamed revival of neo-pagan ideals for the fulfilment of
eir aspirations.

The history of the succeeding centuries is the record of the
rting asunder of those who still remained faithful to the mediaeval
al of the Papacy as the centre of Christian unity and the fount
spiritual jurisdiction from those who sought the restoration of a
ore primitive or less authoritarian type of Christianity, and of the
orious efforts of men of good will both within and without the papal
mmunion to repair the shattered fragments of God's ἐκκλησία,
ich 'the gates of hell' might shake but could not utterly destroy.

VII

The Papacy and Modern Europe

Nunc patimur longae pacis mala, saevior armis
Luxuria incubuit victumque ulciscitur orbem.
JUVENAL, *Saturae*, iii, 292.

1 Macc. IV, 60, 61. 'At that time also they builded up the mount
Sion with high walls and strong towers round about, lest the Gentiles
should come and tread it down, as they had done before. And they
set there a garrison to keep it, and fortified Bethsura to preserve it,
that the people might have a defence against Idumaea'.

How 'the kingdoms of this world' are to become 'the kingdoms
of our Lord and of his Christ' is a crucial problem which has confronted the Church from the day of Pentecost until now. It was
certainly not peculiar to the Middle Ages nor to the Papacy. Yet we
shall do less than justice to the policy of the mediaeval Popes if we
do not regard it on the whole as a sincere, even if unsuccessful,
attempt to achieve a solution. In accounting for its failure it is easy to
attach the greater part of the blame to their temporal power. Yet
other considerations such as the economic position of the Roman see
during the period have to be taken into account if we are to find
a wholly satisfactory explanation.

As the Middle Ages pass into the Renaissance, problems of secular
government loom increasingly large in the papal outlook, and particularly, once the danger that the Empire might become paramount
in Italy has been finally removed, the question how the Papacy
itself can be assured of a unchallengeable position among a multitude
of secular states and princedoms. The lack of any trustworthy power
outside Italy and the repeated failure in the past of the policy of
seeking to rely on the support of such a power seemed to have taught
the Popes that there was but one solution—to make the papal
dominions themselves militarily stronger than any of their immediate
neighbours. It is thus that we find the Popes of the Renaissance
appearing in the incongruous guise of military strategists and com-
manders, and the establishment of an impregnable papal sovereignty
in central Italy regarded as almost the sole end of papal policy.

Hence although the temporal power of the Papacy would be con-

:mned by many as a serious evil, it may be held with some justice
at, given the political conditions at the opening of the sixteenth
ntury, it was in some respects necessary if much that was good in
e Italian Renaissance was to be saved for posterity.[1]

I

That the first of the Popes to direct their policy unreservedly to the
-establishment of the temporal power were Sixtus IV and Alex-
der VI will be generally acknowledged. Yet the task to which
lexander set his hand and devoted so much of his care, in spite of
nsiderable success, remained unaccomplished at his death. And if
: had hoped that the outcome of his policy would be the creation
a Borgia dynasty, sovereign in Rome, predominant in Italy, and
pported by the ready compliance of a *fainéant* occupant of the
rone of St. Peter, the election of the Cardinal della Rovere as
lius II spelt disaster to his ambitions.

Unlike Alexander, of whom it has been said that 'he did not know
1at a principle was',[2] Julius was not wholly devoid of an ideal even
it was no more than to see the Papacy fulfil the part of a unifying
rce in Italy. In consequence of his diplomacy, or perhaps rather of
s military conquests, the Papal States after the treaty of Noyon
510) became, perhaps for the first time, a consolidated entity.
:t, for all his energy and undaunted courage, it can scarcely be
ubted that his achievement was aided by several strokes of un-
pected fortune, and that he was no more successful than his less
litant predecessors in being able to rid the Papacy of its unhappy
pendence on foreign support, a weakness which before long would
d indirectly to the loss of the allegiance of a considerable part of
rthern and north-western Europe.

Almost the only event of any ecclesiastical significance in this
ntificate was the summoning of the fifth Lateran council (1512), the
imary purpose of which appears to have been not so much to take
y real step in the direction of the now much needed reformation,
: which the best minds in the Church had been pressing for so
1g, as to serve as a counter-move to the schismatic council of
sa, the assembling of which had been brought about mainly by a
mbination of French and Spanish influence. Those who responded

[1] Creighton, M., *History of the Papacy*, 1919, vol. v, p. 191.
[2] *C. Mod. H.*, vol. i, p. 242.

to the summons to Rome were relatively few in number, in fa
almost without exception Italians, and in spite of a strong plea ma
by Egidius of Viterbo in his opening sermon[1] for the serious unde
taking of reform, not least in the direction of the recovery of re
sanctity, it soon became evident that Julius II was indifferent if n
actually hostile to any such project. In fact, even the more pr
gressive elements in the council seemed pathetically unaware of tl
dangers now beginning to threaten the Church on all sides.

How real were those dangers had been realized almost half
century before by Cardinal Cesarini, when he wrote to Po
Eugenius IV in the following words:

'When the heresy of Bohemia is quenched, another still mo
dangerous will arise . . . who can fail to see that there is danger
a total subversion? Woe to the ecclesiastics, wherever they may I
found. . . . They will be declared incorrigible, decided as they a
to live in shameful depravity, cost what it may. . . . The minds
men are full of what they are preparing against us. . . . They w
believe they are offering to God a pleasing sacrifice in despoiling ar
killing priests. . . . They will cast the fault and the shame on tl
Court of Rome, for in that court they will see the cause of all the il
of Christendom. . . . The princes of Germany will rise up again
us. . . . I see it, the axe is at the root, the tree is leaning and inste
of supporting it so long as we can, we cause it to fall to the ground'

Even if Julius II paused to notice the writing on the wall, it w
in any case meaningless to him, and his successor Leo X remain
deaf to its interpretation. It was scarcely to be expected that
descendant of the Florentine Medici would welcome any measur
which, though beneficial to the Church as a whole, might invol
some curtailment of opportunity for outward display or luxurio
self-indulgence such as the papal office of the time provided. Nor d
it augur well for the prospects of reform that the new holder of th
office was talking openly about 'enjoying' it.[3]

The Lateran council, which now resumed its labours, held fo
further sessions and was brought to an undistinguished conclusi
in 1515. Its claim to be reckoned among the series of oecumeni
councils is not impressive. In fact, the best that can be said of

[1] Creighton, *op. cit.*, vol. v, p. 171.
[2] Quoted by Sturzo in *Church and State*, Eng. Transl., 1939, p. 192.
[3] Creighton, *op. cit.*, vol. v, p. 208.

that it testified to the prevalence of a 'feeling that the evils of the
resent time were due to ecclesiastical lenity; but there was no
cognition of the fact that papal interference had broken down the
clesiastical system, and that the system could only be restored by
readjustment between the relations of the Papacy and the episco-
ate'.[1]

In due course, and only after considerable delay, the council of
rent was to turn its attention to the possibility of such a readjust-
ent, but by that time the evil resulting from the almost complete
cularization of the Papacy had permeated the whole Church. It is
a fact essential for a right understanding of the apparent impotence
f the Popes in the earlier half of the sixteenth century that we
hould appreciate the extent to which their spiritual office had been
rostituted to the attainment of purely secular ends. The victory
f the Papacy over the Empire had been followed by a reassertion
f its supremacy over councils, and although the spirit of Gerson
nd of the Pragmatic Sanction of 1438 continued to survive, it
cked a means of expression sufficiently effective to check the
nhappy consequences of papal absolutism.[2] The claim to supremacy
ver all temporal princes, at first asserted within the limits of the
piritual sphere *ratione peccati*, had long since been expanded so as
o include the whole range of politics, and was now being used, no
onger for the high purpose of maintaining a Christian ethic, but
olely in accordance with the political expediency of the moment.
Not even the internal government of a nation was exempt from papal
ntervention. The custom of sending legates, which the reforming
Popes of the eleventh century had considerably developed and
xtended, had now been transformed into an established right, so
hat few sovereign states were free from the galling presence of a
apal official, whose inquisitive behaviour might often seriously
ndanger either unity or independence, even where it did not actually
hreaten to infringe the royal prerogative.

The claim first made by the Avignonese Popes to enjoy unlimited
ights in the free disposal of all ecclesiastical benefices had become
he means of providing the Papacy with an assured and ever-
ncreasing source of revenue, and even if certain countries like Eng-
and and France had been successful in checking the drain on national

[1] Creighton, *op. cit.*, vol. v, p. 233.
[2] *C. Mod. H.* vol. i, p. 653.

and ecclesiastical resources arising from such a system, it persisted in Spain down the middle of the sixteenth century. Unhappily for the Church, the only power competent to resist such encroachments was a strong monarchy, such as France possessed under Francis I, with the result, not altogether satisfactory, that rights regained from the Pope were not restored to the Church, but usually, at least in practice, remained vested in the Crown.

A not less serious distortion of the papal primacy of jurisdiction was to be found in the extent to which it had come to be invoked, not only in defence of the so-called 'Benefit of Clergy', of which a particularly scandalous abuse had occurred in the relations of Sixtus IV with Florence,[1] but also for the protection of lay offenders against the proper course of secular justice. It was Sixtus IV again who exceeded the pretensions of all his predecessors in this connexion, by asserting an appellate jurisdiction over all the criminal tribunals of Christendom, a claim which was developed a stage farther under his successors, not only by releasing the purchasers of the indulgences for the erection of the new St. Peter's from all spiritual penalty, but by forbidding their prosecution in secular courts.

Added to this the papal right of arbitration founded on the apostolic authority to bind and loose had itself been degraded into an instrument of mere political expediency, so that it was being repeatedly used to evade obligations and to dissolve pacts, whether in the interests of the Papacy itself as a secular state, or of the states which happened for the moment to be its allies. In view of this we can scarcely be surprised that the Roman see gradually forfeited not only the respect but even the trust of contemporaries, so that when the army of the Catholic Empire forcibly entered the papal capital in 1527, scarcely a finger was seriously raised in its defence. Yet, if selfishness was predominant in the outlook of sixteenth-century Europe, it can always be said that the Popes had only their own example to blame.

[1] *C. Mod. H.*, vol. i, p. 661 f.

II

In tragic contrast to the moral and spiritual bankruptcy of the papacy at this time stood the growing strength of the secular monarchies. The relative failure of the fifth Lateran council to make any considerable progress in the direction of reform seemed to mean that the only hope for the removal of inveterate abuses lay in finding a leader who had the requisite gifts to head a movement of revolt, which with the support or acquiescence of the secular power would end by throwing down a challenge to the papal monopoly of ecclesiastical authority.

Such a leader now appeared in Martin Luther. It must not, however, be supposed that he was the sole originator of the movement for reform in Germany. From the time that the New Learning had first reached that country from Italy it had found its way into educated circles. In Italy the old order had had little difficulty in coming to terms with the newcomer and eventually in effecting its absorption. In Germany, on the other hand, a spirit of criticism and fresh seriousness of outlook, in sharp contrast to Italian moral indifference, had come into being. So early as the first quarter of the fifteenth century Johann Wessel had expressed criticism of current ideas regarding purgatory and indulgences,[1] and to such effect that Luther himself wrote afterwards: 'If I had read his works before, my enemies might have thought that Luther had borrowed everything from Wessel, so great is the agreement between our spirits.' Since that time Humanism, of which Wessel was one of the precursors, had made steady progress in the German universities and towards the close of the century could boast of the favour of the Emperor Maximilian.

The chief responsibility for forcing the German Renaissance into direct conflict with the Papacy rests with Johann Reuchlin.[2] An ardent philologist and a pioneer in the study of Hebrew, he had been led by his researches to doubt the validity of the exegetical methods of St. Augustine and the literary accuracy of St. Jerome, complaining in particular of the 'innumerable defects' in the Vulgate. His work brought him into controversy with the fanaticism of a converted Jew, who, finding an appeal to the Emperor Maximilian somewhat barren of positive results, had recourse to the less progressive theological

[1] Creighton, *op. cit.*, vol. vi, p. 7.   [2] Id., *op. cit.*, vol. vi, p. 36.

faculty of Cologne. On the condemnation of one of his wo
by that body, and with a prospect of being summoned before
Inquisition at Mainz, Reuchlin directed an appeal to Leo X hims
which was immediately followed by a counter-appeal from
German Inquisitor-General. Although the papal commission
ported in Reuchlin's favour, Leo, who was probably far too mu
engrossed in 'enjoying the Papacy' really to grasp the seriousness
the case, insisted on final judgment being deferred. Its seriousne
lay not so much in the matter originally in dispute as in its notorie
which had by this time evoked the interest of Erasmus and oth
outstanding advocates of the Humanist outlook. In the end t
Inquisition triumphed, and in 1520 Reuchlin was formally co
demned to silence.

At the time when the sentence on Reuchlin was issued, scarce
three years had elapsed since a young Augustinian friar had issued
challenge to debate to the purveyors of papal indulgences, then bei
energetically hawked in southern and western Germany in t
interests of the rebuilding of St. Peter's. Contrary to popular beli
however, it must be realized that his famous gesture in affixir
ninety-five theses to the church door at Wittenberg[1] had no mo
significance for his contemporaries than the posting of a subject f
discussion by the Oxford Union would have to-day. The theses d
not repudiate the validity of indulgences or even their usefulnes
their sole aim was to guard against a current misunderstanding
their true character as a means to the remission of penalties impos
as a condition of satisfaction for sin. An interesting sidelight
Luther's earlier attitude towards the Papacy is to be found in t
fact that he could actually express anxiety lest undue popularizati
of the system of indulgences might expose the Roman see to ridicule

In sharp contrast to this attitude was the utter inability of t
Roman theologians to grasp the realities of the situation. This is
be seen most clearly in their answer to Luther's invitation to a
academic discussion, in which they were content to observe that t
Popes were accustomed to grant indulgences and that, being a pap
custom, it had the force of ecclesiastical law. The time was rapid
passing when a reply of this kind would be regarded as sufficient.

Yet, in spite of their highly unsympathetic attitude, Luth
pursued his study and in the following year issued a documente

---

[1] Mirbt, *op. cit.*, No. 415.   [2] Creighton, *op. cit.*, vol. vi, p. 79.

statement of his theses. His opponents, by declining his invitation
debate and by appealing *tout court* to papal authority in order to
eclose the argument, might well have provoked a direct refutation.
stead, Luther was content to maintain an objective attitude and,
ough he rejected the views of the schoolmen on the subject under
scussion, insisted that he believed in the uprightness and learning
Leo X. 'I listen to the Pope as Pope', he said, 'that is, when he
eaks in the canons, or according to the canons, or determines with
council'.[1] Yet it is to be noticed he denied that the Pope in him-
f had the power to make new articles of faith. If the greater part
Christendom agreed with the Pope, said he, it would not be
retical to dissent till the matter had been decided by a general
uncil. He persisted, however, in affirming that he was only seeking
learn the truth and professed his absolute willingness to submit
authority. The document in which these statements were em-
died was addressed to the head of his order, but it was followed
a private letter to Leo, in the course of which, after describing
e scandals alleged to be created by the system of indulgences,
ther declared with an almost engaging frankness and with what
ght appear to some praiseworthy humility: 'I will acknowledge
ur voice, the voice of Christ presiding and speaking in you'.[2]
At certain earlier junctures in the course of papal history other
kers after truth had uttered words of this kind, and had received
nsiderate treatment at the hands of the Roman see. Had Leo now
haved in like manner towards Luther, and not as a proud secular
nce apparently indifferent to all values except his own worldly
erests, much subsequent misfortune might have been spared not
ly to his see but to the whole Church. For it must not be forgotten
at as yet the dogmatic aspect of indulgences had not been seriously
nsidered, and that consequently it was not an unreasonable request
Luther's part that doubts and hesitations on the subject should
examined. The real difficulty appears to have been that Leo and
 Curia were too much preoccupied with the amenities of their
ice to give serious attention to the demands of reason and honest
estigation.

That the friar of Wittenberg had not yet abandoned loyalty to the

A striking appeal to the primitive conception of the Papacy. Quoted by
ighton, *op. cit.*, vol. vi, p. 83.
Id., *op. cit.*, vol. vi, p. 84. Cf. the appeals of Eutyches and Theodoret above,
06.

Roman see, as distinct from submission to the private opinions
an individual Pope, is evident from the language used in his 'Rep
to Prierias', where he says: 'You call the Roman church the rule
faith; I have always believed that the faith was the rule of t
Roman church. The Roman church has preserved the faith becau
it has held by the Scriptures and the fathers of the Church'.[1] Y
such words were pregnant of far-reaching possibilities. Luther no
acknowledged that he had always believed that the faith was t
rule of the Roman church. But might not this imply the dawning o
conviction that it had already ceased to be so?

It would have been in accordance with Leo's temperament if
had allowed the controversy to run its course, as a purely academ
discussion confined to Germany. No doubt his private inclinati
lay in this direction, but there remained one very relevant fact whi
in his official capacity he could not well ignore. Doubt cast upon t
justifiability of indulgences would inevitably affect their marketat
value with the alarming consequence of a diminution of pa
revenue. We may therefore suppose that considerations of this ki
were uppermost in his mind when he cited Luther to appear in Ror
to answer a charge of heresy. After some hesitation about proced
the case was ultimately assigned to Cardinal Cajetan to be examin
at Augsburg. It was unfortunate that the legate's behaviour reveal
his almost complete unawareness of the real gravity of the positi
and of the extent to which Luther actually represented put
opinion in Germany. Nor was this all. Amicable discussion of d
puted points was excluded from the first by the Cardinal's attitu
and negotiation appeared to take the form of a plain demand
unconditional surrender.

The proceedings, in spite of being somewhat protracted, remain
inconclusive, but it is remarkable that Luther still persisted in p
fessing his readiness to submit to the judgment of the Church a
in giving an assurance that he followed the Roman church in
things.[2] It is possible that had the affair been left in the hands
Cajetan, who at least was not altogether devoid of a sense of humo
or of the papal commissioner Miltitz, who as a German was certai
well aware of the strength of Luther's position, the situation ev
at this eleventh hour might have been saved. In so momentous
issue it is particularly lamentable that when the crisis came it v

[1] Creighton, *op. cit.*, vol. vi, p. 86. [2] Id., *op. cit.*, vol. vi, p. 95.

ecipitated largely by the jealousy of an academic rival in the person Johann Eck.

Yet the trial at Augsburg had at least one unfortunate result. In the urse of the argument the question of the grounds of papal autho- y had arisen, and this had led the incriminated Luther to re- amine the decretals. His discovery that they contained not a little at was apocryphal or at least open to doubt on historical grounds ust have contributed much to the formation of an opinion that the oman primacy itself could no longer be treated as common ground tween himself and his opponents.[1] It is not surprising, therefore, at the fruitless outcome of the Leipzig Disputation soon made it ident not only to Luther himself but to a considerable part of ermany, that a final break with the Roman see was now only a uestion of time. With the public burning of Leo's bull *Exsurge omine*[2] the revolt, culminating in Luther's assertion at the Diet of orms that he could accept the decision of neither Pope nor council, d already begun. A Lutheran church, founded not upon the jective authority of historic Christendom but on the subjective octrine of Justification by Faith, was now about to come into being. uther the academic disputant, Luther the reformer, driven by the mpelling forces of his own sincerity and his opponents' total lack comprehension coupled with an overbearing assertion of authority, d become Luther the rebel. Given the conditions it may be said at the outcome was inevitable. Yet the real tragedy lay in the fact at a deep-rooted moral degeneration had largely deprived the hurch of the power to adapt itself to the changed conditions. The iritual prestige which had enabled it to absorb the vital energy of rancis and Dominic in the thirteenth century had for the past two undred and fifty years or so been squandered in the interests of cular ambition. A treasury of merit had been liberally dispensed it there was an alarming overdraft, and the coin now being dis- ursed was at last recognized as counterfeit. But by the time it was alized that the credit of the Church had been exhausted the situa- on was beyond remedy. Did Leo ever actually read Luther's last opeal, it is difficult to believe that even a Medici was not moved by me feelings of remorse for the sin which had brought such ruin pon his heritage.

The utter impotence of the Roman see in the situation created

[1] *C. Mod. H.* vol. ii, p. 135.   [2] Mirbt, *op. cit.*, No. 417.

by Luther's condemnation, as well by the Pope as by the n
Emperor Charles V at Worms, was brought into startling prominen
by the outspoken utterances of Leo's successor, Adrian VI, the l
non-Italian Pope.[1] The possibility of having recourse to a gene
council as a means of ending the troubles created by the unfortun
policy of his predecessor was freely discussed, and among the voic
raised in favour of prosecuting an active programme of reform w
once more that of Egidius of Viterbo. If views such as his had p
vailed earlier, Luther's revolt might well have never taken pla
Adrian showed himself most favourably disposed to his suggestio
and is said to have seriously contemplated making a beginning w
the reconsideration of the grounds on which dispensations we
being given in matrimonial cases. Significant of his desire th
reforms should begin in Rome itself was his curtailment of pa
and curial luxury, and the willingness with which he listened to t
advice of Aleander, urging that if the canons and institutes of t
fathers were duly observed the threatened evil might be averte
Yet the dead weight of opposition to such measures proved too gre
and when Adrian died, after occupying the papal throne for lit
more than a year and a half, he had barely touched the fringe of t
tremendous task now relinquished to his successors. It was piti
that one who so clearly saw the need so conspicuously lacked t
qualities as well as the means necessary for its fulfilment. With t
election of Clement VII, a descendant of the Florentine Medi
scion of that house which had already exercised so baneful an inf
ence on papal fortunes, once again wore the tiara. It was certainly
unhappy augury of future events that the first five years of his pon
ficate, largely occupied with futile attempts to escape from t
unwelcome tutelage of the Emperor Charles V, led to the disastro
sack of Rome by German troops under the leadership of an imper
general, and to the precipitate flight of Clement from a Rome n
completely under imperial domination. In such a political situati
it is easy to realize that the Papacy found itself deprived of a
effective liberty of action, and that under pressure of the urgent ne
of securing his personal freedom Clement might well allow t
problem of the Church's reform to be indefinitely postponed.

[2] Mirbt, *op. cit.*, No. 420.

III

t is against such a background that we must follow briefly the
rse of 'the king of England's business' and note its unfortunate
come for the future unity of the Church. To learn of its origin
have to retrace our steps to the beginning of the century. April 2,
2, witnessed the untimely death of Arthur, eldest son of Henry
and heir apparent to the English throne. The event was no doubt
ause of deep sorrow and disappointment to his father, but to
vate grief was added the anxiety of public financial embarrass-
nt. Only five and a half months had elapsed since Arthur's mar-
e to Catherine, daughter of Ferdinand and Isabella of Spain,
niece of the Emperor. Up till now only a proportion of the
ole dowry promised by her father had been received by the
glish treasury, and with the death of her husband Henry was
d with the alarming prospect of a demand for repayment.[1] It
ame, therefore, urgently necessary to prevent Catherine's return
her native country, and it was eventually agreed that she should
married to Arthur's younger brother, the future Henry VIII. In
course the necessary dispensation from the first degree of affinity
obtained from Pope Julius II, the effect of which dated from
ember 26, 1503. It was given in the form of a brief addressed to
ella just before she died, and also in a bull subsequently issued
Henry VII. The importance of the brief lies in its evidence that
Pope had no doubt that the former marriage had been consum-
ed, and although some hesitation has been felt about its authen-
ty, there is no serious ground for not supposing it to be genuine.[2]
n spite of the dispensation, the validity of which no one at the
e dreamed of calling into question, the young king's marriage
h Catherine did not take place till more than five years later. As
y as 1514 rumours were current abroad that Henry intended to
ulate Louis XII of France and to obtain an annulment of his
rriage in order to contract an alliance with the daughter of the
ke of Bourbon. Whatever truth there may have been in them, it
not till some thirteen years later that the urgent question of
cession to the English Crown caused Henry to consider means
which he could be provided with a male heir; and in this

Constant, G., *La Réforme en Angleterre*, I, Eng. Tr., *The Reformation in Eng-
*, p. 36.
Id., *op. cit.*, pp. 38, 64.

connexion his infatuation for Anne Boleyn naturally played a important part in leading him to desire an early annulment of h marriage with Catherine.

The first move was to endeavour to obtain a cancellation of th original dispensation from Cardinal Wolsey, acting in the capaci of papal legate.[1] Dispensations of that kind had been revoked befor and there seemed no reason that the process should not now b repeated. Wolsey urged that Henry should have direct recourse the Pope but it was not till some three months later that this w done. There are even grounds for believing that in the first instan the king was seeking for a dispensation to commit bigamy, a reque which argues a strangely large view of papal jurisdiction. In the en however, Henry sought and obtained a dispensation from affini contracted by his earlier relations with Anne Boleyn's elder sist Mary. It is remarkable that for the moment neither he nor Cleme seemed to have given attention to the one matter which alone cou render this dispensation operative. But Clement was much pr occupied at the time with the question of his own personal safet and Henry probably supposed that there would be little real difficul in obtaining an annulment of his marriage with Catherine.

When, however, shortly afterwards a petition for annulment w coupled with the demand that Wolsey should be empowered settle the question finally without right of appeal, Clement sudden drew back before so obvious an infringement of the papal prerogati by explicitly reserving to the Roman see the final verdict. Eventuall after a month's haggling, he conceded the power of pronouncing decision to Wolsey and his legate Campeggio acting together, or need be severally. All the same, Wolsey, for his own securit managed to procure secretly a decretal which laid down that certa defects, such as had been adduced against the validity of Julius II dispensation, would suffice as grounds of nullity in regard to any bu existing on the subject. Yet before Campeggio reached England it w clear that under pressure from Charles V, who naturally support the cause of his aunt Catherine, Clement was doing everythir possible to delay the examination of the case.

Both Wolsey and the king, however, were determined that r hindrance should stand in the way of a speedy decision. Unhappi for them both Catherine proved most unwilling to aid their proje

[1] Constant, G., *op. cit.*, p. 53, n. 65.

and a rumour was already current that the cause would shortly be cited to Rome. When the legates' court opened, therefore, there was every reason for haste. It is remarkable that throughout the proceedings the legate Campeggio shows every sign of having endeavoured to act impartially and strictly in accordance with the principles of Canon Law, but it is also clear that he committed a fatal error of tact when in the presence of the king himself, on the tenuous plea that Roman custom prescribed the beginning of a period of vacation, he suspended the proceedings of the court.

By the end of the year the disgrace of Wolsey suggested that a direct attack on papal authority was impending; in fact, there is evidence that already in the November following Campeggio's unfortunate act of adjournment, Henry was being advised to consider the possibility of cutting the Gordian knot by a complete repudiation of all papal jurisdiction.

Not more than a few days after the closing of the legatine court a priest, who held the post of private tutor to an Essex county family, Thomas Cranmer by name, hinted to two of the king's intimate advisers who happened to be staying in the house that it might be advisable to ascertain the opinion of the English and Continental universities on the 'king's matter'. The plan commended itself as being of the nature of an appeal to a 'dispersed' council and was immediately put into effect. The universities returned a verdict in favour of the king and against the validity of the dispensation, with gratifying though perhaps suspicious unanimity. But it must be realized that the decision depended on the view that marriage with a deceased husband's brother was forbidden by divine law, and that such an impediment could not be removed even by papal dispensation.

Yet we must not forget that this view about the divine origin of the impediment was open to some doubt. Admittedly such marriages had been forbidden by the council of Elvira (306), and the prohibition had been subsequently upheld on the ground that it was based on Leviticus XVIII, 16 and XX, 20. But what of Deuteronomy XXV, 5, which not only permitted such a marriage but even enjoined it as a positive obligation? It had therefore come to be taught, e.g. by Duns Scotus, that the impediment was not of divine but of human origin. Earlier Popes who shared this view, such as Martin V, had been prepared to allow such a marriage, and Alexander VI had given a

dispensation in the case of Catherine's elder sister Mary in order
that she might marry Emmanuel of Portugal. In the face of these
important precedents, therefore, it was obviously most difficult for
Clement VII to declare the annulment of Henry's marriage. Nevertheless so late as 1530 the king persisted in hoping for a papal decision
in his favour. As to the Pope's attitude, it is by no means fair to
allege, as is often done, that Clement withheld a favourable verdict
solely out of fear of consequences, more particularly having regard
to the relationship of the Emperor Charles to Catherine. The most
careful and painstaking researches (unusual perhaps in a Medici), for
the fact of which there is reliable evidence, had convinced him that
Canon Law would not permit Henry's marriage to be declared void.
The pity of it was that Henry preferred the satisfaction of his pleasure
and the security of his dynasty to the unity of the Church. Yet we
shall do less than justice to Clement if we refuse him the respect
which he has not always received, for having throughout remained
unswervingly true to his convictions.

As yet, however, there was no open evidence of the coming breach
even as late as June, 1530, Henry did everything possible secretly or
openly to persuade the Pope to give a decision in his favour.

In spite of the extreme difficulty of his position between the
Emperor on the one side and the king on the other, Clement, as we
have seen, appears to have made a real effort to arrive at a just view
of the case, but it is likely that he had already reached the conclusion
that he could not rightly declare Henry's marriage void. He therefore adopted measures which in plain fact amounted to a delaying
action. Of such a nature were his two admonitions and bulls of the
two following years, the chief object of which was to prevent Henry
marrying again, though the English Parliament succeeded in preventing their publication. By now Henry's patience was exhausted.

Early in 1531 an important measure aimed at limiting or destroy-
ing papal authority was passed by the Convocations of the English
church, declaring, though with evident signs of hesitation, that the
recognized the king's majesty as 'the only protector, unique and
supreme lord, and also, so far as the law of Christ allows, the supreme
head of the Anglican church and clergy'. It was followed by a Act of
Parliament abolishing annates, and by another withdrawing the
power from the Convocations to legislate without royal licence.
Other acts more decisive in character prohibited all appeals to the

pal court, thus dealing a final blow against the recognition of a
pal primacy of jurisdiction in England. In the course of the next
ree years further measures followed, one being tantamount to a
nial of the Pope's doctrinal primacy, but all aimed at removing
e last vestiges of papal authority in this country.[1] The royal
premacy was now an accomplished fact. The Papacy was de-
roned and a specifically English form of Caesaropapism set up in
stead. Yet the one thing which could not be said was that the
urch in this country gained any increase of freedom in virtue of
withdrawal from papal control. Doubtless this is not the place to
scuss the advantages or disadvantages of the change, yet the event
elf was sufficient to show that at least under the Tudors, if not
er, the Church of England had exchanged a vexatious suzerainty
r an oppressive tyranny.

Henry VIII thus possessed himself of spiritual authority such as
ilip the Fair never enjoyed and perhaps had never wished to
quire. Yet it must be remembered that his 'ecclesiastical preroga-
e was a personal and not a parliamentary one.'[2] The rule of Parlia-
nt over the church in this country was yet to come.

IV

We must now watch the steps by which the Papacy, disowned or
uted in the greater part of Europe, began gradually to recover
mething of its lost prestige and then slowly to re-establish its autho-
y, not only over churches which had remained faithful to its alle-
nce, but even in territories where it had been temporarily
carded.

If Paul III can be called the last Pope of the Renaissance, with
ich he was associated by his worldliness and nepotism, he is also
e first of the reforming Popes in virtue of his concern for the
storation of discipline and morals. His task as the successor of
ement VII was unenviable. Rome was in ruins, the Papal States
re reduced to penury. Yet, in spite of his advanced age, he shoul-
red with singular courage and determination the heavy burdens
ich he had inherited, and at his death Julius III might indeed

Constant, G., *op. cit.*, p. 113.
[2] Id., *op. cit.*, p. 128. Many of the difficulties of the Church of England at the
sent time arise from the fact that constitutional evolution has endowed Parlia-
nt with prerogatives originally vested personally in the Sovereign. See Henson,
H., *The Church of England*, pp. 20–22.

complain that the papal treasury was heavily in debt, but he cou
not reasonably say that its revenues had not been well or usefu
expended.

It has been alleged that Paul's main interest in promoting t
assembly of a general council was not reformative but dogmat
and that he conceived of it solely as an instrument for use in deali
a mortal blow against the Lutheran heresy. His undoubted zeal f
the establishment of Catholic orthodoxy must be acknowledged;
the same time the view just mentioned seems to leave unexplain
his deliberate choosing for high office those who, besides favouri
a conciliatory attitude towards the dissidents, were known to be whol
heartedly in favour of a radical reformation of the Church, not ev
excluding the Papacy itself. Evidence of the sincerity of this gro
of progressives, under the active leadership of Cardinal Contari
soon appeared in its report published in 1538 under the title Cc
silium . . . de emendanda ecclesia, the most significant recommend
tion of which was that 'the Vicar of Christ should never consid
himself at liberty to use the power of the Keys for gain'.[1] Other pr
posals were that the evils of pluralism and non-residence should
put down, and that greater care should be taken in the selection
candidates for admission to clerical status.

Before considering the extent to which these hopes were realiz
by the work of the council of Trent, we must call attention to tw
other developments, each of which contributed materially both
the purification of the Church and to the restoration of papal prestig
The first of these was the foundation of a number of new religio
orders, no longer with the monastic ideal of achieving sanctificati
by casting aside all contacts with a fallen world, but with a new a
more practical aim as befitting men in a more practical age, that
to say, the sanctification of the world by peaceful or even forcil
penetration. Most notable among the new orders was the Society
Jesus, founded by Ignatius Loyola in 1534.[2] Its rule, consisting sol
of the three evangelical counsels of poverty, chastity, and obedien
but with this important difference that in the last named spec
prominence was given to absolute obedience to the Roman see, w
approved by Paul III six years later. So phenomenal was its progr

[1] Mirbt, op. cit., No. 427. See also C. Mod. H. vol. ii, pp. 33, 233, 624 ff.; Ki
B. J., The Counter Reformation, 1933, p. 12 ff.
[2] Mirbt, op. cit., No. 430.

at within twenty years of its establishment it included thirteen
ovinces exclusive of the Roman and fifteen hundred members,
ile individual missionaries belonging to the order, like Francis
vier, had travelled to the remotest parts of the earth.

The second development to be mentioned here is the establish-
nt of the Roman Inquisition (1542).[1] The use of compulsion as a
ans to the suppression of heterodoxy had been recommended,
ugh apparently not without reluctance, by Augustine of Hippo,
d had been adopted by Leo I; yet in both cases, it should be
membered, only because it was believed that the heresy in question
permitted to grow with impunity would undermine the social
ric. It was not till the time of Innocent III that the possibility
applying to the crime of heresy the death penalty inflicted by the
ate was envisaged as part of normal procedure. Henceforth the
pal Inquisition entrusted to the Dominicans and Franciscans, and
rking in co-operation with the local episcopal jurisdiction, acted
her on the principle that heresy was the most serious of all crimes
d therefore merited the most severe punishment. The activities
the Dominican Inquisition had declined, however, during the
cceeding centuries in all countries except Spain, where alone it
d acquired a fresh and perhaps unfortunate prominence through
e control over it exercised by a narrowly orthodox Spanish
onarchy.

Thus it is not without significance that the suggestion for its estab-
hment at Rome came from Cardinal Caraffa, who had himself been
ined in the Spanish institution. The principle on which the new
ganization was based was, like that of the Jesuits, one of absolute
bordination to the Papacy, yet with the highly important additional
oviso that no one, whatever his rank in the hierarchy, should be
empt from its authority. Thus if the Jesuits represented, so to
eak, an extension of the papal primacy of doctrine, the Inquisition
ght be described as an analogous extension of his primacy of
risdiction.

It may be regarded as probable that Caraffa's influence was chiefly
sponsible for a perceptible narrowing in Paul III's outlook during
e last seven years of his pontificate. At the same time, in spite of
ery possible discouragement, the aged Pope adhered with dogged
rsistence to his original plan of assembling a general council, in

[1] Mirbt., op. cit., No. 429.

the sincere hope, in which few of his contemporaries shared, that
might procure the reunion of western Christendom.

Summoned at last by a bull of 1536 to assemble at Mantua, tł
council was about to come into being. Unhappily the refusal
Luther's adherents to meet on Italian soil and the advice of Charles
combined to effect its transference to Trent, a city largely Italian
character but actually within the Emperor's dominions. But if tł
Papacy was now prepared for reform, the Church generally remaine
indifferent.

It seems indicative of a widespread lack of enthusiasm for tł
conciliar project or else perhaps of a general disregard for Pap
authority, that although from the side of the Pope preparations we
fully made, even to the extent of providing as president-legates m
of a progressive type known to be disposed towards conciliation, suc
as Cardinals Parisio, Pole (subsequently archbishop of Canterbur
and Morone, the actual number who responded to the Papal sun
mons was so small that Paul's third successor, Pius IV, was oblige
to adjourn the proceedings.

Thus it was not till after an interval of some years that, being
last confident of the support of the Emperor, the Papacy took ı
the project anew and issued yet a third summons. It was unfortuna
that in the interval Roman opinion had hardened towards tł
Lutherans to such an extent that of the original group of legates on
Pole was renominated; moreover, as we shall see, there is eviden
that meanwhile the papal attitude itself had also undergone a cor
siderable change. In spite of all these preparations, widespread luke
warmness towards the Pope's wishes still prevailed and the numbe
of bishops who assembled at Trent on March 15, 1545, remaine
pathetically and disquietingly small.

From the day on which the council actually began its work :
December of that year onwards, it was perfectly evident that tł
effective handling of conciliar business was securely placed under tł
control of the Roman see. This had been ensured partly by the rule
of procedure, partly by the adoption of a system of voting b
numerical majorities, rather than by nations, as at Constance ar
Basle, thus tipping the scales in favour of Italian opinion with i
numerous and papally-dependent episcopate. In spite of the effor
of the conservatives to give precedence to dogma and postpon
questions of reform, it was decided under pressure from the Emper

deal with problems under either heading side by side. Naturally
e general effect of the dogmatic decrees was to restate traditional
ctrine, and this meant that no real concessions could be made to
e scruples of the Lutherans; in fact, the impossibility of bridging
e gulf between the Catholic and Protestant standpoints became
parent at the very beginning, or at least so soon as discussion turned
the indispensability of tradition for the interpretation of Scripture.
was in the course of one of the earlier debates that even Pole
clared himself emphatically opposed to concession, and in so
ing set the standard followed generally by the council in its later
liberations.

The council sat for just over twelve months, in the course of
hich a number of dogmatic and disciplinary measures were adopted.
ost important for our purpose are those which bear on the question
reform, the chief tendency of which was in the direction of in-
eased centralization and a consequent subordination of the episco-
te to the Papacy,[1] a bias which becomes still more evident in the
cisions adopted by the council in its later stages. It is also worthy
notice that in spite of the excellence of the measures taken with a
ew to the removal of such abuses as pluralism and episcopal
glect, the introduction of the excepting clause *salva semper in
nibus sedis apostolicae auctoritate* left the papal power of dispensa-
n unimpaired, with the unhappy consequence that possibility of
asion remained alarmingly wide.[2]

The subsequent suspension of the council and its transference to
ologna was a direct result of renewed hostility towards the Papacy
the part of Charles V, who did his best to maintain the session at
rent in being and even published on his own account under the
le of the *Interim*, in complete disregard of papal authority, some
portant measures bearing on reform.

Pope Julius III now took alarm at the evident eagerness of the
mperor to compromise with Protestant demands and in 1552 made
political pact with Henry II of France. Henry in his turn effected
alliance with disaffected elements in Germany, and the strong
ti-imperial combination thus resulting reduced the Emperor to
actical impotence. The council, which since the previous May had
sumed its deliberations in Trent, after sitting at intervals over a
riod little short of seven years, was finally prorogued in April, 1552.

[1] Kidd, *op. cit.*, p. 66.   [2] Id., *op. cit.*, p. 68.

Very nearly ten years were now to elapse before a fresh assemb
would prove to be possible, and during the interval the alrea
existing situation naturally tended to become stabilized. If anythi
the position of the Papacy in its general relation to Christendo
steadily deteriorated. Lutheranism was dominant in a considerat
part of Germany. England with the accession of Elizabeth on
again repudiated papal authority. Spain was subject to a Catho
form of Caesaropapism under Philip II, and from Geneva Calvinis
was steadily extending its influence over France where, by means
the Huguenot schism, it already held the balance of power. Thus t
Roman church itself was being steadily forced on to the defensiv
The election of Cardinal Cervini as Marcellus II gave brief but ill
sory promise of a more liberal outlook. Although he had many
the qualities of a peacemaker, and is said to have 'well understo
the maxim that on occasions more prudence and less piety was bett
than more piety and less prudence',[1] his pontificate lasted no mo
than three weeks, and with the accession of Paul IV the policy
solving the problems of reform by means of papal authority alo
regardless of the co-operation of a council once more becar
dominant.

It was due to Paul's initiative and foresight that the earliest pla
were laid for the forming of those Roman Congregations which
this day continue to be the backbone of papal administration. But t
failure of his attempt to break the yoke of Spanish influence and t
unpopularity of his measures of reform, many of which, though lo
overdue, seemed likely seriously to curtail the financial resources
the Curia, led to a reaction. It was chiefly as a consequence of t
that his successor Pius IV found himself from the moment of l
election firmly committed to a policy of resuming the interrupt
council. Among other considerations which appear to have prompt
action of this kind was the not ill-founded belief that if nothing we
done the French church might follow the Church of England
abandoning its allegiance to the Papacy.

When at last the council was reassembled its debates bore
marked resemblance to the earlier proceedings. For in spite of t
presence of a representative body of French bishops under t
leadership of the Cardinal of Lorraine, Spanish influence, disti
guished by a rigid conservatism, was more than ever apparent. Y

[1] *C. Mod. H.* vol. ii, p. 673.

or all that a serious if unsuccessful attempt was made to find a
olution of the problem regarding the relation of the episcopate to
he Papacy. Nevertheless, it now became clear that the council was
10 longer interested in the question of the European schism. The
•nly thing which still mattered was to set in order those churches
vhich remained faithful to the Roman see, lest further disaster should
.efall a distracted Christendom.

As was to be expected the Catholic powers themselves were
.ivided. Germany and France were still hopeful for concessions
vhich might unite to the Church the moderate Protestants and dis-
ffected Catholics, and consequently there was a strong desire that
he council should take up its work *de novo* as a distinct assembly.[1]
To this view Spain was strongly opposed. Though agreeing that a
horough reform of the Curia and a diminution of papal authority
vere urgently needed, the Spanish bishops were insistent that no
hanges in the discipline and practice of the Church ought to be
1ade, and consequently held that the new assembly ought to be
egarded simply as a continuation of the previous sessions. As it
urned out, the question was allowed to remain open, but it was the
•panish view which actually came to prevail.

We must naturally restrict our consideration of the work of this
hase of the council to the question of its attitude to the Roman
rimacy. If all those who took part concurred in accepting the
rimacy as a fact, there was by no means unanimity about its inter-
retation. The battle cry of the supporters of the conciliar move-
1ent, the superiority of a general council over the Papacy, had
ever been effectively silenced. Thus, if it was pointed out that the
uestion had been finally settled in favour of the Papacy at Florence,
1e supporters of the conciliar theory were always ready to reply
1at the Florentine decree had been drawn up for the benefit of the
yzantines and that in any case it was of doubtful oecumenical
alidity.[2] In their efforts to limit papal authority the French bishops
ould always count on some support from their Spanish colleagues,
et because the latter were primarily concerned rather with definition
1an with limitation, there remained a subtle difference quite suffi-
ent in such an assembly to be productive of serious disagreement
hen proposals of a practical nature were under discussion.

The Spaniards, who had their own problems of Caesaropapism

[1] *C. Mod. H.* vol. ii, p. 675.   [2] *D.T C.* vol. xiii, col. 319.

at home, were for their part supremely anxious to secure as a weapon against the theory of the divine rights of kingship the divine right of the episcopate. Closely connected with the establishment of this principle was recognition of the divine origin of the obligation of residence, scarcely as it would seem to us a matter for debate, yet of supreme importance when a programme for reform had to fight its way against a phalanx of vested interests and inherited abuses. Inevitably also the question about the source of episcopal jurisdiction came to be raised. Was such jurisdiction actually immediate, or only mediate through the Papacy? And if it should be declared immediate, might not this seem to challenge accepted views on the extent of the Roman primacy, for which precedent could be found even so far back as the fifth century?[1]

On the papal side weighty authority for a theory of derived jurisdiction was cited, and even the view that bishops could be called the successors of the Apostles met with some objection. Nor were the advocates of an extreme Papalism blind to the possibility that the thorny question of residence, if settled in accordance with the episcopalian standpoint, might by establishing a kind of episcopal freehold give rise to a dangerous independence of papal authority.

General agreement, as might have been expected, on some form of papal primacy, and even the papal right to confirm conciliar decisions, was not difficult to obtain, but it was only after a heated debate that the fathers consented to define the obligation of episcopal residence in the following terms:

'It has been enjoined by divine precept on all to whom a cure of souls has been committed that they should know their sheep and offer sacrifice on their behalf and feed them with preaching of the divine word and administration of the sacraments'.[2]

As to the question of the divine right of the episcopate, it was laid down that a hierarchy of successive orders exists under the Pope, to which was added:

'Bishops who have succeeded to the place of the Apostles belong to this hierarchical order, and being established by the Holy Ghost as the (same) Apostle says, rule the Church of God'.[3]

When the relation of the episcopate with the Papacy had come up

---

[1] See the present writer's *Life and Times of Leo the Great*, p. 69 f.
[2] Mirbt, *op. cit.*, No. 466. See *D.T.C.* vol. ix, col. 321.
[3] Id., *op. cit.*, No. 465.

r discussion, it is important to realize that but for the opposition
f the French bishops, who only arrived when the question was
ready in the course of debate, a formula declaring at one and the
me time the divine origin of the episcopate and the derivative
ature of its jurisdiction, assigned by the Roman Pontiff *in partem
llicitudinis, non autem in plenitudinem potestatis*, would probably
ave been included in the conciliar definitions. As it was, however,
e controversy about the divine origin of the episcopate became a
ubject of acrimonious arguments, and one speaker even went so far
 to tax the supporters of such a view with heresy, so that in the
nd agreement could only be reached on the basis of a formula
hich evaded the real point in dispute.[1]

The surprising feature of the Tridentine definitions in their final
orm is that if they fail to include any decisive assertion of the divine
nstitution of the episcopate, they are equally silent about the precise
ature and extent of the Roman primacy. It is probable that this
mission was due to the explicit instructions of Pius IV himself, who
ished at all costs to preserve the moral unanimity of the council.
 this is true, he appears to have set an example which might have
een followed to the advantage of the Church on a later occasion.

Considerable credit for steering the barque of Peter with success
hrough the shoals and reefs of this sea of controversy is often given
 the sincere and devout Charles Borromeo, papal Secretary of
tate and archbishop of Milan. Yet it must be remembered that
harles himself was not primarily a theologian. In such circum-
ances, without the prudent and diplomatic guidance of Pius himself,
ncerity alone could have achieved little.[2]

Of the practical results of the council undue prominence has
erhaps been given to the Index and the Profession of Faith.[3] The
tter, imposed on all recipients of benefices, greater or lesser, in the
orm of an oath to be taken as an indispensable condition of admis-
on, by anathematizing all recent as well as ancient heresies, finally
osed the door on any possibility of reconciliation between Roman
atholicism and Protestantism; while the former had the unfortu-

---

[1] *D.T.C.* vol. ix, col. 324. It is clear from the evidence set forth in Cross, F. L.,
arwell Stone, 1943, p. 308 ff. Letter No. 76, that this ambiguity remains to some
tent unresolved to this day, in spite of the enlightened attempt of the scholarly
ope Benedict XIV in his great treatise *De synodo dioecesana* to evaluate afresh the
lace of the episcopate in the Church.

[2] D.T.C. vol. xii, col. 1636.   [3] *C. Mod. H.* vol. ii, p. 687 f.

nate result of checking a free interchange of ideas and must be hel
chiefly responsible for the comparative sterility of Italian culture i
later times. Great minds such as that of the learned Jesuit Canisiu
freely recognized the unwisdom of slamming the door on reconcilia
tion, though it might be said that given a situation such as prevaile
at Trent a doctrinal formula like the creed of Pius IV was probabl
inevitable. More hopeful of positive achievement were the task
assigned by the council to the Papacy of revising the Missal an
Breviary, of publishing a Catechism and of undertaking the restoratio
of the text of the Vulgate. Yet it must be admitted that a certain lac
of liturgical and historical knowledge, by no means peculiar to Italy
inevitably limited the qualifications of those to whom the work wa
committed.

The situation in Europe in 1563 as regards the Roman see ha
been summarized by an eminent historian in the following words
'At the time of the death of Paul IV, Scandinavia and Great Britai
had wholly gone; Germany was predominantly Protestant; Bohemi.
Hungary, and Poland were in tumult; in France and the Netherlanc
numbers were gathering under the banners of Geneva. Only Spai
and Italy stood firm to the Papacy'.[1]

Thus, if the Roman see had succeeded in regaining in a conside
able measure its earlier prestige, the actual area within which i
authority was now recognized was seriously diminished.

While the later phases of the council of Trent had the effe
of erecting an insuperable barrier between Roman Catholicism an
Protestantism, it also marked the beginning of that epoch in tl
history of the Papacy which might be described by the term 'siege
minded'. Just as in times of severe national crisis the Roman republ
had been in the habit of suspending the constitution and acceptin
the rule of a dictator with absolute authority, so in the face of tl
disintegrating forces of Protestantism the churches which still r
mained in communion with the Papacy seemed now to be driven
accept papal absolutism as a condition of their common survival.

The analogy between the condition of the Papacy in the Count
Reformation period and that of a besieged city is remarkably con
plete. Everything is there; the hasty reconstruction of dogmat
fortifications, the imposition of a strong centralized discipline, eve
the erection of formidable outworks and strong points by the creati

[1] Kidd, *op. cit.*, p. 119.

f the new religious orders, especially the Company of Jesus, which
om time to time would make determined and often effective sallies
ito the enemy's territory, while gradually becoming the dominant
ower in the fortress-citadel itself.

V

The Papacy under Pius V, in spite of the bitter experience of
lement VII and Paul III, almost seemed to show, as it was said of
ie Bourbons at a later date, that it had learnt nothing and forgotten
othing. No doubt it is true that an almost puritanical austerity was
placing the former worldiness, and the well-tried nepotism of the
enaissance Popes could now be regarded as a thing of the past. Yet
a many respects, and those the more marked in the eyes of its in-
eterate opponents, the old claims remained unabated, and were
heerfully and even fanatically reasserted.

The reversal of the pro-papal policy of her half-sister and pre-
ecessor by the English Queen Elizabeth was unproductive of any
nmediate reaction at Rome. Invitations were even sent to English
ishops for the Council then about to resume its sessions, and it
ems as though Pius IV continued to hope that a reconciliation
iight yet be possible. His successor, however, had no such patience
r illusion. By launching his bull *Regnans in excelsis*[1] Pius V made
ie breach between Canterbury and Rome complete. For all her
iatement of the title 'Supreme Head' by 'Supreme Governor'
lizabeth's control of the English church was not less effective than
er father's, while her practical expulsion of the Marian hierarchy,
nd its replacement by one of Puritan or at least anti-papal sympa-
iies, made the later act of repudiation of papal authority far more
ronounced than the earlier. Pius V might flatter himself that he
ad revived the policy of Hildebrand. But this time there was to be
o Canossa. In fact the only practical result of his action was to pro-
ide Philip II with a religious pretext for an enterprise, the chief
iotive for which was far less the restoration of papal authority in
ngland than the removal of the stranglehold of English sea power
n Spanish commerce.

Gregory XIII, though in some respects a contrast to his pre-
ecessor, was the first Pope since the sixth century to treat England
 a missionary country, and there are reasons for believing that, like

[1] Mirbt, *op. cit.*, No. 490.

Sixtus IV in the previous century, for the furtherance of his proje
he was prepared to regard 'tyrannicide' as a virtuous act. But it wa
Sixtus V who more than any other carried through to its logical con
clusion the centralizing policy of the Counter Reformation Papac
Few Popes before or after him held so grandiose a conception
their office, yet he was before all else a realist and had a fine sense
the diplomatic adroitness necessary to preserve the balance of pol
tical power in Europe. Moreover, it may even be said that the king
dom of France owed its recovery and later ascendancy at least
some measure to his favourable attitude towards the Protesta
Henry of Navarre. But he is chiefly to be remembered for the ze
with which he carried through to completion the task of revising th
text of the Vulgate version of the Bible committed by the council
Trent to his predecessors.[1] When at last the work was finished an
the fine Sixtine edition emerged from the Vatican press in 1590,
was accompanied by the bull *Aeternus ille*, imposing the severe
possible ecclesiastical sanctions on any who should venture to tamp
with the restored text. But like all attempts to produce a revision
Holy Scripture, including even the Vulgate version itself on its fir
appearance, the new edition encountered such a solid weight
conservative opposition that on the advice of Robert Bellarmi
Clement VIII recalled all copies which could be traced, and a furth
revision known as the 'Clementine' was put forth. Provided with
preface by Bellarmine, which attempted to evade the censures
Aeternus ille by excusing the fresh edition as necessitated by t
abundance of printer's errors in its predecessor (though in actual fa
they were remarkably few), it serves to provide unique documenta
evidence of the possibility that even the Roman see can change
mind. Yet the fact has subsequently been obscured, for when t
new edition appeared in 1592 it was boldly and somewhat dis
genuously presented to the world as the 'Sixtine' Bible. If the nar
of Clement was later introduced, it scarcely served to atone for
strange feat of literary dishonesty, nor to conceal the truth that t
Roman see had so far yielded to popular clamour as to treat one of
earlier decisions as reversible.

It is relevant to notice and perhaps not a little surprising that t
same writer who had been chiefly responsible for this revision, al
undertook a systematic restatement of the official doctrine of t

[1] *H.D.B.* vol. iv, p. 881a.

Papacy. Although his work covered almost the whole field of Catholic dogma, it is this aspect in particular which has rendered Bellarmine's name justifiably famous.

Starting from the fact of the Church, Bellarmine argued that it was in essence a monarchy tempered by aristocracy. For although he assigns the greatest possible importance to the papal primacy in virtue of which the Pope is to be regarded as the Church's supreme head and pastor, he affirms that the bishops are by divine right true pastors and princes in their own churches, and not merely vicars of the Roman see.[1]

In his view the first duty of the Roman Pontiff is to teach. In his capacity as universal teacher in proclaiming a doctrine regarding faith or morals to be held by the whole Church, Bellarmine holds the Pope to be incapable of error. To him all general councils are subordinate, and his confirmation is indispensable if they are to acquire the character of infallibility. Nevertheless, this quality, he says, does not belong to papal decisions which affect plain questions of history as distinct from questions of dogma. Still less does it belong to utterances of the Pope speaking or writing as a private doctor.[2]

Bellarmine stoutly repudiated the contention that infallibility must involve impeccability, nor would he allow that in making an infallible pronouncement the Pope can be confident of a special revelation or rely on his own unaided personal judgment. On the contrary, he was dependent on the normal methods for attaining knowledge of the truth.

The Pope's second duty is to rule the Church. For the performance of this function he enjoys the plenitude of ecclesiastical jurisdiction. The nature of his power differs from that of all other bishops both in extent and in origin. His is immediate, theirs only mediate through him. If the bishops are real judges of the faith, their judgment is essentially subordinate to his. Nor is the Pope liable to judgment by others; if the case of a Pope who has fallen into heresy constitutes an exception to this principle, it is such in appearance only. For his heresy would *ipso facto* exclude him from the Church and the function of a council would be no more than to certify the fact of his lapse.

Among the spiritual powers assigned to the Pope, Bellarmine includes the right to impose laws on all the faithful and to compel

[1] *D.T.C.* vol. ii, col. 589.
[2] Mirbt, *op. cit.*, No. 500; *D.T.C.* vol. ii, col. 590; Butler, *Vatican Council*, vol. i, p. 36 ff.

obedience even by means of the death penalty; the judgment of greater causes, especially appeals; the summons of and right to preside at councils; the election or confirmation of bishops; the canonization of saints; the approbation of religious orders and the publication of indulgences.

In regard to the authority of the Papacy in temporal matters, while he held firmly to the primacy of the spiritual power, Bellarmine denied that it belonged normally to the Pope as a matter of ordinary jurisdiction to depose kings even for a just cause, as he might depose bishops; to interfere in civil legislation or to judge temporal matters. If he did so intervene, it could only be in the interest of the salvation of souls and within certain limitations. He might only transfer the crown to a legitimate successor; and however severe a sentence he might impose, the execution of the temporal punishment must belong to others.

It was alleged by Barclay that Bellarmine was inconsistent, 'because at one time he asserts, and at another denies, that secular and ecclesiastical societies are separate bodies'.[1] The charge of inconsistency is perhaps less than justified, and due to a failure to appreciate the significance of his insistence on the real subordination of the temporal to the spiritual, as for example in his analogy of the relation of the body to the soul. His chief contribution to thought lay in his theory of the 'indirect power', which though far from limiting papal jurisdiction in temporal matters to a merely directive or advisory authority, tacitly involves the abandonment of the claim to direct sovereignty asserted by the mediaeval Papacy at the height of its development. The civil power is not to him the consequence of the evil in man's nature nor is it only a passive instrument in papal hands: it possesses a real status and because it has God as its source belongs to the realm of natural law. Yet its form, unlike the ecclesiastical monarchy which exists *iure divino*, is a matter purely of human convenience and concerns the nation, not the Church. In this respect as in some others, Bellarmine was notably in advance of his time.

Any one familiar with the subsequent development of Roman Catholic thought and doctrine can scarcely fail to notice the extent to which it has been anticipated by this author, so that it may be agreed in the words of a Roman Catholic historian 'that the definitions of the Vatican Council on the Pope hardly go beyond Bellar-

[1] Quoted in *C. Mod. H.* vol. iii, p. 509.

mine's formulation of the Ultramontane doctrine, and indeed are practically the same as it; so that there has been, it may almost be said, no advance in the three hundred years.' [1]

The words quoted seem to imply a startling admission, probably quite unintended, yet not insignificant if it be remembered that those three hundred years included a social and political upheaval affecting not only the country of its origin but the whole fabric of the social, political, and economic structure of Europe. For if it be true that in the formulation of its more distinctive dogmas there was 'no advance' in Roman Catholic thought in those three hundred years, we seem to be faced with a very serious indictment of Roman Catholicism itself.

VI

How a movement which seemed at first to promise some 'advance' made headway only to be checked and then ultimately stifled, will be seen if we turn from Bellarmine to consider the rise, development and ultimate collapse of a rival theory of the relation between the Church and the Papacy, loosely and inexactly described as 'Gallicanism'.

It is important to realize that the term has been used to cover two distinct, though interconnected sets of ideas, which may be distinguished by the terms ecclesiastical and political. The former denotes what may be called a constitutional theory of the relation of the Church to the Papacy and as such has a special claim on our attention. The latter, describing a conception of the relation between Church and State, which may be characterized as a moderate Caesaropapism, will not immediately concern us here, though we shall have occasion from time to time to notice its influence on the parallel movement.

Ecclesiastical Gallicanism as a theory of church order is, of course, not confined to the period which elapsed between the Tridentine and the Vatican councils, still less to France. Marked by a repudiation of papal absolutism, an attachment to synodical and representative systems of church government and an emphasis on the relative independence of the episcopate, its origins may be found in the primitive ages of the Church. If its supporters were mistaken in regarding the protest of Irenaeus against the supposed papalism of Victor I as its earliest appearance, they were certainly right in finding

---

[1] Butler, *op. cit.*, vol. i, p. 38.

ideas analogous to their own in the attitude of the African Church
towards Popes Zosimus and Boniface I in the golden age of Aurelius
and Augustine. Thus from the church of Africa in the fifth century,
through Caesarius of Arles, Hincmar of Rheims, Gerson, Pierr
d'Ailly, and the Cardinal of Lorraine it is possible to trace a clea
almost continuous sequence of thought.[1]

We have now to see how this conception of church order cam
into collision with papal absolutism as revived and restated in th
period following the council of Trent.

During a considerable part of the sixteenth century Frencl
Catholicism was engaged in a death struggle with Huguenotism, anc
it was only with the establishment of a strong centralized nationa
government under Richelieu that a fresh assertion of its independence
in relation to the Papacy became once more possible. Although the
repudiation of the Tridentine decrees by the French government was
resisted by a considerable proportion of the French clergy, the movement against papal centralization gathered force and, stimulated by
the laxist teaching of Jesuit moral theologians, found doctrinal
expression in the doctrines of Jansen and his following.[2]

For the immediate antecedents of Gallicanism in this form we
have to go back to Michel de Bay or Baius, doctor of Louvain university.[3] Judged by a number of his works on human nature, his teaching
represented a pronounced reaction in favour of the determinism of
Augustine, with a marked bias in favour of belief in the total depravity of the human will. Following the earlier condemnation of his
writings on these subjects by Pius V in 1567,[4] he turned his attention to questions regarding the relations of the Church and the
Papacy and, while insisting on the immediate and divine origin of
episcopal jurisdiction, denied the doctrinal infallibility of the Pope
This led to a fresh condemnation pronounced by Gregory XIII in
1579. Yet, although Baius openly professed his submission at the
time, the fact that eight years later the university of Louvain cen
sured the teaching of Lessius, one of his principal opponents, showed
that his teaching was far from having lost its influence.[5]

The link between Baius and Jansen was Du Vergier of Hauranne
abbot of Saint Cyran. Together the two friends entered upon a

---

[1] *D.T.C.* vol. vi, col. 1102.　　　　[3] *D.T.C.* vol. ii, col. 42.
[2] *D.T.C.* vol. xiii, col. 328.　　　　[4] Denzinger, *op. cit.*, No. 1001.
[5] Id., *op. cit.*, No. 1080; *D.T.C.* vol. ii, col. 57.

tensive study of Augustine's works with the deliberate object of
fecting a revival of Catholicism by substituting for scholasticism
atristic study, and above all by restoring a purer doctrine of grace. In
)26 Saint Cyran delivered an open attack on the moral theology of
.e Jesuits, and six years later published his *Petrus Aurelius*, in which
e defended the thesis that the Church is not a monarchy but an
istocracy; and thus, in relation to the bishops who are his equals,
.e Pope enjoys simply a primacy of honour.[1] The purpose of this
ork was evidently to win as much episcopal support as possible
r the forthcoming *magnum opus* to which it was originally intended
• serve as a preface.

After striving in vain to win the help of that great apostle of the
)or, Vincent de Paul, Saint Cyran established his influence over
.e celebrated convent of Port Royal, with its unique superior Mother
ngelica. The intensely religious clientèle which quickly gathered
)und the convent and its much admired director adopted his
istere teaching with enthusiasm. Gradually they came to regard
.emselves almost as an *ecclesiola*, confident in their possession of a
nique grace, to be jealously preserved by a life of rigorous penitence
; an indispensable condition for the attainment of ultimate salva-
.on. But it must have come as a rude shock to this haven of piety
• learn that Saint Cyran had been interned at Vincennes by order
f Richelieu himself, where he was to remain for the next five years
. a state of honourable captivity till after the death of the great
linister of State.

Jansen himself had returned to Louvain in 1617. It is some index
f the state of his mind at this period to learn that he read with
pproval the *De republica ecclesiastica* of that egregious prelate Mark
.nthony de Dominis, in which vigorous episcopalianism and extreme
rotestantism were found to share an uneasy partnership. With tire-
:ss industry he persevered in the completion of the study of Augus-
ne in spite of innumerable distractions. Among these the composi-
on of his *Mars Gallicus* against the employment of French soldiery
. the service of the Protestant Prince of Orange must be accounted
ne of the more important, as it constituted a direct attack on the
rench monarchy and evoked considerable hostility among the
rench clergy. His elevation to the see of Ypres in 1636 was short-
ved, and when he died eighteen months later, the *Augustinus* had

[1] *D.T.C.* vol. viii, col. 321.

not yet appeared. Whatever there was to be said later against t
orthodoxy of the book, there can be no reasonable doubt that Jans
himself died in the peace of the Church.

The *Augustinus* itself was published in 1640 and at once acquir
a remarkable notoriety. The first part of the work was devoted
the history of Pelagianism and Semi-pelagianism and was intend
to exhibit the essential affinity between these heresies and the teac
ing of Molina, so strongly in favour with the Jesuits of that day. T
second and third parts embraced the system of orthodox doctri
according to the principles of Augustine as interpreted by Jansen,
which the chief characteristics are depreciation of human free w
and emphasis on the irresistibility of divine grace, leaving little
any room for individual responsibility.

The Jesuits naturally gathered their forces to strangle the ne
born prodigy. Yet the day of their triumph was still far ahead, a
they must have found little cause for satisfaction in the bull
eminenti of Urban VIII, which though condemning the *Augustin*
imposed silence on their own propositions.

The work of Jansen was continued by Antoine Arnauld in I
Fréquente Communion, which caused a considerable stir, not least
account of its assertion that St. Peter shared the primitive oversig
of the Church of Rome with his co-apostle St. Paul, a view whi
was considered sufficiently unconventional at the time to merit
explicit condemnation by Innocent X.[1] However remarkable th
papal declaration may have been as an indication of seventeent
century Roman ignorance of history, it was completely ove
shadowed by the constitution *Cum Occasione* issued by the san
Pope in 1653, condemning five propositions believed to be discer
able in the *Augustinus*. It is said that Innocent made this pronounc
ment against his personal inclination; if this is indeed a fact,
certainly marks him out as among the more prudent holders of h
office.

The publication of the new constitution in France with the su
port of Mazarin was at first received with submission by all partie
not excepting the Jansenists. But it soon became apparent that t
latter accepted it with a difference. They willingly condemned t
five propositions which the constitution repudiated, but denied th
these were to be found in the *Augustinus* according to the sense whi

[1] Mirbt, *op. cit.*, No. 528.

Pope appeared to assign to them. This, of course, amounted to a
rect challenge to papal authority, as it called in question the cor-
ctness of the Pope's judgment on a question of fact, and the
rbonne demonstrated its disapproval by formally censuring those
ho upheld this distinction, including the redoubtable Arnauld
mself.[1]

It was at this stage that Pascal, now an enthusiastic adherent of
rt Royal, entered the lists on the Jansenists' behalf, and in his
mous *Lettres à un Provincial* delivered a vigorous attack on the
pposed Pelagianism of Jesuit moral theology.[2] A further bull of
exander VII endorsing the earlier decision had little effect,
hough it was followed by a formula to be subscribed as a con-
tion of remaining in communion with the Church.

Hitherto the Papacy had been able to count on the support of the
ench monarchy. Jesuit influence had been paramount in the
ench court and ensured the total subordination of its nominees
the French episcopate to the papal and royal wills. But the attitude
four bishops in requiring only respectful silence in regard to
cent papal pronouncements marked the beginning of a new phase.[3]
meant that the problem of papal infallibility, not only on matters
fact but in regard to dogmatic truth, was beginning to be re-
amined. After some protracted negotiations the new Pope Clement
, who was evidently no friend of the Jesuits, agreed, on condition
a formal condemnation of the five propositions, to acquiesce in
e distinction between fact and right.[4] Those who regarded the
eace of Clement' as something in the nature of a papal retracta-
n were perhaps not far from the truth.

By this time the influence of French nationalism had begun to
ake itself felt in ecclesiastical affairs, as was shown by the Declara-
n of the Sorbonne in 1663, that the Pope had no authority over
e king of France in temporal concerns, and in its denial that the
ope was above a general council or was infallible without the
nsent of the Church. During the 'Peace of Clement' Gallicanism
thered fresh strength and it was in this period that the erudite
nonist and patristic scholar Pasquier Quesnel composed his
éflexions morales.

---

[1] Nielsen, F., *History of the Papacy in the XIXth Century*, Eng. Tr., 1906
l. i, p. 6.
[2] *D.T.C.* vol. viii, col. 504.   [3] *D.T.C.* vol. iii, col. 89.
[4] Neale, J. M., *History of the Jansenist Church*, p. 32; *D.T.C.* vol. xiii, col. 1480.

To make matters worse for the Papacy in the struggle whi
followed between Louis XIV and Innocent XI on the *droit de réga*
namely, the right claimed by the French king during the vacancy
a bishopric to receive its revenues and to nominate to the benefi
dependent on it, until the bishop-elect had made his oath of fidel
to the Crown, the leading French Jesuits who saw in the royal cla
an opportunity for extending their influence against the Jansenis
paradoxically were found on the side of the monarchy and agai
the Pope.

Innocent XI, previous to his assumption of the tiara, had sho
himself a competent administrator. As Pope he set his face agai
every form of financial and moral corruption and laboured witho
ceasing for the better religious education of youth.[1] Hence it v
natural that a Pontiff of his character would not refuse the appeal
the bishops of Alet and Pamiers against the decisions of their resp
tive metropolitans, pronounced against them for their hostile view
the 'regalian' claims now being put forward.[2] Although he refrain
from extreme measures, the Pope by his attitude sufficiently alarmed t
king to make him recognize the desirability of assuring himself of t
support of the entire French clergy. Obedient to his wishes a meeti
of Gallican bishops under the presidency of Harlay de Champvallo
archbishop of Paris, decided to request the king to summon a natio
assembly to consist of two bishops and two priests from each provin

When it met in Paris, October 30, 1681, the assembly consisted
thirty-six bishops and thirty-eight representatives of the infer
clergy. They were divided into three parties: a strongly anti-pa
group led by Harlay, a moderately pro-papal one represented
Bossuet, and an intermediate section of whom the archbishop
Rheims was the most outstanding.

In spite of appearances the assembly was by no means complete
subservient to the king's wishes. It obtained royal consent to
modification of the *droit de régale* so as to prevent nomination
benefices without the consultation of the ecclesiastical authorit
concerned. Unaware perhaps of the strength of Gallicanism in Fran
at this time the Pope nevertheless declined to accept the assembl
request for approval of this act, and preserved an attitude of hostil
which played into the hands of the anti-papal groups.

[1] *D.T.C.* vol. vii, col. 2006.
[2] *D.T.C.* vol. iv, col. 186.

Such, then, was the situation which led to the adoption by the
ssembly on March 19, 1682, of the famous four Gallican articles.[1]
hese may be briefly summarized as follows:

1. The power of the Papacy derived from God is limited to the
iritual sphere. As a consequence kings are not subject to any
clesiastical power by God's ordinance, nor may the power of the
ys be exercised to depose them either directly or indirectly, nor to
lease their subjects from their obedience.

2. The decrees of the fourth and fifth sessions of the council of
onstance remain in force regarding the extent of the *plena potestas*
the Papacy, and are not to be regarded as limited in their scope to
e period of the schism.

3. The use of papal authority is to be subject to the canons of the
hurch, and the regulations adopted by the kingdom and the church
France and with the consent of the apostolic see are to remain
tact.

4. In questions of faith, though the principal part in their settle-
ent belongs to the Supreme Pontiff and his decisions are applicable
all churches, such decisions are not to be regarded as irreformable
less the approval of the Church given to them.

This statement, however much it might appear to commend itself
in accord with reason and the evidence of history, was highly
nacceptable to the Ultramontane spirit then in the process of gaining
n ascendancy at Rome. For the moment, however, in France its
ominant ideas were triumphant and the Declaration was published
a law of the State. France seemed unanimous and the only quarters
om which unfavourable reactions came were the universities of
aris and Douai.

The policy adopted by Innocent, however, of refusing canonical
onfirmation to candidates nominated by the king from among those
ho had taken part in the assembly proved effective in quickly under-
ining the credit of the Declaration. By 1687 there were no less than
irty-three dioceses without bishops. Louis was thus being driven
desperation, and at the time of Innocent's death the possibility of
expedition against Rome coupled with an appeal to a general
ouncil was being seriously considered.

After protracted negotiations which outlasted the short pontificate
f Alexander VIII, it was agreed by the king to suspend the observ-

[1] *D.T.C.* vol. iv, col. 195.

ance of the Declaration, while each of the bishops nominated sir
1682 was obliged to present to Innocent XII a signed retractati
Nevertheless, this withdrawal had a private and 'unofficial' charac
which scarcely sufficed to undo the impression created by t
publicity given to the Declaration itself.

Strangely enough the Jansenists, who had no particular interest
the 'regalian' question, had for the most part supported the pap
side in the recent controversy. It was now their turn to be attack
afresh. This time the king ensured himself of papal support a
procured a decisive condemnation of the heresy in the bull *Vine*
Domini Sabaoth. The total dissolution of the convent Port Royal c
Champs followed immediately, but even before its buildings h
been destroyed and its cemetery desecrated, the Jesuit ascendan
at Rome had secured a further victory by procuring a pronoun
ment from Clement XI against Quesnel's *Réflexions Morales*.

The power behind these new attacks was the Jesuit Le Telli
now confessor to the king. The same person is believed to have be
the chief agent in obtaining the last and best-known denunciation
the Gallican Quesnel's work in the bull *Unigenitus* published Se
tember 8, 1713.[1] It is said that Clement only consented to issue t
bull with great reluctance and that he had himself been in the ha
of using the book for his own edification. If this is true, it shows t
Jesuit opinions were by no means so popular at Rome at this tir
as one might be led to suppose.

This final condemnation of Jansenism aroused bitter oppositi
all over France and drew a semi-eclipse over the closing years of t
Roi Soleil. In fact with the adhesion of the Sorbonne to the app
of a group of dissentient bishops against the papal decision it ev
seemed possible that something in the nature of a national schi
was impending.

At this stage we may turn aside for a moment to notice the u
happy effect of ill-informed papal intervention in the affairs of t
Catholic church of Holland. In 1685, as a consequence of the revoc
tion of the Edict of Nantes by Louis XIV, there occurred the last
a series of persecutions directed against Catholics by the Protesta
government of the Dutch States-General. The reigning archbish
of Utrecht, John van Neercassel, had recently published his *Am*
Paenitens, a work which was directed against the laxist morality

[1] Mirbt, *op. cit.*, No. 542.

Jesuits, but which received the approbation of a representative
mber of French and Belgian bishops. The Jesuits had demanded
immediate condemnation, but Innocent XI contented himself
th remarking, so it is said, 'Il libro é buono e l'autore é un Santo'.[1]
exander VIII, however, was less tolerant and issued the requisite
ndemnation just before Neercassel's death.

As a further consequence of Jesuit interference, papal confirma-
n was refused to Van Heussen, whom the Utrecht chapters had
osen to fill the vacant see. The electors then nominated three other
ndidates without, however, withdrawing Van Heussen's name. Of
ese, after some delay, the name of Peter Codde was approved and
was consecrated February 6, 1689. Yet even this act of submission
papal authority did not satisfy the Jesuit 'underworld' and in the
d, in spite of an earlier acquittal, Codde was cited to Rome on
spicion of having approved the Declaration of 1682 and of Jansenist
nings. Though a further acquittal followed, the archbishop was
oitrarily suspended from his office, and it was only by the inter-
ntion of the States-General that his return to Holland was pro-
red, but in compliance with the Roman decision he never again
ercised episcopal functions.[2]

The tactless and overbearing conduct of the papal Internuncio at
ologne caused the greatest indignation among the Dutch clergy,
o now flatly refused to accept his nominee to the vacant see. With
e support of the University of Louvain it was decided to continue
resist all such unwarranted acts of aggression on the liberty of the
utch church, and in 1719, after uniting with a group of Gallicans
opposition to papal authority, the church of Utrecht appealed,
t only against the bull *Unigenitus* but against Roman injustice, to
uture council. By a strange series of accidents it became necessary
invoke the aid of Varlet, coadjutor bishop of Babylon, who had
mself been suspended on grounds which are said to have been
garded even by some Ultramontane canonists as insufficient, and
was eventually through his intervention that Cornelius Steenoven,
ving been duly elected archbishop, was consecrated at Amsterdam
October 15, 1724.

Notice was duly sent to Pope Benedict XIII of his consecration, a
stom which was actually continued without interruption down to

[1] Neale, *op. cit.*, p. 189.
[2] Id., *op. cit.*, p. 207.

the year 1853, and only ceased by the consummation of the schis
through Pius IX's action in introducing a fresh hierarchy into t
country. The only papal answer, however, was a declaration of t
nullity of the election and of the irregularity of the consecratio
Nevertheless the Old Catholic church of Holland continued to exi
and remains to this day as a standing witness not so much again
the Papacy as 'Papalism', and as a protest against double deali
in high places.

We must now go back to describe the ultimate collapse of Jansenis
At the beginning of the new reign under the Duke Regent, Philip
Orleans, there opened a regime of tolerance, with marked favour f
the Jansenists. The question regarding the orthodoxy of Quesr
once more gave place to the far more serious problem about t
doctrinal infallibility of the Papacy. If its attitude towards the b
Unigenitus was any test, there could be no doubt in which directi
the opinion of the majority in the French church was now tendir
Alarmed, however, by the growing dissension, the Duke Rege
preferred the advice of Dubois to that of Saint Simon. Yet, aft
receiving a strongly worded encyclical from Clement XI, in whi
the doctrine of papal infallibility was plainly asserted, thus arousi
the most determined opposition from the Sorbonne and the Fren
Parlements, the Regent's policy once more inclined in favour of t
Jesuits. In this way the Company quickly regained its ascendan
over the Court and a thoroughly reactionary policy was adopte
Before the first half of the century was out the victory of *Unigenit*
seemed to be complete. The archbishop of Paris, the Sorbonne a
the University, all had acknowledged defeat. The Jesuits were to
appearances supreme. Yet for the moment Gallicanism was su
pressed rather than destroyed. As for Jansenism, it was now f
degenerating into the creed of those who were disposed to look f
ward to the possibility of a revolution not only in the Church but
the State as well. Thus to many there seemed no choice betwe
submission to Ultramontanism on the one side, and open avowal
secularism on the other.

Of the prevalence of the latter, whether in the form of Monte
quieu's philosophical scepticism or of Voltaire's polemical an
clericalism, by the middle of the century there was only too mu
evidence. There were even those who hinted by implication, if th
did not say so openly, that it soon would not be so much a questi

hether a man ought to believe what the Pope said as whether he
ould believe anything at all.

Meanwhile the work of the Encyclopaedists, the effect of whose
ritings had been seriously to undermine the faith of a large section
 the French people in spite of all that the Government could do to
ippress their publication, continued to flourish. Yet even when
nfronted by the growing success of their activities, the Jesuits
eferred to concentrate their attention on the extermination of their
llow Christian Jansenists and nearly anticipated the now imminent
volution by prevailing on Louis XV to suspend the Parlements, a
easure hastily taken which was almost as hastily withdrawn.

It was probably this action which, as much as any other on their
irt, settled the fate of the Order in France. In other countries too,
ch as Portugal, it had aroused the keenest resentment, and in the
d discontent and openly expressed indignation in most of the
itholic countries of Europe determined Clement XIV to decree the
olition of the Order.[1]

It was perhaps well for the prestige of the Papacy at this juncture
at he did so, as the constitution *Apostolicum pascendi* delivered in
vour of the Order by his predecessor Clement XIII had reduced
e general credit of the apostolic see in Europe to something like the
el which it had reached in the days of John XXIII or Clement VII.
radoxically, as it seemed, the sceptical philosophers were the most
tspoken in their sympathy with its downfall. Yet actually it was
ey who derived the greater benefit from the event, as they were
w able to extend their influence further into the French educational
tem. Thus by a strange turn of fortune one of the most important
d unhappy results of the bull *Dominus ac redemptor* was to leave
 field of Continental education to an almost unchallenged
cupation by the apostles of the 'Enlightenment'.

VII

We must now consider the work of a contemporary writer who,
ile the struggle for and against the bull *Unigenitus* was proceeding
 France, had himself evolved a 'constitutional' theory of papal
hority. This was Nicholas Hontheim, a disciple of Van Espen at
uvain, and later coadjutor bishop of Trier. In his *De statu praesenti*

---

[1] Mirbt, *op. cit.*, No. 548.

ecclesiae published in 1763 we find an enthusiastic, though not alway
consistent defence of the rights of the episcopate, and of the ind
pendence of the State in relation to the Papacy. Febronius, to gi
the author his better-known pseudonym, believed that the futu
prosperity of the Church depended on a fresh and unequivocal asse
tion (such as had been evaded at the council of Trent) of the divir
origin of the episcopate.

Yet he was sufficient of a realist to expect that little serious atte
tion would be given to his appeal for a speedy return to the state
the Church in the first four centuries by the Papacy itself. As Gall
canism had found its support in the claims of the French monarch
so now this German reformer looked to each territorial prince
enforce his rights. By this means he proposed that the papal aut
cracy was to be destroyed and bounds finally set to its authority t
the Catholic rulers acting through a general council or at least
national synods. In particular he urged that all papal claims base
on the *False Decretals* must be utterly abandoned.

The book at once achieved a remarkable popularity and in spi
of its condemnation by Clement XIII, who was evidently anxio
to avoid giving it too much publicity, quickly went through a numb
of editions both in German and in other languages. We cannot, hov
ever, regard the author as wholly disingenuous or even sincere, f
he not only denied his identity with Febronius but eventually,
1778, issued a recantation. Yet as he was then of an advanced age h
contemporary Pius VI could scarcely congratulate himself on a ve
remarkable triumph. For it was certainly true, as the author himse
is alleged to have remarked, that though his recantation might plea
the Roman Curia it could not alter the fact that his book had bee
widely read and approved.

Only five years after its appearance responsible people in Germar
were considering means by which Febronius' ideas might be giv
practical expression, and though the *Articles of Coblenz* were di
creetly shelved by the Emperor Joseph II, they prepared the w
for concrete measures at a later date. In any case, and perhaps as
immediate consequence of the suppression of the Jesuits, a serio
re-examination of the papal position in history, especially in relati
to the now almost defunct Holy Roman Empire, was widely unde
taken and the theory of an 'omnipotent State' began to be taug
publicly in Vienna.

On the death of his mother Maria Theresa in 1780, Joseph initiated various reforms of a liberal nature. In particular he endorsed a decree which forbad the publication of papal bulls without the *placet* of the government and ordered the removal of the bull *Unigenitus* from the service books. To limit the subordination of the Austrian episcopate to the Papacy he insisted that bishops should issue matrimonial dispensations without obtaining the usual quinquennial faculties from Rome, and imposed on them an oath of loyalty to himself to be taken before their oath of obedience to the Roman see.

Though Catholicism remained the dominant religion of the State, Protestants and even Jews were given wide tolerance. Supposedly redundant or indolent monastic establishments were dissolved, thus reducing the total number of such institutions in the country by about a third, while its economic stability was considerably improved by a judicious paring of the considerable proportion of landed property in the hands of the Church. But perhaps the most important of his reforms in its effect on the internal life of the Church was the Emperor's creation of national seminaries under the direct supervision of the State.

Naturally such action aroused the greatest possible indignation and even alarm at Rome, so much so that it even seemed necessary to attempt to check further progress of the Josephist movement by resorting to the expedient of a visit to Vienna by the Pope in person. Not since the beginning of the Avignonese Papacy had the world seen the successor of St. Peter on such an errand. Pius lost no opportunity of a theatrical appeal to turn the situation to his own advantage, but the eccentric Emperor held his ground, and the only tangible result of the Pope's visit was the grant of an empty imperial title to his nephew.

Joseph continued his reforms. If the pace was slower than before, the thoroughness of his measures remained undiminished. At one time it is said that he seriously contemplated a complete renunciation of papal authority, but there are signs that towards the end of his reign his attitude became more restrained.

His brother, the Grand Duke of Tuscany, who succeeded him as Leopold II in 1790, had already done a good deal to introduce similar reforms within his own domains and found an enthusiastic if somewhat reckless supporter of his programme in Scipione de Ricci, Bishop of Pistoia. Ricci's study of the New Testament and of Gallican

Canon Law had led him to adopt Jansenism and Febronianism a
articles of his creed. He quickly roused a storm of opposition, bot
among the Dominicans, who since the suppression of the Jesuits ha
once more come into power, and also among the secular clergy. H
most startling success was achieved at his diocesan synod, wher
approval was given to a considerable programme of Josephist reform
as well as to the four Gallican articles, in addition to a definition (
the infallibility of the Church in a strictly limited sense.

Leopold now committed the false step of summoning a nation,
synod at Florence, which showed clearly that the majority of tl
Tuscan episcopate was united in its opposition to the measure
proposed by the Grand Duke and his reforming bishop.

When Leopold succeeded to the imperial throne, Ricci's chief sup
port was gone. The new Emperor's eagerness for reform quick
abated and Ricci found himself deserted and alone. He resigned h
bishopric in the following year and when Pius VII was in Florenc
on his return from Paris in 1805 he presented a mild form of recant;
tion. It was a pathetic anti-climax to a programme which obvious
needed a greater man than the bishop of Pistoia to carry it int
effect.

A further but even more abortive movement in favour of a 'co:
stitutional' Papacy developed from those *Articles of Coblenz*, whic
we have already noticed, and arose from the papal proposal to estal
lish a Nuncio at Munich. The archbishop of Salzburg, and tl
electors of Mainz, Trier, and Cologne, feeling that such an appoin
ment would impose a limit on their influence in Bavaria, agreed 1
send representatives to a congress held in 1786 at Ems. The issu
of the congress was the publication of a series of points which full
embodied the chief principles of Febronius, recognizing the pap
primacy but rejecting the powers supposed to have been acquired i
virtue of the *False Decretals*. It was also decided to ask the Emper
to make an immediate reform of ecclesiastical abuses possible and 1
urge upon the Pope the acceptance of the 'points'. In the event (
his persistent refusal, the Emperor was advised to call a nation
council to ensure their fulfilment.[1]

Unhappily for the success of this 'paper' reformation, the unden
able fact remained that among the principal ecclesiastical abuse
most deserving of reform was the secular status of the archbishoj

[1] Mirbt, *op. cit.*, No. 553.

lectors themselves. Hence it was easy for the opponents of their
ideas to suggest that the real motive underlying their proposals was
not reform but the stabilization of their own secular authority. It was
not difficult, therefore, for the newly appointed Nuncio not only to
in a considerable measure of support from the inferior bishops,
who as often before in history preferred the intangible authority of
distant Pope to immediate overlordship of a local metropolitan.
Not unnaturally the congress of Ems was soon discredited, and with
the outbreak of the French revolution found itself consigned to the
mbo of good causes defended for wrong motives by insincere
advocates.

VIII

Although it may well be true that the French church in the latter
half of the eighteenth century was not the mass of corruption pic-
tured by some historians, we can scarcely deny that its condition was
such as to render it singularly ill-fitted to meet the storm which was
soon to burst upon it.[1] The economic condition of the country and
the fact that so much of the nation's wealth was locked up in ecclesiastical property, which through the law of exemption was not liable
to taxation, made it inevitable that disendowment of the Church
should be regarded as a reasonable way of solving current financial
problems. But disendowment when it came was only the beginning.
Thus the cancellation of tithe and the confiscation of all ecclesiastical
property in 1789 led immediately to the adoption of the *Civil
Constitution of the Clergy* in the following year.

Up to this time the Concordat of 1516 had remained in force, in
virtue of which the king was recognized as having the power to
nominate bishops, abbots, and priors, while the right of giving
canonical institution was strictly reserved to the Pope.[2] As a result
all through the centuries the royal power had acted in some degree
a restraint on the avowed Gallicanism of the Parlements and the
legal profession. It was therefore only to be expected that once the
power of the monarchy had been broken, parliamentary Gallicanism
should be triumphant. Thus the Civil Constitution may be viewed
rightly as a sign of its victory and the high water mark of its achievement.

[1] Phillips, C. S., *Church in France*, p. 1, to which the present writer is indebted
for much of the following summary of developments in the French church.
[2] *D.T.C.* vol. iii, col. 1537.

By its provisions the organization of the church was to be com
pletely reconstructed according to the new civil circumscriptions.
Instead of twenty-four archbishoprics and one hundred and twenty
four bishoprics, which were either wholly or in part included in
French territory, there were to be ten metropolitan areas and eighty
three sees. Some of the most ancient archbishoprics like Narbonne
Sens, Tours, Embrun, and Vienne lost their metropolitical status
the only see to acquire it was Rennes. Eight new sees were created
and sixty-one suppressed. In cathedral cities the bishop himsel
became as a rule the *curé* of the cathedral church, which also was t
serve as a parish church of the chief parish in the locality, assisted
by a staff of twelve to sixteen *vicaires* according to the population o
the place. A town parish normally comprised a population of not les
than six thousand. In addition, attached to each see there was to b
a diocesan seminary with a staff of four clergy. These together wit
the *vicaires* of the cathedral church composed an episcopal counci
which the bishop was bound to consult before performing any ac
of jurisdiction. All capitular offices, canonries, chaplaincies an
other ecclesiastical titles were totally abolished. A right of appea
against an episcopal verdict lay to the metropolitan synod. To th
metropolitan bishop belonged the right of confirming a bishop-elect
which in the case of a metropolitan-elect was assigned to the senio
bishop of the 'province'. Although the constitution described th
Pope as the 'head of the universal Church', he was a head deprive
of any executive authority, with whom the new church of Franc
was associated only 'by unity of faith and communion'.

In line with ideas of democracy now dominant it was provide
that bishops were to be elected on the same lines as officials of th
civil administration, that is to say, by the whole electorate of th
departement concerned, without distinction of creed. Confirmation o
a bishop-elect was not to be sought from the Pope, who was simpl
to be informed by letter of the fact of his election, but from th
metropolitan, or, if the metropolitical see itself was to be filled, fror
the senior bishop. The only oath to be required of him was a pro
fession of the Catholic, apostolic and Roman religion. Should th
metropolitan refuse confirmation, an appeal was to lie to the civ
power. At the time of his consecration the bishop-elect was to swea
solemnly to guard with care the faithful of the diocese committed t

[1] *D.T.C.* col. 1552.

im, to be faithful to the nation, the law and the king, and to main-
in with all his power the Constitution decreed by the assembly and
ccepted by the crown.

The election of the *curés* was regulated on similar lines. If the
ishop should refuse institution, an appeal, as in the case of an
piscopal election, might be made to the civil authority.

The two remaining sections of the Constitution fixed the amount
f episcopal and clerical stipends and the law of residence, the latter
roviding that no bishop or other cleric might be absent without
pproval of the ecclesiastical and civil authorities for more than
fteen days at a time.

The Civil Constitution no doubt had the merit of providing power-
ul safeguards against current abuses, but the fact that it was imposed
y civil authority without any form of consent on the part of the
hurch was bound to make it unacceptable to a considerable pro-
ortion of the clergy. Among the various criticisms which were made,
 was said that the civil authority ought not to assume the right to
nange the boundaries of dioceses or to suppress episcopal sees with-
ut reference to papal authority. To the claim that the new electoral
ystem was simply a reversion to the primitive practice of the Church,
 was replied that to assign the choice of bishops and *curés* to the
hole civil electorate meant that in future schismatics and un-
elievers would have the same rights in the selection of Catholic
astors as the faithful themselves. The Church would thus be com-
elled to receive its clergy at the hands of its inveterate enemies. It
as also objected that the Constitution was essentially presbyterian
 character; for not only had it raised the status of the *curés*, but,
y subjecting him entirely to a majority vote of his council, actually
ade the bishop no more than a chairman of his clergy without
ghts of nomination or executive power. The supporters of the Con-
itution endeavoured to cite patristic and even scriptural evidence in
s defence, but they could scarcely ignore the contradiction between
s terms and the Tridentine decrees. A more serious objection in the
yes of some was its disregard of papal authority. Even among those
ho were most ardent in its defence was felt the need of giving
me public reassurance on this point:

'We recognize the Pope', they said, 'as the visible head of the
hurch, as the heir of the primacy of Peter, as the centre of unity
ccording to the saying of Bossuet, as the guardian of the canons . . .

we believe with St. Jerome that Jesus Christ has established a hea
to maintain the unity of faith, *ut, capite constituto, schismatis tolleretu
occasio*. That is why we have written to him as a testimony of com
munion. We shall show him submission and deference each time w
render him this homage without doing violence to the canons, th
laws of the kingdom and the rights of the episcopate. We are there
fore in no way schismatics. If schism comes about, which God for
bid, it will be the Pope who separates himself, and we shall remai
always linked with the heart of the Catholic, apostolic and Roma
church'.[1]

The opponents of the Constitution naturally replied that the effe
of the proposed measure was to reduce the office of the Pope to a
empty title. The Church, on the contrary, assigned to him a primac
not merely of honour but of jurisdiction, and only those were to b
accounted Catholics who recognized his supreme authority. In favou
of their view the powers assigned to the Papacy by the Declaratio
of 1682 were cited together with the famous sermon of Bossuet o
the *Unity of the Church*. The Pope's jurisdiction, they said, wa
exercised in two ways: by the canonical institution given to bishop
and the pronouncement of a final judgment on appeal. As, howeve
by the Civil Constitution both these rights were taken away, the Pop
in their view would become no more than *primus inter pares*, an
thus no longer the effective head of the Church.

The most serious objection of the new measure, it was argue
attached to its theory as to the source of jurisdiction. Whence wer
the new diocesans supposed to have derived their rights? Was it i
virtue of popular election? Yet, if that was so, how could a civ
power give what it did not possess? The Constitutional party replie
that jurisdiction was not given by the civil power but was receive
from Jesus Christ, and went on to argue that the spiritual needs o
of the faithful were sufficient to validate the ministrations of the ne
hierarchy.

To sum up, the Constitution was attacked, especially by the gre
majority of the episcopate, as schismatic, because it separated Franc
from its legitimate bishops and from the Pope, and also as heretica
because it denied in practice dogmas such as the papal primacy, th
necessity that bishops should possess jurisdiction given by th
Church and distinct from the power of Order, the hierarchic

---

[1] *D.T.C.* vol. iii, col. 1568.

periority of a bishop to a priest, and finally the right of the Church
govern itself.

The Constitution was adopted by the National Assembly on
uly 12, 1790, and although Louis XVI did his best to persuade
ius VI to give his assent before according the royal sanction, he
aturally failed. Pius promised to refer the question to a commission
f Cardinals, but before their report was received, the king found
imself unable to withhold his assent any longer.

By a further decree the Assembly imposed the oath required by
he Constitution on the whole of the French clergy under penalty of
eprivation for refusal. Once more after a feeble show of resistance
he king gave in.

The effect of this measure was practically to divide the church of
'rance into two parts, but, at least so far as the episcopate was con-
erned, into two very unequal ones. Thus out of one hundred and
hirty diocesan bishops, not more than four were found who were
villing to take the oath, and these included the sceptic Lomenie
e Brienne and the renegade Talleyrand. In spite of some doubt on
he point, it seems generally agreed that the inferior clergy were
livided more equally; in country districts it is likely that a large
umber accepted the oath without realizing fully its implications; in
owns, on the other hand, with the exception of Paris itself, non-
urors were in the majority.

It was not till April 13 of the following year that in the brief
Charitas the Constitution was officially condemned by the Roman
ee, which suspended all those who had taken the oath and declared
ll elections which had taken place under it null and 'constitutional'
onsecrations illicit. In spite of this the supporters of the Constitution
ersisted in protesting that it was not their intention to abandon the
²apacy, and they protested that they held the Pope to be worthy of
ll respect, short of actual obedience.

The schism between the two sections of the French church was
10w complete. The non-jurors were naturally excluded from the
arish churches but continued their ministrations in spite of the law
n private chapels. This state of affairs continued till the Legislative
\ssembly, after overriding the royal veto, imposed a modified form
of the oath, but made the penalties for non-compliance more strin-
;ent. By the middle of 1793 further laws were being passed making
10n-juring clergy who remained in the country punishable with

death. Yet the end of the constitutional church was also alread in sight. By the last months of the year the Paris Commune ha virtually succeeded in securing its suppression, and the examp of the capital was being widely followed in the larger centres population.

As a result both the constitutional and non-juring clergy alike no became victims of the most vexatious and persistent measures persecution. This lasted nearly two years. The year 1795, howeve saw the beginning of a reaction in favour of toleration, and in th course of the next few months many churches were being once mor used for public worship. So rapid was its progress that by the end the year it is probable that mass was again being said in 30,000 ou of the 40,000 French parishes. At the same time a tendency w: already observable among the constitutional clergy to desire recor ciliation with the Papacy, if only on the basis of the Gallican Declar: tion of 1682.

Yet peace was not yet in sight. The Directory which now came i power further antagonized Catholic opinion by adopting a policy reducing the number of church buildings. Under their inspiratio not less than one hundred parish churches in Paris and many famou abbeys perished. At the same time a rival cult to Catholicism was de vised under the name of Theophilanthropism. We shall not be sur prised that, in spite of active support from the government, it mad little headway.

The first real beginning in the direction of Christian revival wa made by the National Council assembled two years later under th leadership of a group of constitutional bishops. It adopted a decre of pacification, which acknowledged the Pope as the visible head the Church *iure divino*, while insisting on the maintenance of Gallica liberties. Naturally it evoked little sympathy from the non-jurors who disliked its Republicanism as much as its Gallican principle Peace was brought nearer by a further modification of the oath loyalty to the Constitution, following the *coup d'état* of the 18t Brumaire, so that it became possible for all but the more extrem supporters of the *ancien régime* to co-operate in the restoration of th Church. Meanwhile, the government had now undertaken th formidable task of subduing the Papacy to its will.

We must now go back for a moment to trace the course of papa history following the death of Clement XIV. With the election o

ius VI in 1775 a reaction had set in in favour of the Jesuits, and
though the Pope was not able to act freely in the matter for fear of
disapproval on the part of France and Spain, he secretly fostered the
revival of the Order, while refraining from committing himself
openly to such a policy. Nevertheless, in defiance of the bull of
Clement XIV, the resumption of Jesuit work in Russia under
Catherine II was being encouraged. Strangely enough there appeared
to be signs that the Papacy was disposed to take a favourable view of
the movement towards democracy. Nevertheless, the belief that this
was so and that its influence was behind certain liberal movements in
Tuscany and Belgium did not save it from the intervention of the
French Republic in the affairs of the Papal States.

In 1796 General Bonaparte had occupied northern Italy as far as
Bologna, and by the middle of the year Pius was compelled to make
humiliating terms of peace with the invader. As a gesture of reconciliation, however, he addressed a brief to French Catholics in which
he pointed out that it was the teaching of the Roman church that all
civil authority is derived from God. Although the address of the
brief made it doubtful whether it was directed also to those who had
taken the oath, it caused considerable satisfaction to them and some
uneasiness among their opponents. Consequently efforts were now
made to persuade the Pope to confirm the Civil Constitution and
negotiations were so far successful, as it seems, that the papal envoy
in Paris received definite instructions to get into touch with the
constitutional party.

Moreover, although counsels evidently remained much divided at
Rome, a serious attempt was made by the Spanish General of the
Dominicans to persuade Pius to withdraw all expressions in previous
bulls and briefs adverse to the Revolution. A period of negotiation
followed, but as soon as the Pope felt assured of a defensive alliance
with the kingdom of Naples he decided on resistance. It was, of
course, utterly futile and only led to the imposition of more rigorous
terms of peace than before.

Yet, in spite of everything, a majority of the Cardinals persisted in
believing that intervention by Austria or Naples would save the situation. Their dreams were quickly shattered when the revolutionary
party in Rome gained control, and on February 20, 1798, the Pope
and the whole Curia were expelled from the city. Pius was at first the
guest of the Grand Duke of Tuscany, but in the following year he

was removed by French intervention to Valence in Dauphiné, wher
on August 29 he died.

His successor, who took the name of Pius VII, was elected unde
singular conditions in the monastery of San Giorgio at Venice, an
when the election was over arrangements were made through th
influence of the Austrian government for the new Pope to return t
Rome. Pius re-entered his capital on July 3, 1800, and a month late
appointed Cardinal Consalvi as his Secretary of State. The choice wa
a happy one. Consalvi had had a distinguished career in the servic
of the Papacy and combined a realist outlook with remarkable gift
of statesmanship. He was therefore particularly well fitted to be th
chief adviser of a Pontiff who, though by no means devoid of firmnes
and personal courage, had had a monastic training and in some re
spects was more at home in a cloister than in an audience chamber.

When the Roman people greeted their new Sovereign with tha
fickle enthusiasm which has characterized them throughout history
barely three weeks had elapsed since Bonaparte had won his victor
over the Austrians at Marengo. His message to the Pope from Vercell
was an open profession of his intention to restore Catholicism ir
France, and of his determination to suppress the constitutiona
church. While he lent his support to a project for a clean sheet ir
ecclesiastical affairs involving a reduction in the numbers of the
French episcopate in which there would be room for neither Gal
licans nor reactionaries, he promised that the Pope should have free
dom for the exercise of his spiritual jurisdiction, that his right o
giving bishops canonical institution should be recognized, and, wha
is more, that his temporal power should be completely restored.

We see presently how far the Emperor Napoleon honoured Bona
parte's undertaking. As to his latest attitude, there must have been a
least a few who remembered that scarcely three years had elapsec
since that distinguished personage had publicly classed religior
among the 'prejudices' which the French nation must overcome. Nor
could it be said that the 'deism' which he had acknowledged on more
than one occasion was easily reconcilable with the traditional theism
of the Church. The fact was, as his behaviour in Egypt showec
clearly enough, that he regarded the establishment of organized re
ligion not so much as an end in itself as an indispensable part of his
policy. Thus it has been said: 'A national religion was to his mind a

[1] Nielsen, *op. cit.*, vol. i, p. 208.

rm of inoculation which might satisfy mankind's love of the miracu-
us'.[1] Though he had once said that on the death of Pius VI the
ection of a new Pope ought to be prevented, according to his later
ords, 'If there had not been a Pope, it would have been necessary to
eate one for this occasion'. In view, therefore, of his earlier religious
hases, it must have seemed puzzling to learn that the French
atholicism which he now aimed to restore was not the Catholicism
f the constitutional Abbé Gregoire but of Bossuet the moderate
allican.

Negotiations for the conclusion of a Concordat began late in 1800.
here were three principal points on which it was difficult to recon-
le the old and the new standpoints. These concerned the episcopate,
isendowment and the choice of a suitable formula to describe the
elation of Catholicism to the French State. As to the first, the com-
lete restoration of the royalist episcopate was unthinkable; the hand-
ig back of endowments was by now utterly impossible and it was
idely felt that merely to describe Catholicism as the religion of the
aajority savoured unpleasantly of fresh intolerance such as had pre-
ailed under the *ancien régime*.

In spite of the diplomatic finesse of Cardinal Consalvi, to whose
ompetent hands they had been entrusted, the negotiations proved
ery protracted. More than once the First Consul threatened to cut
ie knot by establishing a non-papal Catholicism, but in the end
onsalvi succeeded in obtaining the introduction of a qualifying
hrase into the final form of the Concordat which seemed a sufficient
afeguard against improper State interference with the Church's
omestic affairs. Ultimately the agreement was approved by both the
ontracting parties.[2] As finally drawn up it provided first for the re-
istribution of episcopal sees, envisaging the possibility of the resigna-
on of the existing episcopate, the nomination of a new episcopate
y the First Consul and its institution by the Pope, the taking of an
ath of allegiance to the Republic by all bishops and priests, the
election of parish priests by the bishops from men who were accept-
ble to the government, the restoration of church buildings without
rejudice to the occupiers of confiscated ecclesiastical property, the
aitable payment of the clergy, and finally the assignment to the
irst Consul of the same privileges as those which had been enjoyed
y the monarchs of the *ancien régime*.

[1] Nielsen, *op. cit.*, vol. i, p. 226. [2] Mirbt, *op. cit.*, No. 558.

The only one of these provisions which may appear to involve
surprising concession to papal authority is the one allowing for th
collective resignation of the French episcopate. But under the existi
circumstances such a measure was inevitable, and even if it involv
in practice an implicit recognition of Bellarmine's theories of pap
supremacy, there was some justice in the words uttered by Bonapar
on the eve of the solemn publication of the Concordat: 'It was to th
Pope that the example of centuries and reason, bade us go, to mak
peace between divided opinions and to reconcile estranged heart
Yet there were perhaps some grounds for believing that in the end th
Revolution had sold the French church into the hands of the Papac

Bonaparte, however, had his own way of safeguarding the indepen
dence of a French institution. It was the bold if not strictly ingenuou
method of appending to the Concordat after signature the notorio
Organic Articles.[1] These provided a number of guarantees again
papal and episcopal abuse of authority, and actually included th
provision that the Gallican Declaration of 1682 was to be taught
seminaries. Such a measure was naturally highly offensive to the Pop
though for the moment he could not do other than acquiesce in
purely unilateral act. Yet by a singular paradox the very subordin
tion of the parish clergy to the bishops which it encouraged w
itself responsible indirectly for assisting the progress of Ultramo
tanism in France.

Bonaparte had laid the church of the French people at the feet
the gentle Pius, and for the moment a torrent of expressions of goo
will and mutual esteem passed between Rome and Paris. But tho
who knew recent history and had not forgotten the past were boun
to ask, 'How long will this kind of thing go on?' For it must hav
been only too evident that the Altar was now uneasily balanced o
the Consular Throne.

The coronation of the Emperor in Paris, with its strange blendir
of deference and insult to papal majesty, served as an occasion fo
ineffectual requests on the part of Pius for a modification of the Co
cordat and particularly of the Organic Articles. As such it marked th
beginning of the rupture which was to lead to a papal captivity, le
rigorous indeed than that of Liberius or of Martin I, but certain
far more effective in winning Catholic sentiment to the support
the Roman see.

[1] Mirbt, *op. cit.*, No. 559.

It is clear that after the coronation Napoleon had hoped to be able
to retain the Pope in France, and that so soon as it became evident
that Pius had made up his mind to return to Rome, the cordiality
which had hitherto marked their relations began to cool. The first
clash of interests arose in connexion with the papal refusal to sanction
the divorce of Jerome Bonaparte, and the event made it still pain-
fully obvious even to the most uncritical admirers of the Emperor
that 'religion, then as always, was to Napoleon only a weapon for
momentary use'.[1]

By the beginning of 1806 Napoleon was openly complaining of the
Pope's unreasonableness and ingratitude, and showed that he was set
upon a plan of reducing the Supreme Pontiff to be a mere bishop of
Rome. In an outspoken letter to Pius early in the same year he wrote
of the necessity that papal policy should conform to his own and
made it obvious that if Pius wished for peace he must get rid of
Consalvi. Clearly Napoleon was demanding nothing less than an open
recognition of himself as Roman Emperor.

Such a demand was firmly rejected. But as a gesture of friendship
to the French State Consalvi's resignation followed shortly afterwards. By this time, however, Napoleon had gone too far for any
reconciliation to be possible, and more and more he began to assume
the position of an *imperator sacerdos*. True to type, he set about imposing religious uniformity in France in accordance with the Organic
Articles, of which the re-edited form of Bossuet's Catechism now
made obligatory throughout the French church was a significant
example.[2]

Then, following the passage with papal permission of General
Liolli's army through the Papal States, and the virtual occupation of
Rome, Pius took the courageous step of recalling his diplomatic
representative from Paris. The breach was now complete. The Pope
became a prisoner in the Quirinal with Cardinal Pacca as his sole
companion. The Curia was dispersed. It was not long before the
climax came with the publication of the bull *Quam memoranda*, by
which Pius declared the Emperor excommunicated. The arrest of the
Pope, his eventual internment at Savona following a strangely round-
about route passing through Genoa, Turin, Grenoble, Avignon, and

---

[1] Nielsen, *op. cit.*, vol. i, p. 284. It is instructive to compare the attitude of Italian
Fascism towards religion, see e.g. Binchy, D. A., *Church and State in Fascist Italy*,
1941, p. 100 ff.
[2] Id., *op. cit.*, vol. i, p. 281 ff.

Nice, though suggesting that Napoleon himself was undecided about the best means of disposing of his embarrassing captive, calls for no detailed description. Possibly it was the Emperor's intention to make the fact of the Pope's humiliation widely known in France. If so, he certainly succeeded, though whether it produced precisely the effect which he had desired may be open to doubt.

How little Napoleon could have really understood the spiritual power of the Roman see, and the impossibility of making it bend before his absolutist claims, may be seen in his expectation that Pius would be willing to bless his marriage with Marie Louise. The removal first of the French and later of the Italian Cardinals to Paris led to a further impressive demonstration of the Emperor's relative impotence in the refusal of the 'thirteen' to be present at the wedding. Napoleon's action in 'decardinalizing' the recalcitrants showed that in an incredibly short time he had believed himself to have succeeded in reducing Pius to the status of bishop of Rome, and was now attempting to assume the role of Supreme Pontiff himself. It was therefore a mere matter of detail that newly elected bishops were being empowered to take over their dioceses without canonical institution, in spite of the provisions of the Concordat.

Meanwhile the real Pope remained a prisoner at Savona, and in spite of all the pressure brought to bear upon him by means of every form of outrage and petty persecution that absolutist ingenuity could devise, remained impervious to threats and entreaties alike. He did not even hesitate to declare Maury, whom the Emperor had appointed archbishop of Paris, deprived of all authority. But if Napoleon thought that Pius could be deposed by taking away from him his Fisherman's Ring, his books and writing materials, the event was to prove him mistaken.

Ultimately, however, the Pope's resolution began to give way, and in return for a promise of liberty and independence he assented to some concessions in the matter of canonical institution of bishops. Napoleon's plans for a non-papal church were now well in hand, and it was clear that with the assembly of the council of Paris in 1811 he hoped to carry through his programme without any regard for the captive at Savona. In this, however, he encountered a formidable opponent in his own uncle Cardinal Fesch, whose strangely diversified career had not deprived him of his conviction that spiritual allegiance was still owed to the Roman see. All attempts to dragoon

ιe council into independent action utterly failed, so that in the end
εpudiation of the papal right of confirmation was only obtained by
ιeans of taking a vote under imperial pressure.

It was now decided that in view of the forthcoming absence of the
mperor during the campaign against Russia, it would be wise to
ave the captive Pope in immediate proximity to the capital. He was
ιerefore brought to Fontainebleau. Napoleon's star was already be-
ınning to wane, yet this did not prevent him from making demands
νen less temperate than before. A meeting between Pope and
mperor led to the signing of a fresh Concordat in which new and
ιore stringent conditions were accepted. But the ink of the agree-
ιent was scarcely dry when Pius, supported by the presence of his
ardinals now released from internment, showed amazing boldness.
ι spite of the evident consequences, a letter, composed under con-
ιtions of the greatest difficulty, was sent to the Emperor formally
εpudiating the new Concordat.

The significance of this courageous act was that it marked the
ırning of the tide. By May 13, 1813, the Pope had declared all
shops recently installed to be intruders, and early in the following
ιar the Emperor confessed his defeat by giving orders for the Pope
be taken back to Rome. He remained at Savona for nearly two
onths more and finally, on May 24, 1814, with something of the
ιture of a triumph re-entered his ancient capital. Whatever else the
ptivity of the Pope at Savona and Fontainebleau had to teach him,
apoleon must have learnt that in his endeavour to compel the
ιpacy to be an instrument of his policy he was confronted by an
stitution of a character very different from that of the thrones and
ngdoms which had crumbled to dust at his approach. It was the
nperor himself who is reported to have said 'the power that rules
er souls has a greater sway than that which rules over bodies'.[1]

Pius survived his return by more than nine years. During that
εriod, partly as a consequence of the deep impression left upon the
mantic imagination of the period by the picture of a 'martyr' Pope,
d partly by means of the statesmanlike diplomacy and government
Consalvi, the Papacy regained in spiritual prestige far more than
had lost in temporal authority. The only forces which actually
oved too strong for Pope and statesman alike were those of reaction.
An unmistakable sign of this defeat may perhaps be seen in the

[1] Nielsen, *op. cit.*, vol. i, p. 339.

submission of the Papacy to the demand for the complete rehabilitation of the Jesuits. Certain steps, as we have seen, had already been taken in the time of Pius VI in this direction. Now by the bull *Sollicitudo omnium*[1] the measures taken by Clement XIV were reversed and the Roman church found itself once more under the control of a society whose methods in the past had seldom ministered to its true welfare. There is reason to think that some like Consalvi, regarding whose loyalty to the Papacy and desire to promote the well-being of the Church there was no shadow of doubt, were seriously uneasy about the wisdom of this step, not least because it involved the complete reversal of an act solemnly and publicly carried out by a previous occupant of the papal throne.

At once the full tide of reaction began to set in. Social improvements at Rome introduced by the French were banished. The Inquisition and the Index, intolerance and even anti-Semitism came into their own again. Yet in spite of these unfortunate measures for which Cardinal Pacca's influence, to the exclusion of the prudent and temperate Consalvi, must be held chiefly responsible, the former Secretary of State obtained considerable success on the Pope's behalf at the Congress of Vienna. Some of his ideas, such as the view that the Holy Roman Empire ought to be restored, may well run the risk of being regarded as chimerical and lacking in realism. But it could at least be said that he was possessed of political vision conspicuously lacking in the majority of statesmen of the time. In consequence of his work the Papacy regained by far the greater part of its territory; in any case most of what it lost, such as Avignon and Venaissin, it had no conceivable chance of being able to hold in the face of public opinion.

The real and immediate problems which now confronted the Roman see were chiefly financial. Reforms in administration were being urgently demanded, but with a huge papal debt and diminishing resources, they were utterly impossible of execution on anything like adequate lines. Instead of Rome providing for the provinces, the city was now economically dependent on them. It was not surprising therefore that discontent rapidly took hold of the inhabitants of the Papal States, and movements favouring independence of the Roman see made perceptible and disquieting headway.

From the point of view of relations of the Roman see with the non-Roman churches Pius quickly lost any sympathy which his unhap

[1] Mirbt, *op. cit.*, No. 564.

ptivity may have won for him by his hostile attitude to the Bible
cieties,[1] for which Jesuit influence seems to have been chiefly
sponsible. Yet, even if such hostility may have been justified in
ew of the tendentious or inaccurate character of certain vernacular
anslations, it played into the hands of those who were eager to
ow that the Papacy, in spite of its misfortunes, had reverted to the
pport of a reactionary obscurantism.

IX

The period after 1815 was marked by an attempt to resume a policy
Concordats. On all sides, however, and not least in France under
ouis XVIII, the Papacy was confronted with serious opposition;
Austria the persistence of Josephism actually prevented the con-
usion of any agreement whatever. To make matters worse, when
e death of Pius VII came in 1823 it was already clear that a fresh
riod of political uncertainty was beginning. It was an additional
isfortune that Consalvi's influence, which had served to balance
e steadily increasing power of the Jesuits in papal counsels, now
me to an end, and for nearly a century the Roman Curia would
ck any statesman capable of offering any positive contribution to
e political problems of the time. For it was already increasingly
ident that, however much the forces of reaction at Rome and else-
ere might desire to put the clock back and restore the conditions
the eighteenth century, the existence of the secularized state could
ly be ignored at the price of abandoning the Church's mission to
ristianize human society. The tragedy lay in the absence of anyone
influence in the Curia to whom this almost self-evident fact
med in any way apparent.

Before passing on to consider the nature of those developments
ich took place under the immediate predecessors of Pius IX, we
st notice briefly a group of French writers of this period whose
ork serves to illustrate a pronounced current of thought in the
tholic world during the earlier half of the nineteenth century,
rticularly strong in France.

Joseph de Maistre, the first of these who claim our attention, had
ent his earlier days in the service of the kingdom of Sardinia, and
was not till the last four years of his life that he wrote the works

[1] Mirbt, *op. cit.*, Nos. 568–9.

for which his name has become famous.[1] His conception of human
nature is fundamentally pessimistic. All ideas of democracy and freedom are utterly abhorrent to him. Absolutism is divinely instituted
and must operate in the temporal and spiritual spheres alike. But the
sole true end of all human endeavour is unity, and for de Maistre this
is only capable of achievement by the complete subordination of the
temporal to the spiritual. Thus, if a temporal monarch abuses his
power, resistance can only be offered in the name of the higher
authority reposing with the Pope.

De Maistre, however, was not primarily interested in theology but
in social reconstruction. He had no use for Gallicanism and no real
trust in the monarchist revival. For him the existence of the Pope
was so necessary that, like Napoleon in his earlier years, he was prepared to say that if Christ had not instituted the Papacy, it would be
necessary to create it.[2] But a Papacy which was open to criticism
could be no final authority. Therefore nothing less than an infallible
Papacy would suffice. In fact, it is scarcely too much to say that
de Maistre found in it a complete and sufficient *anacephalaeosis* of
Christianity.

The second of this group of writers, Louis de Bonald, was wholly
in agreement with de Maistre about his views on sovereignty. Like
him he had no use for man's rights. He insisted on the necessity for
unity in religion as an indispensable condition of social order, though
it is doubtful whether he really believed in religion as an end in itself.
He differed chiefly from his contemporary in his attitude towards the
Papacy, which found a place in his scheme merely as an incidental
feature of Catholicism, itself the only safeguard against the in-
dividualism and anarchy of Protestant cults.

Lamennais, who shared the contempt of de Maistre and de Bonald
for the ideas of the Revolution, had been brought up in a very different social environment. His distaste for a commercial life led him
to embrace with enthusiasm the romantic ideals of his elder brother
who was a priest. Though frequently a victim of the deepest pessimism and melancholy, he felt himself to be driven towards seeking
the priesthood. But even after his ordination he retained a morbid
outlook, and it was under its influence that he wrote his celebrated
Essai sur l'indifférence. In this work he attacked three different views
of religious truth: that which treats it as useful in the interests

---

[1] Mirbt, *op. cit.*, No. 576.　　　　[2] Cf. Butler, *op. cit.*, vol. i, p. 143.

public order; that which, while admitting its necessity, repudiates revelation; and, finally, that which acknowledges revelation but denies all but certain fundamentals. Thus he argues in turn against Theophilanthropism, Deism and Protestantism. The *Essai* made Lamennais' literary reputation and for a time he wrote eagerly in defence of the monarchy as the chief means to the restoration of religion. Gradually, however, he turned towards Ultramontanism, the name now generally given to curialist views on papal authority, as the only way to secure for religion its necessary freedom. He appealed to the universal testimony of mankind and pointed to the Papacy as the ultimate means of interpreting that testimony. It is difficult, however, not to feel that his impatience with rationalism had only led him into the opposite extreme of irrationality.

His later writings, such as the *Défense de l'Essai* and *De la religion*, showed how far Ultramontane ideas had come to dominate his outlook. It was the infallibility of the Pope which appeared to be the only really secure basis for Christianity in the future. But the author had already drifted far apart from his original supporters, and in complete contradiction to his earlier principles now appealed to the judgment of democracy in support of his thesis. With this end in view the ill-starred adventure of the periodical *L'Avenir* began. Its policy was an alliance between Pope and people, including the complete severance of the bond between Church and State, openly declaring itself in favour of free education, liberty of the press and freedom of association.

It was not surprising that Lamennais made enemies, not only of the supporters of absolute monarchy but even of the Constitutionalists who had dethroned Charles X. But by now two other prominent figures in the French literary world of the day, the abbé Lacordaire and the layman Montalembert, had joined forces with him. Both alike fell completely under the spell of Lamennais' galvanic personality, and laboured ceaselessly to commend their programme to French public opinion. But the world of Louis Philippe had little use for unrestricted freedom, perhaps still less for a papal autocracy, and the confiscation of *L'Avenir* by order of the government showed clearly that unless the literary triumvirate could manage to score an overwhelming success quickly, they had little hope of ultimate triumph. Faced with almost certain defeat it was decided to appeal to the Pope for support. But an abject address to the shrewd Gregory

XVI only met with a very chilly reception, which was followed by
plain warning to keep silence. Undeterred by his rejection at the bar
of what he regarded as the supreme court of appeal, Lamennais per
sisted. At long last the Vatican gave utterance and in the encyclica
Mirari vos of August 15, 1832, the chief ideas to the propagation of
which *L'Avenir* had been dedicated were formally condemned.

It was the parting of friends; much more, it was the parting of
Lamennais with Catholicism. His idol had failed him in refusing to
fulfil the role which he assigned to it, and though he gave in his sub
mission his spirit rebelled, and in his *Paroles d'un Croyant* he de
liberately broke the silence imposed upon him. An explicit condemna
tion of his work was not slow in appearing. Lamennais was hence
forth lost to the Church and the Papacy. Thus the most fervent
critic of individualists proved himself an avowed prophet of indi
vidualism.

After the breach between Lamennais and his allies, Lacordair
found an outlet for his talents in the famous *conférences* which, begin
ning with addresses to a limited audience in the Collège Stanislas
developed into the great sermons preached at Notre Dame befor
immense audiences. Even so the great preacher encountered con
siderable hostility and was more than once delated to Rome. But he
weathered the storm and contributed in a considerable measure to
the great religious revival in France which marked the middl
decades of the nineteenth century.

The conclave which issued in the election of della Genga as Le
XII was a victory for the *Zelanti*. It was therefore also a victory fo
the Jesuits. That this was so was clearly shown in the first encyclica
Ubi primum[1] which sweepingly condemned religious tolerance an
'indifferentism,' in terms amounting to a denunciation of liberty c
conscience and religious freedom, and also in the privileges no
showered upon that Order. The new Pope's rule was marked by
peculiarly vexatious interference in the liberties of his political sub
jects and certainly prepared the way for the movement aiming a
achieving union with the Italian kingdom. In general he was unfor
tunate in making a great many enemies, and much that had bee
gained by the statesmanlike diplomacy of Consalvi was thus need
lessly thrown away. The outstanding event of his pontificate was th
Jubilee of 1825, but the number of pilgrims who visited Rome fron

---

[1] Mirbt, *op. cit.*, No. 577.

ountries other than Italy during that period was disappointingly
mall, and the moral tone of the celebrations in many Italian cities did
ttle to increase the public confidence of Europe in the Roman see.

His successor Pius VIII, who reigned for no more than twenty
nonths, owed his election chiefly to a desire on the part of the Con-
lave to conciliate French and Austrian opinion. His encyclical
raditi humilitati[1] betrayed no sign of originality, being merely a
epetition of the now familiar condemnation of 'indifferentism' and
ible societies. If on his death the Jesuits were in fact in a somewhat
tronger position than before, in other respects the general situation
emained unchanged.

In Gregory XVI the papal throne had an occupant whose early
raining had been on strictly monastic lines, though its narrowness
ad been modified by his experience as abbot of St. Gregory's on the
aelian and later as prefect of the Propaganda. Nevertheless, it was
egrettable that a Pontiff with an outlook which could have but little
ympathy or understanding for the liberal movements of his day
hould have been at the Church's helm, at the very time when a
nore courageous policy might have made good use of such oppor-
unities as lay to hand.

All Italy was in a ferment, and encouraged by the recent success
f revolution in France those who were impatient of traditional in-
titutions such as the temporal power of the Papacy openly began
ne attack, even in Rome itself, and took the opportunity of reminding
ne Pope that, though Christ had indeed granted St. Peter the keys
f spiritual authority, He had nevertheless declared that His kingdom
as not of this world. That the Papal States could defend themselves
a such a situation was, of course, out of the question. An appeal for
elp addressed to Austria, eager to establish itself wherever possible
n Italian soil, was readily answered. But it soon proved a mixed
lessing, and only led to the need for reforms long overdue but of an
mbarrassing nature being insistently pressed upon the Pope's
ttention.

With the advent of Lambruschini to power as Secretary of State,
iregory XVI submitted to the control of an astute politician and a
etermined reactionary, who, if he hated France, regarded Italian
ationalism with an implacable hostility. The whole apparatus of
etty interference with civil liberties, which had so seriously under-

[1] Mirbt, *op. cit.*, No. 578.

mined the popularity of the Papacy under Leo XII, was now restored to the full. Social progress, science, and the improvements of modern civilization were alike treated as subversive of authority, and as if to fling down a challenge to critical investigation the canonization of Alfonso dei Liguori was decreed. Perhaps it was not insignificant of the general trend of thought in Roman circles that the possibility of defining the doctrine of the Immaculate Conception was being openly discussed. A decision on the question, which in his constitution *Grave nimis*[1] Sixtus IV in the fifteenth century had prudently declared to be not yet determined, was evidently near at hand.

Meanwhile Italian nationalism was quickly gathering strength. Yet it was clear that Mazzini's anticlerical republicanism was still in advance of his time, and in the neo-Guelph party of Gioberti public opinion, which saw no future for Italy as a nation without the Pope was still strongly represented. At first federalist ideas prevailed, and the ultimate goal of the most ardent Italian patriots of the day seemed to be a union under the hegemony of the house of Savoy with the friendly co-operation and blessing of the Church.

But by 1843 revolution was once more raising its head in the Papal States and severe measures were immediately taken for its suppression. Sympathy with the rebels was widespread and found open expression in the writings of Capponi, who made the not unreasonable proposal that while the Pope should remain head of the State, its government should be in the hands of laymen. But it was not to be imagined that an obstinate supporter of the Temporal Power like Lambruschini would give his assent to such a plan, and there were many Lambruschinis in mid-nineteenth century Rome.

When Gregory was dying, he had a deep foreboding of a greater storm to come, and it is alleged that he expressed the wish to one who had enjoyed his special confidence that after his death a history of the secret societies in his time should one day be written. The wish was never fulfilled. Had that history been written, the cause of truth perhaps of the Papacy and the Church itself, might have been served

We have seen in the course of our survey of papal history from the sixteenth to the nineteenth century the consummation of that revo against the spiritual authority of the Roman see, of which traces are already to be found at least two centuries earlier. It has been possible

[1] Mirbt, *op. cit.*, No. 407.

o mark the consolidation of that authority by means of a process of
ncreasing centralization, beginning with the council of Trent and
:ontinuing through the agency of the Jesuit Order down to the
:limination of Gallicanism in its various forms under the double
)ressure of the forces of monarchical absolutism and social revolution.
But the march of events by replacing Caesaropapism by an 'indif-
'erent' secularism opened a new front against papal authority and
:hallenged not its spiritual might, which the new order despised or
gnored, but its temporal power.

The sovereignty of the bishop of Rome had come into existence in
the ninth century. Its survival in the nineteenth was widely and not
unreasonably felt to be an anachronism. Yet, if the Papacy were
deprived of its temporal inheritance, how could its sovereignty, essential as it was believed to be in Roman circles to its supranational
mission, be preserved? Such was the 'Roman question' which, though
ostensibly solved by the Lateran Treaty of 1929, may seem to us now
still to be awaiting its final settlement.

More serious still was the question about the future attitude of the
Roman see to intellectual progress. Could the Church of the nineteenth century make its own the critico-historical outlook of the time
without repudiating much of the past? Criticism was raising doubts
and uncertainty on all hands. As a result the need of an authority to
provide final and irreversible decisions on disputed points of faith
and morals was never more strongly felt. Could it be that in the
primacy of the Roman see, in doctrine and jurisdiction, such an
authority was to be found ?

It had long been held that the dogmatic decisions of the Church
were immune from all error. But the question whether council or
Pope had the last word in giving utterance to such decisions had
remained undetermined. No doubt it was widely believed that the
Pope in his official capacity as teacher of the whole Church was
specially endowed in delivering his dogmatic or moral verdict with
a certain infallibility. But could this be held to be actually a matter
of faith?

It was left to Gregory's successor to bring this question to a head,
and as though in compensation for his territorial loss to enjoy the
credit, if such it was, for the establishment of the dogma of the Infallibility of the Roman Pontiff as part of the official creed of the
Roman Communion.

VIII

The Papacy in the Nineteenth Century

The dawn is overcast, the morning lowers,
And heavily in clouds brings on the day,
The great, the important day, big with the fate
Of Cato and of Rome.

JOSEPH ADDISON, *Cato*.

Rom. XIV, 19. 'Let us therefore follow after the things which make for peace and things wherewith one may edify another'.

In the course of our survey of nearly two thousand years of history, we have traced the development of the Papacy from its earliest origins down to the middle of the nineteenth century. Starting as the episcopate of a small and obscure community in the imperial city of ancient Rome, the Roman see grew in oecumenical significance as it came to be recognized as a centre of reference and appeal for the Christian world as a whole. Thus a primacy of 'honour and leadership' was realized in a primacy of doctrine and jurisdiction. Following the impact of a semi-orientalized Caesaropapism and the emergence of the grand though speedily abandoned ideal of a Christian Empire, the Papacy had to struggle with every means at its disposal to uphold the pre-eminence of the spiritual over the temporal. Unhappily it acquired in the process, as we have seen, a preponderatingly secular character, which for a time at least partially obscured its true spiritual mission, so that even when at last a real effort was made to recover as much as possible of its lost heritage, the fatal entail of temporal sovereignty continued to impair its true freedom.

The effect of the French Revolution and of the rise of nineteenth-century liberalism had been to show the hopelessness and even the folly of attempting to preserve the outworn categories of a vanished social order. Yet in the person of Pius IX the Papacy was to cling desperately to the remnants of its temporal authority, till in the end all but a fragment of its territory was finally wrested from its grasp by superior force.

The latest tragedy of its history seems to lie in this, that the vain attempt to save what had long ceased to be valuable contributed to its failure to appreciate the opportunity for fulfilling its world-wide mission as a centre of unity and order for Christian society as a whole under the changed conditions, and led only to a comparatively sterile reassertion of its primatial status. In this way it may be said that a temporal sovereignty was exchanged for a new form of spiritual absolutism, and the occasion for defining afresh the proper relation between the Papacy and the Church was neglected in the interests of providing some compensation for the loss of a shadowy Italian princedom. During the seventy years or so which have elapsed since that time, there has been opportunity enough for both papal and non-papal Christians to appreciate the unhappy effects of the precipitate action of the Vatican council, and at the same time to recapture a vision of the ideal of a reunited and reintegrated Christendom. Is it too much to hope that both alike may use the occasion of the present world catastrophe to review the problems of Christian Reunion in a new light, and without abandoning conscientious convictions to 'follow after the things which make for peace'?

I

When Giovanni Mastai was elected to the Roman see on June 16, 1846, the friends of liberalism, tolerance and social reform believed they had secured a Pope after their own heart. Nor, at any rate at first, did the attractive and popular Pius IX disappoint their expectations. Though there are grounds for believing him to have been swayed by impulse and sentiment rather than principle, and to have possessed few of the qualities which make either a great diplomatist or a successful administrator,[1] there can be little doubt that he began his pontificate with a sincere purpose of effecting long overdue reforms, particularly in the governmental affairs of the papal dominions. If his attitude towards contemporary politics tended to be erratic, it is to be credited at least in part to the fact that the Papacy had scarcely as yet grown accustomed to treating with the phenomenon of the 'laical' state, so familiar to-day, but at that time of comparatively recent growth, though we must not ignore the possibility that lack of consistency may have been due in his case to a chronic physical ailment.

Petitions for administrative and judicial reforms began to pour

[1] Cf. Nielsen, *op. cit.*, vol. ii, p. 123; Binchy, *op. cit.*, p. 21 f.

into Rome, and were rewarded by the first-fruits of the new regime in the shape of a general amnesty to political offenders recommended by the recently appointed Council of Supervision. Such action provoked a remarkable outburst of popular enthusiasm, which was noticeably increased by the knowledge that a member of the party of conciliation in the person of Pasquale Gizzi was to be papal Secretary of State.

All this was extremely agreeable to Pius. But he was soon to discover that popularity could scarcely survive a failure to translate fair promises into concrete action. Before twelve months were out there were not lacking signs of a change of opinion among the fickle Roman populace, and already the keen eyes of the Austrian Premier Metternich were on the watch for any undue concessions to liberalism or to Italian national sentiment. Nevertheless progress was being made. The month of October, 1847, saw the establishment of a representative body, which marks the beginning of the first and last attempt to give to the Papal States something resembling a constitutional government. But others, besides Metternich, were clearsighted enough to recognize that absolute monarchism, such as the temporal rule of the Papacy necessarily presupposed, and free representative institutions were difficult, if not impossible, of reconciliation.

Meanwhile the republican doctrines of Mazzini were making rapid headway, not least in Rome itself. Everywhere, even in Naples, liberal constitutions were being granted by the local Italian governments. Pius at first showed his characteristic lack of decision, then took the plunge. A papal constitution was in being. But an Upper Chamber of papal nominees, with a Chamber of elected deputies, dominated by the college of Cardinals (who possessed an absolute power of veto), forbidden to discuss ecclesiastical or 'mixed' questions or indeed any measure which might be at variance with the law of the Church, was after all no more than a paper constitution. Nor was the situation really improved by the exclusion of the Jesuits from Rome.

On the outbreak of war between Piedmont and Austria, the Pope committed yet another of those indiscretions, soon to be so familiar, by giving colour to a belief that he wished to pose as the leader of Italian nationalism, and then promptly repudiating any such desire. Yet if its effect on the stability of the new constitution was serious, its repercussion on the Pope's position as Sovereign was even more so. Separation of the spiritual and temporal power of the Papacy was now being openly advocated even by its friends, such as Gioberti and Rosmini, while the latter, besides stressing the need of a really constitutional government, openly pointed to the urgency of numerous administrative and internal reforms in the Church itself, using as his model the famous *Consilium . . . de emendanda ecclesia* of 1538.[1]

Papal ministries fell, were reconstituted, and fell again with disconcerting rapidity, until at last, with the former French ambassador Rossi responsible for the Home Office and the Treasury, it seemed possible that an effectively stable government had been found. Rossi saw perfectly clearly that Pius had only two alternatives; to place himself firmly on the side of the national movement in Italy, or to resign himself to the loss of his temporal sovereignty. But it was not long before it was being said that the Papal States had exchanged a constitution for a dictator, and, with the new minister's assassination at the hands of the Radical party, revolution was soon in full possession of Rome. Within ten days Pius was in flight to Gaëta within Neapolitan territory. The days of the Temporal Power were already numbered.

Meanwhile a Roman republic had been proclaimed, much to the satisfaction, as it appears, of the former minister of finance, Cardinal Antonelli, who saw in it an opportunity finally to destroy any liberal intentions which the Pope may have continued to cherish, and at the same time to render himself supreme in the counsels of the Papacy. By the middle of the following year (1849), Pius was openly avowing himself an enemy of the constitution, and firmly repudiated the efforts of the moderate constitutionalist Rosmini, to whom he had formerly listened with eagerness, to turn him aside from a policy which could only end in disaster.

After the defeat of the Sardinian army by Austria, the powers in support of reaction lent their aid to Antonelli's plans in favour of an unconditional restoration of the Pope. But in this they were forestalled by France, which responding at long last to an invitation sent by Pius as far back as June of the previous year, in accordance with an almost traditional papal policy, landed at Civita Vecchia on April 26, and after encountering some resistance occupied Rome. This done, the city was handed over to a papal commission, and after

[1] Mirbt, *op. cit.*, No. 427. See above, p. 446.

the Pope had published a revised constitution, even less liberal than its predecessor, plans for his return were set on foot.

Pius seemed to have discovered at least one thing during his absence : his mistake in cutting himself loose from the influence of the Jesuits. The resumption of his friendly relations with that powerful Order was marked by the publication of the first number of the *Civiltà Cattolica*, which remains to this day the semi-official organ of Vatican opinion.

It was some further index of a change of policy that the same year saw the re-establishment of a Roman Catholic hierarchy in England, a measure which was soon followed by various others indicative of future religious intolerance and repression in Italy. In the Papal States themselves the new constitution was flagrantly disregarded, and all traces of popular representation obliterated. Meanwhile Cardinal Antonelli lost no time in an attempt to stabilize papal finances, and incidentally to improve his own.

As to the interested powers, Louis Napoleon was engaged in establishing his position following the *coup d'état* of 1851, Austria was on the point of accepting a remarkably reactionary concordat as the price of papal support in the task of maintaining the semblance of internal unity in its heterogenous empire, while the Piedmontese government under the new king Victor Emmanuel II, who was personally by no means averse to an accommodation with the Papacy, was preparing a number of liberal measures calculated to restrict the privileges of the clergy.

A new turning point in the tortuous politics of the time was reached, when, by an agreement between the Piedmontese Prime Minister Cavour and Napoleon III, the support of France was secured against Austria. In the peace following the battle of Solferino, Napoleon gave proof of his new alignment by attempting to induce Pius to accept reforms, and later again to effect a regeneration of Italy by forming an Italian federation with the Pope as its president. For such proposals, however, Antonelli and Pius had no use whatever, and even in France the prospect of the loss by the Papacy of its sovereign independence gave rise to emphatic protest. Yet Napoleon remained convinced, not without good reason, that any attempt to restore papal sovereignty, as it had been re-established in 1815, would now be utterly futile.

Meanwhile Cavour continued to labour for the unification of Italy with papal co-operation. To all suggestions and proposals, however,

Pius remained obdurate, when suddenly a diversion was created by the rising of Garibaldi. Rome was already in a ferment of military preparations, but the initiative was taken by the Piedmontese army's invasion of the Papal States from the north. The only outcome of the Roman venture was that of the twenty provinces ruled by Pius IX at the beginning of his reign there now remained only five. A more serious situation arose from the fact that the lost territory included the richest provinces in the papal dominions, so that the papal finances, already in jeopardy, were now rapidly approaching the danger point.

Cavour then outlined a new policy: Italian independence and unity with Rome as the national capital. As a compensation for the surrender of the temporal power, it was promised that the last traces of Josephism were to be swept away from those provinces where it still survived. To these proposals a considerable body of moderate French opinion lent its support, with the addition of the concrete plan that if Rome was to become the seat of the Italian government, the Pope should remain sovereign of the Leonine district of the city. Cavour's project was actively fostered by three outstanding Italian clerics, Pappalettere, abbot of Monte Cassino, representing the Neapolitan kingdom, Cardinal Santucci, and Padre Passaglia, who had the confidence of the Italian government. For a time it seemed that Antonelli himself was ready to make terms, though it afterwards emerged that his transient enthusiasm had been derived from considerations mainly of a personal nature.

Yet once more the forces of intransigence triumphed. Pappalettere was deposed, Santucci disgraced and Passaglia peremptorily ordered to leave Rome at short notice. As the official mouthpiece of the *Zelanti*, Antonelli made the bold but not really helpful declaration, 'We will never make a compact with robbers'. But behind all this, the person actually responsible for slamming the door on any attempt at conciliation was not far to seek.

It was unfortunate that at this stage Cavour, the advocate of the most promising formula *libera chiesa in libero stato*, was removed by death. With him the last real hope of terms between Turin and the Papacy may be said to have died. Occasional attempts to revive negotiations were made, but even their most fervent advocates can scarcely have believed any longer in the possibility of ultimate success. The only real barrier to the final achievement of Italian national ambitions still remaining was to be found in the attitude of France.

It was now the turn of that country to essay some sort of mediation, and when this failed negotiations with representatives of the Italian government led to the signing of the 'September Convention'. In virtue of this agreement Italy engaged herself not to attack the remainder of the Papal States, while France for her part promised to withdraw her troops, with the further conditions that the Pope should be permitted to organize an international force for his own defence, and that the Italian government should make itself responsible for a proportion of the papal debt.

The Convention was regarded by many in Italy as a betrayal, and as involving far too generous a concession to French Catholic opinion. To them, therefore, the news that the seat of government was to be transferred to Florence brought some relief and a renewal of confidence. Still deeper feelings of satisfaction were experienced when it was learnt that on December 15, 1866, the last French troops had evacuated Rome. But the unsettled state of southern Italy in consequence of the revolutionary activities of Garibaldi and his supporters soon provided a reason or a pretext for fresh intervention, and within twelve months there was once again a French force in the Papal States. Napoleon, it must be remembered, depended to a considerable extent for the stability of his regime on the support of the French clericals, and therefore had his own reasons for wishing to bolster up papal sovereignty. At the same time, in the face of the growing strength of Prussia in central Europe, he did not lack cause to conciliate Italian opinion, all the more so because Prussia had given it to be understood that it would not oppose an Italian occupation of Rome.

Following the final withdrawal of the French, events began to move to a climax. Yet in spite of strong pressure from the Left the Italian government continued to hesitate. There is even evidence that up to the last moment, when the final decision to occupy Rome was taken on September 5, 1870, its stability remained in the balance.[1] A formal announcement of its intentions joined with a final appeal was delivered to Cardinal Antonelli three days later. The papal answer simply amounted to the usual *Non possumus*. Every inducement was used to persuade Pius to surrender without fighting, but

[1] Nielsen, *op. cit.*, vol. ii, p. 385.

t was only after a breach had been made in the walls by the attacking
rmy that the order was given to the papal forces to open negotiations.

It was agreed that the whole of Rome with the exception of the
Leonine city should be handed over, and the papal troops disbanded.
Yet before long, following the withdrawal of this force, it became
vident that order could only be maintained in the papal quarter
by means of an Italian occupation. Thus within a few days of the
apitulation nothing remained to the Pope but the Vatican and St.
Peter's. The Temporal Power, as it had existed for over a thousand
ears, was at an end.

II

It has been necessary to describe in some detail the events of
Pius IX's pontificate which led up to this historic event, since it is
nly against the background of contemporary secular history that
we can rightly appreciate the significance of the ecclesiastical develop-
nents which make the period so remarkable in papal annals. In fact,
t is scarcely too much to say that the general ecclesiastical policy of
he Pian regime is best explained as a reaction to the prevailing
olitical situation.

There is some reason to believe that the humiliating experience
f his flight to Gaëta, following the unsuccessful attempt to estab-
sh a constitutional government in the Papal States, convinced
he Pope of the paramount importance of winning supernatural
elp for his cause. It was therefore with the definite intention of
suing a final decision on the long debated problem regarding the
mmaculate Conception of the Blessed Virgin, that is to say the
elief that she had been preserved from the time of her conception
rom the blemish of original sin, that he circulated a letter early in
849, to all Roman Catholic bishops, inquiring whether or not it was
esired that the belief should be recognized as a part of revealed
ruth.[1] It is beyond doubt that the whole weight of Jesuit influence
as behind the plan, and no one who was aware of the extent of that
nfluence in nineteenth-century Roman Catholicism could seriously
oubt the possibility of its ultimate success.

No description need be given here of the spurious support brought
rward in the defence of the dogma in the later sixteenth century,

[1] In so far as there was any real demand for the dogma to be proclaimed there is
vidence that it came chiefly from Italy. See *D.T.C.* vol. vii, col. 1195.

which had been plainly denounced as forgeries by two of Pius IX'
predecessors. It was urged, however, that a serious difficulty in th
way of its proclamation lay in the absence of direct Scriptura
testimony. Yet to the Roman Catholic world, long habituated t
allegorical interpretation and to an uncritical outlook, such
difficulty presented no real obstacle. More solid objections from th
Catholic standpoint lay in the fact of a divided tradition. Nevertheles
from all sides there came enthusiastic expressions of approval, an
such opposition as there was contented itself for the most part wit
the general observation that dogmas ought not to be proclaime
without real necessity.[1]

Pius, as was his wont, listened only to the chorus of approval, an
paid no serious attention to the objections. Yet even so they were nc
immediately silenced, as was shown by the fact that of the theologic;
commission appointed for the express purpose of expressing a
opinion as to whether or not it was expedient to define the dogm;
at least three out of twenty gave a negative vote. After some delay
new commission was entrusted with the task of drawing up the bull c
definition. It was here that the difficulty regarding tradition was en
countered. In the end all obstacles were removed by the expedier
of defining certain negative principles, among which it was state
that neither the absence of Scriptural witness nor the lack of a con
tinuous or unanimous tradition ought to offer any hindrance to
definition of this kind. Among the more positive arguments the viev
was put forward that any doctrine which had an undoubted con
nexion with existing dogmas or which was evidently presupposed b
current practice, might reasonably be regarded as requiring definitior
the convenience of which under the circumstances was only to
apparent.

The final stage was reached when in the latter half of November
1854, the Pope assembled a group of forty bishops to hear the term
in which the dogma was to be published. Some of those preser
ventured to object that many of the texts quoted from patristic c
other ecclesiastical writers had little if any bearing on the doctrin(
To this it was replied that, if they did not apply to it directly, ;
least it could be said that they did so indirectly. But criticism wa
at least successful in preventing the assertion that the belief ha
been the constant teaching of the Church from the first, and by th

[1] *D.T.C.* vol. vii, col. 1198.

ame means the admission was obtained that revelation in this case
ad been implicit rather than explicit. It is no part of our purpose
ɔ examine the truth of the dogma, but it is scarcely possible to leave
he subject without calling attention to the fact that of all the argu-
ients adduced in its support, the greatest weight appears to have
een attached to one which in the last resort cannot well be more
han a matter of opinion, namely, its appropriateness to what has
therwise been revealed of the relations between God and man.

The significance of the act of definition which took place on
December 8, 1854,[1] is, for our purpose, overwhelming. For, as con-
mporaries were not slow to recognize, it could evidently have but
ne logical issue, namely, the promulgation of the further dogma of
apal infallibility to the exclusion of any degree of dependence on
he decision of such a body as an oecumenical council.

III

Before describing the process leading to this further step it is
ssential to give some account of the famous encyclical *Quanta cura*
nd its accompanying *Syllabus* or 'Collection of modern errors'.

There is evidence that, soon after the failure of the papal experi-
ient in constitutional government, a proposal was mooted by some
talian bishops that Pius should issue a formal condemnation of
urrent errors regarding the Church, society and economics. At the
me of the proclamation of the dogma of the Immaculate Con-
eption a commission was entrusted with the task of drawing up a
st of erroneous opinions already reprobated by papal authority. Yet
ɔr some years the project appears to have hung fire, and it might
erhaps have been abandoned but for the open defence of Liberal
Catholicism put forward by Montalembert at the Congress of Malines
1 1863. The theme of the Congress, Catholicism and liberty, was
self significant, and the speeches of Montalembert, which quickly
cquired a remarkable notoriety, amounted to a direct appeal for an
ccommodation of the outlook of the Church to the dominant ideas of
emocracy.[2] Only by means of such an accommodation, it was said,
ould the progress of the Church be assured, and at the same time

---

[1] Nielsen, *op. cit.*, vol. ii, p. 194 f, points out that between the promulgation
nd the official publication of the dogma certain corrections were made in the text.
: is said that the Pope consoled himself with the thought that these tended to
1ow 'that the Jesuits were not absolute masters at Rome'.

[2] Phillips, C. S., *Church in France*, vol. ii, p. 116.

democracy itself be saved from the evils then besetting it. In addition
while upholding without hesitation the claims of the Church i
the sphere of dogma, Montalembert urged that it was neither possibl
nor right to refuse liberty of conscience. If the Church demande
freedom for its own members to practise their religion, it could no
in justice refuse to concede the same freedom to others. Thus, h
concluded, the Church can rightly come to terms with moder
civilization founded on freedom of conscience, and ought not t
insist that loyalty to the old order of things was alone consistent wit
Catholic orthodoxy.

There was, of course, an element of inconsistency in Montalem
bert's exposition. He unhesitatingly expressed his personal preferenc
for the new order, and yet insisted that it was not his intention t
condemn the old. As a result, his utterances at Malines met with
somewhat mixed reception. Nevertheless, while many Liber;
Catholics hailed them as a proclamation of Christian freedom
Ultramontanes displayed an undisguised hostility.

Meanwhile the Roman commission had been pursuing its tas
of drawing up an authoritative pronouncement on the relation of th
Church to the modern State. Its members had probably been stimu
lated, if not assisted, by the appearance of a list of present-day error
issued in 1860 by an Ultramontane French bishop, Gerbet of Per
pignan, from which there emerged a series of 'theses', presentl
submitted to a gathering of bishops at Rome.

Opinions were by no means unanimous regarding the wisdom o
publishing such a document at this time. Dupanloup, bishop o
Orleans, for example, openly deprecated the plan, and begge
Cardinal Antonelli to consider the unfortunate effect which it migh
be expected to create. In fact, some very frank criticism both i
France and Italy caused its publication temporarily to be withheld.

It is possible that nothing more would have been heard of th
Syllabus but for Montalembert's speeches at the Congress o
Malines. At once that ardent Ultramontane, Monsignor Pie, bisho
of Poitiers, who was later to fulfil the role of leader of the Infallibilist
at the Vatican council, descended into the lists, and urged th
Congregation of the Index to issue an unequivocal condemnation o
Montalembert's opinions, declaring that they were in direct con
tradiction to the official decisions of the Roman see. Pius IX showe
himself not unfavourable to the demand, and made it perfectly clea

at he strongly supported the attitude in regard to the question of
tolerance which Montalembert had declared to be unjust.[1] He
admitted that he desired that there should be freedom of conscience
in states, such as Sweden and Russia, where Roman Catholicism was
in a minority, but only in order, as he said, that the truth might have
free course in those countries.[2] On the other hand, he did not hesitate
to affirm that the Church could not allow it to be a good thing, or
right in principle, that errors should be permitted to be taught in
those states where a Catholic element was predominant. His view
represented the outlook which had prevailed since the Reformation.
It was precisely the same standpoint as the one adopted by Urban
VIII in his bull *Coena Domini*[3] or by Innocent X in his repudiation
of the Peace of Westphalia.[4]

In the end Pius decided that the most politic course was to refrain
from condemning Montalembert openly. The denunciation *nominatim*
of one who had adopted Cavour's maxim *libera chiesa in libero stato*
as the title of his Malines speeches might have unfortunate reper-
cussions when published. A personal letter from Cardinal Antonelli
under the circumstances was therefore held to be sufficient. Nothing
further was necessary so far as Montalembert himself was concerned;
but so indirect a method of attack was scarcely calculated to satisfy
the now dominant Ultramontane party.

Thus, although it has been suggested[5] that the September Convention of 1863 was directly responsible for the publication of the
encyclical *Quanta cura*[6] with its appended *Syllabus* in the following
year, it is much more probable that the immediate cause was the
Malines Congress. At the same time it may well be true that the
opportunity provided by the encyclical was taken to declare the
official papal attitude towards the principles underlying the Convention.

After declaring that no compromise could be made with
'naturalism' as a principle of social order, in virtue of which it was
believed that civilized progress required the regulation of human
society without regard to the authority of religion and without distinction between one religion and another, the encyclical denounced
'liberty of conscience and worship', together with freedom of speech

[1] But see Phillips, *op. cit.*, p. 119.
[2] Nielsen, *op. cit.*, vol. ii, p. 263.
[3] Mirbt, *op. cit.*, No. 513.
[4] Id., *op. cit.*, No. 529.
[5] Phillips, *op. cit.*, p. 121.
[6] Denzinger, *op. cit.*, No. 1688.

and of the Press, released from all restraints of ecclesiastical or civ
control. It pointed out that the present demand that the 'will of th
people' should be recognized as the highest arbiter of right an
wrong was tantamount to preaching a gospel of the *fait accompl*
and after deploring the attacks of secularism on the religious order
it inveighed against any attempt being made to restrain Christia
almsgiving or to abolish official recognition of feast-days, as day
to be marked by freedom from servile work. Next it affirmed tha
the effect of socialism and communism was to lead to the exclusio
of the Church from any part in education. Finally, it condemne
certain opinions specially characteristic of Liberal Catholicism, fc
example the view that assent and obedience 'to those judgmen
and decrees of the apostolic see, the object of which was declare
to pertain to the general good of the Church, and to its legal principl
and discipline, might be withheld without sin and without an
sacrifice of Catholic profession provided that they did not embod
dogmas of faith and morals'.[1]

Two documents were appended: first a chronological list of th
allocutions, encyclicals, and briefs of Pius IX, from which th
Syllabus was derived, then the *Syllabus* itself. This latter documen
comprising eighty numbered paragraphs, covered a considerab
variety of subjects, ranging from pantheism and absolute rationalis
to the relations of Church and State and the value of the tempor
power of the Papacy. It concluded with a section directed again:
'modern liberalism', in which the opinion was repudiated that ':
the present day it is no longer expedient that the Catholic religio
should be regarded as the only religion of the State to the exclusic
of all other cults, and that consequently it is very properly provide
by law in certain areas having the name of Catholic that persons wh
immigrate there shall each enjoy the exercise of his own cult
Finally, it denied that 'the Roman Pontiff can and ought to reconci
himself and make terms with progress, with liberalism and wit
modern methods of government'.

The *Syllabus* naturally evoked a great deal of interest, though i
Catholic circles it was not unmixed with some measure of alarn
For the latter the form of the document was no doubt in some degre
itself responsible. Dupanloup, who may be taken as representativ
of its more moderate critics, published a pamphlet on the encyclic.

[1] Denzinger, *op. cit.*, No. 1698.

as a whole, in which he called attention to the need of interpreting
the language of the several views condemned in the light of their
proper context. But what many of its detractors failed to appreciate
was that the real object of the Pope's attack was not freedom but
licence, not reason but rationalism, not state sovereignty but secularism. It is also not irrelevant to notice that the distinction made by
Dupanloup in the course of his exposition between *thesis* and *hypothesis*, between the ideal and the actual, was later formally endorsed
by Pius IX's successor Leo XIII.[1] And even if it is true that Dupanloup was less concerned to say what the encyclical was than what it
was not, it is at least noteworthy that Pius himself commended his
work. If the more determined critics of the nineteenth-century
Papacy could have foreseen the present-day progress of secularism,
they might have been more willing to recognize that the *Syllabus*, in
spite of its evident limitations, had as its purpose that characteristic
aim of Roman pronouncements, namely, the preservation of a *via
media* amid the conflicting claims of modern society, between
absolutism and anarchy, between theocracy and atheism. Indeed, it
is not difficult to find in this supposedly reactionary document a
few at least of the principles on which a modern enlightened democratic regime is based.[2]

IV

Shortly before the appearance of *Quanta cura* Pius IX took the
opportunity of a meeting of the Congregation of Rites to inform
the Cardinals that he had been considering for some time the
possibility of assembling an oecumenical council.[3] When the project
was later submitted to certain representative bishops, they were
invited to suggest subjects for consideration. A wide range of topics
was proposed, including the request that current errors should be
examined and condemned; in addition suggestions were made that
a Catholic answer should be given to the problems created by the
growth of a critical attitude towards Holy Scripture. Some of the
bishops favoured a more positive policy, including a restatement of
theism and of the fundamental dogmatic basis of Christianity.
Others, again, urged that the idea of the Church should be re-
formulated, though significantly enough not more than eight of those

---

[1] *D.T.C.* vol. ix, col. 594.   [2] Phillips, *op. cit.*, p. 122.
[3] *Collectio Lacensis*, vol. vii, col. 1013.

then consulted held that nothing less than an unequivocal definition of papal infallibility would satisfy the needs of the time. Support was also found for the proposal that the council should aim at the recovery of separated Christians to the unity of the Church. Other recommendations included some of a directly practical nature, such as the revision of the Catechism, the revival of spiritual life among clergy and laity and the reform of Canon Law.

A period of uncertainty and hesitation followed, occasioned at least in part by the political situation, but also perhaps to be explained by a division of counsels in Rome itself.[1] Hence it was not till June 26, 1867, that the Pope made a public announcement of the project in his allocution of that date. If there had been already signs of disagreement about its expediency, still clearer evidence of lack of unanimity among the Catholic episcopate was revealed in the difficulty of producing a reply in a form acceptable to all the five hundred bishops present in Rome at the time. This in its turn unmistakably pointed to the existence of divergent trends of opinion which in the course of the council itself were to lead to a sharp cleavage of policy. The significant feature of the address[2] was that, in spite of all that it had to say in favour of the papal prerogative, it made no mention of infallibility, though much of its language seemed logically to imply its acceptance.

There can be little room for doubt that in the selection of persons to whom it was intended to assign positions of special responsibility in connexion with work preparatory to the council, preference was given to bishops of known Ultramontane sympathies. Yet it must be acknowledged, on the other hand, that the chief part in the definition of procedure was assigned to the great conciliar historian, Hefele, bishop of Rottenburg, whose outlook was notoriously averse to any definition of papal infallibility.

It was decided that in accordance with a principle held to be *iure divino* all diocesan bishops of the Roman communion should be summoned, and that in addition all Cardinals, even those who were not bishops, should be entitled to take part in the council and to vote. Eventually, after some hesitation, it was agreed to invite all titular bishops, whether exercising jurisdiction or not, and that they should be given the privilege of voting like the rest. Finally, abbots with independent jurisdiction, such as the abbot of Monte Cassino, and

---

[1] Butler, *op. cit.*, vol. i, p. 84.   [2] *Coll. Lac.* vol. vii, col. 1033.

he heads of monastic congregations and of religious orders were ncluded. Proctors of absentee bishops were to be admitted, but vithout the right to vote.

In the hope that the council might lead to some measure of eunion with separated Christian bodies, formal invitations were ent to all eastern churches not in communion with the Roman see[1] ind to the 'Jansenist' church of Holland, and a special brief was ddressed to ' all Protestants and non-catholics'.[2] Various Protestant ;roups drew up replies; some even took the opportunity of calling ittention to certain outstanding causes of their separation from the Roman communion,[3] but the eastern churches preferred to remain ;ilent.

The first clear indication of what the summoning of such a council eally portended was given by the *Civiltà Cattolica* early in 1869.[4] There the wish was openly expressed that papal infallibility would)e defined by acclamation. Butler in his history of the Vatican :ouncil, readily admits that 'the idea . . . was surely a regrettable idventure',[5] a view with which even the most loyal supporters of :he dogma must concur, for the practical effect of openly expressing ;uch a hope was to give rise to a deeply felt sense of resentment, even where it did not evoke the strongest expressions of indignation. Of the latter feeling the book *The Pope and the Council* by 'Janus',[6] in spite of the evident *parti pris* confronting the reader on almost every page, was a striking and possibly significant expression. For although it was anything but an essay in objective history, it served to show how deeply Catholic sentiment had been shocked at so gross an attempt to prejudge the issue, particularly by a semi-official organ of Vatican opinion.

Of far greater weight and importance was the document issued by the conference of the German bishops at Fulda, in which it was affirmed that they 'regard the present time as somewhat inopportune for the definition of the infallibility of the Supreme Pontiff, so far as it concerns the German State'.[7]

As the argument that a definition was inopportune was the one

---

[1] *Coll. Lac.* vol. vii, col. 7.   [2] *Op. cit.*, vol. vii, col. 9.
[3] The attitude towards the Roman see of the theologians of Groningen (*op. cit.*, vol. vii, col. 1124 ff, esp. 1128) is of special interest.
[4] Nielsen, *op. cit.*, vol. ii, p. 299 ; Butler, *op. cit.*, vol. i, p. 108.
[5] Butler, *op. cit.*, vol. ii, p. 109.   [6] Eng. Transl., 1869.
[7] *Coll. Lac.* vol. vii, col. 1196.

most frequently emphasized in the course of the later conciliar debates by the minority opposed to it, and by none more persistently than Dupanloup, bishop of Orleans, it will be as well at this stage to take account of some words of his written more than twenty-five years before.

'The mind of the Church is implied in a definition *ex cathedra* which is always in conformity with it. The Pope recognizes it and defines it. He is *caput ecclesiae*'.[1]

It should be noticed that although this statement appears to imply an acknowledgment of papal infallibility, it is infallibility conditioned by 'conformity with the mind of the Church', a condition which the writer postulates will always of necessity be present. We shall appreciate the importance of this limitation at a later stage, but we need to bear it in mind if we are to account both for Dupanloup's attitude of opposition and also for his subsequent assent to the dogma.

Yet while allowing the sincerity of the greater body of the inopportunists, it must be admitted that the book *Du Concile Général*, which had been published early in the previous year by one of their number, Monsignor Maret, dean of the Sorbonne, was not content to declare a definition 'inopportune', but openly and unequivocally affirmed, first, that it would be 'a novel opinion in the Church, denied by the saints, unknown by the greatest among the doctors for ten or more centuries; ignored and violated by all the oecumenical councils'; secondly, that it involved 'a radical and essential revolution in the constitution of the Church'; and, thirdly, that it was 'contrary to Holy Scripture, the fathers, the councils, the evidence of history, in a word, to the universal tradition of the Church'.[2]

In sharp contrast to the scepticism of Maret, certain prominent members of the French liberal school, such as Montalembert, issued a statement which affirmed that they did not share the fears of those who anticipated that the issue of the council would be the imposition of an unmitigated absolutism on the Church. As to the question of infallibility, though they preferred that it should not be defined, they were prepared to acknowledge that it must be found in 'a conciliar decision clothed with the pontifical assent, or a pontifical utterance corroborated by the consent of the episcopate',[3] or else

---

[1] Quoted by Butler, *op. cit.*, vol. i, p. 116.
[2] *Coll. Lac.* vol. vii, col. 956.   [3] Butler, *op. cit.*, vol. i, p. 122.

nowhere at all. The outlook of this group, though entirely opposed to the extreme Ultramontanism of Pie of Poitiers and Manning of Westminster, remained unreservedly optimistic about the outcome of the council.

A further declaration, also by Dupanloup, issued on the eve of the council, calls for brief notice. Published under the title of *Observations sur la controverse soulevée relativement à la définition de l'infaillibilité au futur Concile*, it enumerated a formidable series of reasons against the opportuneness of any definition of infallibility, of which perhaps the most penetrating was the argument that it was impossible in practice to distinguish between those of the Pope's utterances which were fallible and those which were infallible.[1]

Whatever subjects might have been included in the conciliar agenda, it was perfectly clear long before the bishops actually assembled at Rome that the definition of infallibility would be the one which before all else would engage attention, not only within the council but in the world outside.

Of the Ultramontane Majority the most outstanding bishops were Dechamps of Malines and Manning of Westminster. Yet in saying this it must not be supposed that there was absolute unanimity of view within that party. Manning was prominent among those who, like Senestréy of Ratisbon, exerted every effort to secure a definition of infallibility as comprehensive as could be got through the council. Dechamps, on the other hand, could be classed as a supporter of a more moderate Ultramontanism, which hoped to see the dogma properly safeguarded against exaggerated use by means of restrictive clauses, of which *ex cathedra* is certainly the most characteristic. His point of view was, in fact, essentially the same as that of Bellarmine.[2] No doubt there were also other differences, not least those which distinguish aggressive intransigence from an uncontroversial and conciliatory spirit.

The chief strength of the Majority, however, lay not in scholarship or even in perspicacity but in numbers, of which the Italian bishops formed the largest proportion, and in estimating the extent to which the ultimate decision of the council represented a free vote some allowance must be made for the fact that out of the 744 bishops and

---

[1] Butler, *op. cit.*, vol. i, p. 124.

[2] The author of the article *Ex cathedra*, *D.T.C.*, vol. v, col. 1731 ff, states that the expression is not used by Bellarmine, and mentions Melchior Cano, *De locis theologicis* (1563), VI, vii, as probably the first to use it in a technical sense.

others who eventually assembled, perhaps not less than 300 were directly, personally and even financially dependent on the goodwill of the Roman see.[1] It may therefore be said without unfairness that once the personal wishes of Pius IX were generally known (and as we shall see no considerable pains were taken to conceal them), the policy corresponding to them was certain of a substantial nucleus of support.

Those who formed the 'inopportunist' Minority, on the other hand, were almost without exception non-Italian in origin, and, as we have previously pointed out, included the occupants of the most important sees in Christendom, as well as some who like Hefele, enjoyed an established reputation in the world of scholarship. Gifts of this kind, to judge from the speeches made and the arguments put forward in all seriousness by the Majority were, as we have already suggested, by no means conspicuous among the supporters of infallibility. This was to say the least regrettable, for whatever may be said as to a choice of 'the foolish things of the world to confound the wise', the question at issue could scarcely be discussed with intelligence by anyone possessing no more than an ordinary text-book knowledge of ecclesiastical history. Like the Majority, the party of the Minority revealed certain signs of inner cleavage. Several bishops like Strossmayer tended to speak more as free lances than as members of a group, and if a few like Hefele stuck rigidly to questions of principle, there were others, of whom Ketteler of Mainz is typical, who appeared to be swayed chiefly by considerations of expediency.

It is not possible, nor would it serve our purpose, to survey the whole of the conciliar proceedings. We may therefore confine our attention to the stage which was concerned with the Constitution *Pastor Aeternus*, including the definition on the infallible *magisterium* of the Roman Pontiff.

As we have already seen, the Ultramontane Majority secured an initial success in the fact that the deputation *de fide*, to which, in virtue of the papal brief *Multiplices inter*[2], all proposals in regard to any scheme submitted to the council which involved questions of doctrine were to be referred, was with a single exception[3] (due, it is

---

[1] Nielsen, *op. cit.*, vol. ii, p. 324.   [2] *Coll. Lac.* vol. vii, col. 17 ff., 22 f.
[3] Simor, primate of Hungary. Cf. *Coll. Lac. ibid.*, col. 1296 ff., and see Phillips, *op. cit.*, p. 147; Butler, *op. cit.*, vol. ii, p. 306, n. 1.

said, to a misapprehension), made up entirely of members of that party. There can be little doubt that the chief responsibility for the 'intrigue' which procured this result must be assigned to Manning. Even so definite a supporter of infallibility as Pie of Poitiers had been seriously disquieted by the use of methods which seemed to him to savour of the 'caucus' devices of parliaments and municipal governments.[1] Above all, Pius IX himself had openly expressed his wish that representatives of the Minority, among whom he desired the inclusion of Dupanloup, should have some places on the deputation.[2] Butler significantly comments on Manning's behaviour in this respect:

'One cannot but think it regrettable that Manning's Ultramontane principle, "sentire cum Papa", did not on this occasion make him bow to the Pope's wish'.[3]

No doubt it is true that the Minority had a fair representation on the remainder of the deputations, namely, those for Discipline, for Regulars, and for the Eastern Churches and Missions, but this did not alter the fact that its representatives were virtually excluded from the most important one of the four. Yet the election served to reveal that it was simply untrue to describe the opposition to infallibility as 'microscopic' and that a party which would muster as many as 200 supporters was certainly a force of which some account was bound to be taken.[4]

It has been seriously argued that various circumstances contributed to impair the full freedom of the council, and it is difficult not to feel that there is some truth in the contention. Mention has already been made of the very real personal dependence of nearly half the bishops on the Pope. This factor, perhaps, might not have been of much importance if Pius' own attitude had been unmistakably neutral. In actual fact, however, no one could have had any reasonable doubt almost from the very first which of the two parties corresponded to Pius' personal standpoint in the great question.

One of the earliest 'incidents' of the council took place at a private interview between the Pope and Ketteler, *doyen* of the German bishops and a pronounced inopportunist, in the course of which Pius appears to have indicated that he regarded 'inopportunism'

---

[1] Mourret, *Concile du Vatican*, p. 152.
[2] Id., *op. cit.*, p. 150 f.
[3] *Op. cit.*, vol. i, p. 174.
[4] Nielsen, *op. cit.*, vol. ii, p. 324.

as a personal attack on himself. In spite of this Butler affirms that 'at first Pius took up a neutral attitude, saying that he left the matter to the council'.[1] But as we have already seen, consistency was not one of his strong points. Hence it is with no surprise that we find the same author making the following significant admission: 'That at the final stages he exerted his personal influence to the utmost, cannot be questioned, for it was quite open. Even though the charges of direct intimidation and bribery, not of course by money, but by prospect of ecclesiastical promotion, red hats—be set aside, it might with show of reason be held that many of the bishops were swayed by what is known as a reverential fear towards a beloved Superior, an old man, the object in a very unusual measure of the devotion and affection of all'.[2] Moreover, he adds at a later point, 'There can be no doubt that "as private theologian", Pius was a pronounced neo-Ultramontane'.[3]

In this connexion it is not unreasonable to suggest that the contrast between the alleged liberal attitude of the Pope at the beginning of the council and his subsequent whole-hearted partisanship of infallibility finds an unmistakable parallel in the contradiction between the constitutional policy adopted with such eager enthusiasm during the first two years of his reign and his subsequent intransigence. The claims of Italian unification and the pleadings of the inopportunists were in the end confronted alike with the same obstinate *Non possumus*, an attitude which rendered compromise and conciliation utterly impracticable.

On the whole, it may be said that the Cardinal presidents appear to have conducted the debates with scrupulous fairness, though there is reason to believe that the acoustic defects of the conciliar *aula* and the unfamiliarity of a large proportion of the assembled bishops with the methods and procedure of representative government, combined to deprive the debates of any serious value. Yet it does seem possible that the ever-increasing pressure exerted by high authority to expedite the proceedings led to an application of the 'closure' in debate, which effectively though perhaps unintentionally prevented

---

[1] *Op. cit.*, vol. ii, p. 199.

[2] *Op. cit.*, vol. ii, p. 198 f. Cf. Nielsen, *op. cit.*, vol. ii, p. 357; Phillips, *op. cit.*, p. 154.

[3] *Op. cit.*, vol. ii, p. 202. Gregorovius, F., *Roman Journals*, Eng. Transl., 1907, p. 351, attributes to Pius the following: 'In former times before I was Pope, I believed in the Infallibility; now, however, I feel it'.

some at least of the more weighty, if somewhat more verbose, inopportunist pronouncements from getting a fair hearing or even any
hearing at all.[1]

V

We have already described both the conciliar procedure and the
general character of the *schema De Ecclesia Christi*,[2] as well as the
protracted discussion which intervened between its first publication
on January 21 and its final adoption on July 18, and it would be
redundant to add anything here to what has already been said on that
score. We may, however, consider in greater detail the evolution of
those chapters which are directly concerned with the authority and
privileges of the Roman see.

In the *schema* as originally presented, two chapters only were
devoted to those subjects, namely XI and XII, and three, XIV–XVI,
of the appended canons.[3] Chapter XI, entitled 'Of the Primacy of
the Roman Pontiff', opens with the declaration that Christ instituted
in St. Peter a perpetual source and visible foundation of corporate
unity in His Church, by conferring on him a primacy of jurisdiction,
in support of which *Tu es Petrus* and the Johannine commission are
cited. Consequently views which do not differentiate between the
primacy entrusted to St. Peter and the authority of the rest of the
Apostles, or which hold that he derived his special power only through
the Church as its minister, are to be rejected.

The necessity of providing for the abiding welfare of the Church
demands that what was given to St. Peter should be permanent, and
therefore whoever succeeds him in the Roman see must receive
the same primacy which was originally given to him. Consequently
the apostolic see and the Roman Pontiff hold a primacy in relation
to the whole world, and that he 'is in fact the supreme father, teacher,
and judge of all Christians'. Moreover, his power of jurisdiction is
'ordinary and immediate' over all local churches, so that 'the Church
of Christ may be one flock under one supreme Shepherd'. Hence it
is denied that the privileges conferred on St. Peter were merely
personal, or that papal authority over local churches is applicable to
individual churches only and not to all as a whole, or that there lies

---

[1] Cf. Butler, *op. cit.*, vol. ii, pp. 46–55.
[2] See above, p. 13 f. ; *Coll. Lac.*, *ibid.*, col. 567 ff.
[3] *Coll. Lac.*, *ibid.*, cols. 571, 577.

an appeal against the judgments of the Roman Pontiffs to a general council.

In chapter XII[1] it is argued that for the proper exercise of his primacy the Roman Pontiff requires such safeguards as correspond to contemporary conditions and needs. Divine providence has ordained that the Roman church should possess a temporal dominion, and it is only by means of such sovereignty that the Roman Pontiff can exercise his influence for the profit of the whole Christian common-wealth. Hence it is altogether false to say that it is contrary to the Law of God that temporal sovereignty should be united to spiritual power in the Roman Pontiffs, nor can the opinion be tolerated that it is not the business of the Church to give an authoritative pro-nouncement on this subject.

Such were the relevant chapters of the *schema De Ecclesia* in its original form. The controversial nature of its contents and the improbability that it would be accepted without very considerable modifications were shown by the fact that, by the time it had been in the hands of the bishops for barely more than a month, the total number of critical observations submitted to the deputation *De Fide* reached the astonishing figure of six hundred. Certain groups of bishops, notably the Germans under the leadership of Ketteler of Mainz, were so thoroughly dissatisfied with it that in some cases they went to the length of drawing up what was in effect a completely new document. The extent of their industry serves to illustrate the urgent need for a searching reconsideration of the doctrine of the Church, and more especially of the theological basis of the Roman primacy.

Unhappily, as it now seems, their labour was largely in vain. By this time those who had made up their minds that, come what may, the council could not be allowed to come to an end without producing the much desired definition of papal infallibility, had apparently succeeded in convincing the authorities, from the Pope himself downwards, that the chapters on the Roman primacy must be taken out of order, while the rest of the *schema* might be postponed to the more remote future. The congregation *De Postulatis* had been kept busy since the beginning of the year in dealing with endless petitions and counter-petitions, and the fact that the infallibilist Majority held twenty-three out of twenty-six seats ensured a decision in favour of this change of tactics. It is only surprising that though this had

[1] *Op. cit., ibid.*, col. 572.

already been reached on February 9, it was not till March 6 that it was made public,[1] by the issue of an appendix to the *schema* in which papal infallibility was defined in the following terms:

'The holy Roman church holds the supreme and complete primacy and supremacy over the whole Catholic Church, which it acknowledges truly and humbly that it has received with the fulness of power from the Lord Himself in blessed Peter the chief of the Apostles, whose successor is the Roman Pontiff. And, just as it is bound before all others to defend the truth of the faith, so whatever questions may arise regarding the faith ought to be defined by its judgment. Moreover, since the saying of our Lord Jesus Christ may not be passed over, namely, "Thou art Peter, etc.", the words spoken are shown to be true by actual results, because in the apostolic see the Catholic religion has always been preserved without blemish and the holy doctrine has always been proclaimed; therefore, with the approval of the holy council, we teach and define as a dogma of faith that it is by means of divine aid that the Roman Pontiff, to whom in the person of blessed Peter it was said by the same our Lord Jesus Christ, "I have prayed for thee, that thy faith fail not", cannot err; when in performance of the office of supreme teacher of all Christians he defines in virtue of his authority what is to be held by the universal Church in matters of faith and morals, and that this privilege of inerrancy or infallibility of the Roman Pontiff reaches to the same limit as that which marks the extent of the infallibility of the Church. If, however, anyone shall presume to gainsay this definition of ours (which may God forbid), let him know that he has fallen away from the truth of the Catholic faith and from the unity of the Church'.[2]

It will be observed that these words include two quotations, the former from the profession of faith made by the representatives of the eastern churches at the second council of Lyons (1274), and the latter from the formula or *libellus* of Hormisdas, as it was adopted by the fourth council of Constantinople (869/70), with some seemingly unimportant alterations.[3] It should be noticed that apart from the indirect support derived from these conciliar definitions,

---

[1] Butler, *op. cit.*, vol. ii, p. 26.   [2] *Coll. Lac.*, *ibid.*, col. 641.·
[3] From the former the expression 'sive vertice' is omitted; in the latter 'immaculata' is substituted for 'citra maculam', and 'et sancta celebrata doctrina' is added. One can only speculate on the motive behind these changes.

34

which are simply quoted without any mention of the councils t
which they belong, the sole independent Scriptual authority cite
is that of Luke XXII, 32. Further, although the scope of papa
infallibility is definitely limited to that of the Church, no mentio
whatever is made of the means by which the Pope is believed t
acquire the knowledge necessary in order to define a doctrine to b
held by the universal Church, with the exception of the vague claus
'by means of divine aid' (*per divinam assistentiam*).

The new *schema* had no sooner been distributed among the bishop
than the disquieting rumour began to revive that the dogma was t
be proclaimed by acclamation. Whatever Manning had to say late
to the effect that the promoters of infallibility had no thought o
such a thing, could not alter the fact that the plan, as we have seer
had been originally suggested by the *Civiltà Cattolica*, a semi-offici;
and therefore presumably responsible journal. But its only effec
now was to stiffen the attitude of the opposition. Some went so fa
as to say that if this were done they would leave the council at onc
and publish their reason for so doing.[1]

Eventually, on April 29, it was made known that as soon as it wa
complete there would be introduced a new *schema*, which would tak
account of the comments already received by the deputation *De Fic*
on the original document. These were published on the following day
Then at last, on May 8, when the work of redrafting had been finishe
the new *schema* together with the report of the deputation on th
bishops' comments made its appearance.

It is clear from the details set down in the diary of Senestréy c
Ratisbon[2] that even the deputation itself, of which he was a membe
had not found it easy to reach unanimity regarding the form whic
the new *schema* should take, and that both he and Manning wou
have preferred either the original formula or else a statement whic
did not limit infallibility to definitions *de fide*. Probably if thes
advanced Ultramontanes had had their way, infallibility would ha\
been defined as embracing even the most unimportant papal *obit*
dictum on religious matters. It was largely due to the common sens
of Cardinal Bilio the president and Dechamps of Malines that suc
extravagant wishes were overruled.

The revised *schema*, which was the product of these divide
opinions, showed clear evidence of the triumph of the moderat

---

[1] Butler, *op. cit.*, vol. ii, p. 34. [2] *Coll. Lac.*, vol. vii, col. 1695 ff.

party. It consisted of a prologue and four chapters, to which were appended three canons. The crucial chapter, headed with the words 'Of the Infallibility of the Roman Pontiff', reads as follows:

'Moreover this holy see has always maintained, the unbroken usage of the Church confirms, and the tradition of the oecumenical councils themselves has proclaimed, that within the supreme power of apostolic jurisdiction, which the Roman Pontiff holds as the successor of Peter, the chief of the Apostles, in relation to the entire Church, is included also a supreme power of *magisterium*'.[1]

Then a passage from the formula of Hormisdas is quoted in the same form as before,[2] followed by the same citation from the second council of Lyons, but with the addition of a passage from the dogmatic decree of the council of Florence.

Then comes the definition itself in these terms:

'Wherefore, with the approval of the holy council, we teach and proclaim as a dogma of faith, that the Roman Pontiff, to whom in the person of blessed Peter it was said by the same our Lord Jesus Christ among other things: "I have prayed for thee, that thy faith fail not, and do thou, when once converted, strengthen thy brethren", by the power of divine aid promised to him, cannot err, when in performing the office of supreme teacher of all Christians he defines in virtue of his apostolic authority whatever in matters of faith and morals is to be held as of faith or to be rejected as contrary to faith; and that decrees or judgments of that kind, irreformable of themselves, are to be received and held with complete obedience of faith by every Christian, once they have become known to him. And since infallibility is the same, whether it be considered as in the Roman Pontiff as the head of the Church, or in the entire Church teaching in union with its head, we define further that this infallibility also extends to precisely the same limit'.[3] A minatory clause as before concludes the chapter.

The following additions or changes are to be remarked. First, as against Gallican teaching the absolute finality of papal decisions is proclaimed; secondly, the duty of the complete submission of the individual to such decisions is categorically affirmed. But the most important addition is to be found in the introduction of the words 'as of faith', 'as contrary to faith'. These words were clearly intended to impose a precise limit on the infallible *magisterium*, and to confine

---

[1] *Coll. Lac.*, vol. ii, col. 272.   [2] See above, p. 517.   [3] *Ibid.*, col. 273.

it to acts by which a particular belief or practice was declared to be part of or in accordance with the *corpus* of divine revelation or the reverse. It is easy to see that such 'hedging in' of infallibility must have been highly unacceptable to those who like Manning and Senestréy were by no means content with a *magisterium*, the function of which was simply to check the consistency of this or that new idea with the original *depositum*, or (to use the primitive term) *paradosis*, but desired an infallibility which in the manner of an oracle would turn out an immediate answer to every new problem. The real difficulty underlying the proposed definition was that, although everyone took for granted the infallibility of the Church, there was by no means general agreement about its limits. Hence the anticipation of the chapters on the Roman primacy and the postponement of the rest of the *schema De Ecclesia* had the unfortunate effect of leaving those who were opposed to an 'oracular' infallibility in the air. While not themselves disbelieving in papal infallibility of some kind, they were evidently not only unwilling but quite unable to conceive of it as other than the already generally accepted infallibility of the Church. Hence they recognized that only a definition of the former in such terms as would show that it was co-extensive with the latter had any hope of winning general acceptance by the council. Yet the difficulty remained that the precise content of the common belief in the infallibility of the Church had never been defined. It is easy to see, therefore, why the extreme Ultramontanes greeted the new *schema* with dismay, since they believed that the acceptance of the formula would involve the adoption of a minimizing view of infallibility, whether of the Church or of the Pope, and that in this way Catholicism would be defrauded of its proud claim to be in possession of an 'oracular' voice.[1] Hence they attempted by every means to procure the restoration of the original formula, which by saying much less left a far wider loophole for a 'maximizing' interpretation.

The actual debate on the revised *schema* began on May 14 and lasted until June 3. An examination in detail of the utterances of some sixty-four speakers would add little to our understanding of the significance of the new dogma and may therefore be omitted. The chief value of the debate lies in the extent of disagreement which it reveals regarding not only the opportuneness of the definition, but also its precise content. By the time some fifteen days had been spent

[1] *Coll. Lac.*, vol. ii, col. 1704.

on discussion, patience on both sides was well nigh exhausted and little real progress in the direction of elucidating the real significance of papal infallibility had been achieved. It is said that the demand for the application of the 'closure' in accordance with the decree of February 20 represented the wishes of a considerable section·of the Minority as well as of the Majority.[1] Whether this was so or not, it certainly created a good deal of bitterness. But, as Butler points out, the discussion which had taken place 'would surely be deemed a very ample Second Reading debate in the House of Commons'.[2]

Three days later the committee stage was begun. Controversy gathered chiefly round chapters III and IV of the *schema*, those which defined respectively the primacy and the infallible *magisterium* of the Pope. The chief objections to chapter III arose in the main from the absence of any allusion to the hierarchy or to the episcopate, and among those who called for amendment in this regard were not a few who belonged to the Majority. Similarly, the description of papal jurisdiction as 'ordinary' (*ordinariam*) evoked lively criticism, and it was urged that the statement should be so modified as to make it clear that the sense in which the term was used did not mean 'normal' as opposed to 'abnormal', but 'original' as opposed to 'delegated'.

It was not till July 5 that the work of examining the seventy-two amendments proposed was complete. In the end only four were adopted and those by large majorities. Serious division of opinion, however, was caused by the proposal made by the deputation to interpolate a section on the plenary character of papal jurisdiction into canon III. Although it had never been actually proposed as an amendment, its advocates, such as Zinelli, attempted to argue that it was only a modification of one which had been submitted. No doubt it was true, as he said, that the interpolation was already covered by the contents of the relevant chapter, but his justification of the deputation's action is not very convincing.[3] There is reason, however, to believe that the introduction had the support of very high authority, and thus eventually, in spite of the irregularity involved, the council agreed to its adoption.

By far the most important modifications were those affecting chapter IV, the debates on which had begun on June 15. Once more

---

[1] Butler, *op. cit.*, vol. ii, p. 55.   [2] Id., *op. cit.*, vol. ii, p. 57.
[3] *Coll. Lac.*, vol. vii, col. 345, No. 72; col. 368 ff. Butler, *op. cit.*, vol. ii, p. 87.

Cardinal Bilio's influence made itself felt and it was probably his formula which was formally proposed by Cullen of Dublin.[1] In fact it appears to have provided the material for the ultimate form of the chapter, and thus was the source of the phrase 'enjoys that infalli-bility with which the Redeemer willed that His Church should be provided'. In view of the fact that the precise content of the infalli-bility of the Church had not then and has not since been defined, the expression was ambiguous enough to satisfy all parties. A good deal of concern was shown to secure that the definition paid some regard to the necessity for the Pope to take account of the expert opinion of theologians, historians and canonists before issuing a decision which was to be binding on the whole Church. Rauscher of Vienna, a prominent member of the Minority, proposed to introduce a formula to ensure this, derived from Antoninus of Florence, who had taken a prominent part in the council held there in the fifteenth century. Similar proposals were made by Guidi of Bologna, the object of which was to exclude at all costs the doctrine of personal infallibility It was in the course of a subsequent interview with the speaker that Pius made his famous retort 'La tradizione son' io'.[2] He was evidently impatient of any restrictions, theoretical or practical.

The fact that absolutism was not without its advocates is shown by the evidence that some support was found for including a state-ment to the effect that the infallibility of the Church, so far from conditioning that of the Pope, is itself derived from papal infallibility. On the other hand, there were those who wished it to be affirmed that papal infallibility was the same as that of oecumenical councils.[3]

As a way out of this conflict of opinion, Cullen's formula, already mentioned, was found to be highly suitable, but not without at least one important change, namely, the introduction of the pregnant phrase 'when he speaks *ex cathedra*', to which the clause 'in per-forming the office of supreme teacher' was appended by way of an explanation.[4] The intention of those who advocated the use of this phrase was possibly to meet the objections of those who feared that, apart from careful safeguards, an infallible *magisterium* might be abused in the interest of arbitrary and even capricious definitions.

[1] *Coll. Lac. ibid.*, col. 382, No. 68; cols. 1701, 1645. Butler, *op. cit.*, vol. ii, p. 85.
[2] Quoted by Bury, J. B., *History of the Papacy in the XIXth Century*, 1930, p. 124. There is some doubt regarding the precise form of this saying.
[3] *Coll. Lac. ibid.*, col. 1692   [4] *Ibid.*

As to its meaning the comment of Gasser of Brixen is relevant. His exposition, which as spokesman of the deputation *De Fide* he delivered on July 11, stated that its object was to limit infallibility to those definitions in which 'the Pope speaks not as a private doctor, nor as bishop of a diocese, but as exercising the office of supreme pastor and teacher of all Christians', and that for the necessary condition to be fulfilled the Pope must himself make it clear that he is acting in that capacity.[1]

The Deputation began its work on the amendments on July 7. As a result the title was modified so as to read 'The infallible *magisterium* of the Roman Pontiff'. Further, to allay the apprehensions of the Minority, a historical preamble was introduced, drafted by Martin of Paderborn, in which it was explicitly stated that 'the Holy Ghost was not promised to the successors of Peter, that they might make known by His revelation new doctrine, but that, by His aid, they might dutifully safeguard the revelation handed down by the Apostles, or the deposit of faith, and faithfully expound it',[2] to which it was added that 'this see of St. Peter has always remained untarnished by any error', a statement which was justified on the ground of the Lucan promise to the Apostle (Luke XXII, 32). Next the new and amended form of the definition was adopted and finally the canon was put under form of anathema like the rest.

We have now reached the stage in the council's proceedings described in the first lecture,[3] and there seems no need to repeat what has already been said, beyond recalling the fact that although the revised *schema* in its latest form (now become the Constitution *Pastor Aeternus*) was passed by a substantial majority at the general congregation held on July 13, and adopted all but unanimously at the fourth public session on July 18, it remains a fact (to which attention has already been called) that many of the more outstanding personalities of the Roman Catholic episcopate in one way or another refrained from voting in its support. It must, however, be mentioned that after the suspension of the council by papal bull on October 20, those who had resisted, for whatever reason, the definition of the new dogma, eventually signified their adhesion,[4] though it is perhaps not without significance that one of its most formidable opponents, Hefele, the great historian, was not finally

[1] Butler, *op. cit.*, vol. ii, p. 134.
[2] *Coll. Lac. ibid.*, col. 387.
[3] See above, pp. 2 f., 9 ff., 16 ff.
[4] *Coll. Lac. ibid.*, col. 995 ff.

persuaded to do so till April 23 of the following year.[1] Butler speaks in this connexion of 'silent pressure . . . by withholding dispensations . . . in marriage cases', and adds no doubt quite accurately that 'there was a period of hesitation and interior struggle and conflict, that had to be battled through, before Catholic principle came out victorious over private judgment'.[2]

We began our study of the Church and the Papacy with some discussion of the conversation between bishop Dupanloup and archbishop Haynald on their return journey from Rome following the crucial vote of the general congregation on July 13, and drew particular attention to Haynald's words 'Nous avons fait une grande faute', which we held to refer, not to the resistance of himself and his companion, together with their supporters, to the definition of the dogma, but to their failure to record a negative vote at the final session of the council.

In addition to the reasons already mentioned, which Haynald, as a prominent member of the Minority, may have believed sufficient to justify an implacable opposition even in public to the adoption of the Constitution *Pastor Aeternus*, two others may be mentioned at this point. Following the decision of the general congregation, a deputation from the Minority, which included Darboy of Paris, Scherr of Munich and Ketteler of Mainz, obtained a special audience of the Pope in the hope that something might be done to appease their scruples and thus ensure unanimity at the public session. Three requests were made: first that the interpolation into the third canon, which as we have pointed out had been irregularly introduced, should be removed; second, that a phrase qualifying the expression 'when performing the office of supreme teacher', such as 'relying on the testimony of the churches' (*testimonio ecclesiarum innixus*) or 'without the exclusion of the bishops' (*non exclusis episcopis*), should be inserted; and finally that the description of the power of jurisdiction assigned to the Pope, as 'genuinely episcopal' (*quae vere episcopalis est*), should be removed, since it seemed to be capable of an exclusive sense, and to imply that the jurisdiction of other bishops was something less than 'genuinely episcopal'.[3] Pius

---

[1] *Coll. Lac. ibid.*, col. 1004.   [2] Butler, *op. cit.*, vol. ii, p. 187.

[3] The problem regarding the relation of the Pope to the bishops has never been satisfactorily solved. See Cross, F. L., *Darwell Stone*, 1943, p. 308 ff., Letter No. 76, where examples of divergent views among Roman Catholic theologians are given.

declined to intervene and contented himself with pointing out that the decision of such questions must rest with the council. Yet in view of the known composition of the deputation *De Fide*, this was tantamount to a blank refusal.

So far from conciliating the Minority, the congregation held on Saturday, July 16, introduced at the last moment a phrase qualifying the final clause of chapter IV, so as to read 'wherefore decisions of the Roman Pontiff of that sort (sc. *ex cathedra*) are irreformable of themselves, and not as a consequence of the consent of the Church (*non autem ex consensu ecclesiae*)'.[1] This was doubtless the work of the extreme Ultramontanes, who were determined to make the best possible use of this last opportunity to deliver a mortal blow against Gallicanism, and to exclude so far as was possible any 'minimizing' of the conciliar decree.

That section of the Minority which had persisted in its opposition up to and including the congregation of July 13 had every reason therefore to share a deep sense of indignation at the disregard by the Majority for their sincere convictions, so flagrant as almost to suggest contempt. It therefore seems most probable that Haynald believed that after all conduct of this kind ought not to have been allowed to pass without formal protest. Hence it would appear all the more likely, as we have already suggested, that it was to the failure of himself and of his companions in this respect that he was alluding when he spoke of 'une grande faute'.

VI

Here then is a decision by which more than three hundred million of our fellow-Christians have been committed, as it seems, finally and irrevocably to the attribution to the Roman see of a primacy of doctrine, believed to be capable, given certain conditions, of delivering decisions on matters of faith and morals, which by their very nature are incapable of restatement (*irreformabiles*), and of a primacy of jurisdiction, which is not only coextensive with the Church, but which is ordinary, direct, and immediate over each and every one of the faithful. As we look back on it, at a distance of some seventy years from the events which we have been describing, we may well ask in the interests of Christian unity, the need of which has been seldom more apparent than at the present time, what sort

[1] *Coll. Lac. ibid.*, col. 1695.

of hope can exist that the ideal set forth by representatives of successive Lambeth Conferences, in words already quoted in the first lecture,[1] can ever be translated into reality.

There are indeed not lacking signs that liberal Protestantism is coming to recognize the barrenness of a purely ethical, non-dogmatic interpretation of the Gospel, but the indications that the great mass of non-papal Christians are ready to accept an authoritarianism so absolute as that presupposed by the Constitution *Pastor Aeternus* are few indeed.

In undertaking an examination of that document in order to discover to what extent it appears to be open to criticism by those who disclaim the Roman allegiance, we shall naturally give particular attention to the Anglican standpoint. By this means we may be able to discover how far any measure of *rapprochemeut* towards the papal position is possible, at least on the part of Anglicans, and in what respects if any the ineluctable demands of history or reason, in the light of the foregoing study of the relations between the Church and the Papacy, appear to require its rejection. Some very familiar controversial ground will be covered, but it may be hoped that certain new points will emerge, sufficient at least to justify a more positive attitude than has hitherto normally been recognized as possible.

Beginning with the prologue to the Constitution, it is possible to say that no Anglican could rightly reject those statements in which it is affirmed that it was our Lord's own intention to create (or perhaps better, to recreate) one universal society of the people of God. Equally, if we take careful account of its formularies, we have every reason to hold that the Church of England endorses the belief that the divine purpose included provision 'that there should ever be pastors and teachers in His Church to the end of the world'. As to the origin of the existing Catholic ministry, the Constitution has little to say except by implication, and this finds a parallel in the Anglican reluctance categorically to assert the divine institution of the episcopate. On the other hand, to the more positive affirmations of the council of Trent on that subject, which even themselves, as we have seen,[2] fall short of downright assertion, we may adduce as a parallel the statement prefaced to the Ordinal appended to the Book of Common Prayer, which reads :

[1] See above, p. 6.　　　[2] See above, p. 453.

'It is evident unto all men diligently reading holy Scripture and ancient Authors, that from the Apostles' time there have been these Orders of Ministers in Christ's Church; Bishops, Priests, and Deacons'.

These words do not constitute in themselves an assertion of 'divine institution', but they can scarcely imply less than 'divine providence'.

As to the status of St. Peter, bearing in mind the relevant warning of the late Professor Turner already mentioned,[1] even if the validity of the interpretation of the New Testament evidence set forth in the second lecture be regarded as open to doubt,[2] we cannot in loyalty to that evidence deny that Peter received at our Lord's hands a certain preference (*caeteris apostolis praeponens*), and that he was declared by Christ to be meant in his own person, and not only in virtue of his faith, to become the visible foundation of His ἐκκλησία. Of belief in some such 'preference' the Church of England seems to testify when in the proper collect for the Communion assigned to June 29 mention is made of the Apostle's endowment with 'many excellent gifts'.

The first chapter of the Constitution, which, as we pointed out in the first lecture, is devoted to the Petrine primacy of jurisdiction, makes use of the familiar texts *Tu es Petrus* and *Pasce oves meas* in order to prove that 'such a primacy in relation to the whole Church was immediately and directly conferred by Christ the Lord on the Apostle. . . .' It may be said that the Church of England provides no 'official' interpretation of these texts, though it might be argued that the words, also occurring in the collect just cited, 'commandedst him (sc. St. Peter) earnestly to feed Thy flock,' appear to presuppose that in virtue of *Pasce oves meas* St. Peter is held to have been endowed with a special measure of responsibility for the *whole* Church of God. As to the canon with which this chapter concludes, it would seem impossible to allow that so far as the evidence of the New Testament carries us, St. Peter was usually acknowledged by his contemporaries as possessed of more than a priority of judgment, to which they did in fact normally defer. Speaking more generally, it may be said that the chapter appears to share a defect common to the Constitution as a whole, of interpreting the whole early history of the Church in the juridical language of a much later period.

[1] See above, p. 53.   [2] See above, p. 64.

It is in the second chapter that we begin to find ourselves on more controversial ground. Thus in the first place we should not find it easy to concede the logic of the argument which infers the perpetuity of the Petrine primacy from the promise of the keys of the heavenly kingdom made to him as *major domo* of the Dominical household. On the other hand, the evidence of the first three centuries appears to show that *in fact* the Roman see was regarded as in some sense a centre of reference, particularly in matters of doctrine, but also on occasion in those which concerned discipline as well, and that when the question began to be asked why this was so, non-Roman as well as Roman Christians usually replied that it was due to the connexion of that see with St. Peter as one of its co-founders. It is perhaps unfortunate that the only example of this primitive attitude towards the Roman Church cited by the Constitution is the famous passage from St. Irenaeus, which is used by its compilers to prove the 'moral' necessity for conformity with the Roman church, for, as was pointed out in the third lecture,[1] in our view, such an interpretation arises from a complete misunderstanding of the author's argument.

As to the question raised by the accompanying canon, whether or not St. Peter has perpetual successors in his primacy *iure divino* and that his successor is in fact the Roman Pontiff, it may be said that Anglicanism has no 'official' doctrine on these points. That it was believed that the Christian ministry of the sub-apostolic period had succeeded to the authority of the Apostles *iure divino* was demonstrably the belief of the author of the *First Epistle of Clement*. His view was probably shared by Ignatius. In this way at least it may be allowed that the *episcopi* of the primitive Roman Christian community succeeded to St. Peter's position in Rome, as the *episcopi* of the Corinthian community succeeded St. Paul in Corinth, and thus at least it may reasonably be conceded that the succession took place 'by divine providence'. If it be said that no evidence for this can be found in Holy Scripture, we can well reply that such evidence as we possess is at any rate secondary only to Scripture itself, and ought to be regarded as a not less trustworthy witness to beliefs current in the first and second generations of Christians.

The third chapter defines the scope and character of the papal primacy. As to the definition of the council of Florence with which

[1] See above, p. 113, n. 2.

it begins, its limitations as a statement of belief, really representative of universal Christian tradition, should not be forgotten. For in spite of the fact that it was approved at the time by the Emperor, the patriarch and other representatives of the Byzantine church, it loses some of its value as a witness to a really sincere conviction, if the political situation prevailing at the time be born in mind. The claim that the Roman church possesses a *principatus* over all other churches, to be understood here no doubt in its later sense of 'supremacy', and that the juridical authority of the Roman bishop is 'immediate', seems at first sight entirely unacceptable to Anglicans. Some allowance, however, should be made for the peculiarities of patristic diction, which is liable to create an exaggerated impression, if not correctly interpreted. As to the question of the direct authority of the Pope over each and all of the faithful, one of the speakers at the council endeavoured to show the propriety of acknowledging such authority by asking whether any bishop would say that the Pope would have to get his permission to preach, or hear confessions, or administer the sacraments in his diocese. The fact that it was greeted with laughter seemed to show that such an idea was unthinkable.[1] Yet the immediate jurisdiction of the Pope over all churches and their faithful is not only not self-evident to Anglicans; it has even been formally repudiated, though some would argue that such repudiation applies only to civil and not to spiritual jurisdiction.[2]

There can be little doubt that any suggestion of domination by a foreign power, even a spiritual one, is highly uncongenial to the greater part of a nation which has long prided itself on the precious possession of freedom from foreign intervention and on its national independence. Nor is it easy to feel satisfied that the attribution of such authority to the Papacy does not deprive episcopal jurisdiction of almost all its reality. No doubt it is true, as we have seen, that at least from the fifth century onwards individual Popes, such as Leo I, intervened *motu proprio* in the affairs of local churches, but it is natural to share the wish expressed by Rauscher of Vienna that the word used in the definition to qualify papal jurisdiction might not have been '*ordinariam*', an epithet quite innocent in itself yet which by its very ambiguity seems to imply that such intervention was to be treated as 'normal' rather than as 'exceptional'. It may well be a fact that the modern Papacy has on the whole refrained

---

[1] Butler, *op. cit.*, vol. ii, p. 86.   [2] See below, p. 531.

from an arbitrary exercise of its jurisdiction; nevertheless safeguards seem necessary against arbitrariness no less of Popes than of bishops.

The fourth section of this chapter, dealing with the right of the Roman Pontiff to communicate without hindrance with the pastors and flocks of the whole Church, is the only part of the Constitution which touches directly the relations of Church and State. Reference to contemporary history makes it evident that it was the peculiar relations prevailing at the time between the Roman see and the Italian government which seemed to render such a declaration necessary. But in relation to countries such as England, in which Roman Catholicism had long enjoyed the same tolerance and recognition as had come to be extended to all religious bodies, such a declaration was largely irrelevant. It therefore need not detain us here.

The assertion with which the third chapter concludes, that the Roman Pontiff is the supreme judge of all Christians in ecclesiastical causes, and that his decision is not open to reconsideration even by an oecumenical council, simply formulates afresh a claim on the part of the Roman see made in principle at least as early as the fifth century. Yet even if the view that the Papacy constituted a final court of appeal in cases involving the judgment of bishops had been generally conceded by that time, at any rate wherever the influence of Caesaropapism had not made itself felt to any marked extent, the same does not appear to be true of the absolute superiority of a papal judgment to the authority of an oecumenical council. It was certainly not accepted by those who took part in the second council of Ephesus (449), which styled itself oecumenical; even at Chalcedon, the orthodoxy of which every Pope from Leo I onwards upheld with the utmost zeal, it is quite clear that the papal Tome was only adopted after it had been very carefully examined, and then not without a certain measure of opposition.[1]

Nevertheless, as we have seen, in the pre-Nicene period there are signs that Roman judgments were regarded as possessing general validity and a universal significance which not even the imposing machinery of an oecumenical council could normally ignore. Moreover it needs to be borne in mind that it was never quite clear whether such a council owed its authority to the fact that it expressed the will of the Emperor for the time being, or that it was subsequently confirmed by the Pope.

[1] See the present writer's *Life and Times of St. Leo*, pp. 292, 300 ff.

The Church of England has stated not only that general councils have erred 'in things pertaining unto God', but also that local churches, including the Church of Rome, have erred even 'in matters of faith'.[1] It has also been declared that 'the bishop of Rome hath no jurisdiction in this Realm of England'. It has sometimes been represented that these words applied solely to a usurped jurisdiction in civil causes, on the ground that the title of the Article of Religion in which it occurs (Article XXXVII) is 'Of the Civil Magistrates'. But the text makes it clear that not civil jurisdiction alone is in question by saying :

'The King's Majesty hath the chief power in this Realm of England, and other his Dominions, unto whom the chief Government of all Estates of this Realm, whether they be ecclesiastical or civil, in all causes doth appertain, and is not, nor ought to be, subject to any foreign jurisdiction'.

The same view is also affirmed in the language of the Bidding Prayer, which speaks of :

'The King's most excellent majesty . . . over all persons, in all causes, as well ecclesiastical as temporal, throughout his dominions supreme'.

This repudiation of the ecclesiastical jurisdiction of the Papacy is further borne out by the rubric in the Edwardine Ordinal of 1550, directing that the bishop :

'Shall cause the Oath of the King's Supremacy and against the usurped power of the bishop of Rome to be ministered unto every one of them that are to be ordered'.

The oath itself is as follows :

'I from henceforth shall utterly renounce, refute, relinquish, and forsake the bishop of Rome, and his authority, power, and jurisdiction. And I shall never consent nor agree that the bishop of Rome shall practise, exercise, or have any manner of authority, jurisdiction, or power within this realm or any other of the King's dominions, but shall resist the same at all times to the uttermost of my power'.

It may, however, be pointed out that there were Anglicans in the seventeenth century like James I and archbishop Bramhall who did not regard these formulas as inconsistent with recognition of the Pope as the head of the Church, nor as excluding a distinction

[1] Articles XIX and XXI.

between the temporal and spiritual claims of the Papacy.[1] It may also be said not only that, as the oath just mentioned is no longer taken, it may be treated as obsolete, but that with the substitution of assent to the Thirty-nine Articles for formal subscription, the Anglican clergy have ceased to be bound by the same stringency in their regard. Nevertheless one must admit that without some positive act of repudiation the Church of England remains in some sense committed to her own past. It is true that at the time of the Reformation, as we have shown, the Papacy had come to be regarded more as a political than as an ecclesiastical institution. In fact, its political associations were so far bound up with its primacy that it may well have seemed natural to reject both at the same time. On the other hand, now that the dust of late mediaeval controversy has settled, there is less hindrance to a more generous recognition of the strictly spiritual functions of the Roman see.

VII

But in what sense is such recognition possible? If, as here, we take *Pastor Aeternus* as a representative and authoritative statement of the papal position, we have not only to make terms with its definition of a primacy of jurisdiction, a task which as we have seen is by no means devoid of difficulties, but we must in addition formulate our attitude towards the doctrinal primacy as defined in its fourth and last chapter.

Here we read:

'That in the apostolic primacy, which the Roman Pontiff as the successor of Peter the chief of the Apostles holds in relation to the whole Church, is included the highest power of *magisterium*, this Holy See has always maintained, the unbroken custom of the Church proves, and the oecumenical councils themselves, particularly those, in which the East met together with the West in a union of faith and charity, have proclaimed'.[2]

If the argument of our third lecture holds good, there is more evidence for the general acceptance of such a primacy in the primitive Church than has been generally recognized, at least by the majority of Anglican historians, and even if it is true that from time to time

---

[1] Rees, A. H., *The Faith in England*, p. 95 ff.
[2] *Coll. Lac.* vol. vii, col. 485.

in the post-Nicene period it had to face a serious challenge, yet this challenge for the most part may be seen to coincide with those periods in which some form of Caesaropapism was predominant. If we cannot acknowledge that recognition of it amounts to an unbroken tradition, we cannot fairly deny that it was remarkably widespread. The appeal to the testimony of the oecumenical councils, however, is not so easy to justify. In the case of the two first councils, those of Nicaea and Constantinople (381), we have nothing to show that in their dogmatic decisions they were consciously accepting the Roman primacy of doctrine, even if it were argued that they did so in fact. Moreover, it is certainly unfortunate that the compilers of the Constitution could find no conciliar statements more apposite for their purpose than an extract from the formula of Hormisdas as accepted by the fourth council of Constantinople, and the decrees of the second council of Lyons and of Florence. As we have already pointed out in the sixth lecture, it is evident that it was political expediency rather than theological agreement which dictated the short-lived reunions of the Greek and Latin churches which issued from the two latter assemblies, while, so far as the first of the three mentioned is concerned, recent historical research, to which we have drawn attention, makes it reasonably probable that this council only acquired oecumenical rank by a blunder of the eleventh-century canonists, who were ignorant of its annulment by papal authority, so that so far from deserving to rank as an example of one in which 'the East met together with the West in a union of faith and charity', it rather testified to a widening of the already existing cleavage between the sees of Rome and Constantinople.

The section in the fourth chapter which follows was introduced into the original draft chiefly in order to reassure those who feared that the declaration of papal infallibility would be equivalent to a definition of the Pope's personal inerrancy, and would entitle him to proclaim new dogmas to be accepted by the whole Church. That such fears were by no means groundless may be readily discovered by consulting such a work as Manning's *Vatican Council and its Definitions*, in which infallibility is held to extend to dogmatic facts, censures less than convictions of heresy, canonization of saints and approbation of religious orders, in spite of the fact that the official spokesman of the deputation *De Fide* had insisted that such matters were not covered by the definition contained in the Constitution. If,

35

however, we care to examine a pamphlet published by Fessler of St. Polten, who had acted as General Secretary to the council, we are met with a very different interpretation. Fessler insists that infallibility is closely restricted to a definitive exercise of the papal *magisterium* and affirms:

'The Pope in his doctrinal utterances only speaks what he finds, under the special divine assistance, to be already part of the truth, revealed by God, necessary for salvation, which He has given in trust to the Catholic Church (i.e. in the divine *depositum fidei*)'.[1]

The same view was held by Bishop Ullathorne, who writes:

'It is not "new doctrine" or any new revelation, but the "deposit of faith delivered to the Apostles", which, not by inspiration, but by the guiding assistance of the Holy Ghost, the Popes are able to keep inviolable, and to expound without error'.[2]

It is also relevant to add that if one consults such a work as Butler's *Vatican Council* or Dublanchy's important article in the *Dictionnaire de Théologie Catholique*[3] it is remarkable how very restricted and in some respects indeterminate the modern interpretation of this chapter of the Constitution has become. After pointing out that 'we are not so sensitive or so exacting in this matter of infallibility as our forefathers were', Butler says:

'Nowadays Catholics have, for the most part, settled down into a middle position, and are prepared to accept as right and true a great body of teachings and judgments of the Popes, without requring to know that it is guaranteed infallible'.[4]

Later on he even goes so far as to admit:

'Rather does it (sc. the modern Catholic attitude) seem to give point to Salmon's gibe—or was it Whateley's?—that the Pope is infallible so long as he defines nothing'.[5]

If this be true, it is indeed a strange commentary on the heart-breaking struggles with conscience, of which we have been to some extent the sympathetic witnesses in the course of our study of the proceedings of the council at which the doctrine of papal infallibility was solemnly proclaimed.

Yet definition of the conditions of infallibility is by no means the only difficulty raised by this chapter. There is the further question

---

[1] Butler, *op. cit.*, vol. ii, p. 215.
[2] Id., *op. cit.*, vol. ii, p. 211 f.
[3] Vol. vii, col. 1638 ff.
[4] *Op. cit.*, vol. ii, p. 227.
[5] *Ibid.*, p. 228.

about the relation of the Pope in the exercise of his *magisterium* to the witness of the Church. In spite of the fact that an attempt was made, as we have seen, so to word the definition as to assert that the infallibility of the Church is derived from and depends on that of the Pope,[1] the formula actually adopted by the council appears deliberately to avoid such a view, and to be content with the affirmation that such infallibility as is assigned to papal decisions is co-extensive with that of the Church (*ea infallibilitate pollere, qua . . . Redemptor ecclesiam suam . . . instructam esse voluit*). Another recent commentator even asserts the precise contrary to the extreme Ultramontantist view mentioned above by saying:

'Though Popes and General Councils may be looked upon as the proximate principles or organs of the Church's infallibility, yet it is true to say that in a certain sense infallibility resides primarily, not so much in Popes or in General Councils, as in the Church'.[2]

In the face of these opinions it would seem therefore that if we are rightly to understand the meaning of the final chapter of *Pastor Aeternus* we must first of all discover what is meant by the infallibility of the Church. It is certain that at the time of the Vatican council no one dreamed of questioning the latter, but perhaps only the more theologically minded bishops had any very exact idea regarding its meaning.[3]

It is often supposed that infallibility must mean the capacity to deliver an immediately true answer to any given question, after the manner of an oracle (hence the phrase 'oracular infallibility'). But in view of what has already been said, we can be quite confident that, however much certain of the more extreme section of the Ultramontanes may have desired a definition acknowledging such an infallibility, the plain meaning of the chapter on the papal *magisterium* altogether excludes anything of the kind.

Are we justified, therefore, in supposing that the word denotes no more than 'immunity from error'? Those who are impatient of any minimizing of the Church's authority will not readily accept so negative a concept, and will insist that something more positive is demanded if any belief in the finality and completeness of the revelation of God and Man in Jesus Christ is to be maintained. To the Church was committed the original revelation or *paradosis*; the doctrines which form part of this revelation, together with certain

---

[1] *Op. cit.*, vol. ii, p. 130.   [2] *Ibid.*, p. 231.   [3] *Ibid.*, p. 123.

relevant and connected historical truths, such as the facts of the Incarnate Life, constitute the *depositum fidei*, which must necessarily remain constant and thus be incapable of expansion or diminution.

But does not this mean that there can be no such thing as development? So far as the *depositum fidei* itself and its historical setting, there can *ex hypothesi* be none. But in every generation, and in fact to every individual, both must be interpreted, and it is in the process of interpretation or elucidation that error may arise. Moreover, it is necessary for the coherence and integrity of the Christian revelation that truths shall be related to one another, and hence if distortion or exaggeration is to be eliminated, systematization of some kind is unavoidable. It is not that such interpretation constitutes an addition to the *depositum*; the content of the faith is there already; the interpretation is no more than its exterior form. Hence belief in the infallibility of the Church seems to amount to this; it is the conviction that those interpretations to which the consensus of the Church has been given will correctly mediate the original *depositum*, and therefore cannot mislead. The essence of this belief is that the consensus, of which we have just spoken, is a sufficient guarantee that a particular interpretation or expression of doctrine corresponds with the continuous, uninterrupted and general experience of the living society which is the Christian Church itself.[1]

At first sight it would seem that the Vatican Constitution denies the need for any such consensus, by affirming that 'decisions of the Roman Pontiff of that sort (sc. *ex cathedra*) are irreformable of themselves, and not as a consequence of the consent of the Church'. There can be no doubt that this phrase was intended to exclude the view that papal definitions acquired their finality only if the *subsequent* consent of the Church was forthcoming. On the other hand, considerable care was taken, as we have already pointed out, to introduce a section into the earlier part of the same chapter, the object of which was to call attention to the fact that the Popes had always been in the habit of ascertaining, by means of councils or other methods, the nature of the Church's tradition, before actually issuing a decision in its name on a point at issue. If, as was true, Pius IX when about to proclaim the doctrine of the Immaculate Conception had taken

---

[1] On the infallibility of the Church, see *D.T.C.* vol. iv, col. 2175 ff.; Beevor, H. and Rees, A. H., *Infallibility of the Church*, London, n.d.; Hood, F., *Authority and Freedom*, in *Union of Christendom*, 1937.

certain precautions to ascertain the existing mind of the Roman
Catholic episcopate, it might be reasonably expected that his successors would do the same. Yet even if this insertion was intended to
provide a guarantee that what had been done in the past would
continue in the future, it is difficult to see that it could be regarded
as in the strictest sense binding on future Popes, since it was actually
no more than a statement of historical fact and did not itself form
part of the actual definition.

In spite of this, however, it remains true that the ultimate dependence of the Roman see in issuing a definition of the consensus of
the Church, as judge of the consistency or inconsistency of a particular
dogma with the original depositum or *paradosis* of the Christian
revelation, is recognized in some sense even in the Vatican Constitution, and that thus we are once more referred back to the pre-
condition of the infallibility of the Church. That such a conclusion
is possible appears to provide fresh justification for the view that
archbishop Haynald was right in saying that he and his sympathizers
among the minority at the Vatican council had in fact committed
'une grande faute' in not remaining and recording a plain *Non
placet* at the final Session. The crucial defect of the Constitution
Pastor Aeternus lies in the fact that it attempted to define that the
Pope was the infallible organ of the Church's infallibility without
first re-examining the question of the precise sense in which such
a characteristic could rightly be ascribed to the Church.

We have already made some attempt to meet this problem. Yet it
is not difficult to see that whatever character may be assigned to
decisions or definitions which represent the consensus of the Church,
we have still to answer the question 'what is the Church?'

The familiar definition of Article XIX: 'The visible Church of
Christ is a congregation of faithful men, in which the pure Word of
God is preached, and the Sacraments be duly ministered according
to Christ's ordinance in all those things that are of necessity requisite
to the same', is evidently incomplete in itself and leaves a great many
questions unanswered. As a commentary on it the declaration of the
Lambeth Conference of 1920 is relevant:

'We acknowledge all those who believe in Our Lord Jesus Christ
and have been baptized into the name of the Holy Trinity, as sharing
with us membership in the universal Church of Christ which is His
Body'.

With this affirmation we may compare the definition of the council of Florence, which says:

'By baptism we are made members of Christ and of the body of the Church'.

The difficulty in formulating any precise definition of membership, however, was felt as early as the time of Robert Bellarmine, who, though by no means a typical 'liberal', was sufficiently tolerant to recognize some value in the Augustinian distinction between membership of the 'body' and of the 'soul' of the Church. Yet it does not need much reflexion to realize that such a distinction is in itself by no means satisfactory.

Nor is it difficult to see that baptism alone cannot be a final test of membership. For not only has there been widespread recognition of the sufficiency of so-called 'baptism of desire' as supplying membership, but there must always remain the question how far those who have actually been baptized and subsequently repudiate their membership may be regarded as in some sense continuing to be members in spite of themselves. Moreover, we must not forget the case of those who by conscious and wilful sin forfeit exterior communion with the Church, and yet on repentance are not treated as non-members and rebaptized, but simply reconciled on the assumption that membership, though no doubt impaired, has never actually been destroyed.

In view of these and like considerations we may rightly endorse some recent words of a Roman Catholic writer:

'There is something wrong with the facile assumption that the distinction of Catholics from non-Catholics, of members of the Church from non-members of the Church, is always a manifest one. . . . Certainly the Church is visible, and visible by reason of the visibility of her members and her organization. But the edges are very blurred'.[1]

An admission of this kind is not only significant as proceeding from such a source, but has an important bearing on the whole modern problem of Christian reunion, since those who accept such a view cannot well approach its problems in a wholly exclusive spirit. The obvious inference appears to be that it is impossible to give any absolutely clear-cut answer to the question, 'Who are members of the Church?'

[1] White, V., 'Membership of the Church' in *Blackfriars*, September, 1941, p. 457.

Yet, it may be said, if this question cannot be answered absolutely, at least it must be possible to distinguish between one Christian community and another, as forming part of the Church or not, otherwise we shall be bound to abandon any belief in the Church's visibility. The Roman Catholic test in this connexion is generally believed to be quite decisive; only those groups of Christians are to be accounted part of the Church which are in communion with the Roman see. Yet once again it is significant that a modern Roman Catholic writer makes this striking admission:

'We cannot say that any dissident Christian body whatever is a member of the *Una Ecclesia*. Nevertheless, it would seem to the present writer that the various dissident Christian bodies, each in a very varying degree, may be regarded in some fashion as *elements* of the Church'.[1]

Later the same writer adds:

'We may admit therefore, that while Protestant communities are but "elements" of the Church . . . the Eastern Orthodox communities have a true though incomplete ecclesiastical reality and can be in a sense called Churches'.[2]

If we inquire into the precise ground for this distinction, we find that it lies in the belief that the Orthodox churches possess real sacraments and therefore also a real hierarchy. In fact, some Roman Catholic theologians would go so far as to admit that those churches enjoy an effective though illegitimate jurisdiction.[3]

These admissions may be rare and exceptional, but they may at least suggest that not even Roman Catholicism itself has succeeded in establishing an absolute delimitation of the Church, any more than an absolute distinction between membership and non-membership.

Yet there is evidently common ground between the point of view which finds reason to make possession or non-possession of a real hierarchy a means of discrimination and that of an Anglican writer who affirms:

'There are certain schisms which can only be described, not as schisms *from* the Church, but as schisms *within* the Church in the fullest sense of the word; that is to say, the parties on both sides of the schism may be said to remain within the Catholic Church, not

[1] Congar, M. J., *Divided Christendom*, Eng. Transl., 1939, p. 242.
[2] Id., *op. cit.*, p. 245.   [3] E.g. Congar, *op. cit.*, p. 244, n. 1.

merely in virtue of their baptism (the effects of which are held to persist even in spite of heresy), not merely in virtue of their orthodox profession of faith, but in virtue of their continued communion with a Catholic hierarchy'.[1]

These words occur in the course of an essay in which the author argues that in spite of the breach between the sees of Rome and Constantinople, neither side behaved as though it regarded the other as altogether outside the Church. He produces a *catena* of authorities, eastern and western, showing that in the statements on the Roman side there was much that is inconsistent with the point of view that no body of Christians may be reckoned as part of the Church which is not in communion with the Roman see. The natural inference is, as the writer points out, that communion with a *real hierarchy* can alone be accounted a primary condition of membership. A further consideration bearing on this view may now be mentioned.

In the course of our survey of papal history several examples of schisms in the Papacy from the third century onwards have been cited. In numerous cases no reasonable doubt can be held to have existed as to which of the two or more claimants was the legitimate occupant of the see, but at times his identity was by no means certain. What is more, even if we believe that the Church was right in preferring Callistus to Hippolytus, Damasus to Ursinus, or Symmachus to Laurence, the superiority of the title possessed by the ultimately successful candidate does not seem always to have been universally acknowledged at the time, and there must have been many cases where groups of Christians believed themselves to be in communion with the rightful bishop of Rome, when in actual fact, judged in the light of the subsequent verdict of the Church, they were in communion with a usurper or a schismatic. Perhaps the most striking example of this anomalous and seemingly perplexing situation is to be found in the division of allegiance between the Popes of Rome and the Popes of Avignon in the Great Schism of the fourteenth century. Yet neither in this case nor in any other is there clear and consistent evidence that either side treated the other as in no sense part of the Catholic Church. The explanation of this is clear. Communion with the Roman see might be in a state of suspense, owing to the support given to a bishop who was held by the other party to be no true occupant of that see, yet communion with a real hierarchy remained,

[4] Rees, A. H., *The Catholic Church and Corporate Reunion*, 1940, p. 4 f.

and when at length the schism in the Papacy was brought to an end by the Church's intervention, the Church normally found no difficulty in composing her internal differences without mutual recrimination.

It would seem to follow from this that until the attainment of corporate and organic reunion on a basis which includes a restoration throughout the reunited Church of what is sometimes called 'the historic episcopate', or as we should prefer to say, 'a real hierarchy', some latitude must be allowed to exist regarding the Church's limits and hence a considerable lack of precision in the question of membership or non-membership must be conceded.

It is this inability to draw absolute distinctions in these questions which appears to make it impossible to ascribe an absolute infallibility to the Church as it is to-day. If, however, it be said that to make infallibility of this sort depend on a perfect reconstitution of the Christian ἐκκλησία is equivalent to a denial of its attainability under human conditions, we can only say that this may well be the right answer. To some it may seem reasonable to hold that in a state in which 'we walk by faith, not by sight', absolute infallibility is neither possible nor even desirable. Hence it may well be true that such infallibility is not that 'with which the divine Redeemer willed that His Church should be endowed'.

It has been the aim of the present writer throughout the study now completed to maintain, so far as possible, a strictly objective standpoint. At the same time it has been necessary, if our presentation of the subject was not to consist of a mere catalogue of evidence and historical data, in the manner of a collection of documents, to devote some attention to the task of evolving a balanced interpretation of the evidence. Here no doubt some departure from absolute objectivity has been inevitable. We can only hope that it has not been so great as to render the task of attaining the ultimate truth more difficult. But if our aim is to be pursued to the end, it will be neither necessary nor desirable to draw conclusions such as might serve a controversial purpose. We have not sought to refute one interpretation and to uphold another, but rather to examine the evidence afresh, and by presenting it in a new guise to serve the cause of truth and in the end, as we hope, that of Christian unity.

Yet it would seem impossible altogether to avoid the task of attempting some kind of summary of what we believe to be reasonable inferences from the evidence surveyed, particularly from the standpoint of one who is not himself in communion with the Roman see.

In the first place it would appear that the majority of those Christians, whom for the sake of convenience we may describe as non-papal, have not usually given sufficient weight to the evidence of Holy Scripture, in virtue of which it may be held that a somewhat exceptional place was assigned to the Apostle St. Peter in the divine scheme for the constitution of the Christian ἐκκλησία. We do not believe real justice to that scheme can be done, so long as it is denied that both in teaching and in administration it was St. Peter's voice which was meant to possess a real *auctoritas*. That he was *princeps* of the Church in the sense of being its absolute Sovereign, or that he possessed or was believed to possess an unlimited authority over its members as individuals does not appear to rest on any scriptural testimony. That he was less than *princeps* in the sense of being its chief mouthpiece and spokesman can scarcely be rejected without doing violence to such knowledge as we possess.

That the Roman *episcopi*, whether in plurality or as successive holders of a single office, were held to be and were in fact the heirs of the authority of St. Peter and of his co-Apostle St. Paul in the Roman see seems to be suggested, if not guaranteed, even by such limited evidence regarding the standpoint of the primitive Church as we still possess, though it is equally clear that reflexion on the real implications of the original data was needed before their full significance was generally appreciated. The value of the papal office as the primary centre of unity, as the highest court of appeal, as a custodian of order and a corrector of aberrations from the original *depositum fidei*—all this and much more emerges, as we hope to have shown, only when the Church becomes aware of itself in a fuller sense as a world-wide organization, and when a local and 'parochial' consciousness gives place to an oecumenical outlook. Thus the papal ideal, in spite of the occasional distortion and falsification which it has undergone in the course of its long history, is to be viewed in its perfection not as an instrument for the suppression of liberty, but as a means under Providence for the safeguarding of the ordered freedom of the 'sons of God'.

If it be true that 'absolute power corrupts absolutely' we cannot deny that the Papacy, like other institutions which have acquired such power, has not escaped the consequence of its acquisition. Yet in spite of the occasional failure of individual Popes to uphold a morality consistent with the demands of their high office, it is a strange form of historica blindness which is unable to perceive in its long and remarkable history a supernatural grandeur which no mere secular institution has ever attained in equal measure. Its strange, almost mystical, faithfulness to type, its marked degree of changelessness, its steadfast clinging to tradition and precedent, above all its burning zeal for order and *Justitia* compel us to acknowledge that the Papacy must always defy a categorization which is purely of this world.

Of the future it is not our purpose to speak. If our conclusions are correct, the perfect integration of the idea of the Papacy with the doctrine of the Church, more particularly with episcopacy, has yet to be accomplished, and can be effected only in the light of a fuller knowledge of God's purpose than we can claim to possess at the present time.

Meanwhile it must remain the constant and ineluctable duty of all Christians in their separate groups so to seek by the inspiration of the Holy Ghost better to understand the outlook of others, that when the day of reconciliation is at hand, no ignorance or ill-founded prejudice may be found to hinder the fulfilment of the will of Him who prayed 'that they may be One'.

INDEX I

PERSONS, PLACES AND COUNCILS

Aaron, type of Christian bishop, 143.

Abercius of Hierapolis, visits Rome, 108.

Acacius, Patriarch, attitude to Chalcedon, 314–316; asserts primacy of Constantinople, 317; excommunicated by Felix III, 318–320; also 320, 321.

Acacius of Caesarea, consecrates Felix II, 230n.

Acholius of Thessalonica, 250n, 251, 253.

Acts of Paul, the apocryphal, 73.

Acts of Peter, the apocryphal, 73, 99.

Ad Catacumbas, cemetery, remains of Peter and Paul at, 68, 205.

Adoptionists, the, see Adoptionism.

Adrian I, Pope, earliest papal coins, 371n; relations with Emperor, 372–373; represented at Nicaea, 373–375.

Adrian II, Pope, first to use *False Decretals*, 378; and Photius, 385.

Adrian III, Pope, letter of enthronization to Photius, 386.

Adrian IV, Pope, 404.

Adrian, bishop of Thebes, 357.

Adrianople, 246.

Adversus Haereses, see under Irenaeus.

Adversus Marcionem, see under Pseudo-Tertullian.

Aemilian, revolt of, 168.

Aeternus ille, bull, see under Sixtus V.

Africa, churches of, emphasize Petrine connection with Rome, 106; keeping of Easter, 118; reject Novatian, 161; and Cyprian on Novatianist baptism, 173; general synod of, 177; confiscated property returned by Constantine, 191; *traditores* in, 192; and Donatism, 193, 194; relations with Papacy in fourth and fifth centuries, 278–291; also, 320, 346.

Council of (419), 288, 290.

Agapetus I, Pope, visits Constantinople, 342, 343; also 351.

Agatho, Pope, letter to Emperor and sixth Oecumenical Council, 173n, 365–367.

Ager Veranus, site of memorial to Hippolytus, 135.

Agrippinus, 173n.

Alaric the Goth, 280.

Albornoz, Cardinal, 420.

Aleander, 440.

Alet, bishop of, 464.

Alfonso dei Liguori, 492.

Alexander I, Pope, 88.

Alexander III, Pope, 402, 404, 405, 409.

Alexander VI, Pope, attempts to re-establish temporal power of Papacy, 428, 431; grants dispensation to Mary of Aragon, 441, 443, 444.

Alexander VII, Pope, 463.

Alexander VIII, Pope, 465–467.

Alexander, bishop of Alexandria, censured by Arius, 197; and Council of Nicaea, 198–203; succeeded by Athanasius, 209; also 118, 215n.

Alexander of Antioch, 294.

Alexander Severus, Emperor, allows church to retain property, 127, 190n; increased religious toleration under, 133.

Alexandria, see of, relations with Rome, 178, 179, 292, 293, 295, 319, 321, 325; recognizes importance of Nicaea, 199; allegorists of, 200; sixth canon of Nicaea and, 201–203, 278; relations with the state, 211, 212; Athanasius returns to, 233; primacy over the East, 209, 212, 215n, 216, 250, 252, 305, 308; Leo's estimate of, 278; fight for supremacy with Constantinople, 296, 305, 311.

Ambrose, bishop of Milan, quoted in *Pastor Aeternus*, 18; on *Tu es Petrus*, 95, 97, 260–262; influence on Gratian, 246; and the Council of Aquileia, 253, 259; prestige of Milan due to, 271; also 280, 319.

Ambrosiaster, 74n, 259.

Amphion or Nicomedia, 221.

Anaclitus, 91, see also Aneclitus, Anelitus, Anenclitus, Aniclytus.

Anagni, 417.

Anastasius I, Pope, bishop of Thessalonica, 277; and Donatists, 279; and Alexandria, 292; also 273, 280.

Anastasius I, Emperor, and Gelasius, 322, 326; and Symmachus, 335; death of, 338.

Anastasius II, Pope, 330, 331.

Anastasius, bishop of Antioch, 357.

Anastasius Bibliothecarius, 385.

Anatolius, bishop of Constantinople, 310.

Ancyra, Constantine I dies at, 210; also 198.

Ancyra, Council of, 231.

544

INDEX II

WORDS AND SUBJECTS

PRINTED IN GREAT BRITAIN BY WILLIAM CLOWES AND SONS, LIMITED, LONDON AND BECCLES